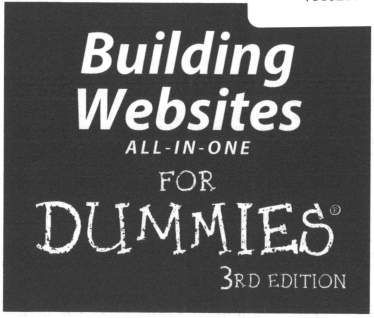

Building Websites

ALL-IN-ONE

FOR

DUMMIES®

3RD EDITION

by Doug Sahlin and David Karlins

WILEY

John Wiley & Sons, Inc.

Building Websites All-in-One For Dummies®, 3rd Edition

Published by
John Wiley & Sons, Inc.
111 River Street
Hoboken, NJ 07030-5774

www.wiley.com

Library of Congress Control Number: 2012942059

ISBN 978-1-118-27003-5 (pbk); ISBN 078 1 118 28348 6 (ebk); ISBN 978-1-118-28482-7 (ebk); ISBN 978-1-118-28725-5 (ebk)

Manufactured in the United States of America

SKY10086712_100224

WILEY

About the Authors

Doug Sahlin is an author and photographer living in Venice, Florida. He is a professional photographer specializing in fine art photography. He also photographs weddings and events and writes books about computer applications like Adobe Acrobat and Adobe Photoshop. Doug's latest books have been about digital photography. In the past years, he's written *Digital Photography Workbook For Dummies, Digital Portrait Photography For Dummies,* and *Canon EOS 7D For Dummies*. To find out more about Doug and see some of his work, check out www.dasdesigns.net.

David Karlins is a web design consultant, author, and teacher, addressing contemporary challenges in digital graphic and interactive design. Visit him at davidkarlins.net.

Dedication

From Doug: For my soul mate Roxanne and Niki, "The Queen of the Universe"

Authors' Acknowledgments

From Doug Sahlin: Two authors wrote this book, but a cast of thousands — okay, maybe hundreds — are responsible for the finished product you hold in your hands. Many thanks to Executive Editor Steve Hayes for making the 3rd Edition of this book possible. Kudos to Senior Project Editor Nicole Sholly for making sure the authors did what they were supposed to do when they were supposed to do it. Thanks to Senior Copy Editor Teresa Artman for peppering the text with insightful comments designed to amuse and otherwise keep the authors on their toes. Thanks to the staff at Wiley for creating an awesome series of books. Thanks to Technical Editor John Chastain for making sure everything was technically accurate. Thanks to Margot Hutchison for ironing out the contractual issues and other such delights.

Thanks to my friends, fellow authors, and family for their continued encouragement and support. Special thanks to Ted, Colin, Karen, Niki the Cat, and her brother Micah.

From Dave Karlins: Bringing this book to life was a collaborative project, with the coauthors; Executive Editor Steven Hayes; Senior Project Editor Nicole Sholly; and literary agent Margot Mailey Hutchinson at the core. In addition, my "pieces of the puzzle" were enhanced by the contributions of a wide range of helpful designers, experts, and reviewers.

A number of creative content developers allowed me to use their inspiring material as models in the book, including: composer Inhyun Kim and Ear to Mind (http://eartomind.com/); graphic designer Emily Strand (http://cargocollective.com/emstranded); and photographer Gary Wahl (www.garywahlphotography.com). I did my best to minimize distorting their content while using it to illustrate techniques in the book, and appreciate their generosity in lending content for that purpose.

Presenting JavaScript and PHP in this comprehensive book posed particular challenges. I was determined to make that material accurate, accessible, and useful while fitting within the constraints and parameters of this book. To that end, I got great assistance from some of the most dynamic innovators in the worlds of JavaScript and PHP. Those who unselfishly shared expertise and advice include Bryn Austin Bellomy (http://signals.io); Jake Brumby (www.MagicToolbox.com); Mary D. (www.WOWslider.com); Alan

Douglas (www.freefind.com); Jonathan Grover (jonathangrover.com); Christopher Heng (www.thesitewizard.com); Torstein Hønsi (highsoft.com); and Orfeo Morello (www.localstreamer.com). None of these experts is responsible for whatever shortcomings there might be in the coverage of JavaScript and PHP in this book, but in different ways they made that coverage much better.

I also appreciate the substantial and detailed responses to questions I posed to the PR and technical staffs at Adobe, Google, Microsoft, and Omni relating to their applications and online tools. It was clear to all involved that no *quid pro quo* was implied in their supplying software and technical support. One of the exciting things about this book is that the content here relating web-design applications is not "sponsored," endorsed, edited, or framed by the providing software publishers.

Last, and far from least, several of my live and online web-design students reviewed the minibooks I wrote for this book, including Yvonne Strassmann, Ernie Crawford, Casey R. Mitchell, and Dawn Andersen. Their detailed, thoughtful, and refreshingly candid insights were always welcome and contributed greatly to my ability to know and speak to our audience. They will recognize their input in the final content.

Thanks, everyone!

Publisher's Acknowledgments

We're proud of this book; please send us your comments at http://dummies.custhelp.com. For other comments, please contact our Customer Care Department within the U.S. at 877-762-2974, outside the U.S. at 317-572-3993, or fax 317-572-4002.

Some of the people who helped bring this book to market include the following:

Acquisitions, Editorial

Senior Project Editor: Nicole Sholly

Executive Editor: Steven Hayes

Senior Copy Editor: Teresa Artman

Technical Editor: John Chastain

Editorial Manager: Kevin Kirschner

Editorial Assistant: Leslie Saxman

Sr. Editorial Assistant: Cherie Case

Cover Photo: iStock 11716379 © iStock / Marcello Bortolino

Cartoons: Rich Tennant (www.the5thwave.com)

Composition Services

Project Coordinator: Sheree Montgomery

Layout and Graphics: Jennifer Creasey

Proofreaders: John Greenough, Jessica Kramer, Christine Sabooni

Indexer: BIM Indexing & Proofreading Services

Special Help
Blair Pottenger, Jennifer Riggs, Rebecca Senninger, Heidi Unger

---

Publishing and Editorial for Technology Dummies

Richard Swadley, Vice President and Executive Group Publisher

Andy Cummings, Vice President and Publisher

Mary Bednarek, Executive Acquisitions Director

Mary C. Corder, Editorial Director

Publishing for Consumer Dummies

Kathleen Nebenhaus, Vice President and Executive Publisher

Composition Services

Debbie Stailey, Director of Composition Services

Table of Contents

Book V: Incorporating Web Graphics and Multimedia.... 319

Chapter 1: Web Media 101 321

Chapter 2: Introducing Fireworks and Photoshop 335

Chapter 3: Creating Buttons and Banners 353

Book VI: Creating Interactive Pages with JavaScript... 447

Chapter 1: JavaScript for Animation and Interactivity 449

Chapter 2: DIY JavaScript. 465

Introduction

*W*ebsites can be very complex or very simple. When you're building a site, you have many decisions to make, all dependent upon the needs of a particular project. Don't become overwhelmed or fret, though, because you have *Building Websites All-in-One For Dummies,* 3rd Edition, to help you. This book is so comprehensive and so flexible that it will help you in all aspects of web design, from the initial planning phases to testing and publishing your masterpiece.

This book can help you take on the role of project manager, graphic designer, developer, or multimedia designer, and offers information about interacting with different specialists on larger or more complex projects. So whether you're undertaking your first web design project or are a veteran taking on a web design team, this book is for you.

About This Book

Here are some of the things you can do using this book:

+ Plan your website project.

+ Assemble and manage a web team or draw on online resources.

+ Create layouts, graphics, navigation menus, and web pages from scratch.

+ Optimize graphic elements for your web pages.

+ Work with HTML, HTML5, CSS, and CSS3 to create and maintain your pages.

+ Add interactive animated menus, navigation elements, and other content with JavaScript and jQuery Mobile.

+ Create forms and manage form input with PHP scripts or online data management tools.

+ Generate and embed search tools for your site.

+ Embed live and streaming data, including RSS feeds and blogs, in your site.

+ Add multimedia content, such as audio and video.

+ Integrate e-commerce into your website project.

✦ Maintain and promote a website.

✦ Explore JavaScript for animation and interactivity and PHP resources for server-side coding.

Foolish Assumptions

We have, perhaps foolishly, made a few assumptions about our readers. We expect that you have basic computer skills (Windows, Mac, or Linux) and a basic understanding of how to use a browser and the Internet. The authors and publisher of this book assume you're a bright, intelligent person who wants to learn but doesn't have the time to read a book from cover to cover. We assume you'll find the information you need by perusing the index and then cutting to the chase to read that section.

If you don't have any prior knowledge of HTML, CSS, JavaScript, PHP, or graphics software, that's okay: We give you the basics here. We do assume that you have more than a passing interest in web design. In fact, this book is geared for web designers, or anyone with aspirations of becoming a web designer. If you don't have any prior experience with web design or managing website projects, that's okay, too. This book starts at the beginning before moving into more advanced topics.

Conventions Used in This Book

By *conventions,* we simply mean a set of rules we've employed in this book to present information to you consistently. When you see a term *italicized,* look for its definition, which we include so that you know what things mean in the context of website construction. Sometimes, we give you information to enter onscreen; in this case, we make **bold** what you need to type. We place website addresses and e-mail addresses in monofont so that they stand out from regular text. Code appears in its own font, set off from the rest of the text, like this:

```
Never mind the furthermore, the plea is self-defense.
```

Throughout the book, you'll find icons such as Technical Stuff, Tips, Warnings, and Remember. These little tidbits are cold, hard facts we found out the hard way. We sprinkle this information liberally so you won't fall into the same chuckholes we did — or worse, end up with egg on your face.

What You Don't Have to Read

We structure this book *modularly* — that is, it's designed so that you can easily find just the information you need — so you don't have to read whatever doesn't pertain to your task at hand. We include sidebars here and there throughout the book that contain interesting information that isn't necessarily integral to the discussion at hand; feel free to skip over these. You also don't have to read the paragraphs next to the Technical Stuff icons, which parse out über-techie tidbits (which might or might not be your cup of tea).

How This Book Is Organized

Building Websites All-in-One For Dummies, 3rd Edition, is split into 10 mini-books. You don't have to read them sequentially, you don't have to look at every minibook, you don't have to review each chapter, and you don't even have to read all the sections in any particular chapter. (Of course, you can if you want to; it's a good read.) The Table of Contents and the index can help you quickly find whatever information you need. In this section, we briefly describe what each minibook contains.

Book I: Getting Ready

This minibook covers all the things you need to do before you start actually creating a website. The topics of planning, managing your project, flying solo on a project, and assembling and managing a web-design team are all covered here. We also include information about creating a site that portrays an organization in a flattering light while providing visitors with content that keeps them coming back for more.

Book II: Designing the Site

Site design is about the nuts and bolts of how a site works and about making the visual aspects work within the technical needs, and this minibook helps you make these two worlds come together. From sketches on the back of an envelope, to working with navigation flowcharts, to generating the perfect color scheme for your style and message, we explore a whole range of options and dimensions to web design. In short, if you're looking for information about creating layouts and planning site structure, implementing appropriate design, and collecting and using feedback, you'll want to read this minibook.

Book III: Building Pages with HTML

HTML is the basic language for designing web pages, and this minibook walks you through generating or coding the basic HTML you need to create pages. Plus, you'll learn to take advantage of HTML5's radically new approach to structuring page content as well as how to create and structure pages in Dreamweaver CS6.

Book IV: Designing Pages with CSS

Modern web pages are designed and formatted using external (linked) CSS style sheet files. This minibook teaches you to format text and images, design pages with columns and boxes, and to apply CSS3 tools to create effects that previously could only be achieved with images or Flash. This minibook also walks you through creating and applying style sheets in Dreamweaver CS6.

Book V: Incorporating Web Graphics and Multimedia

A website without graphics is text, which won't keep a visitor interested for very long. Book V begins with an introduction to web media and the various formats you'll use to incorporate images in your design. Then it's off to the races with Fireworks, Photoshop, and (last but not least) Flash.

Book V also shows you how to add multimedia content to your designs. If you want music or other joyful noise on a website, read Chapter 3 of this minibook. If it's full-motion video your client is after, we show you how to add it in Chapter 4 of this minibook. We wind up this trip down multimedia way with an introduction to Flash CS6 in Chapter 5 of this minibook.

Book VI: Creating Interactive Pages with JavaScript

JavaScript is how you add animation and interactivity to your website. Drop-down menus? Hover-over tooltips? How about a navigation jump menu? Or jQuery Mobile content for mobile sites? All covered. This minibook shows you what JavaScript is, and how to create the elements you need, with three alternatives: writing simple scripts yourself, availing yourself of online libraries of premade JavaScript, and generating JavaScript with Dreamweaver CS6 or online resources.

Book VII: Managing Forms with PHP

Build your e-newsletter list. Provide a helpful search box. Sign up volunteers for your cause. Or collect valuable feedback from happy (or not so happy) visitors. This minibook covers everything you need to design forms with "prompt" text and validation tests (to make sure the data looks right before being submitted). And, we'll show you how to use a wide set of options for collecting form data, ranging from basic PHP scripting to professional (but free!) e-list managers. Bonus: See how to use Dreamweaver CS6 to create validation JavaScript and mobile-specific form elements, such as sliders and switches.

Book VIII: Social Media and Interactive Add-Ons

Social media is a hot topic these days. Businesses use social media such as Facebook and Twitter to get the word out. Social media can also be used to draw visitors to a website. In Chapter 1 of this minibook, we show you how to add a WordPress blog to a website. In Chapter 2, we show you how to incorporate social media with the website and vice versa. If the website you're designing has something to sell, we show you how to integrate e-commerce with a website in Chapter 3.

Book IX: Deploying and Managing the Site

If you build it, they will come. *Not.* The only way to get people to flock to a website in droves is to promote it. We begin this minibook by showing you how to test the site and then upload it. If you've created a good design, visitors will come — and with any luck, the site will catch on. And if the site really catches on, you'll probably need to revise or redesign the site. We show you how to maintain and expand a website in Chapters 3 and 4 of this minibook.

Book X: Case Studies

The final minibook of this lofty tome comprises four chapters of case studies. We learn a lot by surfing the web and dissecting what's good, bad, and downright ugly about what's out there. You can, too. To give you an idea of what goes into planning and then creating a site, we explore the needs of four different clients and the resulting websites, including one case study of a business that incorporated an online newsletter with its marketing efforts.

The companion website

www.dummies.com/go/buildingwebsitesallinone

The companion website contains downloadable code files from the book that you can use for practice.

Icons Used in This Book

For Dummies books are known for those helpful icons that point you in the direction of really great information. In this section, we briefly describe each icon used in this book.

The Tip icon points out helpful information that's likely to make your job easier.

This icon marks an interesting and useful fact — something that you might want to remember for later use.

The Warning icon highlights lurking danger. With this icon, we're telling you to pay attention and proceed with caution.

When you see this icon, you know that there's techie stuff nearby. If you're not feeling very techie, you can skip this info.

Where to Go from Here

Although the book is written so that more experienced web designers can skip around to the parts they need, novice users probably should start with Books I and II, which together provide a good foundation of building websites, before proceeding to the other books. If you're one of those experienced designers, scour the index for the material you need and then read those sections.

Experience is the best teacher. After immersing yourself in those topics you want to know more about, launch your favorite code editor and begin noodling with designs you've created and tweak them, using the information from this book. And if — like the plumber with leaky faucets — your personal website was designed around the turn of the century, by all means spiff it up using the techniques we show you.

Book I
Getting Ready

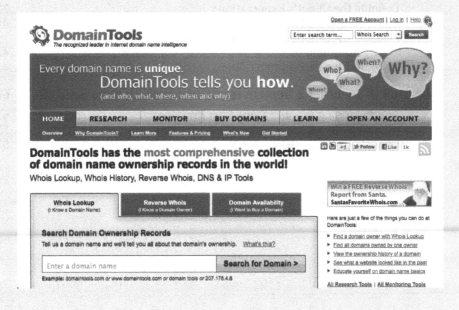

Contents at a Glance

Chapter 1: The First Step in Your Web-Building Journey

In This Chapter

✔ Finding inspiration on the web

✔ Setting goals for the site

✔ Defining the "grand vision"

✔ Making preparations

✔ Implementing changes based on feedback

✔ Reworking an existing site

A website starts as a gleam in someone's eye — a vision of an Internet presence to sell a product, promote a service, or promote an idea. The gleam may be in your eye, or your client's eye, but eventually the vision must be brought to fruition in the form of code, images, and text that are polished into user-friendly pages and then uploaded to a web server for the world to see.

Your mission is simple, kind of: designing a website. You have a good idea of what you or your client wants, and now it's time to start putting your creative spin on those ideas.

Getting Inspired

What your client sees in her mind's eye may be very different from the cold, hard reality of existing websites and what's considered acceptable for a specific type of business. After all, when you go into a five-star restaurant for the first time, you have a certain preconceived notion. If you go inside and smell grease and hear beepers going off ("Fries are ready!"), you'll probably make a quick exit, stage-left.

We recommend going online to do a little research first:

1. **Do a Google search for your company's or client's type of business.**

   You'll come up with quite a few results. You may see some sponsored results at the top of the Google search results. Consider these sites as well. They may be well-heeled competitors.

2. **Start perusing the search results.**

   Visit the sites at the top of the search results page.

3. **Pay attention to the navigation menus and the other elements of each site you visit.**

   Most business websites offer easy-to-navigate menus. Disregard the sites that have navigation menus with cute icons and no text. Navigation menus like that confuse many users. Also disregard any sites that don't look professional or have slow-loading graphics.

4. **Bookmark any sites that appeal to you.**

   If you find a lot of sites that inspire you, consider organizing the bookmarks in a folder, a task you can easily accomplish with most modern web browsers.

Now you have a dossier of sites that you can use and peruse when you need a bit of inspiration. The site you create will have your own unique design style, but this research will steer you in the right direction, enabling you to create a site that has a similar functionality to the sites from companies that perform the same service, or sell the same goods as your client's. Once you know what's expected for this type of website, you can put your own unique spin on it and come up with a unique design that incorporates your company's or client's brand.

You can also surf for inspiration by reading industry trade magazines. Your client probably has a stack of them in her waiting room. The trade magazine will have URLs listed with company profiles or advertisements. Surfing for inspiration is a great learning experience if you've never created a site for your client's type of business before. You discover lots of similarities between the sites that inspire you, and you'll also find some differences.

After you surf for inspiration, let the information stew in your subconscious for a couple of days before writing any code or creating any graphics. You might have your own defined style and way of working, but the additional information gained from perusing websites of the client's competitors and similar companies can help you keep the client's grand vision in check and also help you define what's expected for a website designed for a specific industry or service. It's also beneficial to have the information close at hand. It can help keep you on track.

Setting Goals

Each website needs a purpose. Even if you're designing a small site about your hobby, you need to have a reason for building the site. You also need to decide how you will measure the success of the site. People often talk about a "successful" website, but what does that really mean? Is your goal to raise awareness for a cause, to showcase a service, or to increase sales?

Perhaps the end vision for the site is to cut down on customer service calls, or perhaps obtain a large volume of traffic for a brick-and-mortar business. If a site doesn't have a goal or a definition of success, you won't know how to develop or maintain it. You determine these goals in part by talking with the internal stakeholders of the site (what are their expectations?) and also by determining what it is that the external audience needs. (We discuss these two groups in Chapter 3 of this minibook.)

Usually, a site has more than one goal, so make a list and prioritize your goals. Decide which goals and features are must-haves and which are simply nice to have. Concentrate your efforts on the must-haves first and then create a development game plan to add the nice-to-have stuff. The great thing about websites is that if you plan them well, adding things can be fairly simple.

Another important reason to have goals is that it helps you set project *milestones* — short-range goals that help you measure your project's progress while keeping everyone on track. An example of a short-range goal would be presenting a graphic mockup of the site for approval of team members. When working for a client, having milestones is important because it enables the client to sign off on the progress, showing approval of the work to that point. If the client doesn't approve of the work, you need to get specific feedback regarding what the concerns are, refer to the original plans for the site, and determine whether the requests fit within the original scope of the project. If they do, make the changes and then request a review/sign-off of those changes. This process prevents confusion about whether a client approves of the work and ensures that the client agrees that the product has been delivered as expected. For more about checking your progress at milestones, see the "Revising Your Original Plans: Using Feedback to Improve" section, later in this chapter.

Defining the Scope of the Site

Define your web projects in terms of what features and content you intend to include. Having a general idea of what the site will include isn't enough because everyone has their own vision of that. A well-run project needs good communication right from the start. The success of a project depends on everyone agreeing on what the project includes. This project definition — *scope* — should be clearly written in a *scope document* and distributed to all team members. Any changes to the scope of the project need to be recorded in an amended scope document and then redistributed to team members.

Creating the scope document involves defining what the project is, but don't forget to also define what a project is *not*. For example, if the site will use video but not animations, the scope document needs to say so. Define each element clearly. Simply including "video element," for example, in a list in the scope document isn't enough. With each element, spell out what the project functionality *is* and *is not* in very definite terms. So, to properly reflect the "video element" in your document, you must be specific, like this:

Video element to include product demonstration by Tamara Lush, project spokesperson. Video is to be created by client and rendered as an HD (High Definition) MPEG4 (mp4) file. Web video production will render content into a fast-loading web video.

By being specific, you protect yourself and your client from being unpleasantly surprised when you integrate an element — such as a video — into the site.

All projects suffer to some degree from something called *scope creep,* which happens when people start throwing in little extras that weren't part of the original scope. Keep these things to a minimum. Make sure to discuss the impact of the changes on the timeline and budget with the client immediately. If you need to revise a portion of a project in any substantial way, make sure you amend the original scope document, adjust the timelines accordingly, adjust the budget to reflect the major changes, and then get all the key players to sign off. Failing to rein in scope creep can kill your project, ruin the budget, and ultimately damage your business if you are an independent web designer.

Preparing to Get Started

Your preparation doesn't have to be a giant project. Smaller or less-complicated sites require just a little time — you can accomplish a lot with a couple of hours, a cup of coffee, and a pad of paper. Just sit down and start focusing on the details of the project, such as defining your purpose, coming up with specific ideas, considering budget and timeline, and so on. Of course, you'll need more time and more people on the team if you're planning a large or complicated project — so make that a whole pot of *strong* coffee (and maybe some donuts, too).

Defining why you're doing the project

This might sound obvious, but you should define why you're going to build (or redesign) a site in the first place. Companies commonly start a web project because their colleagues or competitors have websites. While "keeping up with the Joneses" is a reason, it can't be the only reason. Without a strong message or clear direction, your site can end up being a bland imitation of other sites, which is usually counterproductive. A website can be a great tool for an organization if you focus on why you're building it and what can make your site better than everyone else's.

Brainstorming and evaluating your ideas

After the decision is made to create a website, you do your initial research as outlined previously in this chapter, and have a laundry list of things that are needed on the site. Now is the time for all interested parties to get together and have a good old-fashioned brainstorming session. One person can be the moderator and reiterate what's already been decided. You can come up with some wonderful variations or something unique by posing several "What if" questions, such as: What if we added a blog? You can (and in many cases, should) have additional brainstorming sessions with the team. The important thing at this point is to write down everything that pops to mind.

Brainstorming can be done with a pencil and a piece of paper, or with a software application. Many designers like to use a technique called "mind mapping." When you use mind mapping, you start with a clean sheet of paper and then write down the first word that comes to mind. A logical choice would be the name of the website. Draw a circle around the word, and then write down the next word(s) that comes to mind: for example, "color scheme." Draw a circle around that word. When you add additional words, connect the circles with a line to show how the word is connected to the whole. If you're doing mind mapping with a group, one team member is in charge of writing down the ideas and connecting the circles. There are also mind-mapping applications available for the Mac and the PC. Figure 1-1 shows MindNode Pro (www.mindnode.com), a Mac application in action brainstorming a questionnaire for a wedding photographer's website.

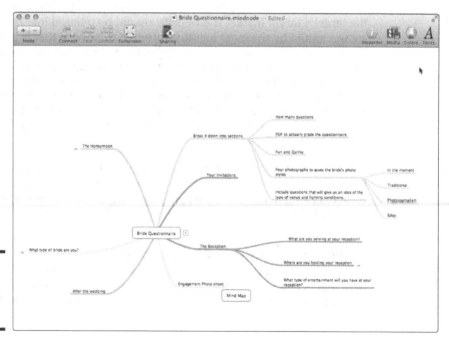

Figure 1-1:
Mind map
your way to
success.

After your brainstorming session, consider the ideas from that session in a more practical way. Compare what you have with your defined goals and reasons and start discarding things that just don't fit. Again, this part of the web project is similar to many other types of projects. Web project managers can easily fall into the trap of thinking that because it's a web project, all the work will be done on a computer, and old-school techniques don't apply. However, resist the urge to fall into that trap. Getting away from the computer and technology can help you focus on the purpose of your project and the content you plan to deliver without the distraction of the computer and technology.

Creating a niche website

If your client has multiple products and services, and you find out that the client also has a diverse target audience, consider creating a website for a portion of that target audience. This enables you to create a highly focused site, a site that will deliver exactly what a specific part of your client's target market wants.

When your research tells you that the client's target market is as diverse as his product line, it's time to schedule another meeting with your client's shareholders. The purpose of the meeting is to decide which portion of the target's target market the website should be tailored for. The obvious answer would be the most lucrative product or service that is purchased by the most affluent part of the target market. If you or your client offer a free service, create a persona for each type of person that will visit the site. You may think you know this information, but only your client can tell you exactly which product and part of her target market generates the most profit. After you're armed with that information, you can use the persona you created for that portion of the client's customer base and begin fleshing out the content for the site.

If your client does consider creating a niche website, you'll have to keep him on track regarding content. If he sends you content that looks like it doesn't belong in the niche site, politely bring it to his attention and ask him whether he thinks it's a good idea to include that information.

Looking at budget and timelines

Even an in-house project has a budget and a timeline. Of course, these parameters can always change during the course of a project because deadlines can't be met or need to be pushed forward. Time and money, as in any project, are tied

While you work on your first web projects, you'll probably find that budgeting time and money is difficult. Projects usually are more complicated than they seem; even small projects need input from multiple individuals, and those individuals will need to agree and collaborate. Although we can't give you a magic formula for calculating how these changes and collaborations will impact your project, keep in mind the following guidelines when you're planning the budget and deadlines:

✦ **Clearly establish deadlines up front, specifying what elements team members will deliver on those deadlines and what resources team members will need from stakeholders for the project to continue on track.** Include information about what will happen if stakeholders or clients delay the project. When a client is responsible for delivering materials (such as photos or text) and those materials don't arrive on time, you can't proceed. Standard practice is to add the number of days the materials are late to the timeline. That is, if your client is two days late with text, the deadline pushes out two days.

✦ **Whether you're working as a freelance web designer or as part of an internal team, put everything in writing.** This way, you avoid the "he said/she said" scenario that causes frustration and is counterproductive.

✦ **Use a rush fee.** This fee is the extra amount that you would charge if the client wants you to deliver the project faster than originally agreed. You can also use a rush fee when a client asks for a project on extremely short notice — for example, a client calls and asks you to create a mini-site in only two days.

Considering collaborations

While you complete your planning, consider the possible reactions to what you're planning. For example, you might encounter opposition from individuals who don't think a website is a good thing. On the other hand, some overly enthusiastic people might want to pitch in and help. Thinking of how (or if) you'll collaborate with those who want to help is a good idea. For more information about possible team members to bring into the project, see Chapter 3 of this minibook.

Revising Your Original Plans: Using Feedback to Improve

As a web project progresses, it moves through a cycle of review, feedback, and revision. Each iteration of the project (hopefully) helps the finished product become better. Establishing project milestones (which we discuss in the earlier section, "Setting Goals") is an important part of the initial planning phases. The milestones provide points along the way when all stakeholders can have a look at the site and give feedback about the progress.

Whether formal or informal, *usability testing* (asking people to play with the site to see what works and what doesn't) at key milestone points can provide useful feedback. To conduct a quick, informal usability test, select some people who are representative of your target audience (preferably, people not involved in the project) and ask them to try to use your site; then have them provide feedback about their experiences. In Book IX, Chapter 1, you can find more information about usability testing and getting feedback.

When you're asking others to preview the site — whether they're usability testers or internal stakeholders — make sure you label placeholder text and graphics clearly to let people know that placeholders are not part of the finished project. *Placeholder* items do just that in a layout — they hold the place while finished text and artwork are being created. A large, red, For Placement Only (FPO) label across a graphic often helps people stay on track while they review a project in progress.

Make sure you show your work to stakeholders whenever you make significant progress or hit a project milestone. They need to know that you're staying on track. Also, keep in mind that some of your stakeholders might not be able to envision the finished product. When you notice someone getting bogged down on a temporary item (such as a placeholder graphic), thank them for their feedback and then try to redirect their attention to items you do need feedback on.

Receiving feedback

If you're looking for a particular type of feedback, make sure you ask specific questions that prompt users to comment on the elements or issues you want to focus on. In general, it's not very productive to just send a link with a note that says, "What do you think?" You'll get vague responses like, "Looks good!," which is great for a final okay before launching a project but is not so good when you're at the midpoint in the project and looking for something more concrete. In some cases, you might even want to direct their attention to a particular piece of functionality, such as the subnavigation or a new animation, and ask them to comment specifically about just that piece. Here are some tips that can help you get the information you need:

✦ **Don't ask for general feedback unless that's what you really want.** The best way to get a group of random comments and personal opinions ("I like it.") is to just send a link without any explanation, or with a vague direction ("Check this out.").

✦ **Make sure you ask for specific feedback from individuals based on their expertise.** Any web project involves many details and many different disciplines working together. Make sure you have experts to help keep you on track. In other words, ask writers to review and editors to proofread your content; trust designers to make sure your colors are working for you. Rely on experts you trust for detailed feedback on details specific to what they know.

✦ **Never assume that a person has nothing useful to contribute.** Although the finer details should be picked over by an expert, a fresh set of eyes is very helpful when looking at the project as a whole. Remember that your actual visitors don't have inside knowledge or expertise and will also be looking at your site from a fresh perspective. We've even gotten great feedback from an 8-year-old child about some icons that weren't working. You never know who will have a useful tip.

✦ **Include a list of what's new since the last time you sent a link for review.** Expecting people to play compare-and-contrast to figure out what you've been up to is neither polite nor productive. Keep in mind that most of your usability testers and sources of feedback are trying to look at your project and return comments between working on their own projects. They won't take the time to help you if you don't take the time to direct their attention to the important issues.

✦ **Make sure you don't ask for feedback if you can't use it.** If you know that you're locked into a particular piece of functionality or presentation, don't ask people to comment on whether it should be there. It wastes their time, and they might not want to help you the next time. Let people know up front about situations that are beyond your control. For instance, if you must display a particular logo in a specific place, include that information in your note requesting feedback.

✦ **Ask open-ended questions.** Try to come up with questions that will make people interact with the site you are designing and really think about what they are experiencing. You need honest input from people even if it's not a bunch of compliments. If you collect useful information and act on it, you will get plenty of compliments when you launch a great website.

✦ **Thank reviewers for their input.** Make sure you thank them for their time because you'll need to call on them again as your project progresses. Keep them interested in helping you. It's easy to forget this little detail when you're wrapped up in your project, but people want to know that their time was well spent. Make sure you send a follow-up after you collect feedback, including a summary of the feedback and what you intend to do as a result of the comments given.

Giving feedback

Giving feedback can be trickier than getting it, so follow these pointers that can help you give feedback without stepping on any toes:

✦ **Take your time.** When you're evaluating a project to give feedback, take your time and look at the site. Your feedback isn't helpful if you immediately start reacting without taking a few moments to look at it and consider what you're going to say.

✦ **Stay polite, and don't get personal in a negative way.** Being polite goes a long way when giving feedback. People often forget that someone has put a lot of time and effort into her work, and no one likes to be criticized. Make sure that when you give feedback, you take that into consideration. Blurting out comments shuts down communications pretty quickly. Ultimately, it's the project that suffers for it.

✦ **Balance positive and negative comments.** Launching into a laundry list of everything that is wrong with the site is a bad idea. After all, a human being did the work — not a machine. The best way to have your suggestions ignored is to sound like you're launching a nitpicky attack. Try to balance your negative comments with positive ones. For instance, instead of saying, "I don't like where the logo is, it's crunched up in the corner," try, "I see that you've put a lot of work into this. It's looking good, but I think I'd like to see the logo with a little more space around it. It seems a bit crowded." The second approach takes a few seconds longer but helps build and maintain a good working relationship. Some web projects take a long time and can be difficult and frustrating. To avoid creating problems, take a few moments to consider delivery of comments.

✦ **If something doesn't look right, ask questions.** Websites go through a lot of changes throughout the design process. If you think something looks wrong, ask what's going on. Sometimes, there is a good explanation for why something looks strange. For example, if the logo is missing, don't just say, "The logo is missing." Instead, try something like, "I noticed that the logo is missing. Why is that?" It could be an oversight, or maybe a new logo is being developed. Again, delivery of critical comments makes the difference between a healthy collaboration and a confrontation.

✦ **Keep your feedback mostly objective.** Remember that the project isn't your personal, artistic statement. If you don't like the color but the colors have already been decided, accept the decision and move on to other issues. It's okay to have some personal reactions to the site and comment on them, but don't be offended if you're overruled. Everyone has something to contribute, but not every idea can be included — or the site will look like a crazy quilt!

✦ **When giving feedback on an interactive piece, be specific!** It's not helpful to look at the functionality of a piece and respond to the developers with, "It's broken." Designers and developers that are working on interactive pieces need specific information about what went wrong. They need to know what you did (for example, "I clicked the Shop Now button."), what you expected to have happen ("I thought it would take me to the shopping cart page."), and what actually happened ("I got a page that said, '404 error — Page Not Found'."). This tells the developer or designer exactly what to look at. "It's broken" doesn't tell them anything. If you encounter an error message or error code, tell the designer/developer what it is — *specifically* — and what action you took right before it occurred. The more information you give, the better. If you don't give specific information up front, you can count on playing a game of 50 Questions later as designers and developers try to wrestle the details from you.

Preparing to Redesign an Existing Site

Most of the preparations that you need to do for a new site also apply to an existing site. Some differences that you should take into consideration as you prepare to redesign a site include these:

✦ **Evaluate the site that you're redesigning.** The first task is to look at the current site and evaluate how well it aligns with your needs, and your client's needs. Look at the content, functionality, and look-and-feel as separate elements. Take each aspect of your site into consideration — technologies used, coding techniques, site structure, colors, style of writing, and so on. List them all and rate them based on whether they can be used on the new site.

✦ **Have experts look at what you have.** Large or complex sites need to be evaluated by selected experts or consultants. In particular, coding and technologies need to be evaluated to make sure that you don't reuse old, outdated technologies (such as a Flash intro or for that matter, any Flash if the site will be accessed by devices such as the iPad) instead of using a redesign as an opportunity to make important upgrades.

Don't get caught up in the "newer is always better" line of thinking because it isn't. You know the old saying — "If it ain't broke, don't fix it." Sometimes that's the best course to take. Make sure you weigh the pros and cons of keeping or replacing code carefully before you dive into revising a site.

✦ **Include all stakeholders in the initial evaluation process.** This step can help you verify that the information on your site is current and accurate. A site redesign is a good opportunity to involve all interested parties in looking at and updating materials that have been posted for a while. It's common for certain types of information to be posted to a site and then forgotten. Be sure to look at contact information and directions pages because they often harbor out-of-date information. Make sure you include appropriate professionals from the client organization in the evaluation. For example, sites that deal with financial, legal, or medical information will need to be reviewed for compliance with laws specific to those industries (Sarbanes-Oxley, HIPAA, ADA, and so on). It is good practice to ask your client about possible compliance issues and have them identify individuals within their organization that will be responsible for reviewing site content in that aspect.

✦ **Check the front-end code.** Look at the code that handles the display of the site interface — HTML (covered in Book III) and Cascading Style Sheets (CSS; Book IV) (if the site has them). These technologies have undergone many rapid changes over the past few years, and many sites could benefit from recoding the pages.

✦ **Gather the data and make decisions.** When the analysis and evaluation are done and you've collected all the feedback from interested parties and *content owners* (people responsible for the content of part or all of a site), start the planning process. Compare what you have with what you need your site to be and then decide what parts of the current site can be used as is, repurposed and used, or thrown out. When you're deciding what to do, keep in mind that it's often better to put a little more effort into recoding or reworking an existing item than it is to roll a cumbersome or badly developed piece of functionality into a new site. One of your project goals is to make the site more efficient. With the analysis in hand, you're ready to start working on meeting with stakeholders and your team to plan your approach.

Chapter 2: Assessing Your Resources

*W*hen you decide to get into the business of web building, you need stuff to design your sites with. We're talking software and apps here: scripting languages, style sheets, maybe a word-processing program. You also need software to create graphics — buttons, banners, footers, for example. In this chapter, we suggest some applications that have stood the test of time and give you the tools you need to create compelling web pages. We also talk about working solo or with a team.

Choosing an HTML Editor

If you're a masochist, you certainly can create web pages in a word-processing program. All you need to know is which HTML tags to use for each section of that document. However, taking this path, intrepid reader, is a very daunting way in which to create web pages. Even the most seasoned web designer uses an HTML editor to create sites. And the granddaddy of HTML editors is Adobe Dreamweaver.

Dreamweaver began life as a Macromedia application in 1997. Adobe purchased Macromedia and added several powerhouse applications to its software lineup, including Dreamweaver. The latest version of Dreamweaver is version 12 and is part of Adobe Creative Suite CS6. Dreamweaver is a WYSIWYG (what you see is what you get) HTML editor that enables you to create HTML documents by inserting objects, such as images and multimedia, into the document. You can also add links, create cascading style sheets (CSS), and much more. We cover Dreamweaver throughout the book as it applies to various stages of the website building process. Figure 2-1 shows Dreamweaver in all its glory with a page under construction.

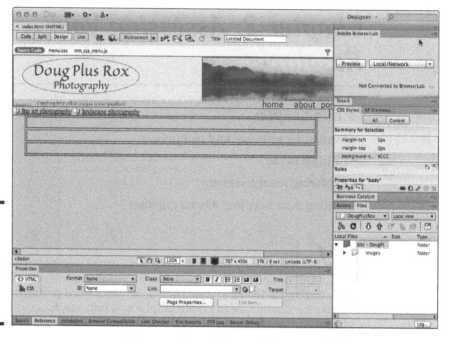

Figure 2-1:
Create
pages in
the Dream-
weaver
HTML
editor.

If you're not a fan of Adobe software, check out Microsoft Expression Web, which is another application you can use to create HTML pages. We do not cover Expression Web in this book, though.

Choosing a Graphics Application

A web page without graphics is, well, text. You get the point. If you build web pages, you need a way of creating graphics and editing them. Clients will send you images that are humongous.

If you're working with one of the CS6 suites, you have some powerful applications that you can use to add multimedia elements, such as images, banners, animations, and so on, to your designs.

Any web designer worth her weight in gold is not satisfied with preset graphics or stock art; she creates her own graphic elements. Adobe Fireworks CS6 is part of the Adobe Creative Suite 6 Design and Web Premium. With Fireworks CS6, you can create banners, navigation menus, and much more. You can export your designs as graphic elements or graphic elements and HTML. For more information on Fireworks CS6, see Book V, Chapter 2.

You can use Fireworks to do your image editing as well, or you can use the acknowledged king and queen of image editors, Photoshop. The current version of Photoshop CS6 gives you the power to fine-tune images for web pages. You can add text to the images, use filters to give images an artsy-fartsy look, and then export them as JPEG or GIF images using the powerful Save for Web command. We introduce you to Photoshop CS6 in Book V, Chapter 2.

With the advent of cable modems and high-speed Internet, video in web pages is a viable option. But the video that comes from a camcorder or an iPhone is not quite ready for prime time on the Internet. It has to be encoded into a web-friendly format and then embedded into a web page. We show you how to use the Adobe Media Encoder CS6, which if you hadn't already guessed, is also part of the Adobe Creative Suite 6 Design and Web Premium suite. Check out Book V, Chapter 4 to find out more about making squeaky clean, fast-loading video.

Some people think Flash content is yesterday's news due to the fact it can't be viewed on devices like the iPad and iPod. Flash, however, still does have a place in web design. Flash Professional CS6 is also part of the Adobe Creative Suite 6 Design and Web Premium suite. We show you how to get flashy in Book V, Chapter 5.

Flying Solo: Skills You Need to Go It Alone

You need many skills to single-handedly undertake a web-design project. Some of these skills are tangible; for example, you must know some HTML and CSS skills as well as how to effectively use Photoshop and other graphics programs. Other skills are intangible: You must be able to provide good service while managing the project and your time and keeping the budget under control. This section lists and describes some of the necessary skills you need to fly solo on a web-design project.

Managing the project

If you're doing most of or all the work yourself, you must be able to work on several aspects of the project simultaneously — requiring your project, time, and money-management skills — in addition to communicating all that to your client. You can make these tasks easier by

- ✦ **Keeping notes:** Document what you've done, when, and what you'll do next.

- ✦ **Making a special e-mail folder for project-related e-mails:** If you can, set up your e-mail to direct all mail pertaining to the project to that folder. (Many e-mail programs, including Microsoft Outlook, Entourage, and Lotus Notes, have this capability.)

✦ **Drawing up a budget:** Your budget should include your fees for doing the work (Hourly Rate × Time = Cost of Work), fees for any contractors you hire, and also fees for project management. You should also include fees for extra services (say, image scanning or writing content) if you want to make those services available to the client. Another possible thing you may need to add is special software or equipment. If your client requires that you buy something, build the cost of it into the budget.

✦ **Establishing a timeline:** Clients often don't understand how much work and time a web project requires — they just know that you make it look simple and easy. Developing a quality site isn't quick, but creating a to-do list for each week (or day) and also marking deadlines on a calendar helps you track what you need to do and when.

✦ **Devising a troubleshooting plan:** Technological issues are inevitable. For instance, multimedia elements sometimes don't download fast enough, certain functions don't work as expected, or layouts have CSS issues. These sorts of problems can take some time to troubleshoot and fix. Your plan for the troubleshooting process should include staying task-oriented and not participating in finger-pointing. During troubleshooting, work with the server administrators of your web-hosting provider and others who are involved with the project to find a solution. Quickly open a line of communication with your client that explains the problem and what you're doing to fix it. Stay calm and confident so that your client feels reassured that you are in control and dealing fairly with her. If you need to bring in help, tell your client whom you're bringing in and why.

The bottom line here is that if you don't figure out how much time you have to complete the project and how much money is in the budget *very early in the process* — and communicate that to your client — you could end up wasting a lot of time and energy planning a project only to find out that the client is unrealistic in her expectations.

Serving your customer

Part of a web project manager's job is customer service. Providing good customer service can help ensure that your clients are happy, which can help you build a solid reputation. The following list describes four important aspects of customer service:

✦ **Communicate often and minimize technical jargon.** You must communicate often about the status of the project so that your client knows what's going on. Communicating with less-than web-savvy clients, however, can be a little awkward. Don't talk down to them, but avoid using a lot of jargon (which can make them feel stupid). Try to ease into the techno-talk gently unless you're sure they speak geek, too.

✦ **Stay professional.** Web jobs can be a lot of fun for everyone if they're well run and everyone has a good attitude. Unfortunately, sometimes you won't mesh well with a client. If that happens, you must keep a professional attitude, do the work, treat the client with respect, and just suffer through it. That's business. However, in rare situations — for instance, if a client becomes abusive — you might find it impossible to continue working with that client. In that case, you must decide how to quickly wrap things up with the client; you can either deliver the unfinished site or hand it off to another designer. Either way, you must carefully explain to the client that he would be better off working with someone else.

✦ **Know when to say "no" to a project.** Accepting every job that comes your way might seem like a good idea. It isn't. Some clients don't have the money or game plan in place to make it worth your time to work with them. If you waste time on someone who can't make a commitment, you could be missing out on a client who is ready and able to start a project. If a client isn't ready right now, stay in touch with him. He will appreciate your interest in his project and might just give you the job when it's time.

✦ **Take only projects that you can execute well.** Your portfolio and reputation are important. Delivering a good product is a great thing, and your client will recommend you to their colleagues, and word-of-mouth advertising is the best form of advertising. Delivering a bad product can have the opposite effect, though, because you might lose that client and any possible referrals. This doesn't mean that you should never take a project unless you can do every part of it. If a project has some components you can't do on your own, call in a specialist — just make sure you let the client know you will be working with a team. The fewer surprises to your client, the better off you'll be.

Dealing with HTML, CSS, and other scripting

Web pages are made of code, so no matter how you look at it, you can't avoid working with code. Luckily, basic Web code — HTML and CSS — is fairly easy to learn. It might seem complicated at first, but with practice and patience, you'll be hand-coding pages pretty quickly. Many tools can help you generate code, but you still have to understand the code because sometimes you have to roll up your sleeves and manually write some code.

Read the fine print

For those rare occasions when a working relationship runs amuck, be sure that your contract allows you to get out of an abusive situation. You also want to make sure that your contract includes a clause so that you're fairly compensated for what you've done. We're not legal experts, so we advise you to check with an attorney to make sure your contracts don't have any loopholes or other problems.

Just bear in mind the following:

- ✦ Even the most sophisticated software package is still just software and can make mistakes.
- ✦ Many advanced techniques require a deeper understanding of the underlying code and how it works.
- ✦ Taking on an existing site to redesign or maintain requires that you know how to analyze the code that's there. If you can't, you might find that you can't work with the site.

Book III covers creating HTML pages with Dreamweaver, and techniques to help you take advantage of both. Figure 2-2 shows an example of HTML code. The first few times you look at the code, it might seem confusing, but it will quickly become familiar.

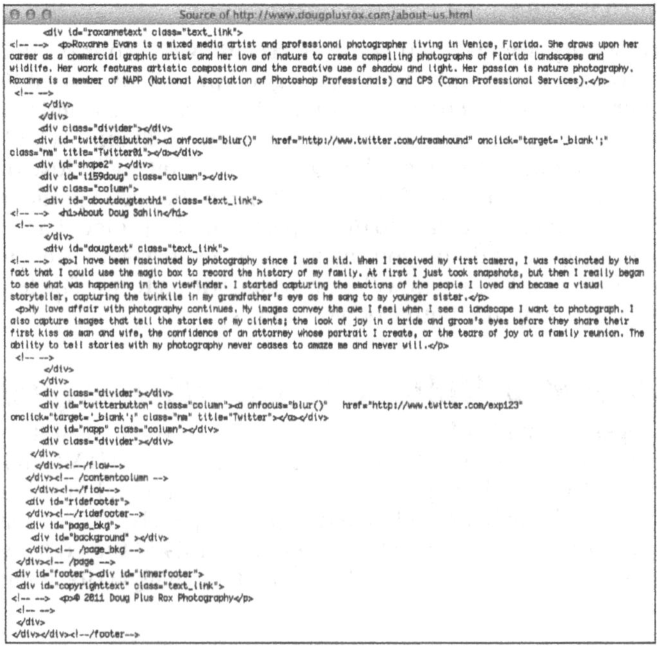

```
Source of http://www.dougplusrox.com/about-us.html
      <div id="roxannetext" class="text_link">
<!-- -->  <p>Roxanne Evans is a mixed media artist and professional photographer living in Venice, Florida. She draws upon her
career as a commercial graphic artist and her love of nature to create compelling photographs of Florida landscapes and
wildlife. Her work features artistic composition and the creative use of shadow and light. Her passion is nature photography.
Roxanne is a member of NAPP (National Association of Photoshop Professionals) and CPS (Canon Professional Services).</p>
 <!-- -->
      </div>
     </div>
     <div class="divider"></div>
    <div id="twitter01button"><a onfocus="blur()"   href="http://www.twitter.com/dreamhound" onclick="target='_blank';"
class="nm" title="Twitter01"></a></div>
    <div id="shape2" ></div>
     <div id="i159doug" class="column"></div>
     <div class="column">
      <div id="aboutdougtexth1" class="text_link">
<!-- -->  <h1>About Doug Sahlin</h1>
 <!-- -->
      </div>
      <div id="dougtext" class="text_link">
<!-- -->  <p>I have been fascinated by photography since I was a kid. When I received my first camera, I was fascinated by the
fact that I could use the magic box to record the history of my family. At first I just took snapshots, but then I really began
to see what was happening in the viewfinder. I started capturing the emotions of the people I loved and became a visual
storyteller, capturing the twinkle in my grandfather's eye as he sang to my younger sister.</p>
 <p>My love affair with photography continues. My images convey the awe I feel when I see a landscape I want to photograph. I
also capture images that tell the stories of my clients; the look of joy in a bride and groom's eyes before they share their
first kiss as man and wife, the confidence of an attorney whose portrait I create, or the tears of joy at a family reunion. The
ability to tell stories with my photography never ceases to amaze me and never will.</p>
 <!-- -->
      </div>
     </div>
     <div class="divider"></div>
     <div id="twitterbutton" class="column"><a onfocus="blur()"   href="http://www.twitter.com/exp123"
onclick="target='_blank';" class="nm" title="Twitter"></a></div>
     <div id="napp" class="column"></div>
     <div class="divider"></div>
    </div>
     </div><!--/flow-->
   </div><!-- /contentcolumn -->
    </div><!--/flow-->
   <div id="ridefooter">
   </div><!--/ridefooter-->
   <div id="page_bkg">
    <div id="background" ></div>
   </div><!-- /page_bkg -->
 </div><!-- /page -->
<div id="footer"><div id="innerfooter">
 <div id="copyrighttext" class="text_link">
<!-- -->  <p>© 2011 Doug Plus Rox Photography</p>
 <!-- -->
 </div>
</div></div><!--/footer-->
```

Figure 2-2: This is an example of HTML code.

Using Photoshop, Fireworks, and other graphics applications

If you're going to do design work, you need some design skills. In addition to understanding how to use color, fonts, and images to support your content and how to use layout effectively, you need to know some basics in a variety of graphics programs, including these three:

✦ **Adobe Photoshop CS6:** This is a great tool for doing practically everything you need to do with web graphics. Photoshop is the industry standard for working with graphics. With Photoshop, you can work with photos and create supporting graphics (such as banners and buttons) and any other graphics you need. If you want to pursue a professional career in design, you need Photoshop skills. See Book V, Chapter 2 for a brief introduction to the Photoshop CS6 interface and Tools panel.

✦ **Fireworks:** Use this web graphics creation tool to manipulate photos and create other graphics. Its strength is in being tightly integrated with Dreamweaver. Fireworks also has great tools for optimizing graphics for the web and a helpful and easy-to-use batch-processing tool (which is good for resizing a large number of photos at once, among other things). Read more about Fireworks in Book V.

✦ **Adobe Illustrator:** With Illustrator, you can create and edit *vector graphics,* which are made up of mathematical information defining points and lines that make up shapes. A discussion of bitmap versus vector graphics is in Book V, Chapter 2. Vectors are great for building graphics with hard lines, such as logos.

You have to convert vectors into bitmaps to use them on a website. Photoshop and Fireworks are primarily bitmap-editing programs; bitmaps are the choice for photographs. Figure 2-3 shows a vector graphic (on the left) and a bitmap graphic side by side. Notice the jagged edges created by pixilation in the bitmap.

Information about how to create, use, and prepare graphics for use on a site is included in Book V.

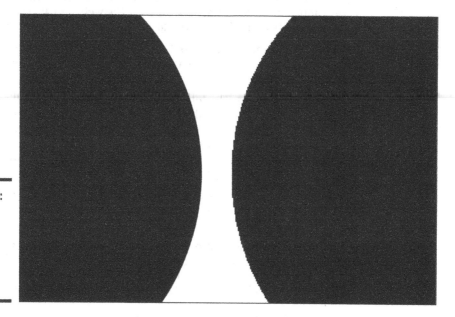

Figure 2-3:
A vector
graphic
(left) and
a bitmap
graphic
(right).

Developing content

Good writing skills are essential for creating a successful website because a site without good content isn't useful to anyone. Whoever creates the site's content — whether you or a partner — must understand how people use websites and why they go to the site in the first place. More importantly, the people who write the content for the site you are designing must understand the site's target audience.

Good writing skills also come in handy when you're preparing presentations and proposals. Almost all projects require some degree of writing skill for preparing contracts, proposals, scope documents, and other communications. Short paragraphs and bullet points help readers find what they need quickly.

Considering basic computer and Internet skills

Not that we want to state the obvious, but you need some computer skills if you're going to design web sites:

✦ **Word processing:** Whether you're using Microsoft Office, Pages (part of iWork, Mac only), or another word-processing program, the ability to prepare documents efficiently ensures that you can prepare contracts and proposals and keep track of the business side of things.

✦ **Creating HTML pages:** If you can't create an HTML page, your career as a web designer will be short lived. Applications like Dreamweaver CS6 make it possible to create HTML pages. See Book III for all things HTML.

✦ **Creating and optimizing graphics:** Web pages without images are almost nonexistent these days. Therefore you'll need to learn how to use software applications to optimize images for the web, and also learn which image formats to use for photo-realistic images and graphics, like logos.

✦ **E-mail/IM (instant messaging):** Communicating with clients is important for your success. With e-mail and instant messenger, staying in contact with clients has never been easier.

✦ **Video conferencing:** The Internet constantly reinvents itself as new technology becomes available. With the advent of fast connections, video conferencing has become a reality. Many applications are available for video conferencing, such as Skype or FaceTime (Mac). Even if your client does business in a distant locale, you can still have a "face-to-face" meeting with this technology.

✦ **Browsers:** Having some familiarity with and testing your site on the popular web browsers (Internet Explorer, Safari, Firefox, and Chrome) ensures that the site will work no matter which application visitors use to view it.

✦ **Windows/Macintosh platforms:** Developing skills on both Macintosh and Windows computers broadens your range and eases testing of your web pages on both platforms. Professional web designers work to make their sites function under a wide range of conditions.

Do not cut and paste text directly from Microsoft Word into your HTML-editing program. Word adds very cumbersome tags to define the original fonts used in Word, which wreaks total havoc in Dreamweaver and other HTML-editing applications. If you're going to use the text directly from Word, copy it into a text-editing application — such as Microsoft Notepad or Apple TextEdit — and then paste it into your HTML editor, which strips out all those cumbersome Word tags.

Incorporating multimedia in your project

If you plan to work with audio or video, you need some multimedia skills. You have a choice of many types of multimedia, and what you use depends on what you're trying to accomplish. Book V has information about technologies and techniques for using multimedia elements, such as audio and video clips, in your project.

Handling a solo project

If you decide to take on a project by yourself, here's a brief list that can help keep you on the right track:

+ **Prioritize your tasks and develop a workflow.** Some parts of the project are more enjoyable than others, but you still have to complete them all. After you do a few projects, you start to develop a workflow that enables you to work effectively through all the parts of the project, even the ones that aren't as enjoyable. Prioritizing your tasks and breaking up creative and analytical tasks (so you don't burn out on one aspect of the project) can help you meet your deadlines.

+ **Establish a point person with your client.** Do this at the beginning of the project. Working with one contact person can help reduce misunderstandings.

+ **Notify your client of personnel changes.** If you need to bring in some help, make sure you let the client know.

+ **Treat your home office like a "real" office.** If you're freelancing from your home, make sure you have a good workspace with all the equipment you need. Treat it like a regular job. Make regular hours for yourself. It's also a good idea to save some days strictly for production and others for meeting days.

+ **Network and market yourself.** Build time into your schedule to look for your next project. When you're writing proposals and discussing projects with clients, don't forget to build "lost" days into the timeline: you know, days spent going to meetings or other events. If you know that you'll need 40 hours to complete a job, don't tell the client that you can do it in five business days — trust us when we say that you won't get it done it that time frame. Those 40 hours is how long you'll spend on the project *specifically;* other related tasks will take up more time. Bottom line: A "40-hour job" can be more like a month-long project.

Getting Some Help

You might hire help for your projects for many different reasons. Some projects might have components that you don't have time to complete yourself, or the site might require things that are beyond the scope of your capabilities. Most folks are good at some aspects of the work but not so good at others. Maybe you're excellent at developing code, but colors and design issues mystify you. Individuals who are great at everything aren't the norm. Even if you're that rare bird who can do it all, working with a team is often more cost- and time-effective.

An effective way of working is to establish relationships with individuals or companies that provide the services you need. After you find people you can work with, you can quickly build project teams that are tailored to the needs of your client. Your "regulars" can develop a smooth workflow. You will also expand the size and scope of projects you take on.

Note: Job titles in the web-design industry vary greatly and even overlap. For instance, a web/new media designer and project manager might both be dubbed "producer." When interviewing people, ask them what their actual experience is and don't rely solely on their job title. Some creative folks don't work and play well with others, so ask a prospective team member whether she has worked on teams and if she likes a team environment. Assembling people who are team players helps ensure that the team will collaborate.

Project manager

A *project manager* for a web project — like the project manager for any project — keeps everyone on the same path and makes sure issues are dealt with as quickly and smoothly as possible. The project manager should be organized and detail-oriented enough to responsibly do the following: make sure members of the team are meeting deadlines, keep track of hours spent on the project, and inform team members of situations that might affect them.

A web project manager needs to know about the workflow and time traps that can accompany the type of project you're planning. Experience working with creative individuals is also important because a project manager must understand each individual's needs concerning workflow and how materials are to be delivered (both to and from team members). The project manager also has to estimate the time needed to complete different types of projects. Familiarity with industry standards and terms can help the project manager when dealing with professional designers. In some environments, the web project manager is sometimes referred to as a "producer."

Web designer/new media designer

A true web designer knows how to hand-code HTML and CSS and might know some other scripting technologies, such as JavaScript. Web designers are also responsible for the visual design of the interface, creation of graphics, and *optimization* (resizing and compressing them for web use) of photos. (Book V, Chapter 2 has more information about optimizing graphics.)

Watch out for web designers who "don't do" code. Web designers who downplay the importance of strong HTML and CSS skills aren't really web designers. They're graphic designers who make graphics that coders can use to create web pages. It will save you time, money, and aggravation if you shop around for someone who can take care of the whole job, as opposed to someone who needs other members of the team to complete the tasks of creating the interfaces.

Web developer/programmer

Web developers and programmers design and create the back-end systems that make your site do more than just deliver static information. A *back-end system* refers to databases and programming that are stored on the web hosting server and are used by the website. If you need or want your website to interact with site visitors, you need databases and the supporting programming to be in place.

Like with web designers, the importance of a good developer is often misunderstood. The availability of point-and-click development tools gives some people the impression that it's simple and easy to create databases and web pages that will work with them. These easy-to-use tools are generally fairly limited in what they can do, though. If the site will have a lot of people interacting with it or if people will be performing complicated functions on the site, hire developers to build your system for you. If you want to add shopping functionality, you need developers who understand how to make a safe, secure, and easy-to-use site, or users won't buy the advertised products.

Point-and-click tools should not be confused with the open source content management systems (CMSes) that have evolved in recent years. Some of the most popular open source solutions include Joomla! (http://www. joomla.org), Drupal (http://drupal.org), and WordPress (http:// wordpress.org). CMSes all come with robust features, can be used to get a dynamic site up and running very rapidly, and can be difficult to manage and customize. If you want to use a CMS, we recommend working with a developer who is familiar with these systems and the development environment (CSS, PHP, and MySQL, all of which are platform independent). To get the best experience from an open source CMS, your developer needs to understand the strengths and weaknesses of these systems and be able to manage the customization and technical support involved.

Content developer/writer

A good content developer or web writer understands that writing for the web is different than writing for other media because visitors interact with websites differently than they do with traditional, printed materials.

When looking for web writers, you want to hire someone who can deliver the following:

✦ **Easy-to-understand information:** Look for a writer who can deliver concise text that has a good tone for the web. Most successful web sites have a more conversational tone.

✦ **A good call to action:** A good web writer can get a site's users to act. Every site has a goal, but without a good call to action, users might not perform the tasks you want them to while on the site. A good call to action is irresistible. A savvy web writer knows how to craft the content so it drives people to the pages and actions that you want them to see and do.

✦ **Organization:** Content developers must understand how to create a flow of information and leverage the nature of the web to provide users and site owners with the best results.

✦ **Search engine optimization (SEO):** Content developers must know how to create text and meta tags that enable users to find the site through search engines. More information about meta tags is in Book III, Chapter 2. Book IX, Chapter 1 covers SEO. You can also read about how important SEO is in tandem with blogs in Book VIII, Chapter 1.

Webmaster/host

Hosting is a service usually provided by a third party. Web hosts own web *servers,* which are computers with server software installed and that are connected to the Internet. For a fee, the owner of the server — the *host* — allows you to copy your website files to the web server so that they're accessible to anyone with an Internet connection.

In addition to owning servers and renting space, web hosts maintain the servers. They might also provide additional software that tracks the number of visitors your site has. Many web hosts also offer URL (Uniform Resource Locator) purchasing services. A *URL* is a website address — for example, www.yourname.com — also known as a "domain name." Most web hosts sell a complete package, including space for your site, e-mail, *traffic reports* (number of visitors to your site), and URL purchasing. Purchasing a domain name and finding a web-hosting service are covered in Book I, Chapter 4.

If your site will include multimedia or dynamic content, consult with your developers and designers before you find and commit to a host. The server software must be compatible with the technologies the team will use to build your site. Many developers and designers will assist their clients with hosting choices or actually offer the services directly or through partnerships.

Other professionals

You should consult with other professionals as you start to work on website projects. Designing websites is just like any other business, and it's important to get some help so that everything runs smoothly. We suggest that you contact the following types of professionals:

✦ **Lawyer:** If you plan to work for clients, you need a copyright and intellectual property lawyer. Make sure you hire someone who specializes in technology and creative industries. A knowledgeable lawyer can prepare contracts that spell out copyrights, address deliverables, and specify timelines, making sure everyone gets a fair deal.

A good contract makes sure that everyone understands the scope of the project, the responsibilities of the parties, and when the project will be delivered and so on. It also spells out how the fees for services work (an hourly rate or a flat fee), which everyone needs to understand and agree upon. Also make sure your contract specifies whether the client incurs the cost if they request or require you to purchase stock photography, extra software, or fonts.

✦ **Accountant:** As with any business, you need an accountant. Seek the advice of an accountant before you start to accept fees or hire others to work for you. Your accountant can advise you how to set up your business so that everything runs smoothly.

Building a Web Team

Sometimes a project is too complex for a single designer, but other times you can create a small web project comfortably with no additional help. The latter scenario occurs when the client (or you, if you're creating the site for yourself or your company) can provide clean text, good graphics, and good multimedia items. But when the project gets complex and you need professionals like photographers, videographers, writers, and copy editors, you need to create a web team. In the following sections, we show you what you need to go it alone, and also show you how to build a proficient web team.

Managing the team

After you assess the needs of a project and call in the necessary team members, have a kick-off meeting. In short, everyone needs to get together and discuss the project, timelines, expectations, and next steps. These two steps are particularly important in keeping the project moving smoothly:

✦ **Establish a point person during the planning phase.** This is especially important if you're working with more than one service provider. Everyone needs to know how to communicate with one another. Will you be using Instant Messenger or video conferencing to stay in touch? Make sure everyone has contact information for each other. Find out what the daily schedules will be to facilitate communications.

✦ **Set up weekly production meetings.** To facilitate the meeting, the project manager should prepare a job grid (Microsoft Excel is a good tool for this) specifying all the tasks, who is responsible for what, expected delivery dates, status, priority, and any contingencies. All team members should update the team on their progress, any issues, and next steps. Make sure that you get good feedback from everyone; vague statements like, "I'm working on it," aren't really helpful. At the very least, find out when each individual expects to finish assigned tasks. After the meeting, send out a follow-up e-mail that outlines what everyone agreed to. Include a new job grid reflecting progress and next steps.

Giving feedback that helps

Web projects have a lot of details to be taken care of. Don't forget to establish a process of asking for and receiving feedback. The project manager should inform members of the team that he is going to send materials to the client for review and await confirmation that everyone is ready for the client to see the work. If some pieces won't be ready on time, don't hold up a scheduled review. Inform the client about the status as soon as you're aware of an issue. Proceed with the scheduled review and be prepared with adjusted timelines.

Establish a contact person within your client's organization and communicate with that person only. It might sound unfriendly, but it isn't. Having only one contact person ensures that there won't be confusion as multiple people give feedback. The contact person should be responsible for asking people in their organization for feedback, getting *signoffs* (formal acceptance of the work as complete), obtaining materials, and communicating with you or your project manager. The project manager is responsible for communicating with the team, presenting materials to the client for review, and making sure the project flows smoothly.

Keeping the team on track

One of the hardest things to control is scope creep: what happens when someone — a client or development team — decides to add "little extras" to make the project better. It's the job of the project manager to keep track of those little extras and make sure that they don't add up to a whole bunch of extra functionality that wasn't in the original agreement or budget.

If the client asks for things outside the scope of the project, you have two options for moving forward:

✦ **Incorporate the extra request into the current plan.** In this case, you have to tell the client that the extra request is beyond the scope of the agreed project and that amending the current scope document (and timeline and budget) is necessary.

✦ **Discuss the additional functionality as a future project.** If the client agrees to hold off on the new idea for later, you can proceed with the project as planned. The good news is that you now have a future job already lined up.

In either case, let the team know about the requests so they can adjust their schedule and workflow accordingly.

If your client decides to amend the scope of the current project, you must prepare a new scope document, timeline, and budget, which your client will have to agree to and sign off of.

Chapter 3: Working for The Man

In This Chapter

✔ Evaluating what the client wants

✔ Selling your idea to the client

✔ Keeping everyone happy

*W*hen you create a website for yourself, the only limiting factors are current technology and your expertise. You do have to create a site that will be well received by your target audience, but you're pretty much on your own. However, when you create a site for a client, or for your company, other people also have a stake in the overall success of the site. You won't have *carte blanche* to add whatever you think should be in the site. You have to please every member of the team and anybody else who has an interest in the outcome of the project. In this chapter, we offer some wisdom for finding out what the interested parties want, selling your plan to the interested parties, and then making sure everyone involved is a happy camper.

Defining the Client's Expectations

Whether your company is the client, or you've been hired to create a website, the first thing you need to do is get on a level playing field and make sure that everybody involved is on the same page. The client may envision a site with bells and whistles, music, mariachi bands, and other visual delights. And when you consider the client's expectations, you must take technology into account. After all, web technology has come a long way, baby, so you must consider the underlying technology of

✦ **The web-hosting company**

Read more about selecting a good web-hosting service in Chapter 4 of this minibook.

✦ **The technology of the end user: namely, your client's clients**

The end user's technology may well be the weakest link in the chain. For example, if the target audience accesses the Internet with a relatively slow connection, adding high-quality video to the website is out of the question.

The best way to define the client's expectations is to have a meeting of the minds. The best place to do this is in a quiet place where you won't be interrupted. The client's office is usually not the best place to do this because of too many temptations, such as the phone on his desk, his computer, and so on. You'll get your best results if you meet your client somewhere with Wi-Fi connectivity, and then you take the lead and gently steer the client — your boss, literally and figuratively — in the right direction! Bring your laptop along so you can visit your client's competitor's sites and other sites that distribute the same product or offer the same service.

You already have the job, so you don't have to sell yourself. However, after you find out what your client expects for the final website, you will probably have to be the voice of reason and tell the client that some expectations might not be possible because the technology available to his target audience. Adding streaming multimedia to a website that will be frequented by visitors with a slow Internet connection is a recipe for disaster.

Bottom-line, defining your client's expectations is a fact-finding mission, and you may have to put on your Sherlock Holmes deerstalker cap and be a bit of a detective.

Here are two simple yet effective ways to keep your meeting productive and fluid. First, on your "Just the facts, ma'am" search, use *your* computer to do the research. If your client offers to use his computer, tell him that you have reference material on your computer that will be needed during the fact-finding mission. If your client uses his computer, he may be tempted to check e-mail during your meeting. Second, if possible, ask the client to put his phone on silent. Yeah, your client may complain if he's used to being in control, but here's where you'll have to be firm and diplomatic while explaining that you'll get more accomplished without interruptions.

Here are some ways to define the client's expectations:

1. **Open a blank document in your word processor and ask your client to start telling you what he expects.**

   A document is a convenient way to keep all this information on your computer. Notes hastily jotted on a pad may be difficult to read and decipher later, and unless you're a meticulous filer, notes can get lost.

2. **Take copious notes as your client tells you what he wants.**

   Make sure you clearly understand his needs. If necessary, ask questions to clarify any gray areas.

3. **Ask your client for the names of his biggest competitors.**

   With this information in hand, you can visit his competitors' websites at your convenience.

4. **Ask your client whether he has a preferred color scheme, or ask for his favorite colors.**

If the client doesn't have a color scheme, you can derive a color scheme from your client's logo. Another alternative is to visit `kuler.adobe.com` and show him some of the popular color schemes. This will give you a starting point.

5. **Ask the client whether he has a domain name.**

If not, start brainstorming domain names. For more information on selecting domain names, see Chapter 4 of this mini-book.

6. **Open a web browser, and ask your customer for the names of some websites he likes.**

7. **Visit the websites and ask the client what he likes about the sites, and add this information to your document, along with the URL for future reference.**

Bookmark the sites that your client likes.

8. **Ask your client about his target audience.**

Get as much demographic information as you can, such as the age range of his target audience, ratio of male to female users, and so on. This will help you determine how technically savvy the user audience is. The website navigation and other factors will be determined by the age group of the audience. For example, if you're creating a website for elderly users, the size of the text will be a consideration.

9. **Tell your client that you need him to get inside the minds of his customers to steer you as to what words they would enter in a search engine to find his product or service on the web.**

This will give you a starting point for creating some relevant keywords.

10. **Ask the client how many pages he thinks he needs and what each page should be called.**

This gives you the rudimentary building blocks for a navigation menu. If the client isn't very web savvy, you'll have to do a little hand holding here and offer some suggestions. You may also have to be the voice of reality and tone down your client's expectations a notch to create a user-friendly website. If the client doesn't have a clue as to how many pages the site needs, you'll have to ferret out the information and make suggestions.

11. **Ask the client for any other information he thinks will be pertinent for the design of the site.**

When the meeting starts winding to a close, you'll have a document that contains enough information to start planning the site construction.

12. **Tell the client what you expect in regard to material from him.**

Unless you're working on a website for your own company, the client or someone on his development team will be preparing the text. Tell your client that the text needs to be in layman's terms with a minimum of technical jargon. It also has to be written in a manner that the client's customers and visitors to the site will understand. If your client expresses any doubts, suggest a good writer with whom he can collaborate.

Your fact-finding mission gives you a lot of information about your client and his needs, but you need to find out more about the target audience for the site, which we discuss in the next section.

Convincing the Client

Unless you're creating the site for yourself, you have other people who will have to approve your grand design for the website. If you're working on a site for your own company, you've got a friendly audience to convince. However, if you're working for a client you've never done work for, you may have to do a selling job. Chances are you'll have to sell your idea to more than one person. In the following sections, we offer some suggestions for getting the project off on the right foot.

Selling the idea

Regardless of whether you work in a large, corporate environment or you're a freelancer/design firm, you need to sell your plan to the stakeholders. Remember that "selling" isn't unto itself a dirty word. You're not trying to get people to agree to buy something they don't need. In fact, if you do your preplanning, your project will actually help the client solve problems.

Be prepared to address the stakeholders' concerns while you point out how your plans will solve problems for them. Don't avoid discussing the negative points or other impact your project might have, such as having to design more than one site if part of the target audience accesses the Internet with mobile devices. You can gain respect and important feedback if you show that you're open to discussion and knowledgeable enough to know that the project is not all about fun and glamour.

In short, present your idea, answer their questions — and be prepared for their concerns.

Holding a kick-off meeting

Another form of selling the idea, a *kick-off* is a meeting to get all the hands-on people involved. This can include other people who will be developing the site with you, the owner of the company for which you're creating the site, the marketing gurus, and so on. The main purpose for this meeting is to explain the project, set expectations among the members of the team, and give them copies of the scope document so they can review and understand fully what is expected. Additionally, open a discussion among team members, giving them an opportunity for sharing ideas and honing the plan.

A *scope document* can be your proposal and contract all bundled into one. Or if you're doing the work for your own company, the scope document shows everyone various things about the project and should include the following:

+ The basic goal for the website. For example, the goal may be to sell more product or introduce people to a service.

+ The amount of time it will take to bring the site to fruition.

+ The stepping stones of the project, such as when you'll deliver the first mockup, when the needed materials from the client are due, when the site will be available for client review, and when the site will go live.

+ Your expectations from the client or team. Tell them when you expect delivery of material like text, images, multimedia, and so on.

+ If you're doing the site for a client, include the payment schedule.

+ List any additional fees you may have to charge the client if the project goes beyond the scope of the document.

When presenting your idea and defining the project, ask the team questions regarding feasibility and capabilities. Also, be prepared for their questions: After all, production people and IT folks need details to do their jobs correctly. Don't misinterpret their questioning as them "being difficult." Also, try to understand any issues that are raised. Sometimes, features or functionality are indeed possible yet just not practical to create or support, so you might need to suggest a compromise. For example, if the client wants a forum, but experience tells you he's not prepared to deal with the work, you can suggest an alternative such as a blog. Work with your team to come up with the best solutions.

At this point, make brainstorming ideas a part of the process. Allow everyone to give input about big-picture concepts on features and functionality. However, when the actual work begins later, respect people's expertise. For example, writers should be responsible for the written content; designers create the designs; developers work with the code. Sharing ideas is great, but a team member doing other team members' jobs is counterproductive. As a web designer and project manager, you should establish that collaboration is good, but second-guessing expertise creates friction and generally hurts the finished project. Make sure you hire the right people and then define the roles and build a good environment for teamwork.

The final task for a kick-off meeting is setting the next steps. Make sure all team members understand what they need to do after the meeting. Be clear about what you expect from each team member and give deadlines. A good way to start the project off right is to follow up by sending an e-mail the day after the kick-off meeting that includes a summary of the meeting, a list of tasks, and an outline of expectations.

Pleasing Everybody from Internal Stakeholders to the Website's Target Audience

Your initial meeting with the client will give you some pertinent information regarding the target audience for the website. However, the website you create has multiple audiences. You must consider everyone when defining your audience and goals for the site. Generally speaking, "everyone" falls into one of two categories:

+ *Internal stakeholders* are the people who work for the company that hired you to create its website — managers, public relations people, IT, marketing professionals, customer service reps, salespeople, and so on. Even if you're creating the website for your own company, you'll have a similar cast of players. All these people have needs to consider when planning and creating the site, and they must all be kept in the loop.

+ *External stakeholders* are website users, who, oddly enough, are often the most overlooked part of the equation. Getting caught up in all the other details of planning and deciding how the site will support the goals of the organization can easily take you away from considering the real needs of the external audience. Often, website visitors are referred to as a *target audience* and are described in very broad terms. Unfortunately, the discussion of a target audience is generally a short one and not very detailed. Failing to think carefully about the needs of visitors will result in a site that looks great to the site owner but probably won't be useful for site visitors.

Each set has its own needs, and in this section we discuss how to find out what those needs are so you can meet them.

Determining the needs of internal stakeholders

You want and need the support of all parties involved, and the best way to gain their support is to do a little upfront legwork. As much as possible, talk to key players and ask them what they want from the website. Doing this helps you make sure that you address their needs and concerns while you prepare to make your formal presentation. It also ensures that when you make the formal presentation of your project, you can speak to their needs and anticipate their questions. Web builders commonly make the mistake of not letting other people have input, thus wasting stakeholders' time by presenting information that doesn't help them decide how to support your project.

Your initial meeting defined the client's expectations. Now it's time to cut to brass tacks and fine-tune your original fact-finding document to flesh out the rest of the information you'll need to create the site. Get the answers to the following questions before starting your project:

✦ What results are envisioned for the site, and what functionality is needed?

✦ Does the client have an existing site? If so, does the client want this to be the basis for the site you create? Or will you be creating a site from scratch?

✦ What printed materials does the client have? The text in those printed materials may be applicable for the website.

✦ Does the client have a corporate brand, logos, and other material that defines the look-and-feel of the client's company? If so, do these need to be incorporated with the site design?

✦ Will people within the client's organization help support the site? If so, what are their roles?

✦ Who is the point person in your client's company?

If, after your initial meeting, you or your client still have some doubts about the ideal website, ask her to spend some time online to peruse existing websites. Tell her to dig deeper and look at other competitors' sites and also at sites that have similar purposes (informational, e-commerce, or whatever) to hers. Ask the client to make a list of things she likes and doesn't like about the site she visits, and make sure she records the URL so you can review the site as well. Set a time for a follow-up meeting to discuss what she finds. When you review the sites, ask her to explain what she likes or dislikes — and why. Digging deeper and analyzing these other sites will help you and your client develop a better vision of what the client needs.

Determining the needs of external stakeholders

To effectively lead a website project, you must be careful to dig a little deeper into what kinds of people make up the target audience as well as what they want; otherwise, the site will try to be everything to everybody instead of being tailor made for the target audience. Luckily, certain techniques, including creating profiles, can help you avoid the common pitfalls of designing a user-friendly site. *Profiles* (also known as *personas*) are detailed descriptions of your users as individuals. While you're developing your content and design, don't forget that the end users are individuals and may fall into a couple of different groups. Generalizing your audience makes it much harder to deliver truly helpful and engaging content. Profiles help you think about your users' needs.

Creating profiles (personas)

Here are some easy steps to help you create a profile:

1. **Start with a general target audience description and then imagine one of those people standing out in the crowd.**

   Refer to the notes from your initial meeting with the client to get a firm grasp of the general target audience.

2. **Create a detailed description of that individual.**

   You can take it one step further by giving the person a name. Attaching a photo that fit the description of the persona to the profile is another way for you to envision this person. Your description of the person includes sex, age, income, buying habits, ethnicity, and so on. In short, you need to consider every possible detail about this person.

3. **Choose several more individuals from that target audience crowd.**

   If your site will service multiple crowds, create several profiles for each crowd. For instance, if you're making a site that helps kids with homework, you need to think of a group of teachers, a group of parents, and a group of kids.

4. **Select just a few individuals to represent the group.**

   Starting with several individuals and then narrowing it down to only a few gives you more information at first, which you can focus on later. If you've really thought about your individuals, you should start to notice patterns that can help you focus on what their needs are.

With profiles in hand, develop a list of how to meet the needs of those individuals. Try to come up with specific ideas of how you will create a site to meet their needs. For example, if you're building an e-commerce site for people who are not so technologically savvy, you need a plan for how to help them use your site. You could plan to include an online tutorial and informational mini-site that explains to them the process and addresses the concerns they may have. Consider a glossary or other materials that would help your users learn about e-commerce. Doing so can help customers feel more confident about doing business with the company.

Personas will also come in handy when you start to brainstorm content for the website. When you know which types of individuals will be visiting the site, you have a good idea of what type of content you need to create for them.

Paying careful attention to your users helps you create a site that delivers what they need and expect. You should be able to develop a good idea of what works well for them. Doing this upfront work helps you decide everything from look and feel to voice and functionality. Making sure your site is what your visitors need and want will help your site be a success.

Getting information from the client's target audience

If your client or your company has an existing client base, this is an excellent resource you can use when planning your design. If your client has a business that has a brick-and-mortar presence, you can get some very useful information from the client's current customers. You may think your client knows his target audience the best, but with a bit of detective work, you can find out a lot of information. As we mention earlier, creating a persona is an excellent way to figure out exactly what your client's customers need and expect on the website you are about to design. If the client has an existing website, create an online survey on the site and ask the customers what they like about the site and what they don't like about the site. Also ask them what features they'd like to see on the new site.

If the client has an existing website, you can learn a wealth of information by examining the site statistics. Many web-hosting companies include a rudimentary method of examining the web traffic. Most web hosting services offer a control panel that gives the website owner lots of options such as setting up FTP access and e-mail accounts. One of the options is generally a detailed breakdown of where visitors come from, referring websites, and so on. Ask your client for access to the control panel so that you can analyze the statistics that tell you where the traffic is coming from, the amount of visits for every day and hour, plus the referring website.

The day and time can tell you a lot about the visitors. For example, if the majority of the visits come during the evening and on all hours of the weekend, you can safely assume the site is attracting people who have a day job. The country from which the traffic originates can also give you some scoop. Say that the client's current site gets lots of traffic from a foreign country whose first language isn't English: Such a client might want to consider offering an option to view the site in the language of the foreign country from which the traffic is coming. This is important info in that a dual-language site will up the price tag for the site. Our recommendation is that you shouldn't consider a dual-language site unless at least 35 percent of the traffic is from that country due to the cost involved in creating a dual-language site.

The *referring website* (the site from which the visitor navigated to the existing website, which in many cases is a search engine) also gives you a lot of information. If the referring sites are search engines, you know that the client's existing site has relevant keywords. You may also see that the referrals came from links at websites related to your customer's business. If the client already has a resources or links page, make sure the referring site is included when you revise the site. If the client doesn't have a resources page, and there are enough referrals from other sites, you need to include a resources page on the new site with links to these referrers.

The client's brick-and-mortar business will also tell you a lot about his target audience. You can find out about the customer's web-surfing habits by having employees ask the following:

✦ Ask the customer whether he uses websites to purchase services or product. If he answers yes, find out what types of products and services he purchases on the web.

✦ If the customer purchases services or product on the web, ask for the URLs of the sites she frequents. Ask her what she likes and dislikes about the sites.

✦ Have your client's employees tell customers a website is being designed, and ask the customers what features they'd like to see on the new site.

✦ If your client has an existing website, ask the customer if she'd consider using the company website to purchase your client's product or service. If she answers yes, find out what type of features she looks for in a website.

✦ Ask the customer if she visits websites of companies that offer the same service and product. If she does, ask her which sites she likes the best.

✦ If the client has an existing site, ask the brick-and-mortar customers whether they know of and use the site. If the customer answers no, ask the customer how she finds out about websites. If she answers that she uses a search engine, you know you'll have to beef up SEO (search engine optimization) for the new site. If she finds out by word of mouth using a social media site like Twitter or Facebook, you know you'll have to ramp up your client's involvement with online media. We discuss social media in Book VIII.

✦ If the customer does know about your client's site, ask her what she likes and dislikes about the site.

✦ If the existing site has items for sale, ask customers whether they purchase items from the site. If so, ask them which items they purchase.

✦ If the current site has items for sale, find out how customers feel about the ease of completing a transaction.

✦ Find out whether the customer can easily locate what she wants on the site.

✦ Ask customers what things they'd change about the current site.

After you or your client gather facts from your client's current customers, you'll have a wealth of information you can use to create a usable website.

You may also find out that your client needs to rethink his original goals if the information gathered isn't congruent with the site envisioned by your client.

Using personas to develop content

When you create a website for a client, part of your job is to identify the client's intended audience. After you find out who the client's intended audience is, find out as much about the audience as possible. Your client should be able to provide you with the majority of the information. Armed with this information, you can tailor the content to the intended audience. In other words, the site you design connects with viewers on a personal level: a task that's easier said than done.

Perhaps your client's goal is to connect with visitors on a *personal level,* such as a politician talking to his constituents. You need to know as much as possible about every member of the target audience. If your goal is a personal-level connection, you can create one or more personas to define your client's archetypical visitors. A *persona* is a hypothetical person whose characteristics and demographics fit your client's intended audience to a tee — and, therefore, has all the information you need to define the audience. When considering what content to use on the site, use the persona to guide you. In other words, tailor your content to the persona, and your client's intended audience will feel as if the content were written personally for them.

Depending on the scope of your client's intended audience, you might have to create multiple personas. For example, if the intended audience is young males between the ages of 24 and 35 with a college degree who live in the United States with income between $65,000 and $95,000 per year, you can get by with one persona. However, if your intended audience is male and female with varying degrees of education and from varied socioeconomic groups, you'll have to create multiple personas.

Defining your client's customers

When creating personas, you have to rely on your client to provide the information. After all, you are a web designer, not a marketing guru. If your client is not familiar with creating personas, here are a few guidelines:

✦ Create a one- or two-page description of each persona. Include information such as gender, age, marital status, ethnicity, education, profession, income, location, and so on.

✦ Include information about the habits and daily routine of each persona.

✦ Identify hobbies and pastimes of each persona.

✦ Denote the buying patterns of each persona.

✦ Determine what computer skills the persona has, as well as whether they access the Internet from a mobile device.

You'll probably end up with between three and six target personas that define your client's customers. If the number gets larger than that, you'll have a hard time tailoring content for such a diverse group. The whole idea behind personas is focusing on the type of individuals who will use your client's product or service, not the general public.

Delivering what they want

With multiple personas defined, your client can begin creating content for the site. Of course, the content that your client provides will be text and possibly images, video, and audio.

The authors will create text that's appropriate for the age, gender, and education level of the personas. Then you'll create a navigation menu and design concurrent with the likes and computer skills of the personas as defined by your client. When you have the initial design nailed, you start adding graphic elements, such as banners and images. If you're using multimedia elements, such as background music, the personas defined by your client will guide you to the proper choice.

The area in which the personas live also governs the content created for the website. For example, if the personas reside locally, you'll want to include information about your client's local events. If the personas live in all areas of the country or world, you can include information about worldwide events pertaining to the client's business or service. If your client hosts *webinars* (web-based seminars), make sure that information is prominently displayed on your client's site.

Another excellent way to figure out what content will be created for the site is to examine the websites of your client's competitors to see what they're delivering. Examine the sites with your client and whether similar content will work for his site. When you're examining the websites of similar businesses with your client, ask whether he offers something that his competitors do not. If so, this is the information you need to focus on. You may also find a specialty that your client offers that none of his competitors offer is strong enough to warrant a niche website. If your client has a bricks-and-mortar business, he'll know whether the product or service is profitable enough to warrant its own website.

To deliver what the client's customers want, examine each product and service and find out what special benefit it offers to the customer. This will be the starting point for the content your client creates and the design you create. The content needs to focus on your client's target market. The target audience for the website doesn't care how many man hours go into creating a product, whether or not your client uses the latest state-of-the art machinery to create the product; the only thing the target audience wants to tune into is radio station WIIFM (What's In It For Me). That's the type of information the site needs to deliver, and it needs to be delivered on your customer's terms.

After defining your client's target audience, ask which portion of the target audience generates the most profit and also which items or services the most-profitable clients purchase. This is additional information that you and your client can use to create content for the site. Your client will probably know the demographics of the most profitable customers. You and your client may decide that the site needs to be tailored for that portion of your client's customers. Armed with demographics, you'll know what type of navigation menu to create, what type of background music to use, and so on.

Handing Off a Project to a Client

Regardless of whether you complete the whole project on your own or with a team, you might need to hand off the project to someone else. When you're planning a project, you need to think about the ongoing maintenance of the website and either include a maintenance agreement in your proposal or outline how you'll hand off the project.

A *maintenance agreement* should outline how much it will cost to maintain the site and what services you'll provide. Clients must know that requesting large additions to the site will require a new proposal, scope document, and contract.

If you're planning to hand off the website to the client, you and the client must agree on the following:

+ **What will you hand off?** If you're turning over development materials, how much are you turning over and in what format?

  The choice of what to do with production graphics is up to you. Some designers keep their original, editable versions of their graphics. Others hand over all the files. Whichever you decide, make sure that the client understands what they're going to get and how they'll get it.

  Whatever you decide as far as the deliverable materials to the client, make sure to keep copies for your own records. Burn the files to discs, collect the site notes, and gather the electronic documents that you've used (e-mails, word-processing documents, contracts, invoices, and so on). Put all the materials together and keep them for your records. Too, sometimes clients will come back to you for follow-up work, so having everything from the first project on file and readily accessible will make the follow-up work flow much easier.

+ **How much transitional support will you give at handoff?** You might want to offer some training if the client doesn't have in-house staff with skills to maintain the site. Make sure you figure any training or transitional support work into your budget.

✦ **How will you transport the material to the client?** Best practice is to deliver the site itself to the client's web server via FTP (File Transfer Protocol). This technique is covered in Book IX. Or you might deliver the site files — and other files, too — on a CD or DVD.

Whatever you decide, make sure you get it all in writing. Make sure that all partied involved understand exactly what you are handing off to the client and in what format. This is especially important if you hire other professionals such as content writers to complete the work. When you work with a web team, all parties must agree, which avoids any potentially unpleasant situations popping up in the future.

Chapter 4: Securing a Domain Name and Web-Hosting Service

In This Chapter

✔ Researching domain names

✔ Securing a domain

✔ Defining your web-hosting requirements

✔ Securing a web host

*T*he preliminary steps for getting a web-design job up and running may seem tedious, but if you and your client get your ducks in a row at the beginning, the work will flow much smoother. As the self-help gurus are fond of saying, "Fail to plan, and you plan to fail." Truer words were never spoken.

Your initial work with the client or your team tells you what you need to know to design the site as well as what content your client or team needs to provide. After the web pages are built, you need a home for them. And then you need a way for the client's potential customers to find the site — and that's where a domain name and URL come in to play. The domain name, of course, is synonymous with the URL. When you pick a domain name such as myfabuolousdomain.com, it becomes a URL: www.myfabulousdomain.com.

In this chapter, we show you how to choose, purchase, and register a domain name for the site, and also how to find a web-hosting service that has all the features needed for the site to run smoothly.

Understanding Domain Name Best Practices

A domain name, like a phone number, is how potential visitors find you — the site you work so hard to bring to reality. Unlike a phone number, though, you do have to purchase a domain name and register it. Domain names have been many things: funny, quirky, long, short, and sometimes just plain weird. Logically, though, the domain name you pick should be the same as your customer's business or service. However, sometimes the logical domain name has already been taken. Or perhaps the name of the business is long enough to induce carpal tunnel syndrome when typed into the address bar of a web browser. Regardless, sometimes you have to choose (and register) a different name other than your first pick.

In a perfect world, all traffic to your client's site would be generated organically through a search engine. However, some visitors come to your site the old-fashioned way by typing the site URL into a browser address bar. That's why you need a domain name that's reasonably short and clear. With simplicity and clarity in mind as a domain name goal, here are some common-sense things to consider when choosing a domain name:

✦ **Keep it simple.** If the business or service for which the website is being designed has a complex name, you don't have to use all of it.

✦ **Abbreviate long business names.** You can truncate a long business name.

✦ **Use hyphens.** If you must use a long domain name with multiple words, separate each word with a hyphen.

✦ **Register misspelled variants.** If the domain name contains a commonly misspelled word, register the misspelled variant of the domain name.

✦ **Purchase a top-level domain extension.** You're likely familiar with top-level domains. For example, `.com` has always been associated with businesses, `.org` has been associated with organizations, and `.net` has been used by a variety of organizations. For a business, your best choice is always `.com` (if available), with `.net` ranking a close second. Use the new `.mobi` extension if your site is strictly for mobile devices. If you're creating a website for a personal project, the obvious answer is the `.me` extension. For flag wavers or to identify your site as one associated with the good old USA, consider purchasing the `.us` extension for your domain name as well.

✦ **Register the name with more than one popular domain type.** When a website starts gaining popularity, the domain name becomes a valuable entity. And you don't want someone cashing in on your success or popularity by registering a name like yours only under a different domain. Say that you are "EggzHead.com." You don't want someone glomming on to your (or your client's) coattails by registering the same domain name as a `.net` or `.info` domain, like EggzHead.net or EggzHead.info.

Registering a domain isn't expensive, so play it safe and cover your bases with registering on multiple domains. And because registering a domain is relatively inexpensive, your client can either park the different domains, or you can use code to redirect the other domains to the client's main (`.com`, most likely) website. When you park a domain, you buy the name, but don't put any content on it. The domain name is protected and reserved for whatever you or your client may want to do with it in the future.

✦ **Choose a domain name that's easy to remember.** If the website domain name doesn't need to include the name of the business or service, brainstorm to come up with a short domain name that can be easily remembered by people who visit the site.

✦ **Choose a keyword-rich domain name.** Your client may want a unique domain name that's consistent with his brand. However, getting traffic is a prime concern with most site owners. Therefore, choosing a domain name that has keywords associated with the business or service presented on the website is an excellent way to generate traffic. For example, if you're in the photography business, including *images, photos,* or *photography* as part of the domain name will vault you closer to the top of the search engine rankings. Use the DomainName online tool to check for available domain names based on the keyword you enter:

    www.domaintools.com/buy/domain-suggestions

✦ **Check for similar domain names.** If you and/or your client fall in love with a domain name that's similar to another domain name, do some research to make sure that the similar domain name is not copyrighted.

Researching and Registering a Domain Name

Now that you know the best practices regarding domain names — practices that are subject to rapid and frequent change as the Internet evolves — it's time to choose a domain name.

Researching the availability of the domain name you want

First things first: As we mention earlier, you need to research whether the domain name that you or your client is absolutely head over heels in love with is taken.

Step 1 is to type the name in a web browser to see whether you get a hit. Don't assume that not getting a hit online is a guarantee that the domain isn't taken, though, because people do purchase domain names and never do anything with them. For example, if a company already has a .com website, they might also purchase the .biz, .net, and .info extensions to protect their brand name and never use (park) the domains.

So, Step 2 — the next way to find out whether the domain is taken — is to go to the website of a company that sells domain names. There, you can typically find a page or section that you can use to determine whether the domain name you want is available. For example, run a search at *domain registrar* (a company that charges you a fee to register the domain of your dreams) GoDaddy (www.godaddy.com) (see Figure 4-1).

Figure 4-1:
Researching a domain name.

You can also use other websites to aid in your search for whether your "perfect domain name" is already taken or free. You can find sites that give you more information about a domain name than a standard registrar. One such site is Domain Tools (www.domaintools.com). The site offers many services, including finding out which domain names are expiring on a specific date, and which domains are for sale (see Figure 4-2). Some of these services are free, and others require you to become a member. The three types of accounts available are Novice (free), Standard ($29.95 per month), and Professional ($49.95 per month). A 15-day free trial is also available.

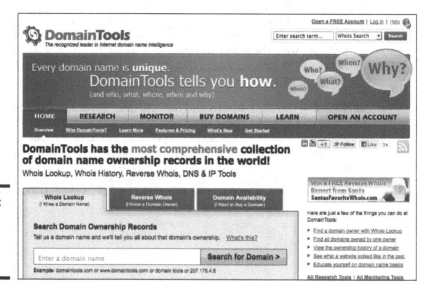

Figure 4-2:
Research domain names online.

If the domain name you want isn't available, consider registering a derivative of the name, or choosing a different domain extension as mentioned earlier in this chapter. Some registrars offer the option to backorder a domain, but if you need the site up yesterday, that's not an option. If the domain name you're after is popular and it's already been taken, the domain name may be up for auction. When you research a domain at a registrar like GoDaddy. com, you'll see alternatives if the domain you want is already registered.

Registering your domain name

When you're certain that the coast is clear and the name you want is indeed available, it's time to register it. When you register a domain name, make sure you register it for at least three years. You can sign up for as little as one year, or go up to ten years. Committing for three years, though, gives your site more prominence with the search engines and also establishes you as a serious player. And most domain registration services offer a discount when you register a domain name for multiple years.

You will find web-hosting services that offer free domain registration. However, you may encounter difficulty down the road if you ever decide to move the site to a different host because the domain may be locked to the web hosting company you contracted with. Check the fine print on your contract with any web-hosting service providing free domain name registration to make sure that it's not impossible to transfer the domain to another server, or whether the service would charge an exorbitant fee to release the domain.

Choosing a Web-Hosting Service

After you choose a domain name and register it, the next step is to find a web-hosting service. These services have computers known as servers that are connected to the Internet. The servers store the HTML documents, images, and other attributes associated with websites. In a perfect world, the servers are up and running 24/7, and visitors can access sites on them quickly. You'll find lots of web-hosting companies competing for their fair share of the market. As with many businesses, the companies vying for your business will have varying degrees of competency and different services and features to offer.

In the following sections, we show you how to assess your hosting needs and how to find the hosting service that's right for your needs.

Determining web-hosting needs

When you create a site — perhaps for a client — you obviously include what is needed: We're talking nuts and bolts, bells and whistles here. So, it only makes sense that when the site going live is a reality, or close to a reality, you and your client need to find a web-hosting service that supports all the functionality you designed into the site.

You can find web-hosting services by doing an online search. There are also sites that rate hosting services, but we take those with a couple of grains of salt due to the fact that some of these sites also sell advertisements, often to the services they rate. However there are still a few rating services that you can trust. One that looks promising to us is `http://webhostinggeeks.com`.

Sometimes the best way to find a good web-hosting service is by word of mouth. If you find a popular website that loads fast, contact the web designer or webmaster and ask her for the name of the hosting service and ask if she's pleased with them. Doug uses a hosting service called HostGator and has had good success with that.

Ask yourself these questions to help you choose what features your potential web-hosting service needs to support your site. Remember to balance hosting service support with cost.

✦ **Will the site have a blog?** If your site has a blog, the web-hosting service needs the latest version of PHP to support the blog code.

The hosting service also needs the latest version of mySQL. The reason we suggest the latest version is for security. Unfortunately, nefarious people in this world think a website is fair game if they can hack it. A web-hosting service with the latest versions of server-side software is obviously better equipped to thwart hack attacks. Also be sure that the server has the ability to quickly and easily upgrade your server to newer versions of protective software when it is released. When you're considering a hosting service, ask them if they can update their servers when new editions of PHP and mySQL are issued.

✦ **Will products or services be sold from the site?** If so, you'll need your web-hosting service to use a secure server. Some sites do use a shared secure server, which is great if the site will use something like PayPal to collect funds.

Side note: We like PayPal because it gives you the option to create a custom payment page. And with that in hand, you can include a logo. If the logo isn't stored on a secure server, or a shared secure server, the visitor will receive a warning that part of the content isn't stored on a secure server. We cover how to install PayPal functionality to a website in Book VIII, Chapter 3.

✦ **Will your pages have any server-side code?** If you create pages that use server-side code — such as Java, ColdFusion Markup Language, PHP, and so on — make sure the service has the software to support the code you create.

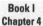

✦ **How much bandwidth do you anticipate using?** If the site features movies and other multimedia content, you need to determine the anticipated bandwidth you'll be using per month. In the beginning, this is just a guesstimation. As a baseline, try to determine the file size of each page of the site, and then estimate how many times the page will be viewed per month. Alternatively, you can search the Internet for a bandwidth calculator. You can find a bandwidth calculator at this URL: `www.ibeast.com/content/tools/band-calc.asp`.

When you do this calculation, anticipate the best-case scenario for the number of visitors per month and then add a fudge factor of 20 percent for growth.

Be sure to check out the fine print on the hosting plan to make sure you or your client isn't charged an exorbitant fee if the usage does exceed the allocated bandwidth.

✦ **How much file storage is needed?** If you have a small website, uploading files to the server obviously won't take up much space. But if you're creating a large website that uses lots of graphics and other multimedia (such as video files), that's probably a different story, so make sure that the hosting plan you choose supports the amount of space that the website files will be using.

Choosing the right web host for your site

After you determine your site needs from the server, it's time to choose a web-hosting service. Like any industry, you'll encounter varying degrees of competency and customer service, so take the time to some research upfront before you commit.

Getting answers to the following questions will help you settle on a dependable and trustworthy service:

✦ **Does the web-hosting service offer a shared server or a dedicated server?** When a host offers a shared server, other client websites share the server with your site. Comparatively, a dedicated server hosts your site on one server dedicated to your site. As you can imagine, a dedicated server is more expensive than a shared server. For example, hosting your site at HostGator can be purchased for as little as $3.95 per month, while a dedicated server with HostGator starts at $139 per month. A pitfall to opting to use a shared server can be poor performance if another site (or several sites) on the shared server gets a lot of traffic. And if you do choose a hosting service with a shared server, check first whether you have the option to have the site moved to another server if you have an issue with performance.

✦ **Does the web hosting service guarantee percentage of uptime?** Many web hosting services advertise that their servers are up a certain percentage of time. Industry standard is around 97 percent.

✦ **How long has the web-hosting service been in business?** Startup companies can have teething problems and may experience technical difficulties. Fairly young companies can also experience cash-flow issues, especially in today's turbulent economy. If a company has been around for a couple of years, chances are that they've got their act together.

✦ **Has there been a recent change in ownership?** Big companies buy small companies. And although change can be good, if the new owners don't have a track record in the industry and none of the old management staff has been retained, this could be a recipe for disaster.

✦ **Do the web-hosting services you're considering have redundancy in case of computer problems?** Most web-hosting services have redundancy in the form of a chain of backup computers on their server in case of a problem. Another important fact to know is whether the service has set up redundant power circuits to the server and a generator, and also how often they check the redundant circuits and generators.

✦ **What is the web-hosting service's backup protocol?** A good web-hosting company will back up its servers on a regular basis. When you're shopping for candidates, find out how often the company backs up its servers. Then, find out how easy (or not) it would prove to get your site restored in the event something goes wrong (which in the worst-case scenario would be a hacker destroying the site). Most services back up their sites once a week.

✦ **Does the web-hosting service allow you to make your own backup?** Even though your web-hosting service backs up their computers on a regular basis, there may be a fee to restore your site should disaster strike. However, many web-hosting services let you create your own backup through the control panel. This gives you the power to create a backup whenever you want, and store it on your own computer.

✦ **Does the web-hosting service have the latest version of server software?** Like all other software, server software is upgraded on a regular basis to support new features, thwart the latest hacking techniques, and so on. Make sure the companies that you're considering have the latest version of the software they use on their server. The service will tell you what version they're using, or you can find it in the site specs. Then you can go online to see if it's the latest version of the software. For example, you can find out the latest version of PHP software (which is currently PHP 5.4.0) by visiting php.net.

✦ **How easy is it to get technical support?** A good web-hosting service will provide a toll-free number that gives you access to 24/7 tech support. Having said that, a toll-free number is fairly useless if you have to wait more than a few minutes to reach a competent specialist.

✦ **How knowledgeable is technical support?** There's nothing more frustrating than being connected to a technical support representative that has no real knowledge and is searching through a database in an attempt to find the answer to your problem. A good web-hosting service will have a system administrator available at all times to solve difficult problems.

✦ **What do people who have used the web-hosting service say about it?** Find out what current and past customers have to say about the web-hosting service. The easiest way to do this is to ask for the URLs of the service's current and past customers. Go to the websites and contact the webmaster and ask for her level of satisfaction. She can also tell you how competent their support staff is.

✦ **Is the web-hosting service flexible?** In this economy, it's never wise to purchase more than you anticipate you'll need. However, you should find the hosting plan that best suits what you anticipate will be the future needs of the site. Make sure you have the option to quickly and easily upgrade or downgrade in the future without having to pay a service fee to change plans. For example, you may not need a blog now, but if you think your site might need one in the future, make sure the web-hosting service you choose can support a blog, and make sure you can easily change to another plan that supports future needs.

✦ **How quickly does tech support solve a problem?** This information may be difficult to acquire when you're looking for a web-hosting service. However, current customers can tell you how competent tech support is and how quickly they solve a problem. When you're looking for a web-hosting service, ask the sales staff for the URLs of sites that currently use their service. Contact a couple of webmasters and ask them for their assessment of the support staff. Another ploy you can try is calling tech support before you choose a service. If you're on hold for a long time, this gives you a clue that they may not have a large customer service staff, or they have lots of customers that are experiencing problems with the service.

✦ **Does the web-hosting service offer e-mail?** Most services do offer e-mail, and you want this functionality. If you are looking at a service that doesn't offer e-mail, disregard it. When you set up a commercial website, you want an e-mail address that's associated with a domain. Visitors and customers feel more confident communicating with bob@*mydomain*.com instead of bob6874@yahoo.com.

Bonus: You can use the hosting service e-mail functionality to make a company appear bigger than it is by setting up several e-mail addresses, such as custservice@*mydomain*.com, info@*mydomain*.com, sales@*mydomain*.com, and so on.

Book II

Designing the Site

The 5th Wave — By Rich Tennant

"Evidently he died of natural causes following a marathon session animating everything on his personal website. And no, Morganstern — the irony isn't lost on me."

Contents at a Glance

Chapter 1: Wireframing and Storyboarding Content

In This Chapter

✔ Learning the art of planning a website

✔ Harnessing the magic of the 960 grid

✔ Designing good-looking pages

✔ Planning user-friendly navigation

*W*hen you plan a site, what do you do first? Do you storyboard the site, which involves creating rough drawings of how the key pages will look? Or do you draw a sitemap that charts the navigation structure of the site?

It's kind of a chicken-and-egg thing. You can't really design pages without having some idea of what links will be in the menu bar at the top of those pages (or some alternate navigation approach). And, you can only get so far in drawing up a navigation structure without knowing how many key pages the site will have or working through what content will be on which page.

We return to the role of wireframes, sitemaps, and storyboarding shortly, and the terms are used differently in different contexts. But here are quick, working definitions to get started:

✦ *Wireframes* are rough sketches of how pages will look, including navigation elements.

✦ *Sitemaps* are flowcharts that demonstrate how pages link to each other.

✦ *Storyboarding* is a less-defined term, taken as it is from the realm of cartooning. But in general, in relation to web design, storyboarding refers to sketching out (in one form or another) key pages in a site, showing how they fit together.

Again, those definitions aren't set in stone. And the process of conceptualizing and planning a site varies depending on the nature of it. A website dedicated to presenting a new movie might just be one page. In that case, planning involves intense design work on that page, and no work in charting navigation to other pages. On the other hand, designing a newspaper website might require only rough wireframes (or sketches) of how different pages will look, but the planning process might focus more on how all those pages and sections of the site will be tied together with navigation.

You can wireframe first, or you can create a flowchart first. In this chapter, we start with wireframing individual pages before focusing on site navigation. But the reality is that as you conceptualize a site, you envision how pages should look and how those pages will interact with each other as a visitor navigates through the site.

Planning a Website

The process of building a website can be described, from concept to implementation, one step at a time. The first step in website building is to conceptualize that website — a process that includes developing a vision for it in terms of the content that should be there, how that content will be presented visually, and how the website will function overall.

The next step in the process is to organize content, design elements, make sure your content will work in a website (for example, images and video have to be in web-friendly formats), and consider your audience in an actual plan for a site. There are different dimensions to this.

As you need to pull together your site's content — text, images, media, and other elements — you need to factor in your audience. Is your intended audience composed of people who speak different languages? If so, you need a plan to translate the site content into the languages your visitors speak. Is your audience a demographic that relies on mobile devices to engage with the web? If so, creating mobile-friendly content needs to be part of your plan.

With your audience in mind, you need to make sure that content you have prepared is web-friendly and web-ready. We walk through the process of preparing and organizing content in Chapter 2 in this minibook.

But here and now, we'll walk you through the pivotal transition between concept and plan, something often referred to as *storyboarding*. That is a term that originated with cartoonists who sketched out how movies would unfold, with the details filled in by armies of animators.

Wireframes, designs, site maps, and flowcharts

As noted, storyboarding generally refers to the process of drawing rough sketches and diagramming navigation between those pages. The combination of rough sketches of pages (often referred to as *wireframes*) and navigation flowcharts (often referred to as *site maps*) lays the basis for building a site that looks the way it's supposed to look and works the way it's supposed to work.

Website *architecture* refers to planning how all the elements of a website — content, *usability* (presenting content in a way that works on the web), *technical planning* (figuring out how the site is going to be built), and *aesthetics* (such as page design, artwork, color schemes, fonts, and other design elements) — will fit together. If you think about website architecture as an analogy to what an architect does in designing a building, a *wireframe* of a web page is similar to a blueprint, and a set of wireframes is analogous to a set of blueprints that sketch how a whole building will look.

Wireframes are *rough* sketches of how a page will look, meaning they usually do not include developed artwork, typography, and colors. Sometimes wireframes are created using Photoshop, Illustrator, or Fireworks. (See Book V, Chapter 3 for an example of mocking up a page in Fireworks.) Whereas wireframes usually demonstrate links to and from pages, *flowcharts* or *site maps* focus on a graphical depiction of a site's navigation arteries.

**Book II
Chapter 1**

**Wireframing and
Storyboarding
Content**

Figure 1-1 shows a *wireframe,* a rough sketch of a single web page. As you see, it has placeholder Ipsum Lorem text (generated Latin text which we grabbed at `http://lorem-ipsum.perbang.dk`). And it has a navigation bar, which indicates the basic navigation flow from the home page, below the logo. This wireframe can be pasted on a wall with other page wireframes to get a feel for how the different pages in the site will look linked to each other and come across to a user as a whole.

And, individual wireframes can be turned over to an artist, who will translate the rough sketch into a full-blown artistic design. For example, the space that has been blocked out for an ad in Figure 1-1 is 324 x 648 pixels (px). Those dimensions will allow a designer to create a web ad that looks good at that size.

In the preceding example, in addition for specs for the ad size, the wireframe might come with notes, indicating that the dashed lines are for location purposes only, that the concept is a 60/40 split between the left and right sides of the page, and that the logo area should be 72 px high.

In the next step in this page's journey, a designer replaces placeholder text with real text, placeholder images with real images, placeholder graphics with real graphics, and so on — pretty much providing a detailed model for the final web page.

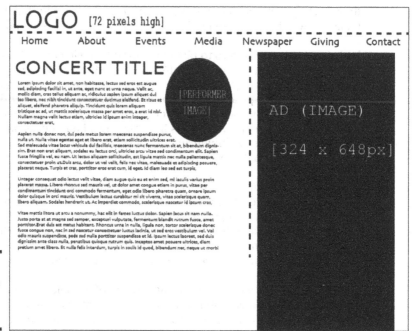

Figure 1-1:
A wireframe of a web page.

Along the way, a designer will make some changes to how content is sketched out in a wireframe. Real life never quite fits blueprints. Content will be longer or shorter than anticipated. Often, when a wireframe is translated into a design, things that seemed like they might work aesthetically in the wireframe end up turn-offs when implemented.

Of course, if your website is a one-person project, you can fill the role of sketching wireframes (and flowcharts) and designing more precisely how pages will actually look.

Figure 1-2 shows what the wireframe in Figure 1-1 might end up looking like after a designer creates a real ad and logo, fills in some real text, and plays around with a possible color scheme.

As we explore in Book I, the arbitrator(s) of how a site is supposed to look might be a client, a collaborative team, or just you. In any of these scenarios, your wireframes and navigation flowchart together serve as the blueprint for your site.

Will you, along the way, make changes to that plan? Of course. But good basic sketches and a basic navigation chart can be the difference between a website plan that meanders forever and one that comes together more or less as envisioned, on schedule, and on budget.

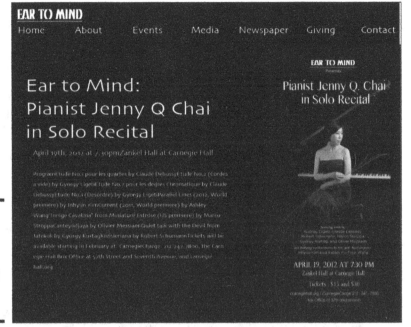

**Book II
Chapter 1**

Wireframing and
Storyboarding
Content

Figure 1-2:
A page
design
based on,
but evolved
from, a
wireframe.

Planning for accessibility

Flash videos don't play on iPads. Sites that rely on huge image files that take a long time to download aren't very effective for people with slow Internet connections. Websites with red text on a green background are the hardest for colorblind people to read.

These and other issues can interfere with how people engage with your website. There are a lot of accessibility challenges, and nobody can memorize or anticipate them all. So, a good rule is that when you organize content or design elements for a site, search to see what accessibility issues might be associated with that content, design approach, or technology.

Throughout this book, we point out potential pitfalls along the way and suggest solutions that make your site as functional as possible in any browsing environment.

Understanding the Constraints of Web Page Design

This chapter focuses on a few basic principles in page design common to most effective sites. Before diving into those suggestions, however, it will be helpful to identify and come to grips with the constraints involved in designing a website. The most fundamental of those is that you can't fix where objects will appear on a viewer's screen. We'll pause while you throw this book against the wall, and wait for you to pick it up and find your place.

Now that you've calmed down, we'll help articulate your outrage: What is the point of designing a web page if you can't define where objects will appear on a viewer's screen? The point is, you *can* define where things appear onscreen, but you can do so only *relative* to the viewer's viewing environment. Even though we all live in a web-centric world, our conceptions of design tend to be framed by print design, where a billboard is always the same size, a newspaper ad is always the same size, and a magazine cover is the same size no matter who is viewing it, or where they are reading the magazine.

However, people see a website's pages in different *viewports* — that is, different-sized screens. And so you have to design pages that will appear in mobile phones and maybe even projected onto wall-sized displays. Figure 1-3 shows a web page viewed on a large screen monitor. Figure 1-4 shows that same site viewed on an iPhone, but with a different design that works better on a small mobile screen.

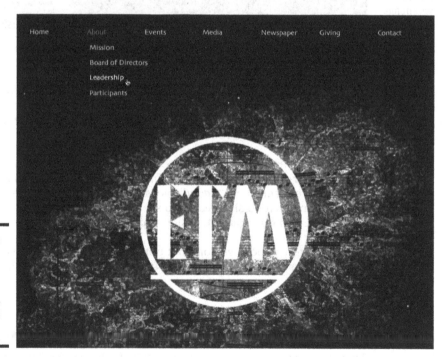

Figure 1-3:
A page designed for, and viewed on, a full-sized monitor,

Figure 1-4:
The same site, but with a design optimized for mobile viewing.

Another constraint of website design is that unlike print designs, where the viewing area of any design is fixed, web users can (and do) zoom in or out as they interact with a web page, changing the size of text and images. And, by the way, different browsing environments handle zoom differently — some enlarge images as text is enlarged, and other times enlarging text doesn't affect other page elements.

Here are three basic techniques for carving out the maximum control over how pages look in different environments:

✦ **Start page design with a container that will hold all your page content.** In the next section, we explore why web designers have standardized on making those containers 960 px wide, and how and why this "960 grid" creates significant freedom for web design.

✦ **Design flexibly.** Account for the fact that viewers will stretch and distort your designs. If you design with flexibility — for example, taking into account that text will expand as a user zooms in on your page — you can create page designs that bend but don't break when they're viewed in different environments.

✦ **Create unique page design or content for full-sized and mobile sites.** That's what we did in the examples illustrated in Figures 1-3 and 1-4. We explore that approach in depth in Chapter 5 of this minibook, and come at it from another angle in Book VI, Chapters 3 and 4, when we look at implementations of *jQuery Mobile,* which is a library of JavaScript that is very easy to use to create mobile web pages.

Harnessing the Power of the 960 Grid

One useful angle from which to carve into the challenge of designing web pages it to start with why web pages are 960 px wide.

But are they? No, not all of them. But there are powerful compelling reasons why web designers are gravitating toward making pages a standard width of 960 px: function and form.

First of all, a very, very wide range of viewports can display a 960 px page. How can both a full-sized monitor and an iPhone display a 960 px page? That question has a two-part answer:

✦ A 960 px page won't fill the entire width of a full-sized monitor — but that's a good thing. A web page that fills the entire width of a large-screen monitor would be too hard to digest. Lines of text would be too long to read. Page content would be too stretched out for visitors to absorb as a unified whole.

✦ Mobile devices have more pixels per inch than full-sized monitors. So even Androids, iPhones, and other small devices can display 960 px pages.

The other attraction of using a 960 grid is that "960" is easily divisible. That means you can break down (divide) your page in manageable chunks — columns — to help plot your design. For example, say you base a design on a three-column approach, each 320 px wide. Figure 1-5 shows just such design: a 960 grid divided into three same-width columns, using Adobe Illustrator as a design tool. In this illustration, a header (in white) fills the top of the screen, and the three columns are placed below the header.

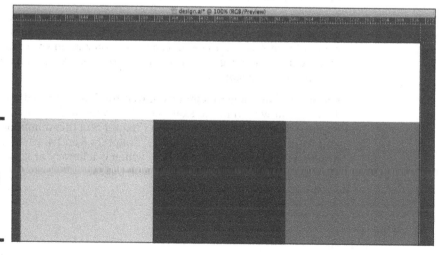

Figure 1-5: Designing with a 960 grid divided into three columns in Illustrator.

Or, a 960 grid can be easily split into eight columns (120 px wide) or 16 columns (60 px wide). Figure 1-6 shows a 960 grid divided into 16 columns. This real estate breakdown makes it easy for a designer (which might be you!) to create appropriately sized artwork for ads, banners, and other content.

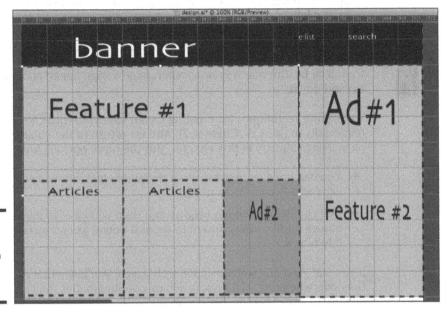

Book II
Chapter 1

Wireframing and
Storyboarding
Content

Figure 1-6:
A 960 grid
divided into
16, 60 px
columns.

In fact, if technical issues were the only issue, web designers could have standardized web page sizes a bit larger than 960 px, and the containers would still fit in mobile devices. Most viewports, including mobile, claim to be at least 1024 px wide — but the value of using 960 lies in the ability to use the "divisibility" of that number in workflow.

The essential point is that designers — using programs like Adobe Illustrator, Adobe Photoshop, or even a sheet of graph paper — can create as many as 16 evenly sized columns (60 px). And, by creating their design on top of that 16-column grid, they then turn the artwork over to a web designer who translates the page to HTML and CSS using a 960 px-wide container, and multiple columns that match those in the original artwork.

Designing pages in columns

Because similar page designs (such as a three-column design) hold different amounts of content, though, you have to plan for where the extra content will go if it doesn't fit within the column.

The simple answer: Down. The point: Scrolling *vertically* (up and down) instead of *horizontally* (sideways) in web pages is much more intuitive and functional. On the negative: Scrolling back and forth, and back and forth, and back and forth (you're getting the point) with a horizontal scroll bar really breaks the flow when people are trying to read a page. In other words, people can much more easily scroll up and down than they can scroll to the right and left.

Although rows (horizontal sets of content) play a role in web page design, columns define page design. A 960 grid page can be as long or short as you want it to be. But one way or another, page design has to allow content to expand down.

We explore techniques for creating layout elements with CSS in Book IV, (especially in Book IV, Chapter 2). And we return to the column approach to page design shortly in this chapter. But the basic options are these:

✦ You can have columns without defined height, allowing content to expand down as far as necessary.

✦ You can define column heights, but then you have to invoke other techniques for allowing content to expand down, like scrollable or collapsible boxes.

If you survey many well-designed web pages, you'll see that not only are they overwhelmingly laid out in 960 px containers, but they're all essentially laid out in either two or three columns.

Really? When you survey a lot of well-designed sites, they won't *appear* to be laid out in two or three columns. They'll look like they're laid out in 5 columns, or 8, or 11. But if you hold a ruler or a sheet of paper up to the screen, you'll see that underlying all the columns in a page is a more basic design.

Take a look at the IMDb (Independent Movie DataBase) page, in Figure 1-7. At first glance, it might appear that this page is laid out in five or even eight columns (if you count the three columns in the lower right). But if you trace a line about three-quarters of the page from the left edge, you can see that underlying the five visible columns (in most of the page) is a more basic two-column structure. That basic two-column division is illustrated in Figure 1-8.

The takeaway is this: When you design pages, it's easy to split columns — to divide them into two, three, four, five, and more columns. However, as we explore in detail in Book IV, Chapter 2, it is technically easy to split page layout elements, but technically difficult to allow content to span across two defined columns. So the rule for technical reasons, is that columns in web design are easy to split but hard to merge.

Figure 1-7:
At first
glance, this
website
appears
to be laid
out in more
than two
columns.

Three
additional
columns

Five columns

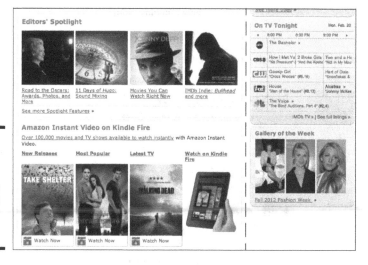

Figure 1-8:
The
underlying
structure is
just divided
into two
columns.

So when it comes time for you to translate a design into a web page, we
recommend that you first divide the page into either two or three columns,
and then further subdivide those columns as needed. For example, Figure
1-9 shows *The New York Times* site, which looks like it's divided into five columns. But when you zoom out and take a look at the page in Figure 1-10, you
can see how underneath those five columns are actually two columns, each
of which is further subdivided into other columns at times. Or, as in the case

of the prominent ad in the right-hand column, content can expand to fill an entire column.

Figure 1-9: This site appears to be laid out in five columns.

Five columns, right?

The masthead is a single-column element.

Figure 1-10: This site is really laid out in two columns.

Just two columns.

There's an exception to the rule here: The main elements of the page are in a two-column layout, but the header (with the *Times* masthead) and the footer (not visible in the screenshots) are single-column elements that stretch across the entire 960 px-wide container that frames the page.

Does this two or three column rule apply only to online newspapers? No. Figure 1-11 shows that Facebook's site is divided into two columns, and YouTube is laid out in three columns. Note that the middle column of YouTube is at times divided in half, into two columns. As you explore the web and identify sites you appreciate, take time to deconstruct how they are structured around either two or three columns.

Two columns

Figure 1-11:
Many sites
use two
or three
columns
as the
foundation
of the site's
look.

Three columns

How a 960 grid puts the pieces together

Whether you sketch pages on paper, or design them in Illustrator, or use another technology, starting with a 960 grid can be the constraint that frames and unleashes creativity. Here's what that means and how it works.

If you design pages in Illustrator (or, if you're more comfortable with Photoshop or other software), you'll find all kinds of 960 grid templates available for download. The 960 Grid System website (www.960.gs) is a one-stop resource for all kinds of 960 pixel grids.

Or, if you prefer to sketch pages on paper, including in a collaborative environment, use graph paper.

You can see how this works by walking through a typical workflow for a website design in an environment with a division of labor between designers, artists, and coders. This scenario is more complex than the one you might be in the middle of, but stick with us for a moment. There's a "bigger point" involved. With that proviso, here's how the workflow for the design of a large scale commercial site might look:

✦ Wireframes (and navigation structures) are sketched out by those charged with conceptualizing the site. Those wireframes are created within a 960 grid.

✦ Designers working in programs like Adobe Illustrator create more developed and detailed page designs. They "flesh out" the wireframes, adding color, fonts, and artwork. They work from wireframes developed and based on the 960 grid, which makes the transition from wireframe to design much more seamless, less stressful, and more coherent.

✦ Photo-editing experts prepare photos for the web using programs like Photoshop. They scale those photos using dimensions framed by a 960 grid. So, for example, if they are creating a "half-page wide" photo, they know that photo should be cropped and resized to about 480 pixels in width. A one-third page photo? 320 pixels wide. And so on.

✦ Graphic designers create artwork and page elements — banners, navigation icons, and logos — using Photoshop, Illustrator, Adobe Fireworks, and other tools. And again, they work within dimensions defined by the 960 grid. A page *banner* — artwork at the top of a page — will typically be designed to be 960 pixels wide. A drop-down menu under the banner might have the same width.

Now, you might well be working with a much less developed division of labor, but here's the important point: Even if you're a one-person team, sketching navigation, designing pages, creating artwork, and putting the pages together with HTML (the markup language for web pages) and CSS (the design language), you still benefit from working within a 960 grid. Everything in this chapter applies with just as much importance in a one-person project. After all, the pieces of a web page — the text, page design, and artwork — still have to fit together.

Designing Globally Unified or Asymmetrical Pages That Look Good

Web design theory, and the larger body of graphic design, is a complex and evolving art. Even a compressed exploration of design theory is quite a bit beyond the scope of what we can offer here. But what we can do is identify a few related — and sometimes contradictory — rules of well-designed sites:

✦ Well-designed sites have a unified global design and maintain continuity in design from page to page.

✦ Well-designed sites use asymmetric (unbalanced, uneven, and somewhat unpredictable) layouts to make content inviting and to lead visitors to explore content.

These two "rules" are somewhat in contradiction to each other. There has to be enough continuity in style and design from page to page for visitors to feel like they're experiencing a unified site. Yet, there has to be enough disequilibrium, unevenness, and distinctness so that visitors don't get bored.

Book II
Chapter 1

Wireframing and Storyboarding Content

Creating a unified global design

In a global design, pages are designed so that visitors to a site feel they are navigating within a unified site, not a bunch of disarticulated, uncoordinated pages. Navigation elements and other global site content help visitors engage with a unified look and feel, and easily find their way around.

This global orientation applies in page design, as well as in common elements (such as header content, footer content, and navigation structures) that appear on all or most pages in a site.

A unified design structure might include these elements:

✦ A page design element that defines the page size width at 960 pixels

We explain how to create these elements in Book IV, Chapter 2.

✦ Header (often with navigation)

✦ Content area

✦ Sidebars

✦ Footer

Figure 1-12 shows all five of these elements in a web page design.

Applying unevenness to page design

In a *symmetric* page, the left and right side of the page are more or less equal in width and prominence. *Asymmetric* page design means designing pages that are unevenly structured. For example, a basic page concept that splits a page into a left side that is two-thirds of the page and a right side that is one-third of the page is asymmetric.

Recommended reading

For an exploration into conceptual approaches to laying out pages, check out Khoi Vinh's book *Ordering Disorder.* Khoi Vinh's work includes a significant role in the design of *The New York Times* website. *Ordering Disorder* avoids any discussion of the technical design tools and methods that we cover in this book, so it can provide a complementary look at the even larger picture of website design. For further discussion, articles, and advice, go to Khoi Vinh's website at www.subtraction.com.

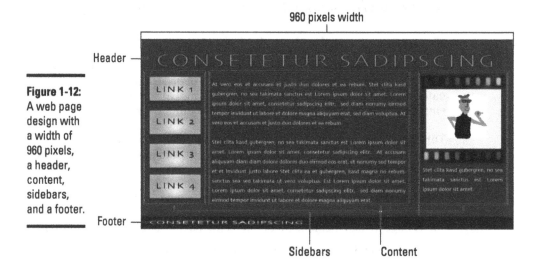

Figure 1-12: A web page design with a width of 960 pixels, a header, content, sidebars, and a footer.

While rules are meant to be broken and all that, as a general rule, a page split of two-thirds/one-third is more inviting, interesting, dynamic, and engaging than one that's split half and half (50/50) or into even thirds. For example, look at Figure 1-13. The sketch on top has three columns of about equal width; the one on bottom is more uneven. Again, spend a bit of time examining web pages you like. Note how the vast majority of them are divided unevenly.

The principle of asymmetry, or unevenness, can be applied on different levels. It can be applied within columns: say, splitting a column into different width sub-columns. It can be applied vertically — so that not all rows are the same height relative to each other.

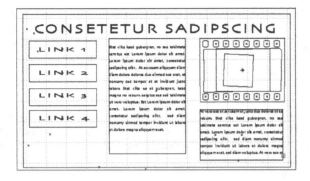

Figure 1-13:
Unevenness
can add
interest.

Developing a Navigation Structure

Alongside page design, a navigation structure is key to planning a website. A navigation structure involves a bit higher level of abstraction than just sketching pages. A navigation flowchart (or sitemap) organizes how you are going to guide visitors through your material.

Did we say "guide" visitors? Yes, we did. You don't want to place hurdles in front of visitors looking for something at your site. You're building your site for a reason (or set of reasons). You have ideas on what material is top priority for visitors to engage with, and what is not. Your navigation flow will reflect those priorities, with the material you want most accessible available from a first line of menu options, with other material accessible through sub-menus or maybe just through links within pages.

In other words, although you want to take your visitors' inclinations into account, you want to provide links to content you want to steer visitors to. For example, if you're selling a product, you want convenient, prominent, even (sometimes) pushy links to the shopping cart at your site.

One good way to conceptualize a navigation structure is to create an out-line. You can do this with a professional outlining program like OmniGraffle (www.omnigroup.com/omnigraffle). You can do it in a word processor. Or, you can grab some scratch paper and sketch an outline of how your site navigation will look.

Figure 1-14 shows a three-level navigation system. The top outline levels (or at least, the top level under the Home page) will be visible when a visi-tor comes to the site and are the key things you want to encourage a visitor to go to. Other menu items (the second level) become visible when a main menu item is hovered over or selected. And sub-submenus provide another level of navigation.

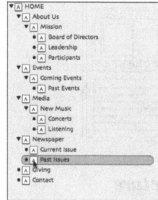

Figure 1-14:
An outline of a navigation system in OmniGraffle.

Creating a graphical flowchart illustrating your navigation structure is often helpful. Such a flowchart is often referred to as a *site map*.

OmniGraffle has both an outline and flowchart view. You can show or hide the outline sidebar. With the outline sidebar active, you can enter flowchart titles, and demote them by pressing Tab (or promote them by pressing Shift+Tab).

Graphical site maps/flowcharts help designers step back, visualize a users's experience with the site, and adjust the navigation flow as appropriate. Figure 1-15 shows a flowchart corresponding to the navigation outline in the previous figure.

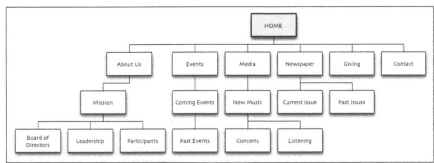

Figure 1-15:
Creating a navigation flowchart in OmniGraffle.

Based on a sketched-out concept for navigation, you (or a designer you work with) can design pages that implement that navigation structure, like the artwork in Figure 1-16.

Figure 1-16:
A page design with a navigation bar.

Chapter 2: Preparing Content

In This Chapter

✔ Preparing text, images, and media

✔ Building your website as part of your web presence

✔ Integrating online resources

✔ Understanding the role of content management systems (CMS)

Content is the essence of a website. If you don't have anything interesting to share with the world, what's the point? On the other hand, if that content is uninviting, or even worse, inaccessible, nobody is going to engage with it.

In this chapter, we walk through preparing content for the web so that when it comes time to pop that content — text, images, video, and so on — into your web pages, that content will *work* on the web. Meaning, the content will open in browsers without creating hurdles that will send people away from your site.

We share a number of tricks of the trade here. Some of those tricks — or better said, *techniques* — are available through different online resources that help you convert content into web-ready formatting.

Another dimension to making your website work is figuring out how your own site can be a point around which people connect with your larger web presence, even beyond your website. For example, you might embed videos that are actually hosted at YouTube or Vimeo (another YouTube-like video hosting site) in your web pages. Or, you might copy and paste a mission statement you have at LinkedIn and recycle that content into your own site.

Getting Text Ready

As much as multimedia has been woven into the web, using text is still the most common way to convey a message. Here are some obvious yet very helpful ways in which text is your friend, both from a design standpoint and for site visitors. Even if your site content revolves around images or video, you are well served to have a text component if you want your content to reach the broadest possible audience, as shown in this list:

✦ **Text can be copied and pasted.** More on that in a bit.

✦ **Text is, well, helpful.**

   • *Advertising an event* can be easily added to a visitor's mobile device calendar.

   • *Providing a location* can be easily used to look up directions with an online map.

✦ **Text can be read in any environment.** It doesn't require earphones to listen to in a cubicle, a café, or a living room; it doesn't require a fast Internet connection to download; it doesn't even require that a user has image display turned on in her browsing environment.

✦ **Text indexes efficiently in search engines.** Online visitors can use search engines like Google and Bing, making text content the best way to connect with people searching for topics online.

✦ **Text offers better accessibility for impaired visitors.** Vision-impaired visitors to your site can use reader software to read text content out loud. (And this aid can help people with different levels of vision impairment, not just those who cannot see at all.) And any hearing-impaired people who might miss out on any audio tracks in your video can read text.

The medium is the message. Or is it?

In the 1960s, communication theorist Marshall McLuhan became famous for his declaration that "the medium is the message." This insight has some value and truth in the sense that evolving media do not just convey a message. The nature of the media conveying a message affects the nature of a message. Live television coverage of the Vietnam War, or the civil rights movement in the United States in the 1960s, for example, had an impact greater than if people just read about those events in a newspaper or heard about them via radio.

That said (and regardless of whether, and to what degree, McLuhan was purposely being a bit of an intellectual provocateur), it's not literally the case that any medium, including a website, is in and of itself "the message"! Just try putting up a website with a nice color scheme and well-laid-out pages but no content — and then see how much impact it has. Okay, maybe the World Wide Web ecosystem would support a couple sites like that as novelties, but overall, the point is: The most important thing about your website is its content.

But this leads us back to the critical importance of accessibility and aesthetic appeal. To put it crudely, if your site is slow, buggy, or ugly, the most important message in the world is going to have a hard time finding an audience.

✦ **All browsing environments support text.** Even an ancient computer, with an out-of-date browser, connected to the Internet with the slowest imaginable connection, will open a page of text quickly.

✦ **Text can be formatted almost infinitely.** Text can be large or small, and even have a whole range of effects applied to it. (For a full exploration of exciting new text formatting available with the latest version of cascading style sheets [CSS], see Book IV, Chapter 3.)

In short, from big page banners to tiny legal disclaimers in footers, from articles to bullet lists, text is the simplest, most flexible, most reliable way to present content online.

Sources for Text

Building on what we mention earlier (that text can be copied and pasted), chances are that the text you want to use in your website already exists. Maybe in a print brochure. Maybe you posted a fundraising pitch at Kickstarter that can be ported into your own website as a mission statement? Maybe you can grab some paragraphs from an e-mail you composed to a client describing what you do. And, very likely, you have material you can use in a word-processing document.

We should note that you might simply not have the text you need ready to go for your website, or that the text you have is not in a copy-and-paste format. In the first scenario, we suggest that you compose text in a word processor and not in an HTML editor. (We explore creating and editing HTML documents in detail in Book III.)

Even if you have text prepared, don't overlook built-in spell checking and other editing tools available in a word processor like Microsoft Word, Google Docs, or Apple's iPages. Or, pony up and hire an editor.

If the text you have is not in a copy-and-paste format — that is, if you have large amounts of text available only in hard copy sources — you can try using a scanner with optical character recognition software to convert scanned images to text.

You have basically two options for moving text from a word processor into an HTML file — which is to say, into a web page:

✦ Save word-processing documents to HTML format, and edit them with an HTML editor

✦ Copy and paste text from a word processor into an HTML editor

Both of these approaches work, but they have distinct advantages and disadvantages.

Saving word-processor documents as HTML files

Nearly every word-processing program can save a document as an HTML file. Here's how for the big guns:

+ **Microsoft Word:** Choose File⇨Save as Web Page
+ **Google Docs:** Choose File⇨Download As⇨HTML Format
+ **iWork:** Choose File⇨Export⇨HTML Export Options

You'll find similar options in other word-processing programs and many spreadsheet and other apps as well.

In many cases, saving or exporting a document to HTML is a good option because it's fast. Within minutes, you can export a document as a web-ready HTML page, retaining much if not all of its formatting.

The downside is that the HTML generated by your word processor applies formatting that don't always mesh smoothly with the standard page design techniques that use external CSS (style sheet) files to apply sitewide styles and design to your pages. We walk through the role of external CSS in Book IV.

That said, the meshing issues are solvable. When you open a document in an HTML editor, you'll see the HTML code generated by the word processor. And you can touch up or edit that code to make the pages mesh better with a global style sheet. The exploration of HTML in Book III and CSS in Book IV will guide you through that process.

Copying and pasting document content into HTML pages

The other option for moving document text into an HTML page is to copy and paste it into an HTML-editing environment. And if you're going to be moving a lot of text content from word processing documents into web pages, consider an investment in Adobe Dreamweaver.

If you're working with large amounts of text, the only really practical, efficient environment where this method works is if you have access to Adobe Dreamweaver or other professional-level HTML editing tools. On the other hand, for smaller amounts of text, some free online tools convert Word documents to HTML. TextFixer.com (`www.textfixer.com`) has free online resources that allow you to copy and paste document text into a box and then churn out HTML. However, free online tools like those available at TextFixer.com maintain only the most basic formatting (such as line and paragraph breaks) when converting text to HTML.

In Chapter 4 of this minibook, we walk you through how to define and build a site in Dreamweaver. But one of the valuable features in Dreamweaver is that it provides a substantial set of options for maintaining (or stripping) formatting from any text that you copy and paste into a web page.

Dreamweaver doesn't provide a specific feature to import word-processing files per se. But it does have a set of options for how text (which can be copied from any program or website) is pasted into the Design window. Figure 2-1 shows those options.

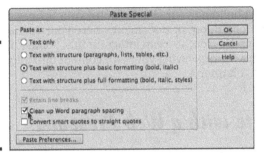

Figure 2-1:
Pasting text into a page in Dreamweaver.

Getting Images and Media Ready

Web images are very different than print images or even images saved on computers or local media (like discs or flash drives). Organizing, creating, and preparing photos, illustrations, and other artwork for the web is an art and science that we explore in Book V, Chapter 3, which specifically covers optimizing images and other artwork. But here we note a few key differences between web and print images:

✦ Web images are usually presented at a lower resolution, 72 *pixels* (dots that make up a screen) per inch, as opposed to 300 dots per inch in a typical print publication.

✦ Web images generally have to be in PNG, JPEG, or GIF formats, whereas print images are often saved as TIFF or EPS (or other vector graphic format) files that are not supported in browsers.

✦ Web images use the RGB color mode that creates colors by combining red, green, and blue backlit pixels (or dots), whereas print images use CMYK color mode that produces a more limited set of colors by combining cyan, magenta, yellow, and black ink.

Again, this list points only to key differences between print and web images, and we walk through these issues in-depth and show you how to convert print images to web-ready graphics in Book V, Chapter 3.

And this is the case for video and audio as well. Video and audio have to be prepared for the web, taking into account what formats are supported in different environments, and the challenges of compressing audio and video into files small enough to download into a visitor's viewing environment in a reasonable length of time. In Book V, Chapter 4, we walk through how to create and present media in your website.

In the early stages of building your site, organize your images and media into folders on your computer, or document where your media is available online. And then, step by step, you can integrate that content into your site. We discuss strategies for organizing your site content into folders on your computer in Book II, Chapter 4.

Comparing a Website with a Web Presence

In organizing and preparing content for your website, think about the difference between your web*site* and your web *presence.* Your web*site* is something you create yourself. You design it. You choose the content. You find a host for it.

That said, your website is probably not going to be the only online presence for you, your organization, product, cause, or company. Your website will likely exist in a larger milieu that constitutes your web presence, and that larger milieu might well include videos at YouTube, a photo gallery at Flickr, social networking at LinkedIn or Facebook, or a blog at WordPress.

In thinking about how your website fits into this big picture, keep in mind that you have qualitatively more control over how people connect with you, your content, and your project when they're at your website.

In your own website, content isn't framed with context-sensitive ads for products that are selected and delivered via Facebook or YouTube. Information gleaned from searches people perform on your website doesn't get marketed by Google (unless you sign up for a Google search tool that turns that information over to them — see Book VII, Chapter 3 for an in-depth exploration of search box options for your site). And, in your own website, your color scheme isn't selected from a handful of themes you share with 9 million other people.

Plus, your own website allows you to put together a whole, unified presentation of your product or message — all in one place.

Here are a few examples of how people or organizations handle the relationship between an online presence, across all kinds of venues, and their own website. Musician Miley Cyrus promotes her videos on YouTube, as shown in Figure 2-2. And that YouTube web presence includes YouTube-provided content, including suggestions that viewers check out videos by other artists. On the other hand, Miley Cyrus's own site features only her content, as shown in Figure 2-3.

Figure 2-2:
Some musicians promote their music online for a web presence.

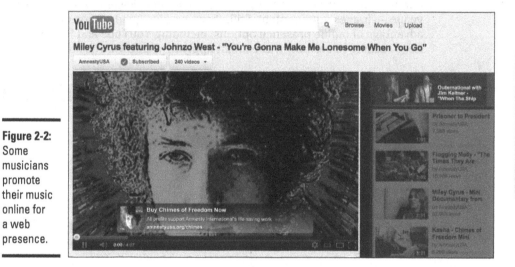

Figure 2-3:
Miley Cyrus's own site promotes material of her own choosing.

Others use Facebook for a web presence, like the Oakland Raiders football team, as shown in Figure 2-4. That presence takes advantage of features the Raiders might feel they need, like being able to have and connect with Facebook friends. At the same time, being on Facebook presents ads that aren't defined by the Raiders, and forces the Raiders to work within a format that includes preset features (like "Friend Activity") that might not necessarily work well with what the Raiders are trying to project.

The Raiders' own website, on the other hand, presents their own content, and they have complete control over what is on that page and what is not. Check it out in Figure 2-5.

You can see where we're going: There are major advantages to building a website of your own, where you — not YouTube, Facebook, or another venue — frames your content. Still, there are also good reasons to take advantage of online presence options, including YouTube and Facebook. Keep reading to see how these might apply to your own website.

Figure 2-4: Some opt for a Facebook web presence.

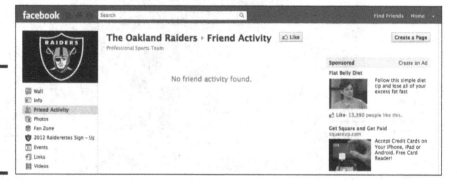

Figure 2-5: The Raiders' own site is defined by their own content and style.

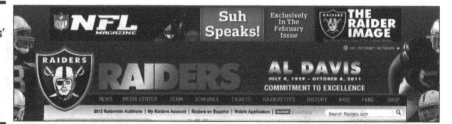

Your web presence beyond your site

Take an example of something that almost nobody is going to create on their own: an e-commerce element for a website. That e-commerce functionality would have to validate and process credit cards, calculate sales taxes and global shipping rates, and maybe even keep track of inventory levels. Creating e-commerce functionality like this requires professional-level programming skills in complex programming languages, as well as — in many cases — access to databases for calculating taxes, shipping, and more. Ugh.

Not a problem, though. Just because you can't build it doesn't mean that you can't use it! By all means, integrate outside content with your own website. Starting with the simplest, here are three basic ways:

✦ **Create links from your site to other elements of your web presence.**
Here are some examples:

  • *eBay:* Click here to buy my sweaters. Let eBay worry about validating and processing clients' credit cards or PayPal accounts.

  • *YouTube:* Click here to watch my new video. Let YouTube worry about streaming your video into a wide range of browsing environments that all require different video file formats.

  • *Blogger:* Click here to read my blog. Let the programming team at Google set up your blog and create and maintain tools that allow you to read and approve (or reject) comments people post at your blog.

  You can choose design themes from sites like these to "match" them, to various degrees, with your site. And, of course, you can include links from those venues to your site.

✦ **Embed content from other sites in your site using different HTML techniques.**

  In Book VII, we talk about the powerful iFrame tag that displays content from other sites within your site.

  If you're building a medium-range website — one with all the features of the most professionally designed sites, but you're hampered by limited resources — this "borrowing" option is often your best bet. See Book VII, where we walk you through how to embed a blog, a search box, a weather update feature, and RSS feeds.

✦ **Hire programmers to develop all the content you need within your own site.**

  We're talking PHP coders and database experts to manage your mail list and search box; video compression experts to present streaming video; PHP coders (again) to set up an on-site blog; and so on. Be prepared to shell out many tens of thousands of dollars. Maybe you're lucky enough to have a whiz-kid programmer for a child or a geeky friend who can do high-level coding for your site.

If you're a little light on funds or resources, using some combination of the first two options might serve you well.

Don't reinvent the wheel

Here's the larger point: Don't build what you don't have to build. If someone has already created a good resource for sharing video online, consider how you can integrate that into your overall web presence before you sign up for

Book II
Chapter 2

Preparing Content

a six-month course in creating video for the web. The same logic applies to including a blog or any e-commerce elements.

If you try to develop a concept and plan for your site, and also collect material with the expectation that everything you need will be created from scratch at your own site, you're going to dig yourself a deep hole from which you might emerge frustrated and without making a lot of progress.

Instead, as you plan your website, think about things you can outsource, so to speak, to other online resources (such as video hosting, e-commerce, and blogging).

And then, assess your capacity to integrate these elements into your website. You might start with more links to external resources (the "Click here to read my blog" approach), and later embed that content into your own site as your website-building skills and resources increase.

Integrating Online Resources

By linking to or integrating online resources, you can deliver content to your site visitors that might normally not be within reach.

Here's how that fits into the process of preparing content for your website: Much of the content you want to include in your website might already exist online, in places like LinkedIn, YouTube, or Blogger. And you can quickly and easily make that content available to visitors of your website by linking to your pages at those sites.

Earlier in this chapter, we emphasize the downside of linkages with sites like Facebook and YouTube — namely, that you can't control the other content on such social networking sites. So the challenge is: How do you take maximum advantage of content hosted at other sites while keeping as much control as possible over how that content gets framed and presented through your own site?

In Book VII, Chapter 3, we show you how to push the envelope in terms of embedding powerful features available from different online resources into your own site and making that content look and feel like it's part of your site. But even in the beginning stages of planning your site and organizing content, you can factor in the possibility of embedding elements into your site that are actually hosted or managed outside it. Here are some examples:

+ **Mail list management systems:** You can integrate tools like MailChimp to build a database of people interested in your product or project, and then to generate nicely designed e-newsletters targeted to their interests.

✦ **Blogs:** You can set up a blog at Blogger and embed that blog into your own website so visitors feel like they're reading the blog at your site.

✦ **Search boxes:** You can define and make available professional-level search tools from Google or FreeFind and embed them as search boxes in your site.

✦ **Video hosting:** YouTube and Vimeo allow you to post videos to their sites and then embed those videos in your own web pages with the HTML they provide you with.

✦ **e-Commerce:** The best way to have "your own site" with e-commerce is to build your site and then plug in an e-commerce solution with links to it from your other site content and links to your other site content from your e-commerce site.

It's not just small operations that farm out these kinds of website elements. Take that venerable institution the Smithsonian, for example; Figure 2-6 shows what happens if you follow a link from the Smithsonian site to its store. You're actually directed to a different URL (www.smithsonian store.com) that serves as the site's e-commerce portal.

Book II
Chapter 2

Preparing Content

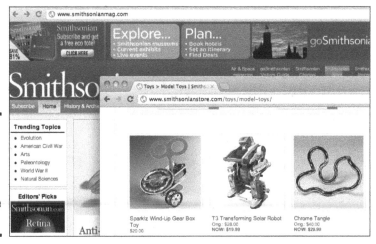

Figure 2-6: Use a different URL to host an e-commerce component.

In short, when you plan and organize content for your website, keep in mind that your content will be of two types: Some of your site content will be text, images, and media that you will create and store in folders on your computer and use to build your website. Other content (such as a blog or video) will reside at remote sites or will be generated using online tools (such as a search box or an e-newsletter sign-up form).

Seeing the role of content management systems

One option for building a website is to use a content management system (CMS). Some of the more popular of these are Drupal (`http://drupal.org`), Joomla! (`http://www.joomla.org`), and WordPress (`http://wordpress.org`).

In general, CMS sites tend to be quick and easy to set up but hard to customize if you want page layouts that deviate from available predesigned layouts and themes (combinations of fonts, color schemes, and page design elements).

If you elect to build your site with a CMS, you'll find it overwhelmingly the case that the challenges and techniques we explore throughout this book apply to creating a CMS site.

Chapter 3: Defining a Color Scheme

In This Chapter

✔ Choosing colors

✔ Discovering the basics of using color on the web

✔ Creating and using a color scheme

*E*very website has a color scheme. Now, we didn't say that every website has a consciously defined color scheme. But consciously or not, every site does have a color scheme. That *color scheme* — the set of colors used in the pages for images, text, links, background colors, and artwork — is critical to how inviting and accessible the site is.

The color scheme applied to a website is part of the message that site conveys: An edgy gray and black color scheme might be perfect for a trendy clothing designer's portfolio, but it wouldn't be so welcoming when applied to a site marketing children's toys.

You should make an informed and conscious decision on the colors used in your website, but you must also consider technical issues (how color works on the web, hexadecimal values, and so on) and how to generate and apply a color scheme. We cover all these points in this chapter.

Finding Colors for a Color Scheme

Before we get into finding colors for a color scheme, we must first cover the most basic rule of color schemes, which is that you have to work with a constrained, small number of colors. Otherwise, your site will simply present a messy cacophony of color. (Yes, a crazy-quilt approach is also a form of a color scheme, but as a general rule is not very effective.) How many colors can you have in your color scheme? Not too many, but just enough:

✦ **Web color schemes typically have five colors.** Five is enough colors to cover a range of site content like background color, text color, link colors, and artwork.

✦ **Neutral colors — white, black, and gray, which are all *shades* — don't count as one of your five colors.** You can use those colors to make your color scheme pop more. For example, if you have a color scheme based on shades of orange, you could use black, white, and the grays for text and other content, letting the shades of orange really glow.

With that basic rule in mind, the next step to creating a web color scheme is to get inspired. Sometimes color schemes seem kind of obvious. The Minnesota Golden Gophers website? Maroon and gold. The Florida Orange Juice growers? If you need help figuring that out, check them out at www. floridajuice.com. On a more serious note, the National Breast Cancer Foundation site color scheme is built around shades of pink, invoking the color used to raise awareness of breast cancer.

So, in some cases at least some elements of a color scheme are almost self-evident. In other cases, that's not the case. What would the natural color scheme be for a website dedicated to humor? Or fencing?

Here are some techniques for deriving color schemes:

✦ **Pull colors from artwork.** If a product, organization, team, or band has a logo or basic artwork associated with it, the colors in that artwork can be the basis for a color scheme. Look for color guidelines from corporate branding documents or colors in logos.

✦ **Use an existing color scheme.** This tact might seem obvious, but it might be the case that the group, school, company, or cause for which you're designing a site for already has a color scheme. In which case, you can use that as a base from which to derive your web color scheme.

✦ **Get inspiration from one of the many sites that provide both technical and aesthetic advice on creating color schemes.** Adobe's Kuler site is the most powerful of these sites, but there are others as well. We show you how to use Kuler and other online color resources a bit later in this chapter. (See the section "Generating and Applying a Web Color Scheme.")

Understanding Web Color Basics

Before jumping to the fun part — picking colors — mull over some technical issues involved in defining colors for the web.

You need a basic understanding of how computers generate color, how colors are defined on the web, and also how to appreciate and address the real challenge of using color while factoring in accessibility concerns. For example, some color schemes make text (such as red text on a green background) unreadable to people who are colorblind. Or, low-contrast color schemes (such as medium gray text on a dark gray background) are hard to read in bright outdoor lighting on mobile devices.

Print color versus web color

In print, colors are created with colored ink. Of course, no print shop can keep in stock all the thousands of colors that can be reproduced in print. Instead, colors are created in print by mixing cyan (a color close to turquoise), magenta (a bright purple), yellow, and black (CMYK). On the web, though, colors are generated by mixing red, green, and blue pixels (RGB involved). The hexadecimal system defines 16 million colors.

Book II Chapter 3

Defining a Color Scheme

Because web colors are generated by mixing red, green, and blue, the code for defining color essentially defines how much red, how much green, and how much blue.

The most widely applied and reliable way of conveying that information is a set of hexadecimal values notation. The "hex" in hexadecimal comes from the number six. Hexadecimal values are six digits and use the first two digits to convey the red value, the second two digits to convey the green value, and the third two digits to convey the blue value.

Hexadecimal values convert RGB values into six-digit codes. In the RGB color mode, the highest possible value attached to a color is 255, and the lowest is 0. So, for example, solid red is defined in RGB as 255, 0, 0 (maximum red, and no green or blue). However, because the hexadecimal system allots only two digits for a value, not three, letters are used to supplement numbers in translating RGB color values to hexadecimals.

When defined in HTML code or CSS style sheets, hexadecimal color values are preceded by a hash tag (#). Some basic colors have easy-to-remember or intuitive hexadecimal values. Black is #000000 (no red, no green, and no blue). Green is #00FF00 (no red, maximum green [FF is the hexadecimal equivalent of 255 on the RGB scale], and no blue).

Veteran designers might store a set of frequently used color values in their heads, but even for them, there is no really intuitive way of remembering the strings of letters and numbers that define how much red, how much green, and how much blue go into any particular color. So, designers use charts found in books, online resources, or graphic design programs (Dreamweaver, Photoshop, Illustrator) to blend colors and then copy the hexadecimal value that corresponds to the value selected.

Figure 3-1 shows a web color being defined in Photoshop. The values in the boxes at the end of the R (red), B (blue), and G (green) sliders define the hexadecimal value for the color. In this case that value is #F90404.

Figure 3-1:
Generating a
hexadecimal
value in
Photoshop.

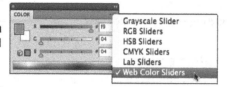

One basic technique for saving a set of colors is to simply copy and paste the hexadecimal values for those colors into a word processor or write them down on scratch paper.

After you have a hexadecimal value for a color, you can use that value preceded by a hash symbol (#F90404) to define the color in HTML or CSS. Or you can copy it into the CSS Rule Definition dialog box, which defines CSS styles in Dreamweaver CS6. Figure 3-2 shows the hexadecimal value generated in Photoshop being applied to create a red page background in Dreamweaver.

Figure 3-2:
Using a
hexadecimal
value in
Dream-
weaver to
define a
color.

We walk through how to define and apply colors in Dreamweaver in Book IV when we explore cascading style sheets. But here we're just "borrowing" Dreamweaver to provide an example of how hexadecimal values derived from a program like Photoshop get applied in a web page.

But here's a quick look at the CSS for applying this shade of red:

```
background-color: #F90404
```

Here are other ways of naming colors:

✦ **Three-digit hex value:** Designers have developed three-digit versions of hexadecimal values although for some reason, as of this writing, the term *tridecimal values* hasn't picked up much traction. The theory behind this technique is it reduces the amount of code in a page, and speeds up download. We're not convinced the world has saved a lot of time because of that, but you'll see three-digit color values used in web design. For example, #FFF is white (maximum red, maximum green, and maximum blue), and #F00 is red (maximum red, no green, no blue).

✦ **Plain color name:** You can also use just plain names for colors, like red, blue, green, aqua, beige. Named colors aren't used widely by designers because support for them is less reliable than hexadecimal values and because those colors that do interpret named colors have limited lists of such colors. But they are awfully easy to remember. For example, the HTML code to define a bit of text as red can be written as

Book II
Chapter 3

```
<font color="red">this text is red</font>
```

✦ **CSS:** A newly emerging method for defining online color is to code color using RGB values. Using that technique, the same red we defined earlier with a hexadecimal value could be applied to a background color with this CSS:

```
background-color: rgb(240,4,40)
```

Again, we cover defining colors in Book IV, but the preceding code is easier to interpret (by humans) because it displays values for red (a big number), green (hardly any), and blue (a little more, but not much).

An advantage of using RGB color values is that in environments with full support for CSS3 (the emerging standard for style sheets), you can add an "A" (for alpha) value that defines opacity: RGBA. An "A" value of 1 defines a completely opaque color, and an "A" value of 0 (zero) means a lack of color — the color is completely transparent. And you don't have to use only 1 or 0; you can use percentages between the extremes.

The following CSS3 defines a background color with the same red we've been using, but at 50 percent opacity.

```
background-color: rgba(240,4,40,0.5)
```

RGBA color isn't supported in older browsers like Internet Explorer versions 6–8. Where it's not supported, browsers ignore the opacity value and display the color without any opacity modification — just the defined color "full strength" with no transparency.

Colors and accessibility

Here are two major accessibility issues associated with using color on websites:

✦ **Color-blind or visually impaired people can have trouble distinguishing a link from regular text and other color-dependent content.** In addition to color coding, use a secondary method of emphasizing information. For example, group content by using positioning, headings, and other visual cues (icons) to separate content. Underlined links, for example, aren't dependent upon whether a user can distinguish colors.

✦ **Outdoor web use on mobile devices requires high-contrast color schemes.** Make sure that the colors you choose have enough contrast so that people can read the text. We're surprised by how many sites sport gray backgrounds with gray text. They might look cool, but for anyone in bright sunlight, text on a page like that is hard to read.

Generating and Applying a Web Color Scheme

Many very useful resources for generating color schemes are available online. These resources allow you to define color schemes based on a color, an image, or even a mood. We'll focus on Adobe Kuler (`kuler.adobe.com`). Adobe Kuler (pronounced **cool-er,** as in, "I'm cooler than you are") is among the top online web design resources. It's free as we go to press, although you have to register with Adobe to use all the features.

And ColorSchemer (a free version available for online use only is at `www.colorschemer.com`) has a clean, intuitive toolset for generating colors based on a starter color, as shown in Figure 3-3.

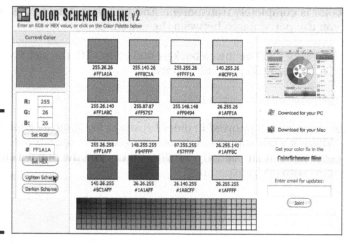

Figure 3-3: Generating a color scheme based on red in Color Schemer.

When you go to Kuler online, you can begin to define a color scheme by entering a color name, a color value, or a word into the search box. In Figure 3-4, we entered "winter" into the search box, and are presented with a variety of winter-themed color schemes.

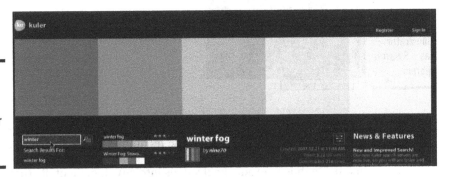

Figure 3-4: Generating winter-based color themes in Kuler.

Clicking the Make Changes to This Theme and View Color Values button in Kuler (as shown in Figure 3-5) displays the values of the colors in your generated color scheme.

Figure 3-5: Accessing color scheme values at Kuler.

After Kuler displays the hexadecimal values for the colors in your color scheme, you can simply copy and paste those values into a text file (using your word processor or text editor) and then copy and paste them into a CSS — something we explore in detail in Book IV.

If you're working entirely within the Adobe Creative Suite system, you can generate an ASE (Adobe Swatch Exchange) file. These ASE files can be loaded into the Swatches panel in Illustrator and other CS6 applications (although not Dreamweaver) and used to create artwork. Figure 3-6 shows a Kuler-generated color scheme imported into the Illustrator CS6 Swatches panel. You can navigate to and display a saved ASE file with Illustrator's Swatch Libraries menu.

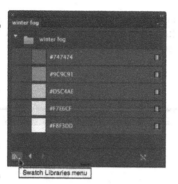

Figure 3-6:
A Kuler
color
scheme
imported
into
Illustrator
as a Swatch
library.

Again, and to be clear, you don't need any Adobe products to grab a color scheme from Kuler. The most basic technique for capturing hexadecimal values generated by Kuler (or any other color scheme tool) is to copy and paste those hexadecimal values into any document file (using Word, Notepad, TextEdit, or anything else) and then save them. Or even, as we have been known to do, scribble them on a scratch pad with a pen and later type them into an HTML file or CSS.

After you define a color scheme, don't lose your set of hexadecimal values! Hang on to them. In Book IV, we spend much time defining and applying hexadecimal values to colors for everything from hovered visited links to page backgrounds. And the hexadecimal values you save from your defined color scheme come into play as you assign colors to different elements of your page design.

Chapter 4: Organizing a Site in Dreamweaver CS6

In This Chapter

✔ Discovering why Dreamweaver sites are important

✔ Organizing site content

✔ Creating a remote server connection

✔ Managing site files

✔ Uploading (and downloading) content

✔ Editing and moving Dreamweaver sites

*W*eb pages appear to the visitor as a single object. But appearances, in this case, are quite deceptive. In reality, behind the scenes, almost every web page is a complex network of many linked files. Orchestrating, coordinating, and ensuring the integrity of links between those files is essential to a functional website. Managing that challenge is the task of the Dreamweaver site.

Take a typical web page. It's likely to be built within an HTML file, but within that HTML are likely embedded images (separate image files). Modern, professional websites rely on external CSS (style sheet) files, so the design and layout of the page will depend on linked style sheets (that control how the page looks). Almost certainly there will be links to other pages. Even more complex pages — like the ones you'll learn to build in the course of this book — include links to JavaScript files (for animation and interactivity), media files (like embedded video), and links to scripts (like PHP) that manage form data.

Seeing the Critical Role of a Dreamweaver Site

Before launching into how you define a Dreamweaver site, zoom out and look bigger-picture on the role that Dreamweaver plays in website creation.

Many people perceive Dreamweaver to be a tool for generating HTML, which is the basic markup language of web pages. Correct! Dreamweaver is indeed the premiere tool for designing websites without coding, and generating HTML (and other page markup language).

And Dreamweaver CS6 includes powerful tools for generating CSS, including the latest version — CSS3 — allowing you to create style sheets without coding. In Book IV, we discuss how to define styles for text, images, and other elements, as well as how to build complex page layouts with CSS.

Even beyond that, Dreamweaver CS6 provides substantial tools for generating JavaScript for animation and interactivity and (as a very significant subset of those tools) jQuery Mobile elements that provide mobile-friendly animation and interactivity. Book VI covers those features. Finally Dreamweaver CS6 even creates basic *server-side* scripts, which are scripts that run on your server and manage sitewide content "served" into pages from a centralized source, a feature we'll examine in Book VII.

First things first, though, and that is the most essential dimension of Dreamweaver in the process of web design is file management in a defined site. Without that, none of these other features work properly!

Defining a Dreamweaver site

A Dreamweaver "site" is a proprietary feature of Dreamweaver. The Dreamweaver Manage Sites dialog box provides tools for creating new Dreamweaver sites and editing Dreamweaver site definitions. After you define a Dreamweaver site, you use it to organize files, keep links between files from getting corrupted, and manage the transfer of files back and forth between a local computer and a remote website. As such, a Dreamweaver "site" can be thought of as a way to manage a website, but don't confuse this with "creating a website." Because a single modern web page can easily involve dozens of files (embedded images and video, linked pages, external style sheets, external scripts, and more), it is essential that the first thing you do when you work on a project in Dreamweaver is to define and work within a Dreamweaver site.

Managing files with Dreamweaver sites

Without careful file management, images on your pages will appear as blank boxes, your videos won't play, your links will lead to error messages, and your creative design and compelling content will all go to waste.

File management is one of the most important things that Dreamweaver does for you. Here's why: You create a website (in Dreamweaver, but this applies more generally) on your own computer. You make the site available to the world by uploading it to a server. That *server* is a powerful computer that stores your site content and makes it available to anyone who visits your website. And one of the things Dreamweaver does is manage the transfer of files from your computer to your remote hosting server, making sure each file gets safely from your computer to the server.

So, before diving into the how-tos of defining and working within a Dreamweaver site, take a minute to see why it's so critical that all your work in Dreamweaver be done within a defined site.

Throughout this book, we'll be referencing and occasionally returning to the importance of working within a Dreamweaver site. But for the most part, after you define a Dreamweaver site, that defined site does its thing invisibly, in the background, making sure that linked and embedded files stay linked and embedded.

We'll walk through the steps involved in defining and working in a Dreamweaver site shortly. But before we do, here's a quick look at some of the work that a Dreamweaver site does, humming along on the background as you define and design web pages.

Book II
Chapter 4

Dreamweaver sites do the following:

Organizing a Site in
Dreamweaver CS6

+ **Manage files.** Dreamweaver sites update links within pages when you rename or move a file, thus preventing embedded images, video, or links from becoming corrupted.

+ **Manage links.** Typically, every page you create in Dreamweaver (and beyond that, any web page in general) involves as many as dozens of *links* — clickable elements (such as text or images) that, when clicked, open other pages within and outside your site. As long as you create and work within a Dreamweaver site, all those links are created automatically.

+ **Upload your site.** When it comes time to upload the site you build on your own computer to a remote server accessible to the world, your Dreamweaver site will manage all the file transfer issues.

+ **Move your site.** If you want to move your local site (the one on your own computer) to another computer, Dreamweaver's site tools make that process smooth and painless.

+ **Manage file transfer.** Dreamweaver sites do the work of FTP (File Transfer Protocol) programs for moving files between your computer and your remote (online) site. So, using third-party FTP programs, like FileZilla, aren't necessary if you're using Dreamweaver.

+ **And more.** Dreamweaver sites enable sitewide tools like spell checking, search-and-replace, collaboration within teams of designers (to make sure two people don't edit the same file at the same time), and error checking.

The integrity of linkages within your site (and between your site and other sites) is ensured if — but only if — you rely on Dreamweaver's site tools. Or you can manually manage these linkages, but that would be a painful and tedious process.

Organizing Content for Your Site

Here we explore the process of organizing all your site content into a single folder, and then within that, subfolders as needed. That process lays the basis for defining a Dreamweaver site because the most important part of defining that site is telling Dreamweaver which folder (and subfolders) holds your web pages and other content.

But wait! Not every file you create in the course of planning and preparing your website actually needs to get uploaded to a remote server. Example: You use Adobe Illustrator to design icons, logos, and banners for your site. You save the file you used to create those images as an Illustrator file (AI format). But you then export the artwork to web-compatible files (in PNG, or possibly JPEG or GIF format). The original AI files can be quite large, and there is no reason to upload them to your server when the time comes to post your site to the web.

Here are more examples of files that should be saved in a different folder than the one that you dedicate to your website:

+ **Photoshop files:** Most photos that you prepare for the web begin as much larger (in file size) image files. In Book V, we explore in detail how and why photos need to be compressed in file size and saved to web-friendly formats before they are embedded in web pages. Original photo files, in formats like PSD or raw photo formats, are very large. Like your original Illustrator artwork files, they should be safely saved — just not in your website folder.

+ **Fireworks files:** In Book V, we explore using Fireworks to create web-compatible navigation and other artwork. Here, too, the original Fireworks files should be saved, but not in the same folder as your website.

+ **Uncompressed video files:** Video files straight from your digital camera or other recording apparatus will likely be edited into shorter clips, and compressed in file size before being uploaded to the web. (See Book V, Chapter 3 for a full discussion of preparing video for the web.) You will *not* want to waste server storage or endure long upload time to send the unedited, uncompressed video files to your remote server.

+ **Text files:** Likely, much of the text content for your site will be extracted or derived from Microsoft Word, Google Docs, or other text formats. The original files should be saved so they can be edited in their original for-mats, but those files shouldn't clutter up your site folder, either.

See a pattern? Many files that are the *source* of web content (Illustrator draw-ings, Photoshop photos, or Word documents) are not actually part of your website. So, keep them in a distinct folder. You won't want to upload them to a remote server, but you will want to access them to generate updated and new content for your site.

Files that do belong in your site

Having sorted out content you that do *not* want to include in your Dreamweaver site folder, here are the content things that you do want to include for your Dreamweaver site:

✦ **Web-ready graphics:** Images that have been exported to web-friendly formats, such as PNG, JPEG, and GIF

✦ **Web-ready video:** In formats like H.264, Ogg Vorbis, and other web-compatible formats

✦ **Web-ready audio:** Saved in web-ready formats, such as MP3

Book V is devoted to a detailed exploration of the process of generating web-friendly graphics and media.

Using subfolders for your site folder

As you can see, your site folder might get a little crowded and untidy. To help keep all your site files organized, consider using a subfolder (and sub-subfolder) structure, just like you probably do every day for documents, photos, and video on your home PC.

You might, for example, have all your images in an images subfolder within your site. Another folder might have all your video. Yet another might have all the audio files you'll include in your site.

Take images, for example. Say you start with a subfolder named images. Not naming it Images (uppercase I) is intentional. More on that in a bit. Then you divide your images into three general sizes and types:

✦ **Thumbnails:** Usually between 60 and 100 pixels (px) wide

✦ **Medium-sized images:** Often something like 300 px wide

✦ **Full-sized images:** Range from 480 pxs wide to 600 px wide

Then you create sub-subfolders for the thumbnail, medium, and large versions of each of your web images.

With image files, you typically create both a working file and a web version of that file. The *working file* is the version that has all the editable pieces still intact. Those files, in Illustrator, Photoshop, or other formats, might include layers (with elements of your graphic on each layer). Those images will be flattened as they are converted to web-ready formats — in other words, the layers no longer exist in that file. That's one reason to maintain your original (working) files, even as you organize your web versions in your site folder.

Especially as your site grows in complexity and size, a rational protocol for where different kinds of files are saved will help ensure that files can easily be found, edited, or moved.

Back to the capitalization of folder names and their children. As you organize your files in preparation for defining a website, the folder structure you create on your hard drive — such as the one shown in Figure 4-1 — should use folder names (and filenames) that are lowercase and also that avoid using spaces or special characters. And by "special characters," we mean pretty much any character other than letters, numbers, the underscore character (_) or dash (-). By sticking to lowercase letters, numbers, underscores, and dashes, you'll ensure that your folder and file names are interpreted correctly in web browsers. That's a very big deal.

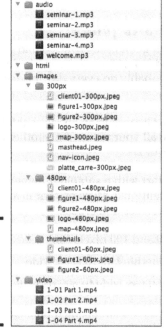

Figure 4-1:
An example
of files and
folders
organized
for the web.

Creating a Site in Dreamweaver

Defining a Dreamweaver site will go more smoothly if you have the files you plan to use in your website organized into a folder. In Chapter 2 of this minibook, we walk through the kinds of files you want to gather together in a folder — with, if you wish, subfolders for images, video, and perhaps other elements like audio.

With your files separated into an organized folder structure, you're ready to define a Dreamweaver site. To do so, just follow these steps:

1. **From the main Dreamweaver menu, choose Site⇨New Site.**

   The Site Setup for Unnamed Site dialog box opens.

2. **In the Site category of the Site Setup For dialog box, enter a name for your site.**

   After you name your site, the dialog box title changes to reflect your site name. If you name your site My Site, for example, the title becomes Site Setup for My Site.

   Contrary to what we preach in the preceding section, this site name doesn't have to be a web-compatible filename — meaning that it can contain special characters (like !@#$,) or spaces. This name is just an internal reference within Dreamweaver and is not shared in any way with visitors to your site. So, pick something descriptive that will help you remember which site this is.

3. **Click the Browse for File icon (it looks like a folder) next to the Local Site Folder field.**

4. **Navigate to the root folder in which you organized your site content, as shown in Figure 4-2, and then click Choose.**

**Book II
Chapter 4**

Organizing a Site in
Dreamweaver CS6

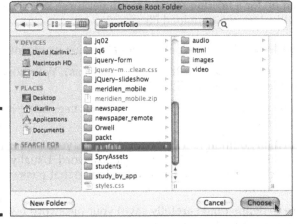

Figure 4-2:
Choose a
root folder
for your
Dream-
weaver site.

5. **Click Save.**

   The Dreamweaver Files panel opens, displaying the content of your site. We'll explore using the Files panel to manage filenames shortly.

Creating a remote server connection

In addition to defining a local "home" folder for your Dreamweaver site, you will, at some point, define a remote location for your site on the Internet as well. You don't have to have a remote location for your site picked out to start building the local version of it, but eventually — to upload your site to the web — you will need to define a remote site location. Both the local and the remote locations become part of a single, defined Dreamweaver site.

Again, to emphasize the point: You don't have to have a hosting service to begin with as you start to build a website on your local computer. You can certainly create site content, test it in a browser, and share it with clients or collaborators (on your own computer) without a hosting connection.

Before you do define a remote location for your site, you need to have arranged with a web-hosting service to upload your site. This is the service that hosts your site on the Internet. In Book I, Chapter 4, we discuss how to choose a web-hosting service.

And, again, you will need a web-hosting service to upload your site to the Internet. So after you acquire a host (relying on the advice in Book I, Chapter 4), you can define a connection to that host in Dreamweaver CS6. And, with that connection defined, you can upload content from your local computer to your live, online site.

When you sign up for a hosting service, you'll get three key pieces of information that will allow you to upload files:

✦ **An FTP address:** This is the path to your Internet site location.

   This is different than your URL (website address). Your hosting service must provide you with an FTP address.

✦ **A user name:** Sometimes called a "login," your user name is required to connect to your server.

✦ **A password:** In addition to a unique user name, your server hosting company will provide you with an initial password. Usually this is accompanied by instructions on how to change that password to one you can remember.

   Make sure to define (and carefully save) your password *before* defining a remote server connection in Dreamweaver.

You do *not* need to have a remote hosting service to create websites in Dreamweaver. If you haven't yet acquired a hosting service, you can simply skip this element of defining a Dreamweaver site and return to it later when you have contracted for site hosting and are ready to upload your site to the Internet.

To define a remote server connection in Dreamweaver, follow these steps:

1. **Choose Site⇨Manage Sites from the main Dreamweaver menu.**

The Manage Sites dialog box opens, as shown in Figure 4-3.

2. **If multiple sites appear in the list in the Manage Sites dialog box, double-click the site you wish to edit to open the Site Setup dialog box.**

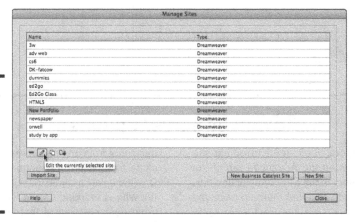

Figure 4-3:
Choosing
a Dream-
weaver
site in the
Manage
Sites
dialog box.

3. **Click the Servers category in the left column of the Site Setup dialog box for your site. Then click the plus sign "+" icon at the bottom of the dialog box to create a new server connection.**

A new Site Setup *[Your Site Name]* dialog box opens with a Basic and an Advanced tab.

The Advanced tab allows you to change how and when Dreamweaver sends files to your server. One of those options automatically uploads saved pages from your local computer to your remote site, which is, generally speaking, a bad idea. Other options enable tools used in collaborative environments. If you're collaborating on a site with other developers and you're all using Dreamweaver to work on the same site, explore the options we discuss in the nearby sidebar, "Advanced server options."

4. **Select the Basic tab (if not selected), as shown in Figure 4-4.**

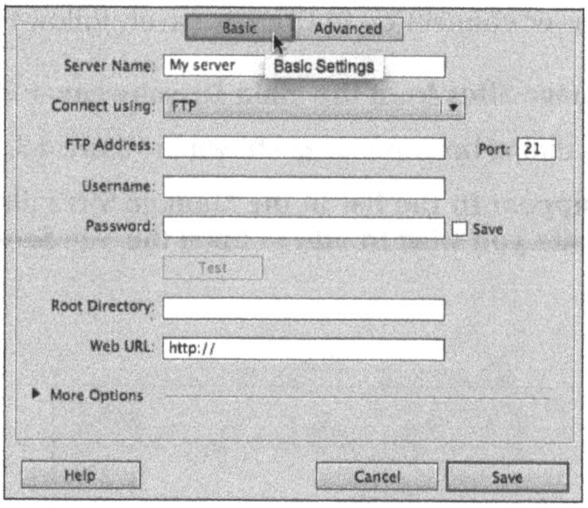

Figure 4-4:
Selecting the Basic tab in the Site Setup dialog box.

Advanced server options

Most developers don't need to adjust the default settings on the Advanced tab of the Servers category in the Site Setup dialog box. But here's what you'll find there, in case you need to:

✔ **Maintain Synchronization Information:** Enabling this check box simply allows Dreamweaver to do the work of comparing files on your computer with those on the remote server, enabling a number of useful features (such as comparing local and remote sites and identifying where the newest version of a file exists), explored in Book IX.

✔ **Automatically Upload Files to Server on Save:** Most designers should avoid selecting this check box. Best practice is to deliberately upload files to the remote server.

✔ **Enable File Checkout:** This option allows multiple designers, using Dreamweaver, to check out files for editing to prevent two designers from editing the same file at the same time. When this option is enabled, Dreamweaver prompts designers to identify who is working on the file and locks other designers out of that file while it's being edited. This is a useful feature in some design environments where large numbers of designers at different sites, perhaps not communicating with each other, are working on a single site.

✔ **Testing Server:** This option should not be enabled or selected. It's used only for complex environments where live data is being accessed from a server. If you're working with a database administrator who has created server-hosted databases and scripts to access them, he will provide you with parameters for defining a testing site. Absent those conditions, avoid defining a testing site.

Relevant elements of these features are explored in more depth and detail in Book IX.

5. Define the server connection by filling in these fields:

- *Server Name:* Enter a name that helps you remember what server connection you're defining. This need not be a regular filename; it can have spaces, uppercase letters, and special characters.

- *Connect Using:* Choose FTP.

- *FTP Address:* As we mention earlier, an FTP address is supplied to you when you sign up for a web-hosting service.

- *User Name:* As we mention earlier, your hosting service supplies you with a user name.

- *Password:* In the Password field, you can create your own.

- *Root Directory and Web URL:* Leave this field blank, unless you get specific instructions from your hosting service to enter a Root Directory.

- *Web URL:* Leave this field blank as well. Entering a wrong URL will corrupt (or mess up) your server connection. The correct URL is calculated and filled in automatically by Dreamweaver when you establish a connection to your remote site.

6. Click the Test button in the Site Setup dialog box.

If all goes well, you'll see the message shown in Figure 4-5.

**Book II
Chapter 4**

Organizing a Site in
Dreamweaver CS6

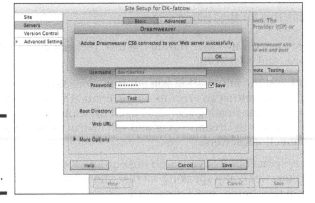

Figure 4-5:
Test your
server
connection.

7. After you successfully test your server connection, click the Save button on the Servers tab of the Site Setup dialog to save the settings.

See the next section for troubleshooting help.

Troubleshooting

Generally speaking, you need to define an FTP address, a user name, and a password in the Servers panel of the Dreamweaver Site Setup dialog box. Other options can usually be left at the default Dreamweaver settings. However, sometimes your hosting service will require additional or nondefault settings for remote server connection options:

✦ **Port:** If your hosting service instructs you to define a nonstandard port (different than the normal setting of 21), you can enter a different value in the Port field.

✦ **Root:** If your hosting service requires that you define a root directory, you can enter the name of that root directory in the Root Directory field.

✦ **URL:** The Web URL field is not required.

✦ **FTP:** If you expand the More Options section of the dialog box (click the triangle), you can change the default settings for Passive FTP (usually selected) and Use FTP Performance Optimization (also usually selected). These default settings work in most environments, but if your hosting service or your local IT administrator instructs you otherwise, they can be deselected.

Other check box options are quite obscure and not required for most host connections. If they are, the settings will be included in the information you get when you sign up for hosting service.

Here are some tips for the testing stage:

✦ If you get an error message during the test, recheck your FTP address, user name, and password.

✦ If you entered the information you got from your host provider correctly but you're still getting an error message, contact your web-hosting service. Any credible hosting service is used to helping resolve server connection issues with Dreamweaver and will instruct you in how to correct your connections settings.

✦ It is the responsibility of your web-hosting service to give you clear login instructions. Generally speaking, all that should be required are an FTP address, a user name, and a password.

Managing Sites

After you define a Dreamweaver site, you have empowered Dreamweaver to protect the integrity of the linkages between files. As you build pages with images, media, style sheets, and scripts, those linkages will be essential to the functioning of your site.

However, Dreamweaver can do its job only if you do all file management in the Dreamweaver Files panel. Luckily, that's easy enough to do.

And here's another nice feature of Dreamweaver's site management toolset: You can move a site from one computer to another by saving all the site definition properties.

The following sections explore both of these valuable features for managing sites.

Managing files in the Files panel

The Files panel is somewhat similar to the file management feature in your operating system (say, Windows Explorer or the Mac Finder). Big deal: When working with files that are part of your site, use the Dreamweaver Files panel instead of your OS tools (or other tools like Adobe Bridge) to rename, copy, move, or delete files from your site.

Like all panels in Dreamweaver CS6, the Files panel can be opened from the Window menu. Choose Window⇨Files from the main Dreamweaver menu. The Files panel has its own fairly powerful toolbar, as shown in Figure 4-6:

✦ **Connect to Remote Server:** Connects Dreamweaver with the remote host, so the Files panel can display both the local version of the site (on your computer) and the remote version (saved at your hosting company's server).

✦ **Refresh:** Updates the display to reflect recent changes in file structure.

✦ **View Site FTP Log:** You can see a record of file transfers to and from the remote server.

✦ **Remote Server Log/Testing Server Log**: These two buttons toggle between viewing your remote site files, and viewing connections to databases at a remote server — the latter being an advanced technique beyond the scope of this book.

✦ **Repository Files:** Displays archived, older versions of a site if Version Control settings are defined in the Version Control tab of the Site Setup dialog box. This is a feature usually associated with complex and large-scale sites and beyond the scope of this book.

✦ **Download:** Downloads selected files from the remote server to your local computer.

✦ **Upload:** Uploads selected files from your local computer to the remote server.

✦ **Checkin, Checkout:** Enables multiple developers working on the same site to check out files from the server, locking other developers out of editing those files while they're checked out. You can then check files back in when the editing is complete.

✦ **Synchronize with Remote Server:** Opens the Synchronize with Remote Server dialog box that provides automated tools for replacing older files with newer ones on either the local or remote site.

✦ **Expand:** Splits the Files panel into two sides: one showing the remote server (generally on the left) and one showing your local files (on the right). Or, when deselected, collapses the Files panel to display only the local, or only the remote, version of the site.

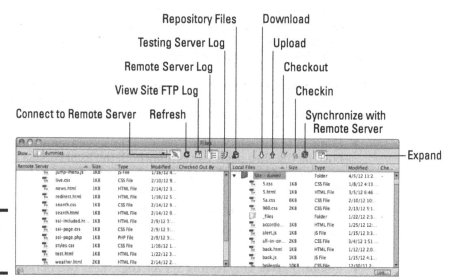

Figure 4-6: The Files panel.

Note the drop-down menu at the top of the Files panel. Here you can choose which of your defined Dreamweaver sites is visible and in use.

Use these tools when necessary to document in minute detail all changes ever made to site content. Both Testing Server and Dreamweaver's automated version control features have rather specialized applicability and are beyond the scope of our exploration of Dreamweaver Sites.

Rename, copy, delete, and open files from the Files panel.

Earlier we advise you to avoid making changes to filenames or locations using your operating system's file management tools. Instead, use the file management tools to rename, copy, delete, and open files that are accessible through Dreamweaver's Files panel. The easiest way to access these features is to right-click (Windows)/Control-click (Mac) a file. The flyout menu will display relevant options for your file, as shown in Figure 4-7. For example, if you right-click an image file — in addition to being able to cut, copy, delete, duplicate, or rename the file — Dreamweaver provides an option to open the file in any of your installed image-editing programs. When you edit the image in your image editor (like Photoshop), saved changes are reflected in the file in your site.

Book II
Chapter 4

Organizing a Site in
Dreamweaver CS6

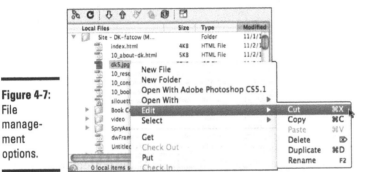

Figure 4-7:
File
manage-
ment
options.

One of the best (or maybe better said, one of the worst) ways to corrupt a website is to mix other file management tools with Dreamweaver's. For example, if you rename a file in Dreamweaver, Dreamweaver will examine your entire site and prompt you to update any pages that rely on that file to work properly. That won't happen if you rename the file using your operating system's file management tool (Windows Explorer or Mac Finder). So, be sure to rely on Dreamweaver's Files panel, not your operating system's file manager, to edit filenames and locations.

Editing and moving Dreamweaver sites

What if your site definition changes? For example, what if you need to save the site content to a different folder or external drive? Or you need to rename a site? Dreamweaver's site dialog box provides tools to manage those events safely.

You can save site definitions and use them to move a site to another computer.

Editing sites

To access Dreamweaver site management tools, choose Site⇨Manage Sites from the main Dreamweaver menu. The Manage Sites dialog box opens (see Figure 4-8).

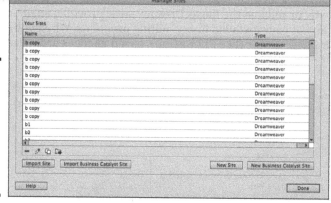

Figure 4-8: Access site management tools in the Manage Sites dialog box.

If you have more than one site, the first step in editing the site is to select the site from the list of sites. Note the four tools at the bottom of the list:

+ **Delete:** At the left is the tool that deletes the selected site.

   Exercise caution before clicking that icon!

+ **Edit:** The second tool re-opens the Site Definition dialog box, allowing you to change the site name, the local site folder, or the remote site definition (as well as more esoteric and advanced features that we explore in Book IX).

+ **Duplicate:** This tool creates a copy of your site definition. It does not duplicate all the files in a Dreamweaver site, only the site definition (including remote server connection information).

+ **Export:** Use this tool to make and send a copy of your site settings to another computer. Find out more in the next section.

And here's where you get your money's worth out of Dreamweaver: If you move a site from one folder to another, Dreamweaver prompts you to make any required changes in your site that might be affected by the change, including updating links, embedded images, and style sheets.

Exporting a site

Exporting does *not* make a backup copy of the entire site. Instead, it makes a copy of the site settings. This is valuable, for example, when you need to back up or restore a site to a new local computer. The saved (exported) site definition allows you to reconnect with a remote server, download the site if necessary, and reestablish other defined site settings.

Follow these steps to export your site definition to a file from which you can restore your site on a different computer:

1. **Choose Site⇨Manage Sites from the main Dreamweaver menu.**

The Manage Sites dialog box opens.

If you have more than one site defined on your computer, click the site you're exporting from the Manage Sites list.

2. **Click the Export tool.**

The Export tool is the last (fourth) tool at the bottom of the Manage Sites dialog box.

3. **In the Exporting Site dialog box that appears, choose one of two export options:**

- *Back Up My Settings:* Selecting this option creates a file (with an `*.ste` filename extension) that can be saved to a flash drive or anywhere else that includes login information to a remote server, as shown in Figure 4-9. This first option is the most valuable and the one you'll use to create a safe, restorable version of your site.

- *Share Settings with Other Users:* Selecting this option shares other site settings but not login and password information. This option has limited value because it doesn't save information needed to connect to a remote server, but it can be used to share where files are saved on a local computer.

Book II
Chapter 4

Organizing a Site in
Dreamweaver CS6

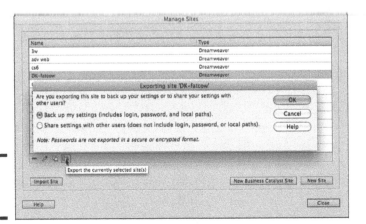

Figure 4-9:
Exporting
a site.

4. **Click OK in the Exporting Site dialog box.**

   Another (similarly named, but different) Exporting Site dialog box opens.

5. **Browse to a folder where you will save the site export settings.**

   This doesn't have to be a folder within your Dreamweaver site. It can be a flash drive, for example, that you store somewhere safe so that you can use the file to restore your site on a different computer if necessary.

6. **(Optional) Change the export site filename by typing a new name in the Save As field in the second Exporting Site dialog box.**

7. **Click Save.**

   The * .ste file is saved.

   The Manage Sites dialog box reappears.

8. **Click Close to exit the Manage Sites dialog box.**

Export your site, and keep the resulting * .ste file somewhere safe. You can use it to restore the site if necessary or to install it on a new or backup local computer.

Chapter 5: Building Mobile-Friendly Sites

In This Chapter

✔ Examining design and technical challenges

✔ Discovering how to approach challenges for mobile content

✔ Exploring the similarities and differences of websites and apps

*I*t's an increasingly mobile world out there. A quick survey of students walking across a campus or professionals at lunch will reinforce what statistics tell us: Mobile is a rapidly growing segment of the online viewing public. But the mobile audience is more important than just the number of people viewing sites on smartphones and tablets. Mobile users are a coveted demographic because studies show that mobile users shop online disproportionate to their numbers (in 2012, most analysts estimated mobile devices accounted for about 5 percent of web browsing activity worldwide).

Statistics are changing rapidly, and much of the emerging evidence is empirical, but, for example, in 2012, the CEO of `Fab.com` (which sells trendy home décor) reported that 30 percent of visits to Fab.com were from mobile devices. An even more striking statistic was that mobile visitors were twice as likely to make a purchase at its company site compared with those visiting on desktop computers. (See `http://gigaom.com/2012/01/11/fab-com-mobile-shoppers-buy-twice-as-often-as-web-visitors/`.)

"Your results" as the TV ads say, "may vary." But the experience at Fab.com gives a sense of the emerging power of the mobile market.

Having mobile-friendly sites remains, at this writing, the goal of websites with a lot of resources to develop alternate content and presentations for mobile visitors. That isn't so in your case, though. Throughout this book, we return to mobile options as they relate to all kinds of design and technical issues.

The point in this chapter is to give you some framework to make *conscious* decisions as to how important the mobile audience is to your site. And then incorporate those conscious decisions as you design pages, embed content, and choose web design technology.

Design and Technical Challenges for Mobile Content

The issue of mobile accessibility emerges in every realm of creating a website, affecting the size and type of images you embed, the color scheme you apply to your site, and what kind of navigational structure you choose.

The point here is not to point out all the different challenges posed by the size of mobile devices. We'll do that throughout this book as we explore the wide range of design and technical challenges in building websites and walk you through solutions. In particular, we show you in some detail how to use two possible solutions for providing web-friendly content:

✦ **Media queries:** You can present the same content in full size and mobile browsers but display that content differently using different CSS style sheets. For example, content presented in three columns in a full-sized monitor can be presented in one column in a (narrower) mobile viewport (screen).

Multiple media queries can be configured for a site. They're defined by the size of a user's viewport. So, for example, you could create one style sheet that displays your site content in tablets, another that displays the site in a mobile phone in landscape (horizontal) mode, and yet another for a mobile phone in portrait (vertical) mode. You're unlikely to create more than two or three versions of your site at first, but the number of styles you can define for a single site is unlimited.

We explore media queries in detail in Book IV, Chapter 2.

✦ **jQuery Mobile:** You can build a completely different site for mobile users. The jQuery Mobile option involves creating separate content for a mobile site than what's presented to full-sized monitor visitors.

We explain how to build mobile sites with jQuery Mobile technology in detail in Book VI, Chapter 3.

If you're reading this book, media queries and jQuery Mobile are within your reach. Neither one requires hiring programmers or advanced knowledge of web design beyond what we cover in this book. That said, when you decide to take the plunge and create a mobile version of your site (using media queries or jQuery Mobile), you'll have to put some time and energy into figuring one (or both) of those approaches.

The point here is to raise consciousness as to how the size difference between a full-sized and mobile viewport affects every aspect of page design and technology, including these issues.

✦ **Small viewports:** The most immediate and obvious difference between desktop/laptop browsing and mobile browsing is that mobile *viewports* (the viewing screens) are smaller. The size difference between full-sized media and mobile devices has radical implications for site design:

- *Mobile pages generally avoid using columns.* As we discuss at length in Chapter 1 of this minibook, building page design with a columnal "understructure" is often essential to making content accessible and inviting in full-sized pages.

- *Links often need to be larger on mobile devices to be accessible.* Tiny links are hard for big fingers to tap, and thus different link techniques (such as large, clickable buttons instead of narrow lines of type) are often used in mobile design.

- *Images must be much smaller in mobile devices.* There is a qualitative dimension when it comes to choosing and cropping versions of images that appear on a mobile site. Designers are often well-served to crop photos tighter for a mobile device. For example, a photo of person from head to toe that works well on a full-screen monitor might be nicer if cropped to just a headshot for mobile devices.

- *Forms are configured differently on mobile devices.* Some form input fields that work okay on a laptop (such as radio buttons and check boxes) are hard to use on a small touch-screen device. Instead, *sliders* (bars with a draggable slider) and *flipswitches* (with a yes/no set of options) make forms easier to fill out on a mobile device. Figure 5-1 shows a mobile-friendly form with a slider and flipswitch.

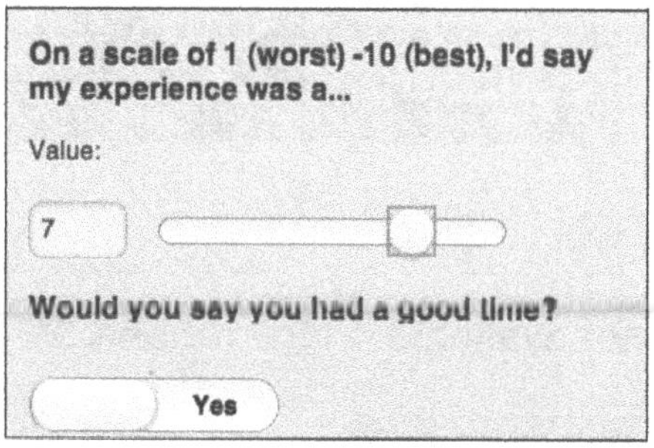

Figure 5-1:
Sliders and
flipswitches
are more
accessible
form inputs
in mobile
devices.

On a scale of 1 (worst) -10 (best), I'd say
my experience was a...

Value:

7

Would you say you had a good time?

Yes

✦ **Lighting and color issues:** Mobile devices are much more likely to be used outdoors than desktops or even laptop computers. And, the lighting intensity on mobile devices is lower than that of bigger screen computers. This poses particular challenges for creating mobile-friendly sites. Color schemes that work well on full-sized monitors — in relatively dark, indoor environments — can prove frustrating or useless on a mobile device in bright sunlight. Avoid color schemes like shades of gray (or subtle shades of any color) on mobile devices.

✦ **Download speeds:** You've heard the ads: "Our 4G is so fast!" Blah, blah, blah. Here's the skinny: Mobile devices, if not running on a Wi-Fi network, load pages much more slowly than desktops and laptops, regardless of whether those larger devices are plugged into an Internet connection or connected through Wi-Fi. And, as you've guessed by now, this has strategic implications for presenting content for mobile visitors. Because mobile pages take longer to load, you want to avoid making users navigate from one page to another.

As noted, we explore the techniques and technology for avoiding making people navigate from page to page in your mobile site in Book VI, where we show you how a technology called *jQuery Mobile* (more on that shortly) and slower download speeds (as well as slower processing speeds) affect the kinds of media (audio and video) you include in your site.

✦ **Mobile plug-ins (and lack thereof):** Perhaps the most widely known difference between mobile and laptop/desktop viewing is that iPhones and iPads don't support Flash video. Yes, Flash Video files (FLV) are widely used to distribute video online, but those files are a no-go for Mac mobile devices. Those users will see a message like the one from Hulu in Figure 5-2.

Figure 5-2:
Videos in
Flash Video
(FLV) format
don't play
on iPhones
or iPads.

Comparing mobile websites and apps

Apps — applications that run on a mobile device without a web browser — perform much the same function as mobile-friendly websites, with a major difference being that apps don't run in a browser window but as free-standing programs. Apps are built with completely different technology and tools than are used to create websites (apps are written in high-level programming languages, such as Objective-C). As such, they fall outside the scope of this book.

Tools are in development that might someday allow a wider range of web designers to generate apps directly from web pages. Most notable is *PhoneGap,* an online resource that originated as an open source (nonprofit, noncommercial) project. PhoneGap was acquired by Adobe, and in Dreamweaver CS5.5, Adobe included the capacity to generate and preview apps for iOS (Apple mobile) and Android (Google's mobile operating system). Dreamweaver CS6 downsized those tools, and Adobe's current course seems to be to encourage developers to go straight to the PhoneGap site and generate apps outside of the Dreamweaver interface.

Addressing the Challenges for Mobile Content

Here are essentially the four approaches you take to making mobile-friendly site content:

✦ **Don't worry about a mobile presence for now.** Not every website needs a mobile presence right away, but you can think ahead and build mobile into your long-term plans.

✦ **Keep your site so simple that it will work in any environment.** This is a less-than-optimal solution because sites that are simple enough to work on a mobile phone that use, for example, a one-column layout aren't going to be very inviting in full-sized screens. But again, there might be situations where this is a working solution, at least for a while. If you go with this approach, keep your site design simple, your images small, your video formatted to work in any environment, your color scheme basic and high contrast, and your fonts large.

✦ **Detect a visitor's media and present the same content, but with different CSS style sheets, depending on the viewport.** This is the media query solution we note earlier in this chapter, and that we show you how to use in Book IV, Chapter 2.

As we note earlier, providing alternate style sheets with media queries allows you to create a single set of web pages, with content, and present them differently (with different color schemes, font sizes, and layouts) in full-sized and mobile viewports.

✦ **Detect a visitor's *media* (their viewing environment) and divert mobile users to completely different content.** This technique relies on JavaScript to detect mobile devices. Or you might need to embed links for visitors to find mobile-friendly content, like the one at the Madison Square Garden site in Figure 5-3.

Mobile-only versions of websites generally are built using a subset of JavaScript — jQuery Mobile — to present content specifically designed to work faster and better in mobile devices. As noted, we explore this option in Book VI.

Figure 5-3:
Offer
visitors links
to mobile-
friendly
content.

Book III

Building Pages with HTML

The 5th Wave — By Rich Tennant

"I can't really explain it, but every time I animate someone swinging a golf club, a little divot of code comes up missing on the home page."

Contents at a Glance

Chapter 1: HTML: What It Is, Why You Need It, and How to Get It

In This Chapter

✔ The foundational role of HTML in web design

✔ Using an HTML editor

✔ Getting HTML from just about anything

✔ Building a basic HTML page

*T*he technology, and the terminology, of web design evolves at a dizzying pace. Last year's content management system (CMS) vanishes into the cloud (applications, services, and data stored and accessed from the web instead of your own computer). Page layout is managed not with tables (grids of columns and rows) but CSS DIV tags (special design rules in a style sheet file). Flash (a technology for presenting video, animation, and interactivity) ruled the web once upon a time, and then it faded. WYSIWYG (what you see is what you get) editors generate web pages from graphical interfaces without the need for coding. And yet, as much as web design continues to evolve, HTML — HyperText Markup Language — remains a foundation of web design. As such, if you want to understand how web pages are built, HTML is your starting point.

HTML is the most essential and fundamental element in creating websites because it defines the structure and content of web pages. By *structure,* we mean that HTML provides a basic framework on which all kinds of web elements — images, audio, video, page design, page formatting, animation, interactivity — are shared on the web. And by *content,* we mean that text, images, and media are placed in pages, in one way or another, by HTML (or with related structured markup languages that we explore later in this chapter).

In the following chapters of this minibook, we dive into the nuts and bolts of coding HTML5 web pages (Chapter 2), explore radical new innovations for structuring content in HTML5 (Chapter 3), and then walk through how to create HTML (and other structured) web pages in Adobe Dreamweaver CS6 (Chapter 4). But before rolling up your sleeves and getting to all of that, it's valuable for you to know how HTML (and cascading style sheets, CSS) fits into the constantly and rapidly evolving world of web design. We also show you options for building HTML. There's actually quite a range of options for generating or coding HTML: You can save word processor documents as HTML files; you can use a text editor (the one that comes from with your operating system) to type and save HTML code; or you can use the Big Tamale (Adobe Dreamweaver).

Exploring the Role of HTML in Web Pages

Take a moment to break down what HyperText Markup Language really means. Sure, you could beef up your ability to bore friends with techno-speak, but when you dissect what HTML is all about you can identify the basic elements of websites and be better prepared to navigate the rapidly changing world of web design.

Where does HTML5 fit in this picture? Like everything in web design, HTML has evolved and will continue to evolve. The current version of HTML is HTML5. Contrary to what you might expect (or might have been led to believe), HTML5 is actually more compatible with browsers than its predecessors (HTML4 and XHTML):

✦ **Browsers are more forgiving of HTML5.** When a browser (like Firefox, Internet Explorer, Safari, or Chrome) opens a page and sees that it's an HTML5 document, the browser will be more forgiving than if that browser encounters an HTML4 or XHTML document. For example, if your page is an HTML5 document and you forget to close a paragraph tag (the HTML element that defines a paragraph), the browser is much more likely to figure out that the paragraph ended when a new tag (like another paragraph or a heading) appears.

✦ **HTML5 is versatile.** HTML5 introduces new (and very cool) elements that aren't supported by older browsers (essentially Internet Explorer 6–8). However, you don't have to use those new elements, particularly if users of very old browsers are a core part of your intended audience. Or, you can use valuable new HTML5 elements in ways that make them optional, so that even if the page is viewed in an outdated browser, the page still "works."

Here's an example: You can create forms with HTML5 that include placeholder text that appears in the form field (like "your name here"). The placeholder text will not appear in outdated browsers but the form will still work, and a label in front of the form field (like "Name:") will make the form accessible in outdated browsers.

✦ **Time is on HTML5's side.** Computers with outdated browsers will not live forever.

The dynamic role of links in HTML

The *HyperText* part of HTML derives from the fact that clickable links have been a defining aspect of web pages since the origin of web pages. And clickable links (associated with text or images) remain a constant and essential element in web pages. Having said that, that hallmark linkability associated with web pages has taken on new dimensions.

Modern web pages — the kind we show you how to build in this book — typically include a dozen, or even dozens, of links! And these links play an even more complex role than links from one web page to another. Consider, for a moment, the kinds of linkages that make a typical web page do its thing:

+ **Links:** The most basic, traditional use of links allows viewers to jump from one page to another, within or outside a website.

+ **Images:** Graphics — including photos, navigation icons, banners, and other objects — are distinct files embedded into web pages. They appear to be part of the page when viewed in a browser, but under the hood, they're really linked files. The placement and display of these images is controlled in large part by HTML. (See Book V for a full exploration of web graphics.)

+ **Audio and video:** Audio and video — so essential to the modern web-browsing experience — are linked to web pages. Like images, they are distinct files. (We explore web media in Book V.)

+ **Style sheets:** External CSS files — distinct files that define the look of a web page — are connected to HTML pages via links.

+ **Scripts:** Animation and interactivity of all kinds — ranging from elements that move about the page to objects that react to a visitor's input (like a form) — are controlled by scripts written in languages like JavaScript (runs in browsers) or PHP (runs on servers that host websites). The pages of coding required to make these scripts work is saved to distinct files linked to an HTML page. (See Book VI for a basic introduction to working with JavaScript, and Book VII for an exploration of using PHP to manage form input.)

When you look at a web page, experiment with trying to identify the different kinds of linked or embedded elements within that page. For instance, the IMDb (Independent Movie Database) page shown in Figure 1-1 has links to other pages (in the navigation bar near the top of the page); images (like those used in the ads); video files a linked style sheet that defines the color scheme and page layout; and scripts, like the one that makes the drop-down menus in the Movie Showtimes section work.

Videos   Links

Figure 1-1:
Different
kinds of
embedded
or linked
content
make this
page work.

Styles   Images   Scripts

There are more ways in which to link or embed content, but Figure 1-1 illustrates how dynamic — interlinked and interdependent — a modern web page is. You can also start to get an inkling of their central, controlling, and defining role of an HTML page. To put it another way, although you *can* build a website without audio, video, style sheets, or scripts, that site wouldn't be very inviting. Generally speaking, though, you can't build a web page without HTML.

HTML, PHP, and ASP pages

When we state that "all" web pages are built on a foundation of HTML, we have to add this caveat: Some pages that are populated with *live data* (content fed from a server) are saved as PHP or ASP pages, depending on the scripting language used on the server to feed content to the page.

Pages built with PHP (or ASP) rely on server-side scripting to manage the page content. *Servers* are huge computers that store tons of data and host websites, and *scripts* are programs. So, a server-side script is a script that runs on a hosting server.

PHP- (or ASP-) based web pages are often referred to as "live" data pages, while pages built with HTML have traditionally been considered static pages.

However, emerging techniques, tools, and technologies have blurred those distinctions. You can embed a lot of live data in a page these days without messing with PHP (or other server-side scripting languages).

Here are four examples of how you can easily embed live data in pages using emerging online resources that do not require you to work with PHP (or other server-side scripting):

✦ If you want to embed a frequently updated blog in your site, you don't have to create PHP programs at your server to manage the blog. You can use a blogging package like WordPress and embed that in your site without resorting to PHP. (See Book VIII, Chapter 1 for the steps involved in integrating WordPress blogs in your site.)

✦ Perhaps you want to stream videos and present them through your site. You can do so by embedding video hosted at sites like YouTube or Vimeo (something we explore in Book VII, Chapter 3).

✦ You can present up-to-the-minute news in your site by embedding live feeds using RSS (really simple syndication) to channel that late-breaking news right into your own pages. We show you how to do this in Book VII, Chapter 3.

✦ If you want to present a frequently updated weather forecast, you can embed tools that do that as well. This, and other techniques for embedding live content with (and without) PHP, are explored in Book VII, Chapter 3.

We're just scratching the surface with the above examples. The fact is, just about any kind of live data can be managed either with server-side programming or with techniques that don't require server-side programming on your part.

In short, HTML pages should no longer be thought of as static, and PHP-based pages shouldn't be thought of as the only option for embedding remote, changing content in a web page.

The nature of a markup language

In the next chapter, we walk through exactly how to create page content with HTML. But before you start typing and examining HTML code, take a minute to review or refresh yourself on the concept of HTML as a markup language and what it does and doesn't do.

In a nutshell, HTML defines content. HTML is a markup language: that is, HTML elements define the nature of different types of content. Those elements — such as <img> (image), <a> (link), or <p> (paragraph) — instruct a browser how to handle each element. In the later sections, "Building a Basic HTML Page" and "Starting Your HTML Document," we delve into the basics of creating HTML pages.

Here's what HTML does *not* do: HTML is not the main way we define how content looks on a page. HTML, when properly used, defines the nature and role of content — picture versus text, for example. For example, we use HTML to assign level one, level two, level three (up to level six) headings to content. Level one headings are more important than level two headings, and so on. But how a level one heading (or a level two heading, and so on) looks is defined by a CSS style sheet. (Read all about style sheets in Book IV.)

However, relying on CSS for page style and design has not always been the case. In the earliest evolutionary stages of web design — when the design factor in web pages wasn't so important — formatting and styling (such as it existed) — was applied with HTML.

Here's an example of this evolution: In earlier eras of web design, tables (rows and columns of data) emerged as a way to present information online. As the importance of web design grew, the format and style of pages became a significant dimension of the web experience, and designers played a larger and essential role, striving to lay out pages in more attractive and inviting ways. And in doing so, they morphed HTML table elements into tools to design pages, cleverly using table cells to place objects on a page.

Thus, inventive designers invoked and stretched the limits of *parameters* (settings) for `Table` tags to accomplish formatting and data present, such as hiding table borders, merging columns and rows, and defining background color of a table (or table cells). As a very rudimentary example, Figure 1-2 shows a page laid out with a three-column, three-row table, but with the column and row borders visible to reveal the underlying structure.

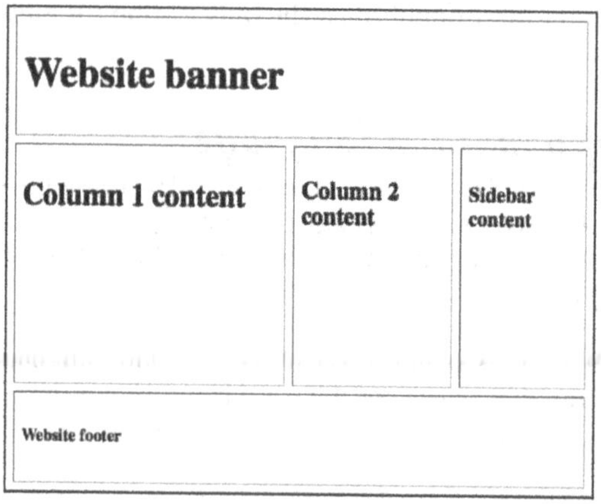

Figure 1-2: Sample basic table layout.

Website banner		
Column 1 content	Column 2 content	Sidebar content
Website footer		

Even though crafting page layout by using HTML Table tags was awkward, at least it showed how you could use tags to denote the type of content (in the case of tables, columns and rows of data) while controlling the display of data.

Without spending a lot of time here walking you through the timetable and steps in the evolution of web design, just bear in mind that the shift is ongoing and fundamental separation of content markup (with HTML) and formatting and styling (with CSS).

HTML isn't a dinosaur, though. Not at all! HTML (or a live data substitute, like PHP or ASP pages, that fundamentally play the same role) is the essential foundation of web pages. And, as you'll discover in this minibook and also in Book IV, HTML and CSS work in close collaboration.

CSS styles are relevant only in relation to HTML tags — they define styles associated with HTML tags.

Evaluating Tools for Creating HTML

Before you start coding HTML, consider the options in terms of a coding environment. There is a wide spectrum of tools, ranging from the free text editor that came with your operating system (like Windows Notepad or TextEdit on a Mac) to professional applications (most notably Dreamweaver) that provide substantial tools to help you write, and test, code.

**Book III
Chapter 1**

HTML: What It Is, Why You Need It, and How to Get It

Code editors

In this section, we survey the three levels of code editors:

✦ **Your operating system's text editor:** Yup, your OS has a text editor built right in. Nice. Here are two great advantages of using the editor built into your OS as a code editor for HTML (and CSS):

  • No cost.

  • The app is already installed on your computer. Done and done.

  This route is definitely the no-frills option, lacking code-hinting and checking features available in free downloadable code editors. Unless you're planning to do only a minimal amount of HTML coding, download a free code editor like Text PSPad or Text Wrangler (see the following bullet).

  Figure 1-3 shows HTML coding in TextEdit, Mac's built-in text editor. And Figure 1-4 shows HTML coding using Notepad, the text editor that comes with Windows 7.

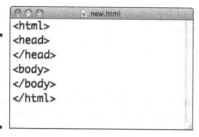

Figure 1-3:
Creating
HTML with
TextEdit on
a Mac.

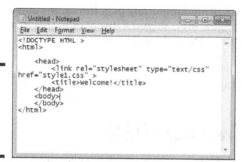

Figure 1-4:
Creating
HTML with
Notepad in
Windows.

✦ **Free, downloadable code editors:** Behind Door #2 are free code editors, like TextWrangler (www.barebones.com/products/textwrangler/) for Macs or PSPad (www.pspad.com) for Windows.

Again, free is good. Those (and other) free code editors include features atop what comes with your OS app:

- *File tabs* that allow you to work with multiple files at the same time. This capability is essential for working with an HTML and a linked CSS file at the same time.

- *Color coding* that identifies coding syntax elements. You'll find this feature very helpful when you've mistyped some code because that mistyped content won't adopt the expected color code. Figure 1-5 shows three open files (accessed using the tab bar on the right) in the free TextWrangler code editor.

- *Spell check* is available in free code editors like TextWrangler and PSPad to help identify misspelled words on the fly. The spell-check feature in PSPad is illustrated in Figure 1-6.

- *Autocomplete* is included in PSPad.

Figure 1-5: Text Wrangler provides color-coding and allows toggling among open files.

Free code editors like TextWrangler (for Macs) and PSPad (for Windows) do not come with WYSIWG graphical windows that display how HTML pages will look in a browser. And they lack the kind of code-hinting options available in code editors that cost money.

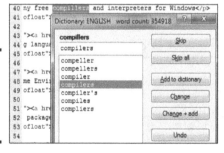

Figure 1-6: PSPad includes a spell-check feature.

Book III
Chapter 1

HTML: What It Is,
Why You Need It,
and How to Get It

✦ **Low-cost code editors:** BBEdit (www.barebones.com), for example (selling for $50 as of this writing), is an enhanced version of TextWrangler. One of the most powerful features of BBEdit is that it can *autocomplete* code — anticipating and filling in the ending of code as you type. Figure 1-7, for examples, shows a range of HTML tags beginning with the letter "h" prompted by typing an "h."

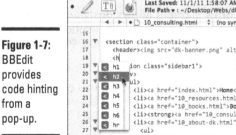

Figure 1-7: BBEdit provides code hinting from a pop-up.

Dreamweaver

The most powerful tool for working with HTML is Adobe Dreamweaver. In addition to the features found in advanced, professional code editors (like spell check and code hinting), Dreamweaver's main attraction is that you don't have to hand-code HTML. You can, instead, use menu options (like "Insert⇨Image") and panels (like the Properties inspector) to generate HTML.

Many people are aware that Dreamweaver can create HTML without hand coding. But what many people don't realize is that Dreamweaver operates in two modes:

✦ **Design view:** In this view, code is generated with menu and mouse actions hidden.

✦ **Code view:** This view provides a full-featured coding environment with code-hinting (as shown in Figure 1-8) and testing for not just HTML but other web design languages like CSS (style sheets), JavaScript (for animation and interactivity), and PHP (for server-side scripts that manage online data).

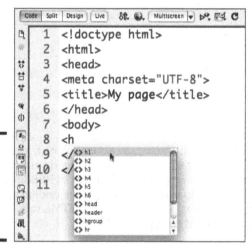

Figure 1-8: Creating HTML with code hints in Dreamweaver.

As noted, Dreamweaver's biggest draw is that it allows designers to generate HTML (as well as CSS and some other coding) in a design window that looks and feels something like other Adobe Creative Suite apps like Photoshop, Illustrator, or InDesign.

Throughout this book, we explore options for generating web content without hand-coding using Dreamweaver.

The "rest"

Many applications can save content as an HTML page. Sometimes that's a good thing. To stretch an analogy from the world of rock music, many successful records were recorded using only primitive home recording devices. There's no rule that a very inviting and accessible web page can't be generated from Microsoft Word, Google Docs, or Adobe Photoshop.

Before we get into the wide range of options for generating uploadable HTML pages, though, we need to qualify what we are *not* talking about here: We are not talking about using tools like WordPress or Facebook to post content to a pre-fab social network or blog. Those options represent a very different approach to creating web sites, with much less creative control for a designer than is available when you create your own HTML — even when that process involves the relatively "quick and dirty" options explored here. (The value and role of websites using social media like Facebook and blogging applications like WordPress are covered in Book VIII.)

The following options for generating HTML web pages from "just about anything" are not presented with the idea that you'll orchestrate a website of hundreds of pages with them. Just bear in mind that there is a role for generated HTML web pages that work just fine as HTML pages when they open in browsers. They might not prove efficient to update, and don't fit well into a major web project, but they are an option.

Word processing programs (like Microsoft Word or WordPerfect) all have some version of a Save as HTML feature that saves the open document as an HTML file. Assuming that you can design a page in a word processor (Microsoft Word, Google Docs, and others), you can easily publish that page as an HTML web page.

On the plus side, web publishing tools in word processors aren't primitive. They generally include features like the following:

✦ **Formatting is robust and transferrable.** Fonts, font sizes, italics, bold, font color, and line spacing are converted to HTML and CSS formatting.

✦ **Images are saved, with appropriate links and HTML coding.** As we discuss earlier in this chapter, images are embedded in HTML pages through links (even though they appear to be "part of the page" when viewed in a browser). When you save a word processor file with images, those images are converted into web-compatible graphic files (using the PNG, JPEG, or GIF formats). And HTML code is generated to make those images appear in the web page.

Book III
Chapter 1

HTML: What It Is,
Why You Need It,
and How to Get It

✦ **You can define web page elements.** A web page title is the content that appears in a browser title bar (the top line of a browser window). When you choose File⇨Save as Web Page in Word, for example, clicking the Web Options button in the Save As dialog box opens a new Web Options dialog box, where you can define a page title and the file format for images.

If you opt to create web pages using a word processor by saving a document as an HTML file, never try to write HTML code in a word processor. Tools like automatic spelling correction and formatting (useful in creating documents) interfere with and corrupt any attempt to actually code with your word processor.

So, why doesn't everyone just create HTML pages in their word processing programs? The major downside is that pages generated from your word processor don't, as they say, "play well with others." The HTML code generated to create these pages is highly nonstandard. Again, this incompatibility isn't an issue if you're simply creating a one-page website and all your content is confined to the word processor document that is the source of your site.

Bottom line, though, is that the nonstandard HTML generated by word processors is too messy to work with or edit in an HTML editor. A single line of text and an image, for example, converted from Microsoft Word to an HTML file, can produce more than 200 lines of HTML code, as opposed to a dozen or so lines of simpler code required to present that content. And the problem of unwieldy, overwrought code is exponentially worse when you try to do page design in your word processor.

Furthermore, HTML generated by word processors breaks the rule of separating content (HTML) from style, which should be organized in a separate, linked CSS style sheet file. When CSS is embedded like this — that is, combined with the HTML in a single file — you lose the ability to define and update global styles that can be applied and updated throughout an entire website. And such external, updatable, linked style sheets are a key element in creating and managing attractive and inviting websites.

In short, the (export to) Save as HTML feature in word processors is appropriate to use *only* when your website will consist of a single page that you will never want to combine with other pages, or update using any tool other than a word processor.

Microsoft Word

Here's how to save any open file in Microsoft Word (2008 or newer) as a web page. Start by opening the Save As dialog box, with its default web settings.

1. **Choose File⇨Save as Web Page.**

The Save As dialog opens, and with file format is preset to the defaults for a web page. You'll be prompted to save the file with an .htm filename extension, but you can change the filename to use .html instead, and that's what we suggest. In Chapter 2 of this minibook, we recommend standardizing your web page file naming with .html filename extensions. Both .htm and .html are acceptable filename extensions for web pages, but you shouldn't mix the two — browsers get very confused when they see both index.html and index.htm, for example.

2. **Navigate to the appropriate folder for your page and associated files.**

You'll be saving your Word document as an HTML file, but if you have embedded images or artwork, you will also be saving that artwork as image files in a subfolder that Word will create within the folder to which you save the page.

3. **Define Web Options.**

At any time during the saving process (until you click the Save button), you can access Web Options by clicking the Web Options button in the Save As dialog. This opens the Web Options dialog. Here are the important available options:

- *Title:* In the Web Page Title field, enter text that will display in the title bar of a browser when the page is opened.

- *Keywords:* In the Web Page Keywords field, enter searchable keywords or phrases, separated by commas. These keywords are important because they are used by search engines to index your page. Figure 1-9 shows keywords being defined.

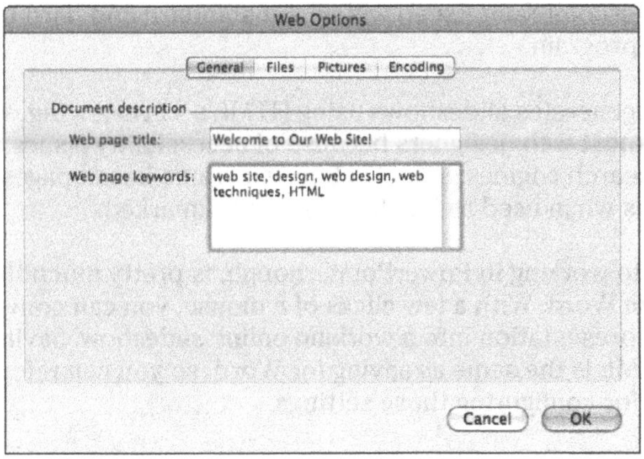

Figure 1-9:
Defining options for exporting a Word file to HTML.

Web Options

General Files Pictures Encoding

Document description

Web page title: Welcome to Our Web Site!

Web page keywords: web site, design, web design, web techniques, HTML

Cancel   OK

- *Graphics:* The Pictures tab of the Web Options dialog box has a couple of useful choices:

  PNG: Selecting the Enable PNG as Output format check box saves images to the widely used and effective PNG image format.

  Screen size: Use the Screen Size popup to define the media (screen size) that you anticipate most of your visitors using to view your page. Based on your selection, Word will scale down your image sizes to fit in a web browser, maintaining the height-to-width ratio so the images don't distort.

- *Files and encoding:* The options on the Files and Encoding tabs of the Web Options dialog box are fine with the default settings. Just leave them as-is.

4. **Save.**

   Click OK, and then click Save in the Save As dialog box to save the Word file and associated images.

You can preview any open Word file in a web browser by choosing File⇨Web Page Preview. Doing so gives you a sense of how the page will look when converted to HTML and displayed in a browser. It may well be the case that your page layout is significantly distorted — remember, even though Word can generate HTML, you have nowhere near the control over how the HTML you do looks if you create your own HTML.

Other Microsoft Office applications

You can also generate HTML from other Microsoft Office applications, even an Excel spreadsheet. More likely, though, you might generate a web page in PowerPoint. Like exporting to HTML from Word, though, the HTML you produce in PowerPoint (and Excel) will be nonstandard and hard to edit outside the original program.

PowerPoint generates slideshows using HTML's < frame > tag, which is avoided by most web designers because of accessibility issues and lack of support in search engines, and also because frame-based pages often present problems when used as link targets or bookmarked.

The upside to working in PowerPoint, though, is pretty much the same as working in Word. With a few clicks of a mouse, you can convert a PowerPoint presentation into a working online slideshow. Saving the presentation to HTML is the same as saving for Word, so you can refer to the previous section for configuring those settings.

In sum, here's when it makes sense to generate an HTML file from a slide-show app:

✦ **You're in a hurry.** Even a veteran designer who needs to quickly convert a large slideshow into an HTML page can publish a PowerPoint presentation as an HTML page.

✦ **You're not combining the resulting HTML page into a larger website that includes other content (like HTML pages you code yourself or generate from other sources, like Dreamweaver).** A presentation exported to HTML would result in a self-contained page, difficult to integrate with other web content, difficult to edit outside PowerPoint, and not really up to conventional standards for web usability and accessibility.

Google Docs

An option to using Office is Google Docs. Just choose File➪Publish to Web in an open Google Docs page, and Google creates an online web presence for you and posts the page there, along with a URL that's a folder in the Google website.

Or, you could save the content of your document as an HTML file that you can work within an HTML editor, or integrate into your own website. To do that, choose File➪Download➪HTML (Zipped). The option is illustrated in Figure 1-10. Then, when you unzip the downloaded file, you get an HTML file, along with a folder that holds embedded images in your page. As with HTML pages generated using Word, you can't expect the generated web page to look exactly like your Google Docs page. And, in fact, it might not look much like your Google Docs page — Google Docs is a "quick and dirty" solution to use when you need a web page in a hurry and you can live with a page layout that might well differ significantly from what you designed in Google Docs.

Book III
Chapter 1

**HTML: What It Is,
Why You Need It,
and How to Get It**

Figure 1-10:
Downloading
a Google
Docs
document
as an
HTML file.

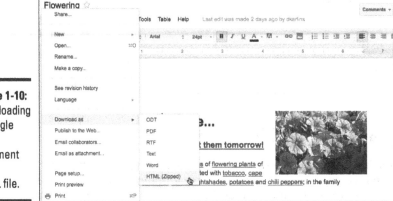

Finding Free HTML Templates Online

You can find a plethora of sites online that provide free HTML template code. Just run a quick search for **"free html templates"**. At these sites, you can download HTML pages and customize the downloaded HTML.

Be sure to note the permission rules at each site. Some such templates are free to use in noncommercial environments — meaning, you have to ante up for commercial use.

And looking at the man behind the curtains is often very helpful. That is, have a look at the HTML of any page you visit to view the source code in your browser, which is a good way to see how others are creating their pages.

To view the source code of a page in Internet Explorer, for example, you can either right-click in your browser window and choose View Source or choose View⇨Source from your browser's menu bar. The location of the View Source option in other browsers might be a little different, but the concept is the same. Figure 1-11 shows an example of the HTML code and the page it produces.

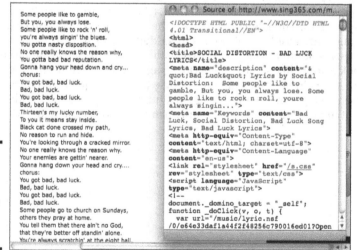

Figure 1-11: A sample of a web page and its underlying code.

Building a Basic HTML Page

Having taken a brief look at the options for creating web pages from popular applications (like word processors or graphics programs), let's turn to the most powerful, flexible, and useful way to build web pages: HTML.

Remember a few "cans" and "cant's" before you start creating HTML code:

✦ You *can* create HTML in the free text editor that comes with your computer.

✦ You *should not* — for reasons we discussed earlier in this chapter — try to create HTML with a word processor.

✦ The best option is to create HTML code either with dedicated code editors, ranging from free ones to professional ones, including Dreamweaver.

If you generate a new HTML page using menus in Dreamweaver (something we explore in Chapter 4 of this minibook), you'll create the same basic HTML code we're about to walk through here.

The four essential elements of an HTML page are

✦ **A DTD:** *DTD* stands for both Document Type Definition and Document Type Declaration. The "declaration" is the line of code that declares what the document definition is. The distinction is kind of a fine point and not worth loosing a lot of sleep over. In either case, the DTD is a line of code that tells a browser, "Hello there, I'm an HTML document."

✦ **An HTML element:** Everything in an HTML page, outside the doctype declaration, is enclosed in the HTML element.

✦ **A head element:** This is content necessary for the web page, like links to a style sheet or an external script. The basic rule is that anything needed to make a page work (and we'll walk through what that includes shortly) but that does not display in the web page itself goes in the head element.

✦ **A body element:** Everything that displays in a web page — text, images, and media — goes in the body element of an HTML page.

HTML elements and tags

Before walking through the coding that defines an HTML page, it will be helpful to sort out the terms *element* and *tag*. These terms are often used interchangeably in talking about HTML. Technically speaking, though, there's an important and interesting distinction: Tags open and close elements.

For example, both the head and body *elements* on a page have opening and closing *tags*. It's helpful to keep this in mind, because on a conceptual level, the fact that elements are framed by opening and closing tags helps visualize how HTML works. Everything on a page is within an element, and the beginning and ending of that element are marked with tags.

Take a very basic example. The four essential elements in an HTML page are defined with the following HTML code:

```
<!doctype html>
<html>
<head>
</head>
<body>
</body>
</html>
```

Note a few things about the elements that form the basic structure for an HTML page:

✦ All HTML elements are enclosed in opening and closing tags.

✦ Opening tags start with the ‹ symbol.

✦ Closing tags (tags that close an element) start with the characters ‹/.

✦ All tags end with the › symbol.

Why doesn't the doctype declaration have an opening and closing tag? Because it's not an HTML element — it's something more basic. The code and syntax for a doctype declaration, including the ! character, transcends HTML, telling browsers "you're about to encounter HTML." In short, the doctype "doesn't count" as an HTML element.

As we explore HTML elements in more depth in Chapters 2 and 3 of this mini-book, we'll some encounter elements that have a single tag. For example, the <br> tag forces line breaks. So, it doesn't enclose anything, and doesn't open or close. And as we'll see later in this chapter, the element that defines a linked style sheet doesn't have open or close tags, either.

But in general, HTML elements have opening and closing tags. Such elements are sometimes called *container elements* because they contain content.

Why do people say "tag" when they mean "element?"

We just made a big deal out of understanding the relationship between HTML tags and HTML elements (elements are enclosed in tags). But in popular discourse, and for shorthand, elements are often referred to as tags.

Is that legal? So far, there's nothing in the legal code of any nation that prevents people from referring to HTML elements as tags. And there are even good reasons to do so. One good reason for using the term "tag" to refer to an HTML element is that the word "element" has a generic meaning beyond HTML.

A web designer, for example, might complain that there are too many elements on a page. In most cases, that designer doesn't mean that there are too many HTML tags on the page. Rather, he means there is too much stuff on the page (too cluttered and busy).

And so, we sometimes use the term *tag* instead of *element* for clarity — including when it's necessary in context to emphasize that, "Hey folks, I'm talking about HTML code here, not just elements in general." And, in that situation, when we say, "Use an h1 tag to define top-level headings," we mean, "Use an h1 element, defined by and enclosed in h1 tags, to define top-level headings."

And in this book, you'll see that we use both ways of referring to HTML elements (sometimes using tag to mean element), especially when using the term "element" would be confusing or ambiguous in context.

Starting Your HTML Document

Having identified the main components of an HTML page, we walk through how these four essential components of an HTML web page are defined in more detail.

The first line in every HTML document is the doctype declaration. In the pre-HTML5 era, it was necessary to include rather long, and convoluted, DTD parameters to help browsers mesh the HTML on a page with other web tools (like scripts). Pleasantly, HTML5 simplifies the process! The only code necessary to identify a document as HTML is this line:

```
<!DOCTYPE html>
```

And, by the way, this line of code is case-insensitive, meaning not that it lacks caring human feelings (which is true, after all, of all code), but that you can use upper-case or lower-case letters. So, you can use

```
<!doctype html>
```

or

```
<!DOCTYPE HTML>
```

Mixing of uppercase and lowercase characters works fine, but DOCTYPE is often written in uppercase as a legacy of previous eras when such things mattered.

Having identified (and celebrated) how simple it is to define a document type in HTML5, and having noted that this code is not actually HTML, but precedes and identifies an HTML document, we now pose another interesting question: How important is it to begin an HTML page with a DOCTYPE?

The answer: Not as important as it used to be but still a good idea. Here's why: In earlier eras of web design and browser development, the DOCTYPE declaration was essential to a browser identifying and interpreting the code that followed. That has changed. Even without the DOCTYPE declaration, a modern browser will probably detect that the code it is encountering is HTML. Or . . . it might not.

If you're not feeling particularly lucky, or (more to the point) if you want to ensure that your page will open as a web page in the widest variety of browsing environments, include a DOCTYPE declaration at the top of every HTML document.

After the doctype declaration, everything else in an HTML page is defined using HTML code.

So, right after your doctype declaration, the first thing in a page is the open <HTML> tag. And the last thing on a page is the close </HTML> tag.

Defining titles and links in the head element

Within the HTML element in a page, there are two main, defining elements. The visible content of the page is enclosed in the <body> tag, and then everything else goes in the head element.

The HTML document head section is where the page title is defined and also where links to files on which the HTML page depends are defined. The HTML elements within the head element communicate important information, such as the name of the site, a description of the site content, and the linked style sheet. This information is used by the browser, search engines, and the site's visitors.

The head section of an HTML typically includes:

✦ The page title

✦ Links to the CSS style sheet file(s) that are used to format the page

✦ Keywords and other "metadata" used in search engines

Time to walk through each of these elements within the head element.

Titles summarize page content

A *page title* displays in the title bar of a browser or browser tab and also in most search engine results lists. Page titles are essential — they should be succinct, but yet summarize page content.

Titles are not filenames. They need not be so *truncated* (short). They can have spaces! Don't create a page title that reads "MyHomePage" or "My-home-page." Just say "My Home Page."

And yes, you can (and often should) use spaces, special characters (like :, !, and ?), and uppercase and lowercase letters to make titles inviting and descriptive.

So, while @#()*&!@ is completely wrong for a filename (filenames should avoid all those characters), "What the @)(*# is going on with my Oakland Raiders?!" would be a technically acceptable title for a page (although you'll have to consider whether it's appropriate from a content perspective!).

On the downside, if you don't define a title, an `Untitled Document` message appears, which is a sure sign of a carelessly designed page. The website in Figure 1-12, for example, is a nicely designed site (we concealed the actual URL to protect the guilty), but the careful design is betrayed by the missing title.

Figure 1-12:
No title: a careless design.

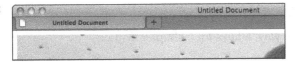

Here's sample code for a page title:

```
<title>Welcome to the Web Collective!</title>
```

Linking CSS style sheet(s)

As noted, links to style sheets also belong in the head element of an HTML page. Remember that formatting is supplied to modern web pages via external, distinct, separate, linked files. Here's how that code looks:

```
<link rel="stylesheet" href="style1.css" type="text/css" />
```

In the preceding example, the linked style sheet is named `style1.css`.

The syntax for a linked style sheet is a bit confusing, so break it down. As noted earlier, the tag that links a style sheet to an HTML page is an example of a non-container element (sometimes referred to as a *void* element). In other words, there is only an opening tag and no closing tag. Instead, this link tag opens with **<** and closes with **/>**.

The syntax for a linked style sheet defines the relationship of the link to the page. Here's how:

✦ `rel="stylesheet"` tells a browser that the relationship between this link and this page is that the linked file is a style sheet.

✦ `href="style1.css"` (or whatever your filename actually is) tells browsers what file to go to for styles for the page (here, `"style1.css"` is the name of the style sheet file.

✦ `type="text/css"` tells a browser that the linked file is a text file used for CSS as opposed to an image file or some other kind of file. The `type` attribute (in this case, `"text/css"`) is not as essential. Like the `DOCTYPE` tag, the `type` attribute is withering away in importance as modern browsers are clever enough to realize whether a link to a style sheet is the same thing as a link to a CSS file. Still, at this writing, it is prudent to include that parameter.

And, by the way, note that if your style sheet is in a subfolder of your site, you need to include the path to that file. For example, if your style sheet is in a folder called "css," you would write the above preceding line of code this way:

```
<link rel="stylesheet" href="/css/style1.css" type="text/css" />
```

HTML5, by the way, allows for a simpler syntax:

```
<link rel=stylesheet href=style1.css type="text/css">
```

In HTML5 (and some other versions of HTML), you can get away with skipping the quote marks around `stylesheet` and the filename for the style sheet (in this case `style1.css`). And, you can end the tag with `>` instead of `/>`. You might run into this alternate way to define a style sheet link. But this is one instance where there really isn't an advantage of using the HTML5 syntax. You want your style sheet to be recognized in the oldest of browsers, and so the few seconds it takes to type the quotation marks and the `/>` characters at the end of the tag are worth the time investment.

Elements, attributes, and values

By the way, or maybe not so by-the-way, in dissecting the link tag for a style sheet, we've introduced the essential syntax you'll find in HTML elements: HTML elements have attributes, and those attributes are defined with syntax that follows the model of `attribute name = "value"`.

To stick with the example of a linked style sheet, the link element had `rel`, `href`, and `type` attributes. Those attributes have both attribute *names* (like `rel`, `href`, or `type`) and *values* (the specific information in quotes that follows the attribute name).

As you beef up your familiarity with HTML in this and the following chapter, and as you explore new and more obscure HTML elements through online resources, you can always break those HTML elements into elements and attributes, with the attributes divided into attribute names and values.

The (less, but still relevant) role of meta tags

Meta tags are optional elements within a head element that convey additional information about a page, including the following:

✦ **Descriptions and keywords used by search engines. For example:**

```
<meta name="Keywords" content="web, Web Design, New York City " />
<meta name="Description" content="The Web Collective designs Webs in New
    York City" />
```

✦ **Additional information about the page, like author:**

```
<meta name="author" content="the web collective" />
```

Like everything else in HTML, the role and value of meta tags is evolving. In earlier eras, meta tags for keywords played a more significant role in search engine optimization (SEO; prominent and accurate display in search engine results).

However, modern search engines (and additional new tags in HTML5) provide alternate and more complex and sophisticated channels for identifying page content and indexing that content in search engines. Still, using meta tags for author (as in the preceding example above), description, and keywords (still sometimes useful for search engines) can still be an important part of HTML head content.

Having broken down the tags within a typical head element, take a look at what a typical opening for an HTML page, including the head element, might look like something like Listing 1-1.

Listing 1-1:   Sample HTML Page Opening

```
<!DOCTYPE HTML>
<head>
<title>Welcome to the Web Revolution</title>
<meta name="Keywords" content="web,Web Design,New York City" />
<meta name="Description" content="The Web Collective designs
    Webs in New York City"/>
<link rel="stylesheet" href="style1.css" type="text/css"/>
</head>
```

The HTML elements within the head element communicate important information, such as the name of the site, a description of the site content, and the linked style sheet. This information is used by the browser, search engines, and the site's visitors.

Figure 1-13 reveals how the pieces of the head element communicate information to the world. You can see the HTML source code for the New York City version of craigslist.com (upper left), along with the defined title, displayed in the title bar of a browser (upper right) and the defined description as it shows up in Google's search result (lower right).

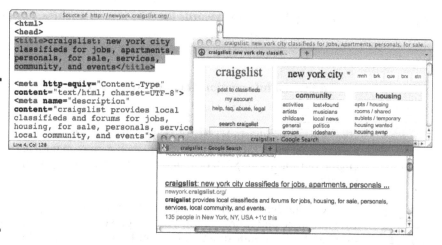

Figure 1-13: Head tag information is used in browser title bars and search engine results.

Page content is in the body element

As we've been pointing to, the content in a web page head element might display in the title bar of a browser, impact the description of your site that displays in a search engine result, or define a link to an external style sheet — but it will not appear in a browser window.

Everything that appears in a browser window is inside the body element of a page. And, as such, the body element is where you'll be using most tags. Tags that create images, links (to pages inside or outside the site), headings, paragraphs, and even page layout elements (a special kind of tag: DIV tags) all fall within the body element. We explore the most important of those elements in Chapter 2 of this minibook.

CSS is used for style

Before winding up our exploration of the essential elements in an HTML page, think about a fundamental concept in modern web design: the separation of content and style.

By moving page styling to separate but linked style sheet files (CSS files), web designers opened the door to radical new freedom to define *sitewide* formatting — formatting that could be applied and updated instantly across hundreds, thousands, and even hundreds of thousands of pages.

This development didn't mandate that every page in a website look the same, but it did create the ability to implement a single (or several) sets of styles that *could* be applied, as needed, in pages throughout a site. With the separation of styles and page content, the role of HTML reverted to its original intent — to organize and structure page content.

Again, to come at it from another angle: HTML pages without associated CSS styles are starkly minimalist — black and white, devoid of layout elements like columns or boxes, and mainly confined to Times Roman font.

As you start to experiment with HTML and create a document, you'll notice that when you *preview* it (open it in a browser), that it's pretty uninviting. The default look of headings and paragraphs can be very unattractive. But that's the way it should be until you link your page to a style sheet. Those style sheets will supply fonts, colors, page layout, and other design elements you need to make your page look good.

The sister CSS file that you later create will take care of all the visual aspects of your page. Some *degraded* (no longer useful) techniques for squeezing limited design features out of HTML (such as using the `<font>` tags) shouldn't be used anymore because those techniques create code that's difficult to edit and update. If you were never trained in this outdated method (of using HTML tag attributes to define styles), lucky you. If you came up "back in the day" when such techniques were in use, you'll quickly come to appreciate the vastly increased power of styling with external CSS style sheet files. We explore those tools in depth in Book IV.

Chapter 2: Building Web Pages with HTML5

In This Chapter

✔ Structuring pages with HTML tags

✔ Creating headings and paragraphs

✔ Formatting lists

✔ Embedding images

✔ Saving and testing web pages

*O*ur approach to explaining HTML coding in this chapter isn't an attempt to provide an encyclopedic definition for every HTML element nor every tag *attribute* (every bit of syntax used to modify how an element works). Doing that would fill this entire book and would require frequent updates to keep up with changing HTML usage and with developments in browsing environments that support, or drop support, for tags.

One body that governs and disperses information about HTML usage is the World Wide Web Consortium (W3C), which we discuss briefly in a sidebar, "Standards are defined at W3C."

Instead, in this chapter, we focus on the concepts behind structuring an HTML page and the key tags used in most web pages.

In Chapter 1 of this minibook, we explore building the basic elements of an HTML page: the doctype declaration, the HTML element, and the head and body elements. On that basis, you can begin to bring a page to life by creating page content, all of which will fall within the body tags.

Why Use HTML5? And What Does That Mean?

In this book, we use HTML5, the current (albeit still-changing) version of HTML. As we note in Chapter 1 of this minibook, HTML5 is actually more widely supported, including in older browsers (such as Internet Explorer 6, 7, and 8), than its predecessors.

Here's the essential point to understand about HTML5: About 99 percent of HTML5 involves the same set of elements that were used by its predecessors, HTML4 and XHTML. (XHTML had more than one version, but we compress that evolutionary stage here under the grouping XHTML.) Those elements worked in HTML4, worked in XHTML, and still work in HTML5. In short, when we create pages in HTML5, we're just creating HTML pages, period.

The other dimension to HTML5, though, is that it introduces some new elements. The most dramatic of these new elements are native video and named page structure elements. We won't go into either of these in any detail here because we explore native video in Book V and page structure elements in Chapter 3 of this minibook. But very briefly, native video allows video to play in web pages without plug-ins, additional software like the Flash Player or Windows Media Player or Apple QuickTime Player. And named page structure elements, like `article`, or `header`, tell a browser "this is an article" or "this is a page header," respectively.

However, when we introduce new HTML5 tags (as we do in Chapter 3 of this minibook), we're creating pages that work best, or in some cases only work, in modern browsers. When we explore those new, added elements in HTML5, in Chapter 3, we also discuss how to approach making those pages accessible in outdated and obsolete browsers (specifically Internet Explorer versions 6–8).

Because you'll run into discussion of which doctype is best, we'll take a brief detour to explain why the XHTML doctype (the version of HTML that preceded HTML5) should be avoided in most cases.

Standards are defined at W3C

The ultimate source for HTML code rules is the `w3c.org` site. *W3C* stands for World Wide Web Consortium, which essentially functions as kind of a United Nations for setting Web standards — with all the good and bad connoted in that analogy. The "bad" is that the W3C brings together competing interests — different browser companies, different technology communities, and so on. The "good" is that to the extent there is a coherent or unified set of standards (found at www.w3c.org).

And W3C sets standards not only for HTML but also for CSS (cascading style sheet) code. Beyond that, the W3C defines standards for supported image formats, video (and audio) formats, scripting, and other dimensions of the web.

A downside to using the w3c.org site as a reference is the overwhelming amount of content. You'll also have to wade through overly complex explanations and formulations that mean something to insiders in the software development community but are hard to navigate for folks looking to find out how to define a link.

The XHTML doctype that preceded HTML5 had stricter rules for page formatting. XHTML (so-named because it facilitated using data organized in a format called XML) made life easier for database programmers using XML (eXtensible Markup Language). But it made life more problematic for web page designers.

What kind of strict rules defined in XHTML interfered with browsers opening pages with flawed HTML code? If you forgot to close a paragraph element with a closing paragraph tag, for instance, XHTML would instruct a browser not to open the page, or if the page opened, to display an error message. The stricter standard for HTML formatting associated with XHTML created annoying browsing experiences, with what appeared to be a barrage of unnecessary error messages popping up in browsers. These issues helped drive the emergence of the current version of HTML — HTML5.

The resolution of these "strict rules" issues in HTML5 has been to simplify HTML syntax, and loosen rules. With HTML5, leaving some tags unclosed is again allowable. (Having said that, best practice is still to close them; it doesn't take a lot of work and helps keep code more organized and comprehensible for troubleshooting.) Further, HTML5 has simplified the code required to define an HTML page. The first line of HTML5 page code is, as we explain in Chapter 1 of this minibook, very simple:

```
<html>
```

Learning resources at w3schools.com

All developers have their favorite source for HTML reference material and tutorials, but you'll find w3schools.com (`http://w3schools.com`; a commercial site with sponsors and ads) on nearly every developer's Top 10 sites list. The site also provides certifications (for a fee). Without passing judgment one way or another on either the ads or the certification programs, we can say that the HTML references material at w3schools.com is comprehensive and reliable, and the tutorials and demonstrations of every HTML tag are highly accessible. The figure, for example, shows an interactive tutorial at w3schools.com for learning how to define links.

Resources at w3school.com aren't as strictly or bureaucratically framed by the various consortiums and industry factions that consult on and approve what the W3C posts online. For example, you might read at w3c.org that a certain tag is "not yet fully adopted," but the folks at w3schools.com will be more candid and explain which browser doesn't support that tag.

Framed by, and in the context of the overview and basic introduction in this chapter, the resources at w3schools.com provide access to the full set of HTML5 tags. You can navigate to those resources at `www.3schools.com/html5`.

Who should continue to use an XHTML doctype declaration at the beginning of an HTML file? The answer: designers working under the direction of XML database managers who insist that the XML element of the pages will only work if an XHTML doctype is declared. Such design environments are rare.

Filling Out Body Content

The "open to the public" part of an HTML page is defined within the body element. This is where all the visible content of a page goes. All the graphics, images, banners, headings, and paragraphs of text must be contained between the <body> and </body> tags.

Before you start coding, organize the content as an outline with a main topic heading and then supporting subheadings under each. Several layers of headings are available. Level one headings are usually used only once on a page. And, theoretically at least, heading twos come next, and under them heading threes and so on. Headings five and six are often reserved for things like photo captions or legal notices.

Viewers like short, easy-to-access information on a web page. The cleaner your outline, the cleaner your page — and the better the experience for site visitors.

Text is organized into headings (1–6) and paragraphs. Text content can also be organized into lists. In HTML-speak, a numbered list is an "ordered list" and defined with the <ol> tag. And a bullet list is an "unordered list" and defined with the <ul> tag.

Images are the other basic element in web pages. They are defined with the <img> tag.

Finally, links are a critical dimension of page content. They can be defined for text or images.

Adding headings

Headings on your page belong between heading tags. These are elements that are used in order of your content structure — <h1>, <h2>, <h3>, and so on. The <h1> tag is for the main heading of your page, <h2> is for subheadings, and <h3> is for subheadings under the <h2> subheadings, and so on. You can see the progression in Listing 2-1.

Listing 2-1: Progression of Head Tags

```
<!DOCTYPE HTML>
<head>
<title>Welcome to the Web Revolution</title>
<meta name="Keywords" content="web,Web Design,New York City" />
<meta name="Description" content="The Web Collective designs
    Webs in New York City"/>
<link rel="stylesheet" href="style1.css" type="text/css"/>
</head>
<body>
<h1>About the Web Revolution</h1>
<p>This page tells the story of the Web Revolution</p>
<h2>Why the Web Collective?</h2>
<p>Because… someone has to do this!</p>
<h3>Who We are</h3>
<p>We are Manny, Moe, and Jack</p>
<h3>Where are We?</h3>
<p>We are located in the "big apple," New York city</p>
</body>
</html>
```

Even though HTML5 is often forgiving of unclosed tags, using closing tags does two important things:

Your code has a better chance of not misinterpreted in a browser.

You can better organize your own thinking: "Okay, now I'm done with the heading 2, that's over and done with, and I'm on to something else."

Coding paragraphs

As you might have noticed in Listing 2-1, the container tags for paragraphs are <p> and </p>, and you use them to separate text into paragraphs. Each paragraph must have its own set of paragraph tags.

As you look at the HTML of different websites, you might notice that sometimes <p> tags aren't used. Instead, you'll see
 (break) tags instead — sometimes several of them — to create the visual effect of having paragraphs.

This is an incorrect use of the break tag and should be avoided. A break tag should be used only when you need a hard break, like in a very long bullet. The reason why using multiple <br> tags is incorrect is that when you apply style sheets, you can get inconsistencies in your design because the style sheet will apply attributes to things like paragraphs. The <br> tags will not get the same attributes unless you clutter your CSS with code to make them the same. Also, coding your site properly will make your content more compatible with other technologies, such as screen readers and handheld devices.

Defining lists

Headings and paragraphs aren't always enough. Sometimes you need lists on your pages, too.

When deciding how to present your data, consider your options. If the text fits into short bullets, present it that way. Bulleted lists work very well on the web where your audience will be looking for quick, easy-to-access information. Using numbered lists can also help your visitors get the point quickly. The code for lists — bulleted or numbered — is fairly simple. You can put the heading for a list in either a paragraph tag or in a heading tag, whichever suits the situation best.

In HTML (and writing and publishing), bulleted lists are referred to as "unordered lists" because they just list items in no order of importance (and use the <ul> tag). Numbered lists, comparatively, are "ordered lists" because order is important; they use the <ol> tag. Items in both kinds of lists, though, are defined by using the list <li> tag.

Take a look at the following example, which creates a simple, bulleted (unordered) list:

```
<p>My list of fruit</p>
<ul>
    <li>apples</li>
    <li>bananas</li>
    <li>oranges</li>
</ul>
```

In the preceding example, note that the paragraph tag is closed before the list tags begin. Note also that the <li> tag is used for each list item.

To turn this list into a numbered list, use <ol> (for *ordered list*) in place of the <ul> tag — and don't forget to close it with the </ol> tag.

Sometimes a list has nested sub-items in it. The code to make that happen looks like this:

```
<p>My list of fruit</p>
<ul>
    <li>apples
    <ul><li>red</li>
       <li>green</li>
       <li>yellow</li>
```

```
    </ul>
    </li>
    <li>bananas</li>
    <li>oranges</li>
</ul>
```

In a browser (and without defined styles), that list looks like the one in Figure 2-1 with bullet points, and indents for sub-bullet points.

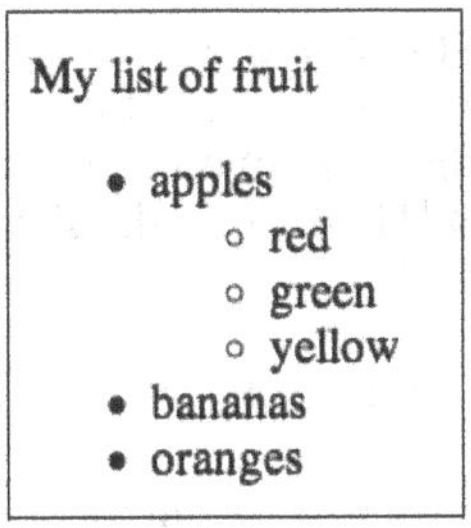

My list of fruit

- apples
  - red
  - green
  - yellow
- bananas
- oranges

Figure 2-1:
A two-level
bullet list as
displayed in
a browser.

The sub-items in the `apples` item are part of a second unordered list. Notice how the sub-items list begins and is closed between the `<li>` and `</li>` of the `apples` list item. The browser displays them as indented items under `apples` in the main list.

Vertical spacing in HTML

At this point in our exploration of applying HTML tags to content, we can anticipate that many of you are asking: "How do I get rid of that (vertical) spacing?" between paragraphs. Or, "How do I add (vertical) spacing between list items?"

First, it will be helpful to understand where that vertical spacing comes from. Vertical spacing in HTML is associated with every element. Who decided that every paragraph element should have a line of spacing under it? And who decided that lists should not have spacing between lines? We may never know who made that call, but we have to live with it.

Every HTML text element, ranging from <h1> to <p> has a default vertical spacing defined above and below it. Just like every heading element has a default font size. And just like, by default, HTML pages have a monochromatic "color" scheme of black and white (plus colors for links).

So how do you change that? CSS. When you create a style sheet for your site, you can change the default vertical spacing associated with any HTML element using the margin property. We explore this in depth in Book IV.

Defining links

Links, those clickable objects that make the web what it is, are defined with the HTML <a> element. We complete our survey of the most essential HTML tags with an examination of this vital link in web page design.

In Chapter 1 of this minibook, we look at the <link> element as it is used to define links to style sheets (and sometimes other files). Defining links to other pages is done differently, using the <a> tag.

The most essential attribute of any <a> element is the href attribute, which defines the link's destination. But <a> elements also must include some content — for example, some text — that displays in a browser and enables the link to work. For example, the following HTML code displays Search Google and links to www.google.com:

```
<a href="http://www.google.com">Search Google</a>
```

Note that the entire link, including the display text, is enclosed within <a> and </a> tags. However, there is also a closing > after the actual link and before the displayed text.

Links can have defined targets, like the "_blank" parameter used to open a link in a new browser window. To edit the preceding example to open in a new browser window, you would use this code:

```
<a href="http://www.google.com" target="_blank">Search Google</a>
```

Absolute and relative links

Links can be absolute or relative:

✦ **Absolute links,** like the one in the preceding examples, are defined with http:// at the beginning and include the entire URL for the link.

✦ **Relative links** are used within a website. So, for example, if you were linking to a page called about_us.html, you could use

```
Visit my <a href="about_us.html">About Us </a>page!
```

However, the preceding code would work only if the about_us.html page is in the same folder as the page from which it was linked.

You can also define more complex relative links, using / to chart a path to the folder with the link. For example, to link to a file called slideshow. html in a subfolder (relative to the original page) named presentations, you would use this code:

```
Visit my <a href="presentations/slideshow.html">Slideshow</a> page!
```

How links look

When you build a style sheet for your site, you define how links appear in different states: unvisited, visited, active (in the process of being opened), or hovered (hovered over by a mouse cursor). By default, until you create a style sheet, links appear like this in all browsers:

✦ **Unvisited links are underlined and blue.**

✦ **Visited links are underlined and purple.**

✦ **Active links are underlined and red.**

> There is no default hover state. And until you create one in a style sheet, hovered links do not change appearance.

Embedding Images

In Book V, we explain how to prepare images for the web and also how to embed them in web pages. But here, we'll note the syntax for the image tag:

```
<img src="image.png"/>
```

In this example, `image.png` is the filename, and of course, you replace this with your actual filename.

There are several important image element attributes that are usually added to an image tag:

✦ `Alt`: The `Alt` attribute defines text that displays when a browsing environment can't display images. While images will display without a defined `Alt` attribute, it's bad practice to not define one. Software that interprets web pages for vision-impaired people reads `Alt` text out loud. Search engines use `Alt` text to index images and make them searchable. And `Alt` text displays when images are loading with slow Internet connections. Figure 2-2 shows `Alt` text displayed at Wikipedia in place of an image of a flower.

✦ `Align`: The `Align` attribute can have two useful values: left or right. When you align an image left, text and other content flow around the image to the right. When you align an image right, text and other content flow around the image to the left. Figure 2-3 shows an image right-aligned.

✦ `Height` and `Width`: The `Height` attribute defines the vertical size the image will display at in a browser, and the `Width` attribute defines the horizontal size. The unit of measurement for the height and width values is, by default, pixels.

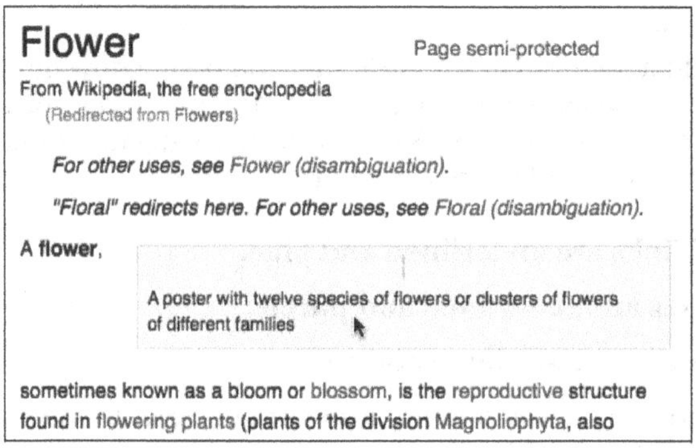

Figure 2-2:
Alt text
displays
when an
image is
slow to
load into
a browser
window.

Flower   Page semi-protected

From Wikipedia, the free encyclopedia
(Redirected from Flowers)

For other uses, see Flower (disambiguation).

"Floral" redirects here. For other uses, see Floral (disambiguation).

A **flower**,

> A poster with twelve species of flowers or clusters of flowers
> of different families

sometimes known as a bloom or blossom, is the reproductive structure
found in flowering plants (plants of the division Magnoliophyta, also

Figure 2-3:
A right-
aligned
image with
text flowing
to the left of
the graphic.

EXPERIENCE:

SENIOR ART
DIRECTOR -
FREELANCER

Here's how those attributes look when defined for an image that is sized at
100 pixels high, 400 pixels wide, and right aligned:

```
<img src="image.png" alt="an image" height="100" width="400" align="right"/>
```

Saving and Testing Web Pages

As soon as you begin to construct web pages, you'll want to save them as
HTML files. If you're creating HTML pages using a coding application, all
you see is code. And, until you save your code and open it in a browser, you
won't really know what it looks like.

By the way, even when you type or generate HTML in Dreamweaver, you'll
still want to preview your pages in a browser. Dreamweaver's document
window has a "Live view" mode (something we explore in Chapter 4 of this
minibook). But even Live view can't really simulate how a page will look in
different browsers because every browser has some unique ways of interpreting HTML.

In short, the process of building HTML pages involves jumping back and forth between your HTML coding (or generating) environment and testing your pages in a browser (or several browsers).

Naming HTML files

You can't open your code in a browser until you save it with a filename extension of .html (or .htm).

In Chapter 1 of this minibook, we discuss the difference between a file name and a page title. Remember that page titles display in a browser title bar or tab bar. Titles are really how your page is "identified" to the world. The page filename, though, is more an internal part of the site.

Filename rules

Filenames are not kept secret from the public; they appear in browsers' address bars. And an emerging approach in file-naming is to create more intuitive (and longer) filenames, like

```
this-is-a-page-about-me.html
```

The next time you do some web browsing, survey this trend by noting the file names that appear in the address bar of your browser as you visit pages. Figure 2-4, for instance, shows a typical filename assigned by *The New York Times* — essentially it's the article heading but with lowercase characters and dashes instead of spaces. That filename will help optimize how the page is detected and promoted in search engines. (For a full exploration of search engine optimization, see Book IX, Chapter 1.)

Book III
Chapter 2

Building Web Pages with HTML5

Figure 2-4:
An optimized filename.

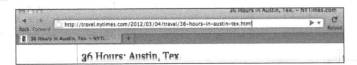

Regardless, the most important consideration for an HTML page filename is that it works and follows necessary file-naming rules.

HTML files should be saved with all lowercase letters and no special symbols (except letters and numbers) except for - (dash) and _ (underscore), concluding with the extension .html.

Alternatively, `.htm` can work as an extension, but whatever you do, don't mix the two. Files named `about_me.htm` and `about_me.html` saved to the same folder will cause havoc and confusion for you, your server, browsers, and visitors.

Similarly, the price for breaking the rules on using uppercase letters and special characters (aside from - and _) can be steep. Filenames with spaces, for instance, get translated into filenames with `%20` where the space was, and tend to get corrupted when saved, forwarded, or linked to. Filenames with a mixture of uppercase and lowercase letters (camelcase) can confuse browsers and servers: for example, avoid having two files named `about_me.html` and the other named `About_Me.html` in the same folder.

And sure, you will indeed encounter HTML pages on the web with filenames that include spaces and uppercase letters. But as you do, you will smile the knowing smile of a battle-scarred veteran designer, feeling comfortable in the knowledge that your own pages are more reliably named.

A special name for a home page

If the page you are creating is going to be the home page for your site, you should name it `index.html`.

You might think of a home page as the page visitors arrive at first when they come to your site. And you are correct. But how does a browser know that when your visitors enter "pat.com" (assuming for the moment that you are Pat and pat.com is your site), which of the many HTML pages at your site to open first?

Browsers detect your home page by looking for a file called `index.html`, which plays a special role. By default, when a browser is directed to a URL (like `davidkarlins.com`), the browser looks for a file called `index.html`. In other words, `index.html` serves as the home page within any folder. And in your site's root folder (your URL), the `index.html` file serves as the site home page.

Previewing web pages

In Chapter 1 of this minibook, we examine a wide variety of tools for creating HTML, and some of them (like Dreamweaver) have preview windows that provide a rough estimate of how your page will look in a browser.

But as noted earlier, you will want to test your page in more than one browser early and often. To see what your code looks like as an actual web page, save the document with an `.html` file extension instead of `.txt`. Then open the document in a browser.

One way to do that is to install as many browsers as you can on your own computer, but it's not possible to install every browser on your computer —

some are no longer downloadable. Others work only in certain operating systems: Internet Explorer, for example, isn't available for Macs.

In addition to testing files in your own browser, you can use online resources that identify which HTML elements are supported in which browsers. One such site is `http://caniuse.com.`

The most powerful tool for previewing pages in browsers is Adobe BrowserLab. BrowserLab is free, but you have to upload pages to a server to test them. Or, you can test pages before you upload to a server if you have Dreamweaver. See Chapter 4 in this minibook for instructions on previewing pages in Dreamweaver, and see Book IX, Chapter 2 for advice on uploading pages to a server.

No matter how you preview your page, until you add CSS formatting, your pages will look rather barren. However, you will be able to see what parts of this code are visible on the page, which parts are in the title bar, and which parts are invisible. You will also be able to see what the different heading types look like by default (before styling).

Don't worry! Your page won't look "naked" like this for long. But like an electrician examining wiring before the walls go up, you can examine the content without the overlay of styles. And if you stripped the CSS off of any site, it too would have the bare-bones unstyled look of pure HTML. eBay, for example, has a very inviting set of attached styles, but without them, it would look like the page in Figure 2-5.

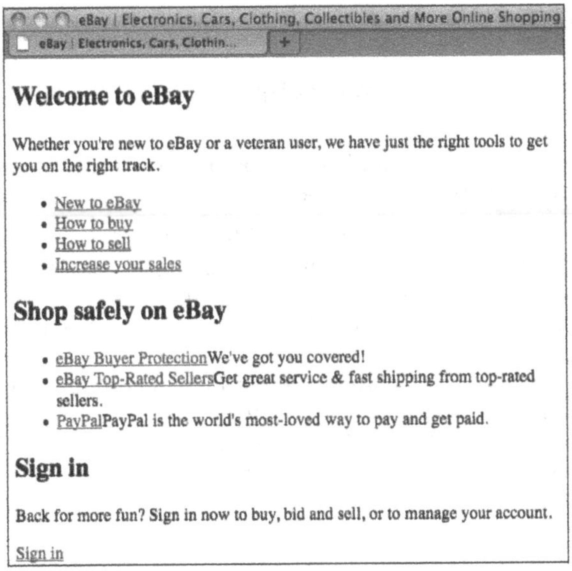

Figure 2-5:
eBay
without CSS.

The Expanding and Evolving Set of HTML Tags

In exploring the head and body elements of a web page, and looking at key tags within the body element (headings, paragraphs, lists, and links), you can get a pretty good idea of the essential elements — that is, the basic rules used to define tags within the body tag apply globally — of a web page. However, we have scarcely scratched the surface of the universe of web design.

You can go a long way in constructing HTML pages with headings, paragraphs, lists, and links, particularly when it comes to organizing and presenting text on a page. As you learn to create additional page content — such as images or video — or special elements called DIV tags that are used for page layout — you'll be applying these same basic rules. We explore relevant HTML tags in the course of covering different web design techniques throughout the book. In particular, we walk through how to design pages with DIV tags in Book IV, Chapter 2. The following list notes a few more generally universal features of elements:

✦ **Elements typically open and close with tags.**

Exceptions include

the <br> tag, which forces a line break

The <img> tag that defines an image

The <a> tag that defines a link

Armed with the basic understanding of HTML elements and syntax we cover in this chapter, you can access a complete list of HTML tags and their syntax, attributes, and range of values at www.w3schools.com/tags.

✦ **If an element encloses content displayed in a web page, it will be encased inside body tags.**

✦ **Many elements are defined with *parameters* — additional code that refines how the element functions.**

The particulars will be different for different kinds of elements. For an image tag, to take an example we looked at earlier in this chapter, parameters define the source (the image file), and additional parameters might define the height and width for how the image displays.

Throughout this book, we explore a wide range of content that might be defined in an HTML page, and as we do, we introduce additional tags and explain how they work. Beyond that, the list of HTML tags that have been adopted widely enough to enjoy critical mass support among browsers continues to grow and evolve.

HTML5 is very much a work in progress. And as you expand your web design capacity, you'll tune in to sites like `www.w3c.org` to see what elements have become endorsed and available to present content. (Find out more about W3C online in the sidebar elsewhere in this chapter.)

In particular, the HTML5 tags that we discuss in this minibook are in the process of being adopted. As of today's writing, older versions of Internet Explorer that have been an impediment to the global adoption of new HTML5 tags are being phased out, and Microsoft will encourage (or even force) users to update their browsers to more standards-compatible versions of IE. And so the process continues.

Helpful Development Practices

Having walked through the process of creating and saving a basic HTML file, there are a few things you should be aware of that don't strictly speaking fall in the realm of coding but are important — even critical — parts of the process.

Some peripheral tips for effectively creating web pages you already know instinctively, such as having a good cup of hot coffee or your favorite tea nearby, along with tasty snacks for when you run up against really hard challenges. Beyond that, we'll share some techniques that can help you while you work on your website projects and help you avoid unnecessary drama, trauma, and stress.

**Book III
Chapter 2**

**Building Web Pages
with HTML5**

Use comments in your code

Comments are notes to yourself and other people who might have to work with your files. Whether you're working alone or in a group, commenting your code is an important habit to develop.

The syntax for a comment is pretty simple. Comment tags open with `<!--` and end with `-->`. And there are no attributes to worry about. Here's an example:

```
<!--The following code needs to be tested before the site is uploaded-->
```

Common things to include in comments are when the code was added to the document, what the piece of code does, who added it, and so on.

Make sure that your comments are clear and concise to avoid confusion and frustration. Too, some comments will be visible if someone looks at the source code for your web page, which is something every browser allows people to do — so don't type things you don't want the general public to read.

Use version-control protocols

Plan ahead for those, "Pshew, that saved my bacon" episodes. How? Use version control.

✦ **Scenario Part 1:** You worked 12 hours perfecting the HTML for your site home page. You saved it as `index.html`. The next day, sleep still in your eyes, you open that file, accidentally delete all the content, and save a blank file as `index.html`. Yikes! You just wiped out 12 hours of work, and you might not be able to remember what it was you lost!

✦ **Scenario Part 2:** After a moment of panic, you remember that you backed up your work onto an external hard drive the night before. You plug in the hard drive, copy last night's version of `index.html` back into your site folder, and go on with your work.

How do you ensure that scenario part 1 is followed by scenario part 2? Here are some basic protocols to implement in one form or another:

✦ **Prevent overwriting #1:** Make sure your mechanisms are in place to prevent you, or members of the team from overwriting each other's work. Dreamweaver and other professional code-authoring programs offer version control tools. These tools warn or prevent other designers from opening and working on files that are open and being edited. These code editors all work a little differently, and some are more effective than others. That is, they might prevent more than one person from opening and working on a file instead of just issuing a warning that someone else is working on the file but letting a second person work on it anyway.

✦ **Prevent overwriting #2:** Other version- and source-control features include warning a user when she is trying to post an older version of a file to the server when the file currently on the server is newer and presumably has been posted by someone else very recently.

✦ **Prevent overwriting #3:** Another way to make sure files don't get overwritten is to limit the number of people who have the power to publish files to the site. The designated person acts as a gatekeeper, making sure that members of the team don't overwrite each other's work.

Most importantly, even if you do none of the above: Make backups. Even if you're working solo, accidentally overwriting a file is easy. Make sure you have backups so you can recover the work if something does happen.

Because you should keep all the files for any website in a single folder (which can be divided into subfolders), the simplest way to back up your site is to make a copy of that folder at the end of each session and then save it somewhere. That "somewhere" can be on a thumb drive, a backup drive, or your cloud (online storage space). Decide consciously how often you and/ or your team should back up work, and stick to that protocol.

Organize your supporting files

While you work on a site, you'll accumulate files that aren't actually part of the site. For example, much of the content for a web page might well come from a word processing document that has your mission statement/price list/tour schedule/call to action, or whatever text content is essential to a page in your website. That word processing file is not really part of your "website." That is, it's not an HTML file (or an image or a video, or any other file that will be viewed by visitors to your site). Yet, it is essential to your work.

Further, as you create your site, you might well start generating new word processing or image documents. If, for example, you craft an "About Us" statement for a site, you will want to compose it using a word processor that checks spelling and has other editing tools. With the document saved, you can then copy the text into an HTML file. But you'll want to hang onto the word processing document in case you need to do substantial editing to your statement.

To organize these kinds of files, make a folder named something like Production Files to keep track of all these files. You can keep this folder with the site folder, but don't post it to your live site.

Chapter 3: Structuring Content with HTML5

In This Chapter

✔ HTML5 — the big new thing

✔ The impact of HTML5 video and CSS3 effects

✔ Structuring pages with HTML5 elements

✔ Using HTML5 for search engine optimization (SEO)

✔ Understanding and managing HTML5 compatibility issues in outdated browsers

*A*s we discuss in Chapters 1 and 2 of this minibook, HTML5 is the current version of HTML, the language that structures the basic content in most web pages. In those chapters our exploration of HTML is pretty much version-free. That is, the HTML5 techniques we cover in those chapters could, for the most part, have been written the same way if we were showing you how to structure web pages with earlier versions of HTML. The HTML5 we cover in Chapters 1 and 2 of this minibook works in every browser, even outdated browsers (such as Internet Explorer versions 6, 7, and 8).

But HTML5 has also added new (and quite valuable) elements. Those elements include more accessible forms (something we cover in Book VII, Chapter 2) and *native* video (video that runs without a plug-in like the Flash Player, QuickTime player, or Windows Media Player).

Perhaps most fundamentally, HTML5 introduces a new way to organize your page content with elements like header, article, section, footer, address, and time. Those new elements — for the first time in web history — give all of us a coherent, logical, and standardized way to organize our page content! That's an exciting development, making it easier to design pages. And, it holds the potential to make your page content much more searchable and accessible because it's clearer to search engines what kind of information is being *indexed* (organized into a search database).

In this chapter, we examine many of these new features in HTML5 and walk through the process of building web pages using HTML5's new page structuring elements.

Understanding the Big New Things in HTML5

Our exploration of HTML5 runs through this whole book. When we explore collecting data in forms, for example (in Book VII), we look at how new HTML5 attributes allow you to *validate* form data (test it to see if it looks right) before a form is submitted. And when we walk through how to embed video in your site (in Book V, Chapter 4), we explain how to use the HTML5 video tag. So, in that sense, this is not "the end-all, be-all" HTML5 chapter in this book. That said, there should be one place where you get a good overview of the scope of HTML5 and what it has to offer — and this is that chapter.

In addition, in this chapter, we focus on building basic web pages using HTML5's new page structuring elements (like header, article, section, and footer). Read on to discover the basic contours of what HTML5 brings to the web-design world:

+ **How video is presented on the web:** One of the most dramatic changes reflected in and implemented through HTML5 is how video is presented on the web. Book V shows you how to create and present web video (and audio). There, we explain how to use the HTML5 `video` element to embed native video that plays without plug-ins. This radical development in how video is presented online has particular importance if you're creating sites that will have significant audiences using Apple's iPhone or iPad, which don't support Flash Video (FLV) files. Again, we cover this challenge in depth in Book V.

+ **CSS3 development:** Much of the hype and buzz around HTML5 is really based on developments in CSS — and specifically *CSS3*, which is the emerging new standard for designing and formatting with style sheets. CSS3 is emerging alongside of — and intersecting with — HTML5, and thus dramatic new features of CSS3 are sometimes lumped together in popular discourse in terms of "what you can do with HTML5." We show you how to take advantage of exciting new CSS3 *effects* (things like drop-shadows, rounded corners, and transparency) and *transforms* (like rotation and skewing) in Book IV, Chapter 3.

+ **A new way to structure page content:** The third dimension of HTML5 is that it presents web designers with a whole new way to structure page content. New HTML5 tags (such as `header`, `article`, `section`, `aside`, `nav`, and `figure`) make laying out pages much easier for designers, and ultimately will have a big impact on how people search for and see content in their browsing environments. For example, search engines will be able to identify that search results include content from an article, a figure caption, or a navigation bar. Such features are, at this writing, a work in progress, but hold great potential. This aspect of HTML5 — structured layout elements — is covered in detail in the latter sections of this chapter.

Throughout this section, we look at each dimension more closely. First, however, we want to point out the overall impact of HTML5, which is, in a sense, bigger than the sum of its parts. HTML5 represents a different approach to presenting web content, an approach that is simpler, easier, and more intuitive, both for users and designers. This approach anticipates the next steps in the evolution of the web, and builds in more powerful and effective search tools that provide more helpful search results. We address this subject more fully in the "Looking at HTML5 Metadata Tags" section later in this chapter.

The wild world of native video

Users have two ways of viewing video on the web: through a plug-in (like Flash Player) or through their browser. *Native* video (and audio) refers to embedded media files that play in a browser without the need for a plug-in player.

Until the advent of HTML5, viewing video in a browser required installing one or more *plug-ins* (applications that "plug in" to a browser and run in the background while the browser is open). The main plug-ins were the Flash Player (used to play Flash Video), Windows Media Player (used to play a variety of media formats associated with Microsoft Windows), and the QuickTime Player (used to play media associated with Apple products).

As of this writing, the "web world" is in a chaotic transition from plug-in based media to native media. Currently, vast amounts of web video are available online in the Flash video (FLV) format, and they will be available in that format for years to come. These videos require that a viewer have the Flash Player plug-in installed. Meanwhile, Apple digital devices like iPads and iPhones don't have and never will have Flash Player support. This means that a significant portion of users — in number as well as in purchasing power and trend-setting impact — will never need Flash to view video files.

Plug-ins were (and still are) often bundled with a browser installation. Apple's Safari browser, for example, seamlessly includes the QuickTime Player, and Microsoft's Internet Explorer installs with Windows Media Player. The Flash Player is relatively easy to install. But nevertheless, folks who want to watch a lot of online video have had to install all three plug-ins, and periodically update them, which can get to be a bit of a hassle.

Native video, on the other hand, does not require a plug-in and thus simplifies the process of watching video online.

The most significant factor driving native video is that for both technical and aesthetic/marketing reasons, Apple chose to not support the Flash Player on its digital devices under the rubric of native video. The appeal is that users don't have to download a plug-in (like the Flash Player, or QuickTime Player, or Windows Media Player) to watch video.

Still, a video player obviously has to be available for the end user to watch a video on a mobile device. Apple adopted one technology for its devices: the H.264 video format (files that often have an .mp4 filename extension). Of course, the makers of Internet Explorer, Firefox, Safari, Chrome, and other browsing environments had to build in support for playing video in their respective browser software as well. As you read in more detail in Book V, every browser has adopted different standards for video presentation online.

As you can guess, the result is a significant amount of chaos in the web video world, with powerful players contending over which video standards will emerge to replace Flash video. In short, while native video may be more convenient for people watching online video, it presents new challenges for web designers. But don't stress — we walk you through a range of doable solutions in Book V.

HTML5's stylish cousin: CSS3

When people talk about HTML5, they often refer to (consciously or not) new features in CSS3. As we mention in the preceding section, the conflict/incompatibility between Adobe (maker of Flash) and Apple (without Flash support on its mobile devices) played a role in setting the stage for the emergence and role of CSS3. Flash video has been a dominant form for delivering online video. Beyond that, though, Flash has also been a significant (probably the dominant) tool and format for enabling web *animation* (motion) and *interactivity* (elements that respond to user action).

That huge online footprint means not only that Flash videos don't play on iPads (and Apple cousins), but also that animated and interactive ads, games, cartoons, and page layouts don't work on Apple devices. No good. This incompatibility has contributed to the urgency and energy with which developers are implementing CSS3, which presentation-features developers might have earlier used Flash for effects and transforms. CSS3 effects and transforms can also be combined with *JavaScript* (a programming tool that provides some of the functionality of Flash). And so, CSS3 can create web pages with some of the animation and interactivity formerly provided by Flash.

The rotated, rounded-corner box with drop-shadows shown in Figure 3-1 gives a feel for the kind of formatting that is newly available with CSS3. And keep in mind that an effect like this is accomplished simply with fast-loading style sheets, not images (except for the photo) or Flash.

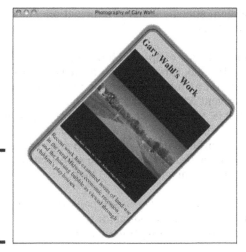

Figure 3-1:
CSS3
effects
applied
to a box.

Here's the takeaway: Because HTML5 provides an alternative to Flash video, and CSS3 opens the door to alternative animation and interactivity, you might people say, "I hear HTML5 is replacing Flash." That's an oversimplification but has some basic truth to it.

HTML5: Standardizing content organization and page layout

HTML5 provides a whole new way to structure page content. The impact of this aspect of HTML5 is less dramatic, at least on the user end. In fact, visitors may well not notice any difference between an "HTML5 page" and a page structured with earlier versions of HTML. The biggest impact of new HTML5 page structuring tags, at this point, is on designers.

However, that change is radical: HTML5 completely changes how you structure page content — and here's how. Pre-HTML5 tags were overwhelmingly content-neutral. For example, the HTML heading tags (h1, h2, and so on) have no connotations as far as what kind of content they represent. Sure, an h1 element denotes that the enclosed content is a heading, and is superior (hierarchically) to an h2 element. But is that content an article headline? A headline for a section within an article (a subhead)? A sidebar headline? A footer headline? Until HTML5 emerged, tags provided no such clues.

HTML5 introduces a set of new elements — for example, article, section, aside, header, and footer — that are content-associated. These new HTML5 elements are assigned in accord with the actual content they enclose, and that's a good thing. Other HTML5 elements, such as time or `address`, serve to highlight specific kinds of information, like the time of an event or the location of a business.

This is a significant shift in terms of approach to web design. Take the `time` element, for example. In HTML5, this new element marks times of events or activities. Now, a website for a club, organization, or business can enclose the time of a scheduled event within `<time>` tags that don't even need any display attributes — that is, someone reading that web page won't see the time displayed differently than other text. Under the hood, though, search engines, social media, and other emerging tools and apps can exploit a time tag to identify events, and use that information to show lists of "things you can do in the next hour in your neighborhood." Nice.

The full implications of HTML5's content-based page structuring tags are yet to be realized, but we see great potential for this approach to radically change how people find and use information on the web.

One of the most immediate impacts of new HTML5 page-structuring tags is on designers, and that change is HTML5 elements replacing traditional HTML `DIV` tags to demarcate sections of a web page.

Until the advent of HTML5, web designers relied on the ubiquitous and generic `DIV` (division) tag to mark off blocks of content. Those `DIV` tags were then associated with *classes* (styling elements that can be used multiple times on a page) or *IDs* (styling elements used just once on a page).

As it turned out, and not surprisingly, most web designers tended to come up with the same names for these `DIV` tags–based formatting containers. For example, most of us named the ID style that defined our page headers as "header." Same thing with "footer." But header and footer were not HTML elements: They were just randomly and nonstandardized names that most of us ended up using because they were intuitive.

The game has changed a bit now because HTML5 uses a `<header>` and `<footer>` tag. And the changes go beyond that — HTML5 `<article>`, `<section>`, and `<aside>` tags compel web designers to organize content in a *structured* (organized, hierarchal) way.

Keep reading as we show you how the HTML5 structured page layout works with the examples in the rest of this chapter.

Introducing Key HTML5 Elements

Here's one of the nice things about the new HTML5 structuring elements. We've noted several of them already, and the names are pretty self-explanatory! The following elements are the key HTML5 elements used to organize page content:

✦ `<header>`: This element holds content at the top of a page. This content often includes a graphical or text page banner, perhaps a search box, sometimes content introducing the page, and often a navigation bar. As noted earlier, the `<header>` element is not the same as a heading tag (h1, h2, and so on). We explain how to apply heading tags (which are not replaced by, but are different than `<header>` elements) in Chapter 2 of this minibook.

✦ `<nav>`: This element holds navigation content, and can be (but does not have to be) embedded with other elements (like a header or footer).

✦ `<article>`: This element defines a specific article within a page. And, within an article, `<section>` elements enclose subtopics within that particular article. *Note:* You never use a section element outside an article element.

What constitutes an "article" or a "section" of an article? This is a judgment call for content creators. Newspaper, magazine, or blog articles are — rather obviously — *articles.* In a newspaper, magazine, or blog site, each article should be inside its own `<article>` element. And subheadings should demarcate sections in that article. In other text content, deciding what constitutes an article, or sections within an article, is an editorial call.

✦ `<aside>`: This element describes sidebar content, usually within an article. Sidebar content is content associated with an article, or an article section, but which stands on its own. Traditionally, sidebars are run on the side of an article (usually on the right side) in online and print publications.

✦ `<footer>`: This element holds typical footer content at the bottom of a page. That might include legal notices, and secondary navigation content (which should be organized into a nav element within the footer).

The page layout (with placeholder text and a bit of minimalist styling added) in Figure 3-2 gives a sense of how HTML5 elements fit together on, and frame, a page.

**Book III
Chapter 3**

Structuring Content
with HTML5

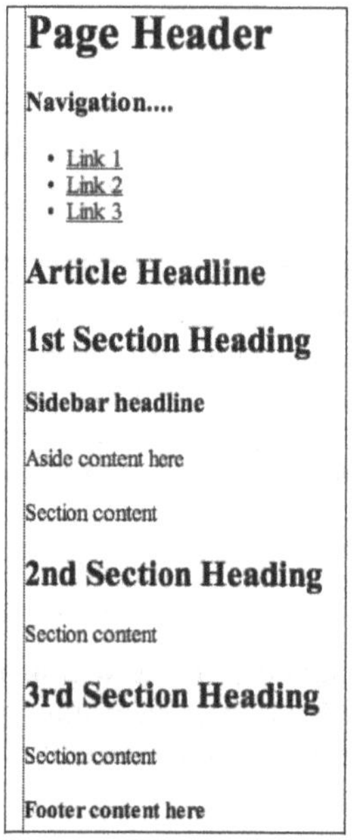

Page Header

Navigation....

- Link 1
- Link 2
- Link 3

Article Headline

1st Section Heading

Sidebar headline

Aside content here

Section content

2nd Section Heading

Section content

3rd Section Heading

Section content

Footer content here

Figure 3-2:
HTML5 page
structure
elements.

Integrating Traditional HTML Tags

Overwhelmingly, new HTML5 elements expand the scope and range of HTML. That is, they don't replace older tags (for the most part). So, for example, the legacy HTML six heading tags, the paragraph tag, and links are all used in HTML5 essentially in the same way that they were in previous versions of HTML. If you know something about HTML tags, don't use that neuralyzer device they used in the "Men in Black" movies to wipe your memory of that information. And by the same token, don't tear out and shred Chapters 1 and 2 of this minibook, the ones that introduce basic, traditional HTML tags and *syntax* (rules for using tags). You still need that information.

✦ HTML5 elements add content-based structuring tools: As a general rule, HTML5 page structure tags structure — that is, they contextualize older, traditional tags. They frame those tags within more-defining elements. For example, a single HTML5 `article` element might well have different levels of headings, paragraph tags, links, images, video, and so on.

✦ Here's an example of how that works: An HTML5 `aside` element can be used to indicate that "this information is a sidebar to (associated with) the article it is embedded in." And that `aside` element, in turn, can include traditional HTML tags like headings, paragraphs, and links.

Beyond that, this `aside` element can also include new HTML5 tags like a `nav` element (to enclose navigation content) and an `address` element (to demarcate the physical location of the business or organization served by the website).

✦ Here's another example of how HTML5 tags can be used within either other HTML5 elements, or within traditional blocks of HTML: You can use the `<address>` and `<time>` elements to help search engines recognize your address (which can be a physical or virtual location — a street address or a URL). And those `<address>` and `<time>` elements can be inserted anywhere within traditional blocks of HTML. A `paragraph` element, for instance, can include an HTML5 tag demarcating a physical address, and an HTML `time` element denoting the time an event starts.

To summarize the point here, new HTML5 elements can be mixed into, and integrated with, traditional HTML elements.

Building a Page with HTML5

Time to walk through the entire process of building an HTML5 page from start to finish. We'll draw on the basic HTML we cover in Chapters 1 and 2 of this minibook, but we'll add HTML5 elements to the mix. In doing so, we'll rely on HTML structure elements like `header`, `footer`, `article`, `section`, and `aside` to structure the content. And we'll use HTML5 elements like `time` and `address` to make relevant content (like event times or addresses) more accessible to search engines.

HTML5 web pages use the same filenaming and basic page layout rules as all HTML pages. As we discuss in Chapters 1 and 2 of this minibook, at the most basic level, they're organized into head and body content, and they begin with a document type declaration.

Here's how to begin:

1. **To start a new HTML5 page using any of the tools and techniques that we cover in Chapter 2 of this minibook, begin the file with this standard code:**

```
<!DOCTYPE HTML>
<html>
<head>
<title> </title>
</head>
<body>
</body>
</html>
```

2. **Enter *title text* — text that will display in a browser title or tab bar — between the title tags.**

   For example, if you want the message Welcome to our site! to appear in the title bar of a browser, you'd use this code:

   ```
   <title>Welcome to our site!</title>
   ```

   That's it! You created an HTML5 page.

3. **Save the file with an .html filename extension.**

   Always save with an .html extension. Alternatively, you can use .htm, but you should stay consistent throughout your site in filename extensions. As we explain in Chapters 1 and 2 of this minibook, mixing .html and .htm filenames can confuse browsers and make the wrong page appear.

So far, your HTML5 page could be any HTML page except that we're using the simpler, more-accessible document type declaration associated with HTML5 — the same document type declaration we introduce in Chapters 1 and 2 of this minibook:

```
<!DOCTYPE HTML>
```

The fun (and value) of HTML5 begins next as we show you how to structure your page with HTML5 elements.

Defining a header

The HTML5 header element is typically the first element after the beginning of the body element in an HTML5 web page.

Don't confuse the <header> element, which we are introducing here, with the <head> element. The <head> element is used to define parts of your HTML document that will not show up in a browser (like the page title). On the other hand, the <header> element defines content that does appear in your page, within the body of the page.

A header element encloses all the content that goes at the top of a web page. And we mention earlier, you use HTML elements like <p>, <h1>, and so on to define content within the header element.

Here's how the HTML5 code would look for a simple, basic HTML5 header:

```
<body>
<header>
<h1>Header Content Goes Here</h1>
</header>
</body>
```

This snippet includes an <h1> tag (and some placeholder text) within the header.

Adding nav elements

Along with text (often in <h1> tags), or a graphical banner, HTML5 headers typically include a navigation bar of some type. Wherever navigation content appears in HTML5 page, that content should be enclosed between <nav> and </nav> tags.

Note: We're not talking about a link, or an e-mail address, as a navigation aid. Some links and e-mail addresses should be enclosed in HTML5 <address> tags, but that's different and something we explore later in this chapter.

nav tags should go around more organized navigation bars like the ones you might typically see at the top of a page (like in Figure 3-3), at the bottom of a page, or in a side column. And that is the case when such navigation content is embedded in a header (or footer).

Navigation content

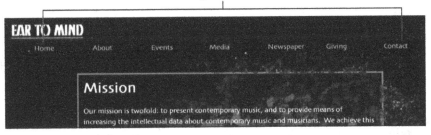

Figure 3-3:
The navigation bar in a web page.

Here's an example of an HTML5 header element, with a simple welcome message (tagged as an h1), with a basic navigation bar:

```
<header>
<h1>Welcome to Our Site</h1>
<nav>
<h5><a href="index.html">Home</a> | <a href="#">Page 1
    </a> | <a href="#">Page 2</a> | <a href="#">Page 3</a>
</h5>
</nav>
</header>
```

That code (and how it looks in a browser) is illustrated in Figure 3-4.

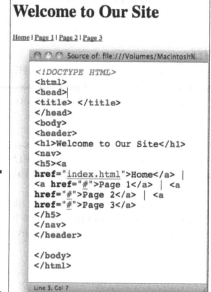

Figure 3-4:
Applying
the HTML5
nav element
to define a
navigation
bar.

As you can see, this sample code applies <h5> tags to links, and the <h5> tags and the links are all enclosed within HTML5 <nav> and </nav> tags. Also, without styling applied, neither the header nor the nav HTML5 elements have any particular default display characteristics.

Enclosing the header content in the HTML5 header element doesn't change how that content is displayed, so you might wonder why you need to bother with placing navigation content within the HTML5 nav element. Here's why: Embedding content in HTML5 tags improves search engine optimization (SEO), and that's a big deal because you want your pages to show up in search engines, and you want the information that's displayed by search engines to be accurate and helpful.

Also keep in mind that you can define CSS styles for these HTML5 tags (and other HTML5 tags, too), which applies uniform styling to their appearance throughout your site. You want that! We explore CSS styling in Book IV.

Organizing header content with hgroup

HTML5 includes an hgroup element, and its purpose is to make header content inside a header more easily categorized by search engines. Like all the page structuring elements we're exploring here, the hgroup element is new to HTML5.

All content within an `hgroup` element should have heading tags applied (`<h1>` on down to `<h6>`).

The purpose behind subgrouping header content with an `hgroup` is that heading content — say, subheadings, alternative titles, or taglines — should be grouped, within the header, for easy access.

For example, if a header has a page title (like "Big Al's Down Home Countryfried Logos"), it might also have a subheading ("Berkeley Office"); an alternative title (like "One-stop shopping for funky logos"); a tagline (like "Serving the community with happening logos since 1969"). You can clue search engines in to the fact that all these components are part of the page heading by including an `hgroup` element.

Other content, like a graphical or text banner or a navigation bar, should not be included in the `hgroup` element — that content is not part of your page heading. A navigation bar, for example, serves a different purpose than introducing your site and should be defined with an `hgroup` element, as discussed earlier in this chapter.

For example, in the following example, the two heading lines have been wrapped in an `hgroup` element. But the navigation content, although part of the header, is not included in the `hgroup` element.

```
<header>
<hgroup>
<h1>Page header</h1>
<h2>Header 2 </h2>
</hgroup>
<nav>
<h5>Navigate: <a href="#">Page 1</a> | <a href="#">Page 2
   </a> | <a href="#">Page 3</a></h5>
</nav>
</header>
```

By the way, you'll notice that the code above uses an h5 element to define the navigation bar content. There's no rule that you have to use an h5 element or any other element. The general rule is that larger, more important headings have lower heading values (h1 or h2), while smaller and less prominent content has higher numbered headings (like h4, h5, or h6).

Defining articles, sections, and asides

Perhaps the most significant content structuring element in HTML5 is the `article` tag. We understand that devotees of headers, footers, and even the relatively obscure `time` tag will be furious at us for suggesting that the article tag is the big attraction in HTML5, but we love it because you can employ the article tag to organize page content into basic "chunks," for lack of a better word. The necessity to structure page content into articles is a positive factor in forcing content developers to organize ideas in a coherent way. And the article tag provides the framework for sections (within the article) and asides (sidebars to the article).

Dividing articles into multiple sections

The following code defines an article and two section elements. It also includes some placeholder text and headings. And, continuing our example, you inserted it after the closing </header> tag.

Note: Although you can technically embed a single section within an article, the concept of articles divided into sections is more effective if that's avoided. A basic rule of editing (and you can ask anyone who edits text for a living, and they'll go on and on about this) is that if you're going to divide an article up to make it easier to digest, it doesn't help the reader organize his thinking to have only one subsection within a section of content. So — when sections are used — it's best to have at least two sections placed within <article> tags.

```
<article>
<h2>Article headline goes here</h2>
<p>First article content goes here</p>
<p>more article content goes here</p>
<section>
<h3>1st section heading goes here</h3>
<p>1st section content goes here</p>
<p>More 1st section content goes here</p>
</section>
<section>
<h3>2nd section heading goes here</h3>
<p>2nd section content goes here</p>
<p>More 2nd section content goes here</p>
</section>
</article>
```

This code creates a page like the one shown in Figure 3-5.

Adding an aside element

As with all HTML5 page structure elements, the aside element is intended to be associated with a certain kind of content. Content such as images, text, or videos in an aside element should be dependent upon — that is, related to content and contributing to — an article or section of an article.

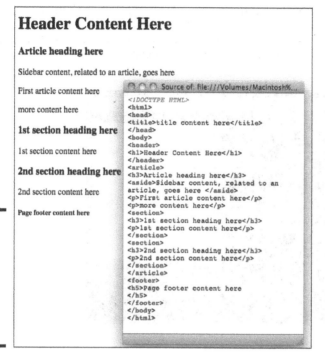

Figure 3-5:
HTML5
elements
used to
structure
an article
with two
sections.

Should you use an `aside` element to enclose a navigation bar? Generally, no. Instead, navigation content should be encoded with the `nav` element, which we discuss a bit earlier in this chapter.

Some CSS styling attributes that are normally applied to HTML5 `aside` elements. As you can likely intuit, `aside` elements are generally laid out as sidebars. So, when you define a CSS style for the `nav` element (something we cover in Book V), you use the CSS `float` property to allow the `aside` element to display as a right- or left-aligned box around which article content can flow.

The following code provides an example of an `aside` element within an article:

```
<article>
<h3>Article heading goes here</h3>
<p> Article content goes here </p>
<aside>Sidebar content, related to the article, goes here </
    aside>
<p>More article content goes here</p>
</article>
```

As noted, you'll want to combine HTML5 structure elements with styles that format the location, font, color, and other style attributes applied to these elements. Figure 3-6, for instance shows how an aside (KUDOS) might look next to the article with which it is associated (Experience).

Figure 3-6:
An aside
(KUDOS)
formatted to
display as a
sidebar with
an article
(Experience).

Creating a footer

A footer element is placed at the end of an HTML5 page. It holds "end of page" stuff, like navigation bars (which, as we mention earlier, should be enclosed in HTML5 <nav> tags, within the header).

Here, again, don't expect the footer element to look like much of anything until a CSS style is defined. Even without a defined style, HTML5 footers demarcate content to facilitate SEO. When we discuss that (soon), we show you how to define properties like height and background color to make the footer look like a distinct box at the bottom of the page.

The following code provides an example of a footer element after the closing of an article, and before the closing <body> tag:

```
</article>
<footer> <h5>Page footer content goes here</h5></footer>
</body>
```

An instant HTML5 starter page

Listing 3-1 more or less pulls together the various components of an HTML5 page that we've shown to this point into a document. You can use it as a template to build HTML5 pages, substituting your own content.

Listing 3-1:   HTML5 Starter Page

```
<!DOCTYPE HTML>
<html>
<head>
<title>title content here</title>
</head>
<body>
<header>
<h1>Header Content Here</h1>
</header>
<article>
<h3>Article heading here</h3>
<aside>Sidebar content, related to an article, goes here </
    aside>
<p>First article content here</p>
<p>more content here</p>
<section>
<h3>1st section heading here</h3>
<p>1st section content here</p>
</section>
<section>
<h3>2nd section heading here</h3>
<p>2nd section content here</p>
</section>
</article>
<footer>
<h5>Page footer content here
</h5>
</footer>
</body>
</html>
```

Book III
Chapter 3

Structuring Content
with HTML5

By the way, an examination of this code poses from another angle a theme we've been harping on somewhat throughout this chapter. And it gives us a chance to review and emphasize what a radical development HTML5 structure elements represent: HTML5 elements (like `article` and `section`) are supposed to be rigidly hierarchical. You can and often should have two sections in an article, but you're not supposed to have two articles within a section. You can have an aside associated with an article (or a section) but you should not have an article inside an aside. These elements (`article`, `section`, and `aside`) connote the relationship of content within a page.

Articles are something larger and more expansive than sections of an article. And asides are comments that add peripheral content to either articles or sections. Search engines will assume this is the case and process the content appropriately.

But that isn't the case with traditional HTML headings. Yes, it's generally accepted best practice that a heading 1 might include some heading 2s, heading 3s, or heading 4s. But that kind of structure is not mandatory, not really followed that carefully, and it doesn't mean much to a search engine. And, to be clear, there's no rule or convention that mandates that you can't place a heading 3 after a heading 1 without having a heading 2 in between them.

Contrasting the role of traditional HTML headings, and HTML5 structure elements, and noting that HTML5 structure elements are, well, *structural* (they define how different parts of a page fit together) is a helpful way to understand and appreciate how new and significant HTML5 structure elements are.

Looking at HTML5 Metadata Tags

To this point in this chapter, we've looked at the structuring role of HTML5 from the perspective of more or less outlining page content. That is, we use HTML5 elements to create sections of a document, within which old-fashioned HTML (or anything else, like JavaScript) is enclosed.

And, again, when you employ HTML5 layout elements to organize page content, you're building in support for search tools and other ways that HTML5 will facilitate a user's search to finding particular content.

And in addition to page structuring elements like headers, footers, articles, sections, and asides, other HTML5 tags are available to enhance SEO yet play a somewhat different role. These HTML5 tags, such as `address` or `date`, operate in a more narrow sphere, enclosing and identifying content types within another tag. Here we examine a couple of examples to show you how this works.

Assigning figures and captions

The `figure` and `figcaption` elements identify a figure or associated caption, respectively. And as with HTML5 elements in general, assigning these elements to content helps content aggregators and indexing programs (like search engines) interpret your page content and make it more accessible.

You might, for example, have a `figure` element wrapped around both an image and the caption (`figcaption`).

Tagging date and time

Date and time information can be enclosed in HTML5 <time> tags. For example, if your web page is promoting a show at a club at midnight next Saturday night, you can use the <time> element to make that information more available to young people using their mobile devices to search for something to do this weekend.

You can use a time element anywhere in a web page — in the middle of an article in an aside, or even in a footer (you might do that, for instance, if you announce in your page footer that an upcoming event is at midnight).

The basic syntax for the time element is

```
<time>14:30</time>
```

Time is indicated with a 24-hour clock. So, in the preceding example, 14:30 represents two o'clock in the afternoon. Six a.m. is 06:00, noon is 12:00, six p.m. is represented with 18:00, and so on.

Here's how you might use the time element in context:

```
<p>The fun starts at 11 at night!<time>23:00</time>. Be there!</p>
```

When you use the time element, you can use the datetime parameter to the actual date and time, as shown in the following example:

```
<p>Save the date! New Year's Eve <time datetime="2009-02-18"></p>
```

If you combine a date and time, a "T" character is used to separate the date from the time, as in the following example:

```
<p>Mark your calendar: 11PM on New Year's Eve!
    <time datetime="2013-12-31T11:00"></time>.</p>
```

Book III
Chapter 3

Structuring Content with HTML5

Using the address element

The address element in HTML5 is used to signify either a physical or virtual address. For example, you can enclose your site's URL within an address element. Or, use the address element to demarcate an e-mail address. The address element follows traditional physical address logic and order, as in 1 Times Square, New York, NY, 10036.

An address element can, and often will, be embedded in a footer element, but you can use it anywhere. To define content as an address, simply enclose it in open and close address tags.

The following example shows an `address` element within a footer:

```
<footer>
<h6>
(c) 2013, Emstrand Graphics<br>
</h6>
<address>1 Times Square, New York, NY 10036</address>
</footer>
```

Deploying HTML5 in Non-HTML5 Environments

HTML5 elements are the most rational way to structure page layout. They make life easier for designers, with tags like header and footer that clearly indicate what kind of content goes in which element. And as search engines learn to recognize and incorporate HTML5 structure elements, they'll make content more accessible for people looking for information online.

But are they supported in all browsers? Before we look at the list of browsers that don't support HTML5, look at the list of browsers that do:

✦ Internet Explorer (Version 9 and newer)

✦ Firefox

✦ Chrome

✦ Safari

✦ Opera

✦ iOS Safari (for Apple mobile devices)

✦ Opera Mobile (for mobile devices using the Opera browser)

✦ Android Browser (for Android mobile devices)

In short, every current browser supports the HTML5 structure elements we have explored in this chapter.

What about older browsers? The only problem here is Internet Explorer versions 6, 7, and 8. Because of Microsoft's (shall we say "unique"?) upgrade policies, people with older Windows computers are in some cases locked out of updating their versions of Internet Explorer. This isn't an issue for other browsers. Firefox, Chrome, Safari, Opera, and mobile browsers make upgrading free and simple, and besides, their current versions all support HTML5 structure tags. But not everyone with an older Windows computer has installed Firefox, Chrome, Opera, or Safari (all of which have Windows versions).

And so, because of Microsoft's policies, and because there remain sections of the browsing public who have not installed modern browsers on their computers, it will remain the case for some time that people stuck with old, outdated versions of Internet Explorer will have problems opening pages structured with HTML5 tags. If styles are assigned to these tags (something we explore later in this chapter), and those styles are relied on for page layout and design, then IE 6–8 visitors will see pages with collapsed and corrupted page layout, an unacceptable experience.

Because this significant, yet declining, section of the "browsing public" will have problems viewing pages with HTML5 structure elements, many web designers and coders have developed work-around solutions for IE 6–8 users that enable them to experience modern web pages that use HTML5 structure tags. Those workarounds are pretty simple to implement. You'll find them by searching the Internet for "HTML5 IE workaround" (and you'll see several million results).

One of the most tested, easy-to-use, and widely applied of these workarounds is a JavaScript called "HTML5 enabling script." HTML code that links to this script can be copied and pasted into a page from remysharp. com. The complete URL for the script is at

http://remysharp.com/2009/01/07/html5-enabling-script

The required code should be copied and pasted into the <head> element of your page. It links to a JavaScript (called html5.js) that allows outdated versions of IE to interpret HTML5 structure elements.

The following code shows a <head> element with the HTML that links to html5.js:

```
<!doctype html>

<html>

<head>

<!--[if lt IE 9]>
    <script src="http://html5shiv.googlecode.com/
    svn/trunk/html5.js"></script>
    <![endif]-->

</head>
```

By the way, if you create an HTML5 page in Dreamweaver CS6, the link to this script appears in the <head> element of your page automatically. We address working with HTML and HTML5 in Dreamweaver in Chapter 4 of this minibook.

Adding this code in the head section of your pages ensures that folks using IE6, IE7, and IE8 will be able to experience your pages as you designed them.

Applying HTML5 to Page Layout

HTML5 elements (like header, footer, and article) structure page content. That is, they organize it into rational chunks. But they don't, on their own, supply page formatting.

To take an example, the <aside> element (used to create content that's in many ways the same as what are thought of as "sidebars") doesn't, by default, align content inside the element on the right side of the page. It doesn't, in other words, create a "sidebar" box.

To make an HTML5 page look good, you need to define CSS styles that match the different HTML5 elements. So, to pick up on our previous example, you might very well want to define a CSS style that assigns a width to the <aside> element. You might also *float* (align) the <aside> element to the right side of a page. And you probably want to define margins around the element, and padding within it.

Here, we'll refer you to Book IV where we explain how to define CSS styles for elements (including HTML5 elements). And we will again emphasize that until you define CSS styles for them, HTML5 structure elements don't define *styles* for content — they don't define how content appears in a page. But with CSS styles defined, HTML5 structure elements determine not only how content is organized, but how it looks.

At the same time, it's both technically and practically incorrect to merge concepts and refer to HTML page-structuring elements as "HTML5 layout elements." For one thing (as we discussed), in and of themselves, HTML5 elements don't function as page layout tools. Only when HTML5 elements are associated with CSS styles does any HTML5 page-structuring tag take on page layout features.

Another reason why it's misleading to speak of HTML5 page-structuring elements as "layout" elements is that at least one essential layout challenge isn't addressed with HTML5 elements of any kind, and that's creating a container to enclose all the page content, and constrain at least the width of that content (typically to a universally applied container width of 960 pixels).

Our point is that HTML5 — and HTML5 page-structuring tags in particular — aren't designed to, nor will they, solve all page layout issues. And although perhaps 90 percent of all `DIV` tags become redundant with the implementation of HTML5 page-structuring tags, you'll still need to use some `DIV` tags for page layout. Most especially, you still need to make up the name of a `DIV` tag for a container that will enclose your entire page and also constrain page width. We detail creating a container `DIV` tag in detail in Book IV, Chapter 2.

Chapter 4: Creating HTML5 with Dreamweaver CS6

In This Chapter

- ✓ The role of Dreamweaver in page design
- ✓ Touring the Dreamweaver interface
- ✓ Creating pages and dependent files in Dreamweaver
- ✓ Testing your pages and validating the code

Dreamweaver generates HTML code as you interact with a graphical and menu-based interface. That's the main reason why designers like Dreamweaver so much — you can design pages and leave the HTML coding to Dreamweaver.

So, Dreamweaver is a page-design program. But that's not all! It's also a file management system and FTP (File Transfer Protocol) program for synchronizing files between your local computer and a remote, Internet-accessible site. Dreamweaver also generates CSS (covered in depth in Book IV), JavaScript (Book VI), and even some PHP (Book VII).

In short, there's a lot to Dreamweaver. In this chapter, in the context of this minibook exploring HTML (including what's new in HTML5), we look at how Dreamweaver creates HTML pages and generates formatting tags (like paragraphs and headings), lists, boldface, italics, indenting, and links. Before we do that, though, we introduce you to the Dreamweaver CS6 interface.

 Before you begin to build HTML pages in Dreamweaver, you need to know that such pages depend on working in a defined Dreamweaver site. This is something more specific and proprietary than just "a website": It's a relationship defined in the Dreamweaver Site Definition dialog box. Setting up a Dreamweaver site is explained in depth in Book II, Chapter 4. Do *not* proceed with the rest of this chapter until you follow the steps in Book II, Chapter 4, to define a Dreamweaver site.

Note: When we work with Dreamweaver in this book, the specific steps and feature descriptions in this book match those in Dreamweaver CS6. However, most (not all) of these features and steps are quite similar or identical in Dreamweaver CS5 or CS5.5. Where we specifically reference CS6

(as in, "with Dreamweaver CS6, you can . . ."), we are generally referring to features in CS6 not available in earlier versions, particularly in versions that predate version CS5.5.

Dreamweaver CS6: An Overview

For such a powerful application, Dreamweaver's interface is refreshingly manageable. While other Adobe applications like Photoshop or Illustrator require you to bounce in and out of dozens of *panels* (little windows that hold the key to the programs' features), you can access almost anything you need in Dreamweaver from the main menu, or from three power panels: the Properties Inspector (it's a panel, but the name carried over from earlier pre-panel versions of the program); the CSS panel; and the Files panel.

In fact, the names of these three panels kind of clue you in to how Dreamweaver works:

✦ **Properties Inspector:** You assign properties to elements in the Properties Inspector. From here, you apply elements like headings, paragraph tags, lists, indents, and links to selected content.

✦ **CSS panel:** You define, link, and edit CSS styles in the CSS styles panel. In Book IV, we break down how Dreamweaver works with CSS.

✦ **Files panel:** You can guess what this does — it lists all the files in your site and provides tools for editing and uploading those files.

In this chapter, we focus on applying HTML tags in with the Properties Inspector and accessing additional HTML elements with the Insert menu in the main Dreamweaver document menu bar.

With that as a preview, take a walk through all this in a bit more detail.

The Welcome screen

When you launch Dreamweaver, the Welcome screen appears. The left column in the Welcome screen lists recent files and appears differently each time you launch Dreamweaver. The right column promotes new features in Dreamweaver CS6.

You'll find the most useful and essential elements of the Welcome screen in the Create New (middle) column, as shown in Figure 4-1. (Your Welcome screen will look different than ours because the Welcome screen saves recent files in the left column.) Clicking the HTML button at the top of the column creates a new HTML file, using default settings for an HTML file.

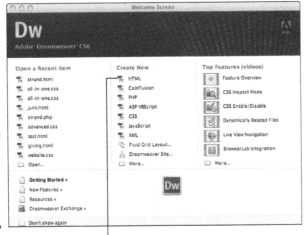

Figure 4-1:
The Dream-
weaver CS6
Welcome
screen.

Click to create a new HTML file.

By default, Dreamweaver creates a new file using the HTML5 doctype. (For an explanation of the significance of the HTML5 doctype, see Chapter 1 in this minibook.)

Most of the time, the defaults settings (an HTML5 document) are fine. But just for your reference, in case you elect to use another version of HTML, you can change these default settings. Here is how to see, or change, the defaults:

1. **Choose Edit⇨Preferences (Windows)/Dreamweaver⇨Preferences (Mac).**

   You can also press Ctrl+U (Windows)/⌘+U (Mac).

   The Preferences dialog box opens.

2. **Click the New Document category on the left, as shown in Figure 4-2.**

3. **Choose a document type from the Default document popup. If you wish to change the version of HTML you use to create new files, you can choose a version of HTML from the Default Document Type (DTD) popup.**

4. **Here's another feature you might want to customize: The Show New Document Dialog Box on CMD+N check box is selected by default, but you can change that.**

   If you deselect this check box, when you press the shortcut keys to open a new document (Ctrl+N for Windows or ⌘+N on a Mac), that new document opens with your default settings, and you will not see the New Document dialog box.

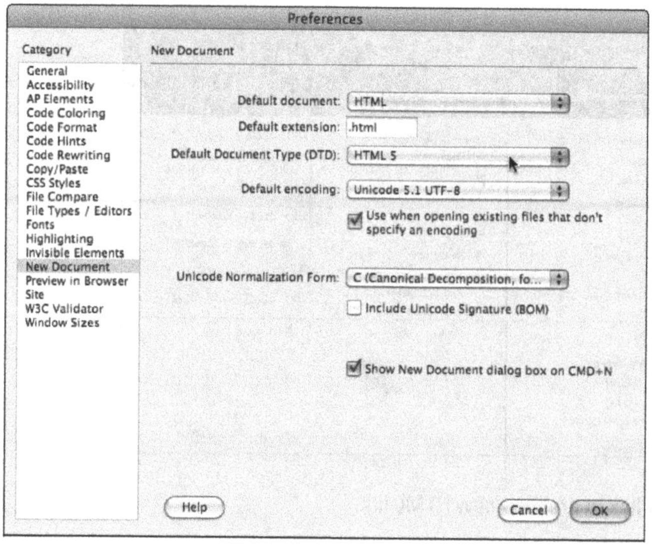

Figure 4-2: Set preferences to create a new HTML5 document by default.

The Document window

As soon as you create a new HTML page in Dreamweaver, the Document window launches. This is the work area where you design and code web pages, create and edit text, and insert and (within limits) edit images.

The appearance of the Document window changes, as we'll see shortly. Design view hides all code. Code view displays just code. And Split view, shown in Figure 4-3, displays both code view (normally on the left) and design view (normally on the right). As noted earlier, you don't really need to use a lot of panels in Dreamweaver. A good option for familiarizing yourself with Dreamweaver's work space is to choose Show Panels to toggle all panels off, which hides all panels until you need one.

In essence, the Document window is your easel, your artboard — your digital design studio. And even if you're inclined to create web pages by hand-coding in Dreamweaver (typing HTML, as we cover in Chapters 1, 2, and 3 of this minibook), you still use the Document window — you can enter code in either Code view or on the Code view side of Split view.

The best way for you to work in the Document window depends on your task and your comfort level. As noted, you have three views you can choose from:

✦ **Code view:** You see the underlying code of your page. Use this view if you're comfortable with hand-coding or want to see the code you generated using Dreamweaver.

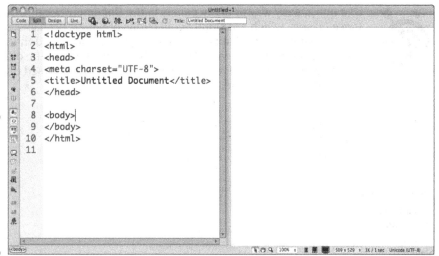

Figure 4-3:
Dream-
weaver's
Document
window
with panels
hidden, in
Split view.

✦ **Design view:** You see only the visual aspects of your page, which can be helpful if you're not as comfortable with code or if you need to see your design.

✦ **Split view:** The best of both worlds, where you see your code at the top of the screen and your design at the bottom.

For more about these views and the Document window's features, see the later section, "Generating HTML."

Dreamweaver's omnipotent panels

Many of the main features of Dreamweaver are accessed through panels, which are ubiquitous to Adobe Creative Suite (CS). Dreamweaver's panels are viewed, moved, and stacked in similar ways in Dreamweaver, Photoshop, Illustrator, Fireworks, and other CS siblings.

You'll find this commonality helpful as you (as designer) integrate Dreamweaver with Illustrator, Photoshop, and other CS6 applications. If you haven't been exposed to other Adobe apps, the basic concept is you can view (or hide) panels by selecting them from the Window menu, and you can drag them around on the screen by clicking and dragging on the panel's title bar (the strip at the top of the panel).

All panels are accessed from the Dreamweaver Window menu. As you traverse this book, you'll see different features accessed through different panels. For example, in Book IV, check out the Dreamweaver CSS-generating tools via the CSS Styles panel.

One quick, easy way to array panels in the Document window is to use *workspace layouts,* which are simply collections of panels prepackaged by Adobe. Choose Window➪Workspace Layout for your choices, and the submenu shown in Figure 4-4 appears. The panels associated with the different workspace layouts vary, as does the location of the panels, based on what workspace layout you choose.

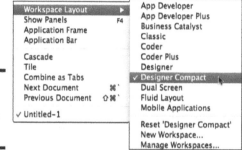

Figure 4-4: Choosing a workspace layout.

You can also customize and save your own workspace layout by simply positioning objects where you want them by choosing Window➪Workspace Layout➪New Layout. When you do that, the Save Workspace dialog box appears, and you can create a new workspace layout by entering a name in the Name box. For example, if you want to define a workspace with just the CSS Styles panel and the Properties Inspector, you can view those two panels and then define them as a workspace, as shown in Figure 4-5.

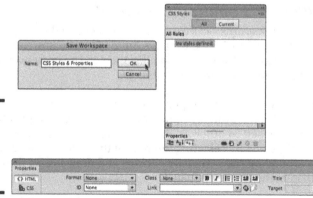

Figure 4-5: Defining a custom workspace layout.

The Properties Inspector

The Properties Inspector is used to apply many of the most useful and commonly used HTML tags to selected content, and, to define parameters for those tags.

The Properties Inspector is *context-sensitive,* meaning that its tools and features vary depending on what type of element is active in the Document window. If you have an image selected, for example, the Properties Inspector provides tools to size, align, or set spacing around it, as shown in Figure 4-6. Similarly, if you have text selected, the Properties Inspector provides formatting tools you can use to, say, assign a heading or paragraph tag to that text, make it part of a list, apply boldface or italic, and indent.

Figure 4-6:
The full
Properties
Inspector
with text
selected.

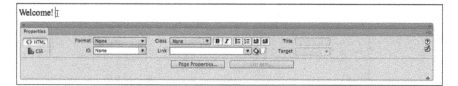

The Insert menu

The Insert menu, shown in Figure 4-7, provides another way of generating HTML (as well as other content). For example, you use the Insert menu to place images on a page, to design forms (something we explore in Book VII, Chapter 4), and to define links.

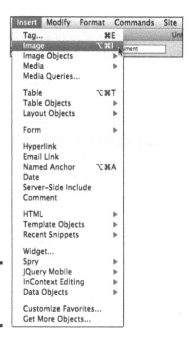

Figure 4-7:
The Insert
menu.

Setting preferences

Throughout this chapter (and elsewhere in this book where we talk about Dreamweaver), we recommend using settings in the Dreamweaver Preferences dialog box shown in Figure 4-8. We don't have the space to list them all, though. And most of these settings are intuitive enough that you can figure them out.

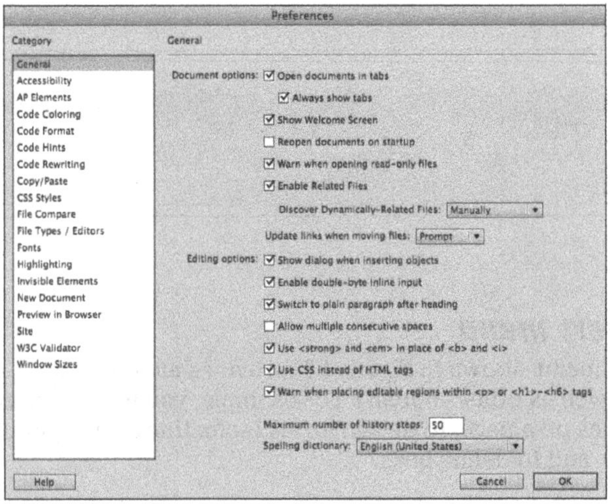

Figure 4-8:
The
Preferences
dialog box.

Having said that, if you're using Dreamweaver as your primary web design tool, take a little time upfront to peruse the options here for customizing your Dreamweaver installation. The Preferences dialog box is available by choosing Edit⇨Preferences (Windows) or Dreamweaver⇨Preferences (Mac). This dialog box has many settings that you can adjust; the best way to become familiar is to explore them. We highlight just a few of the features here.

The General category is where you can turn the Welcome Screen on and off. You also see options to adjust settings for how Dreamweaver handles spell checking and updating links. This is also the place that gives you the option of setting Dreamweaver to warn you when you're opening *read-only files* (files that are locked and can't be edited, just viewed).

Other categories in the Preferences dialog box enable you to customize how you handle accessibility features (on the Accessibility tab), what colors are used when displaying code (on the Code Coloring tab), and how your code is formatted (on the Code Format tab).

If you plan on doing much hand-coding in Dreamweaver's Code view, you should check out the options in the Code Hints category. Here you can manage how Dreamweaver displays hints when you begin typing tags. Among the options are when to display a hint (you have choices as to what typed characters prompt a code hint) and what time delay Dreamweaver will apply before displaying a hint. Or, you can turn off code hinting here. But with code hinting enabled, Dreamweaver attempts to finish tags while you type them to remind you of proper syntax or parameters available for that tag. Also, this feature shows a list of styles available if you have CSS set up for the page. And, of course, if Dreamweaver's code hinting creates code you didn't intend, you can always use the Delete key on your keyboard to undo that code.

Creating an HTML Document

Assuming that you're working in a defined Dreamweaver site (explained in depth in Book II, Chapter 4), you're ready to create a new HTML page. You can do that by choosing HTML from the Create New column on the Welcome screen that appears when you launch Dreamweaver. As we note earlier, this opens a new HTML5 file by default.

You can also choose File⇨New from the Dreamweaver main menu, which opens the New Document dialog box.

New Document options

As you can see in Figure 4-9, the New Document dialog box has four main areas: choices on the left that determine the type of file (HTML, CSS, or any of a large set of possible other file types), whether you're using a sample or template to generate your page, and other options.

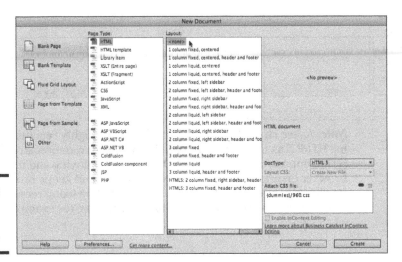

Figure 4-9:
The New Document dialog box.

The Page Type column is where you choose a file type (HTML if you're creating a new HTML web page). The Layout column is where you choose from available samples or starter pages (or choose none to start with a blank page). The preview area in the upper right of the dialog previews how your page will look if you use a layout. In the lower right of the New Document dialog box, you can change the doctype (we recommend sticking with the default, HTML5), and you can use the link icon (it looks like a chain link) to attach a CSS style sheet (something we explore in Book IV).

To begin creating a page, you click the appropriate item from the choices on the left side of the screen:

✦ **Blank Page:** Choose this to create a basic, blank HTML page. Choose HTML as the Page Type, <none> as the Layout, and then HTML5 as the declared document type (from the DocType popup in the right column) as shown in Figure 4-9. Click the Create button, and you see what's shown in Figure 4-10.

Figure 4-10:
Start with a
new, blank
HTML page.

Note: As we stress throughout this book, we highly recommend choosing HTML5 as the document type because older, deprecated versions of HTML impose out-of-date rules that trigger annoying and unnecessary browser errors. Using HTML5 avoids all that and keeps browsers from intelligently interpreting page content including fixing recognizable errors (like a missed closing tag on a paragraph, for example). For more discussion of the advantages of creating pages in HTML5, as well as for an understanding of how to avoid compatibility issues with older browsers, see Chapter 3 of this minibook.

✦ **Blank Template:** This category provides a set of sample Dreamweaver Templates. See our warning at the Page from Template bullet.

✦ **Fluid Grid Layout:** Dreamweaver CS6 users have an additional category tab for creating what Dreamweaver calls *Fluid Grid Layouts* or *Multiscreen Projects.* These are pages with more than one associated CSS style sheet: that is, pages that display differently depending on the size of the media (screen) in which they are viewed. We explore various options for using such *media queries* — code that identifies screen size and presents appropriate content — in Book IV, Chapter 4.

✦ **Page from Template:** Generate new pages from existing Dreamweaver Templates.

Dreamweaver Templates are not generic sample layout-builder pages. For that, Dreamweaver supplies sample or starter pages. Dreamweaver Templates is a proprietary tool that governs sitewide page elements of Dreamweaver and isn't usable if you want to integrate other web-design tools. We recommend not using Dreamweaver Templates because they are nonstandard (see the "Dreamweaver generates clean code, except . . ." sidebar), easily corruptible, and not really suited to sitewide updating in large sites. The functionality provided by Dreamweaver Templates is better managed with external CSS style sheets and other nonproprietary tools.

✦ **Page from Sample:** Sample pages are different than Dreamweaver Templates, and more useful. They come packaged with CSS styles that provide formatting and placeholder text and images that you can replace with your own content. You can preview samples in the preview area of the New Document dialog box to get an idea of whether or not you want to use one of the available samples to start creating your own page.

✦ **Other:** The Other category has options for creating complex, advanced, or obscure file types, with an emphasis on obscure. Among the more used options, you can create a Flash ActionScript file (ActionScript is the programming language used by Adobe Flash) or a page coded in Microsoft's Visual Basic programming language.

If you select an HTML file as the Page Type from the second column in the New Document dialog box, the Layout column displays a variety of CSS-based page designs. The fourth column in the New Document dialog box displays thumbnails of the page-generated layout for whichever layout you select.

Book III
Chapter 4

Creating HTML5
with
Dreamweaver CS6

Dreamweaver generates clean code, except . . .

Dreamweaver is not the only tool in the shop for generating HTML. In Chapter 1 of this mini-book, we survey a wide range of options for generating HTML, including creating HTML from Microsoft Word files, or Google Docs.

Dreamweaver, however, stands head and shoulders above those tools in two ways:

✔ Dreamweaver provides far more powerful tools for creating a wide variety of web content, ranging from web-ready images to JavaScript.

✔ The code, including HTML code, created in Dreamweaver is *clean code,* close to or adhering to best practice standards. Should you elect to edit the HTML you create in Dreamweaver in another environment, like a straight code editor (BBEdit, for example), you won't see a bunch of weird, redundant, nonstandard and hard-to-interpret HTML.

We want to add our opinion again, though, that Dreamweaver's clean, standard code becomes essentially corrupted if you implement Dreamweaver Templates or Library items (a feature that embeds content in a way similar to the way Illustrator or Flash use symbols — content that's embedded in pages but saved and edited elsewhere). Without going into detail, suffice it to say that these tools do not generate standard HTML (or any other kind of) code, can't really be edited outside of Dreamweaver, and have corruptibility issues within Dreamweaver. Suggestion: Avoid Dreamweaver Templates and Library items.

Refer to Figure 4-2 to see that not only does the New Document dialog box preview how a selected layout will look, but that it also provides three options in the Layout CSS popup: Add to Head, Create New File, or Link to Existing File. The first option (Add to Head) embeds CSS in your HTML file, something we generally advise against because it keeps you from sharing your style sheet with other HTML pages in your site. The Create New File option, on the other hand, generates an external style sheet that can be linked to from many pages in your site. The Link to existing file option allows you to substitute your own, already created CSS file for the one associated with the sample — which is kind of an odd option since it pretty much undoes the sample package of HTML and CSS.

As we discuss in several chapters in this and other minibooks, modern web pages derive their formatting, style, and layout from linked, external CSS files. And the options in the Layout CSS popup provide choices for how to manage that — including the Add to Head option, which is not recommended because it isolates the defined style to a single page.

In this chapter, though, we focus just on creating HTML content. So even though it might be handy, you might want to generate an HTML page with CSS all in one step — but later, when you're comfortable with both HTML and CSS and how they interact. However, that's not the approach we take here because creating HTML and CSS are two distinct processes, and you can examine and understand each of them if you focus on one or the other. That said, after you read Book V (where we explore how CSS fits into the picture in detail), you might well want to avail yourself of Dreamweaver's sample layouts, particularly the two HTML 5 layouts at the end of the list that create pages using HTML5 structure (something we cover in Chapter 3 of this minibook).

Saving pages

We can't stress this enough: *Before you create content on a Web page in Dreamweaver, you should save the page as an HTML file.*

As you generate HTML, Dreamweaver will use the name and location of the HTML file (in your site file structure) to generate appropriate code. And it can't do that if the page isn't saved. For example, you can generate *relative links* in Dreamweaver — links that don't contain a full URL (like www. dummies.com) but simply point to a filename — and, if necessary, a folder location (like about_me.html). Generating those relative links works *only* if Dreamweaver knows the HTML page's filename and location. And that is very, very important.

So, save your page off the bat. It's easy, and you will thank yourself (and maybe us) many times later:

1. **Choose File⇨Save.**

2. **Click the Site Root button in the Save As dialog box that appears to quickly navigate to the root folder for your Dreamweaver Site, as shown in Figure 4-11.**

Book III
Chapter 4

Creating HTML5 with Dreamweaver CS6

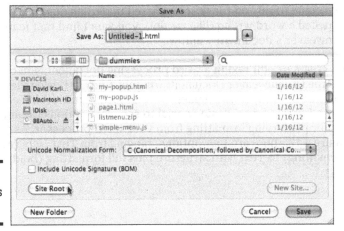

Figure 4-11: The Save As dialog box.

3. **Enter a filename in the Save As field. Leave the filename extension at the default .html, and click the Save button.**

Working with Text and Image Tags

Now that you've walked through the process of creating and saving a blank HTML page in Dreamweaver, how about we walk through how to add some content?

The most basic HTML page content icomprises text; formatting with paragraph, heading, or list tags; and images defined with the HTML $<img>$ tag. Start with creating those elements.

Adding and editing text

To add text, just type (or copy and paste) text into an open Dreamweaver document just as you would in a standard word processor.

You can do this either in Split view or Design view. If you're working in Split view (with code on one side, and Design view on the other), be sure to paste text into the Design view side of the Document window. Otherwise, if you paste text into Code view (or the Code side of Split view) Dreamweaver will think you're copying HTML code, which you're not.

Normal editing techniques like Find and Replace (found on the Edit menu) or spell checking (buried unintuitively at File⇨Check Page⇨Spelling submenu) are at the ready.

If you have major document editing to do, we suggest you do that in a word processor. Dreamweaver's editing tools are okay, but just okay. If you've come to rely on those squiggly red underline markings that show you spelled a word wrong (like we do!), you won't find that feature in Dreamweaver's document window.

If you create or edit text in a word processing document, you can easily copy it into the Dreamweaver Document window. Click in Design view (remember: not Code view, or you'll paste your copied text as HTML code, which it's not). Choose Edit ⇨Paste Special to see what options Dreamweaver offers for preserving formatting from your word processor. As you can see in Figure 4-12, there are four options, ranging from Text Only (which strips all formatting) to Text with structure plus full formatting (bold, italic, and styles).

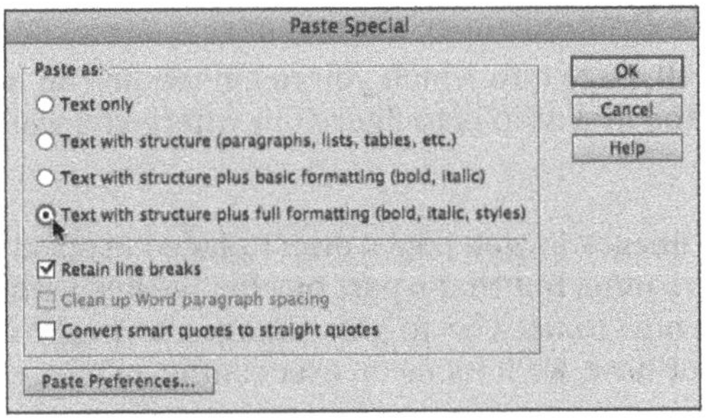

Figure 4-12:
Set how much formatting to preserve in pasted text.

We could explain what each paste special option does, but that would actually be misleading. The results you get from different paste special options vary rather widely depending on the source of the text. So, instead we suggest you start with the forth option, the one that preserves the most formatting. If it doesn't work well (like if it pastes in text with too much formatting or features that weren't really part of the original formatting), try different options. Avail yourself of the Dreamweaver Document menu's Edit⇨Undo feature if the paste results don't do a good job of preserving your formatting.

Inserting and editing images

Time to back up a step. You don't create images in Dreamweaver. For that, Adobe provides Illustrator (for artwork, graphical text, page background images, navigation icons, and so on) and Photoshop (for preparing photos for the web), as well as other tools.

As a general rule, stick with preparing images for the web in those programs, using the techniques we cover in detail in Book V. That said, Dreamweaver's minimalist image editing tools allow you to perform rudimentary image editing, such as resizing and cropping. You find those tools in the Properties Inspector.

We're getting a little ahead of ourselves, though. Start by inserting an image. Here's how.

First of all, make sure you're working in Design view (or, in Split view with your cursor in the Design side of the window). You have two basic paths: Insert from your machine or use a copy-and-paste technique. In either case, you need to be in Design view (choose View⇨Design; or, for Split view, choose View⇨Code and Design) to see images as you paste or embed them.

Inserting images in Dreamweaver documents

Chances are the HTML page into which you're embedding an image will have some text on it. So, the first step is to figure out where you want the image to appear.

Unlike print design, images in web pages aren't placed in specific locations. That drives designers nuts, but that's part of what we live with in design. In Book VI, we explore how to use CSS to place images, as best as can be done in a web page. But for now, we'll focus on associating an image with a paragraph of text.

So, to insert an image file from your computer into an open HTML web page in Dreamweaver, follow these steps:

1. **Click in the Document window at the point where the image is to be inserted.**

In this step, you locate where in your HTML code the image will be inserted. Again, where and how the image is displayed will be defined with CSS.

2. **Choose Insert➪Image.**

3. **In the Select Image Source dialog box that opens, navigate to and select any file on your computer.**

If the image you select is outside your site folder, a helpful dialog box (with no title, but displayed in Figure 4-13) appears, prompting you to save a copy of the image to your Dreamweaver site's root folder.

Figure 4-13: Copying an image to your Dreamweaver site folder.

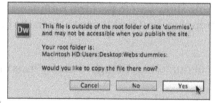

a. *Click Yes.*

b. *Click Save in the Copy File As dialog box.*

4. **Define accessibility attributes.**

By default, the Dreamweaver Image Tag Accessibility Attributes dialog box appears before an image is finally inserted into a page.

The Alternate Text field shown in Figure 4-14 is most important of the two options in this dialog box. It displays text that's read aloud in reader software for vision-impaired visitors, and also that displays in browsing environments where image display is disabled. Alternate text can and often should include uppercase and lowercase letters, spaces, and special characters.

If vision-impaired visitors or people in browsing environments that do not support images are part of your target audience, you might consider creating HTML files with more substantial image descriptions. Such files are linked to the image by defining a link in the Long Description box in the Image Tag Accessibility Attributes dialog box.

Figure 4-14:
Define
accessibility
attributes
for an
image.

Book III
Chapter 4

5. Click OK to insert the image.

At this point, you've only inserted the image. Page design, including placing images and flowing text around them, is managed with CSS, something we cover in Book IV.

Pasting images into Dreamweaver

You can also paste images from your operating system's Clipboard into Dreamweaver documents. This works with images copied to the Clipboard from some, but not all, browsers (Safari being one) and for some but not all non–web-friendly file formats. Any image that you can copy into your operating system's clipboard can be pasted into an open HTML page in Dreamweaver.

Copying images from browsers is a bit different depending on the browser, but the basic technique is to right-click/Control-click and choose an option like Copy Image from the context menu that appears. Or you can copy and paste artwork from programs like Illustrator, Photoshop, or Word.

With an image copied to the Clipboard, follow these steps to paste the image into Dreamweaver and then save it as an image file in your site:

Creating HTML5
with
Dreamweaver CS6

1. **Click in the Document window at the point where the image is to be inserted.**

   How the image displays will be defined with CSS, so don't obsess on that at this stage.

2. **Choose Edit⇨Paste.**

   What happens now varies significantly depending on your version of Dreamweaver although the basic concepts are the same:

   a. *You choose an image file format and a few other image attributes.*

   b. *You assign a filename.*

   In pre-CS6 versions of Dreamweaver, a somewhat complex Image Preview dialog box opens. In CS6, the image appears in the Document window, and a greatly simplified Image Optimization dialog box appears, as shown in Figure 4-15.

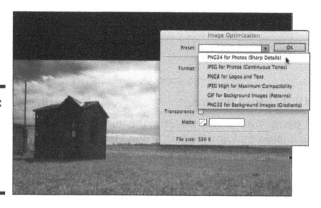

Figure 4-15: Choose a format and settings for a pasted photo.

Default image format settings in the Image Preview dialog box can be changed by choosing image file format and optimization settings (filters like transparency, contrast, and brightness) from the Preset popup. In Book V, we explore optimizing images for the web (making images work well and look good in web pages) in depth.

3. **Make your choices in the Image Optimization dialog box (assuming that you're in CS6) and then click OK.**

4. **In the Save Web Image dialog box that opens, enter the image name.**

   As with all web filenaming, avoid using spaces and special characters, and do not replace the filename extension (.png, .jpeg, or .gif).

5. **Save the file to your site root folder by clicking the Site Root button.**

   Saving to the site root folder is always a safe bet. If you're comfortable with managing file folder structures, feel free to save images within sub-folders inside your site folder, though.

6. **Click Save.**

   The image is saved, and the Image Description (Alt Text) dialog box appears. In this dialog box, you define accessibility attributes.

   You can enter alt text (text that will be read out loud to describe the image for vision-impaired visitors by reader software, or that will display in browsing environments where image display is disabled) in the Alternate Text box in the dialog.

7. **Click OK to insert the image.**

   The image will be visible on the page in Design view.

Defining image attributes

As noted earlier, Dreamweaver's Properties Inspector is context-sensitive, meaning that when you click an image, HTML attributes for that image are displayed and editable.

Some of the editable image attributes are more "technical" than design factors. For example, the image ID is used when images are connected to JavaScript programs or databases. Other image attributes in the Properties Inspector comprise a limited set of actual image editing tools. Those tools include cropping, editing contrast, and sharpening images. Take a look at the most important of these options:

✦ **Map area tools:** The Map area tools create clickable hotspots on the selected image and define separate links for different hotspots. A *hotspot* is a section of an image that serves as a link. You can use the Rectangle, Circle, and Polygon hotspot tools to draw sections on a selected image, and then assign specific links to those hotpots in the Properties Inspector. The fourth tool in this set, the Pointer Hotspot tool, is used to select, move, or edit existing hotspots.

✦ **V Space and H Space:** Define horizontal and vertical spacing around the selected image.

✦ **Align:** Use this popup to choose between left or right alignment. (Other options are technically available, but they're remnants from an era when text-sized graphic symbols were inserted directly into lines of text and aren't used today in image alignment.)

✦ **Src:** This field identifies the embedded linked image.

✦ **Alt:** Change the text that displays, or is read out loud, when an image isn't visible.

✦ **Border:** Define border width (0 pixel, by default), or 1 pixel if the image serves as a link.

✦ **Link:** Define a link that opens when the image is clicked. If a link is defined, you can set the link to open in a new browser window by choosing _blank from the Target popup.

✦ **Class:** Use this popup to assign CSS class styles if any are defined in or linked to the page.

✦ **W (width) and H (height):** Resize the image. Deselecting the Toggle Size Constraints icon unlocks the linkage between height and width, allowing you to stretch or squish the image rather than maintaining the original height-to-width aspect ratio as you resize. You can also resize interactively by clicking and dragging the lower-right corner handle of a selected image. Hold down the Shift key while you resize to maintain height-to-width ratio.

✦ **Resample:** New tools in CS6 allow you to resample a resized (smaller) image. Resampling eliminates unneeded data and makes the image file smaller, and that means the image can download faster. Select the Commit Image Size check box (shown in Figure 4-16) to resample the image, or click the Reset to Original Size button next to it in the Properties Inspector to undo resizing. (For more exploration of how and when to resample images, see Book V.)

Figure 4-16:
Resample an image to reduce download time.

Applying HTML tags with the Properties Inspector

As you can read to this point of the chapter, the Properties Inspector can be used to define both text and image attributes. Up to now, we have focused on images. Now turn your focus to how the Properties Inspector applies tags to text.

As we discuss in Chapters 2 and 3 of this minibook, and as we go into depth in Book IV, most of the formatting that's applied to text is handled with CSS style sheets. By default, for example, a heading 1 tag makes text larger and applies boldface. But it's an attached CSS style sheet that adds font color, font style, alignment, and so on (and a CSS style sheet can even "overrule" the text default text size for a heading 1).

In short, both tags (like headings, paragraph, or lists) and styles (defined by a CSS style sheet) work together to determine how text looks. It was worth taking a moment to sort that out because Dreamweaver's Properties Inspector has both an HTML and a CSS tab. The CSS tab is one of many ways Dreamweaver provides access to CSS styles (something we cover in Book IV, Chapter 4). If you want to apply or edit the HTML tags applied to text in Dreamweaver, you have to be sure you have the HTML tab — not the CSS tab — selected, as shown in Figure 4-17.

Figure 4-17: Select the HTML tab.

Book III
Chapter 4

Creating HTML5 with Dreamweaver CS6

Applying paragraph and heading tags

To apply an HTML tag (like paragraph, link, bullet list, or indent), click a paragraph of text and then choose a tag from the Properties Inspector. And yes, paragraph and heading tags apply to (and only to) entire paragraphs. You apply paragraph or heading tags to a selected paragraph from the Format popup (as shown in Figure 4-18). To create distinct formatting for parts of a tag, you use Class CSS styles, explored in Book IV.

Styling is — for the most part — done with CSS (style sheets), so your applied HTML tags will have very minimalist appearance attributes.

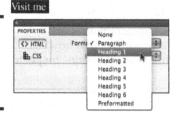

Figure 4-18: Assign tags from the Properties Inspector.

Defining links

Links are an essential element of web pages. In Chapter 3 of this minibook, we explore different options and approaches for defining links. Here, we build on that and walk through how to define links and link attributes in Dreamweaver CS6.

You have a few methods for defining links, depending on what type of link you're creating, how you want the link to look, and where the link is linking to:

✦ **Link text box:** Define links from selected text or images to targets outside your site by typing a URL (starting with `http://`) in the Link field of the Properties Inspector.

> Type the full URL; don't skip to the `www.` part.

✦ **Browse for File icon:** If the link is to a file within your defined Dreamweaver site, on your computer, click the Browse for File icon (shown in the margin) and then navigate to a file within your Dreamweaver site, as shown in Figure 4-19.

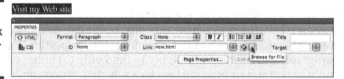

Figure 4-19: Define a link via Browser for File.

✦ **Point to File tool:** You can also define links to a file within your site using the Point to File tool, which looks like a clock or a small crosshair (and shown in the margin), located to the right of the Link text field. To use the tool, click and drag the clock to the file in the Files panel to make a link. A line drags from the box to the file you point to. This is a quick and easy way to make a link, saving you time when linking to files within your site.

Link targets

The default is for pages to load into the same window as the page you're already viewing, replacing the current page with the new page to be viewed. For some links, though, you don't want the new page to replace the one that the visitor is viewing. For example, when you link to another site, you probably want that to open in a new window so that the visitor can easily return to your site.

In that case, you want to choose _blank from the Target drop-down list to the right of the link box. This opens the new page in another window. When the user is done viewing the linked page, she closes that window, and the original page is still there in its window. Use this technique sparingly, though, because visitors can become annoyed if your site launches a lot of windows.

These techniques for defining text links also work for assigning links to selected images using the Properties Inspector.

Link titles

Link titles can also be defined in the Properties Inspector. A link title is popup text that displays when someone hovers over a link.

Link titles can be helpful — they provide additional link information. However, they can also be distracting, cluttering up the page with obvious or redundant information. Figure 4-20 shows a displayed link title.

**Book III
Chapter 4**

Creating HTML5
with
Dreamweaver CS6

Figure 4-20:
Displaying a
link title.

To define a link title in Dreamweaver CS6, enter link Title text in the Title box in the Properties Inspector.

Applying boldface, italics, lists, and indenting

Assign boldface, italics, unordered (bulleted) or ordered (numbered) lists, and add or remove indenting (blockquote) using the icons in the Properties Inspector. You can get help from hover-activated tooltips if necessary. Figure 4-9 shows an unordered (bullet) list applied in the Properties Inspector.

We explore ordered and unordered lists in a bit more depth in Chapter 3 of this minibook, but in a nutshell, unordered lists are bullet lists, and ordered lists are numbered lists. You can apply either unordered list tags or ordered list tags by clicking the Unordered List button (shown in Figure 4-21) or the Ordered list button (just to the right of the Unordered List button), respectively.

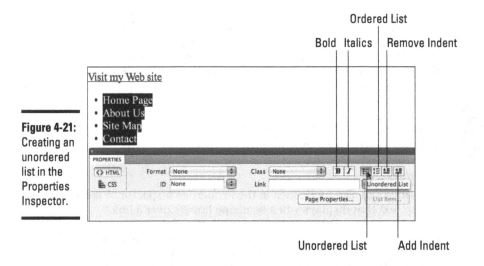

Figure 4-21: Creating an unordered list in the Properties Inspector.

You can apply a blockquote tag (that indents text) to any selected paragraph or set of paragraphs by clicking the Blockquote button in the Properties Inspector (the right-most of the set of small buttons, shown in Figure 4-22). You remove blockquotes using the button to the left of the Blockquote button.

The easily recognizable "B" button applies boldface (technically speaking, the HTML `<strong>` tag) to selected text, while the "I" button applies italics (the HTML `<em>` — short for emphasis — tag).

Figure 4-22: Formatting buttons in the Properties Inspector.

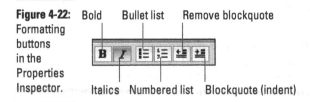

Generating HTML

Inserting code in Dreamweaver often happens "behind the scenes." For example, earlier in this chapter, you can see how Dreamweaver places images in pages, including when you copy and paste an image into the Design view or when you choose Insert⇨Image from the menu. When you use these (or other) techniques to place an image on a page, Dreamweaver generates an HTML <img> element.

Here are three different techniques that Dreamweaver offers for creating HTML elements: the Insert menu, the Insert panel, and then stripping away those interface elements and just entering HTML code directly in Dreamweaver's Code view.

Which approach is best? Well, they all have advantages. Code view gives you the most control over exactly what parameters you apply to an HTML tag, but you have to remember all those parameters and type them. The Insert menu and Insert panel are faster to use and don't require you to memorize code, but sometimes it's not clear exactly what code you've generated when you create content with these tools. Thus, the "best" approach is probably "all of the above" as they say in the multiple-choice testing world. We often generate content using Dreamweaver's menus and panels and then examine and (where necessary) tweak the generated code in Code view.

 No matter which method you choose for generating HTML, check over your code with a validator (covered later in this chapter) before you go live with the page. A *code validator* is a test that you can run on a page's code to make sure it's written properly. The test results alert you to any issues so that you can fix them.

From the Insert panel

The Dreamweaver Insert panel (choose Window⇨Insert) provides quick access to many of the most useful HTML elements. The popup at the top of the dialog box organizes features into categories, as shown in Figure 4-23.

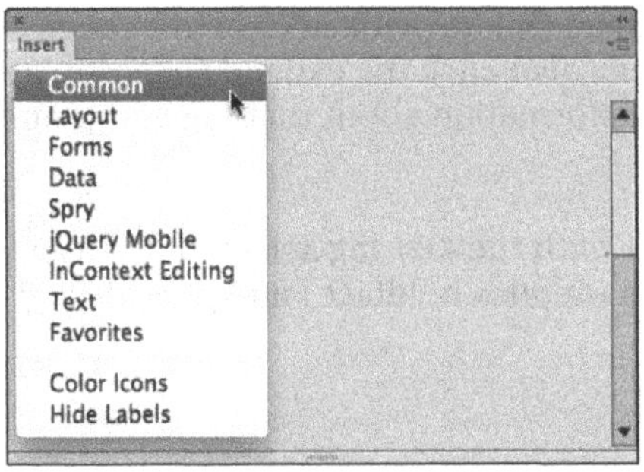

Book III
Chapter 4

Creating HTML5 with Dreamweaver CS6

Figure 4-23: Categories in the Insert panel.

Insert

- Common
- Layout
- Forms
- Data
- Spry
- jQuery Mobile
- InContext Editing
- Text
- Favorites

- Color Icons
- Hide Labels

This panel has several categories of tools for elements that you might want to quickly and easily add to a page. Some items in the default set include the following:

✦ **Common:** Includes basic elements: link, e-mail link, *anchor points* (invisible links that make it so people can jump from place to place on your page), table, image, date (which has several options for formatting), and comment (for adding a code comment).

✦ **Forms:** Inserts the elements you need to build web forms. (See Book VI for details about how to make a form.) The elements found under this toolbar are radio buttons, check boxes, and text boxes. Each has special attributes that you can set via the Properties Inspector after you add them to the page.

✦ **Text:** This group, shown in Figure 4-24, is another place with options for formatting text. Special types of formatting are available here, such as headings and definition lists.

All the elements available on the Insert panel are available via the Insert menu.

Figure 4-24:
Assign a
Heading 3
(h3) tag from
the Insert
panel.

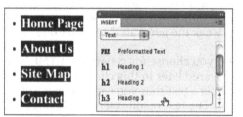

From the Insert menu

Some commonly used HTML elements (like images or forms) are inserted directly from menu options in the Insert menu. But you can also insert any HTML tag from the menu by choosing Insert⇨Tag and expanding the HTML tags folder.

Doing that displays subfolders that provide access to a range of tags. When you click on any tag, you can also click the expand (triangle) symbol in the Tag Info button to display information about that tag and examples of how to use it.

For example, in Figure 4-25, with the <b> tag selected, the Tag Info area explains what this tag does (applies boldface) and provides an example.

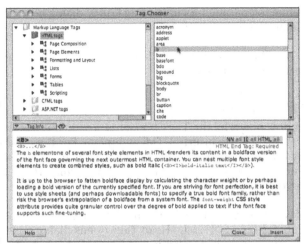

Figure 4-25:
Inserting
a boldface
element
from the
Dream-
weaver Tag
Chooser.

Using the Tag Chooser

To use the Tag Chooser panel to apply tags, first select text and then click
the Insert button. You can keep the Tag Chooser panel open as you edit your
page, and select text with the panel open.

When you click the Insert button in the Tag Chooser panel, the Tag Editor
dialog box opens. Here, you can define parameters for your tag. In Chapters 2
and 3 of this minibook, we explain how tags are modified with parameters,
and you can define parameters for the tag you're applying with the Tag Editor
dialog box. For example, in Figure 4-26, we're applying a `Title` attribute
(popup text) to the <b> tag.

Book III
Chapter 4

Creating HTML5
with
Dreamweaver CS6

Figure 4-26:
Defining tag
parameters
in the Tag
Editor.

After you define tag parameters in the Tag Editor dialog box, click OK to apply the element to selected text.

In sum, the Tag Chooser panel is a full-featured reference and assistant for choosing and applying HTML.

The Insert HTML menu

Having seen how powerful the Tag Chooser is, you might wonder why Dreamweaver also has an Insert⇨HTML submenu. For the most part it's an evolutionary holdover from earlier versions of Dreamweaver. But sometimes the HTML submenu provides quicker access to common HTML elements than the encyclopedic Tag Chooser.

One of our favorite options here is getting quick access to a web page's head content. Choosing Insert⇨HTML⇨Head Tags opens dialog boxes for defining metadata, such as page description and keywords. (See Chapter 2 of this minibook for a discussion of the role of metadata.)

In Code view

Code view (shown in Figure 4-27) is a window that reveals the underlying code of your page. This view is appropriate if you're comfortable with hand-coding your pages or you want to see the code you generated using Dreamweaver menus and the Properties Inspector.

The downside is that you can't see the end results of what you're coding without previewing in a browser or switching to a view that includes Design view.

Figure 4-27: Code view in Dreamweaver shows you just the code.

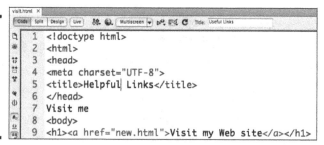

```
visit.html  ×
 Code  Split  Design  Live   ⟨⟩ ⟨⟩  Multiscreen ▾  ⟨⟩ ⟨⟩ C  Title: Useful Links
 1  <!doctype html>
 2  <html>
 3  <head>
 4  <meta charset="UTF-8">
 5  <title>Helpful Links</title>
 6  </head>
 7  Visit me
 8  <body>
 9  <h1><a href="new.html">Visit my Web site</a></h1>
```

Options for displaying code are available from View⇨Code View Options in the main Dreamweaver menu. These include the following:

✦ **Word Wrap:** Without this, the code and content can stretch out for miles. Word Wrap keeps text all in the visible window without affecting the code.

✦ **Syntax Coloring:** This presents different elements of HTML (and other code) syntax in different colors. By default, for example, tags are displayed as blue, making it easy to tell whether you correctly (or not) typed a tag.

✦ **Code Line Numbers:** Displays numbers in the left margin of the Code view window.

✦ **Highlight Invalid Code:** This one highlights errors in the code with bright yellow, which is very handy!

To change the how way code displays in Code view, including to make it larger, choose Edit⇨Preferences/Dreamweaver⇨Preferences, and select the Fonts category. Here, you can change the default font and font size for code that displays in Code view.

The vertical bar of tools on the left side of Code view provides an alternate set of controls over how code is displayed, providing access to code display features available from the menu. Hovering over these tools reveals helpful tooltips that explain what each tool does.

In Design view

In Design view, you see only the visual aspects of your page, which can prove helpful if you're not as comfortable with code or you need to see more of your design for a moment.

The downside to using this view is that you can't see what's happening with your code. Sometimes, edits that you make in the Design view can produce issues in the code, such as *empty tags* (tags that are left behind after the content in them has been removed). Split view mode is really the best of both worlds, which we discuss next, because you get Code view at the top of the screen and Design view at the bottom.

Working in Split view

In Split view, you can hand-code or make edits in the design window. It allows you to see the effects of your edits right away, whether you make them in the Code portion of the view or in the Design portion of the view.

As you edit code, Dreamweaver will display a Refresh button in the Properties Inspector, as shown in Figure 4-28. Clicking this button updates the display on the design side of the screen. Or, you can update the display of code in Design view by choosing View⇨Refresh Design View from the main Document menu.

The downside to Split view somewhat depends on your design environment. If you're working on a 27", 2560 pixel-wide monitor, you've got plenty of real estate to share between design and code. In that environment, there might not be any downside to working in Split view.

If, on the other hand, you're designing a website in Dreamweaver with a laptop, you're going to have a hard time viewing both code and how your page will look at the same time.

Figure 4-28:
In Split view, refresh the display in the Design window.

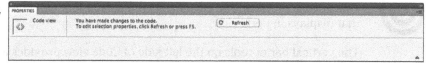

Different Way to View Pages

In addition to Code, Design, and Split view, Dreamweaver provides a range of other ways to view your pages. Why? Aren't three views enough? Not really.

First of all, Design view only approximates how your pages will look in a browser. Live view does a better job of showing you how your page will look in a browser. Later in this chapter, we'll explain why even Live view has limits, and how to preview in browsers, but for now suffice to say that Live view does a much better job approximating how a page will look in a browser than just viewing a page in Design view (with Live view off).

Other view options in Dreamweaver make it easier to identify what code is responsible for which elements in the Design window. This can be awfully helpful when you have a lot of code, or as you are learning to identify how HTML code works.

Beyond that, as your pages get complicated and begin to include linked JavaScript and CSS style sheet files, Dreamweaver helps you identify and examine (or edit) those files as well.

Take a look at these view options.

Examining associated files

As noted, when you add JavaScript to your pages, or link to a CSS style sheet, those associated files are accessible in the Document window.

At the top of the Document window, near the Code View, Split View, and Design View buttons, are the Live View and Live Code buttons. You'll also find Source Code and the names of all the linked script and CSS files that you used in the document.

Figure 4-29 shows three associated files linked to the open HTML file. Clicking any of them opens those files in the Document window.

Figure 4-29:
Viewing associated files for an open HTML file.

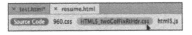

Previewing with Live view

Live view gives you a preview of what your page will look like in a browser, directly in Dreamweaver, which is helpful when you'd rather just get a look at the page without really previewing your page in a browser. You can't edit pages in Live view, though, so, the typical workflow involves toggling between Live view (to see how a page will look) and Live view off (to edit content in Design view).

Live view also lets you turn off JavaScript or plug-ins to see what your page looks like when visitors without those functions load your page.

Here are two big things to always keep in mind.

✦ In this era of competing browser standards, different browsers display different features differently. For example, CSS3 effects and transforms are handled differently, depending on the browser. The standard used by Dreamweaver is the Safari browser.

✦ Using Live view is not as accurate as using the File⇨Preview in Browser option from the Dreamweaver menu and previewing pages in one of your computer's installed browsers. We return to this near the end of this chapter.

Finding code with Live Code

With Live view active, you can click the Live Code button to highlight all the Live View source code. The Live Code button background turns gray when it's selected. The highlighting is visible in Split and Code view modes.

With the Inspect button selected, in Split view, code is highlighted on the Code side of split view when objects are hovered over in the Design site, as shown in Figure 4-30.

Figure 4-30: Highlight code with the Inspect button on in Live view.

Visual aids

Dreamweaver's array of visual aids allows you to see various parts of your page more easily. Some of the options available are CSS layout outlines, table borders and widths, image maps (graphics that have areas that are clickable links), and invisible elements like scripts.

These visual aids are most useful when you're designing pages with CSS styles that are applied to special HTML tags known as DIV tags. We explore this process in depth in Book IV, but while we're exploring view options in Dreamweaver, it's worth taking note of these aids.

On the top in Figure 4-31 is a page in Dreamweaver with all visual aids selected. Those visual aids, in different ways, help distinguish the borders of DIV tags used for page layout. On the bottom in Figure 4-31 is this same page open in a browser, where the visual aids do not display.

You can enable any or all the visual aids to help get a better idea of what's going on "behind the scenes" of your page.

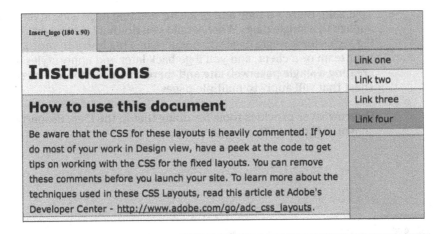

Figure 4-31:
Viewing a
page with
and without
visual aids
turned on.

Defining Head Content

As we explain in Chapter 2 of this minibook, HTML pages are essentially divided into head content and body content. *Head content* contains code that does not directly appear on the page, like the page *title* (text that appears in a browser title bar or tab), links to style sheets, and *metadata* (content used by search engines to find and describe page content).

Setting page properties

Dreamweaver presents different options for defining head content. One of them involves an approach we generally advise against in this book: embedding styles within a page. Instead, we generally steer you toward creating *external style sheets* — style sheets that are separate files that can be linked to (applied to) multiple pages within a website. We explain why this is the best approach for most web projects and how to create and link external style sheets (including using Dreamweaver) in Book IV.

That said, there's a time and place for defining page-wide styling that only applies to a single page. When would you do that? You might resort to defining styles for a single page when you're in a big hurry to prototype a page for your team or a client, and you'll go back later and apply styles. Or, if you're creating a single-page web site and there's no need for an external style sheet that will apply to multiple pages.

Dreamweaver provides tools for doing that in the Page Properties dialog box shown in Figure 4-32.

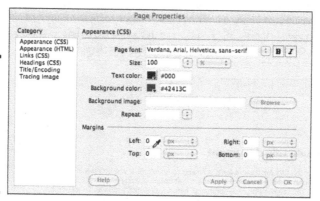

Figure 4-32: Setting a page background color in the Page Properties dialog box.

To open the Page Properties dialog box, click the Page Properties button on the Properties Inspector or choose Modify⇨Page Properties. The Appearance (CSS), Appearance (HTML), Links (CSS), and Headings (CSS) tabs generate head code that defines how different elements on the page appear. The options are intuitive. On the Appearance tab, for example, you can define text font, size, and color as well as background color (or image) for a page. Figure 4-32 shows background color being defined. Other tabs of the Page Properties dialog box provide similarly intuitive options for defining features, such as how links display and how headings look.

In its attempt to make web design easy, and to shield designers from what's "under the hood," Dreamweaver offers options that generate CSS style sheet code "unconsciously." For example, when you use the features in the Page Properties dialog box, you might not realize that as you define properties like a page background or font style, you're really generating CSS code — but you are. Because of this relationship between CSS and HTML, this "on the fly" approach to generating CSS might prove useful. But, again, before you start juggling HTML and CSS, you want to be grounded in the basics of CSS that we cover in Book IV.

Defining a document title

One definable element from the Page Properties dialog box doesn't relate to generating embedded CSS but defines an essential part of the head code in any web page: the Title tag.

You can define a page title from the Page Properties dialog box Title/Encoding tab. This tab also offers options for changing the Document Type (DTD) as well as nonessential Encoding and Unicode Normalization Form settings. Default settings (UTF-8 and C, respectively) provide the widest support for special characters and symbols in your text.

Defining a document title is not an option, so using these settings is important. Page titles are not like filenames. They are meant to be descriptive and can (and often should) have spaces and special characters (such as !, @, #, $, and so on).

In addition to using the Title/Encoding tab of the Page Properties dialog box, you can also type a page title directly into the Title field in the Document toolbar at the top of the Document window, as shown in Figure 4-33. If the Document toolbar isn't displayed, choose View⇨Toolbars⇨Document.

Figure 4-33: Entering a page title.

Book III
Chapter 4

Creating HTML5 with Dreamweaver CS6

About titles

Like admirers of tradition who embrace and uphold titles like King, Queen, Duke, and Lord, we agree that titles are essential — in web documents, that is. Remember that the page title shows in browsers and in search engines, so make sure you give your page a title that makes sense.

You can hand-code a title in any HTML page by typing **<title>My Title Here</>** in the head section of the HTML document. Dreamweaver automatically adds the title tags in the correct place if you create your HTML documents via the New Document dialog box. Simply replace the default `Untitled Document` with the title of your choice. And now you know why so many pages out there seem to be titled `Untitled Document`.

Testing Pages and Validating Code

As you enter the world of coding in Dreamweaver (as opposed to just creating HTML with menu options and panels), you'll want to test that code to see if you did something wrong.

Another source of "bad" code is text copied and pasted into Dreamweaver from Microsoft Word. We advise using Word (or other word processors) for serious text editing and copying text into Dreamweaver's Design window as the best way to create and edit text for your pages. But that process can generate "bad" code (code that's unnecessary to convey the content and style of the text and creates larger files that load more slowly in browsers).

Dreamweaver provides state-of-the-art tools for testing code and fixing errors, whether of your own making or due to pasting in Word text.

Preview in Browser

You can preview a page in Dreamweaver using any browser installed on your computer. And remember, looking at a web page in Browser is really the only way to see what your page will look like in any particular browser.

To preview a page in a browser, choose File⇨Preview in Browser, and select a browser from the submenu, as shown in Figure 4-34.

Figure 4-34:
Previewing
in a
browser.

Although Design view shows a close rendition, different browsers display things a little differently. You need to preview your pages in the actual browsers you're designing for.

Clearly, in this multimedia era, nobody can preview web pages in every browser, browser version, or device. Depending on an assessment of your audience, you should make decisions about what environments are critical. If the significant audience of people using Internet Explorer 6–8 is critical to your mission, test on those browsers. If iPad users are most important, you might need to get your hands on an iPad.

You can use the Adobe BrowserLab option in the Preview in Browser submenu to avail yourself of Adobe's (at this writing, free) online utility that simulates how pages will look in various browsers. It doesn't test for mobile devices, but it does test how your pages will work in older browsers (as well as current versions of full-sized browsers).

BrowserLab is a valuable resource because no designer will have access to actual working versions of older browser versions. Figure 4-35, for example, shows a page being tested in Internet Explorer 6.

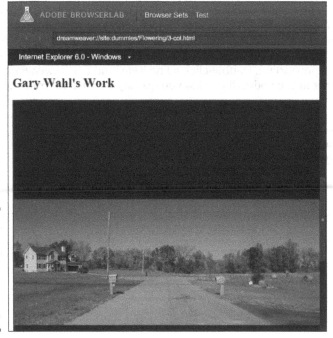

**Book III
Chapter 4**

**Creating HTML5
with
Dreamweaver CS6**

Figure 4-35:
Testing a
page in
Internet
Explorer
6 using
BrowserLab.

The Validation panel

W3C is the organization and website (`www.w3.org`) that defines standards for HTML code. It provides tools for testing HTML to see if the code complies with W3C rules.

To submit an open page in Dreamweaver for validation, choose File⇨Validate Current Document (W3C). When you do, the W3C Validator Notification dialog box appears, as shown in Figure 4-36.

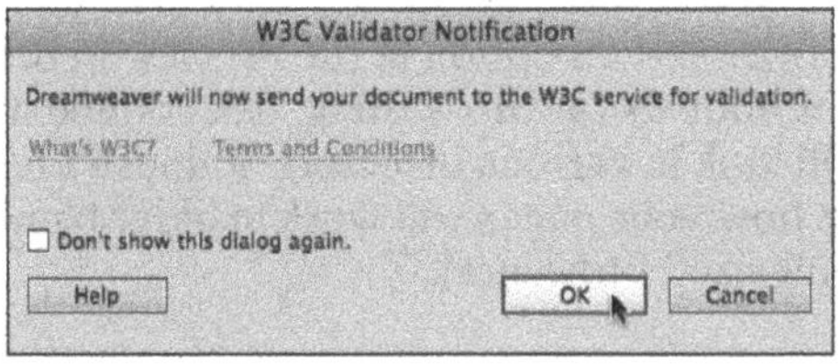

Figure 4-36:
The
Validator
Notification
dialog box.

Click OK to submit the open page to W3C's validation tools. The results appear in the Validation panel.

You can hide (or reopen) the Validation panel by choosing Window⇨Results, the Validation panel. That panel (shown in Figure 4-37 with test results) automatically launches when you run validation. This is where the results of the tests and validators are displayed, along with additional information where appropriate. Double-click a line item, and Dreamweaver takes you to the error in the code; this helps you quickly locate and fix issues.

Also, the Validation panel can give the code line numbers for each error that it finds. Just turn on the code line numbers in the Code View Options by choosing View⇨Code View Options⇨Line Numbers. The line numbers are displayed in the margin of Code view.

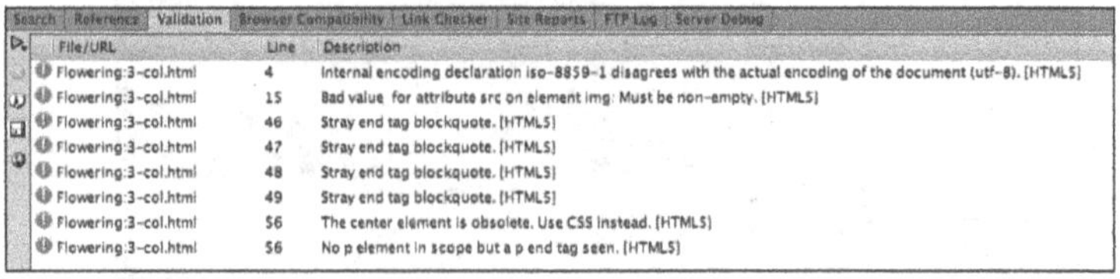

Figure 4-37:
The
Validation
panel can
display
HTML
errors.

The Validation panel also has options to test your links. An easy way to do that is to select File➪Check Page➪Links. A report appears in the Reports panel.

Clean-up tools

Another helpful set of tools for checking code are the Clean Up HTML tools. These tools are available from the Command menu. Choosing Command➪ Clean Up HTML opens the Clean Up HTML/XHTML dialog box, which displays a set of common errors. Selecting any (or all) of those errors and clicking OK prompts Dreamweaver to automatically correct those errors and display a results dialog box that lists all the corrections made. Figure 4-38 shows the results with one empty tag removed.

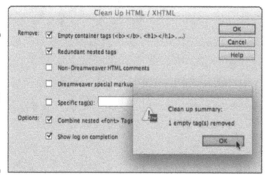

Figure 4-38: Using the Clean Up HTML dialog box to clean up common coding errors.

Book III
Chapter 4

Creating HTML5
with
Dreamweaver CS6

The Clean Up Word HTML (accessed by choosing Command➪Clean Up Word HTML) is similar to the Clean Up HTML command but it has special tools to detect and eliminate nonstandard and redundant (that is, unnecessary) HTML generated when you paste Word text into Dreamweaver.

There are many check box options for what to test for, but by default all are checked, and you should leave them checked to let Dreamweaver detect all nonstandard and redundant Word HTML. Doing this does not remove content or formatting, it just removes tags that don't do anything and that add to file size. Figure 4-39 shows the results of cleaning up a paragraph of text copied from Word into Dreamweaver.

Figure 4-39:
Using the
Clean Up
Word HTML
dialog box
to clean up
unnecess-
ary code
generated
when
Word text
is copied
into Dream-
weaver.

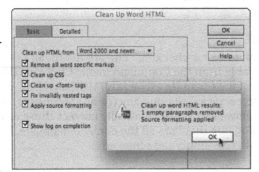

Book IV

Designing Pages with CSS

Contents at a Glance

Chapter 1: Styling Text with CSS

In This Chapter

✔ Understanding modern web design

✔ Creating a CSS document

✔ Defining colors for the web

✔ Setting CSS text properties

✔ Creating styles for a link state

✔ Nesting and grouping styles

✔ Using templates

*I*n Book III, Chapter 2, we break down the role of HTML documents — the basic foundation for web pages. But an HTML page without a style sheet is like a model without a wardrobe. Like a football player without helmet, jersey, and pads. Like a mime without face paint. Like a sumo wrestler without . . .okay, we've gone far enough with analogies here. But they illustrate the relationship between HTML and CSS. Without CSS, web pages have no style.

This chapter shows you how to create a cascading style sheet (CSS) file that defines the style and layout of your HTML pages. By style, we mean color scheme, font size and format, and other elements that bring your site to life. By layout, we mean columns, rows, boxes, and other elements that define where content (such as text, images, or video) appears on a page.

Style sheets are written in CSS — a relatively simple and accessible language that's a flexible and powerful way to control the layouts of your web pages. As your site grows, you'll see huge benefits in the ease of maintenance and the ability to repurpose or redesign sections of your site very quickly.

Before we jump into the mechanics of creating a web page layout with HTML and CSS, we want to show you some reasons why using CSS is a good thing. Next, we tell you how you can use the View Source feature of a web browser to examine other developers' code. View Source provides a valuable way to see how things are done right (or wrong, as the case may be).

And in this chapter, we walk through how to create and attach style sheets that format text and links, align content (left, right, or centered), and create spacing within, and between, containers that hold content.

Understanding How Modern Websites Use CSS

External style sheets are files outside of (but linked to) HTML pages that supply style and layout to web pages. Cascading style sheets are one example of external style sheets. The following are reasons why including external style sheets is a good thing:

♦ **CSS styles are much more powerful than older, HTML-based tools for page design.** For example, the layout with HTML tables requires designers to contort table rows and columns into containers for content. With HTML, you have little control over parameters like the spacing between and within those table cells, or the specific borders on the top, bottom, or sides of the table cell. CSS, on the other hand, can turn a rather generic HTML tag — a DIV tag — into an almost infinitely formattable container for any kind of content.

♦ **CSS classes and IDs are special styles that are at the heart of modern page design.** These CSS classes and IDs have replaced HTML tables as the standard technique for laying out web pages. Tables used cells, created by the intersection of rows and columns, as placeholders for content. This technique was clumsy and limited, compared to the freedom available with ID- and class-defined page layouts.

♦ We explore using classes and IDs for page layout in Chapter 2 of this minibook.

♦ **External style sheets, such as CSS, allow for *global* styling, which has common elements across all the HTML pages in a website.** Need to change the color scheme on 17,412 pages in 5 minutes? No problem with an external style sheet — you simply update the CSS file, and all the HTML files that link to that style sheet instantly update in browsers.

Breaking that down a bit more, we examine in more depth why people use CSS for page styling. When using CSS, you can

♦ **Easily make global changes to how your content is presented.** If styles are applied using external style sheets, they can be used to instantly change the appearance of every page to which they are linked. This is an indispensable productivity tool in large websites. Imagine having to find all the font tags and change them in an extensive website. Using a simple Find and Replace effort often doesn't work because of the inconsistent way tags are coded. It's possible to have hundreds of variations of the font tags — that all look the same on the web page but are coded differently — which makes using Find and Replace utilities useless.

✦ **Easily discern the original meaning of your content.** When working with older, "anything that makes it look good" type techniques that employ HTML tags for formatting and design, you often can't tell what the different parts of the page content are just by looking at it. Old-style HTML allows for using tags improperly, such as applying properties to a font tag that makes a paragraph tag display as though it were a heading. Not easy to fix. If you manage to strip out the old font tags, you also strip out the visual cues that can help you to re-code the page properly.

For example, if you set up your page as a block of content with `<br>` tags to separate it visually into paragraphs and `<font>` tags to make headings look different, it's difficult to figure out what it was if the tags are disrupted or deleted.

✦ **Make your site friendly to all who visit — no matter where they are or what their situation is.** Increasingly, people using the web don't use a traditional computer. Instead, they use tablets, smartphones, and other digital devices. With CSS and HTML, you can detect a visitor's browsing environment and provide different style sheets that display content in a form appropriate to the visitor's media.

✦ **Relying on CSS and HTML also makes sites more accessible to hearing- and vision-impaired users,** who have reader software or other special tools that work better if you avoid using HTML tags for formatting.

Again, some users will have customized style sheets so they can use the Internet. Someone might need to enlarge font sizes or to specify how a screen reader aurally signals different parts of a document to compensate for visual impairments. Information about aural style sheets can be found on the World Wide Web Consortium (W3C) site at `www.w3.org/TR/REC-CSS2/aural.html`.

You might be asking yourself: "Why are style sheet files dubbed cascading style sheets (thus the "C" in CSS)?" *Cascading* refers to how styles are applied and in what order — that is, which styles take precedence over others. CSS can be implemented in three ways — alone or in combination with each other — on your pages:

✦ **Inline:** Inline CSS refers to styles that are directly in the content. This method is the least desirable because it affects only the content that the styles are directly associated with.

✦ **Embedded in the head of the HTML document:** Like inline styles, embedded styles are defined right in an HTML page, and not through an external style sheet. However, these styles offer more flexibility because they can be applied to many elements within that single page, such as all the paragraphs, in the document. These styles do not, however, affect parts of other HTML pages in your site; they apply only to the document in which they're embedded.

✦ **External:** External CSS affects all the pages of a site. You need to create an external CSS file and then link to that file in the head section of your HTML documents. This way enables you to take advantage of the quick sitewide layout control we discuss earlier in this chapter.

We further explain each method — with code examples — in the following sections. Now that you know the ways CSS can be implemented, keep in mind that the style that's closest to an element takes precedence. For example, say you have styles set up for paragraphs in your external CSS file and you decide that you need a special treatment for paragraphs on just one page of your site. You can set up those styles in the header. The CSS in the header takes precedence over the CSS in the external CSS file because it's closer to the paragraphs of that page. If you then decide that one paragraph in that same document needs a third treatment, apply inline CSS to just that paragraph. That paragraph — and only that one — will be styled by the inline style.

It is unlikely you will work with (or create) pages that combine inline, embedded, and external style sheets. But if you do, inline styles will trump both embedded and external styles, and embedded styles will trump external styles. That might sound confusing, but keep a couple things in mind: It is (as we noted) unlikely you'll find pages that combine all three approaches to style sheets, and you can simplify all this by remembering "local trumps global" when it comes to what style applies.

Inline styles

Inline styles are coded directly into the body of your document. For example, look at the following HTML for a paragraph:

```
<p style="color:#000000;">This would be black text</p>
```

Although inline styles are quick to add on the fly, we don't recommend this technique. In essence, you're trading an old style of coding that created hard-to-maintain sites for a new flavor of the same thing. For example, in the code that follows, you can see that this style is applied directly within the <p> tag and will affect only this one instance of a paragraph. No other paragraphs will take on the attributes unless you apply the same style attributes to them.

```
<p><font color="#000000">This would be black text</font></p>
```

The problem with coding this way is that if you decide you want to change the color of the text on your site — or anything else coded with inline styles — you have to find *all* the places that you used these inline styling techniques and change them. Inline styles also make a lot of clutter that isn't necessary.

Styles embedded in the head of the document

When you *embed styles,* you create your CSS styles in the head portion of your HTML document and refer to them in the HTML, like this:

```
<head>
<title>Welcome to Our Site!</title>
<style type="text/css">
<!--p {color: #990099}-->
</style>
</head><body><p>This text would be purple</p></body>
</html>
```

The advantage to using this technique is that you can have some specialized styles embedded in just one HTML document. This can come in handy if you want a special page for an event. The other pages of your site aren't affected by styles that are embedded this way or created inline.

If you're creating styles that you intend to use throughout your site (which is most often the case), don't use this technique. You'll end up with a site that's a pain in the neck to update because you'll have to open each document and edit each embedded style individually.

External style sheets

Using an external style sheet is generally the preferred method, especially if you want to implement your styles across the whole site. All the CSS style information is created in an external file(s). The file is linked to the HTML document in the head portion of the HTML, like this:

```
<head>
<link rel="stylesheet" href="style1.css" type="text/css" />
</head>
```

This code links the CSS file to the HTML document. The CSS file is `style1.css` and is in the same folder as the referring HTML page.

Note: The external style sheet's file extension is `.css`. When a visitor goes to your site, the CSS is loaded along with the HTML, and the page looks great. As we mention earlier, the major advantage to this technique is that if you want to change anything about your design or layout, you can make a sitewide change by changing the styles in the CSS file. You don't need to open the HTML files to edit them. Of course, you need to preview your pages before publishing them, but that's the rule for all web pages.

You can also create multiple style sheets and link them to the same HTML document, like this:

```
<head>
<link rel="stylesheet" href="style1.css" type="text/css" />
<link rel="stylesheet" href="style2.css" type="text/css" />
</head>
```

With this technique, your site can have a unified look and feel, and still have the freedom to have specialized style sheets for particular sections of a large website. To take the earlier example, `style1.css` might define page background, fonts, and colors and be applied to every page in your site, whereas `style2.css` might have some particular styles used just in pages that present videos. In this instance, `style1.css` would be applied to every page in your site, but `style2.css` would be applied only to pages with video.

Creating a CSS Document

A *CSS document* is the external style sheet file where the styles you create are kept. Because the real power of style sheets is implemented with external CSS files, the examples given throughout this section refer to external styles.

You create CSS documents using your code editor, in the same way you create HTML files. The first difference, though, is that CSS files are always saved with a `.css` filename extension.

The term *CSS* can refer to the CSS document or to the actual styles.

Although not required by modern browsers, CSS documents are usually saved with the following first line of code:

```
@charset "UTF-8";
```

And that's it! After you save your CSS file — and avoid uppercase, spaces, or special characters other than dashes (-) or underscores (_) in the filename — you're ready to start building a bunch of styles.

Defining styles

Unlike HTML files, CSS files are not structured or broken into sections (such as head or body sections in an HTML document). You simply define as many styles as you wish.

CSS styles are made up of three parts:

✦ **A selector:** Specifies what the style will affect. The most basic type of selector is one that applies to an HTML style, such as h1, h2, p, body, or li (for list).

✦ **A property:** Indicates what exactly will be affected (such as the font, color, background, and so on).

✦ **A property value:** Indicates how the property will be affected (such as fonts will be black and bold).

As noted, the most basic CSS selectors define how HTML tags (`<p>`, `<table>`, `<body>`) appear. Other, more complicated CSS selectors are classes and IDs. We explain how to use classes and IDs in Chapter 2 of this minibook. Here, we focus on styles that define how HTML tags look.

The *syntax* (or grammar) for writing CSS is

```
selector {
    property: value;
    property: value;
    property: value;
}
```

A style can have several `property: value` pairs, or just one.

Note: Properties are divided by semicolons, and a colon is between the property and the value.

What if you want to define a style that applies to more than one element; for example, a font and font color that apply to headings 1, 2, 3, and 4?

To do that, you create a set of selectors divided by commas. For example, the style that follows has four selectors, and applies to headings 1–4:

```
h1, h2, h3, h4 {
    font-weight: bold; color: #990000;
}
```

In the preceding example, it is important that commas separate each heading that's part of the combined style. If the commas are missing, the code wouldn't work as intended.

Defining basic styles

Keep in mind, a good starting place when creating a style sheet is to define styles for basic elements, such as the body and paragraph tags as well as headings.

The single most powerful style is the one you define for the body tag. In Book III, we identify the framing role of the body element in HTML. Web pages are divided into a head region, which contains content that doesn't display on the page, and the body element, which contains everything that displays on a page. Thus, the properties you define in the CSS body tag apply to all the visible elements on a page. Typically, a body tag style defines a page background color (or image) and basic font attributes (such as the font face and color).

Here's an example of a body tag style definition:

```
body{
      font-family: Verdana,Arial,sans-serif;
      color: #000000;
      margin: 0px;
      padding: 0px;
      background-color:#ffffff;
}
```

The preceding code does the following:

✦ Uses Verdana as the default font, Arial as the second choice if Verdana isn't available, and a sans-serif font if Arial isn't available.

✦ Specifies that the default text color is black (#000000). Here we use a *hexadecimal* (six-digit) code to define the color. For an exploration of web color coding, see "Defining Web Colors" later in this chapter.

✦ Specifies that the HTML document should entirely fill the browser window with no margin (0px) or padding (0px) (*px* stands for *pixels*) between the edge of the browser window and the content of the page.

✦ Creates a default background color of white for the whole site (#ffffff).

Use three font options because your preferred font may not be installed on a visitor's computer.

As noted earlier, the basic tags that are generally defined in style sheets include:

✦ **Paragraph:** For example, a paragraph style with a defined font family (Verdana, or if that's not supported in a browser, use Geneva and then sans-serif), font size (12 points), a line height of double-spacing, and the color gray would be defined with the following CSS:

```
p {
   font-family: Verdana, Geneva, sans-serif;
   font-size: 12pt;
   line-height: 2;
   color: #6A6A6A;

}
```

✦ **Headings 1–6:** For example, a heading 1 (h1) style that displays yellow text on a gray background could be defined using the following code:

```
h1 {

    color: #FFFF42;
    background-color: #7F7F7F;
}
```

✦ **Lists:** For example, a list (li) style definition that formats lists with square bullets instead of round ones would look like this:

```
li {
    list-style-type: square;
}
```

Commenting CSS

Each type of coding has its own language style, or *syntax.* You must use the proper syntax when creating any code. If you don't, the code won't work, or it might do unexpected things. Even comments have proper markup and/or syntax.

Code comments are notes to yourself, or other developers. If you don't create code comments correctly, the browser might see them as content or code and treat them as such instead of keeping them hidden. And you don't want that — comments aren't secret. They aren't hidden from your fellow coders who examine your source code to learn from your work. But they are internal notes for yourself and other coders and don't display in a browser window. In CSS, comments look like this:

```
/* Heading 1 style - creates background and border- this is a
    CSS Comment*/
h1 {
width: 100%;
background-color: #000000;}
color: #fff;}
border-bottom: 1px #33333 solid;
}
/*End Heading 1 style - this is also a CSS Comment*/
```

Comments are between the /* and */, which signals to the browser that the information contained is a comment and is meant to be hidden.

Defining Web Colors

We illustrate the basic syntax for defining the color for a selector in the following example:

```
h1 {
     color: red;
}
```

In this example, the selector is the h1 tag, the property is `color`, and the value is `red`.

The following example illustrates how to define a background color (with the `background-color` property) and border color (black) for the preceding h1 tag:

```
h1 {
     color: red;
     background-color: silver;
     border-color-bottom: black;
}
```

The preceding style properties use color names (red, silver, or black): a silver background with a black border color (and red type) for h1 tags. Color names are an alternative to hexadecimal values, and an easy way to define colors in CSS.

Color naming works only for a limited set. That works for the following colors, including:

✦ Black, silver, and gray

✦ White

✦ Maroon and red

✦ Purple and fuchsia

✦ Green, lime, and olive

✦ Yellow

✦ Navy, blue, teal, and aqua

✦ Orange

As noted *hexadecimal* (six-digit) values can be used to define a wider range of colors. A search for *hexadecimal color values* yields a plethora of online charts that define color values as hexadecimal, or *hex* values (for short). One such chart, nicely organized, is at `www.w3schools.com/cssref/css_colors.asp`.

What about web-safe colors?

In earlier eras of the web, designers were constrained in the set of colors they could use by the limited number of colors supported on the earliest computer monitors. Those 256-color monitors (with 40 of those colors off-limits to designers because they were reserved for the system interface) are largely in recycling bins today.

Modern desktops, laptops, and mobile devices support at least 16 million colors. That means you can use the entire spectrum of hexadecimal colors.

CSS3, the latest version of CSS, introduces new ways to define colors and new color properties. The most substantial of these new features is the ability to define a transparency level for a color. This has significant design implications for background colors, which when semitransparent, allow part of the text, images, or other graphic elements underneath them to show through. We explore defining color transparency in Chapter 3 of this minibook.

Setting CSS Properties for Text

You can do more with font than formatting size, color, and style (see the preceding section). You can also add backgrounds, indent, customize horizontal and vertical spacing, and use borders. For example, a heading might have a background color, lists might be indented, paragraphs (to which the <p> tag is assigned) might have line spacing defined (a line spacing value of 2, for example, creates double-spacing, an option we note earlier in this chapter), borders might be defined in a list, and so on. Using formatting tools like these is an effective way to make headings look like page design elements.

Stylish headings

One interesting thing you can do with CSS is add some style to your heading tags. You can, for example, add a border and/or a background color to a heading:

```
h1 {
        font-family: Verdana, Geneva, sans-serif;
        color: #666;
        background-color: #CCC;
        border-right-width: thin;
        border-bottom-width: thin;
        border-bottom-style: solid;
        border-bottom-color: #333;
        border-right-style: solid;
}
```

Web font aesthetics

Several examples of formatting techniques you can apply to text with CSS are indent, border, background color, line spacing. But one thing to avoid, as much as possible, is the use of font effects (such as fonts that are not supported in many computers, or italics). Keep in mind that many formatting techniques that work well in print, such as italics, or fonts that depend on high-resolution printing will degrade into grainy, blurry, uninviting text when applied to web type.

Why? Because the typical resolution of a print document is three or four times as high as the typical resolution of a web page. Print documents, even those created on home printers, create fonts with 300 dots per inch, whereas monitors generally have resolutions ranging from 72 to 96 dots (more specifically pixels) per inch. And that makes a huge difference in font display. That is why, even with emerging technologies for presenting customized fonts in web documents, it is still important to stick to relatively simple, basic fonts for web pages.

Figure 1-1 shows how this code affects the <h1> tag in the HTML document. Note how the bottom border extends beyond the end of the text, and a right-edge border displays, creating a drop-shadow effect and making the heading a nice, page-separating device.

Figure 1-1:
This h1 headline is styled with borders and a background.

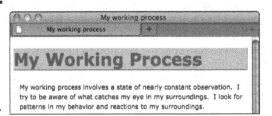

Spacing paragraphs

An underrated technique for making text inviting and attractive is to carefully tweak horizontal and vertical spacing.

The padding and margin properties can be defined in just about any unit of measurement including pixels (px), points (pt), or ems (em, which represents the width of the letter *m*). Pixels and points are considered *absolute* units of measurement because a pixel is a pixel (a dot on a computer screen) and a point is a point (a standard unit of type measurement — there are 72 points to the inch). But the em unit of measurement is considered a *relative* unit of measurement because the letter *m* can be different sizes depending on what formatting has been applied to text.

Although these properties are more often used to creating spacing outside of a box *(margin)* or within a box *(padding)*, they can also be used to indent text and control spacing between lines and paragraphs.

In the following example, the `line-height` property creates additional spacing between lines; the `padding-left` property indents paragraphs; and the `margin-top` property slightly reduces the default spacing between paragraphs (normally one line of type in height) with a negative value.

```
p {
    font-family: Verdana, Geneva, sans-serif;
    font-size: 12px;
    line-height: 18px;
    padding-left: 12px;
    margin-top: -3px;
}
```

Figure 1-2 shows how that paragraph text looks in a browser.

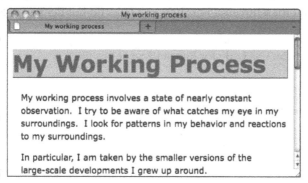

Figure 1-2: Paragraphs with indentation, line spacing, and compressed top margin.

Creating Styles for Link States

A *link* is what a user clicks to go somewhere else on your website. A link is denoted by the <a> tag and has various *states,* such as whether a user has clicked it, for example, or hovered over it.

You can set a specific color for everything that has an <a> tag (links are created in HTML by using `<a href="http://www.`*linkgoeshere*`.html">`), like so:

```
a{
    color: #CC0000;
    text-decoration: none;
}
```

This style automatically works on all link tags in your HTML document because it uses a tag selector.

Or you can spice up the way your links look by creating styles for the different states:

+ **Link:** The default state of a link. The CSS selector for this is `a:link`.

+ **Visited:** A link is considered visited when the user has clicked it. The CSS selector for this is `a:visited`.

+ **Hover:** A link is in the hover state when the user's cursor moves over it. The CSS selector for this is `a:hover`.

+ **Active:** A link is active the moment it's clicked. The CSS selector for this is `a:active`.

By default, if you don't define custom styles for links, they display with underlining: blue for unvisited, purple for visited, and red for active. There is no default for a hovered link; hovered links do not display differently than other links.

Here's what the CSS code for link settings looks like:

```
a:link{
        color: #000000;
        text-decoration: none;
}
a:visited{
        color:#009900;
        text-decoration: none;
}
a:hover{
        color: #000000;
        background-color: #CCC;
        text-decoration: underline;
}
a:active{
        color: #990000;
        text-decoration: underline;
}
```

Figure 1-3 shows how the regular (unvisited) and hover states look with this style applied.

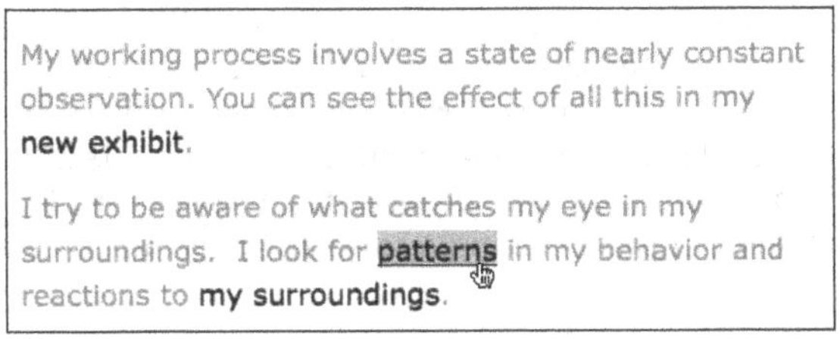

Figure 1-3:
A hovered
link with
underlining
and a
background.

My working process involves a state of nearly constant
observation. You can see the effect of all this in my
new exhibit.

I try to be aware of what catches my eye in my
surroundings. I look for **patterns** in my behavior and
reactions to **my surroundings**.

Styling Lists and Menus

Like all HTML tags, lists — including both *ordered* (numbered) and *unordered*
(bullet) lists — can have CSS styles defined for them. On a basic level, that
means you can define fonts, margin, padding, color, and so on for lists just as
you would for any other text tag. But designers often use CSS applied to lists
to create *navigation menus* (maps that help guide visitors through your website or to other websites). In doing so, you can turn a regular unordered list,
that can be edited simply in HTML, into a more inviting navigation menu.

For example, the following HTML code creates an unordered list with links
to the site's home page, plus links to a few popular sites:

```
<ul>
    <li><a href="index.html">Home</a></li>
    <li><a href="http://www.google.com">Google Search</a></li>
    <li><a href="http://www.ebay.com">eBay</a></li>
    <li><a href="http://www.amazon.com">Amazon</a></li>
    <li><a href="http://www.craigslist.org">Craigslist</a></li>
</ul>
```

That unordered list, unadorned with any CSS style, looks like the bullet list
in Figure 1-4.

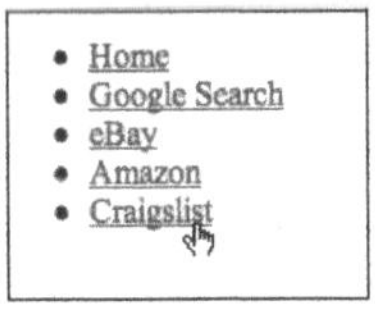

Figure 1-4:
An
unordered
list with
links.

- Home
- Google Search
- eBay
- Amazon
- Craigslist

With just a few CSS properties, you can convert this list into a more inviting
menu that displays the links, with what appear to be hoverable buttons (buttons that change display when hovered over), in one line.

One of those properties is the `display` property. With an `inline` value, this property eliminates line breaks within the tag to which it's applied. By defining a `display:inline` property and value for lists, in the following example, line breaks are eliminated within lists. That is a technique sometimes used by designers who find it helpful to create a list of links, but then display that set of links in a single row on a page, such as at the top or bottom of a page.

The rest of the following code uses very basic CSS properties explored earlier in this chapter, such as color, background color, padding, and `none` as a `text-decoration` value to eliminate the default underlining in links.

```
li{
    display: inline;
}
li a{
    text-decoration: none;
    color: #CCCCCC;
    padding: 12px;
    background-color: #333333;
}
li a:hover{
    color: #fff;
    background-color:#999999;
}
```

The result is a simple but inviting menu, as shown in Figure 1-5.

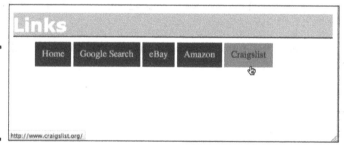

Figure 1-5:
A menu
based on an
unordered
list.

Grouping and Compound Styles

Complex page designs use grouped and dependent styles:

✦ *Grouped* styles are styles that apply to a set of tags. For example, you might define a similar property, such as a font, border, or background color, for all headings.

✦ *Compound* styles are styles that apply only within another tag. For example, you might define link styles for a menu that apply only within an HTML5 header tag (an example we explore shortly).

Grouping styles

Grouping styles is an efficiency technique that saves designers valuable time. For example, the following code has a solid, black, 1-pixel border below four heading tags:

```
h1, h2, h3, h4 {
    border-bottom-width: 1px;
    border-bottom-style: solid;
    border-bottom-color: #000000;
}
```

The result, as shown in Figure 1-6, has the bottom border applied to all four heading styles, even though each of those heading styles also has unique attributes defined separately for each.

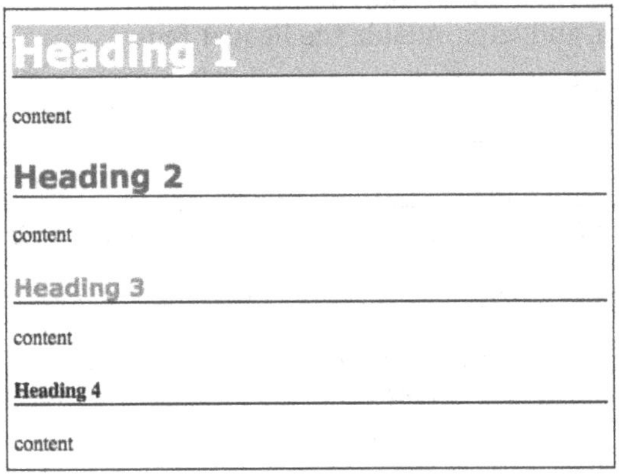

Figure 1-6: A group style applies the bottom border to four heading tags.

Heading 1

content

Heading 2

content

Heading 3

content

Heading 4

content

Compound styles

Compound styles are styles that apply only when the tag to which they're applied is nested inside another tag. Why would you want to do that? We return to the example of formatting a list to look like a menu bar (see the section "Styling Lists and Menus" earlier in this chapter). There, we define a style for lists that converts a list into a menu bar. If we made that a compound style — for example, within a header element — only lists that *were* inside a header or footer would display as menu bars.

Taken from another angle: What happens when you want to create a list in your document that's just a list? That challenge can be solved by nesting the definition for lists within the HTML5 header tag so that the only time the style applies is when a list appears inside a header.

The following CSS takes the properties defined throughout this chapter for a list and nests those properties within the header selector so that they apply only when a list is inside a header:

```
header li{
      display: inline;
}
header li a{
      text-decoration: none;
      color: #CCCCCC;
      padding: 12px;
      background-color: #333333;
}
header li a:hover{
      color: #333333;
      background-color:#999999;
}
```

The following HTML code shows the same list of links, first enveloped in HTML5 header tags, and later outside the header tags:

```
<header>
   <h1>Link Central</h1>
   <ul>
      <li><a href="index.html">Home</a></li>
      <li><a href="http://www.google.com">Google Search</a>
      </li>
      <li><a href="http://www.ebay.com">eBay</a>
      </li>
      <li><a href="http://www.amazon.com">Amazon</a></li>
      <li><a href="http://www.craigslist.org">Craigslist</a>
   </li>
   </ul>
</header>
<p>Welcome to link central! Your home for the most useful
   links...</p>
<h2>Here are some useful links:</h2>
<ul>
   <li><a href="index.html">Home</a></li>
   <li><a href="http://www.google.com">Google Search</a></li>
   <li><a href="http://www.ebay.com">eBay</a></li>
   <li><a href="http://www.amazon.com">Amazon</a></li>
   <li><a href="http://www.craigslist.org">Craigslist</a></li>
</ul>
```

Figure 1-7 shows a page with the same list used twice, once inside the header tags and once outside those tags.

Figure 1-7:
A list nested in a header applies different styling than the same list outside the header.

Working with Borrowed Styles

Many talented people have put many hours into creating style sheets. You can use free templates, or buy commercially distributed ones and customize them for your site. You can also view the CSS files for websites and learn from the techniques and approaches in them.

With the basic CSS techniques explored in this chapter, you're well positioned to adopt and adapt template style sheets that you can find online.

Using templates

A quick search for *CSS templates* or *free CSS templates* yields links to hundreds of sites that provide downloadable CSS templates that, with the techniques covered in this chapter, you can dissect, learn from, or edit to suit your own style requirements.

Commercially distributed CSS templates, and some free ones as well, provide models for you to examine before you buy (or download) the CSS file. And they often include helpful tips on how to customize and apply them. Figure 1-8 shows custom style sheets available at www.csstemplatesweb.com.

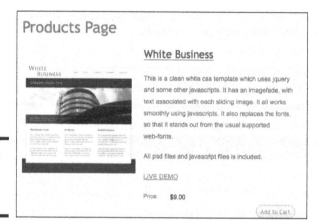

Learning from examining other people's CSS files

You're not the only one creating CSS files to format pages! We know, that's not a big surprise. But here's the useful part: When you see a site you like, you can examine the CSS that goes into making that site look the way it does.

To examine the CSS of a page, in Internet Explorer (IE) for example, either right-click in your browser window and choose View Source or choose View⇨ Source from your browser menu bar. (You can also view source with other browsers. The location of the View Source option might be different, but it's found under a similar view-type menu.) Look for a line of code in the <head> section of the page that refers to the CSS file or look for the actual CSS in the head of the file. If you find a reference to the CSS file, you can use your browser to view the file (more about that in a minute). CSS can also be applied within the document itself, but that method defeats one of the main strengths of CSS: namely, the reusability of code that's kept in only one place.

When you view the source, look for a link to the site's CSS, such as the one in Figure 1-9.

You can examine that CSS file by typing the URL of the CSS into your browser window.

To see a lot of examples of the power of using CSS to control your visual display of a page, visit the CSS Zen Garden at www.csszengarden.com. This project, created by Dave Shea, encourages and supports the usage of CSS design. Here you find a series of page designs that are all very different in appearance, but they all share the same HTML code; only the CSS changes from design to design.

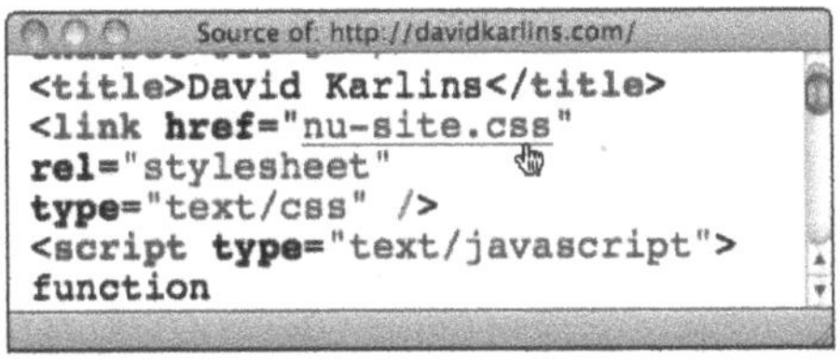

Figure 1-9:
Locating a
link to a CSS
file in the
source code
viewed in a
browser.

```
Source of: http://davidkarlins.com/
<title>David Karlins</title>
<link href="nu-site.css"
rel="stylesheet"
type="text/css" />
<script type="text/javascript">
function
```

Following links to the CSS file opens a page's linked CSS file in your browser. On that page, you can examine, learn from, or grab (and edit) the CSS code, as shown in Figure 1-10.

Obviously there are ethical, if not legal, issues involved in simply stealing CSS code from another site without permission or attribution. But studying and learning from such code is as much a part of the process of developing as a web designer as listening to great music is to developing as a composer.

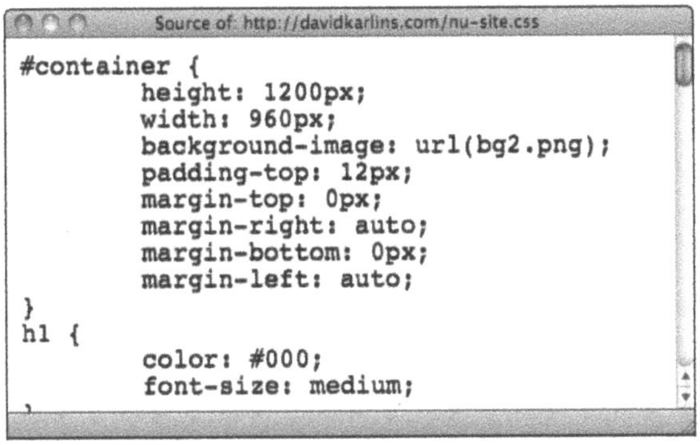

Figure 1-10:
Examining a
CSS file in a
browser.

```
Source of: http://davidkarlins.com/nu-site.css
#container {
        height: 1200px;
        width: 960px;
        background-image: url(bg2.png);
        padding-top: 12px;
        margin-top: 0px;
        margin-right: auto;
        margin-bottom: 0px;
        margin-left: auto;
}
h1 {

        color: #000;
        font-size: medium;
```

Chapter 2: Designing Pages

In This Chapter

✔ Setting CSS for boxes

✔ Creating page layout elements with ID styles

✔ Using class styles for layout

✔ Working with media queries

*T*he secret behind web-design technique is that most web pages are essentially laid out in a two- or three-column format, using the 960-pixel-wide grid that we discuss at length in Book II, Chapter 1. With that concept in mind, this chapter explains how to design pages with CSS. We break down the CSS properties required to create page layout elements that locate and shape content on a page. And we show you how to use *ID* and *class* selectors, special selectors that are applied to DIV tags in HTML documents, to define page design elements.

CSS for Page Layout Elements

As we allude to in Chapter 1 of this minibook, CSS is where it's at when it comes to designing page layouts. Not only can you style text (with fonts, colors, spacing, and so on), but you can also define page layout elements — essentially boxes that hold page content using CSS.

How is that done? Any HTML tag can have attributes attached to it with CSS that turns it into a page layout element (or box) that holds page content. Those box attributes generally include the following:

✦ **Width** defines how wide something is — makes sense, right? Web designers never know what the "page size" will be when it's viewed. Nor can you control a user's browser settings, which might include preferences like enlarged type. Page design elements (boxes) often have defined widths, but height is left undefined so that if content needs to expand, the content expands down, not sideways.

✦ **Margin** refers to the space between the edge of one layout element and the edge of the layout element next to it. For example, if you're using CSS to define styles for a three-column layout, you'd use the `margin` property to define the spacing *between* columns.

✦ **Padding** refers to the space that divides the content of a page layout element from the edge of that element. In a three-column page layout, the space *inside* the column, between the column content (text, images, or video), and the edge of the column is defined with padding.

✦ **Border** defines the thickness, style, and color of the border around any element (see Chapter 1 of this minibook).

✦ **Float** is the alignment that allows content to flow to the right or left of the page layout element.

Setting width and height

To define a 480-pixels wide and 100-pixels high property for the HTML5 aside element, use this CSS:

```
aside {
        height: 100px;
        width: 480px;
}
```

Height and width can be defined in all kinds of units of measurement including px (pixels), pt (points), cm (centimeters), in (inches), and em (the width of the letter "m"). When height and width are defined with absolute values like these, pixels is the most often used because it corresponds to the physical units that make up device screens. And, as we note earlier in this chapter, designers generally work with a 960-pixel-wide framework, which requires that elements with that framework be defined in pixels as well.

However, you can also assign a percentage to a height or a width. Percentages are rarely applicable to height values but are often used to create a column that is, for example, half the width of the enclosing box (50 percent).

Defining padding and margins

Padding and margins can be defined in CSS for all four borders of a box. To build upon CSS that turns an HTML5 aside element into a box, use these properties and values to add 2 px of padding to the right of a box, 4 px to the left, 6 px on top, and 2 px on the bottom:

```
aside {
    height: 100px;
    width: 480px;
    padding-right: 2px;
    padding-left: 4px;
    padding-top: 6px;
    padding-bottom: 2px;
}
```

Then buffer that box with a 4 px margin on the left by adding this code:

```
aside {
    height: 100px;
    width: 480px;
    padding-right: 2px;
    padding-left: 4px;
    padding-top: 6px;
    padding-bottom: 2px;
    margin-left: 4 px;
}
```

CSS, the era of the box model bug

Internet Explorer 6 does not interpret width, padding, and margins in the standard way. As a result, some page layouts that rely on CSS (as all modern ones do) can appear distorted in environments where users still have IE6 installed. Viewed in that version of Internet Explorer, for example, a three-column layout might display as two columns side-by-side, with the third column pushed below them. For a period in the history of web design, this problem was referred to as the Internet Explorer box model bug.

Contemporary web designers need to be cognizant of compatibility issues when using, for example, new elements in HTML5 (see Book III, Chapter 3), or the fun and dynamic CSS3 effects we explore in Chapter 3 of this minibook. When you use those new HTML5 elements, or new CSS3 effects, you have to implement them in ways in which, if those elements or effects are not supported in a browser, the page still

"works" even if a particular effect doesn't enhance the page. And as we explore emerging features in this series of books, we address specific compatibility challenges that might be involved in using them.

But the standards for CSS layout you apply in this chapter were adopted by the *W3C,* the so-called governing body for web standards, in 1996. That was a long time ago in web design years! At a certain point, web designers had to draw the line at how far they'd go to make pages display perfectly in very old browsers. Some time ago that line was drawn and crossed. Unless there are specific demands from a client, or a particular audience that warrants such adjustments, designers create pages that will work in browsers that comply with standards for CSS set in 1996 and do not design for browsers that do not comply with those standards.

Using margins to center elements

One of the most frequently asked questions in web design is how to center something. The `text-align:center` CSS property and value applies to text, not boxes. However, you can center an element within its constraining element by assigning the value `auto` to the left and right margins. For example, if the `aside` element is inside a box, you could center that `aside` element with this CSS:

```
aside {
    height: 100px;
    width: 480px;
    padding-right: 2px;
    padding-left: 4px;
    padding-top: 6px;
    margin-right: auto;
    margin-left: auto;
}
```

The math of margins and padding

You might expect that if you created two, 480-pixel-wide boxes and put them side by side inside a 960-pixel-wide page layout element, they'd fit. But chances are, they won't. That's because, oddly enough, margin and padding values are added onto the width of a page layout element. In this example, if both columns have margins of 10 pxs on the right and left side, they have to be 460 pixels wide each to fit. And if the enclosing box has padding defined, that also has to be accounted for.

Because of calculating margins and padding, testing page layouts, adjusting values when those page layouts collapse, and converting two-column layout into two columns stacked on top of each other vertically on a page, web designers always have a calculator handy.

Creating custom borders

CSS allows you to define separate style properties for the width, style, and color for all four borders around any element:

✦ `border-top`

✦ `border-right`

✦ `border-bottom`

✦ `border-left`

And each of these properties can be modified with color, width, or style, such as dashed or dotted. Style is almost always a solid, but you can adjust thickness. Dashed or dotted styles are supported unevenly in browsers. But width and color can be, and often are, defined separately for different borders. In the following example, the HTML5 `aside` element takes on style attributes that create a drop-shadow-like border (see Book III, Chapter 3 for an exploration of the `aside` element and other HTML5 layout elements):

```
aside {
    height: 100px;

    width: 320px;

    padding-right: 24px;
    padding-left: 6px;
    padding-top: 6px;

    margin-right: auto;
    margin-left: auto;

    border-top-width: thin;
    border-right-width: medium;
    border-bottom-width: thick;
    border-left-width: thin;

    border-top-style: solid;
    border-right-style: solid;
    border-bottom-style: solid;
    border-left-style: solid;

    border-top-color: silver;
    border-right-color: black;
    border-bottom-color:black;
    border-left-color: silver;

}
```

See Figure 2-1 for the `aside` element, with height, width, padding, margin, and border properties.

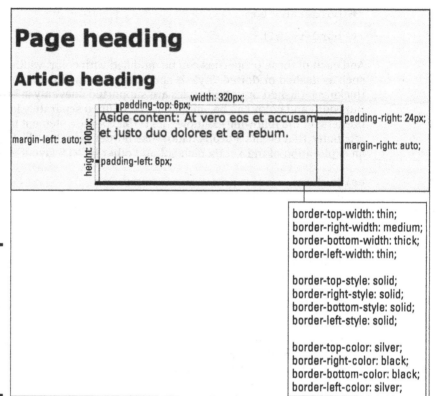

Figure 2-1:
An aside element with height, width, padding, margins, and border properties.

Figuring out float

Earlier in this chapter in the "CSS for Page Layout Elements" section, we introduce the main CSS properties used to define styles for page layout elements and note that the `float` property can have a value of either `left` or `right`. But to expand on the concept, floated elements are often *stacked* horizontally. That is to say, they're lined up in a row, with their left and/or right edges touching other page layout elements.

Here we examine the example HTML code with three `aside` elements, one after the other:

```
<aside> <h1>First aside element, floated left</h1> </aside>
<aside> <h1>Second aside element, floated left</h1> </aside>
<aside> <h1>Third aside element, floated left</h1> </aside>
```

With a width of 200 px and a `float` value of `left`, the `aside` elements in this HTML code stack up against each other, as shown in Figure 2-2.

Figure 2-2:
Three
elements,
floated left.

First aside element, floated left	Second aside element, floated left	Third aside element, floated left

To break a sequence of floats, use the value `float:none`. Figure 2-3 shows the same aside elements from Figure 2-2, but with a value of `none` assigned to the `float` property.

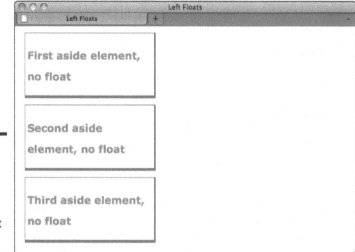

Figure 2-3:
The same
three
elements,
with none
for the float
property.

The `clear` property clears any inherited floats that an element might adopt from previous elements. The following line of CSS removes all `float` properties from an element:

```
clear:both;
```

Special Layout Elements: ID and Class Selectors

With the advent of HTML5, you can define CSS layout properties for elements, such as `header`, `footer`, `article`, `section`, and `aside`. By defining CSS elements with height, width, margins, padding, borders, and float, you can create a basic page layout, like the one shown in Figure 2-4.

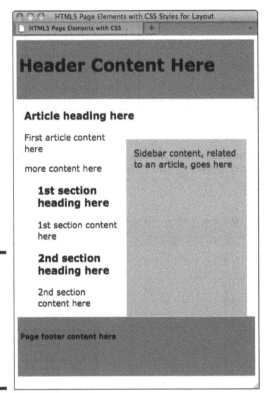

Header Content Here

Article heading here

First article content here

more content here

Sidebar content, related to an article, goes here

1st section heading here

1st section content here

2nd section heading here

2nd section content here

Page footer content here

Figure 2-4:
A page layout created by assigning CSS to HTML5 elements.

The page design shown in Figure 2-4 is serviceable, but it could be further enhanced by defining styles, such as heading tags (h1 through h6) and lists, which we explore in Chapter 1 of this minibook. This design carries some limitations, however, that are solved by the ID and class selectors, which are special styles that can be assigned to any DIV tag. Before we get to the limitations and the solutions, though, look at Listing 2-1, which shows the HTML code for the page in Figure 2-4, and Listing 2-2, which shows the linked CSS for the same page.

Listing 2-1:   HTML Code for a Basic Page Structure

```
<!DOCTYPE HTML>
<html>
<head>
<title>title content here</title>
</head>
<body>
<header>
```

```
<h1>Header Content Here</h1>
</header>
<article>
<h3>Article heading here</h3>
<aside>Sidebar content, related to an article, goes here
    </aside>
<p>First article content here</p>
<p>more content here</p>
<section>
<h3>1st section heading here</h3>
<p>1st section content here</p>
</section>
<section>
<h3>2nd section heading here</h3>
<p>2nd section content here</p>
</section>
</article>
<footer>
<h5>Page footer content here
</h5>
</footer>
</body>
</html>
```

Listing 2-2:   CSS for a Basic Page Design

```
@charset "UTF-8";
/* CSS Document */
body {
      font-family:  Verdana, Geneva, sans-serif;
}
header {
      height:  100px;
      background-color:  gray;
      padding: 5px;
}
article {
      padding-left: 15px;
      background-color: white;
      border-top: 1px black;
}
section {
      padding-left: 25px;
      background-color: white;
}
footer {
      height: 100px;
      background-color:gray;
      padding: 5px;
}
```

(continued)

Listing 2-2 *(continued)*

```
aside {
        float: right;
        width: 200px;
        background-color: silver;
        margin: 15px;
        padding: 15px;
        height: 300px;
}
```

The HTML and CSS in these listings create a working, basic page design. But it has some limitations we need to note:

◆ **All elements, such as all the aside elements, must have the same styling**. Any style applied to an element (like the aside element) affects every instance of that style.

◆ **You can't assign the same style to different elements**. For example, you can't create a generic "box" style that works on *any* block of content, no matter what elements define that content.

◆ **You can't assign styles within a tag.** For example, you can't assign highlighting or a distinct font color to text within a paragraph element.

◆ **None of the element styles serve as a page layout element to hold all the page content within a 960-pixel-wide frame.**

The solution to these, and other design issues, lies in ID and class styles. ID and class styles can be applied to any tag and are often applied to DIV tags, which have no default properties of their own until a style is assigned to them.

The main distinction between ID and class selectors is that ID selectors are applied only once in a page, whereas class selectors can be applied multiple times.

How class and ID styles work become clearer as we walk you through a code example in the upcoming sections.

Creating boxes with ID styles

Because any particular ID selector can be applied only once on a page, they define page layout elements that constrain all the page content.

When you look at the code of an HTML document that works with CSS, you might see code enclosed between two page layout elements with an

ID style named `"container"` (ID styles can be named anything that helps you remember what purpose they serve, as long as the style name doesn't include spaces or special characters, except underscore or dash):

```
<div id="container">
The rest of the page content goes here
</div>
```

In CSS, ID selectors are indicated by starting with a hash tag (#). An ID selector named `container` that has a width of 960 px and is centered looks like this:

```
#container {
    width: 960px;
    margin: auto;
}
```

Enveloping the rest of the page code within a `DIV` element, to which the `container` ID is applied (illustrated in Figure 2-4), constrains all the page content within a 960-pixel-wide, centered box, as shown in Figure 2-5.

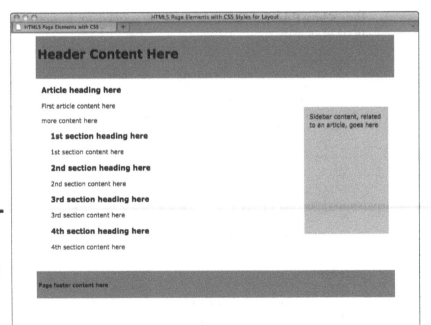

Figure 2-5:
A page layout constrained and centered in an ID style.

Using class styles for layout

Because class selectors can be used multiple times on a page, they're more flexible than ID styles and are a widely implemented tool for page design.

For example, a class style with a property of `width:30%` could divide a page layout element into three columns, and it could be used within a column to further divide that column into thirds. Here's what the CSS for that looks like:

```
.third-column {
        width: 30%;
        height: 300px;
        float: left;
}
```

Note that the class selector begins with a period (`.`). And `30%` is, of course, not exactly a third; it's a bit less. But by defining the width of the class selector at 30 percent (less than the 33 percent you want), you provide a bit of wiggle room for whatever margins and padding might be assigned to the elements enclosed within the class selector.

Here's how this class selector would be applied, for example, to three sections of an article:

```
<article>
        <h3>Article heading here</h3>
        <p>First article content here</p>
        <p>more content here</p>
        <section class="third-column">
        <h3>1st section heading here</h3>
        <p>1st section content here</p>
        </section>
        <section class="third-column">
        <h3>2nd section heading here</h3>
        <p>2nd section content here</p>
        </section>
        <section class="third-column">
        <h3>3rd section heading here</h3>
        <p>3rd section content here</p>
        </section>
</article>
```

Note the syntax in the HTML: the `class=` code (followed by the name of the class style in quotes) attaches a class style to a tag.

Figure 2-6 illustrates how this combination of HTML with class selectors looks in a browser.

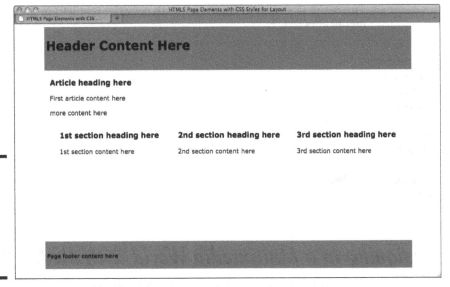

Figure 2-6:
A three-
column
layout
defined
with class
selectors.

Using class styles for formatting spans

In addition to their value in page layout, class styles can apply formatting to just part of an element, or to multiple elements. Applying a style to just a *part* of an element, and not the entire element, is done with HTML *spans*. For example, if you wanted to place a border around some text inside a paragraph element, you could do so with a span element inside that paragraph element.

Spans are also used to apply class (or ID) styles to more than one element. For example, say you want to put two paragraph elements in a single box. You could wrap both paragraph elements inside a single span element and apply a box style to both paragraphs.

Here's another example: You might create a highlight class selector that applies a yellow background to text. In the code following, that selector is named .highlight:

```
.highlight {
        background-color: yellow;
}
```

A span element inserts this style into any selected section of HTML. For example, the following code applies the .highlight class selector only to the word *section:*

```
h3>1st <span class="highlight">section</span> heading here</h3>
```

**Book IV
Chapter 2**

Designing Pages

The result is shown in Figure 2-7, with only the text within the span elements affected.

Figure 2-7:
A span element applies a class highlight style to selected text.

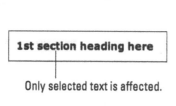

1st section heading here

Only selected text is affected.

Designing in a Multimedia World with Media Queries

Web design, as opposed to design for print media, has always been aimed at a moving target, not only just in the realm of time — where features and techniques emerge, get adopted, and are then superseded at a fast pace — but also in the sense that web designers have to create pages that work in a wide range of media. With the proliferation of tablets and the widespread reliance on smartphones for browsing, this issue has become more challenging and has taken on new importance.

Features that are essential to an inviting desktop or laptop web presence, such as hoverable elements (something we explore in Chapter 3 of this minibook) or columns, don't work (because hover doesn't exist on tablets or cellphones) or are unattractive and dysfunctional. Tablets, and especially cellphones, don't have the horizontal real estate to support multicolumn layouts. On the left in Figure 2-8 is the Google News page, laid out in three columns with hoverable links (that appear underlined when hovered over). The mobile version of the same site, as shown on the right, however, dispenses with columns. And there is no hover state for links because there's no hover option in mouseless mobile devices. Book II, Chapter 5 contains more information about designing for smartphones and tablets, as well as a discussion of general mobile design considerations.

Part of the solution is scientific audience evaluation. Who are you designing a site for? If your site is aimed at people viewing it on a laptop or a desktop, and mobile device users are only a minor niche in who comes to the site, design accordingly. And conversely, if your online shop relies almost completely on late nighters with iPhones, avoid columns and hover elements.

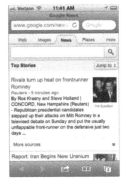

Figure 2-8:
The Google News page displayed on a laptop and on an iPhone.

But the reality is that most websites have to serve laptop and desktop users, as well as mobile device users. The solution to this web design problem is the *media query,* which analyzes the browsing environment of a visitor and presents the HTML page with a specific style sheet that matches that environment. (We discuss creating media queries in Dreamweaver in Chapter 4 of this minibook.)

The media tag in HTML defines the media, such as a screen, or print output:

```
<HTML>
<HEAD>
<TITLE>Media Example</TITLE>
<LINK REL="stylesheet" TYPE="text/css" MEDIA="screen" HREF="style1.css">
</HEAD>
<BODY>
</BODY>
</HTML>
```

The default media value is `screen`. The preceding example identifies a media (screen), but even if it didn't, browsers would assume the linked style sheet applies on computer screens.

The two most widely used other options are

✦ **Print:** Styles for printer output

✦ **Handheld:** For mobile devices

Other options range from Braille devices to monochrome monitors.

So, to create three style options, you could expand the preceding example to the following:

```
<HTML>
<HEAD>
<TITLE>Media Example</TITLE>
<LINK REL="stylesheet" TYPE="text/css" MEDIA="screen" HREF="style1.css">
```

```
<LINK REL="stylesheet" TYPE="text/css" MEDIA="print" HREF="style2.css">
<LINK REL="stylesheet" TYPE="text/css" MEDIA="handheld" HREF="style3.css">
</HEAD>
<BODY>
</BODY>
</HTML>
```

In the preceding example, a visitor using a laptop or desktop monitor would see the page with `style1.css` applied. If the page was printed, the file `style2.css` would define formatting for the printed output. And if a visitor's device was detected as a handheld device, he'd see the page with the CSS file `style3.css` applied to it.

CSS3 media queries

With the explosion of mobile devices, the old handheld value for a `media` property became too vague. There is a big difference between designing pages for a 300-pixel-wide cellphone, a 7-inch-wide reader, and a 10-inch-wide tablet. CSS3 addresses this challenge with new media queries. They include

✦ **Width and height of the viewing area:**

- *Width options:* `width`; `min-width` (minimum width); `max-width` (maximum width)

- *Height options:* `height`; `min-height` (minimum height); `max-height` (maximum height)

✦ **Whether the device displays color**

✦ **The shape of the viewing area**

✦ **Orientation:** Whether a mobile phone or tablet is held in portrait or landscape view; the value can be portrait or landscape.

The most widely applicable of these properties is `min-width` because it can define media queries for different devices based on their width. For example, the following code defines a media query that displays the `laptop-tablet.css` style sheet unless the user's media is less than 481 pixels wide (the width of many smartphone viewports). If the user's viewport is 480 px or less, in width, the `mobile.css` style sheet is in effect:

```
<html>
<head>
<title>Media Query example</title>
<link href="laptop-tablet.css" rel="stylesheet" type="text/css" media="only
    screen and (min-width:481px)">
<link href="mobile.css" rel="stylesheet" type="text/css" media="only screen and
    (max-width:480px)">
</head>
```

More CSS3 media queries

You can find a complete, updated list of CSS3 media queries at www.w3.org/TR/css3-mediaqueries. But keep in mind that these media queries depend on browsers recognizing the targeted media. And in the ever-evolving world of new media, that doesn't always happen. If you target a particular device, such as an Apple iPad, research online to find media queries that work with the latest version and operating system.

Media query techniques

To create sets of style sheets that work in both full screen and mobile devices, we recommend keeping these points in mind:

✦ Mobile devices need different versions of web pages than desktop/laptop media.

✦ The tool for converting site content into mobile-friendly content is a media query, such as the `max-width` property in the preceding section.

✦ Both style sheets need to have the same set of CSS selectors, but those selectors will have different values for the web and mobile versions.

✦ The main elements of restyling for mobile devices are constraining width, including high contrast colors, and eliminating floats to get rid of columns. The following examples cover these elements.

Some examples:

✦ A defining `#container` ID selector might be sized at 960 pixels wide for a desktop/laptop style sheet, but at 480 pixels wide for the mobile device version.

✦ A color scheme for a laptop/desktop style sheet might include subtle color contrast, whereas the colors (as defined in the `body` tag, headers, and the `paragraph` tag) for a mobile device would have much higher contrast.

✦ A `float:right` property that aligns a sidebar to the right in a desktop/laptop style might be changed to `float:none` for the mobile style sheet to eliminate columns.

Chapter 3: Effects and Transforms with CSS3

In This Chapter

✔ Discovering how CSS makes development easier

✔ Getting the lowdown on CSS3 browser support

✔ Applying effects and transforms

✔ Determining whether customizable fonts are right for you

✔ Using hover states for interactivity

C SS3 — the current (and still evolving) standard for cascading style sheets — creates radically new options for applying effects like transparency, shadows, and rounded corners on boxes, along with transforms like scaling (sizing), rotating, and moving objects on a web page.

In this chapter, we briefly explain why this new development is so significant, and then dive into how to define and apply these effects and transforms to text and to containers that hold content.

New Design Tools, New Styles

Web designers have long been able to place rotated graphics, semi-transparent backgrounds, drop-shadows, or rotated objects on web pages. You can also animate these types of effects and transformations. Therefore, a mouse hovering over an object on a desktop or a tapped element on a mobile device screen can activate effects and transforms.

Before the advent of CSS3, achieving these kinds of effects had several drawbacks:

✦ You had to use graphical elements — PNG, JPEG, or GIF image files — which had to download into a browser. You couldn't copy and paste these elements like you could text. Graphics hindered search engine optimization (SEO) because graphics are not recognized by search engines.

✦ Flash was the most applied tool for adding animation and interactivity to such effects or transforms, but it had accessibility issues with Apple devices, demanded substantial system resources, and required the Flash Player plug-in. On the designer end of the process, you needed the resources and skills to create animated and interactive graphics with Flash and its ActionScript coding language!

So what's the big deal about achieving these effects in CSS3? CSS3 makes graphical effects cheaper and easier to create, faster to download on web pages, and more accessible in all kinds of environments and search engines. For example, the skewed text (and enclosing skewed text box) in Figure 3-1 is not a graphic; it's text that you can copy, and it's *indexed* (or put into a database) by search engines, can be read out loud if speech software is installed in a browser or operating system, and does not have to download into a page.

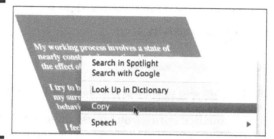

Figure 3-1: Text that can be copied and pasted with CSS3 effects and transforms.

TIP

Judiciously employed, animation and interactivity with CSS3 can bring a page to life, adding dynamism and energy. But like any design technique, CSS3 effects and transforms can be overdone. The point is this: Just because effects and transforms are now easy to create without any software, that doesn't mean you should load your pages with gratuitous effects. The skewed box and circle in Figure 3-2 can grab the eye and provide formatting treatment previously available only as a graphic image or Flash.

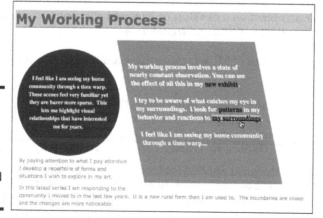

Figure 3-2: A CSS effect (the circle) and a transform (the skewed box).

Here are the two basic techniques for animating and making CSS3 effects interactive:

✦ **Using pseudo-classes:** One technique relies on associating CSS3 effects and transforms with CSS pseudo-classes. You use pseudo-classes in Chapter 1 of this minibook, when you assign different states (including a hover state) to links. A hovered link represents the simplest form of CSS interactivity with an effect like underlining or causing a background color to appear when a link is hovered over. We expand on that technique later in this chapter in the section, "Implementing Interactivity with Hover States," to animate and make interactive CSS3 transforms.

✦ **Combining CSS3 with JavaScript:** A technique for managing interactivity and animation with CSS3 styles (or any other styles) is combining CSS3 with JavaScript. We explore that process in-depth in Book VI.

The Wild World of CSS3 Browser Support

The current state of standards for web browser support for CSS3 effects and transforms is in flux. Most likely, over time the powers-that-be in the browser world — those who publish Internet Explorer, Safari, Firefox, and Chrome (and others) — will come to some common agreement on how to code for CSS3 effects. But right now, they haven't come to such agreement. That means that, at least at this writing, these cool new effects have to be defined separately for different browsers.

Here's what you need to know about CSS3 and browser support:

✦ CSS3 effects and transforms are supported in *current* versions of all major browsers, but Safari, Firefox, and Opera require different code prefixes to make CSS3 effects and transforms work in their browsers. We explore this issue in more depth after this bullet list.

✦ Three-dimensional (3D) transforms, which we explore later in this chapter (see the section "Experimenting with @font and 3D Transforms"), are not supported by browsers except Safari and Chrome, and because they rotate objects along the x-axis (horizontal) or y-axis (vertical), they don't do much without additional JavaScript to animate them. That said, the world of CSS3 transforms is in constant flux and development, and 3D transforms may gain broader support and become more accessible to developers.

✦ As we go to press, CSS3 effects and transforms work well in every modern browsing environment. You just need to include redundant versions of each effect, with different browser prefixes, in order to make them work in every browser.

✦ Some obsolete browsers don't support CSS3 effects and transforms at all (see the nearby sidebar, "Are old versions of IE a big problem for CSS3?").

Use CSS3 effects and transforms in such a way that even if a browser doesn't support CSS3, the page content isn't corrupted. Figure 3-3 shows the rounded-rectangle effect from Figure 3-2. On the right, the browser supports CSS3 effects, and on the left, the browser doesn't support them. In both environments, you can read the content, and some design effects, such as the box and font color, are supported.

Figure 3-3:
CSS3 in a
browser
that doesn't
support
CSS3 (left),
and in a
browser
that does
(right).

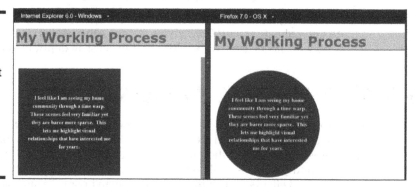

Because every digital device comes with copy-and-paste tools, the work-flow involves creating one effect or transform property, and then creating a set of copies with different prefixes. We explore examples of that process in this chapter.

The following is the CSS3 code that created the skewed text in Figure 3-1. Note that five lines of CSS are necessary to define the same skew effect for Firefox, Safari, Opera, Internet Explorer, and a generic version. (The people who make browsers seem to gravitate toward the generic version, but this isn't adopted universally.)

```
.skew {
    background-color: #999;
    height: 300px;
    width: 300px;
    -moz-transform: skew(12deg,0deg);
    -webkit-transform: skew(12deg,0deg);
    -ms-transform: skew(12deg,0deg);
    -o-transform: skew(12deg,0deg);
    transform: skew(12deg,0deg);
    color: white;
    padding: 15px;
```

```
        float: right;
        margin-top: 6px;
        margin-right: 100px;
        margin-bottom: 6px;
        margin-left: 6px;
}
```

Four of these variations of the CSS3 transform have prefixes (`-moz`, `-webkit`, `-ms`, and `-o`); the generic version doesn't have a prefix. Each prefix applies to different underlying engines in these browsers:

✦ The `-moz-transform-skew` code applies to Mozilla Firefox.

✦ The `-webkit-transform-skew` code applies to Safari and other browsers that adhere to the WebKit standard (which includes the Dreamweaver CS5 Live view).

✦ The generic `transform: skew` code applies to "everyone else," including most iterations of Internet Explorer 9, which doesn't require a browser prefix to interpret this (or other) effects. However, some versions of IE9 require the `-ms` prefix. So, it is a good idea to include the `-ms` prefix just in case.

✦ The `-o-border-radius` code applies to the Opera browser.

Are old versions of IE a big problem for CSS3?

Microsoft's Internet Explorer isn't the only browser with a legacy of older versions that don't support modern web-design tools, such as CSS3 effects and transforms. Older versions of Firefox, Safari, and so on also have similar issues. The difference is that because of the way other browsers are distributed and supported by their vendors and publishers, they more forcefully compel users to upgrade to the current version.

Internet Explorer comes installed on Windows computers. Because many older computers operate with older versions of Windows installed (and because of a complex web of marketing and culture factors), Microsoft doesn't compel, or even make it possible for users of older IE versions to easily upgrade their browser.

Gigabytes of online bandwidth are consumed with debate over the necessity of designing sites that work well in pre-IE9 versions of Internet Explorer:

✔ Some want to place a priority on designing sites tailored to older versions of IE because of the continuing large numbers of installed copies of older IE browsers.

✔ Others argue that IE9 should be the focus because Microsoft has increased its emphasis on encouraging browser updates. Plus, machines with earlier versions of IE9 will probably die off in the coming years.

Applying CSS3 Effects

As we state earlier, CSS3 effects and transforms are new. And fun. And exciting. Designers are really in the early stages of experimenting with the four available transforms (scale, translate, rotate, and skew) and effects (such as rounded corners, shadows, and transparency).

CSS3 transforms, and especially CSS3 effects, are rapidly being integrated into web page design, and designers are coming up with some exciting and creative ways to apply them. In this section, we examine three of the most useful: border-radius, shadow (for boxes and text), and transparency/opacity. Figure 3-4 illustrates a page with all three effects applied to the banner at the top. The rounded corners have a defined border-radius, the drop-shadow is created with a box-shadow style, and the semitransparent white background that allows the page background image to partially show through is produced with the opacity effect.

Figure 3-4: Border-radius, shadows, and opacity (transparency) applied to a drop-down menu.

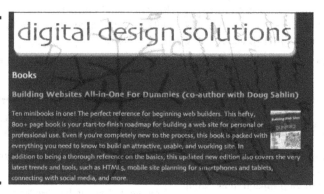

Border-radius

The CSS3 border-radius effect defines rounded corners. And, as we allude to earlier in this chapter, you need to use browser-specific prefixes when defining a border-radius.

Here a few rules for defining a border-radius:

✦ **You can't apply a border-radius to a selector (a CSS style) that doesn't have either a defined height or width (at least one or the other).**

✦ **The basic property for a border-radius in CSS3 is `border-radius`, followed by a value.** For example, `border-radius:12px;` creates rounded corners on all four corners of the element to which it is applied. And the "rounding" of those corners will extend for 12 pixels from the corners.

✦ **You can define separate radii for each corner of a border.** For example:

```
border-top-left-radius:1px;
border-top-right-radius:2px;
border-bottom-right-radius:3px;
border-bottom-left-radius:4px;
```

Take the following example: a class style that defines both borders and border radii. The following CSS style creates a .borders class that applies both borders and border radii to any element to which it is applied:

```
.borders {
        border:12px solid gray;
        border-top-left-radius:48px;
        border-top-right-radius:24px;
        border-bottom-right-radius:12px;
        border-bottom-left-radius:6px;
        padding: 12px;
}
```

The outcome of the preceding code, as shown in the Chrome browser in Figure 3-5, depicts the class selector (style) with a defined border and defined border radii properties.

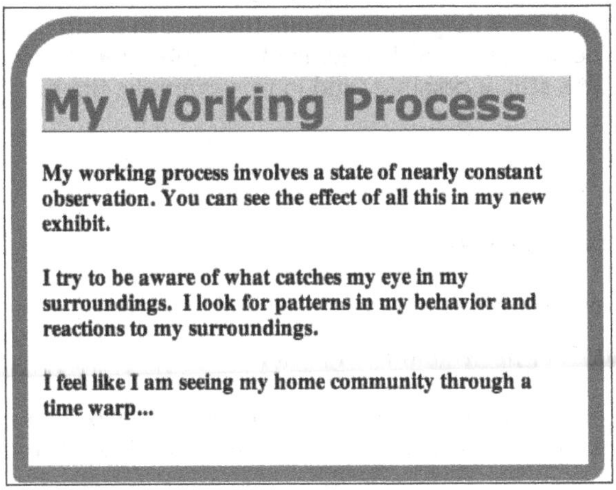

Figure 3-5:
Rounded corners in a browser that supports CSS3.

> # My Working Process
>
> My working process involves a state of nearly constant observation. You can see the effect of all this in my new exhibit.
>
> I try to be aware of what catches my eye in my surroundings. I look for patterns in my behavior and reactions to my surroundings.
>
> I feel like I am seeing my home community through a time warp...

The rounded corner (border-radius) code works fine in contemporary versions of IE and Chrome because those browsers do not require a prefix for this effect. But to make border-radius work in Mozilla Firefox, WebKit browsers like Safari (for desktop/laptop and mobile), and some versions of Opera, you have to make three copies of the border-radius code with the appropriate prefixes, like this:

```
.borders {
        border:12px solid gray;
        border-top-left-radius:48px;
        border-top-right-radius:24px;
        border-bottom-right-radius:12px;
        border-bottom-left-radius:6px;
        -moz-border-top-left-radius:48px;
        -moz-border-top-right-radius:24px;
        -moz-border-bottom-right-radius:12px;
        -moz-border-bottom-left-radius:6px;
        -webkit-border-top-left-radius:48px;
        -webkit-border-top-right-radius:24px;
        -webkit-border-bottom-right-radius:12px;
        -webkit-border-bottom-left-radius:6px;
        -o-border-top-left-radius:48px;
        -o-border-top-right-radius:24px;
        -o-border-bottom-right-radius:12px;
        -o-border-bottom-left-radius:6px;
        padding: 12px;
}
```

Only with four versions of the CSS style definition will this border work in all major, current browsers.

Folks viewing the page in older browsers have to forego the enhanced design experience they'd get if they were viewing the page in a current-generation browser. But because the CSS3 effect isn't a requirement to view the actual page content, it's still accessible (and in this example, the border still appears).

Shadows

CSS includes two shadow effects:

✦ **Box-shadow** is applied to borders around selectors.

✦ **Text-shadow** applies shadows to text.

Both shadow effects require at least two properties: horizontal and vertical shadow dimensions. Using box-shadow as an example syntax looks like this:

```
box-shadow: h-shadow v-shadow;
```

Positive h-shadow values generate a shadow to the right of the text, whereas negative h-shadow values generate a shadow to the left of the text. Positive v-shadow values generate a shadow below the text, whereas negative values create a shadow above the text. Values are normally defined in pixels.

Shadows also often include a `blur` property. The `blur` value defines the thickness of the `blur` element of the gradient — essentially how widely to space the gradient in the shadow. A higher `blur` value creates a, well, blurrier effect, whereas a lower `blur` value creates a crisper, sharper drop-shadow. The `blur` value appears after the `h-shadow` and `v-shadow` values in the style definition, like this:

```
box-shadow: h-shadow v-shadow blur;
```

You can also define a shadow color (if no color is specified, a browser default color appears). So, for example, in the following code example, the box-shadow is defined with a horizontal shadow extending 3 pixels to the right, 6 pixels down, with a medium blur effect, one that applies to create a gradient-like blur that extends 3 pixels into the drop-shadow. And a color has been assigned to the box shadow (silver).

```
box-shadow: 3px 6px 3px silver;
```

Spread defines the size of the shadow. By default, the shadow is the same size as the element to which it's applied but you can make that shadow larger (or smaller) by adding a `spread` value to the style definition.

Adding the `insert` value to a shadow definition inverts the shadow, placing it inside instead of outside the box.

Here's an example of a `box-shadow` definition that creates a shadow that extends 12 pixels to the right and 18 pixels down, is 25 pixels larger than the original element to which it is applied, and is silver in color:

```
box-shadow: 12px 18px 12px 25px silver;
```

Applied to a box, the values in the preceding example look like Figure 3-6.

Figure 3-6:
A drop-shadow applied to a box with defined size and color.

Finally shadows can be *inset* — that is, placed inside the element to which they're applied. Figure 3-7 demonstrates how inset impacts the same box-shadow in Figure 3-6.

Having explored the basic syntax and role of CSS3 shadow effects, we zoom in on how to create box-shadows and text-shadows, and how you might use them.

Creating a box-shadow

As we note earlier, box-shadow effects are defined with two essential parameters: horizontal and vertical offset.

For example, to create a class style that generates a box-shadow with 6 pixels of horizontal offset and 12 pixels of vertical offset, you'd use this code:

```
box-shadow: 6px 12px;
```

If you wanted to define the length of the blur, you'd add a third value. And if you wanted to define the color of the shadow, you'd add that color value:

```
box-shadow: 6px 12px 9px gray;
```

You need to do more work if the box-shadow is going to work in every modern browser. Chrome, Opera, current installs of Firefox, and IE9 support the box-shadow effect with no prefix. But you still need to create prefixed versions of the code for older versions of Firefox and, at this writing, all versions of Safari. The following code defines a class selector named box_ shadow that works in all current-generation browsers and has some padding and margin values:

```
.box_shadow {
    box-shadow: 6px 12px 9px gray;
    -webkit-box-shadow: 6px 12px 9px gray;
    -moz-box-shadow: 6px 12px 9px gray;
    padding: 9px;
    margin: 24px;
}
```

And remember, you've defined a class style. To apply that class style, it still has to be attached to an HTML element. For example, you could apply the class style defined in the preceding batch of code to a paragraph tag with the following HTML:

```
<p class="box_shadow">
content goes here
</p>
```

Figure 3-8 shows this box-shadow applied to a paragraph in the Safari browser.

Figure 3-8:
A box-shadow applied to a paragraph element.

In this latest series I am responding to the community I moved to in the last few years. It is a new rural form then I am used to. The boundaries are closer and the changes are more noticeable.

In particular, I am taken by the smaller versions of the large-scale developments I grew up around.

I feel like I am seeing my home community through a time warp. These scenes feel very familiar yet they are barer more sparse. This lets me highlight visual relationships that have interested me for years. I tend to take lots of study prints that act as sketches for the "official" exposures. At a certain point I will reach a critical mass of ideas where I need to go out and collect the images I have been thinking about. When I find one of these veins my work progresses rapidly. It is incredibly rewarding to see find the pre-visualized situations, commit them to paper and then appreciate them out in the open.

Applying shadows to type

The text-shadow effect, oddly enough, is supported in browsers (except for IE) with no prefix required.

The basic, essential syntax for creating a text-shadow is

```
text-shadow: h v color
```

In this syntax, *h* is the horizontal offset; *v* is the vertical offset; and `color` is the color value.

The following example creates a class selector (`.text_shadow`) that applies a text-shadow with a 4-pixel horizontal offset, a 1-pixel vertical offset, the color dark gray:

```
.text_shadow {
        text-shadow: 4px 1px gray;
}
```

Text-shadows are sometimes applied to white type for a clean, inviting effect. Figure 3-9 demonstrates the `text_shadow` class style defined in the preceding code to white type.

Effects and
Transforms
with CSS3

Figure 3-9:
A text-
shadow
applied to
white type.

My Working Process

Opacity

In CSS3, transparency is defined by assigning a value to the opacity property. A fully opaque object completely obscures whatever is behind it; objects that aren't fully opaque are partially see-through, or *transparent*. Defining semitransparent backgrounds for page layout elements with CSS3 presents some exciting options for web designers. Semitransparent backgrounds are often used, for example, in drop-down lists, as shown in Figure 3-10. There, the drop-down menu elements have .5 opacity assigned (they are 50 percent transparent). As a result, the underlying page content remains visible when a menu drops down.

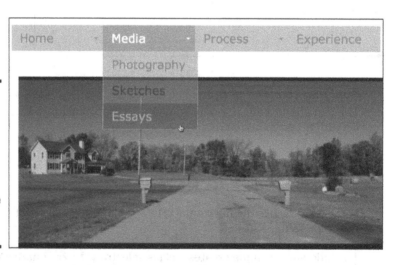

Figure 3-10:
With the
opacity
property
set to .5,
the photo
remains
partly visible
behind
the list.

The opacity property is defined with a value ranging from *0* (completely invisible) to *1* (fully *opaque;* not transparent at all). So, for example, an opacity value of .8 makes an object 80 percent opaque, and so on.

The opacity property does not require prefixes for different browsers. The syntax is simple:

```
opacity: .x
```

The drop-down list in Figure 3-10, for example, is defined as such:

```
.menu_box {
        background-color: #999;
        padding: 2px;
        color: #333333;
        opacity: .5;
}
```

Scaling, Moving, Rotating, and Skewing with Transforms

With CSS3, designers can *translate* (move), *scale* (resize), rotate, or skew boxes. (Remember, CSS3 does this without requiring that boxes be created as graphics; the transformation takes place entirely through CSS.) Translate, scale, rotate, and skew are all values that are defined for the CSS3 `transform` property. Different translate values (translate, scale, rotate, and skew) have their own parameters, but the general syntax is

```
transform: [translate, scale, rotate, or skew] [values]
```

The first value defines the kind of transform, and additional values define the parameters of that transform — that is, how it gets applied. This will become clearer as we explore specific transforms.

The scale transform

The scale transform can be used to change the height and the width of any element. In other words, it can either be used to resize an object, keeping the height-to-width ratio unchanged, or it can be used to stretch an object. In the latter case, you use different values for the height and width values in a scale transform.

In the following simple example, the CSS3 class selector (`.stretch`) rescales an element to retain the original width but stretches it to twice its original height.

```
-moz-transform: scaleX(1) scaleY(2);
```

Figure 3-11 demonstrates how the transform defined by the simple preceding code works; it shows the same text, first without the transform applied and then with the scale transform applied.

Transforms work for tags or class styles

You can apply CSS3 transform properties to any tag, including image or heading tags. However, more typically, CSS transforms, such as scale or rotate, are properties for a class (or ID) style and are applied through assigning the class (or ID) style to a DIV tag.

Figure 3-11:
Applying
a scale
transform
to text.

Heading 1

Heading 1

This example has a -moz prefix. That's because browsers don't support CSS3 transforms without a prefix. The prefixes required are

✦ -moz: Firefox

✦ -ms: Internet Explorer

✦ -webkit: Safari and Chrome

✦ -o: Opera

The following code creates a class selector named .stretch that maintains the width of an object but doubles the height:

```
.stretch {
      transform: scale (1,2);
      -moz-transform: scale (1,2);
      -moz-transform: scale(1,2);
      -webkit-transform:  scaleX(1) scaleY(2);
}
```

Move with translate

The freedom to *translate* (or move) DIV tags that CSS styles have been applied to also opens the door to layering elements on top of each other. When that happens, the CSS3 z-index property defines which of the overlapping objects will appear on top of the others — the higher the z-index value, the higher in the stacking order an element appears.

The syntax for the translate transform is similar to that for the scale transform except that the first parameter, the x-value, defines how far to the right (left, if negative) the object will move; the y-value defines how far down (up, if negative) the object will move. Values are normally defined in pixels.

Here's an example of a class style (.move) that moves an element 12 pixels to the left, and 50 pixels down.

```
.move {
    -webkit-transform: translate(-12px,50px);
    -moz-transform: translate(-12px,50px);
    -o-transform: translate(-12px,50px);
    z-index: 100;
    opacity: .7;
}
```

In the preceding example, we introduce the z-index CSS property. Elements to which styles with higher z-index values have been applied appear on top of, or *stacked* in front of, elements with lower z-index values. The default z-index value is 1.

The z-index property is not new to CSS3, but it takes on more importance now that you can move objects easily, and those objects often end up overlapping with other objects. The z-index property was defined with a value of 100, which places it on top of anything with a lower z-index value.

Also, an opacity property has been applied to the style with a value of .7, making the content 70 percent opaque (or, 30 percent transparent). The result is shown in Figure 3-12; the negative x-value bumped the text to the left, and the positive y-value moved the text down, over the black image.

Figure 3-12: A translate transform has moved the type down and over the black box.

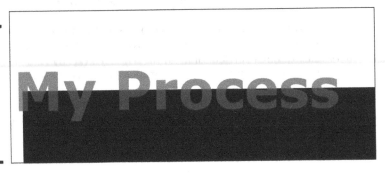

Rotating

The rotate transform has just one parameter: rotation angle. That angle can be positive (applies clockwise rotation) or negative (counterclockwise).

Here's an example of a class selector (.rotate) that rotates an object 12 degrees counterclockwise:

```
.rotate {
     transform: rotate(-12deg);
     -webkit-transform:rotate(-12deg);
     -moz-transform:rotate(-12deg);
     -o-transform:rotate(-12deg);
}
```

The result is illustrated in Figure 3-13.

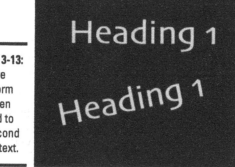

Figure 3-13: A rotate transform has been applied to the second line of text.

Twisting with skew

At the beginning of this chapter, we used a skew effect (refer to Figure 3-1) to show what CSS3 can do. The skew effect can be pretty dramatic. A little skewing goes a long way, and this isn't an effect to overdo.

The skew transform is defined by two parameters, separated by a comma. The first defines the x-axis (horizontal) transform in degrees; the (second) y-axis value defines vertical distortion. When a 0 (zero) value is defined for one of the two axes, the result is a parallelogram, as shown in Figure 3-1.

Here's an example of a class style (.skew) that defines a 300-pixel-wide box with a bit of padding and a thin, gray border, skewed 12 degrees on the x-axis:

```
.skew {
     height: 300px;
     -moz-transform: skew(12deg,0deg);
     -webkit-transform: skew(12deg,0deg);
     -o-transform: skew(12deg,0deg);
     -ms-transform: skew(22deg,0deg);
     transform: skew(12deg,0deg);
     padding: 15px
     border: 1px solid #999999;
}
```

Mixing and matching effects and transforms

You can mix and match any combination of effects and transforms, within the limits of taste. For example, in exploring the translate (or move) transform, we threw in an opacity effect so that the moved content wouldn't completely obscure content below it. Use your imagination and start with designs that include

overlapped, rotated, skewed, semi-transparent, or rounded-corner elements. Then stack effects and transforms (see the earlier example in the section "Move with translate" of combining the opacity effect and the translate transform) as an example and model to work from.

Experimenting with @font and 3D Transforms

Back in its glory days, *Saturday Night Live* had a series of sketches presented by the Not Ready For Prime Time Players, a part of the show reserved to present material that was experimental and a chance for the cast and writers to try things that might blossom into ready-for-prime-time material later. Similarly, a couple of CSS3 features whose practical impact is not yet proven are the @font property (which has generated considerable buzz) and an emerging set of 3D transforms.

If you apply @font for custom typefaces, or 3D transforms, be sure your page works well in browsing environments that don't support these effects. And, because that isn't so easily done with @font or 3D transforms (for reasons we explore in the next sections of this chapter), you might want to consign these options to the not-ready-for-prime-time category to wait and see how they develop. But we explore them briefly here.

@font

The concept behind @font is that developers can finally break free of the tight constraints regarding what fonts can be used in web pages by uploading custom fonts that users then download to view on the page. However, @font is something of a flawed concept, and to the extent it has potential, the implementation is not in place to make this accessible for most web designers. Here are a few of the problems @font comes with:

✦ **Operating systems don't have these fonts installed.** With a resolution (in dots per inch) about four times grainier (or less dense) than print resolution, the web demands fonts that are relatively simple. Creative designers exploit CSS tools for micro-tuning font height and spacing to create unique and intriguing type using standard fonts that are already installed in most computers. In other words, in many cases, designers can use CSS to create unique looking fonts without resorting to asking users to download a font before a page can be viewed.

✦ **Visitors have to download a font into their operating system before the font applies.** Doing so tends to prompt warnings in browsers and requires a process that, in time and complexity, is more likely to drive a visitor away from a site than make her browsing experience more positive.

✦ **Custom fonts have to be purchased.** Licensing legal use of custom fonts involves rather complex licensing contracts, and the costs begin at several hundred dollars (to use a custom font in a single site).

Support for @font is emerging more slowly on mobile devices than it is for full-screen environments. The most popular mobile operating system, Android, for example, adopted full support for @font in version 4, but many smartphones still run on versions of Android 2 and 3.

At times, downloadable fonts can be appropriate. For example, if you're Keith Richards of the Rolling Stones, you can use a downloadable custom font (check it out at www.keithrichards.com, or see Figure 3-14). But if your browsing environment can't handle downloadable fonts, his staff of developers has created scripts that detect that your browsing environment doesn't support downloading the font and supply a graphic image of the type instead. (If you want to examine the fairly complex set of @font CSS styles on Keith's site, check out his style sheet at www.keithrichards.com/_styles/kr_site.css.)

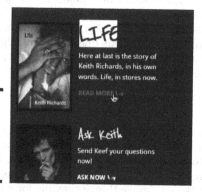

Figure 3-14:
Custom
fonts help
Keith's site
rock.

With all those cautions, if you want to install and apply custom fonts, follow these steps:

1. **Purchase a font or find a free one online.**

Sources like Fonts.com provide downloadable fonts as well as installation tools that help install, implement, and troubleshoot downloadable custom fonts. In many cases, the "steps" might end here — if you can spend in the range of $500 for a downloadable font set (sets include options like italics, bold, and so on), this is probably a good option.

2. **Install the font.**

If the font didn't come with an installation package or instructions, you can install it by saving the TTF or OTF file to your website folder.

3. **At the top of your external CSS file, add this code:**

```
@font-face {
font-family: xxx;
src:url(yyy.ttf');
}
```

xxx is the name you will use in styles to assign the font, and yyy is the TTF (or OTF) filename for the fontface you downloaded.

4. **With the preceding code at the top of your CSS file, use the font name as part of style definitions.**

For example:

```
h1{
font-family: yyy; courier;
}
```

Courier is the backup font that will appear in browsers that don't support your downloadable font.

3D transforms

3D transforms can rotate an object on either the x-axis (horizontal) or y-axis (vertical). Because flipping an object horizontally or vertically has very limited design implications, these transforms are intended to be combined with JavaScript or other animation and interactivity tools to make objects flip and spin. In the following section, we discuss options for applying interactivity to transforms and effects.

Even more limiting is the narrow scope of browser support for 3D transforms. At this writing, only browsers built on the WebKit engine (Safari and some versions of Chrome) support 3D transforms.

With those caveats, here's an example of applying a 180-vertical spin to a class selector (.rotate_3d):

```
.rotate_3d
{
    transform: rotateY(180deg);
    -webkit-transform: rotateY(180deg);
}
```

Implementing Interactivity with Hover States

Having surveyed and walked through the process of creating and applying CSS3 effects and transforms, we turn now to one of the most dynamic aspects of these new style features: interactivity. *Interactivity* means that an object or elements of a page react to a visitor's action with their own action. A visitor hovers over an object, and that object moves, resizes, rotates, skews, develops a shadow, becomes semitransparent, or undergoes some other change. Here are the two basic techniques for combining interactivity with effects and transforms:

+ **Use JavaScript, and write or generate code that combines with transforms and effects.** Combining JavaScript with effects and transforms can be a very powerful technique for creating interactivity on the level that can be generated, for example, using Flash. Actually writing JavaScript on the level of animating 3D transforms is the scope of what we can address in this book.

+ **Use the widely supported and easy-to-use :hover pseudo-class.** If you're familiar with defining a *hover* state for a link (a link takes on a unique appearance when hovered over), you have a basic idea of how this works. And we walk through that in more detail.

Pseudo-classes are CSS modifiers that define the appearance of a web page object depending on the state of an object. They're best known for, and most widely applied as, modifiers on links. By default, unvisited links on a web page display as underlined blue, visited links are underlined purple, and active links are underlined red. These parameters are easily changed in Dreamweaver's CSS Styles panel. And, they're supported in every browser.

But in addition to the :visited, pseudo-class style (pseudo-classes) is another, more dynamic state named :hover. This definable state applies to anything on a page that a visitor hovers his mouse over. By applying effects and transforms to the hover state of an object, you can make it interact in a defined way with a visitor's mouse actions.

The basic concept is that you define a :hover pseudo-class for the object you wish to transform when hovered over. That object can be an HTML tag, such as h1 or a DIV tag (either a class or ID). In the case of the h1 tag, this line of code in the CSS file would define a scale transform with increasing height and width by 20 percent when the image is hovered over:

```
h1:hover  {
      webkit-transform: scale(.2.2,2.2);
      -moz-transform: scale(.2.2,2.2);
      -ms-transform: scale(.2.2,2.2);
      -o-transform: scale(.2.2,2.2);
}
```

Here's another example with a class selector (`.rotate`). The following code creates a class style that, when applied, rotates 45 degrees when hovered over:

```
.rotate:hover {
     webkit-transform: rotate(45deg);
     -moz-transform: rotate(45deg);
     -ms-transform: rotate(45deg);
     -o-transform: rotate(45deg);
}
```

You can apply `:hover` class animation to any transform or effect, or any combination of transforms or effects.

What about mobile devices? Although hover isn't available on most mobile devices, tapping the screen activates the hover state in mobile devices in which 3D transforms are supported. So, for example, you can tap a 3D transform element in an iPhone and experience the same effect as if you hovered over the element in a browsing environment that includes a mouse. The possibilities for highly accessible, easy-to-code interactivity are infinite.

Chapter 4: CSS in Dreamweaver

In This Chapter

✔ Working with the Insert Layout Objects tools

✔ Editing CSS with code hints

✔ Creating, linking, and editing CSS with the CSS Styles panel

✔ Discovering the CSS Rule Definition dialog box

✔ Applying CSS3 effects and transforms

✔ Previewing HTML documents with Multiscreen Preview

✔ Creating media queries

CSS is the heart of web design, and Dreamweaver provides substantial tools for generating, editing, and previewing CSS. These tools were made available through the HTML5 pack for Dreamweaver CS5 and are still available in CS5.5 and CS6. Versions CS5.5 and CS6 also include an intuitive, interactive media query generator. Dreamweaver makes it easy to define CSS, but that obscures what goes on behind the scenes. In reality, you can get lost in a maze of tools as easily as you can define CSS after you open a dialog box. For that reason, this chapter focuses on the big picture: how Dreamweaver generates CSS and what it does with that CSS after you generate it.

Defining CSS styles (or selectors) in Dreamweaver is easy. The CSS Styles panel and the CSS Rule Definition dialog box allow you to define styles, properties, and values with intuitive popups. Dreamweaver provides two sets of tools for creating CSS:

✦ **Code hinting in Code view:** Like code hinting for HTML, Dreamweaver's Code view completes CSS as you type and provides popups to define CSS selector properties and values. The Split view displays both code and a preview screen.

✦ **The CSS Styles panel:** The CSS Styles panel is a quick way to generate CSS styles on the fly in a designer-friendly format that's comparable to other applications in Dreamweaver's Creative Suite.

Dreamweaver's Multiscreen Preview window allows you to see a web page as it appears in different media. Figure 4-1 shows the Multiscreen Preview window with a cellphone, tablet, and desktop/laptop view displayed.

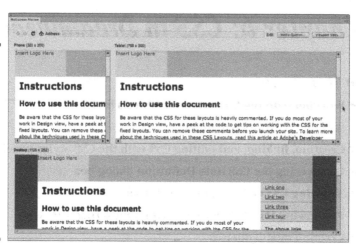

Figure 4-1: Dreamweaver's Multiscreen Preview window shows alternative versions of a page in different devices.

The Insert Layout Objects Set of Tools

As we just noted, you can define CSS styles in Dreamweaver's Code view by entering code — just as you would in any code editor. And, we noted that the CSS Styles panel is an alternate way of defining styles that does not require coding.

Beyond those two options, Dreamweaver has the Insert Div Tag dialog box. The Insert Div Tag dialog box in Dreamweaver is sort of a one-stop shopping terminal for a number of CSS tasks including applying existing styles to page content, creating new styles in existing style sheet files, and creating new style sheets.

To open the Insert Div Tag dialog box, as shown in Figure 4-2, choose Layout Objects Insert ⇨Layout Object ⇨Div Tag.

Dreamweaver's Insert Div Tag dialog box combines many different CSS generating tools in one dialog box, making it a powerful productivity tool and potentially confusing. Figure 4-2 shows the Insert Div Tag dialog box's two basic options:

✦ **Selecting an existing CSS selector (either a class or ID selector) and applying it to selected content.** The Insert drop-down list in the dialog box provides context-sensitive options for how to insert a selector. By *context-sensitive*, we mean that the options vary depending on what you have selected in the open web page document.

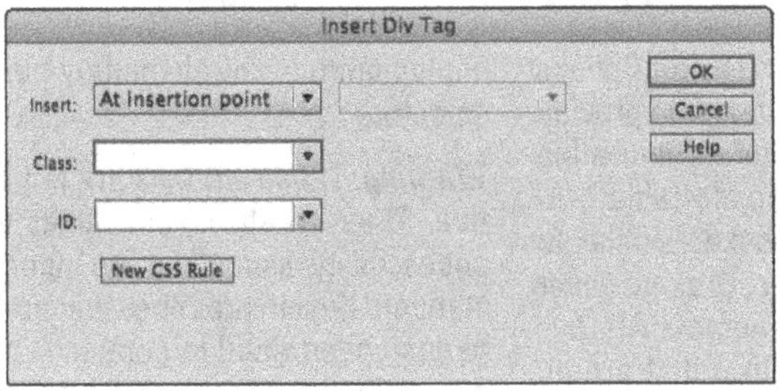

Figure 4-2:
The Insert
Div Tag
dialog box
has options
to apply
an existing
ID or
Class style
selector,
or create a
new one.

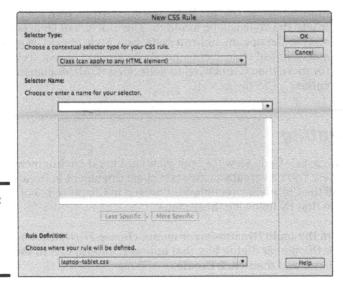

◆ **If you have content selected in the open document, the Wrap Around Selection option is operative.** This option encloses selected content in a CSS selector (a class or ID) that you choose from the Class or ID dropdown lists.

◆ **Other options appear depending on where your insertion point is located.** Those other options are not used to enclose content in a `DIV` tag.

◆ **Creating a new style.** Clicking the New CSS Rule button allows you to generate new styles on the fly in the New CSS Rule dialog box (as shown in Figure 4-3). From this dialog box, you can adjust settings for the following:

Figure 4-3:
Creating a
new style
in Dream-
weaver.

Dreamweaver's AP Divs

Among the options in the Insert Layout Options submenu is an AP Div. In an attempt to provide a design alternative for designers migrating from print design, who feel comfortable creating pages with draggable boxes similar to objects in Illustrator or InDesign, Dreamweaver provides a design tool that generates AP Divs (short for *absolute position Divs*) that are an implementation of absolutely positioned CSS selectors.

Warning: These AP Divs are not a good practice. They create layout boxes with serious accessibility issues and are incompatible with standard design practices that are built around pages constrained in container DIV tags. So our advice here is to avoid AP Divs.

- *Selector Type:* The drop-down list at the top of the dialog box lets you choose four kinds of selectors: Class, ID, Tag, or Compound (styles defined for tags that are embedded in other tags). We explain class, ID, and tag styles in Chapters 1–3 of this minibook. Dreamweaver's Compound option includes styles for links and styles that apply only within other styles.

- *Selector Name:* The Selector Name box is where you name the tag, ID, or class style (again, compound styles are styles associated with tags). You don't need to type a period (".") for a class selector name or a hash symbol ("#") for an ID style, Dreamweaver automatically adds those.

- *Rule Definition:* Use the Rule Definition drop-down list to define where the style will be saved to: This Document Only embeds the style in the document head code; New Style Sheet File generates a new, linked style sheet; and, if you already have a style sheet (or more than one) linked to your open HTML document, you can choose a CSS file as well.

CSS Code Hinting

Dreamweaver's Code view (or Split view) is a great environment for writing CSS styles. You can create a new style sheet document in Dreamweaver and apply all the CSS coding techniques covered in Chapters 1–3 of this minibook. Do that by following these steps:

1. **From the main Dreamweaver menu, choose File⇨New and in the New Document dialog box that appears, choose CSS in the Page Type column, and then click Create.**

Doing this opens a blank CSS page, with some basic code (a UTF declaration) and a comment that the file is a CSS document, as shown in Figure 4-4.

Figure 4-4:
A CSS document generated in Dream-weaver.

2. **Choose File⇨Save to save the style sheet document.**

3. **Enter CSS in Code view.**

   Again, see Chapters 1–3 in this minibook for the CSS techniques that can be created in Dreamweaver's Code view after you create a CSS document.

   As you start creating a style, you can press the spacebar or Enter key to provide quick access to code hinting. *Code hinting* helps complete style definitions and assign style properties and values, as shown in Figure 4-5. In the figure, a popup list displays possible properties for the body tag selector, including `background-color`.

4. **Select a property from a code-hint popup in Code view and press the spacebar to add that property to your CSS code.**

   In some cases, doing so opens a new set of code hint options, and again you can select one of them and press the spacebar to apply that selection and continue coding.

   For example, if you choose Color from the popup list, a color palette opens to make it easy to define a color, as shown in Figure 4-6.

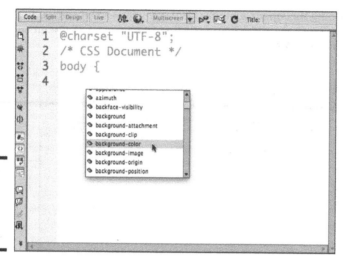

Figure 4-5:
Choosing
properties
for the
body tag.

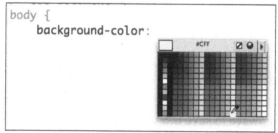

Figure 4-6:
Defining a
background
color
with code
hinting.

Creating and Editing CSS with the CSS Styles Panel

The CSS Styles panel is arguably one of the most useful tools in Dreamweaver. If this panel isn't visible, choose Window➪CSS Styles.

The CSS Styles panel allows you to define styles (or many properties of many styles) in a graphic and menu interface, without coding. The CSS Styles panel generates CSS code in linked files while a designer can remain in Dreamweaver's Design view. (For an extensive exploration of how to use Dreamweaver's Design view, see Book III, Chapter 4.)

Given its value, the CSS Styles panel is worth exploring in a bit of detail. The panel has two tabs near the top:

✦ **All:** The All tab, as shown in Figure 4-7, is used most of the time and provides access to all styles associated with an open HTML document. With the All tab selected, the panel splits into two halves. The top section provides a list of styles, and the bottom section displays the properties and values for the selected style.

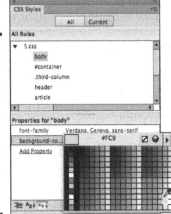

Figure 4-7:
The All tab in the CSS Styles panel identifies where style properties are defined and allows you to edit them.

✦ **Current:** The Current tab, as shown in Figure 4-8, reveals styles associated with whatever content is selected in Design view. The top section summarizes the styles that affect the selected content. The middle section lists all the selectors that impact how the selected content displays. And, depending on which selector is chosen, the bottom section displays an editable list of properties.

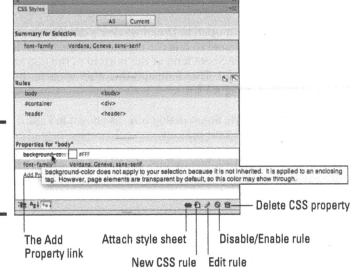

Figure 4-8:
Editing a style in the CSS Styles panel.

The Add Property link

Attach style sheet

New CSS rule   Edit rule

Disable/Enable rule

Delete CSS property

Editing styles in the CSS Styles panel

On the Current tab, click the Add Property link at the bottom of the panel to create new properties for a selected style. From the popup lists in the value column to the right, edit the properties of existing styles (refer to Figure 4-7). In this example, a new background color is being selected for the body tag.

If a property applies to elements that surround the selected element but does not apply to the selected element, the property will display with a line through the type. If you hover over the property, a tooltip appears explaining why the style isn't editable (refer to Figure 4-8). For example, because all tags are inside the <body> tag, the style (including properties like font color and background color) applies to everything on the page.

Another way of putting this is that everything that displays on a web page *inherits* the definition of the <body> tag because everything is enclosed in the <body> tag. However, if a specific style applied to a style within the body tag (like an <h1> tag, for example) and had a different color and background color, the color and background colors inherited from the <body> element are canceled. And on the Current tab of the CSS Styles panel, those canceled styles appear with a line through them. This is a very valuable tool for detective work when you can't figure out, for example, where an element gets its background color from.

Linking a style sheet from the CSS Styles panel

As we emphasize in Chapter 1 of this minibook, a key feature of modern web design is creating and relying on an external style sheet to define how pages look. You attach (or *link*) a style sheet in Dreamweaver through the tools at the bottom of the CSS Styles panel.

With an HTML document open in Dreamweaver's document window, you can use the CSS Styles panel to link (or unlink) an external style sheet. To do so, click the Attach Style Sheet icon at the bottom of the CSS Styles panel (it looks like a link in a chain). That icon and the other tools in the CSS Styles panel are identified in Figure 4-8.

The Attach External Style Sheet dialog box, as shown in Figure 4-9, opens with the following important options:

+ **File/URL:** The File/URL box defines the linked style sheet file. Click the Browse button next to this box to browse to and select a file on your computer.

+ **Add As:** The Add As options determine how the styles are attached to your open HTML page. Typically, select the Link option to maintain a live link to an external style sheet. The Import option copies the styles from the style sheet into your HTML document.

+ **Media:** The Media drop-down list defines a media query. In Chapter 2 of this minibook, we explore how media queries are used to provide alternative styles for different media (such as laptops or mobile devices).

+ **Sample Style Sheets:** Click this link to arrive at a set of sample CSS files developed by Dreamweaver.

Figure 4-9:
The Attach
External
Style Sheet
dialog box.

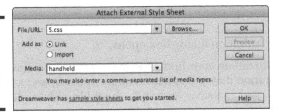

Creating a new style sheet in the CSS Styles panel

When you click the New CSS Rule icon (shown in the margin) at the bottom of the CSS Styles panel, the New CSS Rule dialog box opens (refer to Figure 4-3). The New CSS Rule dialog box combines features for defining styles for existing style sheets and creating a new style sheet.

You can use the New CSS Rule dialog box to add new styles to an existing CSS style sheet file. But you can also use the New CSS Rule dialog box to create a new CSS style sheet file. The latter creates a brand-new CSS style sheet file that we walk you through.

Follow these steps to create a new style sheet from the New CSS Rule dialog box:

1. **With the New CSS Rule dialog box open, choose Tag from the Selector Type drop-down list.**

2. **Choose Body from the Selector Name drop-down list to create a body tag style for your new style sheet.**

Nearly every style sheet includes a body tag style that defines the font, font color, and page background for the entire page.

Later you can create additional styles, but the body tag is almost always a good place to start when creating a new style sheet.

3. **In the Rule Definition area, specify where your rule will be defined by choosing New Style Sheet File.**

Later, when you add additional styles to the CSS file, you will select the open CSS file from this same drop-down list.

4. **Click OK in the New CSS Rule dialog box.**

The Save Style Sheet File As dialog box appears.

5. **Click the Site Root button to save the file in the root folder for your Dreamweaver Site and enter a filename.**

   Dreamweaver supplies the `.css` filename extension automatically.

6. **Leave the Relative To drop-down list set to Document.**

   This option defines a reliable and efficient link between the style sheet file and the open HTML page.

7. **Click Save.**

   The CSS Rule Definition dialog box opens.

   You're ready to define your first style in Dreamweaver. But because the CSS Rule Definition dialog box has so many options, we explore them next. For now, you can save your style sheet file without defining the body tag properties.

Dreamweaver's CSS Rule Definition Dialog Box

After you create your CSS style sheet file, the CSS Rule Definition dialog box opens. Here you access many CSS properties in a friendly, graphical dialog box without coding.

If the CSS Rule Definition dialog box isn't open already, open it by clicking an existing style (like the body tag style) in the CSS Styles panel and clicking the Edit Rule icon at the bottom of the CSS Styles panel. Or, you can create a new style in the CSS Rule Definition dialog box by clicking the New CSS Rule icon at the bottom of the CSS Styles panel.

The CSS Rule Definition dialog box organizes CSS properties into categories on the left. For the most part, these categories are self-explanatory, and you can click each one to see which CSS properties are defined in which category.

For example, the Type category provides access to CSS properties that affect how type looks. The Type category is shown in Figure 4-10.

Figure 4-10: Defining a font style for the h1 tag in the CSS Rule Definition dialog box.

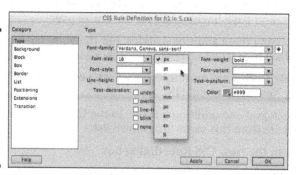

Defining properties for CSS styles

Here are a few tips on how to find and apply particularly useful or hard-to-find CSS properties in the CSS Rule Definition dialog box:

✦ **Type:** Beyond the obvious properties (font-family, size, and color), you can use the Type category to define line height. For example, to add a 1.5 multiple to provide extra spacing between lines of type, enter **1.5** in the Line-Height box, and choose Multiple from the unit of measurement drop-down list next to the Line-Height box.

✦ **Background:** The Background category includes detailed options for control over how a background image *tiles* (or repeats) within a container or on a page.

✦ **Block:** The Block category has text vertical and horizontal spacing tools.

  For example, you can create extra spacing between letters or words by selecting a value of .1 or .2 in the Word Spacing or Letter Spacing drop-down lists, and em, a unit of measurement.

  Extra spacing between words or letters can be effective in "airing out" heading text.

✦ **Box:** The Box category is one-stop shopping for defining boxes: size, float, margins, and padding.

✦ **Border:** The Border category defines style, width, and color for borders.

✦ **List:** Use the List category to change the bullet point and number styles and positioning.

✦ **Positioning:** The most valuable tools in the Positioning category have little, if anything, to do with positioning (those features define absolute positioning, which we suggest you avoid because it matches poorly with standard design techniques). Use the Z-Index drop-down list to move selected elements in front of other objects (by defining a higher z-index value) or behind (by lowering the z-index value). And use the Overflow drop-down list to define how text that doesn't fit in a container displays, including the option of displaying a scroll bar as needed (choose Auto).

✦ **Extensions:** Use the Extensions category to define print-specific styles, such as page breaks.

✦ **Transition:** The Transition category applies timing to animation. This category deserves some special attention. Up to this point, in this chapter, all the CSS rules we've identified in the CSS Rule Definition dialog box are ones we explore in earlier chapters in this minibook. That is not the case for the options in the Transition category. They're worth exploring in a bit more depth, which we do in the next section.

Defining transitions

Transitions apply to animation and interactivity of the kind we explore in Chapter 3 of this minibook. They are defined, in Dreamweaver, in the Transition category of the CSS Rule Definition dialog box.

From the Transition category in the CSS Rule Definition dialog box, you can:

✦ Define a *duration* (how long the effect or transition takes to complete)

✦ Define a *delay* (the time before the transition or effect begins)

✦ Experiment with various ways the transition takes place with the options in the Timing Function drop-down list

We explore 3D CSS3 effects (such as rotation) in Chapter 3 of this minibook. In short, they make objects appear to rotate on either the x-axis (horizontal) or y-axis (vertical) in a browser.

What's cool about the Transition category of Dreamweaver's CSS Rule Definition dialog box is that you can define properties associated with a transition, such as *duration* (how long the transition takes to complete) and *delay* (the time that elapses between the moment a visitor hovers over the element with her mouse or taps the element on her device, and when the transition begins).

Figure 4-11 shows one face of a rotating box, the CSS3 property that rotates it on hover (`-moz-transform`). Of course on the page of a book or viewed as a book page in a digital reader, you can't experience the rotation, but when this box is hovered over, it appears to rotate. And you can see the duration and delay settings for this transition in the figure. A transition duration of 5 seconds and a delay of 2 seconds have been assigned to the transition.

Applying CSS3 Effects and Transforms in Dreamweaver

We cover the CSS3 effects and transforms in Chapter 3 of this minibook, but they can be defined in the CSS Styles panel. Creating a CSS3 effect takes some typing on your part. To add a CSS3 effect or transform to a style definition, follow these steps:

1. **From the All tab of the CSS Styles panel, select the style and then click the Add Property link.**

   A new row becomes active at the bottom of the panel.

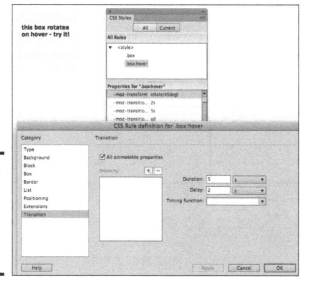

Figure 4-11:
Defining a
delay and
a duration
for a CSS3
rotate
transform.

2. **Choose either an effect from the drop-down list in the first (left) row of the new column or type Transform.**

   • *To apply an effect,* such as `border-radius`, choose that effect from the menu.

   • *To apply a transition,* such as `rotate`, choose Transform from the menu. A second drop-down list then appears in the right column from which you can choose specific transforms (such as rotate, scale, skew, or translate).

3. **Enter a value(s) for the transition or effect in the second column.**

   The amount of help you get varies. For example, if you define a `border-radius` effect, a handy dialog box pops up when you click the second column in the CSS Styles panel, as shown in Figure 4-12. Then click outside the popup dialog to apply the settings you selected.

4. **When you finish defining effects and transitions, choose File⊅Save All to save both your open HTML document and the linked style sheet.**

   You can see the impact of your effects and transitions by previewing your page in a browser (choose File⊅Preview in Browser).

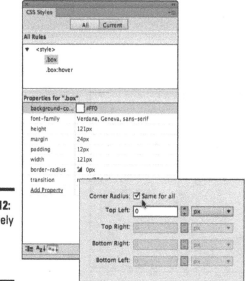

Figure 4-12:
Interactively
defining
a border-
radius.

Previewing HTML Documents on a Cellphone, Tablet, or Laptop in Dreamweaver

One of the celebrated new features in Dreamweaver (first introduced in CS5.5) is the *Multiscreen Preview,* which works in tandem with the interactive Media Query tools in Dreamweaver. Those Media Query tools create different style sheets that apply depending on the media in which a visitor uses to view the site. We explain media queries in-depth in Chapter 2 of this minibook.

As we explore in Chapter 2 of this minibook, designing pages that work well in media, ranging from large projections to tiny screens, is one of the big challenges in the world of modern web design. Multiscreen Previews allow you to see how an open HTML document looks in different media, such as on a cellphone, a tablet, a desktop, or laptop.

With an HTML document open, you can view an open page in Multiscreen Preview by following these steps:

1. **Click the Multiscreen Preview button in the document toolbar, or choose Window⇨Multiscreen Preview from the document window.**

If the document toolbar isn't active, choose View⇨Toolbars⇨Document.

The Multiscreen Preview window opens, with three views, as shown in Figure 4-13.

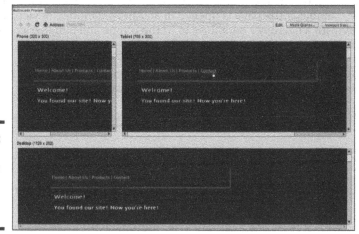

Figure 4-13: Previewing a web page in three different viewports.

2. **To adjust the viewport sizes, click the Viewport Sizes button in the Multiscreen Preview window.**

   The Viewport Sizes dialog box opens. You can edit the values (in pixels) for the width and height at which each of the three preview windows displays. Figure 4-14 shows the Phone view being adjusted to 480 pixels to match the size of popular smartphones.

Figure 4-14: Customizing viewport sizes for Multiscreen Preview.

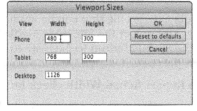

3. **Click OK in the Viewport Sizes dialog box to return to the Multiscreen Preview.**

4. **Exit Multiscreen Preview by deselecting that option in the Dreamweaver document Window menu.**

Don't try to edit content in Multiscreen Preview. This mode, like Dreamweaver's Live view, does not allow editing.

Creating a Media Query in Dreamweaver

Media Query identifies a media (print, screen, handheld device, and so on) and displays the HTML page with a CSS style sheet based on that media. So, for example, if the page is opened in an Android mobile device, it would display with a narrower container to fit the phone and a higher contrast color scheme that worked well in sunlight.

We cover media queries and the approach to creating one in Chapter 2 of this minibook, but to reiterate, here's that process:

1. You need to have at least two CSS style sheets with identical style selectors.

   Not identical selector properties or values; those differ between style sheets.

2. You need to customize each version of the style sheet for the media with which it will work.

3. With at least one alternative, or more, save the style sheets.

You're ready to create a media query in Dreamweaver. To do that, follow these steps:

1. **With your alternative CSS files created and saved, view the HTML page to which they'll be linked in the Multiscreen Preview window (see the preceding section).**

2. **Click the Media Queries button to open the Media Queries dialog box.**

3. **In the Write Media Queries To area, select This Document (to define the media query for the open document).**

   To generate a sitewide Media Queries file that can be applied to other pages in your Dreamweaver site, select the Site Wide Media Queries File option and then click the Specify button to navigate to and select a folder and filename for that purpose.

4. **Click the Force Devices to Report Actual Width check box.**

   A special tag is inserted that produces more accurate width values from queried media.

5. **Click the "+" button to generate the first media query.**

6. **In the Description box, enter a comment that reminds you what this query is for (such as laptops, tablets, mobile devices, and so on).**

For example, if you're defining a style to be used on desktops and laptops, you might describe it as *Desktops and Laptops.*

7. **To define a minimum width for the media query, enter a value in the Minimum Width box.**

   A good minimum width for full-screen layouts is 960 pixels.

8. **Click the Use Existing File button and navigate to the CSS file you want to use in full-sized browser environments.**

   Figure 4-15 illustrates this first defined media query.

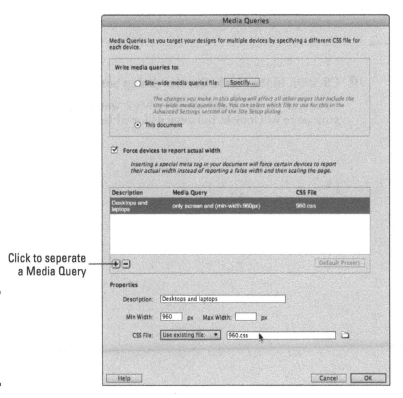

Click to seperate a Media Query

Figure 4-15:
Defining a media query for full-sized media.

9. **Define at least one additional media query by repeating Steps 5–8.**

   For example, if you have a CSS file for tablets and smartphones, make that your second option and define a maximum width of 959 pixels, as shown in Figure 4-16.

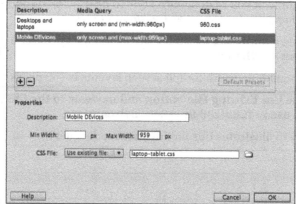

Figure 4-16: Defining a media query for mobile devices with screens smaller than 960 pixels wide.

10. **Click OK in the Media Queries dialog box.**

You return to the Multiscreen Preview window where you can see how your page will look in the devices for which you defined a media query.

Book V

Incorporating Web Graphics and Multimedia

The 5th Wave   By Rich Tennant

"You ever notice how much more streaming media there is than there used to be?"

Contents at a Glance

Chapter 1: Web Media 101

In This Chapter:

- Understanding graphics for the web
- Finding inspiration
- Dealing with copyrights
- Using web-friendly media
- Including readable fonts
- Adding clip art

*B*ack in the Jurassic era of the web, it was indeed a dark and dreary place. Websites were text only, and the web was accessed through a dial-up modem. In short, the World Wide Web was a wonderful place for geeks with pocket protectors and eyeglasses patched together with duct tape, but not a very friendly place for the average person. Then, with the advent of faster computers, lightning-fast Internet connections, and monitors that rival television monitors, the Internet blossomed with colorful graphics, audio, and video. Photographers, artists, and musicians were able to strut their stuff on the net. Graphics online became the norm.

Pretty graphics aren't the only thing you can put on your web page, though. Don't forget about how important text is — pretty, and user-friendly text, that is.

However, you can't just put any old graphic on a web page. The image must be in a web-friendly format, load quickly into the visitor's browser, and be a visual feast as well. That may seem like a tall order, but it's easily achievable. In this chapter, we introduce you to the wild and wonderful world of media on the web.

Getting Inspired

As you begin to design a site, you'll likely look for inspiration. And before you search for inspiration, get a handle on your client's likes and dislikes. When you initially interview a client, we recommend that you always ask for the URLs of your client's competitors' sites as well as those sites she likes.

This can give you an idea of your client's tastes. The client's business and printed material can also give you some ideas. Then, there's the matter of the client's intended audience. If you know the demographics of your client's intended audience, you know their likes and dislikes. If you're dealing with a large company, it probably already has this information. Or perhaps you and your client can create a persona to define the likes and dislikes of your client's intended audience.

If your client likes a clean look with tasteful graphics, you can easily incorporate that in your design. However, if your client likes a web page with lots of images that look like a cluttered clipboard, you'll have to step in and be the voice of reason and arrive at a compromise somewhere between the two extremes. A cluttered web page confuses viewers: They don't know where to focus their attention. If the page is too cluttered, they'll visit a competing website.

Another factor you have to consider is the client's industry. Chances are that the sites associated with your client's industry have a similar look and feel. Stretching the envelope is okay, but it's probably not a good idea to reinvent the wheel. Therefore, your first method of looking for ideas should be to use your favorite search engine into which you enter keywords that relate to your client's business. The top-ranking hits you get (sites) might not be the most inspirational, so randomly pick a few sites from the first few pages of results. Bookmark the ones you like. Let your creative muse stir the porridge for a day or two, and then go back to your bookmarks and make notes of what you like.

After you peruse your bookmarked sites, you might still need additional inspiration. If so, find some portals that link to exemplary websites. One way to find URLs to inspiring websites is to run an online search on something like "cool websites," "100 best website designs," or "best *type of business* websites" in your favorite search engine. You'll come up with a few places to look for inspiration. Here are a few you can try:

✦ *Time Magazine,* **The 50 Best Websites of 2011**

> www.time.com/time/specials/packages/0,28757, 2087815,00.html

✦ *PC Magazine,* **Top 100 Websites 2011**

> www.pcmag.com/article2/0,2817,2397663,00.asp

✦ **Web Marketing Association's WebAward, Best Real Estate Web Sites**

> www.webaward.org/winners

✦ **Planetizen Top 10 Websites of 2011**

> www.planetizen.com/websites/2011

If your search lands you on a site that looks like nothing but advertisements, it probably is. Pick and choose the portals that look like the real deal. Another great source for inspiration is the Adobe Customer Showcase:

www.adobe.com/cfusion/showcase/index.cfm

There, you'll find inspiring designs that were created using Adobe software.

We're not suggesting that you blatantly rip off someone else's design, but rather that you look at as many websites as you can. Incorporate those ideas that you like with your own sense of design. For example, you can use media to make your design different than the ones you like. If your client's business would be better served by video and the sites you like us still images, incorporate video in your version. By doing this, you'll take your design skills to the next level and give your client what he wants: a unique website.

Respecting the Copyrights of Others

It's one thing to mix and match ideas from other designers with your own. However, blatantly copying someone else's design isn't creative. In fact, the copyright of intellectual material, such as photographs and text, is owned by the creator. Websites also fall into this category. Some people might be tempted to steal an image from a website, thinking they'll never get caught. However, always remember that when an image or block of text is saved to a hard drive for the first time, that creator retains copyright to the image. Some images might fall under the Fair Use Clause of copyright law.

However, taking an image (without permission) or repurposing text from one website for use on a commercial website can hardly be considered fair use. If a website owner does give you permission to use his image, make sure you get that permission in writing. Covering thine own posterior is better than dealing with legal fees and a "he said, she said," knock-down, drag-out situation. If your client needs photographs of products for the website, have her contact the manufacturer and ask for images you can incorporate in the design. Most major manufacturers can provide you with a URL to a page from which you can download high-resolution images.

If you or your client need an image that's perfect for your design, consider licensing one from a local photographer or purchasing licensing rights to a photo from a stock agency, such as iStockphoto (www.istockphoto.com) or Jupiterimages (www.jupiterimages.com). You can also set up an account with a stock photography firm. After setting up an account, you can peruse the agency's collection and find the ideal image for a website. When you visit a stock photography site, enter the keyword for the type of photo you're looking for (see Figure 1-1).

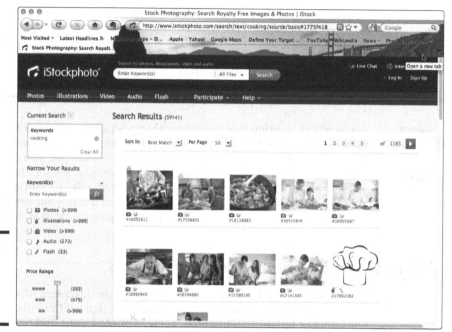

Figure 1-1:
Searching
for the
perfect
image.

Stock photo sites operate differently, and some even have different methods for purchasing images. You may be able to purchase a yearly membership, buy single images as needed, or purchase points that are then used to purchase individual photos. When you purchase a photo, you purchase the rights to use a photo for a certain destination. The price of the photo varies depending on the size and resolution of the photo, and whether you're using it on the web, in printed media, and so on. Many stock houses charge a higher price if more people see the images. The details pertaining to photo usage are generally easy to find on each site or are listed alongside the photo.

And don't forget about logos. Logos also fall under the copyright laws. You might think it's perfectly okay to take a logo from a manufacturer's website and use it in your design because your client is selling that manufacturer's product. However, most manufacturers restrict the use of their logos. To legally use a logo, your client has to accept the manufacturer's terms of use and agree to some kind of licensing. Some manufacturers won't let you alter a logo in any way. For example, you can't get creative in Photoshop with the

MSNBC logo and apply it to an image to make it appear as though it was part of a scene or embroidered on an article of clothing.

If you're designing a lot of sites that do need photos or other elements that you and your client can't supply, consider buying a clip art package of royalty-free images. When you purchase a package like this, you're free to use the image wherever you want. You can find clip art packages at your local office supply store or on the web.

Enforcing Your Own Copyrights

As we clearly mention in the preceding section, you can't copy or use content created by another web designer without permission. Period. However, that same protection applies to the content that *you* create for your client. You own the copyright to all the graphic elements you create for the design, such as the interface and buttons, as well as the layout of the page.

However, the content you create is often mingled with other content, such as images and text created by the client. Therefore, who owns the copyright to what is kind of a gray area. As the web designer, you can claim copyright to the content you create for your design by including the following statement on the bottom of each web page:

> Web Design Copyright © *year your name or company name* All Rights Reserved

Likewise, you should copyright your client's original material with the following statement:

> Content Copyright © *year your client's name or company name* All Rights Reserved

In Adobe Dreamweaver, you can create a Library item for the web design and content copyright information. When the year changes, you change the copyright year in the Library item, and all site pages are updated. Upload the revised files to the server, and your copyright is covered for the new year.

This book is written by web designers, not legal experts. The information presented in this section should not be construed as advice from legal counsel. To fully protect your material and your client's material, you should contact a lawyer whose area of expertise is intellectual property.

Working with Colors (Web-Safe versus Not-Web-Safe)

When you create a website, you strive to create an aesthetically pleasing blend of images, text, and graphics, such as banners and navigation menus. Your design must be harmonious: a careful blend of what the client supplies you and what you create. If your client supplies you with images for the site, you can often choose a pleasing color palette by sampling colors from one of the images. An application like Photoshop makes it easy to sample the exact color and use it for a background color or as part of a banner. If your client has a logo that readily identifies the business, you might be able to create a pleasing color palette by sampling colors from the logo.

When you design a website, the colors must be specified in hexadecimal format, which contains six characters. For example, white is hexadecimal #FFFFFF, and black is hexadecimal #000000. The first two characters are the red color component of the RGB (red, green, and blue) color model, the third and fourth characters are the green component, and the fifth and sixth are the blue color component. To designate 256 hues of a color in hexadecimal format, you specify a value from #00 to #FF. Therefore, pure red is #FF0000, pure green is #00FF00, and pure blue is #0000FF.

Common sense tells you that text color is very important. If you create a site with text that's hard to read, you're not doing yourself — or your client — any good. If you take the Santa Claus approach and slap red text on a green background, you have a recipe for disaster. Traditionally, websites have used black text on a white background. Some designers use a shade of gray for text (for example, #333333 or #666666). If you go any lighter than the latter, though, the text will be hard to read.

The web-safe palette (shown in Figure 1-2) has been around since the early days of the Internet, and consists of 216 colors that any video card can display, on any monitor, by any platform. The web-safe color palette is the default color palette of applications such as Adobe Dreamweaver, Adobe Fireworks, and Adobe Flash. Yeah, Figure 1-2 is in black and white (well, actually grayscale). If you want to see the web-safe palette in live, living, and glorious color, create a new web page in Dreamweaver. Before adding anything to the page, open the Properties Inspector, click Page Properties. Then, in the Page Properties dialog box (also shown in Figure 1-2), click the Background color swatch. Walla! The web-safe, 216-color palette appears.

Click to see the color palette.

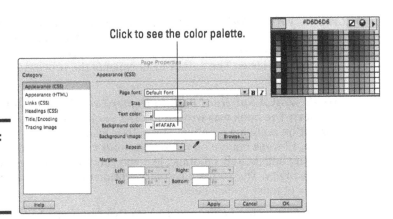

Figure 1-2:
The web-safe, 216-color palette.

Most modern computers have video cards and monitors capable of displaying millions of colors. Therefore, sticking with the web-safe palette isn't imperative. If you like to err on the side of caution, most web applications enable you to create a reasonable facsimile of the desired color by picking its closest counterpart from the web-safe palette. Smaller mobile devices don't sport good contrast and are often viewed in less-than-ideal lighting conditions. This becomes a problem with text. And heaven forbid you design a page with dark blue text elements — that could be mistaken for hyperlinks!

As we mention earlier, many designers use pure-white text (#FFFFFF) on a black or dark gray background. If you use this color palette, increase the line height to a percentage of 130 to 150 percent of the text. This increases the space between lines and makes the text easier to read.

Exploiting Creativity Tools — Color Charts and More

When you design a site from scratch (as we discuss in Book II, Chapter 3), visualizing what colors will look like can be difficult. Fortunately, you can easily experiment with different colors in Fireworks or Dreamweaver when you lay out the elements of your design, such as the banner, navigation menu, text, and so on. But when you're under the gun to create a site quickly, it helps to have a bit of inspiration or a tool to help you in your quest. The following list shows some books you can use to inspire your creativity, aid you in choosing colors, and show you some inspiring design ideas:

✦ *Creativity for Graphic Designers: A Real-World Guide to Idea Generation,* **by Mark Oldach (North Light Books):** This book isn't filled with eye candy. Instead, it guides you through processes you can use to come up with ideas. The author also explains the process of creating a good design.

✦ *Artist's Way: A Spiritual Path to Higher Creativity,* **by Julia Cameron (Tarcher):** The book was written in 1992, yet it still contains a wealth of information on being creative. The author leads you through a comprehensive, 12-week course on recovering your creativity from things such as limiting beliefs, self-sabotage, jealousy, and other things that deter your creativity. The 10th anniversary edition of this popular book is available at most booksellers.

✦ *How to Think Like Leonardo da Vinci: Seven Steps to Genius Every Day,* **by Michael Gelb (Dell):** This insightful book lists seven principles found in Leonardo da Vinci's thinking and creative process and shows how to tap into these principles and use them in your own work.

✦ *Color Index,* **by Jim Krause (How Design Books):** Keep this handy reference on a bookshelf near your computer. The book is divided into several sections that show color combinations for print and web. Each color combination shows a graphic using the colors and swatches that list the components needed to create the color using the CMYK (cyan/magenta/yellow/black) and RGB (red/green/blue) color models. The swatches in the web design section are designated in hexadecimal format and the RGB color model.

✦ *Color: A Course in Mastering the Art of Mixing Colors,* **by Betty Edwards (Tarcher):** This book delves into color theory. Although much of the information is geared toward artists, you can use the information to create harmonious colors for your web designs. The author gives you an understanding of primary, secondary, and tertiary colors, and shows you how to use the color wheel to understand color values and intensity.

If you're really color challenged, consider purchasing an application such as ColorSchemer Studio 2 (www.colorschemer.com). ColorSchemer is an application that features a color wheel and a Photo Schemer section, which enables you to create a color palette using colors from a photo. As of this writing, ColorSchemer Studio 2 retails for about $50.

You can also find some interesting color schemes at Adobe's Kuler website (http://kuler.adobe.com), which we discuss further in Book II, Chapter 3. Here you'll find color combinations created by web designers and graphic artists. If you have an Adobe ID, you can log in and create your own color combinations by modifying an existing one or uploading a photo as reference. Adobe Kuler can also be accessed using Photoshop.

Using Web-Friendly Fonts

If you've been designing websites for a while, you know that not everyone has the same fonts on their computers that you have on yours. When you design a site, you must take this into consideration. If you design a site with a nonstandard font that's not installed on the client's machine, the page will look fine to you, but it won't display like you designed it. Several fonts are commonly used for websites because they can be used on websites that are displayed cross-platform. Your universal font friends are Arial, Times New Roman, Courier New, Courier Mono, Helvetica, and Verdana. You can set the default font by changing the Page Properties in Dreamweaver and set fonts for other elements using CSS as discussed in Book IV, Chapter 1.

In addition, you can specify a serif or sans serif font. For example, Georgia is a serif font, and Verdana is a sans-serif font. *Serif* refers to the decoration at the end of strokes that make up letters or characters, such as the diagonal at the end of the angular ascenders of a capital A. When a font is sans serif, there is no decoration at the end of strokes or letters. Figure 1-3 shows a sans serif and a serif font.

Figure 1-3:
To serif, or not to serif? That is the question.

A A

Georgia
Serif font

Verdana
Sans-serif font

When you create web pages and specify a font, you can specify the default and also alternate fonts for a block of text. That way, if the user doesn't have the default font installed on her machine, the HTML page displays one of the alternate fonts. Fortunately, you don't have to hand-code the alternate fonts. When you use an application like Dreamweaver, you can choose a set of fonts from a popup menu. (See Figure 1-4.)

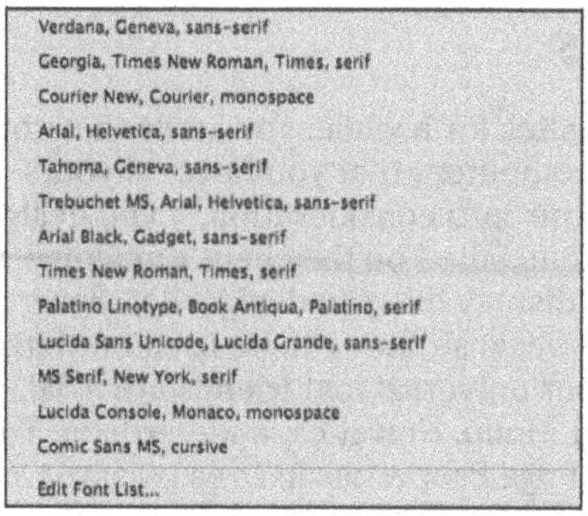

Verdana, Geneva, sans-serif

Georgia, Times New Roman, Times, serif

Courier New, Courier, monospace

Arial, Helvetica, sans-serif

Tahoma, Geneva, sans-serif

Trebuchet MS, Arial, Helvetica, sans-serif

Arial Black, Gadget, sans-serif

Times New Roman, Times, serif

Palatino Linotype, Book Antiqua, Palatino, serif

Lucida Sans Unicode, Lucida Grande, sans-serif

MS Serif, New York, serif

Lucida Console, Monaco, monospace

Comic Sans MS, cursive

Edit Font List...

Figure 1-4:
Vote your
choice!

And just when you think it's safe to make an educated choice, there's another issue to contend with: web browsers. When you use *pixels* (the default unit of measure for text), your text looks fine in the Internet Explorer web browser. However, if you view the same page in Mozilla Firefox, the text appears smaller. The solution is to use points as the default unit of measure for text. Then your text will display correctly in all browsers.

Use a CSS (cascading style sheet) to specify the parameters for text. This saves you from individually formatting each block of text you add to a web page. For more information on using CSS to specify text, see Book IV, Chapter 1.

Print to Web: Making Your Website Work with Existing Materials

What came first, the website or the brick-and-mortar business? In most instances, the brick-and-mortar business. When this is the case, you need to incorporate as many elements as you can from the client's brick-and-mortar business on his website. The obvious way to do this is to use the client's printed materials as a prototype for your web design.

When you're thinking about design elements for your client's site, start with the client's logo, as we mention earlier. That needs to be displayed prominently on every page of the site. If the client has a letterhead with his logo, you can use this as the basis for the site banner. If the client doesn't have a letterhead, use elements from her business card. Figure 1-5 shows a business card for a business coach and the website that was designed using elements from the business card.

Figure 1-5:
A website design, using elements from a client's business card.

Understanding Image Formats for Web Design

When you use images on a website, you have two things to consider: the image format and optimization. When you get these factors spot on, you have a crisp-looking image that loads quickly and looks the same in any web browser. If you get it wrong, you either have an image that loads at the speed of light but looks horrible, or you have an image that looks absolutely gorgeous but takes three forevers to load. In the upcoming sections, we discuss the image formats used in web designs plus the uses and limitations for each.

Using the GIF image file format

An image saved as a GIF (Graphics Interchange Format) file comprises 256 (8-bit) colors. Images saved with the GIF format can be viewed on all current web browsers. The GIF (pronounced *giff* or *jiff*) image format is commonly used for images with large areas of solid color (such as logos or graphic symbols (such as buttons). This file format also works well when the banner is predominantly text.

The resulting file size of the image depends on how you optimize the image. When you *optimize* a GIF image, you specify the number of colors with which the image is saved and the color reduction algorithm. The goal is to optimize the image so that it still looks good and loads quickly. Find out more about image optimization in Chapter 3 of this minibook.

GIF images also support transparency. This option is useful when you're displaying text over a background image. When you create the image, use a background color similar to, or the same as, that of the background image for the web page.

Don't use the GIF format to save photorealistic images with millions of colors. The restrictive color palette degrades the image quality. If you use *dithering* (where colors from the 256 color palette are mixed to create a reasonable facsimile of a color not in the palette), the file size is too large for practical use in a web page.

Using the JPEG image file format

The JPEG (Joint Photographic Experts Group) file format is ideally suited for photorealistic images with millions of colors. The original JPEG (pronounced *JAY-peg*) format also has a derivative known as *JPEG 2000,* which features better image compression that results in smaller file sizes. Unfortunately, as of this writing, JPEG 2000 is supported only by Safari. The JPEG format does its magic by compressing images. When you compress an image, data is lost; therefore, the JPEG format is known as a *lossy* format. Figure 1-6 shows a JPEG image from a photographer's web portfolio.

The image quality is determined by the amount of compression you apply when saving the image. The ideal compression depends on the amount of detail in the image and the size of the image in the web page in which you'll insert it. If the image is small without much detail, you can apply higher compression to the image. If the image takes up a large portion of the web page and contains a lot of detail, you'll have to apply less compression to the image. Otherwise, the detail will be muddy, and the image won't be crisp. Fortunately, most image-editing applications, such as Fireworks and Photoshop, have options that enable you to compare the original image side-by-side to a version of the image with compression applied. The details about image optimization are in Chapter 3 of this minibook.

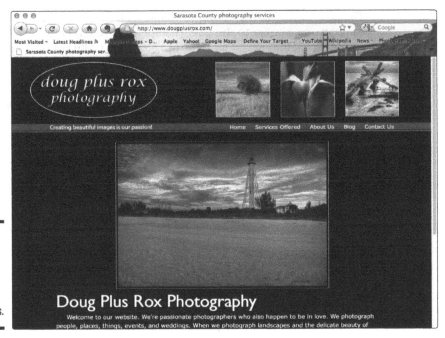

Figure 1-6:
The JPEG
format
is ideally
suited to
photographs.

If you have an image with a lot of text — such as a banner with a text logo and a text tagline — saving the image in the JPEG format will result in text with jagged edges because of the text anti-aliasing blending the edges of the text with the surrounding image. The best way to overcome this is to use an image-editing application (such as Fireworks) that enables you to "slice" an image into sections and then save them in different formats. Save the sliced sections with text in the GIF format and the rest of the image as JPEG files. When you optimize the image, make sure you specify enough colors; otherwise, you'll see jagged edges where the anti-aliasing blends the font to the background.

Using the PNG image file format

The PNG (Portable Network Graphics) format was originally designed to replace the GIF format. For graphics such as buttons and banners, you can save a file using PNG-8 format, which results in an 8-bit file that supports transparency. When you're working with photorealistic images with millions of colors, you can save the files using the PNG-24 format, which saves the file with millions of colors.

The best feature of the PNG (pronounced *ping*) format is that it uses *lossless compression*, similar to the LZW (Lempel-Ziv-Welch) compression used when compressing files saved as TIFFs (Tagged Image File Format). This results in a good-looking graphic with a relatively small file size. The drawback to using the PNG format has been differing levels of support by popular web browsers. Current browsers offer better support for the PNG format, but there are still issues when PNG files saved with transparency are displayed.

Chapter 2: Introducing Fireworks and Photoshop

In This Chapter

✔ Using a color palette

✔ Understanding vector and raster graphics

✔ Create graphics for the web

✔ Introducing Fireworks CS6

✔ Introducing Photoshop CS6

✔ Optimizing for the web

The mission that you accepted was to design a website. You've done your research and arrived at an optimum design for the project. Now it's time to create it. When you create the site, you work with text and images. The images may be photographs; or they may be graphics, such as logos. If you receive graphics from outside sources, chances are that they'll need some work. That is, the objects will have to be resized to fit your design and then optimized for the web. This step is important because if you don't optimize images for the web, they take longer to load.

And in addition to working with images, you may also be required to create web objects, such as banners and buttons. If you're not familiar with the art and science of creating graphics for the web, but you own Fireworks and/or Photoshop, you've come to the right place.

In our humble estimation, if you have to choose one tool for graphics, Fireworks is the one because it integrates seamlessly with Dreamweaver. And with Fireworks, you can create sophisticated graphics, such as navigation menus, and export the graphics with HTML that you import into your Dreamweaver documents.

In this chapter, we also show you how to optimize images for use on your site. The step-by-step instructions are based on Fireworks CS6 and Photoshop CS6 but apply to previous versions as well.

Using a Color Palette

Before we get to graphics and images specifically, think about how those elements will fit in your Big Picture. When you create a website, consistency is very important. Think of designing and decorating a home with many rooms: Each room has a specific function, but the home has an overall style and flow, typically enhanced by a deliberate and harmonious choice of a color palette. Just like using pale blue might be great for an oceanfront home, fire engine red might be perfect for a high-rise loft in a vibrant downtown setting.

Likewise, the same color-choice logic applies to a website. When you create graphics for a different page of the site, changing or deviating colors from what's used on another page isn't advisable. After all, in a home, it's jarring to walk from room to room of red, then light blue, then hot pink, then orange. As we first mention in Book II, Chapter 3, we recommend selecting a set of three to five colors for the site — your *palette* — and sticking with those colors on every page of the site.

You can choose colors from a web-safe palette (as outlined in Chapter 1 of this minibook), or use an application like Kuler, which you'll find in Photoshop and Fireworks. You can also access the Kuler application online at `http://kuler.adobe.com`.

When you access Kuler online, you get a chance to see popular color schemes, and those ideas can often be a starting point for the color palette of the site you're designing.

Introducing Fireworks CS6

You can use lots of applications to create the graphic elements of your web design. However, if the elements are exported only as image files, you have to lay them out yourself in your handy-dandy HTML-editing application. And that means working with tables and images and spacers, oh my!

In other words, the task won't be a whole lot of fun. However, some applications can export your graphic design as images *and* HTML, and you don't have to write the first bit of code. Bingo! That's just the ticket! Enter Adobe Fireworks CS6, which is just such an application that you can use to export a graphic design as images and HTML.

Fireworks has been around for a long time, albeit not quite as long as the Internet. As of this writing, the Adobe Creative Suite 6 has not been released. If Adobe follows suit with CS5, Fireworks CS6 will be part of Adobe Creative Suite CS6 Master Collection, Adobe Creative Suite CS6 Web Design Standard, and Adobe Creative Suite CS6 Web Design Premium.

Understanding Vector and Raster Graphics

Fireworks CS6 is an application that enables you to create vector and raster graphics to create the graphic elements for your web design. This duality is a good thing.

So what's the big difference between vector and raster, and why should you care? Briefly, when you create vector graphics, you have the power to edit and resize to your heart's content. A very good thing.

Vector graphics generated by using math to determine where the points and line segments that comprise paths appear within a graphic. And when you resize a vector graphic, mathematical formulas are used to regenerate the graphic at the larger size with no distortion (unless a gradient fill is applied to the object).

Figure 2-1 shows a vector graphic in Fireworks that was created with the Pen tool. Notice the points. The points have what look like handles: These are *curve points.* The handles are *tangents,* which are used to reshape the curve segment between adjoining points.

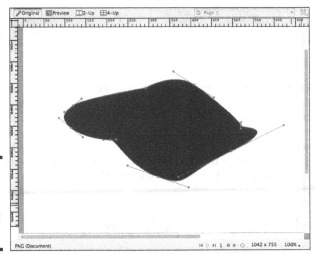

Figure 2-1:
Vector
graphics:
The math all
adds up.

Raster graphics — known as *bitmaps* — are rascals composed of dots of color — *pixels.* You also have something known as *resolution,* which shows how many pixels per inch (ppi) are used to create an image.

So here's the rub. Monitor resolution is 72 or 96 ppi. (And that resolution will work for tablets and mobile devices.) When you create a graphic for print, though, the ideal resolution is 150 ppi or greater.

Now, if you're good at math, you can see the problem when you enlarge a raster graphic. Say, for example, you want to increase the size of an image from 4" x 5" to 8" x 10". You're still working with the same number of pixels per inch; therefore, you're asking the application to double the size of each pixel. The math adds up, but the end result is not very useful, and usually not very pretty. The left side of Figure 2-2 shows a small JPEG image; the rest of the figure shows the same image magnified several times. You can actually see blocks of pixels. Not good.

Figure 2-2:
I've got
pixels. Who
could ask
for anything
more?

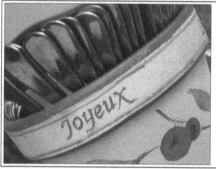

So this is how using Fireworks can save your bacon: You use a combination of raster and vector graphics to create your web designs — in Fireworks. In fact, in Fireworks, you can flesh out the entire web page, leaving placeholders for your HTML text. Stay with us as we show you how to use Fireworks to create site banners and navigation menus. The application has powerful tools to optimize graphic images, slice them into objects (like buttons), and then export the document as images with HTML.

Creating Fast-Loading and Pretty Graphics

One of the worst things that can happen to a website is when it's s-l-o-w loading. And you can be part of the reason for this slowness! Maybe you're trying to cram too many graphics on the page, or you've created a page with beautiful graphics that have a file size slightly bigger than the state of New York.

The trick — the art — of getting a page to load fast is using the right graphics file format and then optimizing it.

As we mention in Chapter 1 of this minibook, GIF is the ideal graphics file format to use when you create objects like banners, or when displaying images with large areas of solid color. You then *optimize* a GIF graphic by specifying the number of colors used to display the image. You can also specify the type of GIF rendering to use. We show you how to optimize GIF graphics in an upcoming section of this chapter.

When you need to display photo-realistic images on a web page, though, JPEG is the obvious choice. JPEG is a *lossy* format, which means that data is lost when the image is optimized for the web. The data that is lost is adjacent pixels of similar color. Instead of rendering every subtle nuance of a color, the adjacent pixels are display with an average color that approximates the shade lost when the image was optimized. The trick is to lose just enough data for a fast-loading image but end up with an image that still looks crisp. We show you how to optimize JPEG images in the next chapter of this minibook.

The PNG file format

Fireworks uses the PNG (Portable Networks Graphics) file format as its native file format. However, it's not the same format as when you export an image from Photoshop or Fireworks using the PNG format. The Fireworks PNG format saves all the layers and elements used to create the Fireworks document. The Fireworks PNG file also has a Web layer, which contains information such as the slices and hotspots you created. (Slices and hotspots are used to add interactivity to a document.) Then, when you export the document, Fireworks takes all the pieces you sliced and diced and houses them in a table. The resulting export is an HTML document and images. You can export the native Fireworks PNG file as one file exported in the format that is best for the content or as slices, and each slice can be optimized for the format that is best for the content.

You can export a Fireworks document or slice in one of the following formats: GIF, which is great for images like logos that have large areas of solid color, or for areas of the document that contain text; JPEG, which is great for photorealistic images such as those captured from a digital camera; or PNG, which can be used for images with areas of solid color or photorealistic images. We cover optimizing and exporting images in Fireworks in upcoming sections of this chapter.

Fireworks interface mini-tour

Fireworks CS6 is an incredible application. You can use it to create all the graphics for your web designs. You can use the application to create complex interfaces, web banners, navigation menus, and so on. If your client has more content than will fit comfortably on a navigation menu, you can even create drop-down menus that — well — actually drop down.

In addition to creating graphics with panache, you also have some powerful export options. After you create the navigation menu or banner of your dreams, you can export the whole kit and caboodle as graphics or HTML, with or without CSS. Now how cool is that? But you get the gist; you can use Fireworks to create some very cool stuff for your web designs. In the upcoming sections, we show you the Fireworks workspace.

The Fireworks work area

Fireworks might look like other image-editing applications you've used. However, Fireworks has a few other elements that are specifically related to web design. For example, in the Layers panel, you find a layer labeled Web layer. You also find an object called the Button Editor, which (you guessed it) enables you to create buttons. Find out more about buttons in Chapter 3 of this minibook.

The Fireworks interface, shown in Figure 2-3, consists of a main window where you assemble the elements of your design, the ever-present menu bar, a toolbar, and the window in which panels are docked. In fact, the panel dock has almost as many panels docked as there are Smiths in the local phone book. The Properties Inspector has different options, depending on the object you selected. When you're creating text, for example, the Properties Inspector is configured as shown in Figure 2-4.

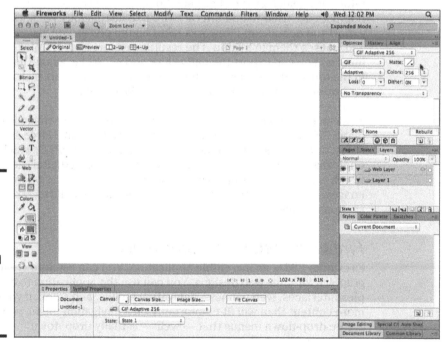

Figure 2-3:
When
you need
sparkling
graphics,
menus, and
other web
delights,
launch
Fireworks.

Figure 2-4:
The
Properties
Inspector is
contextual.

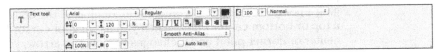

The Fireworks toolbar

Fireworks has a wide array of tools that you use to create and manipulate objects for your web designs. The toolbar shown in Figure 2-5 houses the following tools (described in order from top to bottom).

Figure 2-5:
Got a whole
lotta tools.

When multiple tools reside on a toolbar, the last-used tool is at the top of the heap. When you click the down arrow, the other tools appear to fly out of the last used tool — hence, the term *fly-out menu.*

✦ **Pointer:** Use to select and move objects. This tool has a cohort in crime — the Select Behind tool — that hangs out on the fly-out menu. Use Select Behind to select objects that are hidden partially behind other objects.

✦ **Subselection:** Use to select and move objects within a group or on points along a path.

✦ **Scale:** Use to resize objects and rotate objects. You can resize objects proportionately by dragging a corner point, change the width by dragging a point in the center of either side, or change the height by dragging a top or bottom center point. When you move your cursor toward a center or corner point and it changes to a curved arrow, you can rotate the object. This is the default tool for this little piece of real estate on the toolbar. You can access three other tools by clicking the down arrow at the lower right of the Scale tool icon. They are

- *Skew:* Use to slant objects; you know, get them off kilter. You can also use the Skew tool to rotate an object. If you really get miffed at an object, you can tell it, "Skew you and rotate!" And then you can do it.

- *Distort:* Use to change the shape of objects. With this tool, you click and drag individual points to morph an object into something totally different than you started with.

- *9-Slice Scaling Tool:* This tool displays nine slice guides within a selected object. The slice guides can be moved to determine how the object is transformed when you increase or decrease the size of the object. The center slice scales horizontally and vertically. The top and bottom slices scale vertically. The middle end slices scale horizontally, and the corner slices doesn't change size at all. This is a way of intelligently scaling the object so it's not distorted.

✦ **Crop:** Use to trim the document to a smaller size. Click and drag inside the document to create a cropping rectangle. While you drag the tool, a bounding box appears, showing you the current size of the cropping rectangle. Release the mouse button when the cropping rectangle is the desired size. After creating the cropping rectangle, you see eight small squares that you can use to change the width, height, or width and height of the cropping rectangle. When the rectangle is the desired size, double-click inside the rectangle to crop the document.

- *Export Area tool:* Use to export a select area of a document.

✦ **Marquee:** Use to create rectangular selections. Press Shift while dragging the tool to create square selections. Or click the down arrow in the lower right of the tool icon to select a tool that creates oval selections:

- *Oval Marquee:* Use to create oval selections (or circular selections, if you press the Shift key while using the tool).

✦ **Lasso:** Use to create freeform selections. Click and drag around the area you want to select. Or click the down arrow in the lower right of the tool icon to access this tool:

- *Polygon Lasso:* Use to create selections by clicking to define the first point of the selection and then clicking to define the other points of the selection. Fireworks creates a line segment between points. Double-click to close the selection.

You can add to an existing selection by holding down the Shift key and using one of the selection tools to define the area you want to add. Hold down the Alt key (Windows) or Option key (Mac) while using one of the selection tools to remove an area from a selection.

✦ **Magic Wand:** Use to select areas within a document. Click inside an area to select areas of like color. The tool has a Tolerance value from 0 to 255 that you specify in the Properties Inspector. A low Tolerance value selects hues that are close to that of the area in which you click. A high Tolerance value selects a wider range of colors.

✦ **Brush:** Use to paint areas of color within the document. You specify the brush parameters — such as size, stroke, and edge — in the Properties Inspector. The Brush tool strokes are divided into categories, such as Watercolor and Oil, which enable you to create strokes like those from an artist's brushes. Each stroke has options that enable you to tailor the brush to your liking.

✦ **Pencil:** Use to create freeform lines within a document. You specify the thickness of the stroke within the Properties Inspector. You can constrain the tool to a straight line or 45-degree diagonal by holding down the Shift key while creating strokes with the tool.

✦ **Eraser:** Use to erase areas of color within the document. You specify the shape, diameter, edge, and opacity within the Properties Inspector.

✦ **Blur:** Use to blur areas. You specify the diameter of the tool, softness of the edge, shape, and intensity within the Properties Inspector. This is another spot on the toolbar that is home to many tools. Click the down arrow in the lower right of the tool icon to access these tools:

  • *Sharpen:* Use to increase the contrast between edges, which makes an object look sharper. You specify the diameter of the tool, softness of the edge, shape, and intensity within the Properties Inspector.

  • *Dodge:* Use to lighten areas within the document. You specify the diameter of the tool, softness of the edge, shape, range, and exposure within the Properties Inspector.

  • *Burn:* Use to darken areas within the document. You specify the diameter of the tool, softness of the edge, shape, range, and exposure within the Properties Inspector.

  • *Smudge:* Use to create areas of smudged color within the document. If you've ever dipped your finger into a bucket of paint and rubbed it against a solid object, you have an idea of the effect created with this tool. You specify the diameter of the tool, edge, shape, pressure, smudge color, and intensity within the Properties Inspector.

✦ **Rubber Stamp:** Use to clone areas from one part of the document to another. After selecting the tool, press Alt (Windows) or Option (Mac) and click the area from which you want to clone pixels, and then "paint" in the area to which you want the pixels cloned. This tool comes in handy when you want to retouch images you'll use in a web design. The Rubber Stamp tool is just the tip of the iceberg, though. Click the down arrow at the lower right of the tool icon to access these tools:

- *Replace Color:* Use to replace areas of solid color in the document with another color. In the Properties Inspector, you can choose the color to replace by using the default From option of Swatch and then clicking inside the document to sample a color, or by choosing Image from the From drop-down menu. You then choose the replacement color in the Properties Inspector. Click and drag inside the document to replace color. If you choose the Swatch option, the tool replaces the color that matches the swatch. If you choose the Image option, the tool replaces the area of color you first click.

- *Red Eye Removal:* Use to remove red-eye in images. This tool has two parameters, Tolerance and Strength, which you set in the Properties Inspector. Click inside the red area of the eye and drag to get the red out.

✦ **Line:** Use to create vector-based straight lines in the document. After you begin to draw the line, hold down the Shift key to constrain the line horizontally, vertically, or diagonally on a 45-degree angle. The line is constrained in the direction in which you start dragging.

✦ **Pen:** Use to create paths in the document. Click to create a point and then click to create another point. The resulting path comprises points that are connected by line segments. This tool can be used to create complex shapes. If you click and drag, you create a curve point. Curve points have tangent handles that you can drag to modify the line segment to which the curve point is attached. You can edit paths created with the Pen tool with the Subselection tool. Other path tools can be accessed by clicking the down arrow in the lower right of the tool icon. They are

- *Vector Path:* Use to create freeform paths that you can edit with the Subselection tool. The tool works similar to the Brush tool except that when you release the mouse button, Fireworks creates editable points along the path. You set the tool parameters in the Properties Inspector. The Precision parameter determines how often Fireworks creates points.

- *Redraw Path:* Use to modify a path created with the Pen or the Vector Path tool. You must first select the path with the Pointer tool, then select the Redraw Path tool, and then click and drag along the path to change its shape.

✦ **Rectangle:** Use to create rectangles. Hold down the Shift key while using this tool to create a square. You set parameters, such as stroke shape, stroke diameter, fill, stroke color, and much more in the Properties Inspector. But wait, there's more — three more, in fact, that you access when you click the down arrow at the lower right of the tool icon.

- *Ellipse:* Use to create ovals — you know, those rotund critters that form the basis for your generic smiley face. Hold down the Shift key while using this tool to create a circle. You set parameters such as stroke shape, stroke diameter, fill, stroke color, and so on in the Properties Inspector.

- *Polygon:* Use to created polygons, those multisided wonders that inspired the Pentagon. You set parameters, including the number of sides, in the Properties Inspector. Click and drag to create your polygon. The tool also has an option for creating stars, which is a handy option if you're creating a website for an actor or a rock star.

- *Auto Shape Tools:* These useful critters (Arrow, Arrow Line, Beveled Rectangle, Chamfer Rectangle, Connector Line, Donut, L-Shape, Measure, Pie, Rounded Rectangle, Smart Polygon, Spiral, and Star) are just below the Polygon tool. They work like regular shapes except that you modify them using the Properties Inspector and the Auto Shape Properties panel. The following auto shape tools are available to add artistic shapes to your web designs.

- *Arrow Tool:* Use this tool to create a filled arrow.

- *Arrow Line:* Use this tool to create a line with an arrow at the end. Your website viewers will get the point.

- *Beveled Rectangle:* Use this tool to create a rectangle with beveled edges.

- *Chamfer Rectangle:* Use this tool to create a rectangle with *chamfered* corners — each corner looks like someone punched a quarter of a circle from it.

- *Connector Line:* Use this tool to create a line that can be used to connect two objects. You modify the size of the line by dragging a point.

- *Donut:* Use this tool to create a circle with a hole in the middle. It is rumored that this tool was used to create a website for a legendary police force.

- *L-Shape:* Use this tool to create a shape that looks like the letter L.

- *Measure:* Use this tool to create a line with the measurement from point A to point B in the middle of the line.

- *Pie:* Creates a circular pie with a slice cut out of it. Drag a point on the segment to change the size of a slice. Alt-drag (Windows) or Option-drag (Mac) a point on the segment to create another segment.

- *Rounded Rectangle:* Use this tool to create a rectangle with rounded edges.

- *Smart Polygon:* Use this tool to create a polygon with five sides. The polygon has intelligence due to the fact that you can Alt (Windows) or Option (Mac) drag a segment point to create additional segments.

- *Spiral:* Use this tool to create a spiral shape.

- *Star:* Creates a five-point star. Drag an inside or outside point to change the shape of the star.

When you create a shape using one of the shape tools, you edit the shape by dragging one of the points. The type of edits that you can perform varies depending on the shape you create. On some of the shapes, you pause your cursor over one of the points, and text appears telling you how to edit the shape.

✦ **Text:** Use to add words of wisdom to your client's website. You use the Text tool to add text to buttons and banners as well as add other cool and groovy things to your design. And you guessed it — you set the parameters for the Text tool in Ye Olde Properties Inspector.

✦ **Freeform:** Use to do yet more cool things with paths. This tool modifies vector paths in a freeform manner. For example, select the tool and drag it across a path you made with the Line tool to transform the path from the straight and narrow to whatever you care to conjure up. And yes, Virginia, Fireworks adds the points to define the reshaped path. If you take a good look at Figure 2-5, you might notice that one of those cute little down arrows also resides on this tool. Click the arrow to reveal the following:

  - *Reshape Area:* Use to reshape an area previously folded, spindled, and mutilated by the Freeform tool. In the Properties Inspector, set the Size and Strength and then drag it across the path to reshape it.

  - *Path Scrubber (Additive):* Use to add points to a path created by using a pressure-sensitive tablet. Select the path and then click and drag to redraw the path.

  - *Path Scrubber (Subtractive):* Use to remove points from a path created by using a pressure-sensitive tablet. Select the path and then click and drag to remove unwanted portions of the path.

✦ **Knife:** A clever cleaver of a tool you use to sever (ouch!) a vector object into pieces. Click and drag across the vector object at the point where you want it to split into two pieces. After wielding the knife ("Careful with that axe, Eugene!"), you can use the Pointer tool to move either piece to a different part of the document, or use the Subselection tool to grab one or more points of either piece by the scruff of the neck and modify the shape.

✦ **Rectangle Hotspot:** Use to create *rectangular hotspots,* which are interactive areas of the document. You can use rectangular hotspots for image rollovers and other delights. This tool also has close relatives that you can access by clicking the down arrow in the lower right of the tool icon. They are

- *Circular Hotspot:* Use to create circular hotspots in the document.

- *Polygonal Hotspot:* Use to create hotspots for irregularly shaped areas. Click to define the first point of the hotspot and then click to define the other points of the hotspot. Fireworks connects the dots.

✦ **Slice:** Use to divide (hence the name *slice*) a document into pieces. For example, you can create a slice and use it as the basis for a pop-up menu, image rollover, and so on. Each slice becomes an individual image when the document is exported. Click the down arrow in the lower right of the tool icon to reveal more choices.

- *Polygonal Slice:* Use to create irregular slices by clicking to define each point of the slice. And if you guessed that Fireworks connects the dots, you would be correct.

✦ **Hide Hotspots and Slices:** Use to hide hotspots and slices (designated as light blue and lime green areas, respectively) in the document.

✦ **Show Hotspots and Slices:** Use to reveal hidden hotspots and slices.

✦ **Eyedropper:** Use to sample colors from within the document. This tool is very handy when you need to exactly match a color from an image you've imported into the document. Simply click the color you want to match. You can sample colors for the stroke or fill.

✦ **Paint Bucket:** Use to fill an object with the current fill color. You can also set parameters for the tool such as fill color, tolerance, and opacity in the Properties Inspector. There's another tool lurking with this tool. Click the down arrow in the lower right of the tool icon to reveal

- *Gradient:* Use to fill an object with a *gradient,* which is a blend of two or more colors. You can choose a preset gradient or mix one of your own in the Properties Inspector.

✦ **Stroke Color:** Use to specify the outline color of objects you create with tools, such as the Rectangle tool. Click the swatch to open the Color Picker and choose a color. Alternatively, you can click the icon to the left of the color swatch and then use the Eyedropper tool to sample a color from within the document.

✦ **Fill Color:** Use to specify the color inside of objects you create with tools, such as the Oval tool. Click the swatch to open the Color Picker and choose a color. Alternatively, you can click the icon to the left of the color swatch and then use the Eyedropper tool to sample a color from within the document.

✦ **Set Default Stroke/Fill Colors:** Use to set the color swatches to their default colors: black for the Stroke color and white for the Fill color.

✦ **No Stroke or Fill:** Click the Stroke swatch, and then click this tool to create an object with a fill, but no stroke. Click the Fill swatch, and then click this tool to create an object with a stroke but no fill.

✦ **Swap Stroke/Fill Colors:** Swap the current Stroke and Fill colors.

✦ **Standard Screen mode:** Use to revert to standard viewing mode, the document, tools, and menu.

✦ **Full Screen with Menus mode:** Maximize Fireworks to fill the monitor while displaying all elements of the Fireworks workspace.

✦ **Full Screen mode:** Display the current document surrounded by a black screen.

Press F to toggle through each viewing mode.

✦ **Hand:** Use to pan within the document.

Press the spacebar to momentarily switch to the Hand tool. After panning to the desired area, release the spacebar to revert to the last used tool.

✦ **Zoom:** Use to zoom in on the document. Click inside the document to zoom to the next highest degree of magnification. Click and drag diagonally to zoom to a specific area of the document. Press Alt (Windows) or Option (Mac) to zoom out.

Press Tab to hide the tools and all panels. Press Tab again to display the hidden tools and panels.

Creating Art with Photoshop

As we mentioned earlier, Fireworks is considered the workhorse for creating graphics for Web pages. However, you can create some very artistic elements for your web pages using Photoshop CS6. Photoshop has a Save for Web & Devices command, which is used to optimize images for the web. We show you how to use this command to optimize graphics for the web in Chapter 3 of this minibook. The following sections introduce you to Photoshop CS6.

Adding Photoshop CS6 to your graphics toolbox

Photoshop CS6 is a powerhouse image-editing application used by professional photographers and artists.

The application features an extensive set of filters, tools, and commands to perform functions such as color-correcting images, removing red-eye, creating images that look like paintings, and so on. Many web designers use Photoshop to create content such as splash images and banners. The native Photoshop file format, PSD, supports multiple layers, 16-bit color depth, a unique set of blend modes, and much more. Figure 2-6 shows a banner for a website being designed in Photoshop CS6. Notice the Layers panel, which shows the layers that make up the final image.

The toolset of Photoshop deserves a book of its own. Some of the features appear in Chapter 3 of this minibook (which covers creating a banner and a web gallery).

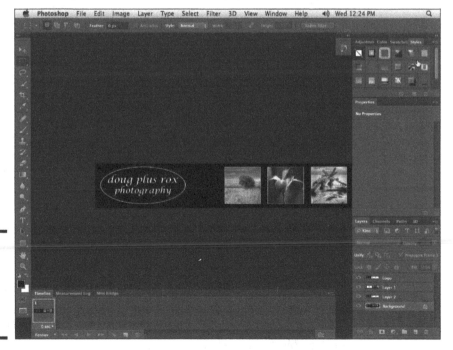

Figure 2-6: Creating web artwork in Photoshop CS6.

Getting images ready for the web with Photoshop

Fireworks is the tool of choice when you're creating graphics for a web page. However, there are still times when you create a document in Photoshop when you need to export different parts of the document with different file formats. For example, if you create a splash page similar to the one in Figure 2-7, you get your best results and the smallest file size when you export the text by using the GIF format, and export the sections with images by using the JPEG format. To get an image ready for the web in Photoshop, follow these steps:

1. **Choose File➪New.**

2. **In the New dialog box that appears, specify the size of the document.**

In most cases, you'll be creating things like banners. Choose Pixels as the unit of measure, and then specify the width and height of the image (see Figure 2-7).

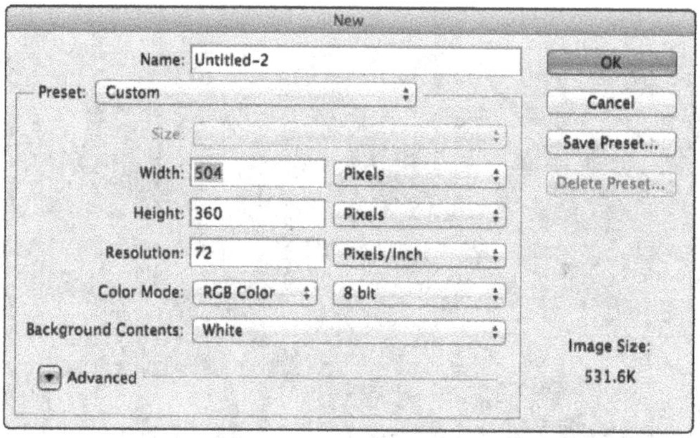

New	
Name: Untitled-2	OK
Preset: Custom	Cancel
Size:	Save Preset...
Width: 504 Pixels	Delete Preset...
Height: 360 Pixels	
Resolution: 72 Pixels/Inch	
Color Mode: RGB Color 8 bit	
Background Contents: White	Image Size:
Advanced	531.6K

Figure 2-7: Creating a document in Photoshop.

3. **Add the objects you need to flesh out the document.**

For example, to add an image, choose File➪Place, and then click inside the document where you want to place the image.

This can involve layers, filters, adjustment layers, as well as adding text.

Mastering Photoshop deserves a book of its own. A good bet is to check out the *For Dummies* series for the one that best fits your needs.

4. **Resize objects as needed.**

a. *Select the object with the Transform tool.*

b. *Choose Edit➪Transform.*

c. *Choose one of the options from the popup menu.* You can scale, rotate, skew, distort, rotate, and so on.

5. **Select the Slice tool.**

   This tool is introverted by nature and shares space with the Crop and Slice Select tool, which is the fifth slot on the toolbar. The last-selected tool appears at the top of the heap. Click the arrow in the lower right of the last-selected tool, and then select the Slice tool from the fly-out menu (see Figure 2-8).

Figure 2-8:
The Slice tool cuts images.

6. **Slice and dice the image as needed.**

   When you first select the Slice tool, the entire image appears as a slice. You then use the tool to select individual layers (see Figure 2-9), and choose export options using the Save for Web command.

Figure 2-9:
Slicing and dicing for the web with the Slice tool.

7. **Continue creating slices as needed.**

   If you're working on a complex image, you might end up with lots of slices. You can select individual slices with the Slice Select tool and then, if needed, resize them by clicking and dragging one of the eight handles that appear around a selected slice. After you slice and dice your image to perfection — which could be a picture of a piece of pizza with pepperoni, say, if you're creating a website for a pizza restaurant — you're ready to save the image, as described in Chapter 3 of this mini-book. This command enables you to use each document slice as an image and also create an HTML file that will assemble them neatly using a table.

Chapter 3: Creating Buttons and Banners

In This Chapter

✓ Creating simple buttons

✓ Creating rollover buttons

✓ From concept to completed page

✓ Optimizing and exporting your Fireworks design

*W*hen you design a website, you create graphics that you use over and over and over and . . . you get the picture. Buttons can range from the mundane to passing-for-sane. In other words, you can have a site with buttons ranging from very utilitarian (you know, functional?) to very cool that are both functional and artistically gorgeous. Buttons are an integral part of your design. This chapter shows you how to create buttons and other graphics for your web design. So roll up your sleeves and get ready for a magical Fireworks tour de force.

Creating Buttons in Fireworks

You have to have navigation for a website. Without navigation, your visitors, looking at the home page, might yawn and say something like, "Is that all there is?" Hopefully not, if you expect to be a web designer for any length of time. It's rare that a client needs a one-page website. When you create a multipage website, you need to provide visitors a way to navigate from page to page. In the old days (before cool applications like Fireworks appeared), navigation menus consisted of underlined text that when clicked, transported the visitor to a related page. Although functional, this method was far from being artistic or compelling. Fortunately, Fireworks makes child's play of creating cool buttons. In Fireworks, you can roll your own, or use button presets.

When you create a button in Fireworks, you create a button symbol and then use the States panel. With it, you can create anything from a simple two-state button to a multistate button used for a navigation menu. Figure 3-1 shows a Fireworks preset button that was imported into the document. Fireworks preset buttons run the gamut from a one-state clickable button that you can modify to a full-fledged, four-state button.

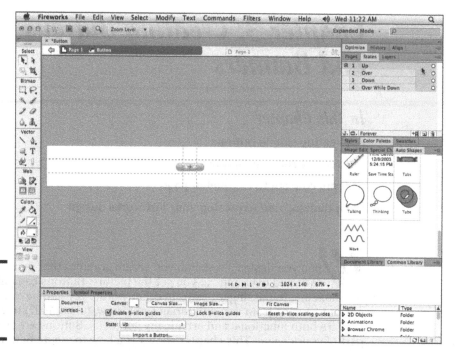

Figure 3-1:
Edit me a
button, my
lovely!

Creating a simple two-state button

The concept of a two-state button is scary, especially if the states are California and Florida. The left coast meets the right coast. Yikes! But we digress. As we mention earlier, a two-state button is the default Fireworks button. You create the graphics and text for *State 1*, which is what the viewer sees when the page initially loads. Then you modify the same graphics for *State 2*, which is what the user sees when hovering the cursor over the button. The different graphics are a dead giveaway that something will happen when the button is clicked. Of course, the site visitor also sees the ubiquitous (default) hand with the pointing finger like he would with a text link, but using different graphics for each button state makes your design much cooler.

Before you can create any button, figure out what size to make it. When you decide to create a website, you do some sort of planning. Whichever method you use, you know how much area you delegated for navigation. If you have only a few links, you can use a horizontal navigation menu. If you have lots of links, though, you need a vertical menu. After you meet with and create a mockup for your client, you should know the title for each button. Your button should be slightly larger than the longest title. With all that figured out, you're ready to create a two-state button as follows:

1. Choose Edit⇨Insert⇨New Button.

The Button Editor appears, with (alas) only guidelines in which to put the button graphics. Your mission, should you decide to accept it, is to populate the button symbol with a shape and text. (See Figure 3-2.)

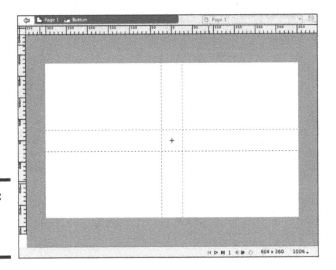

Figure 3-2:
This is the Button Editor.

2. Choose your drawing tool of choice.

The logical choice is the Rectangle tool. If you're creating an oval-shaped button, you can choose the Rectangle tool and then use the Roundness parameter in the Properties Inspector to round the corners of the rectangle.

3. Create a shape with your tool of choice on the document.

4. In the Properties Inspector, specify the width and height of your button and any other parameters, such as stroke color and fill color.

Figure 3-3 shows a button under construction.

5. Center the button.

To center the button, drag the button toward the center of the document until you see a vertical and horizontal crosshair appear in the center of the graphic.

6. Select the Text tool. In the Properties Inspector, specify the parameters for the button text.

Verdana and Arial are both good choices for the font face. Choose a color that's harmonious with your design. The font size depends on the size of your button.

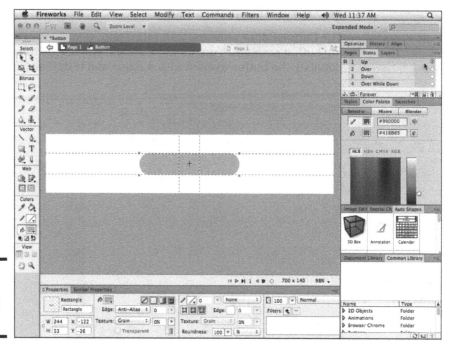

Figure 3-3:
Building
the perfect
button.

Obviously, if you make a small button and try to pack a lot of text on it, the button is hard to read.

7. **Type the desired text on the button.**

8. **Select the text and the button graphic and then choose Window⇨Align.**

   The Align Panel appears (see Figure 3-4).

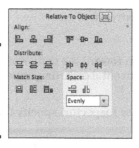

Figure 3-4:
Web
designers
align text,
not wheels.

9. **Align the text to the button by clicking the desired icons.**

   In most instances, you'll want the text aligned to the center of the button, which you can also accomplish by selecting the text with the

Pointer tool and dragging it toward the center of the document until a vertical and horizontal crosshair appear. However, you may want to align the text to the left, right, top, or bottom of the shape. To achieve this result, you use the Align panel.

10. **Choose Select⇨Select All.**

If you're like us and like keyboard shortcuts, just press Ctrl+A (Windows) or ⌘+A (Mac) instead. Selecting everything makes it easy to copy the graphics and text to another state.

11. **Choose Window⇨States.**

The States panel opens in the Panel docker (see Figure 3-5).

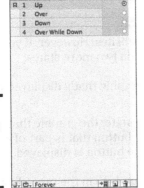

Figure 3-5:
There is not a state of confusion here.

12. **Right-click (Windows) or Control-click (Mac) State 1 to display the contextual menu and then choose Copy to States.**

State 1 is the *Up state* — the state that displays when the page loads.

The Copy to States dialog box shown in Figure 3-6 opens. By default, All States is selected.

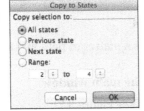

Figure 3-6:
If this dialog box could copy us to another state, we could save lots of gas.

13. **Select the Next State radio button and then click OK.**

You have a carbon copy of the shape and text in State 2, which is the graphic that users see when they pause their mouse over the button.

14. **Select State 2 and then modify or change the graphic you copied from State 1.**

Of course, you could go with a different shape, but that's not practical for a conventional navigation menu button. You modify the button by changing its color and/or the text. For a conventional site, we vote for changing the color of the text.

15. **Click the Back button to return to the main window.**

The button is added to your design.

Creating buttons with pizzazz

Two-state buttons work great for most websites. However, if you want to kick the button up a notch, you can include two more states:

✦ **State 3:** This is the Down state: the graphic that's displayed on the down stroke of a mouse click.

✦ **State 4:** This is the Over While Down state: the graphic that's displayed when a user moves his cursor over a button that is part of a navigation (nav) menu and the page linked to the button is displayed.

To create a multistate button, repeat Steps 1–15 in the preceding steps for creating a simple two-state button, and then continue with these steps:

1. **In the Copy to States dialog box, select the All States radio button and then click OK.**

Right-click State 1 to display the contextual menu and then choose Copy to States.

You have a carbon copy of the shape and text in States 2, 3, and 4.

2. **Select State 2 in the States panel and then modify the graphic.**

As a rule, we change the button and/or text button depending on the site design and the client.

3. **Modify the graphic in States 3 and 4.**

What you do to the shape and text is a matter of personal taste — yours or your client's.

4. **Click the Back button to return to the main window.**

The button is added to your design (see Figure 3-7).

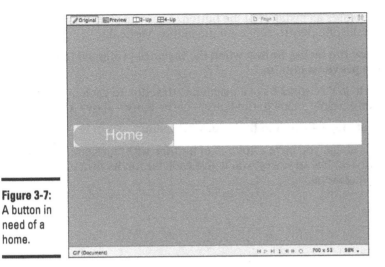

Figure 3-7:
A button in
need of a
home.

Creating a Navigation Menu

A *navigation menu* is nothing but a collection of buttons all lined up neatly horizontally or vertically. In Book VI, Chapter 4, we show you how to insert a navigation menu bar using a Spry widget, which is built into Dreamweaver. But Fireworks is another tool that you can use to create a navigation menu. You do all the grunt work in Fireworks and then add the menu to an HTML document you're creating in Dreamweaver. Talk about your applications that play well with others!

A vertical menu is a good choice when you need lots of menu options that can't be grouped with a drop-down menu. A horizontal menu is the obvious choice when you have a limited number of menu links and want to display them under or with the site banner.

To create a vertical navigation menu, follow these steps:

1. **Create a new document in Fireworks.**

   The document dimensions are the width and height of the area in which the menu appears in your HTML design.

2. **Create a single button.**

   If you fast-forwarded to this section, please rewind to the "Creating Buttons in Fireworks" section of this chapter.

3. **Select the button with the Pointer tool.**

4. **Hold down the Alt key (Windows) or Option key (Mac) and drag down.**

This creates an instance of the button. After you start dragging, hold down the Shift key to constrain the motion vertically.

5. **Release the mouse button when the instance is aligned to the bottom of the previous button.**

   Objects in Fireworks have a magnetic attraction to each other. The button actually snaps to the bottom of the button above it.

6. **Repeat Steps 4 and 5 to flesh out your menu.**

   At this stage, you have a column of buttons with the same title. (See Figure 3-8.) Not to worry; you'll give each button its own identity in the following steps.

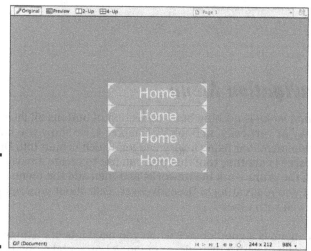

Figure 3-8: Creating instances of the original button.

7. **Select the first button in your menu. If the Properties Inspector isn't already open, choose Window⇨Properties.**

8. **In the Properties Inspector, enter the following parameters:**

   Link: The URL to the page that opens when the button is clicked.

   alt: The alternative text that's displayed in screen readers. alt text is also used by search engines when indexing a site. Certain browsers, such as Internet Explorer, display alt text as a tooltip when a user pauses the cursor over the button.

   Target: The target window in which the linked page appears. In most instances, _top is the proper choice. Your options are

   - _blank: Displays the document in a new and unnamed browser window.

   - _parent: Displays the document in the parent window currently displaying the frame.

- _self: Displays the document in the same window or frame as the link.

- _top: Displays the document in the body of the current window. This option ensures the document called by the form action displays in the full browser window, even if the document was originally displayed in a frame.

Show Down State on Load: Shows the button's Down state when the page to which the button is linked loads.

9. **Select the second button. If the Properties Inspector isn't already open, choose Window⇨Properties.**

   You modify parameters for each button, but you perform one extra step for each button other than those on the home page.

10. **Type the title of the button in the Text field. (See Figure 3-9.)**

    This changes the text that displays on the face of the button.

Figure 3-9:
Change the
button face
text.

11. **Use the Properties Inspector to modify the other parameters of the button.**

12. **Repeat Steps 9–11 for the remaining buttons.**

    The finished menu is shown in Figure 3-10.

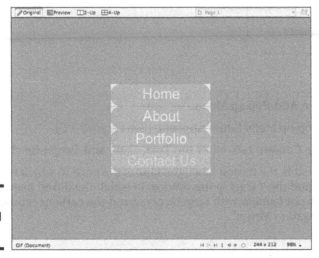

Figure 3-10:
The finished
menu.

You can design horizontal navigation menus in the same manner. Create a document that's the height of your button. The width of the document is the button length multiplied by the number of buttons. After you create the first button, use Alt (Windows) or Option (Mac) to drag the button right while you hold down the Shift key to create an instance of the button.

Creating a Popup Menu

If you have a lot of pages to link to but only a limited amount of space, a popup menu is the obvious choice. A *popup menu,* um, pops up (hence the name) when a site visitor pauses his cursor over the button that triggers the pop-up menu. You might be thinking doomsday thoughts like "JavaScript code," but you'd be only half right. A popup menu created in Fireworks uses JavaScript to create its magic. However, Fireworks writes all the code. To create a popup menu, follow these steps:

1. **Use the Pointer tool to select the button to which the menu will be attached.**

   A white button appears in the middle of the button. This signifies that you can add interactivity to the button. When you create a button, Fireworks creates a slice that conforms to the size of the button. The slice is saved as an image when you export your menu.

2. **Click the white button.**

   A menu appears with a list of interactive behaviors you can add to the button. (See Figure 3-11.)

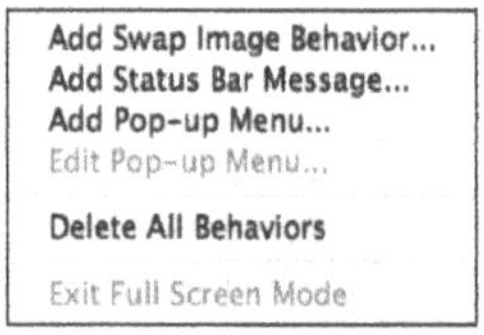

Figure 3-11: Gonna get down, get interactive with the button.

Add Swap Image Behavior...
Add Status Bar Message...
Add Pop-up Menu...
Edit Pop-up Menu...

Delete All Behaviors

Exit Full Screen Mode

3. **Choose Add Pop-up Menu.**

   The Pop-up Menu Editor appears. (See Figure 3-12.)

4. **On the Content tab, enter the Text, Link, and Target for the item.**

   The Text is the button label, the Link is the page to which the button links, and the Target is the window in which the linked page opens. If you're not familiar with targets, check out the earlier section, "Creating a Navigation Menu."

Figure 3-12:
Popups
R us.

5. **Click the plus sign (+) to add another item to the menu.**

   Fireworks adds blank fields for the button's Text, Link, and Target.
   Alternatively, you can press Tab to add another item to the menu.

6. **Repeat Step 4 for this button.**

7. **Continue adding the other items to your popup menu.**

   Figure 3-13 shows a popup menu with several items.

Indent Menu button

Click here to change
the target window.

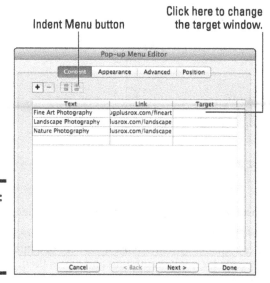

Figure 3-13:
Adding
items to
the popup
menu.

- *To change the order of menu items:* Click an item and then drag it to the desired position.

- *To indent menu items:* Click the Indent Menu button. When you indent menu items, they appear as their own popup menu (or submenu if you prefer) when a visitor pauses the cursor over the parent menu item.

- *To change the target window:* Click inside the Target field (shown in Figure 3-13) and choose one of the following options from the drop-down menu:

  _blank: Opens the link in a new browser window.

  _self: Opens the link in the same frame or window as the link.

  _parent: Opens the link in the parent frameset or window of the frame that contains the link. If the frame containing the link is not nested, the linked file loads into the full browser window.

  _top: Opens the link in the full browser window, thereby removing all frames.

8. **Click Next.**

The Appearance tab of the Pop-up Menu Editor displays. (See Figure 3-14.)

Figure 3-14:
The
Appearance
tab
makes an
appearance.

9. **Specify the parameters for the pop-up menu items' appearance:**

- *Cells:* Select HTML or Image. If you choose HTML, Fireworks creates the code for creating the menu items. If you choose Image, Fireworks creates the images for each menu item and saves them when you export the menu.

- *Menu alignment drop-down menu:* Choose Horizontal Menu or Vertical Menu.

- *Font:* Choose a font set. These are identical to the font options you have in Dreamweaver. The first font is the default. The web browser defaults to the next font face if the default font isn't installed on the user's computer.

- *Font size:* Choose a font size from the drop-down menu.

- *Font style and alignment options:* These are the same options you find in your friendly word-processing application: bold; italic; and left-, center-, or right-align.

- *Up State:* Click the color swatches and choose the color for the cell and text. As a rule, you choose the same colors as the menu to which the popup menu is attached.

- *Over State:* Click the color swatches and choose the color for the cell and text that appear when a visitor pauses the cursor over a menu item.

10. **Click Next.**

The Advanced tab of the Pop-up Menu Editor appears. (See Figure 3-15.)

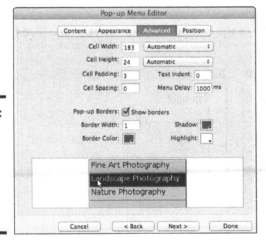

Figure 3-15:
And now for the Advanced properties of your popup menu.

11. **Accept or modify the following parameters:**

- *Cell Width:* Fireworks determines the width based on the menu item with the longest text. To modify the width, choose Pixels from the drop-down menu. This opens the Cell Width text box into which you can enter a value.

- *Cell Height:* Fireworks chooses a height, which can be modified by entering a different value in the Cell Height field. Alternatively, you can choose Automatic from the drop-down menu.

- *Cell Padding:* Accept the default value, or enter a different value. This value determines the area in pixels around the cell text.

- *Text Indent:* Accept the default value (0), or enter an amount by which to indent the text.

- *Cell Spacing:* Accept the default value of 0, or enter a value. If you enter a value, a space appears between each item on your popup menu. We like our menus tight, so we accept the default value of 0.

- *Menu Delay:* This is the amount of time for which the menu appears after a visitor pauses his cursor over the button. If no action is taken within that amount of time, the menu disappears. The default delay is 1000 ms, or 1 second. Enter a different value to increase or decrease menu delay.

- *Pop-up Borders:* The Show Borders check box is selected by default, with a default value of 1. Enter a value to display a bigger border, and then click the applicable color swatches for the border: Shadow, Border Color, and Highlight. This option isn't available if you choose Image on the Appearance tab.

12. **Click Next.**

    The Position tab of the Pop-up Menu Editor appears. (See Figure 3-16.)

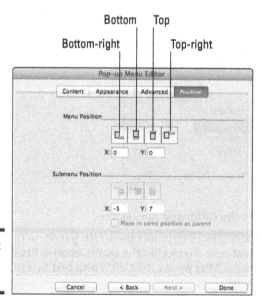

Figure 3-16:
Position is
everything.

13. **Click an icon to align the popup in one of the following configurations: to the bottom-right, bottom, top, or top-right of the slice.**

    After you choose an option, Fireworks inserts values in the X and Y fields. If you want, you can enter different values to further define the positioning of the popup menu. If you have indented menu items, the submenu options appear, which enable you to specify the position of submenus.

14. **Click Done.**

    The popup menu is added to the button.

15. **Choose File➪Preview in Browser and choose the desired browser from the menu list.**

    Your menu appears in the desired browser. (See Figure 3-17.)

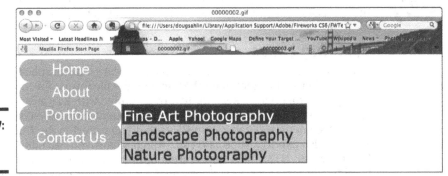

Figure 3-17:
Pop goes
the menu.

Recycling: Reuse Everything

Creating graphics for your web designs is time consuming. When you create something for your own or for a client's site, keep it. Everything you create in Fireworks and save as a PNG file (Fireworks' native file format) is fully editable. For example, if you create a vertical navigation menu in Fireworks, you can change the document size, the size of each button, and the other parameters such as the button text, URL, target window, and so on. If the colors clash with the site where you're going to put them, change the colors. It's a lot easier than creating an item from scratch.

Making a reusable graphic template

Why work harder when you can work smarter? When you create a new web design, you don't have to reinvent the wheel: Just modify it to suit the client. Most designers develop a signature style. If you fall into that category, you can use Fireworks to create templates for the things you use often, such as banners and navigation menus. As we mention, Fireworks documents are saved with the PNG extension. The resulting document is different from the document you get when you save a file using the PNG format in an application like Photoshop. The Fireworks PNG document is fully editable. You can easily use the template for a client's site by doing the following:

✦ **Changing the Canvas size and color in the Properties Inspector**

✦ **Modifying the button color and size by selecting it in the Library, and then double-clicking it to open it in the Button Editor**

If the menu is created using the techniques outlined in the earlier section, "Creating a Navigation Menu," editing the button also changes the color and size of each instance of the button.

✦ **Modifying the text and URL of each button in the Properties Inspector**

Keep a folder of assets that are editable Fireworks and Photoshop files. When you're creating a new site for a client, just pick and choose the assets that you can easily modify to suit the site you're designing.

Creating slices

When you create a *slice* in a Fireworks document, you can specify a specific area in the document and then specify the file format for that slice. For example, if you create a slice for text or a graphic with a large area of solid color, you specify the PNG or GIF format. If you have photorealistic images in the document, you can create slices that you export in the JPEG format. You can also export a slice as HTML, which means you can edit the slice in Dreamweaver. HTML slices are a great option when you create a template and need to add text to a specific portion of a page. Here's how to create a slice:

1. **Select the Slice tool (looks like a knife, and is found in the Web section of the toolbar).**

   The Slice tool is used for creating rectangular slices. You can also create a slice with the Polygonal Slice tool, which makes it possible for you to create a slice around an irregularly shaped area of the document.

2. **Define the size of the slice.**

   If you use the Slice tool, click and drag around the area. If you use the Polygonal Slice tool, click to define the first point, and then click to create a line segment on one side of the slice. Continue adding additional points to define the shape of the slice. After you create a slice, a green overlay appears over the area.

   To create a slice for an existing item in the document, select the object with the Pointer tool, choose Edit➪Insert, and then choose Rectangular Slice or Polygon Slice. After invoking this command, a green overlay appears over the selected object.

3. **To change the size of a slice, select it with the Pointer tool, and then drag a border.**

   When you move your cursor over the border of a slice, a double-headed arrow with parallel lines appears, which is your signal that you can drag the border.

4. **With the slice selected, specify the slice type and export format in the Properties Inspector.**

   You can export a slice as a background image, a foreground image, or HTML.

5. **Continue slicing and dicing until you define every area of the document.**

   If a slice doesn't define an area of the document, Fireworks exports the area using the format you specify for the canvas in the all-powerful Properties Inspector. Figure 3-18 shows a sliced and diced document complete with menu and ready for export.

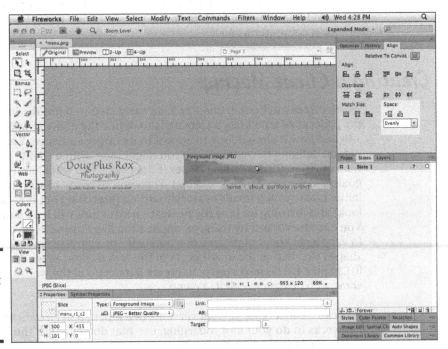

Figure 3-18:
A document sliced and ready for export.

Organizing a site

When you create a single website, you might end up with hundreds of files. Some of them are items supplied by your client that you need to optimize the website. Others are files you create in applications, such as Fireworks and Photoshop. When you deal with that many files, it's definitely in your best interest to be organized. Consider adopting some version of the system we use to organize site assets:

✦ **Client:** This is the main folder for all files pertaining to the website. The folder bears the client's name.

✦ **Client-supplied Assets:** You can lump all assets supplied by the client into this folder. If the assets are of several different types, subdivide the folder keeping all text files in one subfolder, images in another sub-folder, multimedia assets such as video in yet another folder, and so on.

✦ **Assets:** Store all the assets you create in this folder. This folder might also be subdivided. For example, you could keep all Fireworks and Photoshop files in a subfolder named Images, and keep Flash and video content in a folder named Multimedia.

✦ **Site:** This folder contains all the files that you'll upload to the site server. In the main folder, keep all the files that will be in the root folder on the server. Keep a separate folder for images. If the site needs to be subdi-vided into different folders on the server, create those folders on your local computer as well.

Creating a Client Mockup

As we discuss in Book I, Chapter 1, an early step — if not the first one — in the process of a building a website is to define the concept behind the web-site and how it should look to appeal to its target audience. You might be the person defining these things, or you might meet with a client (perhaps more than once) to discuss those issues. Either way, you will identify the site's goals and its general look and feel. Then you're ready to start making the initial plans, which involves storyboarding (sketching out how key pages will look) and drawing up how the navigation structure will look and function. You can storyboard by using an application like Fireworks or by using paper (a very large sheet of paper). In a nutshell, the exercise amounts to creating shapes that define the major parts of the web design, as we discuss in Book II, Chapter 1. The next step is to create a mockup of the website — or, as some web designers call it, a *comp*.

You can easily create several versions of a mockup in Fireworks. If you used Fireworks to do your storyboarding, use that document as the basis for your client mockup. Flesh out the shapes with actual content. If you have assets already created, you can incorporate them into the design. Add link titles to the shapes you created for the navigation menu. Then you're ready to create alternative versions of the mockup. To create alternative versions of your mockup in Fireworks, just follow these steps:

1. **Open the States panel.**

2. **Select the first frame and then click the New/Duplicate State icon.**

Fireworks creates a carbon copy of the first state.

3. **Create a variation of the first state.**

This is the second design you present to the client. You can change how the menu is displayed, placement of objects, choice of colors, and so on.

4. **Create additional states to create different variations of the design.**

5. **After creating different variations of your design, choose File➪Export.**

Fireworks displays the Export dialog box.

6. **Choose the desired file format in which to save the images. Then from the Export drop-down menu, choose States to Files.**

7. **Name the document and then click Save.**

After you export the states, you have multiple files with the same filename, appended by the number of the state. You can now send the individual versions to your client for consideration.

Optimizing Artwork in Fireworks

When you *optimize* artwork in Fireworks, you choose the file format for export and then specify other parameters. The file format in which you export the document depends on the type of artwork you're creating. When you export the document, you specify other parameters, such as the amount of compression applied to a JPEG file or the number of colors and the palette for a GIF image file.

Optimizing GIF artwork

If your design has large areas of solid color and other elements, such as a client logo, the GIF file format is the ideal format in which to optimize your design. Banners and navigation menus are other candidates for the GIF format. To find out more about the GIF format, see Chapter 1 of this mini-book. To optimize an image for export in the GIF format, follow these steps:

1. **Click the 2-Up icon at the top of the document window.**

Fireworks displays two versions of the image: the original and a copy with the current optimization settings applied. Comparing the original with the optimized version lets you decide the best setting for optimizing the document.

The optimized version of the image is what the graphic will export as and also what it will look like on the final website.

2. Choose Window⇨Optimize.

The Optimize panel is displayed. Figure 3-19 shows the document window in 2-Up display and the Optimize panel. The right side of the window displays the image with the current optimization settings applied. Below the image is the file size, number of colors in the palette, and the estimated time to download the file with an Internet connection speed of 56 Kbps.

The Saved Settings menu

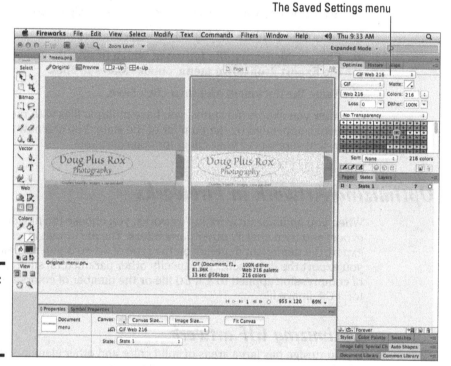

Figure 3-19: Please optimize me — set me free.

3. Choose a preset from the Saved Settings drop-down menu (in the upper right of Figure 3-19).

Preview each setting and pay attention to the right pane of the document window. Choose the preset that's the best compromise between image quality and file size. Your choices are

- *PNG 32:* Gives you the option to export as: PNG, which is an 8-bit image (256 colors) similar to the GIF format; PNG 24, which is a 2-bit image (16.8 million colors); or PNG 32, which has alpha transparency. The last two PNG formats are for photorealistic images.

- *JPEG – Better Quality:* Gives you the option to export as a high-quality JPEG. Use this option for large images or slices where image quality is a deciding factor.

- *JPEG – Smaller File:* Gives you the option to export using the JPEG format and achieving a smaller file size. Image quality suffers when you use this option. We recommend that you use this option only on small slices of the document.

- *GIF Web 216:* Converts all colors to web-safe colors. The color palette contains up to 216 colors.

  Read all about web-safe colors in Chapter 1 of this minibook.

- *GIF WebSnap 256:* Converts non–web-safe colors to their closest web-safe colors, creating a color palette that contains up to a maximum of 256 colors.

- *GIF WebSnap 128:* Converts non–web-safe colors to their closest web-safe colors creating a color palette that contains up to 128 colors.

- *GIF Adaptive 256:* This color palette contains only the actual colors used in the document up to a maximum of 256 colors.

4. **Modify the preset to suit your document.**

   At this stage, if you're exporting a slice or document in the GIF format, you can experiment with reducing the number of colors in the Indexed palette. You can either enter a value in the Colors text field or choose a preset from the Colors drop-down menu. If you notice image degradation, you went too far. When this occurs, choose the next highest value from the Colors menu.

   Make sure you have image magnification set at 100 percent so you see the pixels at their actual size.

5. **If desired, save the modified preset.**

   To save a preset with the current settings, click the icon in the upper-left corner of the Optimize panel and then choose Save Settings from the drop-down menu (see Figure 3-19). After you click Save Settings, a dialog box appears prompting you for a name for the setting. Choose a logical name that reflects what the preset does, or the number of colors and the file format. For example, if you're saving a preset for the GIF format with 32 colors based on Web Adaptive, a logical choice would be GIF Websnap 32.

To export an image with transparency, follow these steps:

1. **Choose Index Transparency from the Transparency drop-down menu.**

   The default is No Transparency, as shown in Figure 3-19. When you choose a transparent color, the background of the HTML document shows through. This is a useful option when you have an image as a background on the HTML page on which the graphic will appear.

2. **Click the Select Transparent Color eyedropper and click inside the document to sample the transparent color.**

   Fireworks displays the transparent area as a checkerboard in the right pane of the document pane when displayed in 2-Up mode. (See Figure 3-20.)

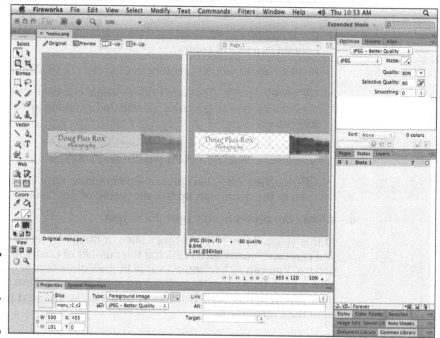

Figure 3-20:
Now you
see me; now
you don't.

3. **You can modify the transparent colors as follows:**

   • Click the Add Color to Transparency eyedropper. Then, inside the right pane of the 2-Up window, click the color you want to be transparent.

   • Select the Remove Color from Transparency eyedropper. Then, inside the right pane of the 2-Up window, click a transparent area. The associated color will no longer be transparent.

You can also find the option for Alpha Transparency, which is only supported by images optimized in the PNG format — and is not widely used by web designers.

Optimizing JPEG artwork

The JPEG format is best suited for artwork that is photorealistic in nature. The JPEG format compresses the file by losing color data; therefore, JPEG is known as a *lossy* format. Your goal is to export the image at the smallest possible file size without noticeable degradation. To optimize a document using the JPEG format, follow these steps:

1. **Click the 2-Up icon at the top of the document window.**

   Fireworks displays two versions of the image: the original and a copy with the current optimization settings applied. Comparing the original with the optimized version lets you determine the best setting for optimizing the document.

2. **Choose Window⇨Optimize.**

   The Optimize panel is displayed. When you optimize a document, you can click the 2-Up button to display two versions of the image. The right side of the window displays the image with the current optimization settings applied, and the left side shows the original image. Below the image is the file size, number of colors in the palette, and the estimated time to download the file with an Internet connection speed of 56 Kbps.

   Make sure you have image magnification set at 100 percent so you see the pixels at their actual size.

3. **Choose an option from the Saved Presets drop-down menu.**

   We recommend starting with the JPEG-Better Quality option. The theory is to start with a high quality and apply compression until noticeable degradation occurs.

4. **Gradually apply more compression to the image by specifying a lower image quality.**

   You can enter a value in the Quality text box or drag the Quality slider. When you see noticeable degradation in the image, gradually bump up the image quality until the end result looks good to you.

If you have to apply heavy levels of compression to get the desired file size, choose an option from the Smoothing drop-down menu in the Optimize panel to smooth out the jagged edges caused by heavy compression.

Optimizing PNG Artwork in Fireworks

PNG browser support first appeared in Internet Explorer 4.0, which is sometime during the Jurassic period of the Internet. The PNG format supports 8-bit (PNG-8), 24-bit (PNG-24), and 32-bit (PNG-32) files. The PNG format offers index and alpha transparency. When you optimize a PNG-8 image and specify Index Transparency, you can specify only one color as transparent, which may cause artifacts around the object that you want to display through the transparency. Alpha transparency combines the image color you choose to be transparent with the background, which effectively eliminates any artifacts, such as jagged edges.

PNG-8 is a good option for documents or images with large areas of solid color. This is an 8-bit file format, which means that the images are exported with a maximum of 256 colors. PNG-8 supports transparency. The file size is similar to the GIF format. PNG supports index, matte, and alpha transparency. With the exception of very small images, PNG produces slightly smaller files than GIF images.

Beware of using PNG-8 to optimize documents that contain graphics with gradients because the gradients will show banding due to the limited color palette.

PNG-24 is an ideal option for photorealistic images. It supports 16 million colors. Like PNG-8, this format works well for areas of solid color and is ideal for documents with gradients. Because of the additional information, the file size is considerably larger than PNG-8.

PNG-32 is also an ideal choice for photorealistic images and supports alpha transparency, which works well when you need areas of the image to be transparent and let the background image or color show through.

The optimization process is identical to optimizing a GIF image or slice (see "Optimizing GIF artwork") except that you choose PNG-32 as the export default and then choose PNG-8, PNG-24, or PNG-32 as the export option. The PNG-8 dialog box is identical to the GIF dialog box. The PNG-24 and PNG-32 dialog boxes have a matte option, which enables you to choose the transparent color.

Exporting Artwork from Fireworks

After you optimize the image, it's time to export it from Fireworks. Exporting images is fairly straightforward; choose File➪Export and then specify the folder in which to save the image. When you export a document like a navigation menu with multiple slices, you export the document as images and HTML as follows:

1. **Choose File➪Export.**

The Export dialog box appears.

2. **Choose HTML and Images from the Export drop-down menu.**

This option exports the document as an HTML file with all the code necessary to reassemble the exported images, create links for navigation menus, and so on. Alternatively, you can export a Fireworks document as CSS and Images, in which case you'll get an HTML document, a CSS (cascading style sheet) document, and images.

When exporting a JPEG image, choose Images Only. Typically, this is selected by default when you're exporting an image without slices or *hotspots* (areas that support interactivity, such as image swapping or a popup menu).

3. **Choose Export HTML File from the HTML drop-down menu.**

   Your alternative is to copy the HTML code to the Clipboard.

4. **Select the Include Areas without Slices check box.**

   This exports the areas of your document, such as the background, that has not been designated as a slice.

5. **Click the Put Images in Subfolder option.**

   This helps keep your files neat and tidy. By default, Fireworks creates a folder named Images. You can specify another folder by clicking the Browse button and then navigating to the desired folder.

6. **Click Save.**

   Fireworks exports the document (as an HTML file) and images to the specified folders.

Creating Banner Graphics

Banners are proudly displayed at the top of just about every website you visit. The banner often incorporates the client's marketing tools, such as the company logo. When you create a banner for a site, you use the company logo and a color scheme that's harmonious with your client's logo. If your client doesn't have a logo, you use your own sense of design to create the logo using the site color palette. Read more about all these baseline considerations in Chapter 1 of this minibook.

Using Photoshop to create a banner

You can create a banner in just about any image-editing application that enables you to create a document from scratch. Photoshop, however, gives you the power to augment your creativity with its rich feature set. Photoshop ships with a set of Adobe Pro fonts that give you the capability to create a very unique banner.

When you design a banner, your first consideration is size. Your client's logo — if she has one — is nestled in the design. Therefore, the banner must be tall enough to prominently display the logo. Fortunately, most professionally designed logos look good in sizes from the sublimely small (the customer's letterhead) to the ridiculously large (a billboard ad). If the client's logo already has text, the logo and a harmonious background color are all you need. If the client logo displays only an artistic arrangement of the client's initials, you have to add text. As a rule, centering banners and site content is preferable.

When you decide on the size for your banner, you must take into account the amount of available monitor real estate for the desktop size of your client's intended audience. A good practice is to optimize web graphics for the lowest common denominator, which is currently 1024 x 768 pixels. In order to keep all your content above the *fold* (the area of a web page that can be seen without scrolling down), you have to deal with an area of 955 x 600 pixels, which is all you have left after browser toolbars, menus, scroll bars, and so on. Therefore, the maximum size of any banner you create should be 900 x 120 pixels. This leaves you room for a navigation menu, images, and text.

Including all the important information

The size of your banner is determined by the amount of information that your client wants to display. Sometimes your client goes over the top and asks you to include everything but the kitchen sink: for example, the name of the company, address, phone number, website URL, and so on. That's simply way too much information, and why most websites include a Contact Us page. In reality, all a banner needs are the following elements:

✦ **Client logo:** If your client has a logo, it should be displayed prominently on the banner. Logos aligned to the left side of the banner look good.

✦ **Company name:** If the client's logo doesn't display the company name, add the company name to the banner. If you're designing a banner for a client who doesn't have a logo, center the company name or website name on the banner. When designing a banner for a client with a logo that doesn't feature the company name, display the logo on the left with the company name immediately following. Leave enough space so that the banner doesn't look cluttered.

✦ **Tag line:** If the company has a tag line, display it below the company name. A *tag line* is a sentence usually less than ten words that describes what the company does. For example, the tag line for Doug's Doug Plus Rox Photography company pages is: "Creating beautiful images is our passion." If the client has a logo with a company name, the tag line is displayed to the right of the logo, centered vertically. If the company has a logo without a company name, the tag line is centered below the company name. The logo is sized to fill the height of the banner.

Working with an existing logo

When you design a banner — or, for that matter, a website — your client's logo plays an important part in the overall design. If the logo is well designed, you can incorporate elements from the logo into your design. The banner and the website should include colors from the client's logo. The screenshot on the left in Figure 3-21 shows a logo being incorporated into a banner design in Photoshop; on the right is the banner being incorporated with the web design.

Figure 3-21: Incorpo-rating an existing logo into a web design.

Complement your style

When you design promotional material to promote a business that's driven by a website, the style of the promotional material should be similar to the style of the website. The printed material should look as though it were pulled right from the web design. Fortunately, this is a fairly easy task if you design the graphic elements of your website using the Adobe Creative Suite, which as of this writing is Version 6, or CS6. This powerhouse application enables the same elements you designed for the website in Photoshop to be used in other applications — such as Adobe InDesign (page layout applica-tion) or Adobe Illustrator.

All applications hinge around Adobe Bridge, which is available from InDesign, Illustrator, and Photoshop. Adobe Bridge enables you to choose saved items and open them in their host application. You can then modify the item for the application in which you'll use it. For example, you can resize a photo for use in a poster you're creating in Adobe Illustrator or for use in a brochure you're creating in InDesign. This capability to quickly access assets designed for the website in other applications lets you create printed material with the same style as your website.

Adobe Bridge is an integral part of your workflow if you use the Adobe Creative Suite to create other materials for the client. You can use Bridge to organize the assets of your project. If the client sends you high-resolution images, you store the originals in one folder and the materials that are opti-mized for the web in a different folder. You can create folders using Bridge.

After you organize your assets in Bridge, you're ready to bridge the gap to other applications in the Creative Suite. For example, you can use InDesign CS6 to create brochures and folders to compliment the website. The InDesign Place command (File➪Place) places the image in the design. The Place command is very powerful because it allows you to shrink the original image to fit into a specific portion of your design. If you later decide to increase the size of the image, you can do so with no degradation. When you lay out a brochure using InDesign, you can take advantage of the powerful Text Wrap panel to wrap text around images in the design. (For all the ins and outs of using InDesign, check out *InDesign CS6 For Dummies* by Galen Gruman, Wiley.)

Creating Fast-Loading, Beautiful Photos

Photos are an integral part of any website. The trick is to display photos that look great and load quickly. You can always tell when you're at a site that wasn't created by a professional designer because the images are either huge and load slowly, or they load quickly but look bad. The next few sections show you how to resize and then optimize your images for the web.

Resizing your photos for the web

If you're working with images supplied by your client or images from a clip art disk, chances are that you're dealing with high-resolution images suitable for print. High-resolution images have large file sizes. The combination is totally unsuitable for display on a website. Granted, you can control the size at which the image is displayed by entering the desired width and height in the `<img>` tag. The file size is still the same, though, and the image will load slowly.

Images for the web need a resolution of 72 pixels per inch (ppi). Some designers insist on 96 ppi, but this is more than you need. Images with a resolution of 72 ppi are sufficient for all modern computer monitors. Images for print have a resolution of 150 ppi or greater.

In addition to resolution, your next concern is image size. The size of the image is determined by where the image will reside. If you're posting the image inline with text, you size the image smaller than you would size an image for a photographer's gallery. Also consider the desktop size of your audience. Keep in mind that many people are still surfing the 'Net with an 1024 x 768 pixel (px) desktop size, which (with a maximized browser) has an available display area of 955 x 600 px. If you resize an image with *portrait orientation* (an image that's taller than it is wide) to 800 px in height, people with an 1024 x 768 desktop size will have to scroll to see the entire image. When you resize images for inline display, a good practice is to never exceed 300 pixels in width or height.

If the image is displayed as a *splash image* (the main image on a page) on a home page or in an image gallery, we recommend never exceeding an area of 600 x 360 px. Granted, this gives the advantage to *landscape* (wider than tall) images, but the available display area in a web browser is also wider than it is tall. You can resize images by using Fireworks or Photoshop CS6, as shown in the following steps.

To resize images in Fireworks, follow these steps:

1. Choose Modify⇨Canvas⇨Image Size.

The Image Size dialog box (see Figure 3-22) appears.

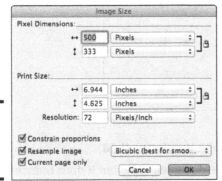

Figure 3-22:
Resizing an image in Fireworks.

2. Enter a value of 72 in the Resolution field.

This doesn't change the print size, but it does reduce the pixel dimensions of the image.

3. Enter the desired width or height in the Pixel Dimensions section.

You can enter either value because the option to constrain proportions is selected by default. We advise that you always keep the Constrain Proportions check box selected because otherwise, the image will be distorted.

Downsizing (reducing in size) an image is okay, but when you try to *upsize* (enlarge) a small image, you're asking the image-editing application to increase the size of each pixel in the document. Image degradation is the unhappy result of trying to upsize an image.

4. Click OK.

Fireworks resizes the image to the desired dimensions.

To resize an image in Photoshop, follow these steps:

1. **Choose Image⇨Image Size.**

   The Image Size dialog box (see Figure 3-23) appears.

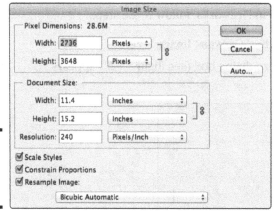

Figure 3-23:
Resizing an
image in
Photoshop.

2. **Enter a value of 72 in the Resolution field.**

   This doesn't change the document size, but it does reduce the pixel dimensions of the image.

3. **Enter the desired width or height in the Pixel Dimensions section.**

   You can enter either value because the option to constrain proportions is selected by default. We advise that you never deselect the Constrain Proportions check box because the image will be distorted.

4. **Click OK.**

   Photoshop resizes the image.

Using professional optimization techniques

As long as you begin with a high-quality image, you can resize and optimize a photo for the web in Adobe Photoshop or Fireworks. Optimizing an image in Fireworks is covered in an earlier section of this chapter. Photoshop CS6 also has a stout optimization algorithm. You can optimize images in GIF or JPEG format.

Using the Photoshop Save for Web & Devices command

Photoshop CS6 gives you all the tools you need to create pixel-perfect images for print as well as for the web. The web has different considerations, though. First and foremost, you must choose the right file format. The next step is to optimize the image — or, if you've used the Slice tool, optimize each slice.

Optimizing for JPEG

To optimize JPEG images you created in Photoshop CS6 for the web, follow these steps:

1. **Choose File⇨Save for Web.**

2. **In the Save for Web & Devices dialog box that appears, click the 2-Up tab.**

This option enables you to compare the original image with the optimized version (see Figure 3-24).

Figure 3-24: Optimizing is so easy when you use the Save for Web & Devices command.

3. **Select the Slice Select tool.**

   The tool allows you to select individual slices in the image and apply different optimization settings to each slice. Steps 3 and 4 are necessary only if you created slices in the image and intend to use different optimization settings for each slice.

4. **In the optimized section (the bottom or right section when you're viewing the image in 2-Up mode), click the slice you want to optimize.**

5. **Choose the desired optimization setting from the Optimized File Format drop-down menu (see Figure 3-25).**

   For the first slice of this image (which is text and a circle), the ideal format is GIF, which is ideal for areas of an image that have large areas of solid color. We show you everything you need to know about optimizing GIF artwork in Photoshop in the next section. For more information on file formats, see Chapter 1 of this minibook.

6. **To optimize an image using the JPEG format, choose JPEG from the Optimized File Format drop-down menu.**

Optimized File Format menu

Figure 3-25: Choose the desired optimization method.

When you choose JPEG, the options shown in Figure 3-26 appear. The default JPEG setting is Maximum when you create an image from scratch in Photoshop; and the Quality is 100 percent, which results in a squeaky-clean-looking image but the file size is way too big for a website. You can modify the Quality setting and other applicable settings as outlined in the next step.

Figure 3-26:
Optimizing
an image,
using the
JPEG
format.

7. **Modify the following parameters if desired:**

    Quality: Enter a value or click the arrow and drag the scrubby slider. Higher values apply less compression, resulting in a better-looking image albeit at the expense of a larger file size. Lower values apply higher compression, resulting in a smaller file size with poorer image quality. You can tell the optimal setting for an image by comparing the original in the left pane if your image is portrait, or in the bottom pane if your image is landscape (as shown in Figure 3-26), with the compressed version in the right pane. When image degradation is noticeable, specify a higher value.

    Progressive: Downloads the image into the user's browser in multiple passes. This option enables the visitor to see a low-resolution version of the image as soon as the page loads. The optimized version appears when the image finishes loading. Use this option for large images, or if your intended audience accesses the Internet with a slow connection.

Optimize: Optimizes the color palette in the image to the degree of compression applied. This option results in better color fidelity.

Blur: If you have to apply heavy compression to achieve the desired file size, enter a value or drag the Blur scrubby slider to blur the image and minimize the appearance of jagged edges.

Matte: Specifies a color to fill pixels that were transparent in the original image. Choose an option from the Matte drop-down menu. Your choices are

- *None:* Choose this option when you don't want to specify a matte color.

- *Eyedropper:* Choose this option, and then click the Matte Color Swatch below the Eyedropper tool on the left side of the dialog box to choose the fill color from the Color Picker.

- *Foreground Color:* Choose this option, and the current foreground color becomes the matte color.

- *Background Color:* Choose this option, and the current background color becomes the matte color.

- *White:* Fill transparent pixels with white.

- *Black:* Fill transparent pixels with black.

- *Other:* With this, you can select a matte color from the Color Picker.

Embed Color Profile: Embeds the current color profile with the saved file. We recommend against using this option; leave it unchecked and use the Convert to sRGB option described in the next step. If the current color profile is anything other than sRGB and you embed it, the image won't display properly on a computer monitor.

8. **Make sure you leave the Convert to sRGB option enabled.**

   If your image was captured from a digital camera using the Adobe RGB color profile, or if you converted the image to the Adobe RGB color profile, you definitely need to have the resulting image converted to sRGB because the Adobe RGB color profile cannot accurately be displayed outside Photoshop CS6, whereas the amount of colors in the sRGB color profile can be displayed accurately when displayed on a web browser.

9. **Choose an option from the Preview drop-down menu.**

   Your choices are Monitor Color, Macintosh (No Color Management), Windows (No Color Management), or Use Document Profile. In most cases, the default Monitor Color options works best.

10. **Choose an option from the Metadata drop-down menu.**

   Your options are None, Copyright, Copyright and Contact Info, All Except Camera Info, or All. Digital cameras add *metadata* to an image when a picture is taken. The information includes the camera make and model, exposure information, and so on. The photographer might have also added copyright and contact info in Photoshop, Photoshop Lightroom, or a similar image-editing application. If the image was supplied by a photographer, leave his contact and copyright image with the optimized image. Adding the camera data isn't necessary, though.

11. Choose the desired options in the Image Size section.

You can resize the image proportionately by entering a value in the W or H text fields. We don't advise clicking the link icon, which makes it possible to resize only the width and not the height, or vice versa. This distorts the image. You can also resize the image by changing the value in the Percent text field or by dragging the Percent scrubby slider. If you resize the image, you can choose an option from the Quality menu. In most cases, the Bicubic option works well.

12. Click Save.

The Save Optimized As dialog box appears.

13. Choose the desired option from the Save As Type drop-down menu.

If you're saving an image for a banner, accept the default Images Only option. If you sliced the image, choose HTML and Images to save an HTML file and image files in the specified file formats.

Optimizing for GIF

To optimize GIF images in Photoshop CS6, follow these steps:

1. Choose File⇨Save for Web & Devices.

The Save for Web & Devices dialog box appears.

2. Select an option from the Preset drop-down menu.

Your choices are GIF Dithered; GIF No Dither with a palette of 128, 64, or 32 colors; or GIF Restrictive.

Dithering mixes colors from the web-safe palette to approximate a color that is not in the web-safe palette.

If you created your design using colors from the web-safe palette, choose one of the No Dither options. Choose one of the Dithered options to export the image with web-safe colors. Any non–web-safe colors in your design are mixed (dithered) using colors from the web-safe palette. GIF Restrictive pulls colors from the web-safe, 216-color palette. Figure 3-27 shows the Save for Web & Devices dialog box after choosing the GIF 128 No Dither preset.

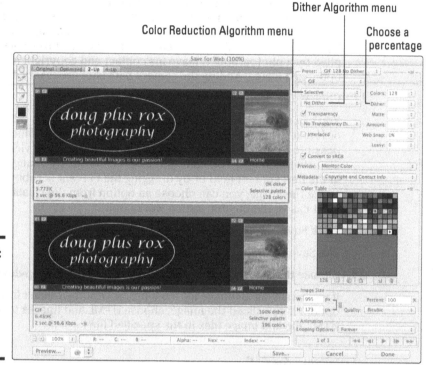

Figure 3-27: Optimizing an image using the GIF 128 No Dither option.

3. **Select an option from the Color Reduction Algorithm drop-down menu.**

The Color Reduction Algorithm determines the method by which the colors for the image palette are created. Your choices are

- *Perceptual:* This creates a color table by giving priority to colors for which the human eye has greater sensitivity.

- *Selective:* The default option creates a color table similar to that created by using the Perceptual algorithm, but it preserves large areas of color in the original image and also web-safe colors. This algorithm creates a color palette that closely resembles the original image.

- *Adaptive:* This creates a color table using the predominant color spectrum in the image. If you're optimizing an image that's predominantly red and orange, the color table is made up primarily of reds and oranges. Choose this algorithm if the image you're optimizing is made up of similar color hues.

- *Restrictive:* This creates a color palette using colors from the web-safe, 216-color palette.

- *Custom:* This creates a color palette that you create or modify. If you open a previously saved GIF or PNG-8 file, it will have a custom color palette.

- *Black - White:* This creates a color palette comprising black and white. Use this algorithm to save images that will be displayed on PDAs (personal digital assistants) that can't display color.

- *Grayscale:* Creates a color palette comprising 256 shades of gray from solid black to white. This is similar to how black-and-white film photos display.

- *MAC OS:* Creates a color palette based on the colors from the Mac operating system (OS) color palette.

- *Windows:* Creates a color palette based on the colors from the Windows OS color palette.

4. **Modify the number of colors in the palette.**

   You can modify the number of colors by choosing an option from the drop-down menu. When you change the number of colors, you see the results in the Color Table. When you reduce the number of colors in the palette, pay careful attention to the optimized image. If you specify a color palette that doesn't have enough colors, image degradation occurs. If this is the case, choose a higher value that doesn't result in image degradation.

5. **Choose an option from the Dither Algorithm drop-down menu.**

   Dithering creates a facsimile of colors in the image but not in the palette by mixing colors in the palette. Your choices are as follows:

   - *No Dither:* The default option uses image colors, which is fine when the image you're optimizing has only a few colors.

   - *Diffusion:* Dithers by creating a random pattern that, in most cases, is less noticeable than Pattern dither. Dithering is diffused across adjacent pixels.

   - *Pattern:* Dithers by creating a pattern that looks like halftone squares to simulate image colors not in the color table.

   - *Noise:* Dithers by creating a random pattern similar to the Diffusion method, but the pattern is not diffused across adjacent pixels. Seams don't show if you use this dithering method.

6. **Specify a Dither value.**

   This option determines the percentage of colors that are dithered. A higher value gives you greater detail at the expense of a higher file size.

Drag the slider to 100% and then to the left until you notice image degradation in the bottom pane of the dialog box, and then drag the slider to the right until the image looks better. This will be the optimal dithering value for the image you're optimizing.

7. **Transparency is selected by default. Deselect this option if you don't want to optimize the image with areas of transparency.**

   Transparency is used when you want areas of the image to be transparent. This option is most often used when you want areas of a tiled background image to show through the image you're optimizing. However, even though transparency is enabled by default, you have to choose the transparent colors by specifying Matte and Transparency colors.

8. **If desired, choose an option from the Transparency menu.**

   You have the following options:

   - *No Transparency Dither:* Doesn't apply dithering to partially transparent pixels in the image.

   - *Diffusion Transparency Dither:* Dithers by applying a random pattern that is, in most cases, less noticeable than Pattern dither. Dithering is diffused across adjacent pixels. When selecting this option, specify a Dither percentage to control the amount of dithering applied to the image.

   - *Pattern Transparency Dither:* Dithers by applying a halftone-like square pattern to partially transparent pixels.

   - *Noise Transparency Dither:* Dithers by applying a random pattern similar to the Diffusion color-reduction algorithm, but the pattern isn't diffused across adjacent pixels. Seams don't show if you use this dithering method.

9. **If the Amount option becomes available — which it will if you select Diffusion Transparency Dither — drag the slider to specify the percentage of dithering applied to the image.** Alternatively, you can enter a value in the text field.

10. **Select the Interlaced option to download the image in stages.**

    This option displays a low-resolution version of the image when the page loads. The fully optimized version is revealed when the image loads completely.

11. **Specify the Web Snap value.**

    This option determines the amount of non–web-safe colors that are shifted to web-safe colors. Choosing a higher value snaps more colors from the original image to the nearest web-safe counterpart.

12. Drag the Lossy slider to reduce file size.

This option discards color data to reduce file size. If you use this option, pay careful attention to the image in the right pane of the Save for Web & Devices dialog box. When the image begins to degrade, drag the slider to the left until you no longer see the degradation.

You can't use the Lossy option if you use the Interlaced option, or with the Noise or Pattern Dither option.

13. Make sure you leave the Convert to sRGB option enabled.

This is the optimal color profile for monitor viewing. If you don't convert to sRGB, the original color profile may contain colors that can't be displayed accurately on a computer monitor.

14. Choose an option from the Preview drop-down menu.

Your choices are Monitor Color, Macintosh (No Color Management), Windows (No Color Management), or Use Document Profile. In most cases, the default Monitor Color option works best.

15. Choose an option from the Metadata drop-down menu.

Your options are None, Copyright, Copyright and Contact Info, All Except Camera Info, or All. Digital cameras add metadata to an image when a picture is taken. The information includes the camera make and model, exposure information, and so on. The photographer might have also added copyright and contact info in Photoshop, Photoshop Lightroom, or a similar image-editing application. If a photographer supplied the image, leave his contact and copyright image with the optimized image. Adding the camera data isn't necessary.

16. Choose the desired options in the Image Size section.

You can resize the image proportionately by entering a value in the W or H text fields. We don't advise clicking the link icon, which makes it possible to resize the width and not the height, or vice versa. This distorts the image. You can also resize the image by changing the value in the Percent text field or by dragging the Percent scrubby slider. If you resize the image, you can choose an option from the Quality menu. In most cases, the Bicubic option works well.

17. Click Save.

The Save Optimized As dialog box appears.

18. Choose the desired option from the Save as Type drop-down menu.

If you're saving an image for a banner, accept the default Images Only option. If you sliced the image, choose HTML and Images to save an HTML file and image files in the specified file formats.

19. **Click Save.**

Photoshop saves the image in the GIF format using the options specified.

The Color Table at the bottom of the dialog box shows swatches of the colors that make up the image color palette. You can modify the palette by adding colors to the palette, snapping colors to the nearest web-safe color, and defining transparent pixels.

Chapter 4: Creating Audio and Video Content

In This Chapter

✔ Discovering audio formats for the web

✔ Encoding audio

✔ Encoding video

✔ Audio tips and tricks

Some people think that websites are just pretty pictures and text. That's all changed, though. You can add sound to a website without breaking a sweat. When you add sound in a web-friendly format to a website, the sound streams into the user's browser. Video is another option for savvy web designers. If a picture is worth a thousand words, a video must be worth at least a million. Before HTML5 arrived on the scene, you had to jump through quite a few hoops to play video in an HTML document. With HTML5, though, you have to worry about only two file formats, and a wee bit of code to display video on a web page. In this chapter, we show you a thing or two about sound and video.

Note: HTML5 is not compliant with older browsers. However, we do offer a thrifty solution for incorporating good-quality video in the websites you design. After reading this chapter, you can create websites that can be seen — and heard.

Exploring Audio Formats for the Web

Audio for websites is saved in formats that enable the sound to stream into the visitor's browser. Streaming sound is similar to an interlaced picture that loads in stages. With streaming sound, the sound begins as soon as enough of it downloads into the user's browser to play without interruption.

With the advent of HTML5, which is supported by most modern web browsers, you don't have to fiddle with a gazillion audio formats like you did in the Jurassic era of web design. The following sections explore video formats that are compatible with HTML5 browsers. The following is a list of audio file formats that are supported by HTML5:

✦ **AAC:** Advanced Audio Coding (AAC) format is the same format used by Apple's iTunes software. It's a *lossy* format, which means that data is lost when the file is compressed. The standard data rate for music encoded with iTunes is 128 kbps (kilobytes per second), which is acceptable for devices like the iPod and an Internet website, yet it is far from audiophile status. With a fast Internet connection, higher data rates can be played with no streaming issues.

To err on the side of caution, we recommend that you encode at lower data rates for the spoken word and don't exceed 128 kbps for music.

✦ **Ogg Vorbis:** This format is the combination of the Vorbis audio compression codec commonly associated with the Ogg *container,* or "player," if you will. The codec is a lossy codec and is suitable for the spoken word. A *codec* compresses video when it's encoded for the web, and the player compatible with the video format decompresses it for playback.

✦ **MP3:** The MP3 audio format is a derivative of the MPEG video format. The MP3 sound format combines excellent fidelity with relatively small file sizes and is the favorite format for audio podcasts. The sound quality depends on the data rate at which the audio file is compressed and played back. When using a higher data rate, the format is suitable for music.

Browser support varies for playing music files embedded into an HTML5 document. Table 4-1 shows browser support for digital audio formats.

Copyright issues

The person who creates a recording (or the recording company) owns the copyright for any original material on the recording. If you use a copyrighted song or recording on a website you're designing, you are in violation of the copyright laws. You might be able to obtain a license from the copyright owner. Another option is to obtain royalty-free songs or recordings. You can find these by typing **royalty-free recordings or royalty free music** in your favorite search engine. Some office supply stores sell royalty-free music collections. Or, if you're the really adventurous and artistic type, you can create your own background sounds using a program such as ACID Pro (Windows; `www.sonycreativesoftware.com/acidpro`) or GarageBand (Mac; `www.apple.com/ilife/garageband`). Both applications enable you to create music by mixing and matching royalty-free music loops.

Table 4-1	Browser Support for Embedding Audio formats in HTML5 Documents	
Browser	*File Format*	*Supported*
Safari 5.1	AAC	Yes
Safari 5.1	Ogg Vorbis	No
Safari 4.1	MP3	Yes
Firefox 8 and 9	AAC	No
Firefox 8 and 9	Ogg Vorbis	Yes
Firefox 8 and 9	MP3	No
Opera 11.1	AAC	No
Opera 11.1	Ogg Vorbis	Yes
Opera 11.1	MP3	No
Chrome 15 and 17	AAC	Yes
Chrome 15 and 17	Ogg Vorbis	Yes
Chrome 15 and 17	MP3	Yes
IE 6, 7, and 8	AAC	No
IE 6, 7, and 8	Ogg Vorbis	No
IE 6, 7, and 8	MP3	No
IE 9	AAC	Yes
IE 9	Ogg Vorbis	No
IE 9	MP3	Yes

HTML5 is powerful, yet it's still in its infantile stage. Browser support will be more robust as time goes on. However, to support all possible browsers, you need to use Adobe Audition (Windows only) or Adobe Soundbooth to export the audio formats that are supported by the browsers used by the target audience for the website you're creating. We show you how to use JavaScript to redirect the user to a different iteration of a web page. In Book VI, we show you how to use JavaScript to create interactive pages.

Embedding Audio Files in an HTML5 Document

When you want to add audio to a web page, you don't have to jump through a bunch of hoops as long as you pick a file format compatible with the browsers used by your target audience. As we mention earlier, support of each web-friendly format varies depending on the browser being used. However, all you need to do is encode the original audio file, which with any luck will be the original recording, into each of the web-friendly formats and embed all of them in the HTML5 document as follows:

1. **Create an HTML5 document in Dreamweaver or your favorite HTML editor.**

2. **Switch to your HTML editor's Code view.**

3. **Position your cursor in the body of the document.**

    That would be anywhere after the <body> tag.

4. **Enter the following code:**

    ```
    <audio src ="/audio/mymusic.mp3", autoplay="true">
    <audio src ="/audio/mymusic.aac", autoplay="true">
    <audio src ="/audio/mymusic.ogg", autoplay="true">
    Sorry, your browser does not support the <audio> tag
    </audio>
    ```

    The first three lines of code will play the file format supported by the user's browser. If the user accesses the page with an older browser, the warning in the fourth line of code is displayed.

5. **Save the document and test it in each browser used by your target audience.**

    If you use Dreamweaver CS6, you can use Adobe Browser Labs to test the document in each browser that supports HTML5. You access Adobe Browser Labs by choosing File⇨Preview in Browser⇨Adobe Browser Lab.

The previous steps are all well and good for background music, but to embed an audio file with controls in an HTML5 document, position your cursor where you want the player to appear in Step 3, and change the code in Step 4 to the following:

```
<audio countrols="controls">
<source src="/audio/mymusic.mp3" type="audio/mp3" />
<source src="/audio/mymusic.aac" type="audio/aac" />
<source src="/audio/mymusic.ogg" type="audio/ogg" />
Sorry, your browser does not support the <audio> tag
</audio>
```

This code enables audio playback in an HTML5-friendly browser. If the site visitor uses a browser that doesn't support HTML5, the fourth line of code is displayed.

Adding Flash Audio to a Page

Flash audio is the perfect solution when your client wants background music on a web page. Although Flash is *not* supported on many mobile devices (such as the Apple iPhone and iPad), you can still use Flash to good effect on pages that will be displayed on laptop and desktop computers. With Flash audio, you can compress music by using the popular MP3 format and then choosing a data rate that assures good-quality sound and a quick-loading file. The next sections cover how to create Flash audio and add it to a web page.

Creating Flash audio

Creating Flash audio isn't rocket science, but you obviously need a copy of Flash unless you're fortunate enough to have a client who sends you the sound file in the SWF format. To create Flash audio, follow these steps:

1. **Create a new Flash document.**

   Accept the default frame rate (24 fps), choose a color that matches the web page into which you're adding the sound, and specify a size of 1 pixel x 1 pixel. We explain why color is important in the next section, "Adding Flash sound to a web page."

2. **Choose File⇨Import⇨Import to Library.**

   The Import to Library dialog box appears.

3. **Select the sound and then click Open.**

   Flash imports the sound to the document Library.

4. **Select the first keyframe on the timeline.**

   You only have one, so it shouldn't be hard to find. For more information on Flash and keyframes, check out Chapter 5 in this minibook.

5. **Open the Properties Inspector.**

6. **Choose the imported sound from the Sound drop-down menu.**

   The filename of the sound file appears in the Name text field.

7. **Accept the default Sync options of Event and Repeat, but change the value of the last option to 0 (zero).**

   These settings play the sound once. If you have a quiet background sound, you might want to change the second option to Loop and then enter the number of times you want the sound to repeat. After you add a sound to a keyframe, your Properties Inspector should resemble Figure 4-1.

   A word of caution is in order here. If the song is too loud or doesn't suit all audiences, looping the sound is a surefire way to have part of your intended audience escape by clicking the Back button.

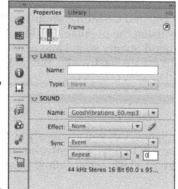

Figure 4-1:
Add
sound to a
keyframe —
the only
keyframe.

8. **Choose Window⇨Library.**

   The document Library opens.

9. **Select the sound file, right-click (Windows) or Control-click (Mac), and then choose Properties from the contextual menu.**

   The Sound Properties dialog box appears.

10. **Choose MP3 from the Compression drop-down menu.**

    The Sound Properties dialog box reconfigures, as shown in Figure 4-2.

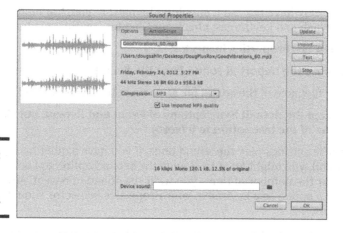

Figure 4-2:
Modify
the sound
properties.

11. Choose an option from the Bit Rate drop-down menu.

This option appears only if you import a file other than an MP3 audio file.

The default option of 16 Kbps works well for simple background music with one or two instruments. However, if you use more complex music to entertain your viewers (or your client is a diva, an opera star, or a rock musician), you need to specify a higher bit rate to get a better-quality sound. When the bit rate is less than 20 Kbps, the file is converted to monophonic (mono) by default. When you exceed 20 Kbps, the sound is still converted to mono, but, if desired, you can convert the sound to stereo by deselecting the Convert Stereo to Mono check box. A higher bit rate does increase the file size, so you can't go too far unless you have a sound clip less than 30 seconds in duration.

If you import an MP3 sound file, a check box appears in the dialog box with the option to use the imported MP3 quality. The Bit Rate options appear if you deselect this option.

12. Choose an option from the Quality drop-down menu.

This option is available if the Use Imported MP3 quality option is not selected. The default option Fast renders the file quickly. However, you get better-quality sound if you choose Medium or Best. The latter options take a while longer to render the sound.

13. Click the Test button to preview the sound clip with the current compression settings.

If the sound isn't to your liking, choose a higher bit rate. If you choose a different bit rate, click the Update button to update the file, and then click the Test button to preview the file with the new settings.

14. After modifying the sound to suit your web page, click OK.

The new settings are applied to the sound.

15. Choose File➪Publish Settings.

The Publish Settings dialog box appears.

16. Deselect the HTML option.

All you need is the Flash SWF file, which we show you how to add to a web page in the next section.

17. Choose File➪Publish.

The SWF file awaits a web page.

Editing sound for fun and profit

If you do a lot of work in Flash with soundtracks or add soundtracks to many of your web pages, consider investing in a sound-editing application, with which you can apply special effects, such as reverb and echo, to a sound to equalize the volume (and much more). You can also use a good sound-editing application to create voice-overs for a video track, record a podcast, and so on. Another definite bonus is the capability to save the sound in just about any format available today. Sony Sound Forge and Adobe Audition are two of the better sound editing-applications. Another option is Adobe Soundbooth, which is cross-platform.

But as Doug's dear mother Inez used to say, "For free, take; for buy, waste money." If you're on a budget, you can get a lot of bang for no buck by downloading the cross-platform Audacity application (`www.audacity.soundforge.net`). Audacity gives you the power to record and edit OGG/Vorbis, MP3, WAV, or AIFF sound files. Try it; you'll like it.

Adding Flash sound to a web page

After you publish your Flash sound as a SWF file, you're ready to add it to your web page. Remember that this file is infinitesimally small, as in really, really tiny. No one will see the file, so you can tuck it in just about anywhere. Adding the file above the header section of the document is generally a good idea. Honestly, who's going to notice an extra pixel, especially when it's the same color as the background? These steps show you how to add the sound file:

1. **In Dreamweaver, open the web page to which you'll add the sound.**

2. **Position your cursor where you want to add the sound.**

   You can put the sound anywhere that's a blank space — say, above the header or below the *fold* (you know, the stuff you can't see in the browser window and need to scroll to).

3. **Choose Insert⇨Media⇨SWF.**

   The Select File dialog box appears.

4. **Select the soundtrack SWF file and then click OK.**

   The Object Tag Accessibility Attributes dialog box appears. This information is used by visually challenged people using screen readers to access the page. For more information on usability and accessibility, see Book II, Chapter 2.

5. **Enter the desired information and click OK.**

   Dreamweaver adds the soundtrack to the web page.

6. **Save the file and preview it in all browsers used by your target audience.**

   The sound will start playing when the HTML document loads. We think you should add a button to control the volume of the sound, or mute it. However, our editors are trying to conserve a rain forest in Brazil — an endeavor of which we approve — and won't allot the number of pages it would take to show you how to add the button.

Delivering Your Message

When you add audio to a website, you're entertaining site visitors or informing them. When you entertain visitors, it can be in the form of music or perhaps comedy. When you inform people, it's generally in the form of the spoken word with, perhaps, some background music. In either event, your goal is to deliver a high-quality audio track that's clear and easy to understand. Here are a few things to consider when preparing audio for a website:

✦ **Go pro.** If your client is recording audio for a website, make sure he uses a professional microphone and application (such as Sony Sound Forge, Adobe Audition, or Adobe Soundbooth) to record the track. If your client is on a budget, tell him about the free Audacity application (`www.audacity.soundforge.net`), which does a stellar of capturing and compressing sound.

✦ **Pop is a no-go.** You should also make sure that your client positions the microphone in such a manner that the sounds of his breath are not recorded. The microphone also needs to be far enough away from his mouth to ensure the plosive sounds from the letters such as P and S are not recorded. Your client can also purchase a *pop filter* to minimize plosive sounds. Pop filters take the form of a screen that is between the microphone and the speaker's mouth, or a foam sock that fits snuggly over the microphone.

✦ **Find the right voice.** If the sound of your client's voice isn't pleasing or if she speaks with a heavy accent, tactfully suggest hiring a professional to record the narration.

✦ **Think small.** When compressing soundtracks for the web, strive for the smallest possible file size, while still maintaining a clean, crisp sound. The MP3 audio format is well suited for web delivery.

✦ **Don't compress.** Don't compress music soundtracks to 8-bit depth. The recording will sound scratchy in soft passages.

✦ **Don't overmodulate.** Make sure that the soundtrack isn't overmodulated. The loudest parts of overmodulated (too loud) soundtracks are *clipped,* which means that the sound is distorted. If your client is recording the track with a good sound-editing application with *VU meters* (meters that visually display the intensity of the sound), tell him to make sure the levels don't go into the red area.

✦ **Don't purloin.** Don't use recordings from other websites unless you can secure a license to use the recording in your web design.

✦ **Watch copyrights.** Don't use digital versions of copyrighted recordings unless you can secure a license to use the recording in your web design. Don't use any application — including iTunes — to create a digital version of a commercial recording for use on your website. This is a clear violation of the copyright laws.

Exploring Web Video Formats

There aren't quite as many video files as Carter has little liver pills, but close. During the infancy of video for the web, video was segregated to platforms. Macintosh users had Apple QuickTime, and Windows users had Windows Media Video. After a while, both platforms could play both formats. But that involved a bit of code and embedding a player in the HTML document. With the advent of HTML5, you can play video in a web page without breaking a sweat. The following is a list of video formats that are supported by HTML5:

✦ **WebM:** This is a video compression format that was developed specifically for HTML5. The development of the WebM project is sponsored by Google. As of this writing, the format is supported by the following browsers: Mozilla Firefox 4.0, Opera 10.6, and Google Chrome 6.0.

✦ **H.264/MPEG-4:** If you've downloaded video podcasts from iTunes or watched them online, you've witnessed this format firsthand. The format was designed to deliver high-quality video at lower data rates, which of course means that the files stream into the viewer's browser more quickly and are a smaller file size. As of this writing, the format is supported by the Internet Explorer 9.0, Google Chrome 5, and Safari 5.

So as you can see, HTML5 video support is a bit of a conundrum. The trick is to encode your video in both formats, and then embed both formats in your HTML document, as shown in the "Adding Video to a Web Page" section.

Encoding video to the WebM format

The WebM video format development was sponsored by Google — you know, the search engine giants. When the lads at Google sponsor something, you can be pretty much assured that the format will stand the test of time and will also gain support when new versions of browsers that don't currently support the format are released.

Therefore, if you're designing pages with video that need to be viewed on devices like the iPad and other devices that don't support Flash video, you'll need to get in the swing and learn how to encode video into the WebM format. The all-singing, all-dancing Adobe Media Encoder doesn't currently support the WebM format. However, the free Miro Video Encoder application (www.mirovideoconverter.

com) encodes video into the WebM format and MP4. Talk about killing two birds with one stone. Miro Video Encoder isn't very sophisticated. You can encode only one video at a time, and the data rate can't be changed from the application default. Still, the encoded video is good quality, and the file size is reasonably small compared with the original file.

We did notice some video artifacts such as visible pixels when compressing a test file to WebM format. However, this file did have video transitions, which generally cause problems when compressed. As long as you're not compressing a movie file with video transitions, the Miro Video Encoder should work just fine. Audio within the video is encoded as well.

Adding Video to a Web Page

Adding video to a web page used to be hard. You'd have to deal with a specific video player, such as RealMedia Player, Windows Media Player, or QuickTime Player. The HTML5 format has a video tag, which enables you to add an .mp4 and .webm video and controls to a web page. The user's browser determines which video plays when the HTML file is loaded. If you include both formats as we show you here, you cover all the bases for HTML5 browsers. To add video to an HTML5 document, follow the bouncing ball:

1. **Encode a video in the .mp4 and .webm format.**

The .webm format is brand-spanking new to HTML5. If you need a tool to encode your video, read the "Encoding video to the WebM format" sidebar in this chapter.

2. **Create an HTML5 document.**

Of course, you may have other goodies in the page. Add them before adding the video to the page.

3. **Switch to your HTML editor's Code view.**

4. **Position your cursor where you want the video to appear and add the following code:**

```
<video width="320" height="240" controls="controls">
<source src="movie.mp4" type="video/mp4" />
<source src="movie.webm" type="video/webm" />
Your browser does not support the video tag.
</video>
```

The first line of code specifies the dimensions of the video, and the fact that controls will be available for the video. The controls vary depending on the video format. The second and third lines of code specify the location of each video file, and the type. The browser determines which video is played when the HTML document is loaded from the website. The final line of code is displayed if the visitor is using a browser that does not support HTML5 video.

5. **Test the file in all browsers used by the site's target audience.**

Working with Digital Video

Today, video is an integral part of the web. Therefore, to be successful as a website designer, you need to know about video and how to incorporate it on your design work. As we mention earlier in this chapter — which was toiled over late in the evening and with great precision — two video file formats are supported in HTML5. Like images, video files start out as something completely different from what you end up putting on a web page. If you're lucky, you have a client or someone in your company who knows all about video and serves up perfectly encoded video all ready to plop onto your web pages. (Right! And we have a bridge in Brooklyn, New York, that we'll let you have for a song.)

The reality of the matter is that you're likely to get a video cassette from your client's camcorder, a flash drive with video — or, worse, a CD with encoded video that's been severely compressed, along with instructions for which bits he wants for the website. When that happens, you have to encode the video yourself or hire a professional videographer to do it for you. And if you opt for the latter scenario, the video has already been compressed, which means the end result won't be high quality. Always start with the highest-quality video you can get your hands on. You get high-quality video from digital camcorders or a high-end digital camera capable of capturing video. And if you think you can get high-quality video from your iPhone, you're sadly mistaken: Garbage in, garbage out.

Capturing video

If your client hands you a cassette tape, or a memory card from a digital camera, you have to get the contents of it into your computer (*capture* it) before you can encode it. To capture video from a cassette, you need either a video capture card or an application such as Adobe Premiere or Sony Vegas. Well, for that matter, Windows Movie Maker and Apple iMovie can also capture video. Most applications capture video in a proprietary, digital video (DV) format. We say "proprietary" because even though the file format name is the same, different applications seem to use slightly different algorithms to capture video as DV files. If you've dabbled with digital video, you're familiar with these terms.

The application itself isn't all you need, though. You also need a connection between the digital video camera or digital video deck and the computer. Most digital cameras and digital video decks use FireWire (IEEE 1394) or USB connections. On the computer side, a FireWire card, FireWire Connection, or video-capture card is required. Capturing video is a fairly boring process because you just can't speed it up. If your client gives you a cassette with 20 minutes worth of video, it takes 20 minutes to capture it. But that does give you an excuse to catch up on something more important, like creating a shag rug with recycled hairballs.

Digital video isn't just limited to devices that use cassettes. Many digital video cameras have built-in hard drives that enable you to capture hours of video before downloading the files to your computer. Most digital cameras also give you the option to capture video, in which case, the video will be stored on a memory card, which you transfer to your computer with a card reader.

In fact, you can even capture video with mobile phones such as the iPhone. The iPod and iPad also have built-in video cameras. The quality of the video from mobile devices isn't quite up to snuff with full-fledged video cameras, but unless the video was captured with dim lighting, the quality may be good enough for use on a web page.

Editing digital video

We know what you're thinking: This is a book about building websites. However, it never hurts to master multiple skills, especially where digital video is concerned. Many video-editing applications are sheer torture to work with. We won't name names, but some video timelines show only the beginning and end of a clip, which makes it pretty difficult to know what to leave in and what to leave out. Other video-editing applications show intermediate frames, and if you zoom in close enough, every frame on the timeline. This makes it easy to slice and dice a video to perfection.

If you've worked with Flash, you're familiar with timelines. Video-editing application timelines are no different. You navigate to a specific spot in the timeline to perform a task, such as splitting a video, inserting a video clip, adding a video transition, and so on. If you use a video-editing application with an intuitive interface, creating a video production can be extremely rewarding.

Encoding video

When you *encode video,* you specify a video codec, such as .mp4 or .webm. A *video codec* compresses the video to the desired data rate, which — when combined with the length of the video — also determines the file size. A higher data rata means better-quality video at the expense of a large file size, and potentially slow loading if a website visitor doesn't have a fast Internet connection. The other end of the spectrum decreases video quality but yields a smaller file that loads more quickly into the visitor's browser. When the encoded video is played, the codec decompresses the video. When you encode video, you specify the frame size and data rate. The data rate is specified in Kbps. Where web video is concerned, data rate is directly related to bandwidth. If you try to cram a video with a data rate of 512 Kbps through a modem with a connection speed of 56 Kbps . . . well, you can see that it just won't happen.

So how do you know what data rate to use? And why do you need to worry about data rate when you already have your hands full with CSS and other HTML delights? Well, you really don't *need* to know a lot — that is, if you have a good application to encode your video. A good video encoding application, also known as a *compression application,* shows you which options to use for a specific destination. We highly recommend the Adobe Media encoder that ships with the Adobe CS6 Creative Suite. If you're preparing video for a client whose intended audience will be viewing the video with a broadband connection, you can choose the proper preset to suit the need.

Creating and Encoding Flash Video

If the pages you're creating won't be viewed on mobile devices (such as an iPad or a smartphone), you can create web pages with beautiful Flash video. Adobe Flash Professional CS6 has its own built-in video encoder. The upcoming sections show you how to encode digital video into the FLV format within Flash.

Full motion video in Flash is a beautiful thing. You tailor the video for the target audience viewing the website. If your target audience accesses the Internet with a slow connection, you create a video with smaller dimensions and higher compression to load and stream without stopping. You can also add a controller to the video, which enables visitors to control playback of the video.

When you need to quickly add a video to a Flash movie, you can do so by encoding the video within Flash. When you encode a video in Flash, you can launch the Adobe Media Encoder, which enables you to encode the file. You then come back to Flash to add the encoded video to your project. These handy steps show you how to encode a video in Flash:

1. **Create a new document the same size as the video you're incorporating on your web page.**

Make sure you match the frame rate of the main movie.

2. Choose File⇨Import⇨Import Video.

The Import Video dialog box (see Figure 4-3) appears.

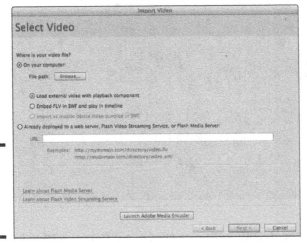

Figure 4-3:
Start by
importing a
video into
Flash.

3. **Click the Browse button.**

The Open dialog box appears.

4. **Select the video you want to import and then click Open.**

The path to the video and filename appears in the File Path field. If Adobe Flash Player doesn't support the video format, a message to this effect appears telling you it's necessary to use Adobe Media Encoder to convert the file to a supported format.

5. **Accept the default Load External Video with Playback Component option unless you have a client who owns several Ferraris and is rich enough to afford Flash Video Streaming Service or Flash Media Server. Alternatively, you can embed the resulting Flash video FLV file into the SWF file.**

6. **Click Launch Adobe Media Encoder.**

Flash prompts you to save the document. After you save the FLA document, the Adobe Media Encoder dialog box appears (see Figure 4-4).

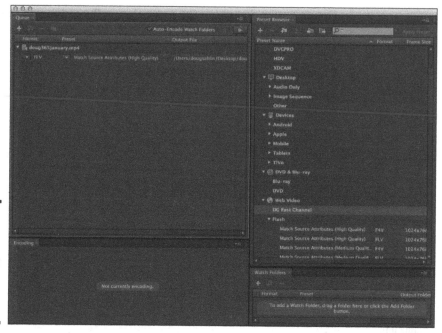

Figure 4-4:
Encode
video into
Flash format
with Adobe
Media
Encoder.

7. **Accept the default setting or choose a different setting from the Settings drop-down menu.**

   After you click Settings, you are faced with a plethora of choices. In most instances, the default preset is right on the mark. However, if you're familiar with video encoding, feel free to choose the setting you deem best for your intended audience.

   If you're familiar with encoding digital video, choose Custom and tweak the settings to suit the web page in which the video will appear. When you modify the settings, Custom, rather than one of the defaults, appears in the encoding window.

8. **Click the Start Queue button (looks like a video recorder Play button).**

   Adobe Media Encoder does its thing. If you have a long video, this would be a good time to grab your favorite snack or beverage. If you did decide to take a break while the video is encoding, you'll know when it's done, unless you're in the next county or do your work in a soundproof room. The Adobe Media Encoder plays a rather distinct sound when encoding has finished. After the video is encoded, you can close Adobe Media Encoder.

9. **In Flash, click Browse.**

   Navigate to the video file you just encoded and open it.

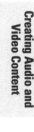

10. **Click Next.**

The Skinning page of the Import Video Wizard appears (see Figure 4-5).

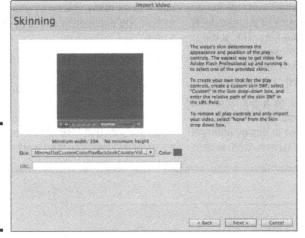

Figure 4-5:
Here's
where you
can add a
cool skin to
your video.

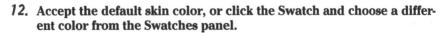

11. **Select a skin from the Skin drop-down menu.**

After you select a *skin* (interface for the video), a preview appears in
the preview pane. Unless you're going to use the video as part of a Flash
website, choose None. All you need is the encoded Flash video. You can
add a skin when you add the video to your web page in Dreamweaver.

The minimum width of the skin is listed after you choose it. If the minimum width is larger than the width of your video, choose a skin that
doesn't have as many controls.

12. **Accept the default skin color, or click the Swatch and choose a different color from the Swatches panel.**

13. **Click Next.**

The Finish Video Import page of the Import Video Wizard appears (see
Figure 4-6).

14. **Review the information and click Finish if you're satisfied.**

If not, click Back and navigate to the page on which you need to make
changes.

15. **Choose Control➪Test Movie to preview your video.**

Encoding video with Adobe Media Encoder

If you're encoding multiple videos, use Adobe Media Encoder, which ships with all Adobe CS6 Suites. This gem gives you the capability of encoding multiple video files. The settings options are identical to those you find when you import video into Flash and use the progressive download method of deployment.

After you apply settings to a file, you can duplicate the file and modify the settings. This option is useful if you need to deploy different versions of the video for visitors who access the web with different connection speeds. You can add as many videos as you want to the queue. The application encodes one video at a time.

Here's a good tip: When encoding multiple videos, set up the application prior to finishing work for the day. Then before you leave, just click the Start Queue button. Unless you're encoding several long videos into multiple formats, the encoded files will be ready to use in a web page when you start work the next day.

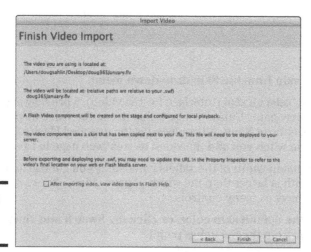

Figure 4-6:
That's a
wrap.

When you encode video via Adobe Media Encoder from within Flash, the video encoder creates an FLV (Flash Video) file with the same name as the source file with the `.flv` extension. You need to upload this file to your web server along with your web page.

Adding Flash Video to a Web Page

Adding Flash video to a web page in Dreamweaver is easy. As an added bonus in Dreamweaver, you can add controls to the video to enable website visitors to start and stop the video as they please. This is much better than having the video loop endlessly while the visitors are trying to pay attention to the other content on the page. To add Flash video to a web page, follow these steps:

1. **Position your cursor at the point in the web page where you want to insert the video.**

2. **Choose Insert⇨Media⇨FLV.**

   If you haven't already done so, Dreamweaver prompts you to save the file. If you've saved the file, or just now save the file at the prompt's behest, the Insert FLV dialog box appears. (See Figure 4-7.)

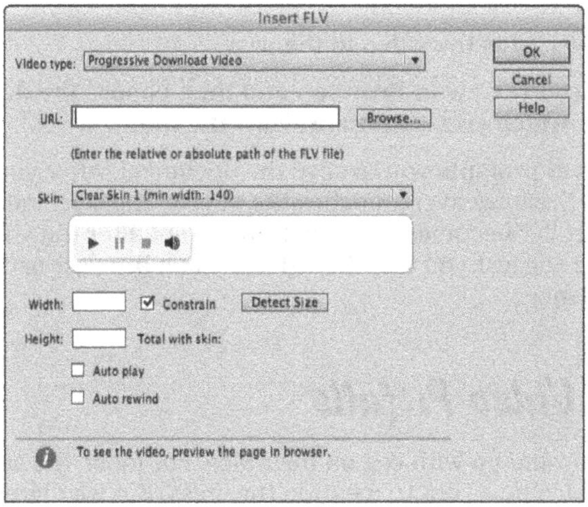

Figure 4-7:
Inserting
Flash video
in a web
page.

3. **Accept the default Progressive Download Video option for Video Type.**

   The other option is Streaming Video, which requires a special server. Servers that specialize in delivering streaming video don't come cheap, but we show you how to get streaming video on a budget in the "Streaming Video on a Budget" section.

4. **Click the Browse button next to the URL field.**

   Navigate to the FLV file you want to add to the web page. If you've been neat and tidy, the file should be in the website folder. If you haven't been neat and tidy, Dreamweaver lets you know by displaying a dialog box offering you the option of copying the file to the website folder. Take it.

5. **Choose a skin from the Skin drop-down menu.**

   There are several options that give website visitors different options, such as playing the video or playing and pausing the video as well as adjusting the sound volume. Each skin lists the minimum width required to display all the controls. Your video width must be equal to or larger than the width of the skin you choose.

6. Enter values in the Width and Height fields.

These are the dimensions of the video you're adding to the page. Alternatively, you can click the Detect Size button to have Dreamweaver fill in the blanks.

7. Choose additional options as needed.

You can have the video auto-play when fully downloaded and auto-rewind when finished. If you choose both options, the video will loop endlessly until the user clicks the Stop button on the skin.

8. Click OK.

Dreamweaver adds the video to the page.

9. Choose File⇨Preview in Browser, and then choose the desired browser in which you want to preview the file.

Dreamweaver prompts you to save the document. After you save the document, Dreamweaver launches the page in the selected browser. The video controller becomes partially transparent after the video begins playing. We suggest you test the video in each browser used by your target audience.

Avoiding Digital Video Pitfalls

Nobody likes to wind up with egg on their face. For most, the additional cholesterol is unwelcome — not to mention the mess. But we digress. Egg on your face where web video is concerned is a file that doesn't play or doesn't play properly. Here are some handy tips and tricks to help you keep your client's web video squeaky clean:

✦ **Don't copy video from other websites and use them on yours.** This violates copyright laws.

✦ **Don't use a video from one of your client's suppliers before reading the licensing rights to the video.** After you read the rights, make sure your client agrees to them. Being named as a second party in a copyright infringement suit isn't a good thing.

✦ **If your client is recording a video for his website, which you or someone else will later compress and encode for the web, make sure he uses a good-quality camcorder and not some el cheapo webcam.** Garbage in, garbage out.

✦ **Make sure your client's intended audience has the necessary plug-ins to view the video.** When in doubt, list the required plug-in and include a link to the website from which visitors can download it.

✦ **Don't use video transitions.** Video transitions look great when you create a video with a high bit rate, but if you compress the video to any degree, you'll see artifacts. When in doubt, use a straight cut between clips.

✦ **Don't embed more than one video per web page.** If your client wants multiple videos to be accessible from a page, use a video editing application to export one frame of the video as an image. Do this for each video the client wants to be accessible from the page. On the web page, each photo serves as a link to the full video. The only exception to this is when you create an HTML5 document for multiple browsers. You'll need to embed an MP4 and WebM version of the video, as outlined in the "Embedding Video in a Web Page" section of this chapter.

Streaming Video on a Budget

As we mention earlier in this chapter, HTML5 makes it easy to incorporate video into a web page. However, not everybody surfs the web with HTML5 browsers. The other option is to encode the video as an FLV file and embed it in a web page. Of course, if your company or client has a website with limited bandwidth, this can pose a problem if lots of people view the video.

The easiest solution we know is to upload the video to a video-sharing site, like YouTube or Vimeo. As of this writing, YouTube is free, and Vimeo Basic is free. YouTube lets you upload videos up to 15 minutes in length. The Vimeo Basic account lets you upload high-quality video but limits you to a maximum upload of 500MB per week and one HD video per week. Vimeo Plus gives you even higher quality video (less compression when the file is crunched by Vimeo), a maximum upload of 5GB per week, and unlimited uploads of HD video.

When you upload a video to either service, you can get the code necessary to embed the video in a web page. We show you how to embed video in a web page in the next section.

Embedding a Video in a Web Page

After you create a YouTube or Vimeo account, it's child's play to add a video from either site to a web page. Vimeo's embed code supports mobile devices like the iPad and iPhone. To embed a video in a web page

1. **Create a new web page in your favorite HTML editor.**

We prefer Dreamweaver, but any HTML editor that lets you work directly with code will do.

2. **Create the content for the page, position your cursor where you want the video to appear, and then switch to Code view.**

3. **Navigate to Vimeo or YouTube and select the video you want to embed.**

4. **Select the option to embed.**

Figure 4-8 shows the Embed This Video dialog box from Vimeo, and Figure 4-9 shows the Embed code from YouTube.

5. **Copy the code.**

Make sure you select all the code. The easy way to do this is to place your cursor inside the text box with the embed code, press Ctrl+A (Windows) or ⌘+A (Mac) to select all the code, and then press Ctrl+C (Windows) or ⌘+C (Mac) to copy the code to the system Clipboard.

6. **In the web page you're creating, position your cursor where you want the video to appear.**

7. **Paste the embed code.**

Press Ctrl+V (Windows) or ⌘+V (Mac) to paste the embed code.

Figure 4-8:
Getting the
embed code
for a Vimeo
video.

Figure 4-9:
Getting
the embed
code for a
YouTube
video.

8. **Save the web page and then upload it to your server.**

9. **Navigate to the web page and preview the video.**

The video will play when you click the play button in the YouTube or
Vimeo player. The beauty of this is that your company or your client's
company doesn't get hit with the bandwidth: Vimeo or YouTube does.

Chapter 5: Creating Content with Flash

In This Chapter

✔ Adding Flash interactivity

✔ Adding Flash navigation to a website

✔ Creating Flash animations

*I*f you need to kick up a web design with some multimedia, Flash is an excellent tool to use. With a bit of imagination, you can use this powerful tool to create websites that make those of your competition look positively lame. This chapter introduces you to the all-singing, all-dancing Flash CS6 workspace. Here, you find out how to use it to create flashy navigation in a flash (almost the same duration as a New York minute), and add animation to your designs. Let the games begin.

Introducing Flash CS6

Historically, Flash has been used to create animated introductions to websites as well as full-fledged websites. However, Flash intros are no longer in vogue, and Flash websites aren't search engine–friendly. Flash has been in a state of decline due to the fact that Flash content isn't compatible with some mobile devices, most notably Apple devices such as the iPod and the iPad. However, for now, Flash does still have a place in the greater scheme of things. If you're creating a website and you want to add Flash interactivity, you can create a version of the site with Flash as well as a mobile version of the site without Flash. Just use JavaScript to determine which device the visitor is using, and then load the correct version of the site. We explore how to do this in Book VI, Chapter 3.

Designers can control the user's experience in a website by how they place items — such as graphics or create interactive forms — on the Flash Timeline. They can also control the flow of a Flash movie by using ActionScript, which is a coding language developed by Adobe that is similar to ActionScript. ActionScript comes in two flavors: 2.0 and 3.0. With ActionScript, you can add interactivity to an application, such as calling up a URL or changing the characteristics of a symbol. A *symbol* is simply a reusable graphic.

When you create instances of a symbol, you can modify each instance, changing its size, color, location, and so on. When you create an instance of a symbol, you don't increase the file size. Flash re-creates the instance using the properties of the original symbol, which you can modify to suit the document you're creating.

Typically, a web designer uses Flash to create animations or navigation menus. A Flash navigation menu consists of buttons that transport the visitor to other parts of the website.

And whether you're creating an animation or a menu in Flash, the end result is an SWF file, which is also known as a "movie." When constructed properly, Flash movies are relatively small files. Still, a designer can go over the top by adding so many graphics and other bells and whistles that the finished product loads at a snail's pace.

The tempo or pace of a Flash movie is defined by the frame rate. The default frame rate of a Flash movie is 24 frames per second (fps), which is fine for most Flash movies. You can also incorporate Flash video (FLV file format) in a Flash project or in an HTML web page, or with the use of JavaScript incorporating H.264 (.mp4) video with the Flash Player. For more information on Flash video and other web video formats, see Chapter 4 of this minibook.

Touring the interface

The Flash interface might seem a little daunting to the uninitiated. We certainly had our doubts several years ago when we launched Flash CS3. However, the workspace is really quite civil after you work with Flash for a while. If you've used Flash CS5, this version will seem familiar to you. However, if you've never used Flash, we bring you up to speed in the following sections. To start the tour, check out the various parts of the Flash interface (see Figure 5-1).

Exploring the Tools panel

The right side of the interface is home to the Tools panel, which is called out in Figure 5-1. This part of the interface is home to the tools you use to create objects and text. For the purpose of this illustration, the Tools panel is floating in a one-column format, as shown in Figure 5-2. You can also use the tools to move and modify objects, or you can choose a different workspace from the drop-down menu to the right of the menu groups. Some of the less-frequently used tools share space in the Tools panel. When you see a right-pointing down arrow, you've found a tool that's subletting space to another. Click the arrow to reveal a fly-out menu that shows more tools.

Stage   Tools panel

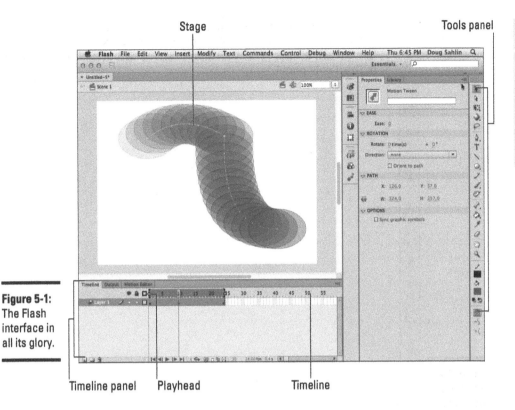

Figure 5-1:
The Flash
interface in
all its glory.

Timeline panel   Playhead   Timeline

The following tools reside in the Tools panel (described here from top
to bottom):

+ **Selection tool:** Select and moves objects.

+ **Subselection tool:** Select points along a path and objects within a group.

+ **Free Transform tool:** Scale objects; change the width or height of an
object; skew an object; change an object's center of rotation; rotate
an object.

  • *Gradient Transform tool:* Transform a gradient that fills an object. This
  tool shares space on the Tools panel with the Free Transform tool.

+ **3D Rotation tool:** Take objects for a spin. Flash isn't true 3D yet, but you
can simulate 3D in an animation with this tool.

  • *3D Transform tool:* This tool has three axes — X, Y, and Z — that you
  use to move an object left and right, up and down, forward and backward. This tool makes it possible for you to simulate 3D in a motion

tween animation. A *motion tween animation* is one where an object moves from Point A to Point B, and Flash creates the objects in the in-between frames. This tool shares space with the 3D Rotation tool in the Tools panel.

Figure 5-2:
Tools you
use for fun
and profit.

✦ **Lasso tool:** Create a freeform selection.

✦ **Pen tool:** Create a path. You can choose other tools from the fly-out menu that enable you to add points to or delete points from a path. There is also a tool to convert a straight point to a curve point and vice versa.

✦ **Text tool:** Add text to a document.

✦ **Line tool:** Create lines.

✦ **Oval tool:** Create ovals. Hold down the Shift key while using this tool to create a circle. The Oval tool shares a one-story walkup with the Rectangle, Rectangle Primitive, and Oval Primitive tools. Note that the tool last used gets top billing on this space in the toolbar.

• *Rectangle tool:* Create rectangles. Hold down the Shift key while using this tool to create a square. You can add a radius to rectangle corners to create rectangles with round corners by clicking the Set Corner Radius button in the Options area of the Tools panel.

- *Rectangle Primitive tool:* This critter is also used to create rectangles and rounded rectangles. The beauty of a primitive shape is that you can edit the shape's attributes at any time via the Properties Inspector.

- *Oval Primitive tool:* Create ovals that can be edited in the Properties Inspector any time after they are created.

- *Polystar tool:* Create multisided polygons and stars. The Polystar tool appears on a fly-out when the arrow in the corner of the Rectangle tool is clicked.

✦ **Pencil tool:** Create freeform lines in the document.

✦ **Brush tool:** Paint objects within the document.

- *Spray Brush tool:* Use to add graffiti-like splashes of color to a document. You can change the color that sprays from the nozzle, or spray a symbol out the tool's nozzle from the document Library. This tool shares the rent with the Brush tool.

✦ **Deco tool:** Use to draw a shape that looks like a flowering vine. You specify the colors in the Properties Inspector, and you can also choose a symbol from the document Library for the leaf and the vine.

✦ **Bone tool:** Use to create an Inverse Kinematics (IK) animation. You use the tool to add bones to the object you're animating. The bones are the Inverse Kinematics chain. You yank a bone with the Selection tool, and the bones that are higher in the chain move.

- *Bind tool:* Use this to fine-tune an IK animation that's not performing up to snuff — "bound up," if you will. You use the tool to bind points from an object with a bone.

✦ **Paint Bucket:** Change an object's fill, which can be a solid color or gradient.

- *Ink Bottle:* Change the color of an object's stroke (outline). The Ink Bottle and Paint Bucket share space in the Tools panel.

✦ **Eyedropper:** Sample a color from an object within the document.

✦ **Eraser:** Erase an area or object within the document.

✦ **Hand tool:** Pan within the document.

 While using any tool, press and hold down the spacebar to momentarily activate the Hand tool. Release the spacebar to revert to the previously used tool.

✦ **Zoom:** Zoom in within the document. Click to zoom to the next highest level of magnification. Click and drag to zoom to a specific area of the document. Hold the Alt key (Windows) or Option key (Mac) and then click inside the document to zoom out to the next-lowest level of magnification.

✦ **Stroke Color:** Click the swatch to open the Color Picker and then choose a stroke color. This color is applied to all the tools that create objects with a stroke.

✦ **Fill Color:** Click the swatch to open the Color Picker and then choose a fill color. This color is used by all the tools that create objects with a fill.

✦ **Black and White:** Click this icon to revert to the default stroke color (black) and fill color (white).

- *No Color:* Click the Fill Color swatch to open the Swatches panel, and then click this icon to create an object with no fill. Or, click the Stroke Color swatch and then click this icon to create an object with no stroke.

✦ **Swap Colors:** Swap the current stroke and fill colors.

✦ **Options:** This part of the Tools panel changes depending on the tool you select. For example, when you choose the Brush tool, you're presented with options that specify how the tool disperses color, the brush size, tip, and so on.

Someone told me it's all happening on the Timeline

You use the Timeline, which consists of frames, to control the tempo of your Flash movie. You add *keyframes* where you want a change to occur. For example, when you create an animation, you add a keyframe and then move the object to a different position.

You create blank keyframes to signify the end of a set of frames. For example, if you're creating a slide show, you add an image to a keyframe where you want the animation to start. The frames downstream from the keyframe duplicate the contents of the keyframe — in this case, the image. The number of frames signifies the length of time for which the image is displayed. We don't show you how to create an animation just yet — that comes later, in the "Creating your first animation" section — but we get you started here:

✦ **To create a keyframe, click a regular frame and press F6.** Alternatively, choose Insert⇨Timeline⇨Keyframe. A keyframe with objects is signified by a solid dot. (See Figure 5-3.)

✦ **To create a blank keyframe, click a regular frame and press F7.** Alternatively, choose Insert⇨Timeline⇨Blank Keyframe. A blank keyframe is signified by a hollow dot. (See Figure 5-3.)

✦ **To create a regular frame, press F5.** Alternatively, choose Insert⇨Timeline⇨Frame. Frames duplicate the content of the previous keyframe. The area between keyframes is a *frame range*. You add frames to increase the duration of a frame sequence. The last frame in a frame range is signified by a rectangle. (See Figure 5-3.)

Blank Keyframe

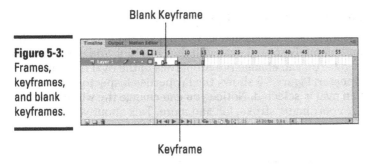

Figure 5-3:
Frames,
keyframes,
and blank
keyframes.

Keyframe

Panels not cast from wood

You use panels to do a lot of your work in Flash. The three panels on the
right side of the interface are the Properties Inspector, the document
Library, and the Tools panel. You open other panels by using commands
on the Window menu. When you use a menu command to open a panel (for
example, Window⇨Color), it appears in the workspace as a floating panel.
(See Figure 5-4.) The Flash interface is customizable. If you don't like the
default layout, choose another preset. You can also modify any preset workspace to suit your working preferences.

Many of the panel names are self-explanatory, whereas others require a little
clarification. You can use Flash Help (F1).

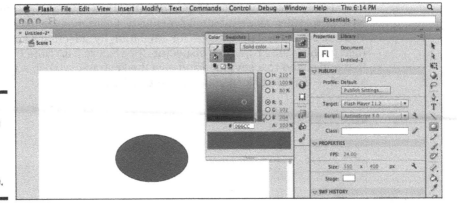

Figure 5-4:
Panels can
be docked
or can
float in the
workspace.

Inspecting the Properties Inspector

Objects have properties. It's a Flash law. When you create an object, such as the lowly and infinitely rotund oval with the Oval tool, you don't have to take what you get. You can change the properties of the oval by using the Properties Inspector. Figure 5-5 shows the Properties Inspector as it's configured when an oval is selected. Notice you can change the width, height, X coordinate, Y coordinate, stroke, fill, and more. Talk about your useful inspectors.

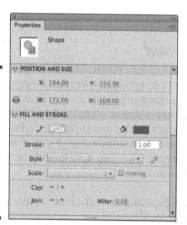

Figure 5-5: The Properties Inspector at work, sans monocle and magnifying glass.

You also use the Properties Inspector with other objects. Keyframes also have properties. As we mention previously, keyframes are used in animation. You can set several parameters for animation by selecting a keyframe and then opening the Properties Inspector. (See Figure 5-6.) Notice the options that add sound to a keyframe and give the keyframe a label. A keyframe with a label — isn't that like giving it a name? Yikes!

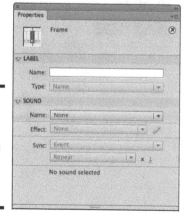

Figure 5-6: The Properties Inspector is used when creating an animation.

Getting comfortable with Flash

Flash is big, huge, vast. Even if you learn just half the bells and whistles in the application, Flash will never be half-vast. But we digress. One chapter just isn't long enough to learn all that Flash has to offer. To do so, you have to get your fingers a little greasy — get under the hood, so to speak. However, the next sections show you the fundamentals for creating a new document, an object, and then an animation. Buckle up and enjoy the ride.

Creating a Flash document

When you launch Flash CS6 for the first time, the first thing you see is a welcome screen that gives you options to create new documents or view tutorials. We generally look at welcome screens once and click anything that piques our curiosity. The next time we launch Flash and the pesky critter appears, we mark the Don't Show Again check box to make the welcome screen exit stage left. Forever.

When you launch Flash, the first thing you want to do is create a document. The interface is pretty, but it won't do you a bit of good without a document. You can create several types of documents. In this section, we show you how to create a basic document with the default document size, frame rate, background color (refrigerator white, which is boring), and so on. It's a good place to start, but you generally need to modify the document to suit the web page in which the Flash movie will be embedded. We're also assuming that you disabled the welcome screen and are using Flash like the frequent Flash fliers do.

To create a Flash document, follow these steps:

1. **Launch Flash and choose File⇨New.**

The New Document dialog box appears (see Figure 5-7).

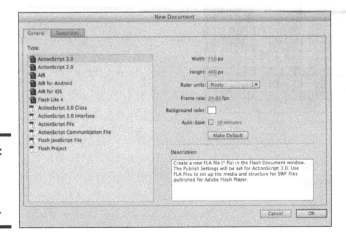

Figure 5-7:
It's time
to create
a new
document.

2. Choose the desired document type.

For a Flash document you're creating for the web, choose one of the first two options. ActionScript 3.0, which was introduced with Flash CS3, is a robust language, but it's not appropriate for casual Flash users. We also don't have the space to give you a proper introduction to ActionScript 3.0. For the purpose of this exercise, create a Flash File (ActionScript 2.0).

3. Enter a value for the Width and Height.

You can enter a value by clicking the field, or by hovering your cursor over the current size until a hand with a pointing finger and a two-headed arrow appears, which in Adobe-speak is known as a "scrubby slider." Drag the slider to set the desired value. The default document size is 550 pixels (px) x 400 px. If you're creating a small animation for a banner, you may end up with a document size of 150 x 90 or something similar. If you're creating a Flash website optimized for a 1024 x 768 desktop, you'll create a document that's 955 px x 600 px.

4. Select an option in the Ruler Units section.

Your options are Pixels (the default), Inches, Inches (decimal), Points, Centimeters, or Millimeters.

5. Enter the desired frame rate in the Frame Rate field.

Alternatively, you can grab the scrubby slider by the scruff of its neck and drag to set the desired frame rate. The default frame rate of 24 fps works well for most Flash movies. If you're streaming video to an audience that has a high-speed cable connection, you can specify 30 fps and deliver beautiful full-motion video.

6. Click the Background Color swatch.

Flash opens the Swatches panel shown in Figure 5-8.

Figure 5-8:
Please, pick anything but white.

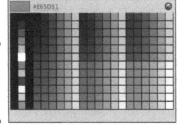

Book V
Chapter 5

Creating Content
with Flash

7. **Select the desired background color.**

   You can choose a color by clicking a swatch. The colors in the default palette are from the web-safe, 216-color palette. (Read all about that in Chapter 1 of this minibook.) Alternatively, you can enter the hexadecimal value for the color in the text field. This determines the background color of the Flash movie as well as the background color of the HTML document in which the Flash movie is embedded.

8. **If desired, select the Auto-Save check box.**

   This option comes in handy when you're working on a complex document. When you accept this option, the document is saved every 10 minutes. You can change the default auto-save time by entering a different number in the field there. Alternatively, you can drag the scrubby slider to set the time.

9. **(Optional) Click the Make Default button if you want these parameters to be the defaults for future Flash documents you create.**

   This option applies all parameters.

10. **Click OK.**

    Flash creates a new document.

Now that you have a new document, you're ready to create something very cool (or not so cool, depending on what your design calls for). The next section points you in the right direction. When you've tweaked your Flash document to perfection, you export it as a Flash movie in the SWF format, which can be embedded in a web page.

Creating an object

After you create a Flash document, you can add objects to it. Objects can be plain old ho-hum static objects, or they can be symbols.

A *symbol* is simply a reusable graphic. When you create a symbol, you create something that can be used over and over and over again. Just drag the symbol from the document Library and drop it in the desired place on the Timeline. When you use a symbol instead of creating a new object, you don't increase the file size of the published movie because Flash re-creates an instance of the symbol using the information stored in the document Library. Symbols come in three flavors: Button, Graphic, and Movie Clip.

These steps show you how to create a Graphic symbol:

1. **In the Tools panel, set the Stroke and Fill colors.**

   Click the applicable swatch to open the Swatches palette. The colors you select are applied to all objects until you change the colors.

2. **Select the Oval tool.**

   This tool gives you the power to create, um, ovals. "Will it go round in circles?"

3. **Click and drag an oval on the Stage.**

   When you release the mouse button, the oval appears on the Stage. The *Stage* is an area of the workspace that is the same size as the document. It has a definite border. The Stage is where you arrange your production.

   Hold down the Shift key to create a circle.

4. **Use the Selection tool to select the object.**

   If you created an object with a stroke, double-click the center of the object to select both the fill and the stroke.

5. **If desired, open the Properties Inspector and change the parameters for the circle.**

   You can change the Width, Height, and X and Y coordinates.

   The X and Y coordinates determine where the object is placed on the Stage. The upper-left corner of the Stage has the following coordinates: x=0, y=0.

6. **Press F8.**

   The Convert to Symbol dialog box appears.

7. **Type a name for the symbol and choose the Graphic option.**

   Flash gives the symbol a default name, but it's not very descriptive. A better idea is to give each symbol a unique name, which makes it easier for you to select the proper object from the Library. This is a distinct advantage when you're creating complex Flash movies with hundreds of symbols.

8. **Click the desired registration point.**

   This determines the center of rotation for the symbol. The upper-left point works well in most instances.

9. **Click OK.**

   The symbol is added to the Library.

Creating your first animation

After you add a symbol to the Library, you have the bare bones needed for a Flash animation. In this case, we show you how to make an oval go from Point A to Point B. It's not the coolest of animations, but it's a start. To create an animation, create a new Flash document and follow these steps:

1. **Create a Graphic symbol, using the Oval tool.**

   Creating a symbol is easy if you know Flash or if you read the preceding section. If neither is the case, please rewind and read the previous section.

   You create all your symbols on Stage.

2. **Use the Selection tool to move the symbol to the desired starting point.**

   To move an object with the Selection tool, click and drag the object to the desired location.

3. **Right-click (Windows) or Control-click (Mac) and choose Create Motion Tween from the context menu.**

   Flash creates 25 frames on the Timeline and positions your cursor in the 25th frame.

   If you don't create a symbol as outlined in Step 1, Flash displays a dialog box telling you the object cannot be used in a motion tween animation, but Flash will convert the option if you click OK.

4. **Move the oval to the point where you want to end the animation.**

   Flash creates a motion path and converts the 25th frame to a keyframe (see Figure 5-9).

   A *keyframe* is where a major change takes place in your Flash animation.

5. **Press Ctrl+Enter (Windows) or ⌘+Return (Mac).**

   Flash displays the animation in another window. You're probably thinking that the animation is pretty ho-hum. You're right. So kick it up a notch. After you get tired of looking at the animation, close the window.

6. **Click a frame between the beginning and ending keyframes. Using the Selection tool, move the object to another position.**

   Flash creates another keyframe when you move the object to another position.

7. **With the Selection tool, move your cursor toward the first half of the motion path.**

   When you see a curve appear under the arrow cursor, you can bend the motion path.

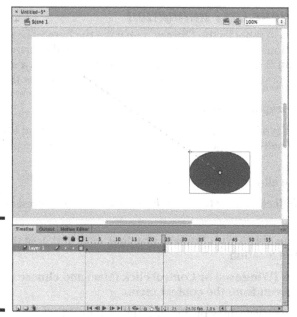

Figure 5-9:
Creating
a motion
tween
animation.

8. **Click and drag the motion path to curve it.**

9. **Repeat Step 8 for the other half of the motion path.**

Your motion path should resemble Figure 5-10.

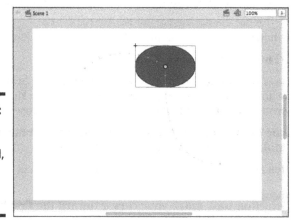

Figure 5-10:
A motion
path that's
been folded,
spindled,
and
mutilated.

10. **Press Ctrl+Enter (Windows) or ⌘+Enter (Mac).**

Now you're cooking. To give you an idea of what you should be seeing, Figure 5-11 was created using the Onion Skin option, which displays multiple frames at a lower opacity. Close the window when you're done patting yourself on the back.

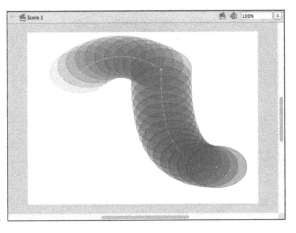

Figure 5-11:
A motion
tween
animation
with multiple
keyframes.

Setting up your workspace

If you're like most designers, you have a set way of doing things. The designers of Flash set up the workspace to suit the needs of most Flash users. However, you can customize the Flash workspace to suit your own working preferences. In this section, we show you a few things you can do to set up the workspace just the way you like it.

Setting Flash preferences

Everybody's got preferences. Doug prefers blondes, but that's a whole different kettle of fish. You can modify the default Flash Preferences for the way you work. We don't go through each and every Flash preference, but we show you a few that we think are important:

1. **Choose Edit⇨Preferences (Windows) or Flash⇨Preferences (Mac).**

Alternatively, you can press Ctrl+U (Windows) or ⌘+U (Mac) to open the Preferences dialog box. By default, the dialog box opens to the General section. (See Figure 5-12.)

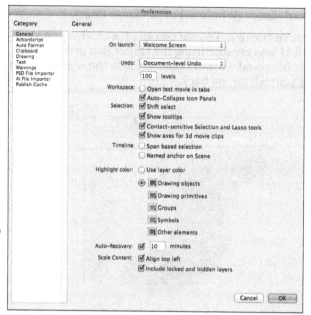

Figure 5-12:
Preferences,
and General
ones at that.

2. Modify the default preferences to suit your working style.

Most of the preferences are self-explanatory. However, we do recommend that you choose New Document from the On Launch drop-down menu. This option creates a blank document with the default document size, frame rate, background color, and ActionScript 3.0 when you launch Flash, enabling you to cut to the chase instead of dealing with the pesky welcome screen. Another option you might consider changing is the number of Undo levels, which by default is a whopping 100 steps. If you have an older computer or limited memory, lowering the number of Undo levels cuts down on the overhead that Flash places on your system.

Before you consider creating a Flash project, or for that matter, purchasing Flash, make sure your system meets the minimum system requirements.

3. Change the remaining preference categories to suit your working style.

The only other change that we recommend you make depends on whether you use ActionScript and whether you have a large desktop size. If both conditions apply, in the ActionScript tab, change the font size from 10 to 11 or 12, but keep the default Monaco font, which has code geek written all over it.

4. Click OK to apply the new preferences.

Modifying the workspace

The layout of the Flash workspace suits most designers. You can certainly choose a different workspace, or create a custom workspace to suit your working preferences. Essentials is the default workspace, but you can also choose from Animator, Classic, Debug, Designer, Developer, or Small Screen. There are also options to reset the current workspace to its original settings. And, you can also modify the workspace by opening panels and docking them or by placing them in a convenient position.

If you really like your changes, you can save them as a custom workspace. This is also a handy option if you work with another designer on the same computer. If the other designer is a gal and you're a guy — you know, the Mars and Venus thing? — you can change the workspace to suit your style of working, save it as a workspace, and then let your femme fatale Flash cohort in crime do the same. Here are a few things you can do to customize the workspace:

 ✦ **Undock a panel.** Click its title and drag it into the workspace.

 ✦ **Dock a floating panel.** Click its title bar and drag it to one of the interface sides. When you see an opaque vertical bar, release the mouse button, and the panel will develop a magnetic attraction to a side of the workspace. When you see an opaque horizontal black bar, release the mouse to dock the panel with the top or bottom of the workspace.

 ✦ **Dock one floating panel with another.** Drag its title bar toward the other panel. When an opaque blue overlay appears over the other panel, release the mouse button; the panels are joined at the title bar. If you see an opaque blue line appear over the panel to which you're docking, the panel you are moving is docked on top of the other panel.

 ✦ **Resize a panel.** Move your cursor toward a corner. When it becomes a line with a dual-headed arrow, click and drag to resize the panel.

 ✦ **Go retro.** (Imagine that you're a Flash veteran who feels bereft because of the new default workspace.) Choose Window⇨Workspace⇨Classic.

When the workspace is just the way you want it, choose Window⇨ Workspace⇨New Workspace, which opens the New Workspace dialog box. Enter a name for the workspace (Doug calls his *Flash Space Nine*) and then click OK. Your new workspace is ready to use and also appears on the Workspace menu.

If someone plays a nasty trick on you while you're at lunch and rearranges your custom workspace, choose Workspace⇨Reset *the name of your custom workspace,* and everything will be where it was when you saved the workspace.

If you feel the need to rename or delete a workspace, choose Window⇨ Workspaces⇨Manage Workspaces, which opens the Manage Workspaces dialog box. Select the workspace you want to manage, and then click Rename to open the Rename Workspace dialog box, or click Delete to delete the workspace.

Building Flashy Navigation

You can do so many things with Flash, and creating a *très* cool navigation is one of them. You can indeed create cool navigation with HTML, but Flash lets you take it a step further. If you want animated buttons (for instance, a button that makes noise), Flash is your answer. In this section, we show you how to create cool (Flash-y, if you will) navigation.

You have options when it comes to navigation menu creation. We show you how to create a navigation menu in Fireworks and then add it to an HTML document in Dreamweaver in Chapter 3 of this minibook. In Book VI, Chapter 4, we show you how to insert a navigation menu bar using a Spry widget, which is built into Dreamweaver.

Creating the navigation menu document

Before you can create a Flash navigation menu, you create a document to be the base for your menu. Before you create this document, though, you must know the size of the area in which you plan to place the navigation menu. Typically, a nav menu is the width of your site banner and the height you want for your menu. Choose a background color that's harmonious with the web page in which the menu will be placed. For this example, we show you how to create a menu 600 px x 25 px with a black background, using the default frame rate of 24 fps. (Variety is the spice of life!)

Figure 5-13 shows the document in the Essentials (default) workspace. Notice that the document is set up for Flash ActionScript 2.0. There are two reasons for this. If you use Flash only for creating animations and navigation, there's no need to learn a new programming language. The second reason is that showing you how to use ActionScript 3.0 would require many more pages than we've been allocated. (If you only knew how huffy editors get when you go over the specified page count. But that's a story for another day.) Now, on with the subject at hand: creating flashy navigation.

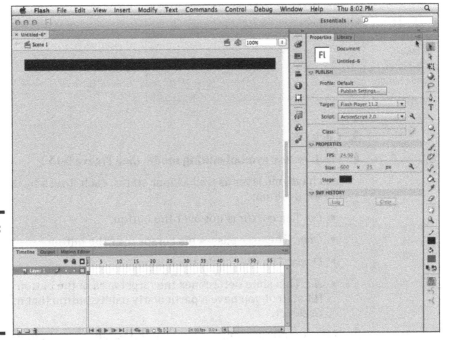

Figure 5-13:
Creating a
document
for the
Flashy
navigation
menu.

Creating buttons in Flash

Navigation menus need buttons. Flash gives you all the tools to create some
really cool buttons. If you haven't created Flash buttons before, consider
this your baptism by fire. To create a button for your menu, follow these
steps:

1. **Choose Insert➪New Symbol.**

The Create New Symbol dialog box appears.

2. **Type a name for your symbol and choose the Button behavior from
the Type drop-down menu.**

You're creating a menu, and the obvious place to start a menu is with
the Home button. Therefore, name the button **Home.** (See Figure 5-14.)

3. **Click OK.**

4. **Flash enters symbol-editing mode. (See Figure 5-15.)**

   You have one layer as well as four states, each driven by the user's cursor position:

   - *Up:* The cursor is not over the button.

   - *Over:* The user passes his cursor over the button.

   - *Down:* The user clicks the button.

   - *Hit:* This state determines the target area of the button. You add the Hit state if you have a particularly dainty button that might be hard to select.

5. **If it's not already open, choose Window⇨Properties to open the Properties Inspector.**

6. **Create the shape size for your button.**

   When creating buttons, use the Rectangle tool with a corner radius of 50 px to get an oval shape. Before creating the shape, change the Rectangle Options value in the Properties Inspector to 50, which gives you a nice rounded edge. Choosing View⇨Rulers enables you to create an object that's the approximate size of the button.

7. **Select the button shape, and in the Properties Inspector, type the desired dimensions for your button in the width and height fields.**

   To figure out what size to make each button, divide the width of your navigation menu by the number of buttons. In this example, we're creating six buttons for a navigation (nav) menu that's 600 pixels wide and 25 pixels high. Therefore, each button is 100 pixels wide and 25 pixels high. (See Figure 5-16.) We don't recommend creating a menu with different-sized buttons.

8. **Select and then align the button to the center of the Stage.**

   If you don't center the symbol when you create it, you have no way of centering it when you add it to your production.

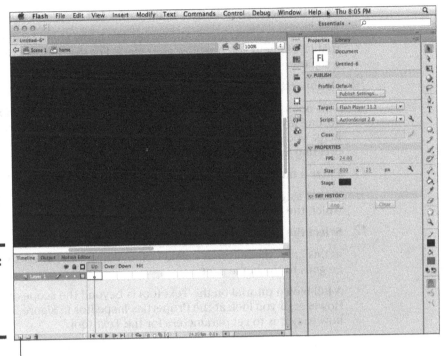

Figure 5-15:
Welcome
to symbol-
editing
mode.

New Layer button

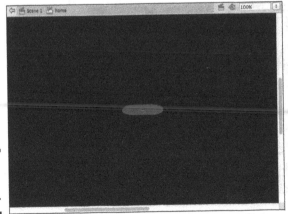

Figure 5-16:
The button
takes shape.

Press Ctrl+K (Windows) or ⌘+K (Mac) to open the Align panel. Select
the To Stage check box, and then click the icons that center the button
vertically and horizontally.

9. Click the New Layer button in the lower-left corner of the Timeline.

Flash creates a new layer. All you need to know about layers for now is that layers help you organize your work. For the button, you're creating a separate layer for button text.

10. Double-click the button text layer title.

This opens a text box into which you can type a new name for the second layer. It's not imperative, but crafting an intuitive name now helps you decipher later which layer is used for what when you're creating a complex movie or symbol.

11. Enter a name for the layer.

Text is as good a name as any. While you're at it, rename the layer on which the button resides. *Button Shape* is a good name.

12. Select the Text tool and type the desired name.

In this case, the button is called Home. When a visitor clicks this button, he goes to the home page.

A full-blown tutorial on the Text tool is beyond the scope of this book. However, if you look at the Properties Inspector in Figure 5-17, you see how easy it is to set parameters for the Text tool.

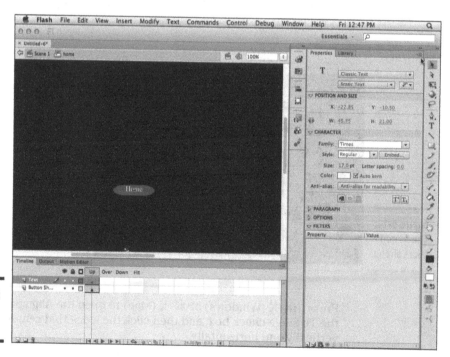

Figure 5-17: Add text to the button.

13. **Press F5 in the Down frame on the Text layer.**

This copies the contents of the Up frame to the Over and Down states.

14. **Press F6 to create keyframes for the Over and Down states on the Button Shape layer.**

Creating keyframes enables you to change or modify the contents of these frames, or make some other change that will notify users they have indeed found a clickable button. The graphic on the Down state appears when users successfully click the button.

15. **Make changes in the Over and Down states for the Button Shape layer.**

For this running example, we changed the color of the button to red in the Over frame and to orange in the Down frame.

16. **Click the Back button (looks like an arrow, and is left of the Scene title above the uppermost layer).**

The button is added to the Library and is ready for use.

Assembling your menu

After you create a button, you can duplicate the button symbol and then change the text to flesh out your menu. If you did the math right, your button is perfectly sized. When you align the buttons end to end, your menu will assembled. To assemble the menu, follow these steps. The first set of steps walks you through creating the rest of the buttons. Then you'll see how to arrange them.

1. **Right-click the symbol in the document Library and then choose Duplicate from the context menu.**

The Duplicate Symbol dialog box appears. (See Figure 5-18.)

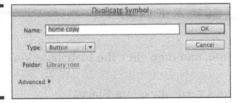

Figure 5-18:
Duplicate
a button to
complete a
nav menu.

2. **Name the symbol.**

The logical choice would be the page to which the button will link.

3. **Click OK.**

Flash duplicates the button.

Sounds like . . .

Kick up a button's cool factor by creating a new layer (named something clever, like *Sound*) and then importing a short MP3 sound clip to the document Library and inserting in the button symbol's Down layer. When the button is clicked, the sound will play.

---

4. Create enough duplicates to flesh out your menu.

For the menu we're creating here, you need four more buttons.

5. Double-click one of the duplicated buttons.

Flash enters symbol-editing mode.

6. Change the button text.

7. Repeat for the other buttons in your menu.

After creating the duplicate, arrange the buttons on the Stage:

1. Select the first button for your menu from the document Library and drag it on the Stage.

You don't have to position it exactly. You can use the Align panel to align and distribute the buttons.

2. Drag the remaining buttons onto the Stage.

Position the buttons end to end.

3. Select all the buttons.

With the Selection tool, simply click and drag around the perimeter of the buttons.

4. Press Ctrl+K (Windows) or ⌘+K (Mac).

The Align panel opens.

5. Click the To Stage icon, and then click the Distribute Vertical Center icon.

Flash aligns the buttons vertically on the Stage.

6. Click the To Stage icon, and then click the Distribute Horizontal Center icon.

The buttons are distributed horizontally to the Stage.

7. **Click the Align Vertical icon.**

Flash aligns the buttons vertically to the center of the Stage. (See Figure 5-19.)

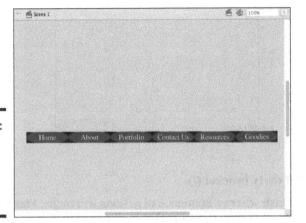

Figure 5-19:
Six little buttons all lined up neatly in a row.

Adding functionality to the buttons

If you test your menu now, the familiar pointer-hand icon appears when you pause your cursor over a button, and the button changes color and makes a noise when clicked. However, the button will do nothing, zilch, nada. Hmm. To make the button truly functional, you need to specify the page to which the button links. To do that, you must venture into the wild and wooly world of ActionScript. As we mention earlier in this chapter, this segment covers ActionScript 2.0. To make the buttons truly functional, follow these steps:

1. **Select the first button in your menu.**

2. **Choose Window⇨Actions.**

This opens the Actions panel shown in Figure 5-20. If this is your first introduction to ActionScript, you might be reminded of Pandora's box. The Actions panel has so many actions that they're divided into what the Flash designers refer to as *books*. When you click a book, you have access to all the actions within that book. And sometimes books open other books.

3. **Click inside the right pane of the Action panel and type** on(release).

This code tells Flash to execute the action when the mouse button is released.

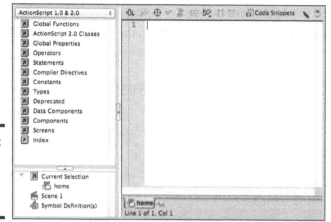

Figure 5-20:
Yikes! Look
at all those
Action
books.

4. **Type a left curly bracket ({).**

   This tells Flash where a sequence of actions will begin. Flash automatically inserts an ending curly bracket on the next line.

5. **Click the Global Functions book, click the Browser/Network book, and then double-click the getURL action.**

   This action tells Flash to navigate to the URL that is typed inside the parentheses.

6. **In the URL text field, type the URL for the web page that opens when the button is clicked.**

   The page you want to open when the button is clicked should be in the same folder as your Flash navigation menu. Therefore, just type the name of the file. For example, if you're creating a button that links to the home page, the link is index.htm.

   Having said that, you'll be creating the document on your desktop or laptop computer. To avoid the hassle of uploading the published movie to your server, consider entering the entire URL. This enables you to test the document from within Flash by pressing Ctrl+Enter (Windows) or ⌘+Return (Mac). This previews the document in another window, with full functionality.

7. **Type a comma, beginning and ending quotes, and then type one of the following options between the quotes:**

   • _self opens the page in the current frame in the current window.

   • _blank opens the page in a new window.

- _parent opens the page in the parent of the current frame.

- _top opens the page in the top-level frame in the current window.

If the button links to a page within the site, choose _self. If you're opening a page from another site, choose _blank. At this point, your Actions panel should look like the one shown in Figure 5-21.

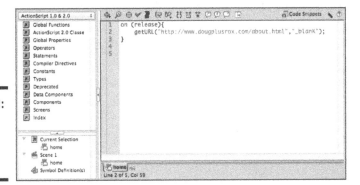

Figure 5-21: The getURL action in action.

8. **Repeat Steps 3–7 for the remaining buttons in your menu.**

You have to select each button in turn, and then add the ActionScript.

To save some time, select the three lines of code for the first button you create, right-click, and choose Copy from the context menu. Select each button in turn, open the Actions panel, place your cursor in the right side of the Actions panel, right-click, and then choose Paste from the context menu. Change the URL in the second line of code to the proper link for the button. Trust us: This saves time and takes less time to do than it does to read this Tip.

9. **Choose File⇨Save.**

10. **In the Save dialog box that appears, enter a name for the file, specify the location where you want to save the file, and then click Save.**

Saving Flash documents in the same folder as the other assets for the website is typically a good idea. Flash files are saved with the .fla extension. You can modify the FLA file at any time by reopening it. All the files you import and objects you create are saved with the file.

Publishing your file and adding it to your page

When you finish your menu in Flash, you publish it as a Flash movie. The default publishing options publish the Flash movie embedded in an HTML document. However, you plan to use the menu in an HTML document with other items. Therefore, publish the file as follows:

1. **Choose File⇨Publish Settings.**

The Publish Settings dialog box appears. (See Figure 5-22.) The default settings publish the file as a Flash SWF movie embedded in an HTML document. However, for a navigation menu that you want to add to an HTML document, all you need is the Flash movie.

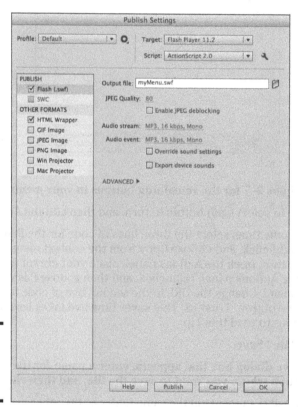

Figure 5-22:
The Publish
Settings
dialog box.

2. **Deselect the HTML option and then click OK.**

You don't need the HTML wrapper when you add a Flash movie to a page you're creating in Dreamweaver.

3. **Choose File⇨Publish.**

Flash publishes the file as a SWF movie.

Adobe Edge: The next-generation animation tool

As of this writing, Adobe is creating a new animation tool called Edge. Adobe Edge gives you the power to add animation to websites using standards like HTML5, JavaScript, and CSS3. Adobe Edge enables you to quickly create an animation without using code. The application supports web fonts and the creation of reusable symbols, which makes it possible to create different iterations of a symbol without increasing the file size. Edge also has Playback Actions, which gives you the power to create sophisticated animations without using code. Edge is compatible with modern browsers and mobile devices. As of this writing, the application is a public beta and not for sale but is available for download at `labs.adobe.com/technologies/edge`.

After you publish the navigation menu as an SWF file, you're ready to add it to your web pages. In Dreamweaver CS6, follow these steps:

1. **Create the document in which you want to add the Flash navigation menu.**

2. **Position your cursor where you want to add the menu.**

3. **Choose Insert⇨Media⇨SWF.**

   The Select SWF dialog box appears.

4. **Select the SWF file and then click OK.**

5. **In the Object Tag Accessibility Attributes dialog box, fill in the desired attributes and then click OK.**

   Dreamweaver inserts the Flash movie in your web page.

6. **Press F12 to test the file in your default browser.**

   Dreamweaver displays the web page in your default browser. We recommend that you test the document in any other browser that the site's target audience may be using.

Using Flash as an Animation Tool

In addition to creating navigation menus, you can use Flash to create impressive animations. The only limit to the capabilities of Flash are your knowledge of the program, Flash ActionScript, and your imagination. For example, you could use Flash to create an animated banner. In a nutshell, you'd create the banner text on one layer, and then create a new layer for the company logo. Refer to the "Creating your first animation" section of this chapter to animate the text and logo. Just make sure you don't have an endless loop lest your visitors become a bit loopy.

Book VI

Creating Interactive Pages with JavaScript

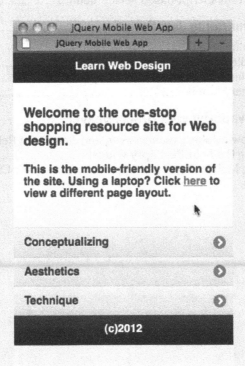

Contents at a Glance

Chapter 1: JavaScript for Animation and Interactivity

*J*avaScript is the main source of interactivity and animation in web pages. And of even greater value, it helps visitors interact with objects. They can click a button, scroll a drop-down menu, choose an option from a drop-down menu, and so on — all user-initiated events trigger an action. That action might be launching a slideshow, or opening a new browser window, or a form being *validated* (the data a user enters is tested before that data is sent to a server).

As such, JavaScript is the third leg of the basic building blocks of modern, inviting, dynamic websites, along with HTML (which we cover in Book III, and throughout this minibook) and CSS (which we cover in Book IV).

Understanding the Role of JavaScript

As you peruse the web to identify the source of various content you want to include in your site, train your brain (and eye) to identify JavaScript objects. You'll find them everywhere. For example, basic fly-out menus, like the one in Figure 1-1 from eBay, are typically created with JavaScript.

Drop-down menus and JavaScript

There are other techniques for creating animated drop-down menus. For example, some are created using only CSS (style sheets). But JavaScript drop-down menus are the most widely implemented, powerful, and accessible in a wide variety of browsing environments.

The JavaScript code that makes drop-down menus work is stored in files with a `.js`

filename extension. If you look at the source code for a website that includes JavaScript, you most likely won't see the hundreds or thousands of lines of JavaScript code that make drop-down menus and other animated, interactive elements do their thing. You will, though, see links to the external JavaScript files that make the drop-down menus work.

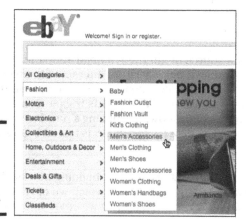

Figure 1-1: Fly-out menus are created in JavaScript.

To have a look under the hood, examine the source code by choosing View⇨ Page Source (or a similar command path, depending on your browser) for `.js`, which is the filename extension for external JavaScript files By the way, we link JavaScript files for the same basic reasons we used externally linked CSS style sheet files (something we explore throughout Book IV). The two main reasons are

✦ External (linked) files can be applied to many pages within a website, not just one.

✦ Organizing the (often large) batches of code that define CSS styles, or JavaScript files into separate, linked, external files helps keep HTML code from becoming bloated, indecipherable, and confusing in a sea of CSS or JavaScript.

JavaScript: Not just for web browsers

JavaScript, by the way, doesn't run only in web browsers. JavaScript (or adaptations of it) is used to write programs that run on *servers* — the big "back end" computers that host websites. However, the most popular application of JavaScript is to create animation and interactivity in websites, and that's the dimension of JavaScript that we explore in this book.

The menus at eBay, for example, are managed with external JavaScript files like the one revealed in the code in Figure 1-2. That HTML code includes the `<script>` element that encloses a link to a JavaScript file.

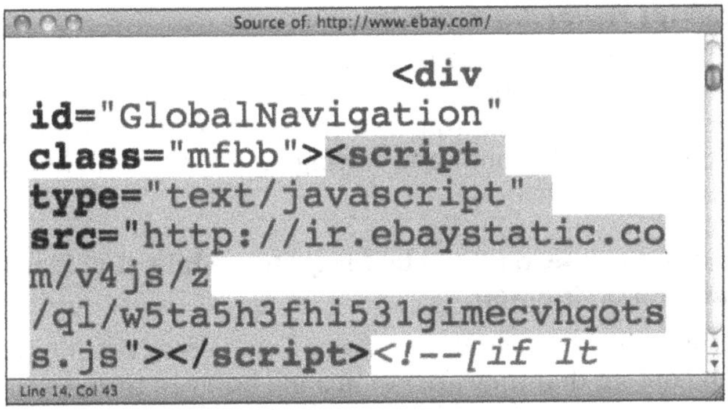

Book VI Chapter 1

JavaScript for Animation and Interactivity

Figure 1-2: Examine the source code to identify links to external JavaScript files.

```
                    <div
id="GlobalNavigation"
class="mfbb"><script
type="text/javascript"
src="http://ir.ebaystatic.co
m/v4js/z
/q1/w5ta5h3fhi531gimecvhqots
s.js"></script><!--[if lt
```

Shortly, we'll break down the code revealed in Figure 1-2, but here are three key things about relatively complex JavaScripts that create interactivity:

✦ **JavaScripts are enclosed in `<script>` and `</script>` tags in HTML.**

Read more about these tags in this minibook.

✦ **JavaScript works closely with CSS selectors.**

In the example code, note the ID selector named `Global Navigation` (you might guess that it has something to do with formatting a navigation bar) as well as the more cryptically named class selector `mfbb`.

✦ **JavaScript, on the level of creating anything substantial like an interactive menu, is saved in separate, external files.**

This underlying mechanism is similar to how CSS style sheets are saved to linked, external files. And, as with CSS, saving JavaScript as external, linked files means that same JavaScript can be applied throughout a website, without having to be re-created individually for every page.

JavaScript and Flash

A client recently posed the following criteria for an online portfolio: It had to be a really inviting, attractive, dynamic Flash slideshow that producers could review on their iPads.

Well, as you might have guessed, there is no such possibility because Flash doesn't play on iPads (or on an iPhone or iPod touch). But the fact that meeting this challenge was technically impossible didn't mean that it wasn't real. People have come to expect a level of animation, effects, and interactivity in certain kinds of web pages (like slideshows) that has historically been provided by Flash.

Is JavaScript replacing Flash?

JavaScript is emerging as the replacement for Flash. We use the present tense "is emerging" as opposed to "has emerged," even with the understanding that hundreds of years from now (okay, a few years from now), people will still be reading this book and relying on it for current information. There are two reasons for this:

✦ **It is still the case, and will be for quite a while, that Flash content will be around on the web.**

Designers have invested time, money, and creativity into building Flash content that they are not in a big hurry to throw away. And Flash has applicability beyond the web. Desktop and laptop browsers will continue to include the Flash Player, and as of this writing, Google is supporting Flash in its Android mobile devices. In short, there is a substantial body of work as well as an established user-base for Flash — and will be for a while.

✦ **At this stage of development, JavaScript does not provide the same level of effects and animation as Flash.** This is due to two factors:

- *Flash is not just a format.* It's a program, an application from Adobe, with sophisticated design tools that are not available (at least as of this writing) in any JavaScript-generating tool. There are apps in development or coming onto the market, like Adobe's Edge, that do generate JavaScript. But at this stage of development, they are not nearly as powerful as Flash, the program.

- *The Flash Player does some of the "heavy lifting" (computer processing) required for really smooth and, well, "flashy" animated effects.*

Flash Player is a *plug-in,* or software that is added to (plugged into) a browser or operating system. In fact, this was one of the reasons why Steve Jobs argued that Apple devices should not support Flash. If Apple allowed the Flash Player plug-in on its devices, that would absorb processing resources (reducing battery time) and interfere with Apple's attempt to maintain a distinct and unique interface in its devices.

JavaScript and CSS3

As we explain earlier, one of the differences between JavaScript and Flash is that JavaScript runs *native* in browsers. That is, it doesn't require but also doesn't have access to additional tools to speed up the resolution of effects, for example.

In design and aesthetic terms, this means that some of the effects that designers and users have come to expect in slideshows aren't really available in JavaScript. Or, they don't work as well. Effects like fades, for example, are choppier in JavaScript than the smooth resolves between slides possible with Flash.

On the other hand, because JavaScript does run native in browsers, without running in a plug-in (like Flash Player), it can more easily access and take advantage of HTML and CSS. And in particular, JavaScript can be (and is often) linked closely with CSS, and with CSS3 effects, like transparency.

The special role of JavaScript in mobile pages

JavaScript plays a particular and growing role in designing pages for mobile devices. Before we get a bit technical, take a quick look at some of the specific challenges in designing mobile-friendly websites.

The challenges in designing inviting, accessible mobile pages include

+ **Small screens:** Mobile pages are small, as small as 320 pixels (px) wide. You can't fit much content on a mobile screen. Even tablets, with widths of 768 px, for example (in portrait mode), have considerably less onscreen real estate than a laptop.

+ **Download speeds:** Mobile pages are often downloaded over 3G, 4G, or other mobile networks that (despite all the claims by competing cellphone providers) are significantly slower and flakier than home or office DSL and cable connections.

Now, think for a moment about how these two challenges interact with each other to create a mega-challenge: You can't put much content on a single mobile page, but if you try to make additional content available through linked pages, users will have to endure annoying waits for those linked pages to open.

The generally applied solution is to use JavaScript — and, in particular, a subset of JavaScript called *jQueryMobile* — to essentially hide, and then display, sections of a web page as a user interacts with the page.

Here, basically, is how that works: Most mobile-friendly sites are composed of a *single* HTML document. That is to say, they are really just a single web page. However, that single HTML document looks like multiple pages to a visitor because those mobile pages contain multiple jQuery Mobile "pages" that open and close in response to users tapping the screens of their mobile devices. The terminology gets a bit crazy, but the basic concept is this: HTML pages can have multiple jQuery Mobile pages within them.

The mobile page in Figure 1-3, for example, appears to include links to three pages (Conceptualizing, Aesthetics, Technique). When a user taps those links on a mobile device, though, what actually happens behind the curtain is that JavaScript closes some content (the home page) and displays other content (one of the three clickable pages).

Figure 1-3: jQuery Mobile, a subset of JavaScript, is key to designing mobile-friendly pages.

We describe how to create jQuery Mobile pages in depth in Chapter 4 of this minibook, through the doorway of Dreamweaver CS6's impressive set of jQuery Mobile–generating options.

Understanding That JavaScript Is a Programming Language

Here's the short version of this section: JavaScript is too complicated for most of us to actually program, so instead, we rely on various tools to generate JavaScript.

That doesn't mean that you can't have dynamic, inviting web pages with all the JavaScript you need. That does mean in large part, though, that you choose menu options from programs and online resources to generate that JavaScript, and then integrate the generated JavaScript and other files (almost always CSS files) into your own site.

HTML and CSS and JavaScript

In Books III (HTML) and IV (CSS), you can learn enough HTML and CSS to jump in and start coding pages yourself, just based on the code in those chapters. You can enhance pages by exploring more HTML tags and more CSS selectors online, but

✦ You can use those additional tags and selectors to write your own code, moving into more complex coding as you gain experience and become more comfortable.

✦ Even if you copy and paste some of that HTML or CSS, you can understand and edit pretty easily.

That's not the case with JavaScript, though. JavaScript is a programming language, requiring much more complex coding than HTML and CSS. You can take the HTML and CSS you learn in this book to create quite a complex website. However, we would have to devote this entire book to JavaScript to cover enough of that language to create usable programs to fulfill the requirements of the JavaScript examples we've explored so far in figures in this chapter (menu bars and slideshows).

Beyond that, coding the JavaScript required for common applications (like validating forms, or presenting slides) would be an exercise in reinventing the wheel. Professional, full-time JavaScript programmers develop and test the code required for these tasks — and make it available: sometimes for free, sometimes for a fee (we're talking in the $35 range for a slideshow script).

The implication of all this? For most JavaScript applications, you either

✦ Copy, paste, and edit JavaScript you get somewhere.

✦ Generate JavaScript using online resources or applications like Dreamweaver, with its fairly developed JavaScript-generating tools.

The role of DIY JavaScript

In this minibook, we explore how JavaScript is used, the basic principles of coding JavaScript, and demonstrate some simple scripts you can create yourself.

So what kind of JavaScript can you code yourself? We code JavaScript from scratch in Chapter 2 of this minibook for two reasons. One is that simple JavaScripts — such as creating alerts (popups), inserting the time, or providing a link that replicates the Back button on a browser — are useful tools and things you can do on your own. The other reason to learn basic JavaScript syntax is that it will help you look at, edit at times, and understand JavaScript that you get from other sources.

But the meat of the minibook is showing you how to access, customize, and apply various available packages of JavaScript, including JavaScript *libraries* (customizable code) and *generators* (applications and resources that generate JavaScript code without coding).

Seeing That JavaScript Is Client-Side Scripting

Client-side scripting is basically a technical name for scripts that run in a browser — meaning, in this case, that JavaScripts run in a browser like Internet Explorer, Chrome, Firefox, or Safari.

What are the real-world implications of this? It means that the things you do with JavaScript are constrained by its inability to send data to, or grab data from, a remote web server.

For example, the scripts (programming) used to handle an order you place for a book at Amazon online or eBay have to run on a *server* — a massive computer that hosts websites and data. Those scripts combine user input (the order you place) with databases that store the price, shipping costs, inventory stock, and other data needed to fulfill your order. We examine *server-side* scripting in Book VI. Those are scripts that manage content on servers, like data submitted in a form.

Where did that name come from?

JavaScript has nothing to do with another programming language called Java. The origin of the name JavaScript is a weird story that can be boiled down to one word: marketing. At some stage of its development, in the course of conflicts between the powers-that-be in the web world (like Oracle/Sun on the one hand, and Microsoft on the other), someone decided calling the language "JavaScript" would cash in on the cache (at the time) of the Java programming language. And the name stuck.

On the other hand, JavaScript manages all kinds of interactivity within a browser, or *client,* to use that technical term for the last time in this chapter.

Drop-down menus that send visitors to pages in your website? Client-side scripting. Pages that allow a visitor to customize the color scheme? Client-side scripting. Popups that provide sometimes annoying warnings when you enter or leave a page? Well, you get the point.

Any script that reacts to a user, but does not send a record of that activity to a server, is a client-side script. And JavaScript is where almost all of them come from.

Seeing How JavaScript Works

Scripts and programs are very different if you go see a play. The script tells the actors what to say, and the program tells you how many acts are in the play and who the actors are. But in web design, a script and a program are the same thing. Scripts and programs (in web design) are batches of computer code that make something *happen.* That something might be a program that reacts to a user's click, or a program that updates the weather in a website.

Websites that are interactive (react to visitors' actions) or animated (have things that move around), or both, are created using a scripting/programming language.

JavaScript is a scripting language *and* a programming language because it's used to write programs that make things happen.

So, then, what is *not* a scripting or programming language? Neither HTML nor CSS are scripting/programming languages. HTML is considered a "markup" language because it is used to define content (like a heading, or a form), but it doesn't ("in the main") *do* anything. CSS is considered a styling language because, in the main, it defines how web page elements look.

Take a look, in very broad strokes, at the "how" of JavaScript. In very basic terms, it might be helpful to think of two levels of JavaScript:

✦ Simple lines of code you can write yourself

✦ Complex combinations of JavaScript and CSS that you would not want to create yourself unless you choose to branch off into learning a full-fledged, complex coding language

We first discuss the simple lines before getting into the complex combinations.

Simple lines of JavaScript code

The most basic application of JavaScript, as we allude to earlier in this chapter, involves lines of code that produce interactive elements that appear onscreen, often in response to a visitor's action.

For example, popups — like the one in Figure 1-4, that appear so frequently as you enter and leave web pages — are JavaScript and nothing but JavaScript. There is no CSS to define how they look and no HTML to create the message in them.

The JavaScript that launches the alert box in Figure 1-4 when a page *loads* (opens in a browser) can be inserted as a parameter for the <body> tag, like this:

```
<body onLoad="alert('Entering commits you to a scary loss of privacy.')">
```

Figure 1-4:
Those ubiquitous popups? JavaScript. Here, viewed in Internet Explorer.

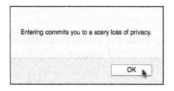

The display of the actual popup box itself is defined entirely by the browser in which the JavaScript opens. So, for example, the same JavaScript popup

that appears one way in Internet Explorer, has the same text content but looks quite different in Safari, as shown in Figure 1-5.

Figure 1-5:
The display of popups is determined by browsers. Here's a popup in Safari.

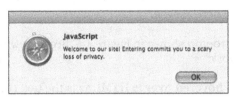

Here are a couple things to digest, in terms of the kind of JavaScript that you write yourself, embedded in an HTML file:

✦ **Simple JavaScripts can be created with just HTML and JavaScript.** And any CSS applied to the page will apply to things like the font applied to display a date.

✦ **Simple JavaScripts don't create the level of interactivity and animation you need for things like slideshows.** That requires both more complex JavaScript coding, and combining that coding with controllable style sheet elements.

JavaScript plus CSS

More complex JavaScript — the kind that creates more dynamic, interactive, and fun elements in a web page — requires some things that simple JavaScript does not:

✦ **Long scripts:** Even a simple tooltip can easily take 1,000 lines of JavaScript.

✦ **HTML:** Works on making interactive HTML elements like text, images, and media.

✦ **Linked style sheets:** Complex JavaScript, used to create things like slideshows, tooltips, and mobile device pages, is actually a combination of complex CSS styles and JavaScript.

Take a relatively simple example of a complex JavaScript (hey, everything is relative) and use it to get a handle on how JavaScript, HTML, and CSS work hand in hand. You can also see how that relationship opens the door to quite a bit of potential for you to customize all manner of JavaScripts without touching the JavaScript, but instead tweaking the HTML content and CSS styles that play a big role in how the JavaScript works and displays.

Every CSS technique we cover in Book IV is applicable to what we discuss here, in terms of modifying the CSS styles that come with complex, generated JavaScript. And, for that matter, the HTML techniques that we explore in Book III are applicable here as well.

Our example here is the tooltip shown in Figure 1-6. Break down the three elements that make it work:

✦ **The link text that is hovered over is HTML** as is the text (the draconian agreement) that appears in the tooltip when that link is hovered over.

✦ **The design of the tooltip box is CSS**, including the light background color (yellow), the rounded corners (a CSS3 effect), and the border.

✦ **The coding that makes the HTML text and CSS formatting appear when the text is hovered over is JavaScript.**

Figure 1-6:
More complex JavaScript elements combine HTML, CSS, and JavaScript.

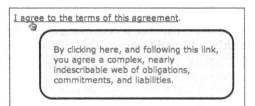

And given that most JavaScript is saved as an external file (that is, linked to the HTML page to which it applies), most pages with JavaScript require at least three files. One of those three files is the HTML file in which, or to which, the JavaScript runs. That HTML file is, of course, created with plain 'ol HTML.

Here is the HTML code that creates the alert in Figure 1-6:

```
<span id="sprytrigger1">
<a href="#">I agree to the terms of this agreement</a>.</span>
<div class="tooltipContent" id="sprytooltip1">By clicking here, and following
    this link, you agree a complex, nearly indescribable web of obligations,
    commitments, and liabilities.
</div>
```

This HTML includes span and DIV tags, which are tools for applying CSS styles that we explore in Book IV. And even if you don't recognize them, it's not hard to figure out which part of this HTML code you would edit if you wanted to change either the triggering link text (I agree...) or the tooltip content (By clicking here...).

And what about the CSS required to make this JavaScript work?

The JavaScript requires a class selector, named .tooltipContent. That CSS class selector can be customized. For example, the CSS code to create a tooltip that looks like the one in Figure 1-6 is

```css
.tooltipContent {
    background-color: #FFFF66;
    width: 320px;
    font-family: Verdana, Geneva, sans-serif;
    margin: 6px;
    padding: 24px;
    -webkit-border-radius: 25px;
    -moz-border-radius: 25px;
    border-radius: 25px;
    border: medium solid black;
}
```

Note that in the HTML example, you see div class="tooltipContent". In the CSS file, add a dot beforehand, to become .tooltipContent.

Nothin' here that isn't covered in Books III and IV. Just some HTML and CSS to edit.

Often, when you generate JavaScript — be it for a tooltip, menu bar, or slideshow — you customize the content and appearance of that JavaScript not by messing with the generated external JavaScript (.js) file itself, but simply by tweaking the HTML and CSS — a much more manageable task.

JavaScript's offspring: AJAX, jQuery, and jQuery Mobile

Because JavaScript does most of its magic by interacting with other elements — especially CSS elements — developers who package JavaScript into editable libraries (to be adapted for all kinds of applications) have developed packages of JavaScript, CSS, and HTML.

The most dominant of those packages is Asynchronous JavaScript and XML (AJAX), which at this point has very little relevance to what AJAX actually does or how it works because AJAX doesn't require the XML (a markup language), nor does it have to be created with *asynchronous* JavaScript (a particular form for interacting with data). A library of AJAX functionality that can be relatively easily adapted is the Spry framework, which is sponsored by Adobe.

To come at this from another angle: Developers have put together packages of ready-to-use JavaScript for things like menus or placing data on a page, and these packages (libraries) are used by other developers. These libraries are more accessible to noncoders than writing JavaScript from scratch, and can be packaged as editable tools for building all kinds of interactive content. What does that mean to you, the noncoder? Mainly, the libraries of editable JavaScript that you find online, and the packages that generate JavaScript, probably use AJAX. Not a huge issue to you, but useful to know.

The most significant JavaScript *library* — set of packaged JavaScript — as of this writing is jQuery. The jQuery library (set of modules that can be put together to make a script) makes it easier to create JavaScript. And, as we discuss earlier in this chapter, a very important offspring of jQuery is jQuery Mobile, with a refined set of tools for mobile web development, like expandable pages and accessible forms.

Discovering Where to Get JavaScript

If you're asking yourself, "Where do I get JavaScript?", you're ahead of the game because you're asking that question instead of, "How do I become a JavaScript programmer?"

In a nutshell, you'll most likely tap into a substantial and growing world of editable JavaScript libraries and JavaScript-generating tools and resources. Read all about that in Chapters 2 and 3 of this minibook.

The enhanced value of Dreamweaver

If you're thinking about designing pages with a lot of JavaScript, that might be an argument for investing in Dreamweaver. If creating mobile-friendly sites with a lot of jQuery Mobile is a high priority, that only enhances the argument for taking up Dreamweaver. And, if you're intent on creating apps that can be distributed through the Apple App Store and the Google Android Marketplace, you have a fairly compelling reason to invest in Dreamweaver CS5.5 or later because the app-generating tools introduced in CS5.5 have been incrementally enhanced in CS6.

Compared with our exploration of HTML in Book III or CSS in Book IV, this minibook on JavaScript puts enhanced focus on techniques in Dreamweaver CS6 for generating JavaScript and jQuery Mobile that are arguably the most valuable tools in Dreamweaver CS6.

Open source and other JavaScript options

Also in your potential arsenal are open source and other commercial alternatives to Dreamweaver for creating jQuery Mobile pages. An emerging tool for generating JavaScript is Adobe Edge, a program that as we go to press is in *alpha* phase (downloadable for people who want to test it, but not close to final release). The concept is that designers who don't want to code will be able to create effects and animation in a WYSIWYG environment, and then Edge will spit out all the HTML, CSS, and JavaScript files required to make that animation work. It's too early to pass judgment on Edge, which is getting mixed reviews at this stage of the game. Free downloads of the preview (in-development) version of Edge are available at `http://labs.adobe.com/technologies/edge`.

**Book VI
Chapter 1**

**JavaScript for
Animation and
Interactivity**

Critics argue the feasibility of creating a wide range of serious animation and interactivity without coding JavaScript. Others look with intrigue and hope for the prospect of a Flash-like program that outputs JavaScript instead of Flash's ActionScript (which was always a cousin of JavaScript). At this point, Edge isn't yet a functional tool for generating JavaScript, but stay tuned as it evolves and emerges.

"Borrowing" JavaScript

As alluded to throughout this chapter, and emphasized here, "borrowing" JavaScript (editing libraries or generating code) is the approach that the vast majority of web designers use. There are many sources for JavaScript packages that can be used to generate everything from drop-down menus to slideshows. And for simpler projects, like popups or *rollover* images (images that change when hovered over), there are a plethora of online sources for easily editable JavaScript code.

Often, developers will add comment lines in their JS files that indicate their stance on the copyright of the code. If the file contains a copyright statement, don't copy any of it. If the file contains a "must include byline" statement, then follow the author's request to include a byline. But don't ignore the original author's ownership rights by indiscriminately copying code!

That said, some basic JavaScript functions can be coded (yes, coded) on the fly without mastering the whole art and science of programming. Here are a few simple examples: a link that works like a browser's Back button, or a script that inserts the current day and time into a web page. We explore those options, and just enough JavaScript syntax to understand the code you encounter, in the next chapter of this minibook. After that, we look at some of the more powerful and accessible tools for generating JavaScript.

For those of you who do want to dive into programming with JavaScript on a deeper level, one starting point is *JavaScript & AJAX For Dummies*.

Chapter 2: DIY JavaScript

In This Chapter

✔ Creating popup alerts

✔ Using buttons with JavaScript

✔ Navigating with JavaScript

✔ Creating and inserting updatable variables

As we touch on in Chapter 1 of this minibook, you can create simple JavaScript yourself to do things like embed the current time and date in a page, or display a popup. We cover this do-it-yourself dimension of JavaScript in this chapter.

We also note that the kinds of complex JavaScript used for things like drop-down menus and slideshows are beyond what's covered in this book. Scripts like that are the products of much work by teams of professional programmers who make them available commercially through packages that generate JavaScript. However, that doesn't mean you can't use and customize complex JavaScript programs. You don't have to code JavaScript to customize JavaScript-based programs. The JavaScript you get from an online source can be customized by editing the associated HTML and CSS that work with that JavaScript. We focus on customizing JavaScript-based animation and interactivity in Chapter 3 of this minibook.

Adding JavaScript to an HTML Page

Learning to create such simple JavaScript code opens the door to include a nice set of handy features in your web pages. But more than that, crafting your own simple code provides you with a basic understanding of JavaScript that allows you to work more effectively with generated JavaScript and editable JavaScript code.

Complex JavaScript should be saved to an external `.js` file, and even simple JavaScript that performs functions like opening a popup or inserting today's date in a page can be saved that way. Later in this chapter, we walk through how that's done. But for now, get your feet wet in JavaScript by simply adding some to an HTML page.

Defining a script

JavaScript (and any script) in an HTML page has to be placed inside
`<script>` tags. Otherwise, browsers will interpret it as HTML and display
the JavaScript code as text on the page.

The following HTML code is the basic framework for including JavaScript in
a page, inside `<script>` tags:

```
<!doctype html>
<html>
<body>
<script type="text/javascript">
[the JavaScript code goes here]
</script>
</body>
</html>
```

Objects, properties, and methods

One of the most basic things you can do with JavaScript is to write to a
document. This simply means, "print the specified on the user's screen."
Although writing to a document doesn't do anything very exciting on its
own, it is a basic JavaScript command used as part of more complicated
(and interesting) scripts.

The syntax for that is

```
<!doctype html>
<html>
<body>
<h1>
<script type="text/javascript">
document.write("This is JavaScript");
</script>
</h1>
</body>
</html>
```

The preceding script simply creates a heading 1 tag with the text `This`
`is JavaScript`. Not that exciting, so far, but it gives you an opportunity
to examine the different elements of basic JavaScript code: In JavaScript,
objects (things like a document), *properties* (that modify objects), and methods are separated with *dots* (periods).

Beyond DIY JavaScript

JavaScript, beyond the "do it yourself" level, uses keywords (such as `var`, `function`, `if`, `for`, `while`, `alert`, `print`); values (such as `null`, `undefined`, `strings`, `numbers`, `boolean` [`true` and `false`], `arrays`); and operators (`+`, `-`, `++`, `--`, `>`, `<`, `>=`, `<=`, `!==`, `===`, `!=`, `!!`, `&&`, `||`, `*`, `/`) to string together `if` . . . `then` statements that evaluate user input or other factors (like what time it is) and then produce different results depending on how values and operators are combined. But, again, stringing together keywords, operators, and values into complex programs is a science and art that requires a high level of programming skill.

In our example, the code includes basic elements of JavaScript, strung together with dots:

+ `document` is a JavaScript *object*, something on a web page (or in this case, the page itself). Other JavaScript objects include images, buttons, links, or class or ID `DIV` tags.

+ `write ()` is a JavaScript *method*, an action performed on the object. And the text inside the parentheses is a *variable* — in this case, simply the text that is written in the `document`.

Don't trip too much on the difference between an object, a property, a method, and a value in JavaScript. These are somewhat flexible and relative terms. JavaScript defines its parts in much more loose and more flexible ways than many other languages.

In JavaScript, most things can be considered objects. If you define a new variable (`var x;`), you're creating a new object. Shortly, we explore *functions* in JavaScript, which do things like calculate and place the current date in a document. These functions could also be considered an object as well.

The final concept we'll throw into the hopper is *event handlers*, which are triggered by actions in a browser. Here are a few examples of event handlers:

+ `onload` triggers a JavaScript when a web page opens.

+ `onunload` triggers a JavaScript when a web page closes.

+ `onclick` triggers a JavaScript when a user clicks an element.

We use these event handlers in the examples we are about to explore.

Using JavaScript Date Functions

Take a minute to quickly revisit the `document.write` example from earlier in this chapter:

```
<script type="text/javascript">
document.write("This is JavaScript");
</script>
```

That code simply prints `This is JavaScript` on a page. However, `document.write` can also be used to write functions on a page.

The `Date()` function in JavaScript is most effectively used as part of complex coding, but it works on its own to display the current date and time, as in this code:

```
<!doctype html>
<html>
<body>
<h3>
The correct time is:
<script type="text/javascript"> document.write(Date()); </script>
</h3>
</body>
</html>
```

This code can make a web page a bit more dynamic because the displayed date and time will update as time elapses.

And this example strings together a JavaScript object (`document`), method (`write`), and value (`date`), all enclosed in an HTML `<script>` element that identifies this as JavaScript for browsers.

Applying JavaScript: Inline, Embedded, or Linked

Having gotten your feet wet with a line of JavaScript (technically speaking, you're a JavaScript coder now!), it's valuable to identify the three ways how JavaScript can be applied in a page: inline, embedded, or linked.

Inline JavaScript is written in the `<body>` section of an HTML page. Early in this chapter, we examine examples of inline JavaScript used to create a "back" link and to embed the date in a document. The examples we explored so far in this chapter were all inline. Inline is the quickest but least reliable and least flexible way to create and apply JavaScript.

A better, more efficient, and more standard (and reliable) way to apply JavaScript in an individual page is to use the *embed* method, which involves defining the JavaScript in the `<head>` element. You can define a JavaScript function, like the ones we created so far, in the <head> element of an HTML document, and then use that script in the body of the document.

Embedded script is more efficient than inline script, but not as powerful as external linked scripting. External scripts can be used on any web page, but embedded scripts can only be used within a single HTML page. On the other hand, embedded scripts are more powerful than inline scripts because you can use them multiple times *within the same HTML page*.

The following JavaScript code uses the history object to create a defined script (within <script> tags) for a Back button in the <head> element of an HTML document and then applies that script twice within the document.

```
<!doctype html>
<html>
<head>
<script type="text/javascript">
function goBack()
    {
    window.history.back()
    }
</script>
</head>
<body>
<h1>Here is a chance to navigate back to your previous
    page:</h1>
<input type="button" value="Back" onclick="goBack()" />
<h1>Here is yet another chance to navigate back to your
    previous page:</h1>
<input type="button" value="Back" onclick="goBack()" />
</body>
</html>
```

The preceding code produces a page that looks like Figure 2-1.

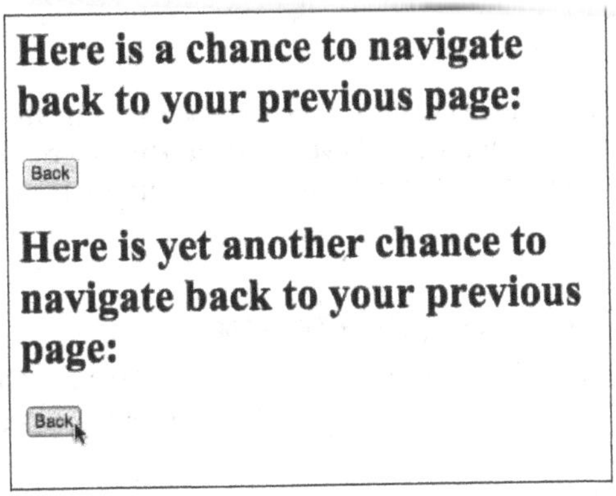

Here is a chance to navigate back to your previous page:

Here is yet another chance to navigate back to your previous page:

Figure 2-1:
Testing a
Back button
created with
JavaScript.

Finally, the most powerful and effective way to deploy JavaScript is to save the script as an external linked file. As noted earlier, external, linked JavaScript files can be applied in any page. Note, though, that JavaScript files don't require a document declaration (like `<!doctype html>` in an HTML document). Instead, they are saved with a `.js` filename extension. We will return to this technique shortly when we start writing scripts.

Looking at Useful DIY JavaScripts

Many common interactive functions can be created with just a few lines of JavaScript. You can, for example

+ Launch a popup alert dialog box.

+ Create a button that works like a browser's Back button.

+ Design a jump menu for navigation.

Even though these are relatively simple scripts, in some cases for the examples in this section, we provide the JavaScript that is saved to an external JavaScript file.

Generally speaking, the process is

+ **The JavaScript itself is saved to a file with a `.js` filename extension.**

+ **Any and all HTML documents that use that script have to include the following in the `<head>` section of the HTML document:**

    ```
    <script src="xyz.js"></script>
    ```

    where `xyz.js` is the filename of the JavaScript. If your JavaScript is saved to a subfolder of the folder in which the HTML file is saved to, you need to include a path to that folder. For example, if the JavaScript is in a subfolder `javascripts/alerts`, the preceding line of code would look like this:

    ```
    <script src="javascripts/alerts/xyz.js"></script>
    ```

+ **In most cases, additional HTML in the body section of the HTML document inserts and configures the JavaScript in the page.** That varies depending on the script, and is explained individually for each example in this section.

Not using or disabling JavaScript

All browsers with any significant user base today support JavaScript, but users can elect to turn JavaScript off in any browser. Some people prefer a browsing experience devoid of any popups or other JavaScript-powered activity. Others have JavaScript turned off by accident.

In any event, you can alert visitors to a page in which their browser configuration has JavaScript turned off by using <noscript> tags in the body element of an HTML document.

For example, the following simple script displays the message, This page requires JavaScript. Your browser has JavaScript turned off. if someone opens the page with JavaScript disabled.

```
<noscript>
<h1>This page requires JavaScript, and your browser
    configuration has JavaScript disabled!</h1>
</noscript>
```

Book VI
Chapter 2

The heading 1 (<h1>, </h1>) tags are optional here, and simply serve to make the display large and impressive, as shown in Figure 2-2.

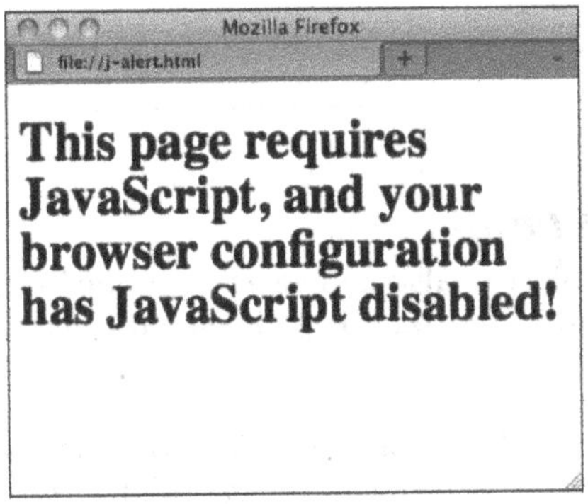

DIY JavaScript

Figure 2-2:
Let visitors know their browser has JavaScript disabled.

> Mozilla Firefox
> file://j-alert.html
>
> # This page requires JavaScript, and your browser configuration has JavaScript disabled!

You don't need to create a JavaScript file to make this work. The <noscript> tag is HTML, and browsers don't need any JavaScript to display the <noscript> text where appropriate (or to hide it if not necessary).

This script won't appear if a visitor does have JavaScript enabled, and it alerts visitors without JavaScript that they're not seeing JavaScript-based content.

The <noscript> element goes in the <body> element of an HTML document — not the <head> element — because it defines text that appears in a browser page (if that browser doesn't have JavaScript enabled).

If you want to test pages in a browser, you can find options in a browser's Preferences dialog box that disable JavaScript. Figure 2-3 shows JavaScript disabled in Firefox, for example.

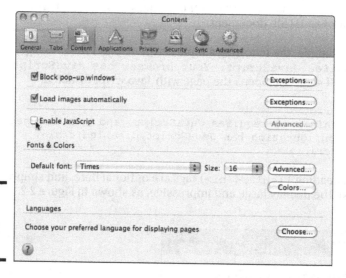

Figure 2-3:
Disabling
JavaScript
in Firefox.

Creating an alert popup

The ubiquitous JavaScript alert — also known as a "popup" — appears on too many websites. You know: *Are you sure you want to leave this page?* An annoying prompt.

On the other hand, alerts can play a valuable role informing visitors of things they need to know before (or after) viewing a page. And, as we shall see shortly, alerts can also be a way of providing sitewide access to updated information, and they also can be a way to present or make accessible globally updatable information.

Launching an alert when a page is opened

You might want to create an alert that confirms to a user that he or she has a JavaScript-enabled browser. For example, you have content at your site that requires JavaScript to be enabled, and you want to give visitors a way to test their browser configuration so they can be sure they have JavaScript "turned on." You could provide a Click Here to See Whether You Have JavaScript Enabled link to take visitors to a page with an alert that reassures them that they have JavaScript turned on and working.

And here's how to do that. To present that alert — one that displays if a visitor has JavaScript enabled — use the following code in an external JavaScript file:

```
alert("You have JavaScript enabled");
```

With the JavaScript file saved as `alert.js`, you can create a link to that script from any page in your website — just make sure that the JavaScript and HTML file are in the same folder on your site.

And the following HTML to display the alert `You have JavaScript enabled` (if a visitor actually does have JavaScript enabled):

```
<!doctype html>
<html>
<head>
<title>Check JavaScript</title>
<script src="alert.js"></script>
</head>
<body>
</body>
</html>
```

Using an alert to provide updated information

In the preceding example, the alert message is relatively timeless. It is interactive in the sense that it displays only if a visitor has JavaScript enabled. But there is another, more powerful dimension to JavaScript that can come into play here: JavaScript can be used to embed updated information throughout a website.

For example, if you need to update announcements across a website, you could do that simply by changing the information in the alert code of the JavaScript.

To take a simple example, say you choose to alert visitors when your city or area has issued some kind of warning — a smog alert in Los Angeles, a gridlock alert in New York City, a fog alert in London, or an air-quality alert in Cairo. You create a JavaScript file (with a filename like `traffic.js`) that displays an alert message, as in the following example:

```
alert("Our city has issued a traffic advisory, please
    consider sharing a ride, biking, or taking public
    transportation!");
```

The preceding code is the whole JavaScript file. To display this alert when a page opens, you can embed a link to that script in the head section of your page. Here's the code for a very basic HTML page with a link to that script:

```
<!doctype HTML>
<html>
<head>
<meta charset="UTF-8">
<script type="text/javascript" src="traffic.js">
</script>
</head>
<body>
</body>
</html>
```

Visitors to your site would see the message in the alert box in Figure 2-4. And, of course, you can change the message when traffic eases up.

Figure 2-4:
Use an alert to provide updated information throughout a website.

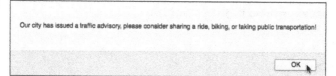

Our city has issued a traffic advisory, please consider sharing a ride, biking, or taking public transportation!

OK

Button-activated alerts

One widely applicable and easy-to-create method for launching JavaScripts is to provide visitors with a clickable button that starts the JavaScript. Explore how this works by adjusting the previous example to make the alert accessible only if a button is clicked. The obvious advantage is that visitors can elect to view the popup information or not.

For example, the traffic alert in the previous example could be adjusted to appear only if a visitor clicks a button. The JavaScript file code is

```
function upDate()   {   alert("Traffic is OK  today")   }
```

And the HTML code is

```
<!doctype html>
<html>
<head>
<title>Traffic Alert</title>
<script src="alert.js">
</script>
</head>
<body>
```

```
<input type="button" value="Traffic Alert Update" onclick="upDate()"/>
</body>
</html>
```

The head section in the preceding JavaScript links to a JavaScript file, `alert.js`. In the `<body>` element of the document, the `input` tag parameters define a button that displays text (the value) as well as the action that the button performs: Namely, when the button is clicked, the `upDate` function in the linked JavaScript script is activated.

The result is an interactive button that provides access to updated traffic alerts, like the one in Figure 2-5. And, of course, this button could be installed in multiple HTML pages, and updated globally by updating the JavaScript file.

Figure 2-5:
Launching
an alert with
a button
to provide
globally
updated
info.

Using JavaScript for navigation

The basic dynamism of the web has always been interactivity. The *hyper* in HyperText Markup Language (HTML) represented the ability to click a link and go somewhere.

JavaScript can make navigation more interactive with buttons that jump a browser back a page (or two, or three), or with jump menus that can pack a long set of navigation options into a single expandable form field. (We show you how to create a jump menu later in this chapter.) Another navigational aid we discuss in this section is the ability to redirect visitors from one page to another.

Creating a Back button

The JavaScript `history` object can be used to create JavaScript for navigation backward or forward in a browser, essentially acting like a browser's Back and Next buttons.

The history object can be combined with the following methods:

+ back(): Loads the previous URL in the history list
+ forward(): Loads the next URL in the history list
+ go(): Loads a specific URL from the history list

The default value of () is 1 although you can certainly change that. For example, to have visitors jump back two pages when they click a Back button, you can use (-2) to jump back two pages.

In the previous example, you can see how a button action can be used to launch a JavaScript function. That's a widely applicable technique to make scripts run in HTML pages, and we'll use that trick again here to create an HTML button that works like a Back button in a browser navigation bar.

The external JavaScript file (again, saved with a .js filename extension) uses the object.method syntax that we discuss at the beginning of this chapter to create a function named goBack:

```
function goBack() { window.history.back() }
```

And here's an HTML page with a button that launches that function, where the linked JavaScript file has been named back.js:

```
<!doctype html>
<html>
<head>
<title>Get Back</title>
<script src="back.js"></script>
</head>
<body>
<p>Click the button to return to the previous page</p>
<input type="button" value="Back" onclick="goBack()"/>
</body>
</html>
```

The HTML defines a button with a value (displayed text) of Back, and a click-triggered action that launches the goBack function in the linked, external JavaScript file (in this case, back.js). And, we added a paragraph element that describes the button. The whole thing looks like Figure 2-6.

Figure 2-6:
A JavaScript button that acts like a browser's Back button.

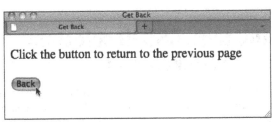

Click the button to return to the previous page

Back

Redirecting visitors to another page

Another useful navigational tool is the ability to redirect a visitor from one page to another. For example, if you've widely distributed the URL xyz.com but later change your company name to abc and set up a new site at abc.com, you can redirect folks who followed your old links to your new site with a JavaScript redirect.

You can redirect visitors to a new site with the location.replace method. Because this script is likely to be placed in a specific page, and is pretty short, we'll just embed it in the head element of an HTML page with the following HTML and JavaScript:

```
<!doctype html>
<html>
<head>
<script type="text/javascript"> location.replace('http://
    buildingwebsitesfordummies.net/'); </script>
<title>Visit our new site</title>
</head>
<body>
<p>Click <a href="http://buildingwebsitesfordummies.net">here</a> for our new
    site</p>
</body>
</html>
```

Note, by the way, that the preceding HTML includes a regular HTML link so that visitors to the old page who don't have JavaScript will have the option to click a link that is supported in any HTML browsing environment.

Embedding an updatable variable in pages

If you've been working through the DIY JavaScript examples so far, you've noted a trend: using JavaScript to supply globally updatable content throughout a site. In an earlier example in this chapter, we use that capacity to create an updatable, button-triggered alert that could be added to any or every page in a website.

HTML DIV tags, CSS ID selectors, and JavaScript

In Chapter 2, Book IV, we explore using HTML DIV tags and ID CSS selectors in depth. There, our focus is on ID selectors as page layout tools. However, DIV tags and ID selectors can also be used to demarcate content elements that are controlled by JavaScript.

In this chapter, we look at using an ID selector with an HTML tag essentially as a "variable"

in HTML documents, with the content supplied by a JavaScript. Even at the level we apply this technique here, it opens the door to powerful sitewide flexibility. An ID selector applied throughout a website can create a globally updatable content element.

Another way to apply this dimension of JavaScript is to define an ID style that draws its content from JavaScript.

This JavaScript file combines the document object with a value — in this case, an updatable color:

```
window.onload = function() {document.getElementById("todaysColor")
    .innerHTML = "Red!"; }
```

The preceding JavaScript could be saved to a JavaScript file called color. js. With that done, the following code creates an HTML file that links to that JavaScript file (color.js) and includes some text to introduce the color of the day, which is displayed by including an ID selector as a parameter of the h1 tag:

```
<!DOCTYPE html>
<html>
<head>
<title>Color of the day is...</title>
<script src="color.js"></script>
</head>
<body>
<h1> Today's color is:</h1>
<h1 id="todaysColor"> </h1>
</body>
</html>
```

If tomorrow, the color of the day is green, you can rewrite the JavaScript variable from "Red!" to "Green!" like this:

```
window.onload = function() {document.getElementById("todaysColor")
    .innerHTML = "Green!"; }
```

And, in doing so, update your entire website, replacing one variable (`red`) with another (`green`) throughout.

Figure 2-7 shows the updatable color-of-the-day script in action, with the linked JavaScript file revealed in a separate window in Firefox — and, with the script applied to a couple of additional HTML pages, all of which update when the JavaScript changes.

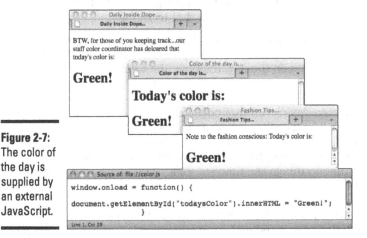

Figure 2-7:
The color of the day is supplied by an external JavaScript.

Using JavaScript Partners: HTML and CSS

Having worked through some basic but useful JavaScripts, you can identify a couple of themes:

+ JavaScript can be used to provide sitewide, globally updatable content — that is, not just global styles (which are applied with external style sheet files) but text or other content.

+ One essential technique for deploying such updatable content is by using an `ID` selector (an element of CSS sheets we cover in Book IV) to serve as a "container" for data fed into the page by a JavaScript.

The basics of complex JavaScript

Right — how can something complex be basic? The point is to have a general understanding of how the tools you're working with in this chapter are built on by professional JavaScript programmers. That helps you find, understand, and customize JavaScript that you get from other sources.

From that perspective, we can point you to and explore a couple of more complex implementations of JavaScript:

✦ Feed data (text, image, media) into an HTML document through ID selectors, like how we show you in the earlier section, "Embedding an updatable variable in pages." The technique we used there involved connecting JavaScript with CSS ID selectors. This is a widely applied technique for creating a definable container to present content supplied by a JavaScript to define styling for externally supplied data. Even non-programmers can take advantage of that technique.

✦ An even more powerful and interactive way to feed data into a page with JavaScript is for that data to be *dynamic* — for example, data that changes depending on the day, the time, the weather, a visitor's input, or all kinds of factors.

Creating interactive JavaScript that collects user input and external data (like that supplied by a traffic alert system or a weather database) and then uses that data definitely crosses the "expert" line. This level of JavaScript requires a very high level of programming proficiency. Designers find or generate scripts that do things like this. We walk you through that process in Chapter 3 of this minibook.

The way this works, basically, is that you get a JavaScript file and then edit the HTML and CSS associated with it. In other words, anyone who knows HTML and CSS, and can recognize ID selectors in JavaScript code, can go a long way in customizing any JavaScript program, simple or complex.

Meshing CSS styles with JavaScript data

To get your arms around the concept of customizing JavaScript by meshing it with CSS styles, go back to the earlier example in this chapter that defines a "color of the day." That project uses JavaScript to embed content within HTML documents, using an ID selector.

You can jump back to the section, "Embedding an updatable variable in pages," a bit earlier in this chapter to review how that works, and you can use the HTML and JavaScript files that we define there to work through this example if you wish. Or, just read along and absorb the concepts.

To review the basic elements of what we did earlier, we created an external JavaScript that defines a value that can be inserted in any HTML document (in your site, or any other one for that matter) using a CSS selector named todaysColor. The JavaScript includes

```
window.onload = function() {
document.getElementById("todaysColor").innerHTML = "Green!";
}
```

And we then link HTML pages to this JavaScript, and popped our color of the day wherever we wanted, in as many HTML pages as we wish, using HTML that combined tags like h1, or p, with the ID selector. For example:

```
<h1 id="todaysColor"> </h1>
```

You might have already suspected or anticipated where we're going with this: You can adjust the font color style for the todaysColor ID selector so that when you update the color of the day sitewide using JavaScript, you also update the style of that color sitewide using an external style sheet. In other words, if the color of the day is green, you can display that, throughout a website, with green type.

**Book VI
Chapter 2**

DIY JavaScript

If you create a style in a linked style sheet called todaysColor, you can use the following CSS to assign a color to that text:

```
#todaysColor {
      color: green;
}
```

Obviously, the example here is simple, requiring the web designer to manually change the globally linked external JavaScript file and the globally linked external CSS file. Still, this basic technique of using JavaScript for global content and combining that with styles assigned to ID selectors used in the JavaScript opens the door to more complex applications.

Creating a JavaScript-based Select Menu

Time to push the limits of DIY JavaScript further: to create and examine a JavaScript-based jump menu, which is a widely applied navigation element.

As a bit of a tangent, veering into aesthetics and design here: Jump menus are an underrated tool for providing a long list of navigation options in a page.

A great thing about jump menus is that they take up hardly any space. Yet, as shown in Figure 2-8 from Amazon.com, a single select menu can provide an almost ridiculously long set of navigation links that pop out or drop down (depending on your lexicon) from a single, tiny select menu.

Drop-down? Popup? Option? Select?

Some folks call them popup menus. Others call them drop-down menus. The technical HTML term is either an "option menu" or a "select menu" based on the fact that they use the HTML `select` and `option` tags to allow users to, well, select an option. We use "select menu" in part because it's technically correct (referring as it does to the defining HTML tag — the `select` tag). But, more importantly, using the term "select menu" allows us to circumvent the emotionally wrenching and potentially explosive divide between those who passionately insist on calling these things "popup menus" and those who just as passionately demand they be called "drop-down menus."

It's all good, but we'll standardize on "select menu" here.

And we also use the term "jump menu" here because the particular nature of the select menu we're creating is one that jumps to a link.

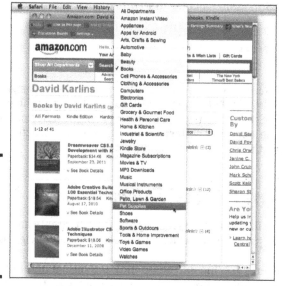

Figure 2-8:
Amazon.
com's
select menu
displays a
long list of
links.

Enough design discussion for the moment; return to technique. In Chapter 1 of this minibook, we explore the two ways how form data is collected and acted on: server-side scripting and client-side scripting.

Pop quiz: Which kind of form management scripting are you creating here? Answer: Client side. The data that a visitor enters into an option navigation menu, managed with a JavaScript, is *client-side scripting*. The data isn't sent to a server (like it would be if someone were placing an order, or signing up for an e-mail list). Instead, the data entered into the form (a navigation link) is managed right in the browser. A JavaScript handles that data.

HTML, CSS, and JavaScript in a select menu

As we walk you through the process of building a JavaScript select menu, we further explore the dynamic interrelationship between HTML, CSS, and JavaScript:

✦ The actual menu *content* — that is, the options that appear in the menu, and the links associated with them to other web pages — will be created with HTML.

✦ The *style* of the menu — how options appear (text color, background color, font and so on) — are defined with CSS.

✦ The coding that makes the menu pop up (drop down) will be created with JavaScript.

Keep reading to see how to create these three files, and then link the HTML file to the external JavaScript and CSS files.

HTML for a jump menu form

We explore forms in more depth in Book VII. There, we look at form design and also how to send form data to a server where it can be used to generate a mailing list, place an order, post content to a blog, and so on. But here, we use three form tags required for a jump menu:

✦ `form`: The `form` element defines a form and also an action that the form carries out.

✦ `select`: The `select` element defines an option form field (a drop-down/ popup menu) within a `form` element.

✦ `option`: The `option` element defines options within the `select` element by defining labels (what displays in the menu) and values (links).

The following HTML code (which should be inserted in the `body` element of an HTML document) defines a five-option drop-down menu:

```
<form method="POST" name="menu" >
<select name="newPage">
<option value = "" selected> Go to... </option>
<option value = "page1.html"> Page 1 </option>
<option value = "page2.html"> Page 2 </option>
<option value = "page3.html"> Page 3 </option>
<option value = "page4.html"> Page 4 </option>
</select>
</form>
```

More complex jump menus

Our project here is a working, functional JavaScript navigation jump menu that really works. That said, it's not the most elegant one ever developed. It includes inline JavaScript, which (as we note in Chapter 1 of this minibook) is less powerful than organizing all JavaScript into external `.js` files. Doing that would require introducing too many new JavaScript concepts than is appropriate or necessary in this compressed exploration of "do it yourself" JavaScript.

Professional JavaScript programmers would also include options for non-JavaScript–enabled browsers in the applications they distribute. Our simpler approach here is to avoid JavaScript that is essential to the page content, along with alerting visitors that the page requires JavaScript and they don't have it enabled. (See the section, "Not using or disabling JavaScript," earlier in this chapter.)

And, a professional-level jump menu includes a "reset" feature that resets the jump menu to the default option when a visitor uses a browser Back button to return to the page.

Such professional-level, more complex JavaScript option menus are available from many online resources, with directions for customizing options. But this is a JavaScript menu you can build yourself, with just a few lines of code, that works well in most browsing environments.

This form displays drop-down options. But before it really works — that is, you can use it to navigate a site — it needs a script that connects with the form and activates the option links.

JavaScript for a jump menu form

The following, very concise JavaScript is one of the easier solutions to creating a jump menu:

```
function gotoPage(newPage)
   {
   nextPage = newPage.options[newPage.selectedIndex].value
   {
   document.location.href = nextPage
   }
}
```

Here is the breakdown:

1. Define a JavaScript function (that we call `gotoPage`) and assign a value to that function (`newPage`).

2. The script defines a variable, `nextPage`, that will be based on the `new-Page` value.

3. The script opens a document using the `document.location.href` that returns the value of the `nextPage` variable (the page that a user selects from the option menu).

The last step in making the form work is to insert a line of JavaScript into the form HTML that calls this script when a visitor chooses a menu option. We add this inline JavaScript as a parameter for the `form` tag by editing the HTML we created earlier to add a JavaScript `onChange` event:

```
<select name="newPage"     onChange="gotoPage(this.form.newPage)">
```

The `onChange` event launches the JavaScript `gotoPage` function when a visitor clicks any menu option. An `onChange` event, by the way, can be triggered by any change to any field in a form, but in this case, the change that will trigger the JavaScript is when a visitor chooses a new option from the select menu. The `this.form` string defines the action of the form — and in this case, uses the data collected in the form to open the page to which the linked JavaScript has assigned a value of `newPage`.

Touching up a form with CSS

All the CSS techniques we explore in Book IV can be applied to our jump menu. And there are a number of ways this could be approached. We could create a new class style that defines fonts, backgrounds, border, and so on, and apply it to a menu. Or, we could create custom CSS styles for the HTML tags used in this menu: `form`, `select`, or `option`.

A nice, simple way to format the whole form is to create a style sheet file with styles for these elements. The following CSS code, for example, *floats* (aligns) the form right, defines a width of 200 pixels (px) with a 5 px margin and padding, a gray background, and a black border. The `select` tag background is set to white, and the `option` tag is set to silver:

```
form {
    background-color: #666666;
    margin: 5px;
    padding: 5px;
    float: right;
    width: 200px;
    border: medium solid #000000;
}

select {
    background-color: #FFFFFF;
}

option {
    background-color: #C0C0C0;
}
```

Some browsers block form styles

Defining styles for the `form`, `select`, and `option` tags *should* be a simple way to style a jump menu. But some browser publishers, particularly the folks at Apple, who distribute the Safari browser, feel that the appearance of a jump menu is essential to the look and feel of a browsing experience, and the Apple browser overrides CSS styles applied to `form`, `select`, and `option` tags. You can circumvent this barrier to some degree by using class styles, which we explore in Book IV, instead of tag styles to format jump menu elements. You can preview some of these elements in Adobe BrowserLab (`https://browserlab.adobe.com`).

In browsers that allow you to define styles for jump menus, the styles in the preceding example produce a jump menu that looks like the one in Figure 2-9.

Figure 2-9: Customize the appearance of a jump menu with CSS.

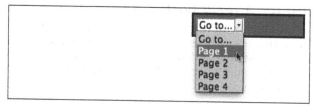

Chapter 3: Generating JavaScript

In This Chapter

✓ Using open source JavaScript to create page elements

✓ Generating more complex JavaScript using online and downloadable apps

✓ Using the jQuery Mobile JavaScript library

As of this writing, an online search for "JavaScript slideshows" turns up something like 65 million resources. And that makes sense: One of the most widely applicable uses for JavaScript is creating slideshows. With the decline of support for Flash (starting with Apple's mobile iOS used for iPads and iPhones), web designers are turning to JavaScript for dynamic, inviting, and intuitive slideshows.

And you can find many online sources for JavaScript to perform other commonly needed scripting, for things like drop-down menus, password-protected pages, and animation.

In this chapter, we do two things: We walk through a dozen or so of the most useful online JavaScript resources and how to use them; and in the process, we explore the methods and techniques needed to find and implement JavaScripts on your own.

Overviewing Online JavaScript Resources

Almost unlimited JavaScript resources are available online, with which you can create content ranging from a simple one-line script to highly complex slideshows and animations. How do you find them? How do they work? What do you need to know to access those scripts? And, oh yes, how much do they cost?

Rock band ZZ Top noted that spectacles that protect your eyes from the sun come in two classes: "rhinestone shades, and cheap sunglasses." Stretching the metaphor, online JavaScript resources also come in several classes:

✦ **Copying and editing code:** The most basic form for sharing JavaScript online is, well, sharing JavaScript online. As in, "Here, dude. This worked for me; you try it." Such scripts are always free (although proper etiquette dictates crediting the author in comments in your code); often require a bit of tweaking; and are highly useful for simple options, such as alerts (popups) and drop-down menus.

✦ **Online code generator:** These resources generate JavaScript files, often along with HTML and CSS files, and provide helpful advice on how to save them to your site. Usually, these scripts are shared without cost.

✦ **Online resources or downloadable applications that are driven by menus, options boxes, and extensive help:** These resources and applications generate JavaScript applications neatly bundled into folders and ready for your website; and code — customized for you based on options that you select in a menu-driven interface — that you copy, paste, and tweak, and save to your site. These options are sometimes free, and sometimes distributed for a licensing fee — typically, less than $100 for unlimited use.

✦ **JavaScript libraries — especially jQuery Mobile:** The jQuery Mobile script is open source and online, and comes bundled with a CSS style sheet. You add the HTML to create custom mobile-friendly content and style. jQuery Mobile is free.

Which option(s) you go with might depend on your project, resources, inclinations, and comfort level with the HTML and CSS.

Copying and editing JavaScript

As we mention, all kinds of free, open source resources for sharing JavaScript are available online. They come with no guarantees, and often only minimalist documentation. However, they are a valuable resource for simple scripts and are often hosted by communities that provide reviews, comments, ratings, and sometimes a support community.

One such site is the JavaScript Kit (www.javascriptkit.com), which we cover in the later section, "Horizontal menu bar from JavaScript Kit."

Keep reading as we explore options for a simple password-protection script and a drop-down menu.

A password-protected page

If you want a quick script to password-protect a page, you can copy and paste a few dozen lines of code (HTML and JavaScript) from the JavaScript Kit site and create a simple password-protection script for web pages like the one in Figure 3-1.

The script is among the collection of scripts at www.javascriptkit. com. The login page you create with this script provides no frills, minimalist instructions on how to adjust the code to change the password, and the page that opens when the password is entered.

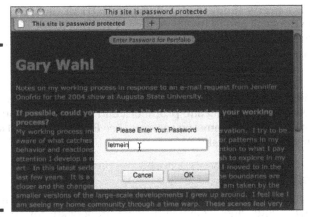

Figure 3-1:
A simple
login
created
with a few
lines of
JavaScript
from
JavaScript
Kit.

Listing 3-1 holds the entire JavaScript.

Listing 3-1:   Simple Password Page

```
<script language="javascript">
<!--//
/*This Script allows people to enter by using a form that asks for a
UserID and Password*/
function pasuser(form) {
if (form.id.value=="JavaScript") {
if (form.pass.value=="Kit") {
location="page2.html"
} else {
alert("Invalid Password")
}
} else {   alert("Invalid UserID")
}
}
//-->
</script>

<center>
<table bgcolor="white" cellpadding="12" border="1">
<tr><td colspan="2"><center><h1><i><b>Login
Area</b></i></h1></center></td></tr>
<tr><td><h1><i><b>UserID:</b></i></h1></td><td><form name="login"><input
name="id" type="text"></td></tr>
<tr><td><h1><i><b>Password:</b></i></h1></td><td><input name="pass"
type="password"></td></tr>
<tr><td><center><input type="button" value="Login"
onClick="pasuser(this.form)"></center></td><td><center><br><input
type="Reset"></form></td></tr></table></center>
```

1. **Change Kit in the JavaScript to your own password.**

2. **Change the password-protected page (the page that opens when a correct password is entered) by replacing page2.html with your own
link.**

Again, this is a pretty simple script. If you know HTML and CSS on the level we cover in Books III and IV, you'll do some tweaking to the code to add your own content, change the button message, or format the page with your own CSS style sheet.

This script, and JavaScript in general, doesn't provide secure protection for sites that hold confidential data! Managing such data requires exponentially more complex programming and protocols, and is handled through professional resources like e-commerce servers. (See Book VIII for a discussion of using e-commerce at your site.)

A drop-down menu

Other free online JavaScript resources combine tutorials, substantial hints on customizing code, and explanation. Iggy Korogodskiy, for example, provides not just scripts but tutorials as well at WebDesignDev (www.web designdev.com). That site includes a tutorial by Brian Cray for a quite complex, interactive drop-down menu, shown in Figure 3-2.

Figure 3-2:
Check out tutorials online to create menus like this.

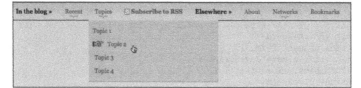

We won't repeat Brian's tutorial here (search the site for "Create the Fanciest Dropdown Menu"), but it is an accessible JavaScript drop-down menu that you can construct yourself. There are three parts to the tutorial: building an HTML file with the text and links that display in the menu, building a CSS file that styles the way that text and links appear, and a JavaScript file that provides the interactive animation for the menu. In that sense, "nothin' new here."

There has been (and will continue to be) a running theme through this mini-book: When people talk about "JavaScript" this or that, they're really talking about combinations of HTML (for content), CSS (for style), and JavaScript for animation. So, as you go through the Fanciest Dropdown Menu, you'll recognize these three elements (and you'll create three separate files: an HTML, a CSS, and a JS file).

Finding generated scripts

One option for creating JavaScript is sites that provide forms that you fill out, and then they spit out customized JavaScript. After you generate a

JavaScript file (and often, accompanying HTML and CSS files) from these sites, you save those files to your own website.

SuperTom.Com (www.supertom.com), for example, is a site that focuses on tools that generate JavaScript. One of our favorite tools there provides a nice, simple online form in which you enter menu options and links and come out the other end with a cascading menu, like the one in Figure 3-3.

Figure 3-3:
Use
JavaScript
for
cascading
select
menus.

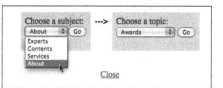

**Book VI
Chapter 3**

**Generating
JavaScript**

You can find the form used to generate this menu at www.supertom.com/menugen. Or, search SuperTom.Com for "menugen". Figure 3-4 shows a bit of the form that generates the menu.

MenuGen

Number of Options for Second Drop Down Box Help

For each option in the first drop down box, there will be a group of options that load in the second drop down box. Please tell us how many options there will be in the second drop down box for each option in the first box.

1st Drop Down Box	2nd Drop Down Box	
About Us	Number of Options:	3
Product line	Number of Options:	3
Staff	Number of Options:	3
services	Number of Options:	3
Contact information	Number of Options:	3

(<<Back)   (Next>>)

Figure 3-4:
Generating
JavaScript
for a set
of linked
drop-down
menus from
a form.

With this menu installed, visitors to your site choose a category from the first select menu, and depending on their section, a defined set of options becomes available in the second menu.

Amazon.com, for example, uses a setup like this to find out what you're shopping for (toys, gadgets, books) and then presents you with a second select menu with options based on your first choice.

Reading Chapter 2 of this minibook, as well as having some comfort level with Book VII, will put you in a good position to choose options from the wizard.

In many cases, the HTML packaged with generated JavaScripts is a bit clunky because JavaScript coders (the folks who are kind enough to create and share these tools) tend not to be designers. They often provide rather minimalist HTML, or use nonstandard techniques for laying out pages (like tables). Where this is the case, designers should see it as an opportunity to clear out the nonstandard code and use modern techniques, like the CSS design techniques that we explore in Book IV.

These online resources are labors of love of programmers, online forums for sharing scripts, and open source communities. They are often sustained by ads, and appreciate you respecting their rules that usually include keeping a comment in your code that credits their site.

Buying professional apps for generating JavaScript

At the "high end" of the scale are many professional application environments for generating JavaScript. The cost of scripts is well less than $100 for an application that, in many cases, you download onto your computer and use as often as you wish. Plus, many offer trial versions as well as free licenses for nonprofits and schools.

Such professional apps are not only easier to use than copy-and-paste-code sites, but they often provide more complex, sophisticated, professional, and reliable JavaScript (and related files).

As noted, these professional apps for generating JavaScript are either downloaded applications (that you buy and install like any other app) or online tools that sell licenses to use their resources. We explore examples of both in the remainder of this chapter. Normally, by the way, if you pay for a script, you're not required or expected to credit the developer (although the programmers often insert credit lines into the code they provide, lines of code that are seen by other curious coders but not by the general public).

Case Studies: Copying, Pasting, and Editing Code

Menu bars that display drop-down submenus when a menu item is hovered over might well be one of the two most widely used JavaScripts (the other probably being slideshows).

Earlier in this chapter, we point you to a very simple, editable JavaScript from JavaScript Kit that password-protects a page. Now we walk you through a more substantial and valuable tool at that site — one that generates a horizontal menu bar. And, in the process, you'll dip more than just your toes in the waters of borrowed JavaScript.

Horizontal menu bar from JavaScript Kit

As we note earlier, you won't find fancy script generators at JavaScript Kit (`www.javascriptkit.com`), but you probably won't need that level of help.

Among the scripts you'll find at JavaScript Kit are

✦ JavaScript clocks, calendars, and timers

✦ Menu and redirection scripts

✦ Forms and form validation

✦ Status bar effects

✦ JavaScript games

JavaScript Kit has some really basic JavaScripts that do things like define an alert popup (an element you can see how to code on your own in Chapter 2 of this minibook) and also a very simple password-protection script for a page we take a quick look at earlier in this chapter.

Here, we explore options at the site for creating a JavaScript menu bar, like the one in Figure 3-5.

Book VI
Chapter 3

Generating
JavaScript

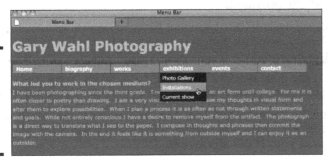

Figure 3-5:
A drop-down menu bar from JavaScript Kit.

Like most free JavaScript-sharing sites, the rule for using scripts from JavaScript Kit is that you must include the commented code promoting their site in your source files. And you may freely use any scripts found in our library on both personal and commercial web pages.

Customizing this script for your own custom content requires the HTML and CSS skills that we cover in Books III and IV, respectively. Later in this chapter, we examine a more sophisticated and elegant tool for generating slideshows that doesn't require any coding at all (at least to create the slideshow itself).

The steps for this menu bar are

1. **Download the two scripts for this menu bar at**

```
http://www.javascriptkit.com/script/script2/
     csstopmenu.shtml
```

You need to download and link two files to the HTML page(s) in which you install the menu. There are links to the CSS and JavaScript files at the menu bar's home page, but for quick reference, the CSS file is

```
http://www.javascriptkit.com/script/script2/
     csshorizontalmenu.css
```

and the JavaScript file is

```
http://www.javascriptkit.com/script/script2/
     csshorizontalmenu.js
```

Save both files in one folder, and use that folder for all the files required for the menu bar.

2. **One by one, right-click the three image files next to the text The three images (resized) and save them to the folder that will contain all the files for the slideshow.**

3. **With the CSS, JavaScript, and image files downloaded into the folder that holds all the files for this project, create a new HTML page, using the HTML provided.**

Create a basic HTML document (refer to Book III as needed) with head and body elements. Save it to the folder that you're using for all the files in this project.

4. **Copy the code marked Add the following code to the <head> section and paste it into the head element of your HTML document.**

5. **Copy the code marked Add the below HTML to your page, which contain your menu links and paste it into the body element of your HTML document.**

At this point, you have a working menu bar, but it has placeholder content for menu options. The menu bar content (the titles of each menu and submenu option, and the links associated with them) are all organized in an unordered list (remember that in HTML, an unordered list — ul — is the same thing as a bullet list), with the CSS ID selector ul id="cssmenu1".

6. **Edit the links in the unordered list to replace the placeholder content with your own content.**

   - *To add menu options:* Copy and paste an unordered list item.

   - *To delete menu options:* Delete unordered list items.

7. **After you customize the menu bar, you can save the HTML page in which it is embedded as a template.**

   You can then later use the template to create more pages that use the menu.

   Save pages you generate from the template with their own HTML file-names. For instance, you could name this file `js-menu.html`.

8. **Customize page content by adding HTML after the `</div>` tag that closes the `class DIV` that defines the menu bar. For example, here is one of the drop-down menu options customized to provide links to a staff directory:**

```
<li>
<a href="#">Staff</a>
<ul>
<li>
<a href="ed.html">Ed "Too Tall" Thompson</a></li>
<li><a href="aliceb.html">Alice B. Jones</a></li>
<li><a href="marty.html">Marty Aneilowitz</a></li>

<li><a href="denise.html">Denise Louie</a></li>
</ul>
</li>
```

Figure 3-6 shows how a customized drop-down menu based on (but customized from) the drop-down menu code at JavaScript Kit.

Figure 3-6: A drop-down menu customized from the code at JavaScript Kit.

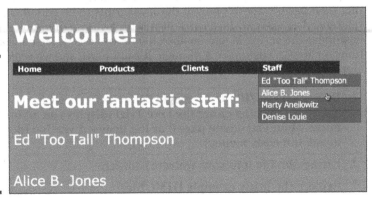

Zoomable image from Magic Toolbox

A valuable download-and-edit code resource is the series of scripts available at Magic Toolbox (www.magictoolbox.com). The scripts offered by Magic Toolbox (like its Magic Zoom tool) can create zoomable images, like the one shown in Figure 3-7. They also provide image slideshow JavaScripts.

These kinds of zoomable images are especially useful for presenting products but can also be used for maps, artwork, or even just regular "zoomable" photos. The ability to rotate images, or zoom in (or out) of an image is a feature that earlier generations of designers relied on Flash for. JavaScript solutions to replace Flash are emerging, and the tools at Magic Toolbox are among the best so far.

Figure 3-7: JavaScript is used for zoomable images using Magic Zoom.

Magic Toolbox's scripts are a little different than copy-and-paste scripting in that their license doesn't permit the JavaScripts to be edited. The scripts are referenced as external JavaScript files, with a choice of optional settings to customize the script. Magic Toolbox hands you the HTML code and instructions on how to customize it, though. It's not hard, and we walk through the steps here.

1. **Download the ZIP file for Magic Zoom (at** www.magictoolbox.com/magiczoom**) using either the Free Trial (displays an ad for Magic Zoom when you create pages) or the licensed version (doesn't display an ad, but costs money)**

2. **Extract the file into your website's folder.**

3. **Explore the many example HTML files.**

360-degree images

Magic Zoom, by the way, provides a choice of two scripts that allow users to interactively rotate images 360 degrees (to see the sides and the back of an object). Implementing these scripts, however, requires a series of photos that have to be carefully created to facilitate the "spin" — a process that basically involves photographing an object from equally spaced angles on a turntable. For example, a shoe designer might want to provide a rotatable model of a new design, like the one in the figure shown here.

The HTML files include links to an external CSS file (`magiczoom.css`) and the external (and not-editable) JavaScript file that makes this all work (`magiczoom.js`). Other HTML is editable, but our suggestion is to test the interactive zoom and then edit the customizable section of the HTML with your own content. That makes troubleshooting easier if you accidently edit the HTML that's required to make the JavaScript work.

4. **You can edit the default CSS file with your own style definitions.**

Don't delete or rename the CSS selectors, though. They're required to make the JavaScript work.

5. **Replace the images in the images folder with your own images.**

You'll find three sets of image files in the folder, with filenames beginning with `r1-black`, `r1-blue`, and `r1-red`.

The more basic examples, the ones without thumbnails on the bottom (like the example shown in Figure 3-8) require two images: `r1-blue-2.jpg` and `r1-blue-3.jpg`.

To customize the zoom, read the directions on the page, and replace the placeholder images with your own images, scaled to match the size of the placeholder images. We cover preparing images for the web, including scaling them, in Book V. You can use PNG, JPEG, or GIF format images.

For example, in the `example16.html` file, you replace `r1-blue-2.jpg` with your own image scaled at 320 pixels (px) x 190 px, and you replace `r1-blue-3.jpg` with your own image scaled at 974 px x 578 px. And you save your images with the filenames of the placeholder files, in the same images folder provided with Magic Zoom.

Hover over the image to examine detail...

Photo

My working process involves a state of nearly constant observation. I try to be aware of what catches my eye in my surroundings. I look for patterns in my behavior and reactions to my surroundings. By paying attention to

Figure 3-8: Customize a Magic Zoom example page with new images and content.

Sizing your images precisely is important. The JavaScript is defined to "zoom" (display a section of the larger image) based on these dimensions.

6. Customize the HTML to replace the default content with your own.

Again, this is a no-frills, do-it-yourself JavaScript. The folks at Magic Toolbox came up with the JavaScript, but rely on you to replace both the sample images they supply and the placeholder text with your own, while not messing with the HTML or CSS required to make the JavaScript work. If you need help, free support is available by e-mail.

If you're up for a bit of trial and error, this is a script that many online marketers and other portfolio designers will find valuable. And the folks at Magic Toolbox tell us that they're working on a service to allow people to upload their images and automatically write all their code for them, so keep checking Magic Toolbox for that.

Using Online and Downloadable Apps

The examples you've looked at so far require you to edit at least the HTML provided with the JavaScript. And, should you wish to customize the look of your menu bar or zoomable image page, you need to edit the CSS style sheet files that come with the JavaScript as well.

There are, however, more user-friendly and elegant options for creating JavaScript. Explore two case studies here. One generates *sliders,* which are animated, interactive JavaScripts that allow a visitor to click and drag to navigate a series of images. The other generates more traditional slideshows using JavaScript.

Presenting images with the WOW Slider

An inviting, dynamic, and widely applied technique for presenting sets of images is to generate sliding horizontal panels, also known as "sliders" or "carousels."

WOW Slider (available from `http://wowslider.com`) generates JavaScript sliders, like the one in Figure 3-9.

Figure 3-9: The WOW Slider includes transition effects and interactive options for navigating slides.

Book VI
Chapter 3

Generating
JavaScript

You can choose from a large set of templates, select effects (Blast, Fly, Blinds, Squares, Slices, Basic, Fade, Ken Burns, Stack, Stack Vertical, and Basic Linear) and generate all the files you need for a JavaScript, Flash-free slideshow that runs in any environment. If you're designing a site in a WordPress or Joomla! content management system (CMS; we discuss WordPress, the most widely used CMS, in Book VIII), WOW Slider comes with plug-ins and modules for those packages.

WOW Slider's package is very user-friendly. You don't have to generate sliders at that site and then download batches of files. Instead, you download and install the WOW Slider application and then create sliders with it on your own computer.

Creating a WOW Slider involves these basic steps:

1. **Add images to a gallery by clicking the Add Images to Gallery button (the + sign, shown in Figure 3-10).**

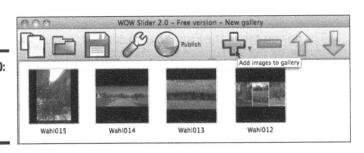

Figure 3-10: Adding images to a WOW Slider.

The Select One or More Images to Open dialog box appears.

2. **Navigate to and select PNG, JPEG, or GIF images, and then click Open to add them to the Gallery.**

3. **Put the images in the order they will display by clicking and dragging them to move them into correct order.**

4. **Click an image and use the Up and Down buttons on the application toolbar to move images forward or backward in the list.**

5. **Define Properties for the slider. Click the Properties tool (looks like a wrench) in the toolbar to open the Properties dialog box.**

   a. *On the General tab of the Properties dialog box, enter a title that will display in the Slider Title.*

   b. *Use the check boxes to choose from options, such as Auto Play Slide Show (the slider starts playing when the page it's embedded in opens) and Show Next/Prev Buttons.*

   c. *Use the Thumbnail Preview select menu to choose where to display thumbnails.*

   Figure 3-11 shows settings that will play the slider automatically, pause when a slide is hovered over, stop the slideshow after it loops once, display descriptions and navigation, and put thumbnails on the bottom of the slider.

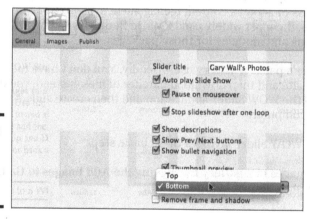

Figure 3-11:
Defining
properties
for a WOW
Slider.

The Images tab of the Properties dialog box provides a set of templates (on the left), image size, check box options for whether and how to resize images, transition options (including the popular Ken Burns effect), and transition effects and their timing.

We recommend not resizing your images, but to choose a size that fits your images (to avoid distortion).

6. **Publish the slider from the Publish tab of the dialog box.**

   The simplest option is to publish the slider to a folder. This generates everything you need to make the slider work, including an `index.html` page that will be the home page of the folder to which the slider is published.

   There are also options for users of the Joomla! and WordPress blogging CMS to add the slider to your blog. When your settings are good, click the Publish button. If you leave the Open Web-page After Publishing check box selected, your slider opens.

WOW Slider is free for noncommercial users, such as school sites, noncommercial blogs, and nonprofit organizations, but the free version generates sliders with a WOW Slider credit line. Commercial licenses are available, and with them, you don't have to display the WOW Slider credit.

Slideshows with Highslide

Highslide (`www.highslide.com`) provides two options for generating JavaScript slideshows that are as sophisticated as any you'll find online, like the one in Figure 3-12.

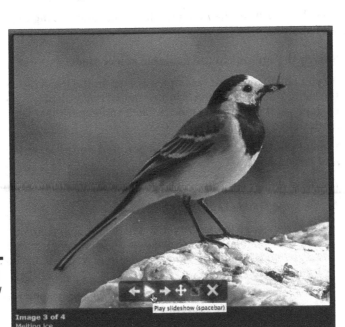

Figure 3-12: A slideshow option from Highslide.

Image 3 of 4
Melting ice

Play slideshow (spacebar)

Highslide provides the option of downloading a set of files (with all the HTML, JavaScript, and CSS you need). Even easier, you can use the online Highslide Editor application (`www.highslide.com/editor`).

The Highslide Editor provides an environment that users of Lightroom, Adobe Bridge, and other Flash-generating slideshow applications will find intuitive. But, to be clear, the Highslide Editor generates JavaScript, not Flash.

Again, what's remarkable about this app is the level of detail available — both in terms of the options available for customizing a slideshow and also in how carefully the slideshows are generated. For example, Highslide Editor takes images you upload and doesn't just resize them: It *resamples* them. We explore this process in depth in Book V, but in short, not just the image dimensions but also the file size is reduced to fit on web pages, and that process is done "intelligently" to maintain the best possible quality photo.

As designed by Torstein Hønsi, the Highslide Editor sends images to a server where a PHP script downsamples them, automatically adjusting image resolution, effects (like Unsharp Mask, to make the image look better online), or JPEG quality settings.

Here are the four basic steps to creating a slideshow using the online Highslide Editor:

1. **Survey the options in the Example select menu.**

   As you check them out, examples appear in the Preview window on the right. And the Preview window doesn't just display a picture of the example — it's a working model. Click and experiment with the different models, like the one in Figure 3-13.

2. **Upload photos in the Image Manager, and define sizes for thumbnails and large images.**

   a. *Select the Gallery tab on the left side of the Highslide Editor window.*

   b. *Keep the Enable Gallery check box selected.*

   c. *Click the Image Manager button and define Thumbnail dimensions (the size of the small, clickable versions of the images), and the size of the Large Images, using the sliders in the top section of the Image Manager window.*

   d. *Click the Select Files to Upload button, navigate to and select photos from your computer, and click the Upload Now! button.*

   e. *After your images upload, click OK.*

   Your own images replace the placeholder images in the Gallery.

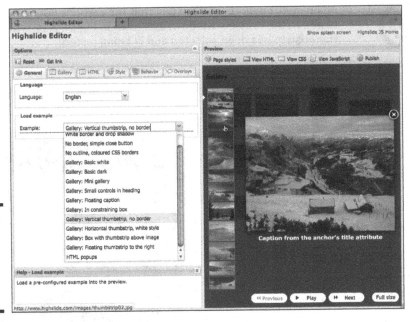

**Book VI
Chapter 3**

**Generating
JavaScript**

Figure 3-13:
Preview
examples
in the
Highslide
Editor.

3. **In the Controls section of the Gallery tab, choose a Preset style from the select menu, and experiment with options available by clicking the Options button.**

The Preview window displays a working, testable version of the slide-show as you define options, so experiment with the options you select.

4. **In the Numbers section of the Gallery tab, choose how to display numbers for your images.**

- *No numbers:* If you don't want numbered slides, choose None from the drop-down menu in the Numbers section.

- *Numbers:* If you do want numbered slides (your slideshow is sequential, and you want to encourage viewers to watch slides in order), choose a position: Heading, to display a large number at the top of the slide; or Caption, to present a smaller number at the bottom of the slide.

Leave the default setting to display no numbers.

5. **Use the options in the Thumbstrip section to define where a strip of thumbnails should appear in the slideshow.**

6. **Use the Behavior section of the Gallery to fine-tune options for transitions between slides, timing when the slideshow runs automatically, and other transition options.**

Again, take advantage of the fact that the settings you choose can be tested in the Preview window, as shown in Figure 3-14, where a vertical thumbstrip has been selected and is being tested.

Figure 3-14: Test slideshow features interactively.

7. **Click the Publish button to generate and save all the files needed for the slideshow images and settings you configured in the Editor.**

   You'll see a dialog box that explains who can use Highslide Editor for free and who should buy a license. Click the appropriate button to either buy a license and generate your slideshow or to generate a slideshow without a license.

   The Publish dialog box provides three options for installing the files generated by the Editor. You can

   • *Upload them directly to a website using the Upload Your Files via FTP link.*

   • *Download a ZIP archive.*

     In most situations, downloading a ZIP file is the easiest option. Save the file to your website folder and unarchive (unzip) it. The unzipped folder, Highslide-custom, has a file `highslide-custom-example. htm` that is the home page for the slideshow.

   • *Copy and paste code.*

8. **Apply HTML editing techniques we explore in Book III, and CSS formatting we cover in Book IV, to customize the slideshow page.**

   The most basic change you'll want to make is to change the content of the `Title` element in the head section of the generated HTML page to reflect your own content.

   And simply redefining the `Body` tag with your own color scheme and fonts can integrate the slideshow nicely into the rest of your site.

9. **(Optional) You can save the page with a different HTML filename as well, as shown in Figure 3-15.**

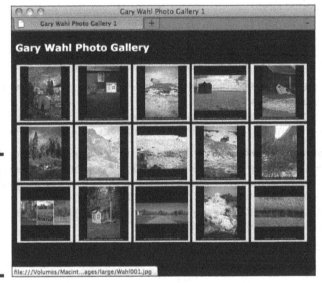

Figure 3-15:
A Highslide
slideshow
with
customized
HTML
and CSS.

Using jQuery Mobile

jQuery Mobile is more than an available online JavaScript resource: It is the foundation of many, if not most, mobile-friendly sites. It provides tools that solve the aesthetic and accessibility challenges involved in designing pages for devices that present web content very differently than even a netbook screen, let alone a full-sized laptop or desktop monitor.

And as culture and technology evolve and mobile devices become more and more central to the web experience, the importance of presenting pages that look good and work well on mobile devices is growing rapidly.

The challenges of mobile design

When you pull your mobile device out of your pocket, backpack, or attaché case, you view web pages in a very different environment than if you were viewing those pages on a laptop or desktop. And more to the point, so do visitors to the sites that you design.

Here are some of the most important differences:

✦ **Size:** Obviously, mobile device viewports (screens) are smaller than those for laptops and desktop monitors.

- Design elements like multicolumn layouts are often inappropriate for mobile sites.

- Text should generally be larger.

✦ **Viewing location:** Mobile devices are much more often used outdoors. That has design and accessibility implications as well.

Avoid using subtle color schemes. For example, using brown type on a beige background may be a perfectly good way to convey an earthtone ethos on a laptop, but that kind of low-contrast color scheme may produce difficult-to-read type in bright sunlight on a mobile phone.

✦ **No mouse:** Mobile devices don't have mice. Avoid relying on hover states, for example, to reveal a link. Hover-activated drop-down menus (like the examples we explore earlier in this chapter) are great for laptops, where the user has a mouse to click (or hover over) menu options. But those navigation techniques (using a mouse and hovering) are generally not available in mobile devices.

✦ **Bandwidth:** Despite the competing, confusing, and exaggerated claims of the 3G and 4G networks, mobile devices open pages more slowly than a laptop or mobile device on a cable or DSL network.

Survey a few websites on your own. Check out a site on a laptop or desktop, and compare it with the same site's mobile presence. The ABC News site, shown in Figure 3-16, for example, has multiple columns, hoverable drop-down menus, subtle gradient backgrounds (in the header), and (we elected not to include them in the screenshot) popup ads.

Now examine a page from the ABC News site viewed on a mobile device, as shown in Figure 3-17. A single-column layout replaces the columns; a high-contrast, simple color scheme replaces the gradients and subtle hues; menus are simpler; and there is nothing to hover over.

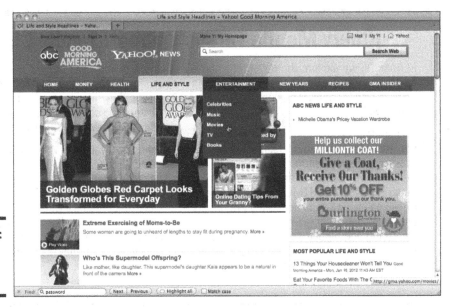

**Book VI
Chapter 3**

Generating
JavaScript

Figure 3-16:
ABC News
full-sized
site.

Figure 3-17:
ABC News
mobile site.

How jQuery Mobile solves challenges

jQuery Mobile provides tools to solve all the issues we just listed. We walk you through exactly how shortly, but first, take a minute to see how this happens on a conceptual level.

jQuery Mobile versus mobile-friendly CSS?

In Book IV, we explore the option of using a media query to assign an alternate CSS style sheet to mobile pages. How does that relate to jQuery Mobile?

In short, these are two alternate ways to present mobile-friendly pages. Using HTML media queries to present alternate style sheets, as explored in Book IV, has the advantage of not requiring separate HTML for full-sized and mobile pages. That technique simply reformats the same content for full-sized screens on the one hand, and mobile devices on the other. And for that reason, media queries require less work and less web design resources than providing jQuery Mobile pages.

jQuery Mobile pages require a whole set of alternate HTML pages for mobile visitors. However, they provide more substantial tools for customizing content presentation for mobile devices that use a media query.

Which should you use? That's a judgment call that should probably be based on how significant your mobile audience is and also your available resources. If a mobile audience is a very high priority, and if you have the resources to create a complete, alternative site for them, jQuery Mobile is a more powerful solution to providing mobile-friendly content.

jQuery Mobile essentially puts the content of an entire site in single HTML pages. Or, at least it's used to minimize the number of HTML pages. It does this by dividing HTML pages into jQuery Mobile "pages."

Yes, the terminology is confusing, but the concept is at the heart of how jQuery Mobile works: When a user taps an element on the screen of a mobile device, JavaScript alternately hides and reveals sections of an HTML page. The regions that are hidden, or displayed, are jQuery Mobile pages. In this way, visitors never have to wait for a new page to load when they tap a link.

jQuery Mobile also comes with a set of mobile-friendly themes that assign high-contrast color schemes to pages.

In short, jQuery Mobile is a very powerful solution for creating mobile pages.

Mobile pages and apps

Before we turn to the nuts and bolts of building jQuery Mobile pages, it's time to address that nagging question in the back of your mind: What's the difference between a mobile page and an app?

Apps run without the framework of a browser window. That means you have some additional freedom to design them because you don't have to leave room for a browser title bar and other elements. And if properly designed, apps run even when you are offline. Other than that, mobile pages and apps look and act pretty much the same. But underneath the hood, apps are written in the Objective-C programming language.

How jQuery Mobile works

Like all pages that use JavaScript, jQuery Mobile pages present content with a combination of HTML (the actual content), CSS (for style), and JavaScript. Two of those elements are fixed. You don't edit them — at least not normally. You simply link to them at the jQuery Mobile site. That site and jQuery Mobile are sponsored by a wide-ranging consortium of software and phone manufacturers.

You can simply link to three scripts hosted there that provide updated, debugged versions of both the JavaScript and the CSS needed to make jQuery Mobile work in a page. Those links are updated periodically, but as we go to press they are

```
<script src="http://code.jquery.com/jquery-1.6.4.min.js" type="text/
    javascript"></script>
<script src="http://code.jquery.com/mobile/1.0/jquery.mobile-1.0.min.js"
    type="text/javascript"></script>
```

The first link is to a special CSS style sheet, again hosted at the jQuery Mobile site, that provides the complex CSS file needed to make jQuery Mobile work. You customize that style sheet within the HTML of your document by defining a theme, a technique we'll return to shortly.

The second two links are to the required JavaScript.

The entire preceding code should be copied and pasted into the head element of your HTML document. So, the basic HTML for a jQuery Mobile page is

```
<!doctype html>
<html>
<head>
<title>jQuery Page</title>
<link rel="stylesheet" href="http://code.jquery.com/mobile/1.0/
    jquery.mobile-1.0.min.css" />
<script src="http://code.jquery.com/jquery-1.6.4.min.js"></script>
<script src="http://code.jquery.com/mobile/1.0/
    jquery.mobile-1.0.min.js"></script>
</head>
<body>
</body>
</html>
```

A jQuery Mobile site must start with an HTML5 doctype to take full advantage of all the framework's features.

Using data-roles

jQuery Mobile pages are built around data-roles. As noted, jQuery Mobile creates its own "pages" that open and close depending on a visitor's touch on a screen (or, if viewed with a clickable device, a click). Those jQuery Mobile pages are defined by using one of several jQuery Mobile data-roles.

jQuery takes advantage of a new HTML5 tag, the `data` element (always followed by a specific data-role like data-name, data-list, or data-theme). The data-tag doesn't have any "built-in" attributes, and in this way, it's somewhat similar to a `DIV` tag. But defined data-roles can be meshed with JavaScript, and that meshing (of the HTML5 `data` tag with JavaScript code) is at the heart of how jQuery Mobile works.

There are additional data-roles, but this basic set of four are used to set up pages:

✦ Page

✦ Header

✦ Content

✦ Footer

Data-roles are defined styles in the CSS style sheet that's part of the jQuery Mobile package. Keep reading to see how to put together a jQuery Mobile site using the four data-roles.

Data-role pages

As noted, the basic technique in jQuery Mobile for organizing page content is using special "pages" that are really data-role pages. All that's required to create a basic, working jQuery Mobile HTML page, with multiple jQuery Mobile pages, is the `data-role` page element.

The basic HTML for a page data-role is

```
<div data-role="page" id="page">
```

Each data-role page has to have a unique ID. So, a second page might have this HTML code:

```
<div data-role="page" id="page2">
```

The significance of assigning a unique `id` to each page is that these are used for navigation. For example, a link from to the `"page2"` id in the preceding would be

```
<li><a href="#page2">Go to page 2</a></li>
```

You can string together data-role pages with such links to create a navigable jQuery Mobile page. The code in Listing 3-2 is all you need for a working jQuery Mobile page.

Listing 3-2: jQuery Mobile Page

```
<!DOCTYPE html>
<html>
<head>
<meta charset="UTF-8">
<title>jQuery Mobile Web App</title>
<link href="jquery-mobile/jquery.mobile.theme-1.0.min.css" rel="stylesheet"
    type="text/css"/> <link href="jquery-mobile/jquery.mobile.structure-1.0.min.
    css" rel="stylesheet" type="text/css"/> <script src="jquery-mobile/jquery-
    1.6.4.min.js" type="text/javascript">
</script> <script src="jquery-mobile/jquery.mobile-1.0.min.js" type="text/
    javascript"></script>
</head>
<body>
<div data-role="page" id="page">
<div data-role="header">
<h1>Site Title</h1>
</div>
<h2>Home page</h2>
<h3>Links:</h3>
<ul>
<li><a href="#page2">Go to page 2</a></li>
<li><a href="#page3">Go to page 3</a></li>
</ul>
</div> <div data-role="page" id="page2">
<h2>Page 2 content here</h2>
</div> <div data-role="page" id="page3">
<h2> Page 3 content here </h2>
</div>
</body>
</html>
```

Figure 3-18 shows this minimalist jQuery Mobile page, with navigation to data-pages within the HTML page.

Adding headers, content, listviews, and footers

The very basic HTML code we just examined creates a very basic jQuery Mobile page. To provide more styling options, other data-roles are usually used inside data-role pages.

Headers at the top of the page, content in the middle, listview styles that format unordered lists inside page content, and footers at the bottom of a page are usually used to create attractive elements within data-role pages.

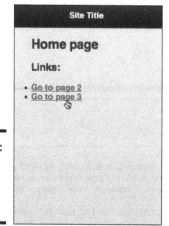

Figure 3-18:
A basic jQuery Mobile page.

Within any data-role page, you include a header, content, a listview style, and a footer. For example, a page with header, content, list, and footer elements would have HTML code like this:

```
<div data-role="page" id="page2">
<div data-role="header">
<h1>Page Heading</h1>
</div>
<div data-role="content">
<h2>Content goes here</h2>
<ul data-role="listview">
<li><a href="#page3">Page 3</a></li>
<li><a href="#page4">Page 4</a></li>
</ul>
</div>
<div data-role="footer">
<h4>Page Footer</h4>
</div>
</div>
```

And each of these elements (header, content, listview, and footer) has styles defined in the CSS style sheet that comes as part of the jQuery Mobile package.

For example, because we are assigning the data-role list to the unordered list on the page (the two links), that CSS style kicks in, providing the more interactive link bar shown in Figure 3-19.

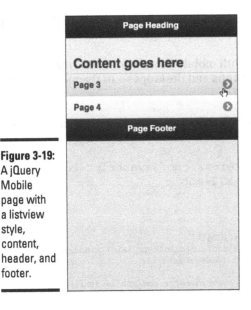

Figure 3-19:
A jQuery
Mobile
page with
a listview
style,
content,
header, and
footer.

You can include as many data-role pages as you wish in a jQuery Mobile site. And you include header, content, listview, and footer data-roles within these data-role pages.

Customizing jQuery Mobile data-themes

The CSS style sheet that's part of the jQuery Mobile package allows you to assign one of five standard data-themes to any data-role. Those data-themes are named a, b, c, d, and — you guessed it, e. They provide different sets of mobile-appropriate (that is, high-contrast) color schemes.

You assign a data-theme to a data-role element by adding `data-theme="a"` (or b, c, d, or e) to the `data-role` tag. For example

```
<div data-role="page" id="page2" data-theme="e">
```

Because there are many elements to each of the five jQuery Mobile themes, and all are in color, it won't work to present them here in the book, but you can see them all illustrated at

```
http://jquerymobile.com/demos/1.0/docs/api/themes.html
```

Scripts to divert mobile users to your mobile page

As we note earlier, you have two basic approaches to providing alternate content for mobile users. One is to use a media query to provide alternate

CSS styles, and we explore that option in Book IV. The other, that we apply in this chapter, is to create a jQuery Mobile page.

But how do you divert visitors with mobile devices from the "regular" page — the one designed for laptops and desktops — to the mobile page built with jQuery Mobile?

You can choose from a variety of JavaScripts online that do that, but our favorite is found at

```
http://localstreamer.posterous.com/javascript-code-
    snippet-how-to-detect-all-mob
```

That script is

```
<script type="text/javascript">// <![CDATA[
    var mobile = (/iphone|ipad|ipod|android|blackberry|mini|windows\sce|
    palm/i.test(navigator.userAgent.toLowerCase()));
    if (mobile) {
        document.location = "http://www.yoursite.com/mobile.html";
    }
// ]]></script>
```

You insert this script into the head element of any HTML document, and replace "*http://www.yoursite.com/mobile.html*" with the URL of the jQuery Mobile page to which you want to divert mobile users. Visitors viewing your page in a nonmobile device won't be diverted to the jQuery Mobile page but stay on the original page.

Chapter 4: JavaScript with Dreamweaver

In This Chapter

✓ How Dreamweaver generates JavaScript (and why)

✓ Creating tooltips, menu bars, and tabbed panels

✓ Embedding live data in pages

✓ Generating jQuery Mobile pages

This chapter meshes with and builds on a bit that we explore in earlier chapters of this minibook. Steeping yourself a bit in those chapters will allow you to get substantially more value from Dreamweaver's JavaScript tools in two ways:

✦ You'll have a basic background and foundation so you understand what Dreamweaver is doing when it generates JavaScript, where that JavaScript is saved to, and what might go wrong (and how to fix it).

✦ You can actually work with and edit JavaScript in Dreamweaver that comes from somewhere else (like the do-it-yourself projects in Chapter 2, or the generated code you see in Chapter 3, of this minibook).

With some background in JavaScript under your belt, you can max out taking full advantage of Dreamweaver's tools for generating JavaScript content.

Seeing How Adobe, Dreamweaver, and JavaScript Relate

To understand how Dreamweaver handles JavaScript, we need to get political for a moment. Got your attention? No, we don't mean political as in elections and all that. But to understand new developments in Dreamweaver's support for JavaScript in CS6 (and CS5.5), it helps to have a sense of why Adobe is so late to the table on JavaScript, and also how Adobe is catching up.

Here's the deal: In many ways, JavaScript and Flash do — or did — many of the same kinds of things, such as animation (things that move onscreen), interactivity (elements that respond to a user's actions at a website), and managing forms. Even Flash's *ActionScript* — the coding language for creating useful projects with Flash — sounds like *JavaScript*. And because of its investment in Flash, Adobe shied away from promoting what was in many ways a free, open source, alternative, and competing technology.

Adobe, JavaScript, and the Spry toolset

With the decline of Flash, especially in the wake of Apple's historic decision to not support the Flash Player on iPhones and iPads, Adobe turned to creating tools that help designers generate JavaScript without coding. There are essentially two tracks to this. One is a set of "not ready for prime time" tools (at least at this writing), like Adobe Edge, which is in testing phases. The second track is building up the toolset for generating JavaScript in Dreamweaver.

Step by step, upgrade by upgrade, Adobe has built a significant set of JavaScript-generating tools into Dreamweaver. Dreamweaver CS5.5 and CS6 add easy access to jQuery Mobile pages. That toolset is organized as *Spry widgets*. As we note throughout earlier chapters, JavaScript applications have been organized into editable libraries, with much of the coding "pre-packaged." Spry is one such set of scripts and related CSS files that Adobe has integrated into Dreamweaver.

In addition, Dreamweaver CS5.5 and CS6 allow you to export jQuery Mobile–based pages into *apps* (programs that run independently of any browser) and can be distributed through the App Store (for Apple devices) or Google Marketplace (for Android devices).

How Dreamweaver generates and edits JavaScript

Throughout the rest of this chapter, we do the following:

✦ Walk through step-by-step instructions on creating the most useful JavaScript objects that you can make in Dreamweaver.

✦ Discuss global points on how Dreamweaver manages JavaScript that you can apply to integrating additional JavaScript elements in Dreamweaver.

✦ Examine how Dreamweaver generates jQuery Mobile pages and publishes them as iOS (Apple mobile) and Android apps

Creating Spry widgets

Take a look at some of the global dimensions to how Dreamweaver generates JavaScript content through Spry widgets, that combine JavaScript, CSS, and HTML that you add to the mix.

✦ **Creating:** You typically begin to create JavaScript by choosing Insert⇨ Spry, or Insert⇨jQuery Mobile, from the main Dreamweaver menu, in an open HTML document. Then you choose a particular widget from the submenus, as shown in Figure 4-1.

As you can tell from the options in the Spry submenu, many Spry widgets are related to validating (testing) form data. We explore those features in Book VII, where we discuss how to generate forms and validation scripts in Dreamweaver.

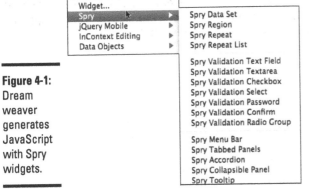

Figure 4-1:
Dream
weaver
generates
JavaScript
with Spry
widgets.

✦ **Saving:** You must save the HTML page that you're working on to a Dreamweaver site before you start generating JavaScript. The Spry widgets generate a number of linked files, and the links between those files and the HTML page can be defined only if the page is saved to a Dreamweaver site.

Linking: The generated JavaScript that comes with a Spry widget will be in a linked, external file (or more than one). In Chapter 1 of this minibook, we discuss how and why most complex JavaScript is not embedded in an HTML page, but saved to an external file. The short explanation is that these are large files, and by making them external (linked) files, they can be used in many pages within a site.

Accessibility: The linked JavaScript and CSS files are viewable, accessible, and even editable in the related files tab above your HTML document, as shown in Figure 4-2, which displays the JavaScript file (`SpryTooltip.js`) and the CSS file (`SpryTooltip.css`) that make a tooltip work.

Figure 4-2:
Related
JavaScript
and CSS
files are part
of every
Spry widget.

You can review the importance of and procedure for defining a
Dreamweaver site in Book II.

✦ **Properties editing:** You can edit many properties of an embedded Spry
widget by selecting the widget in Design view. Spry widgets can be
selected in the document window by clicking the aqua-highlighted code.
In addition to color-coding JavaScript elements, Dreamweaver displays
selected, editable JavaScript elements in a box with a tab that appears in
Design view (with Live view off), as shown in Figure 4-3.

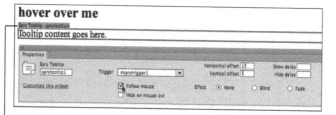

Figure 4-3:
Editing a
Spry widget.

Select the code to edit the widget.

✦ **HTML adaptability:** Some Spry widget content can be edited by simply
creating or changing the HTML in a document. Two examples are

   • *Tooltip trigger text:* You can edit this HTML in the Dreamweaver docu-
     ment window.

   • *Tooltip text:* Such text appears when an object is hovered over, and is
     also HTML content.

✦ **Properties editing:** When a Spry widget is selected, the Properties
Inspector displays editable properties of the widget. Although the
lengthy and complex JavaScript files associated with Spry widgets can
be opened and edited by JavaScript coders, a much easier option is to
edit the properties of the JavaScript in the Properties Inspector.

✦ **CSS editing:** CSS files that are generated as part of the Spry widgets can be edited. Those CSS files are half the puzzle in making Spry widgets work. Again, we want to stress that the links between them and the HTML page will be corrupted and won't work if you don't save your HTML page to a defined Dreamweaver site. (Book IV discusses the CSS skills you need to edit these linked CSS files.) Those CSS files display in the CSS Styles panel, as shown in Figure 4-4.

Figure 4-4:
A style sheet associated with the Tooltip Spry widget.

Here's the condensed version of creating and editing JavaScript in Dreamweaver:

1. You create Spry widgets from the Insert menu.

2. Then you edit them by making changes to the HTML in the Document window, the CSS in the CSS Styles panel, and the JavaScript in the Properties Inspector.

Be sure to upload all the files generated by Dreamweaver to your web host server for your widgets to work correctly on your live site.

Examining the Four Best Spry Widgets

Several useful Spry widgets are built into Dreamweaver. We'll walk through how to use our favorite Top 4, and in the process show you how to navigate the intricacies of creating and editing other Spry widgets.

✦ **Tooltips:** Tooltips are everywhere online. Hulu certainly uses them extensively. (See Figure 4-5.) These popup balloons appear when an object is hovered over, which allows Hulu to pack a ton of information onto a page.

Figure 4-5:
Hulu makes good use of tooltips.

✦ **Menu bars:** We explore in Chapter 3 of this minibook how menu bars and interactive drop-down menus are a bit of a hassle to create if you're editing JavaScript you find online. Dreamweaver menu bars are much easier to generate and refine.

✦ **Tabbed panels:** Also in Chapter 3 of this minibook, we explore why it's so important that mobile websites use JavaScript to cram multiple "pages" (that is, what appear to be pages) into a single HTML document so that users with their mobile connections don't have to wait unbearably long for pages to open. Tabbed panels provide one option for creating multiple panels (that feel like pages to a user) in a single web page.

✦ **Live data:** Earlier in this chapter, we discuss the power of using live data in a website, and Dreamweaver includes a Spry widget that generates pages fed by that live data.

You can, of course, jump straight to using the widget you need right now, but we advise starting with the Spry Tooltip because it provides the simplest example but one that includes all the concepts and techniques involved in creating any Spry widget.

Creating a Spry Tooltip

We have two reasons for choosing tooltips as one of the four featured Spry widgets in Dreamweaver. One, they're fun and useful. Two, they provide the simplest example, and thus a good way to get your head around the concept of creating and editing Spry widgets.

As we mention earlier, all Spry widgets have three components: HTML, CSS, and JavaScript. In this case, the text that appears in the tooltip is HTML. The CSS defines how the tooltip looks. And JavaScript (which can be tweaked in the Properties Inspector) controls effects and time delays for when, where, and how the tooltip pops up.

To create a tooltip, start with a page open, with something on it to which you want to attach the tooltip — typically, text or a PNG, JPEG, or GIF image.

As we caution you earlier in this chapter, remember that for Spry widgets to work their magic and not become corrupted (broken), you must save your page to a Dreamweaver site (we show you how in Book II, Chapter 4) before you start generating the Spry widget.

With text or an image selected, follow these steps to create and configure the tooltip:

1. **Choose Insert⇨Spry⇨Spry Tooltip.**

   Immediately, a tooltip appears on the bottom of the Dreamweaver Document window.

2. **Replace the placeholder content of the tooltip with your own content, as shown in Figure 4-6.**

Figure 4-6:
Customize
your Spry
Tooltip
content.

3. **Turn on Live view and examine the effect as you hover over your selected content. Think about changes you want to make in the appearance and effect.**

4. **Turn off Live view and view the Properties Inspector with the tooltip selected. Here, you can edit the JavaScript in the fields shown in Figure 4-7.**

   If you have trouble viewing the JavaScript options in the Properties Inspector, make sure to click directly on the aqua-highlighted tab to select the tooltip JavaScript — not the text.

Book VI
Chapter 4

JavaScript with Dreamweaver

Figure 4-7:
Customize the JavaScript properties of a Spry Tooltip.

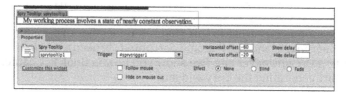

Only a few options in the Properties Inspector are available for configuring the generated JavaScript, and none of them are very important. You can experiment with changing the Horizontal offset and Vertical offset values to move the box to the right, left, up, or down (in pixels).

- *Positive Horizontal* offset values move the tooltip to the right.

- *Negative Horizontal* offset values move the tooltip to the left.

- *Positive Vertical* offset values move the tooltip down. That seems counterintuitive, but that's how it works.

- *Negative Vertical* offset values move the tooltip up.

Feel free to experiment with effects — such as delays and transitions — available in the Properties Inspector. After all, you can always revert a change here.

For aesthetic and accessibility reasons, you want to keep tooltips simple and avoid using a lot of flashy effects. And keep in mind that because they are triggered by a user hovering over them, tooltips aren't appropriate for mobile sites, where users don't have a mouse to hover over anything with.

5. **Edit the CSS that came with the Spry widget in the CSS Styles panel (SpryTooltip.css).**

   Use the CSS skills that we cover in Book IV to format the display and appearance — height, width, fonts, background color, and other properties of the style — of the tooltip, as shown in Figure 4-8.

You edit the Spry Tooltip the same way you create it. Select the text and edit it as necessary in the Document window. Tweak the JavaScript in the Properties Inspector, and then control the appearance by editing the default CSS styles.

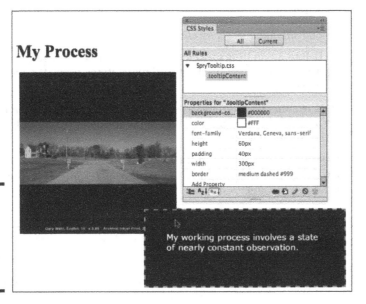

Figure 4-8:
Edit the
CSS style
associated
with a Spry
tooltip.

Defining a Spry menu bar

As we note in Chapter 3 of this minibook, creating menu bars takes a lot of work — so, if you have Dreamweaver, why not let Dreamweaver do that work?

Here's how to insert a menu bar.

1. **Position your insertion point in an open, saved Dreamweaver file.**

2. **Choose Insert⇨Spry⇨Spry Menu Bar.**

   A dialog box appears with the options of a Horizontal or Vertical menu bar. Choosing Horizontal generates a menu bar that runs across the top of your page.

3. **Click OK.**

4. **Click the aqua tab above the menu bar.**

5. **Edit both the HTML and JavaScript in the Properties Inspector.**

   a. *Select top-line menu items from the left side of the Properties Inspector and then rename them in the Text field on the right side of the Properties Inspector.*

   b. *Enter a link for the menu item in the Link field in the Properties Inspector.* You can use the Browse for File icon (looks like a folder) to locate files on your computer.

The Title field is not required.

c. *Add submenu items by clicking the + sign.*

Delete menu items by clicking the – sign. Move a selected item up the list by using the up arrow, and move items down the list by using the down arrow.

Use the same techniques to define secondary menu (submenu) items in the second column, and sub-submenu options (if you really need them) in the third column.

As you edit the content of the menu in the Properties Inspector, you can see the menu evolve in the Document window with Live view turned off, as shown in Figure 4-9.

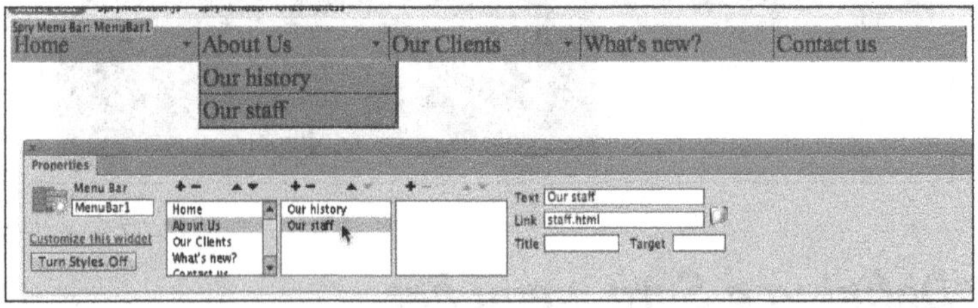

Figure 4-9:
Define the
content
of a Spry
Menu Bar.

6. **Check your progress. Turn on Live view again and examine the effect as you hover over your selected content.**

Think about changes you want to make in the appearance and effect.

7. **Test the menu.**

   • *While still in Live view, test how the menu will look.*

   • *Choose File⇨Preview in Browser to test the actual links.* You can choose a browser from the Preview in Browser submenu that displays all the installed browsers in your system.

8. **To control the display of the Menu Bar, edit the CSS that came with the Spry widget in the CSS Styles panel.**

   Use the CSS skills that we cover in Book IV to format the height, width, fonts, background color, and other properties of the style that defines the appearance of the menu bar.

   Unlike the simple Spry Tooltip widget, the menu bar widget comes with a whole bunch of styles. They control everything from the vertical and horizontal displacement of drop-down menus to the colors in the menu.

   You have two options for identifying which of the many styles controls how different menu options appear:

- *Click the Customize This Widget link in the Properties Inspector, and study the Dreamweaver documentation.*

- *Click the different styles and experiment with changing them, with Live view active in the Document window, as shown in Figure 4-10.* You'll find a couple of styles that control the most significant style attributes in the menu bar:

  ```
  ul.MenuBarHorizontal a
  ```

  This style defines how not-hovered-over navigation elements appear. You can change the color and/or background color of your menu options here.

  ```
  ul.MenuBarHorizontal a.MenuBarItemHover,
  ul.MenuBarHorizontal a.MenuBarItemSubmenuHover,
  ul.MenuBarHorizontal a.MenuBarSubmenuVisible
  ```

  This style defines how hovered-over navigation elements appear. You can change the color and/or background color.

**Book VI
Chapter 4**

**JavaScript with
Dreamweaver**

Figure 4-10:
Edit the styles associated with a Spry Menu Bar.

You edit the text in menu bars either right in the Document window, as shown in Figure 4-11, or in the Properties Inspector with the widget selected.

Figure 4-11:
Edit the content of a Spry Menu Bar.

Simulating multiple pages with tabbed panels

Three Spry widgets — Tabbed Panels, Accordion, and Collapsible Panels — all accomplish similar tasks. You use them to create sections within an HTML page that "open" and "shut" based on user clicks. All three are defined in a similar way. Here, we focus on tabbed panels because they generally provide a more useful and inviting way to put multiple "pages" in a single HTML page, as shown in Figure 4-12.

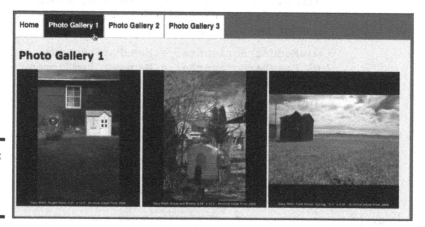

Figure 4-12: A set of tabbed panels.

To insert tabbed panels into a web page (and, of course, this should be a page saved to a Dreamweaver site), follow these steps:

1. **Choose Insert⇨Spry⇨Spry Tabbed Panels.**

When you insert a Spry Tabbed Panels widget, a two-panel tabbed panel is generated.

2. **Define the properties of the panel in the Properties Inspector.**

- *To add new tabs or delete them:* Click the + sign to add a tab, or delete a tab by selecting it and clicking the – sign.

- *To reorder the tabs:* Use the Up and Down triangles in the Properties Inspector, as shown in Figure 4-13.

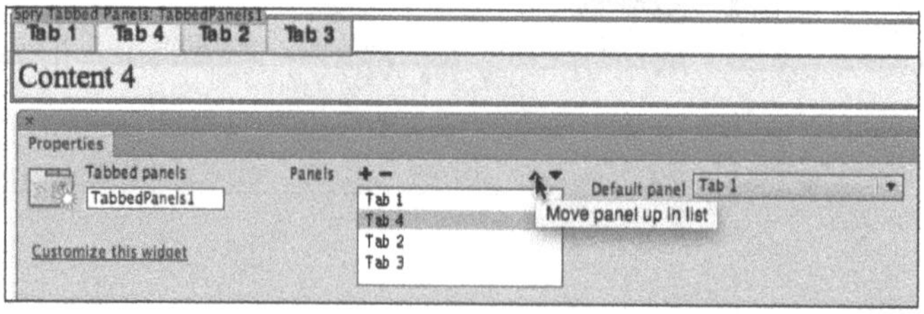

Figure 4-13: Reordering tabbed panels.

- *To change the tabbed panel that is selected, by default, when a page opens:* Change the Default Panel selection in the Properties Inspector.

3. **Edit the content of the tabs and the panels in the Document window.**

   Click and type right in any of the tabs themselves to edit the content of tabs.

   To open a panel for editing, hover over the tab of the panel in the Document window, and click the "eye" icon that appears, as shown in Figure 4-14.

Figure 4-14:
Select a
tabbed
panel for
editing.

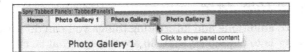

4. **Edit the appearance of the tabs (the colors, borders, and background colors, among other attributes) by editing the SpryTabbedPanels. css style sheet file in the CSS Styles panel.**

   As with other Spry widgets, a substantial style sheet enables the JavaScript. Here are a few key CSS styles in that style sheet that control the main features of the tab display:

   - TabbedPanelsTabSelected class style

     As shown in Figure 4-15, you can edit the borders, color, and background color of this class style to control how selected tabs appear.

Figure 4-15:
Control how
selected
tabs appear.

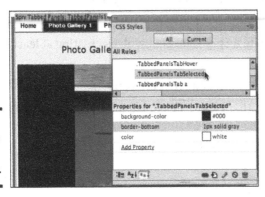

- `TabbedPanelsTabHover` class style

  Edit the borders, color, and background color of this class style to control how hovered-over tabs appear.

- `TabbedPanelsTab` class style

  Edit the borders, color, and background color of this class style to control how inactive (not selected) tabs appear.

- `TabbedPanelsContentGroup` class style

  Edit the borders, color, and background color of this class style to control how the actual tab "pages" — the content of each tab — appears.

Embedding live data

One of the more ambitious and interesting things you can do with JavaScript in Dreamweaver is to embed live data in a web page: that is, data that resides somewhere outside the HTML page and is fed into that page.

Here's an example. You run a shop buying and selling used stringed instruments. You maintain a spreadsheet of inventory, including a few hundred guitars, violins, ukuleles, and an occasional cello or bass. You maintain that spreadsheet, deleting instruments when they're sold, updating the price as needed, and adding instruments when you acquire new ones to sell.

Or, you are presenting an online photo portfolio, but the photos are updated frequently, perhaps by others. You need to define and control the display, but you want to be able to easily update the photos that appear.

Dreamweaver's Spry Data Set works for relatively simple sets of data, like an inventory of 100 items, a staff of dozens of people, or a set of 20 upcoming events. More complex data management requires more complex tools. For major data management, see Book IX's discussion of WordPress.

Dreamweaver generates live data sets using the Spry Data Set widget. Preparing to generate a Spry Data Set involves creating at least two HTML files:

✦ One HTML file has the table that holds the data.

✦ One (or more) other HTML files present that data using a Spry Data Set widget. The widget displays the content of the table in the first page.

And of course, as always, the prerequisite step is that you're working in a Dreamweaver site.

For those sensitive types

Complex, commercial databases, and databases that handle sensitive data are managed with server-side scripts. In Chapter 1 of this minibook, we discuss how client-side scripting (like JavaScript) runs in browsers, and server-side scripts run on remote servers, almost always protected by software that shields that data from hackers.

We explore server-side databases, and scripts that connect them with web pages, in Book VII. There we dive into PHP (both minimalist do-it-yourself programming, and more complex server scripting you contract to use).

Create a data table

A long, long time ago — in web design years, that is — rows and columns in tables were used as design tools. That role for tables has been superseded by CSS style sheets, but tables do continue to play a role in websites as a way to store data in columns and rows (which was the original intent of including `table` tags in HTML).

Data in tables is organized into rows and columns. Each column can represent a *field* — a category. Each row represents a *record,* which is a specific item. For example, a photo database might have three fields (columns): title, description, and the photo itself. Bonus: Table data can include images and video. That table could then have an unlimited number of records (rows) to hold as many photos as necessary. So, when you create a table to be used with a Spry Data Set, you generate a table with sufficient columns for all your fields. It's easy to add rows to a table in Dreamweaver, so there's no need to stress over how many records you'll end up having in your table.

To create a table in an open document in Dreamweaver, follow these steps:

1. **Choose Insert⇨Table.**

2. **Define table parameters in the Table dialog box that opens.**

   - *Fields:* Enter a value in the Columns field to define the number of fields.

   - *Records:* Enter a value in the Rows field to represent the number of rows.

   - *Size:* Make the table 100% in width to maximize the space you have to enter and organize data.

Because this table won't be seen by anyone, and is used only to organize data, Cell Padding (space between the content of a cell and the border of the cell) and Cell Spacing (space between cells) aren't important.

- *Accessibility and Heading options:* Don't worry about these, either. This table isn't for display.

Figure 4-16 shows a table with three columns, which will be used for a database with three fields.

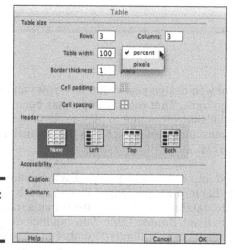

Figure 4-16:
Defining a
table.

3. **In the top row of the table, enter field names.**

   These names won't display in the Spry Data Set widget; they just serve to remind you what's in each column.

4. **Starting in the second row of the table, enter text, images, links, video, or any other content that will be presented in the Spry Data Set widget.**

   In general, we don't recommend applying any styling to the data you enter in the table. Styles will be applied in the Spry Data Set widget.

   Press Tab on your keyboard to move from cell to cell as you enter data. Also, pressing Tab when your cursor is in the last cell in the table adds a new row to the table.

5. **(Optional) Use the Modify⇨Table menu in the Dreamweaver document window to add or delete rows or columns.**

6. **After you enter data (and of course, you can always add more data, or delete data), give the table a name (in the Table field) in the Properties Inspector.**

The context-sensitive Properties Inspector displays Table attributes when you select the table. Click the border of the table, or click the Table tag in the Tab bar at the bottom of the Dreamweaver document window.

Figure 4-17 shows a table, with a name (pics) entered in the Properties Inspector.

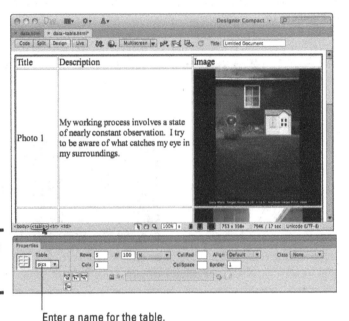

Figure 4-17:
Name your
table.

Enter a name for the table.

7. **Save the HTML page with the table.**

   You're now ready to create a Spry Data Set widget that will display this data in other pages.

Generating a Spry Data Set widget

Many options are available for creating Spry Data Set widgets. Some of them are rather obscure, and we won't dive into all of them here, but instead focus on the essential steps required to generate a working Spry Data Set.

Before you generate a Spry Data Set widget, make sure the page in which it will be placed is saved to a Dreamweaver site. Then, follow these steps:

1. **Choose Insert⇨Spry⇨Spry Data Set.**

   The first window of the Spry Data Set Wizard opens.

2. **Use the Browse button in the Specify Data File box to navigate to and select the HTML page with the table you created to hold the data for the Spry Data Set.**

   Use the Data Containers select menu to choose the named table. If no table names appear, return to Step 6 in the previous set of steps for creating a table, and make sure that you named the table holding your data.

   A view of your data appears in the bottom part of the wizard, as shown in Figure 4-18.

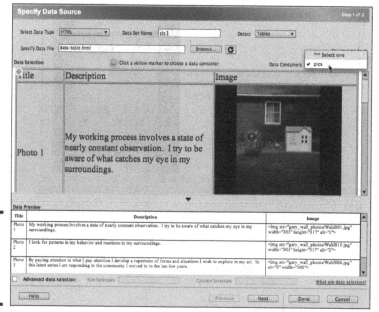

Figure 4-18: Select a table for a Spry Data Set.

3. **Click Next to move to the second page of the wizard, which shows default settings that are fine.**

4. **Leave the Use First Row as Header check box selected, and then click Next.**

5. **On the third page of the wizard, configure how the Spry Data Set will appear in a page.**

   Choose one of the first four options: a table, a master/detail layout, stacked containers, or stacked containers with a spotlight area. The fifth option — Do Not Insert HTML— doesn't create any display.

   The Master/Detail layout option is often a good way to present sets of data, with "master" (basic) information on the left and detail on the right.

Click the Setup button to explore options. A dialog box opens with setup options available to tweak the display of your data set. Generally, the default settings work well.

Click OK in the Setup dialog box to close it when you're done.

6. **Click Done to close the wizard and generate the Spry Data Set.**

Like other Spry widgets, you can't see how your Spry Data Set looks until you turn on Live view in the Document window. But you might find it interesting to note how little "content" there is on this page with Live view turned off, as shown in Figure 4-19.

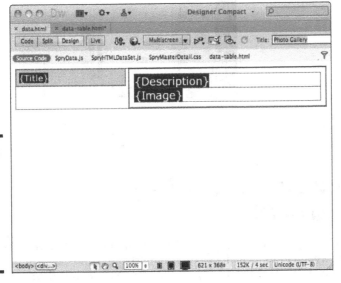

Figure 4-19:
With Live view turned off, very little data shows on the page itself.

You can view your page with data displayed in Live view and then toggle back to Live view off to edit the page.

Unlike simpler Spry widgets, there are no options for editing the JavaScript for the Spry Data Set widget via the Properties Inspector. If you want to try an alternate layout, the best move is to simply delete the generated display and then create a new one with the wizard. And the *data* (content fed into the page) is edited in the table, which is in its own HTML file.

What you can do to control the display of the Spry Data Set is to edit the CSS style sheet that is generated as part of the widget. And you can do that with Live view on, which makes it easier to apply the trial-and error method as you experiment with the generated styles. (These styles vary depending on which layout you choose.)

Figure 4-20 shows a Spry Data Set widget in Live view, with edits made to the CSS styles.

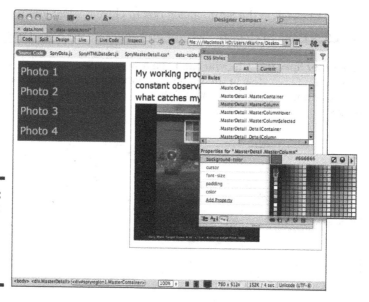

Figure 4-20: Editing CSS styles for a generated Spry Data Set.

Managing Mobile Pages and Apps in Dreamweaver CS6

Mobile pages and apps play similar roles in the world of web design. They work well in mobile devices. Their underlying technical structure is profoundly different, though. *Apps,* which run on a mobile device without a browser, are built with the Objective-C programming language. Mobile web pages are built on HTML, CSS, and JavaScript.

Starting with Dreamweaver CS5.5, and expanded in Dreamweaver CS6, Adobe has integrated PhoneGap (an open source program) into Dreamweaver. Combined with powerful jQuery Mobile–generating tools, Dreamweaver CS6 allows you to save time in generating jQuery Mobile pages and turning them into apps.

For more on how jQuery Mobile works, see Chapter 3 of this minibook.

Creating a mobile-ready page in Dreamweaver

Dreamweaver's jQuery Mobile Starter pages are a good way to quickly generate a mobile-friendly site. The Mobile Starter page creates an HTML5 page with five prebuilt jQuery Mobile *data-pages,* or sections of the HTML page that look and act like "pages" as they appear or disappear within a mobile device. And those starter pages provide a fine starting place for both mobile pages and apps.

Follow these steps to generate and customize a jQuery Mobile page in Dreamweaver:

1. **Choose File⇨New.**

The New Document dialog box opens.

2. **Select Page from Sample in the left column, Mobile Starters in the Sample Folder column, and jQuery Mobile (CDN) in the Sample Page column.**

Avoid using the jQuery Mobile (Local) and jQuery Mobile with Theme (Local) options. These options use versions of the CSS files required for jQuery Mobile pages that come with Dreamweaver CS6 and saved on your own computer. The problem with using these files is that you can easily corrupt them — and if you do that, the jQuery Mobile pages won't display properly.

Choose the first option, jQuery Mobile (CDN).

DOCTYPE is set by default to HTML5, which is required for jQuery Mobile–based pages. The New Document dialog box, with settings for a jQuery Mobile page, is shown in Figure 4-21.

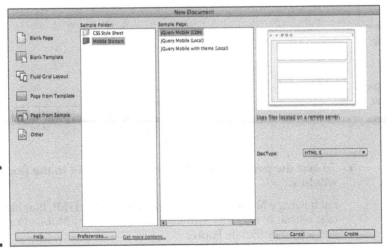

Figure 4-21:
Creating a
new jQuery
Mobile site.

3. **Click the Create button.**

An HTML page appears with four jQuery Mobile "pages."

If you need more pages, choose Insert⇨jQuery Mobile⇨Page to add a new jQuery Mobile `data-page`.

Because the generated page relies on JavaScript, you can't see anything close to the actual appearance without turning on Live view. To get a feel for how the page will look and work in a mobile device, click the Live view button and navigate in the generated jQuery Mobile pages, using the Forward and Back buttons on the Document window toolbar. Use the Window Size option on the toolbar at the bottom to resize the Document window viewport to a mobile device size, as shown in Figure 4-22.

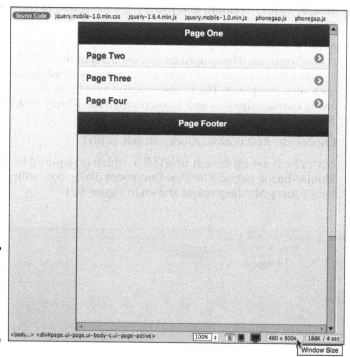

Figure 4-22: Viewing a jQuery Mobile page in Live view.

4. **To edit the pages, deselect Live View, and edit in the Document window.**

   Each jQuery Mobile "page" (within the single HTML file) has three DIV tags within it: a jQuery Mobile Header, a jQuery Mobile Content element, and a jQuery Mobile Footer.

   You can edit the contents of any of the elements in Design view the same way you edit any HTML page in Dreamweaver. (For a basic overview of editing pages in Dreamweaver, see Book III, Chapter 4.)

5. **After you edit the placeholder content, replacing it with your own content, toggle back to Live view to see how pages will look in mobile device browsers.**

Editing themes

The CSS file that enables jQuery Mobile is massive — it has hundreds of defined styles— and editing the CSS styles in a jQuery Mobile–based page is very difficult. And, in the previous set of steps, we advise you to *not* edit that CSS file but instead link to the CDN (remotely hosted, centrally distributed CSS file).

So how do you customize the color scheme of your mobile pages? After all, you don't want your mobile site looking like it came straight out of the box, using the default color scheme that comes with jQuery Mobile.

Answer: Dreamweaver provides an easy, accessible solution. You assign jQuery Mobile *swatches* — themes that are embedded in the CSS style sheet. Dreamweaver CS6 provides access to those swatches through the jQuery Mobile Swatches panel. To view and apply jQuery Mobile swatches, follow these steps:

1. **Open the jQuery Mobile Swatch panel (choose Window➪jQuery Mobile Swatch).**

2. **Click to select any element in a jQuery Mobile page.**

3. **Click a color swatch in the jQuery Mobile Swatches panel to apply that color scheme to the selected element.**

4. **Turn on Live view to see the impact of the swatch you assign to an element, as shown in Figure 4-23.**

5. **Use the same technique to apply jQuery Mobile swatches to any or all elements in your page.**

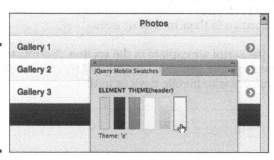

Figure 4-23: Styling a jQuery Mobile page with a swatch.

Publishing apps with PhoneGap and Dreamweaver

Apps — applications that run in mobile devices — are written in the Objective-C programming language, which is a high-level programming language. PhoneGap, an open source project acquired by Adobe, seeks to provide tools to convert jQuery Mobile sites into apps.

It should be understood that apps generated with PhoneGap function almost exactly like the jQuery Mobile page they are created from.

PhoneGap, as embedded in Dreamweaver, does not develop full-fledged animated, interactive apps.

Therefore, given the very limited capacity of Dreamweaver's PhoneGap tools, as well as the major hurdles involved in registering with app developers to enable these tools, generating apps from Dreamweaver is not a recommended workflow.

Saving jQuery Mobile pages

After you edit the content of your jQuery Mobile page, and after you customize the color scheme, you're ready to save the page. But before you do, make sure you assign a title to your page. The title appears in the title bar of browsers. Enter title text (any characters are okay, including spaces) in the Title box in the Document toolbar. (We explore page titles from a number of angles in Book III, Chapter 1.)

When you're ready to save your mobile page, here's a useful file-naming and -saving convention for mobile pages: Create a folder at your website called Mobile and save your mobile page in that folder with the filename index.html. That way, visitors can find the mobile version of your site by going to a URL (like mypage.com).

You can test this out now by going to sites like amazon.com/mobile or disney.com/mobile. If you use this technique, visitors can bookmark *yoursite*.com/mobile in their mobile devices.

And, you can use the script we explain in the section, "Scripts to divert mobile users to your mobile page," in Chapter 3 of this minibook to automatically divert visitors with mobile devices to this page.

Book VII

Managing Forms with PHP

Get on our e-list

* indicates required

Email Address

ilike2buy@me.com   *

First Name

Jay

Last Name

Kaczynski

Tell me about...

☑ sales
☐ new offerings

Preferred format

◉ HTML
○ Text
○ Mobile

Subscribe to list

Contents at a Glance

Chapter 1: Collecting Information with Forms

In This Chapter

✔ The value of data

✔ Interactivity with forms

✔ Designing a form

✔ Collecting form data the easy way

✔ Making forms attractive and inviting

*F*orms are how visitors tell you things: their name, their e-mail address, what they want to buy, who they think belongs on the Top 5 "worst covers of The Beatles songs list," or which of your songs they want to purchase and download.

In this chapter, we walk through how to design a form and a simple (but useful) technique for having that visitor data sent to you. And you see how to make forms inviting and attractive. After all, form data is valuable. So, anything you can do to encourage a visitor to sign up, make a purchase, provide feedback, or donate to your cause is important.

Forms as the Basic Tool for Visitor Interaction

How essential are forms? Imagine Bing (Microsoft's search engine) without a search box. Or Yelp (a popular site for posting reviews) without a form to upload comments. How about an airline booking site without menus to choose your date and place of departure, and arrival?

'Nuff said. In a way. But there's more to the picture. Forms are essential: not just for big corporate sites but for just about any site. If you don't have forms on your website, you're missing out on half the value of having a website.

Three forms that almost any site needs

Take a look at three kinds of forms that benefit almost any site:

✦ **Signup form:** Collects e-mail addresses, interests, demographics (age, gender, and so on), likes, and dislikes from people who want to hear from you.

It's hard to imagine a business, school, organization, activist cause, or even personal websites that can't make use of a list of people who want to hear from you, like those who fill out the form in Figure 1-1 that enlists volunteers and collects information related to a certain cause.

How valuable are lists you accumulate from people who want you to stay in touch with them? The answer is actually quantifiable. When we purchase mail lists for clients to send out e-mails (yes, sorry to disabuse you of any illusions, but people do sell e-mail lists), we pay between $2 and $3 for a single name! And these are names of people who didn't *ask* to be contacted, in most cases.

You'll see how to create a working, basic signup form in this chapter.

✦ **A feedback form:** Collects feedback and opinions. Including a feedback form on your site is like signing up proofreaders, reviewers, beta testers (who can let you know if a tested feature is working or not in their browsing environment), and fact-checkers — but for free. The form in Figure 1-2 lets such volunteers know their input is appreciated.

If fact-check comments or notes on typos or suggestions for improving the site come with an attitude, you can live with that. It's better to be tuned into how visitors are reacting to your site than to be oblivious to how people are engaging with your site.

✦ **A search box:** Helps visitors quickly find things on your site. Only a few sites can't benefit from using a Search feature. The search box in Figure 1-3 will help visitors find videos, even if the site navigation structure confuses them. And as you can see in Figure 1-3, forms can be pretty simple.

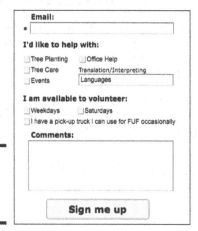

Figure 1-1:
Use a form to sign up volunteers.

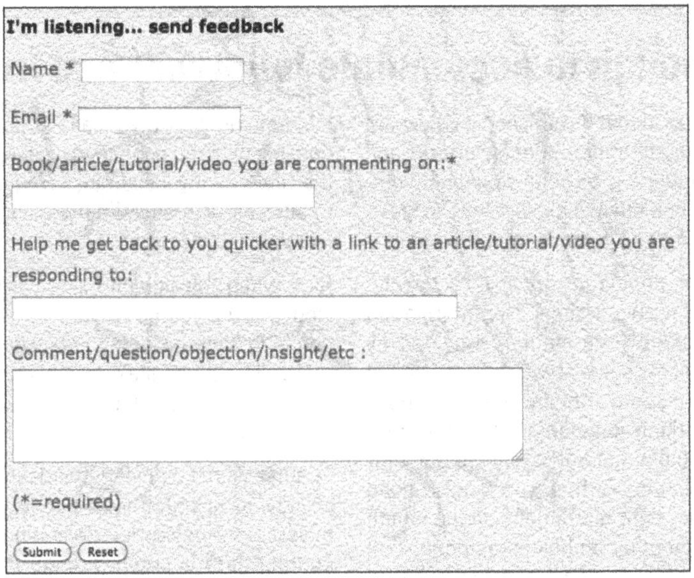

I'm listening... send feedback

Name *

Email *

Book/article/tutorial/video you are commenting on:*

Help me get back to you quicker with a link to an article/tutorial/video you are responding to:

Comment/question/objection/insight/etc :

Figure 1-2:
Welcoming visitor input and feedback.

(*=required)

Submit   Reset

Figure 1-3:
A search box supplements other navigational tools.

Search this site...

videos   search
          advanced

Book VII
Chapter 1

Collecting
Information
with Forms

DIY forms

Here are two things you have to do before you can collect visitor information using a form at your website:

1. Design a working form.

- Forms are designed with HTML tags, like the `form` tag, along with form field tags for individual boxes of information.

- Forms are styled with CSS styles, on the most basic level by defining styles for forms and form field tags.

2. Build in the functionality so that after a visitor to your site enters data in a form, something happens to send that data somewhere.

Is it enough to accumulate followers and friends?

One way to stay in touch with people who want to follow your thoughts, special offers, and calls for volunteers is through social networking sites. In Book VIII, we explore how to maximize the networking potential of those sites.

But there are significant downsides to relying on social network sites. The information (including contact information) provided by people who follow you at Twitter, friend you at Facebook, and so on actually belong to those social networking companies. And the data shared over those networks is absolutely for sale, and not by you. Further, social networking sites have very tight restrictions on the length of postings and other technical restrictions on how many people you can reach, with what.

The names you collect through a signup form, on the other hand, are your property. And maintaining your own mail list puts your relationship with the people who sign up outside of the real privacy issues that are just beginning to surface with social networking forums like Facebook and Twitter.

Plus, when you sign up visitors using your own signup form, you get to decide what information to collect, including detailed, specific info that will help you make sales, organize volunteers, alert clients, or issue selected e-mailings to select audiences.

In other words, social networking has a place in staying in touch with clients, supporters, buyers, and networks. Collecting and saving contact data yourself through forms at your site is more flexible, valuable, reliable, secure, and professional.

There are simple and also complicated ways to solve that challenge. We start with a simple but effective technique in this chapter. We explore more complex approaches (used for things like blogs or order forms) in Chapters 2, 3, and 4 of this minibook.

Sophisticated forms include JavaScript that validates the data before it is submitted. *Validation* means testing the data so that, for example, if someone enters **mickeymouse.con** in an e-mail field, he is reminded that this doesn't look like a valid e-mail address, and please fix it before the form gets submitted. We explore this dimension of form handling in the remainder of this minibook.

On a basic level, we solve both these challenges in this chapter, with an HTML form, styled with CSS, that sends the collected data to an e-mail address. This is a technique that manages relatively small amounts of input, but it works. And it is an effective way to introduce all the basic techniques involved in collecting data with a form.

Examining Server-Side versus Client-Side Data

Before diving into building forms and collecting data, take a minute to walk through the concept of server-side versus client-side data.

Server-side forms collect data that is sent somewhere. For example, data can be sent to

✦ A file or database at the server that hosts your website. You can retrieve that data using tools provided by your web-hosting company, and tools can be quite sophisticated or pretty simple.

✦ You, via the server that manages your e-mail.

✦ A server maintained by someone else, like a company that offers e-commerce solutions, or one that manages large mailing lists and enables you to send out e-newsletters.

As such, server-side form data is different than client-side form data. In Book VI, Chapter 2, we explore the role of JavaScript in taking data entered into a form (like a jump menu) and acting on that data. In the example of a jump menu, for example, a JavaScript program looks at a visitor's selection, and jumps to that page. That data is not sent to a server; it's just acted on in the *client* (browser).

Server-side form data is different, and more powerful than client-side data. Server-side data is saved — you can store it, organize it, study it, and use it. And data sent to, or saved at, a remote server can be protected much more reliably from hackers using server software that is provided by and maintained by the hosting companies that sell you server space, something we cover in Book VIII.

In this chapter, we collect form data using the simplest form of "server-side scripting" known to humanity. We e-mail that form data to an e-mail address — which does send it through, and to, a server where it is saved: namely, your e-mail server.

Book VII
Chapter 1

Collecting
Information
with Forms

Dissecting the Anatomy of an HTML Form

Later in this chapter, we walk through how to build a form in detail. Before we do, zoom the lens out (so to speak) and examine the basic elements of a form.

Forms collect data and send it somewhere. To do that, they almost always require three basic elements:

✦ **The form itself**

You can't collect without defining an HTML form.

A form must include a defined *action* — a parameter telling a browser what to do when someone clicks or presses the Submit button.

The form `method` parameter determines how the form is submitted. This is almost always set to `post`.

The form `enctype` parameter (short for *encryption type*) defines how text in a form is handled, and this is determined by the server and scripts that manage the form data.

✦ **Different fields inside a form**

The *fields* in a form — that is, the boxes within the form that collect data, include text boxes, check boxes, radio buttons, select menus, and so on. Of these, text boxes are the simplest way to collect data, which we discuss further in the later section, "Developing More Complex Form Fields."

Fields don't work unless they are inside a form. A useful metaphor: If you want to send some clothes to someone, you have to put them in a package or you can't ship them. Same thing with form fields: If they're not inside a form element, the content that is entered in them by users won't get sent anywhere.

✦ **A button to launch the form action**

Gotta have one of these so that the data gets sent where it's supposed to go.

You can also add a Reset button to clear a form, clearing all entered content.

Figure 1-4 shows all three of the preceding elements in the search box form at Craigslist:

✦ **The form itself encloses all the form elements.**

Form data gets sent somewhere through a defined *action,* which is a parameter of a form field. A form action either defines a link to a server-side script (usually written in the PHP programming language) that handles the form data (a process we dive into in depth in Chapters 2 and 3 of this minibook), or can simply send the data to an e-mail address.

✦ **Within the form, two form fields collect information.**

A text box collects text, and a drop-down (select) menu allows a user to select categories to search.

✦ **Clicking the small > button submits the form to a server.**

And at this server, millions of elves at Craigslist sort through the submitted data, and come back with a list of useful options that fit the criteria in the search box. (By the time this book is published, those elves are being replaced by computer databases.)

In addition to these critical elements, forms usually include some way to clue a user in regarding what she is to do with the form and its fields. We explore different techniques for providing that help, ranging from *labels* (text associated with a form field) to text that appears in a form field with advice on what to enter, like that shown in a form at Monster.com in Figure 1-5.

Multiple forms on a page?

Technically, you can have multiple forms on a page, but that's usually not a good idea. The more you clutter a page, the less likely someone is to fill out a form. Multiple forms on a page get confusing. When a user clicks Send,

he should have a good idea whether a search is being launched or an order is being placed.

If you must have multiple forms on a single page, make sure you have unique HTML form elements defining each form.

Figure 1-4:
The three main elements of a form that collects server-side data.

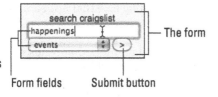

Form fields   Submit button

**Book VII
Chapter 1**

Collecting
Information
with Forms

Figure 1-5:
Form fields can hold instructions.

We want to talk a bit more about labels and the role they play making form fields accessible to vision-impaired users. If you want to collect an e-mail address from a user, you obviously need to indicate that required field: that the user is supposed to enter an e-mail address in the box. This can be done by simply entering some text, like Enter your e-mail address on your page, before you create the text field in a form. Enclosing that text in a <label> tag makes the text more accessible for vision-impaired people who rely on reader software to read page content out loud. That software will identify that the text that describes what to enter in a form field is a label, making it clearer to the user what she is being prompted to enter.

Labels have two properties. One identifies the field with which the label is associated, and the other the text that displays. So, for example, the following HTML defines a text field, named email, with a label:

```
<label for="email">Enter your email address:</label>
<input type="text" name="email" />
```

Labels aren't essential for making forms accessible to vision-impaired users, but they can enhance the ease of form field data entry for users who rely on reader software.

Creating a Simple Signup Form

Time to dive into building a simple, effective, useful, working signup form. You can pop that into your site as it grows, and build up your e-mail list from the start.

As always, when building website content, make sure that you're working in a web page that's been saved to the folder that holds your site content (or a subfolder within that folder). Form elements are defined within the body tags in an HTML document, like everything else that appears to a user in a browser's page.

The following code defines a form, called `signup`, that sends data by e-mail to an e-mail address. Substitute your own e-mail address for *email@email.com*.

```
<form action="mailto:email@email.com" method="post"
    enctype="text/html" name="signup">
</form>
```

The `form action` really works pretty much like an HTML e-mail link. It opens an e-mail in the user's e-mail program, such as Gmail, Yahoo! Mail, Outlook Express, Windows Mail, or (Mac) Mail.

The `enctype` code specifies the kind of content being sent, which in this case is HTML text and identified with the parameter `enctype="text/html"`.

Then, with a form defined, you add form fields to collect data and a button to send it.

A basic signup form requires

✦ **One defined form action**

✦ **One Submit button**

✦ **Two text fields**

   • One to collect a visitor's name

   • One to collect a visitor's e-mail address

Speaking of collecting visitors' input, the most basic, widely used, and flexible way to collect data in a form is through a text field. A text field is defined as an `input type` in HTML, using this syntax:

```
<input type="text" name="field_name" />
```

Styling a form

Later in this chapter, we walk you through how to define CSS styles for particular elements (tags) that make up forms. However, much of the content within a form is simply text: labels that tell a visitor what a form field is, what it does, and how to use it, as in, *Enter your e-mail address here*. And that content is defined by the styles in the external style sheet you create.

Here, `"field_name"` is a placeholder for a real field name, such as `"name"`, `"email"`, `"address"`, or `"phone"`:

Data collected in form fields gets sent to servers, and servers can be fussy about field names so avoid using spaces, uppercase letters, or special characters. To be safe, stick with using only lowercase letters, numbers, dashes, or underscore characters — with no spaces.

Even if you're creating a very basic form, you can invoke optional parameters to define the size of the field in characters as well as the maximum number of characters allowed. So, the syntax for a text field called `"email"` that displays 30 characters and will accept up to 80 characters is

```
<input name="email" type="text" size="30" maxlength="80">
```

Listing 1-1 shows the code for the entire HTML page for the signup form. It has all the main elements of a signup form: a form action, a text field to collect names, a text field to collect e-mail addresses, and a submit button.

**Book VII
Chapter 1**

Collecting
Information
with Forms

Listing 1-1: Signup Form

```
<!doctype html>
<html>
<head>
<meta charset="UTF-0">
<title>Sign up!</title>
</head>

<body>
<h3>Get on our email list!</h3>
<form action="mailto:dkarlins@gmail.com" method="post"
    enctype="text/html" name="signup" >
  <p>Name:
  <input name="name" type="text" size="30" maxlength="60">
  </p>
  <p>Email:
    <input name="email" type="text" size="30" maxlength="80">
  </p>
  <p>
    <input type="submit" />
  </p>
</form>
</body>
</html>
```

Text field length

It's often the case that for design purposes, you'll want to limit the number of characters that display in a text field even while you allow more characters to be entered in the field. For example, almost all e-mail addresses are 30 characters or shorter. E-mail addresses, though, can be up to 384 characters long. Designing a form that displays 384 characters for an e-mail address would be ungainly and unnecessary for the vast majority of users. In those rare cases where an e-mail address is longer, even much longer than 30 characters, you can allow users to enter additional characters. Of course, they won't see the entire e-mail address displayed in the form field, but they'll be able to enter it.

This form (and the entire page) uses very minimalist HTML and no CSS for styling, but feel free to enhance the content with HTML (see Book III) or CSS styles (covered in Book IV).

Listing 1-1 gives you all you need to create a basic signup form to add folks to a relatively small mailing list. Signup info will be sent to you by e-mail, not sent to and saved in a complex online database. Our basic signup form looks something like the one in Figure 1-6. Then, all you have to do is make sure you use the data you collect to do good, not bad, things with it.

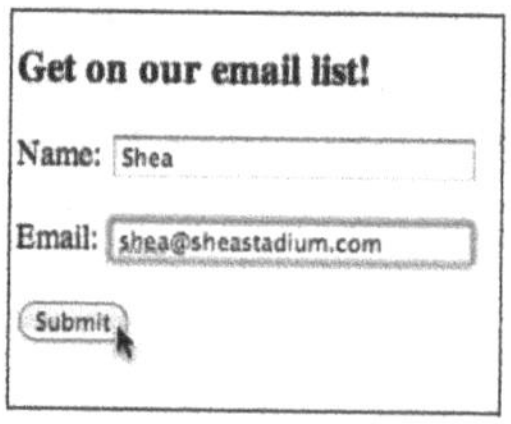

Figure 1-6:
A minimalist
signup form.

> Get on our email list!
>
> Name: Shea
>
> Email: shea@sheastadium.com
>
> Submit

Developing More Complex Form Fields

Different kinds of form fields enable different ways of collecting data in a form. Text boxes are the simplest way to collect data and also the most widely used to collect names, e-mail addresses, phone numbers, addresses, credit card numbers, Social Security numbers, order numbers, customer numbers, and more, including passwords. And there are variations of text boxes, for example, when visitors enter several lines of text, or maybe enter text in password mode, where their entry shows up as asterisks onscreen (******).

Still other kinds of form fields present people with choices:

✦ **Select menus:** Provide menus for choices. For instance, visitors can choose a topic to search for, a job title, or a date to book an airline flight.

✦ **Check boxes:** Check boxes can be singles or hang out in a herd. Use a loner to give visitors the chance to opt in or out of receiving a newsletter. Use groups for when visitors can make multiple selections, like for ordering pizza toppings. Here's the important point, though: Whether grouped or individuals, any check box can either be selected or deselected. Any time you want to provide users with an either/or choice, you can use a check box. The following code creates a check box that allows a user to get on an e-list:

```
<input type="checkbox" name="elist" value="Yes"/> Put
    me on the e-list
```

When submitted as part of a form, a checked check box would send a message: `"elist=Yes"`

✦ **Radio buttons:** This type of form offers a choice bank from which visitors pick only one option. You can use a set of radio buttons to have a visitor rate something on a scale of 1–10, or specify the type of credit card they are using.

Whenever you add a form field, place it between the `<form>` and `</form>` tags.

Here's code that, when placed within a form element, creates a set of radio buttons that allow users to rate something on a scale of 1–5:

```
<p>Rate us on a scale of 1-5 (5 is best)</p>
<input type="radio" name="rating" value="5" /> 5<br />
<input type="radio" name="rating" value="4" /> 4<br />
<input type="radio" name="rating" value="3" /> 3<br />
<input type="radio" name="rating" value="2" /> 2<br />
<input type="radio" name="rating" value="1" /> 1<br />
```

**Book VII
Chapter 1**

**Collecting
Information
with Forms**

Formatting fields to collect phone numbers

When you see text fields that appear to collect a phone number in three parts, with dashes, those are actually three separate fields, with complex CSS styling applied to make them appear to be a single field. Such "three-part" text fields are necessary for forms submitted to sophisticated databases that require identical formats in how phone numbers are submitted. For an organization or business collecting phone numbers for members or customer contacts, for example, you can allow users to enter their phone numbers in any format they choose. In Chapters 2 and 3 of this minibook, we explore a variety of ways to validate form data to make sure, for example, that a phone number "looks like" a phone number in some form before a form can be submitted.

More you can do with text fields

As we note earlier, a simple text box can become a field where visitors can enter multiple lines of text. And text fields that are used to collect private information use password mode.

Using a password format in a text box does *not* provide any real protection for data. It simply conceals the content of what's being entered from anyone "looking over the shoulder" of the person entering data.

Defining a textarea

A textarea field is like a text field but rather than just allowing one line of text, they allow multiple lines of data entry, and thus are great for collecting comments. The syntax for a textarea field requires a name, like all form fields.

The most important optional parameters for a textarea field are the cols (columns) and rows values that define the size of the box. Each col represents a character, so col=40 defines a 40-character–wide field.

The following code defines a textarea field, named comment, that's 40 characters wide (characters are, oddly enough, defined as cols in HTML) and five lines high, along with text explaining to a user what to enter in the field:

```
<p>Tell us a bit about yourself:</p>
<p><textarea name="comment" cols="40" rows="5">
</textarea>
</p>
```

There is no HTML textarea property that limits the number of characters that can be entered into a textarea.

Using a password format

When you apply a password parameter to a text field, the content is disguised on the user's screen. As we warn earlier, this is not a way of encrypting (hiding) data as it travels over the Internet. In fact, when you send password text to an e-mail address, that data shows up just as if it were never concealed.

However, password fields do protect the privacy of a user in the sense that other people can't see what you're typing. Here's the password type parameter added to an email field.

```
<input name="email" type="password" size="30" maxlength="80"/>
```

Figures 1-7 and 1-8 also include the comment field.

Get on our email list!

Name: Shea

Email: •••••••••••

Tell us a bit about yourself:

I'm eight years old, six feet tall, and already I can dunk! Is there any way I can help your girls basketball team?

(Submit)

Figure 1-7: Entering data in a password type field.

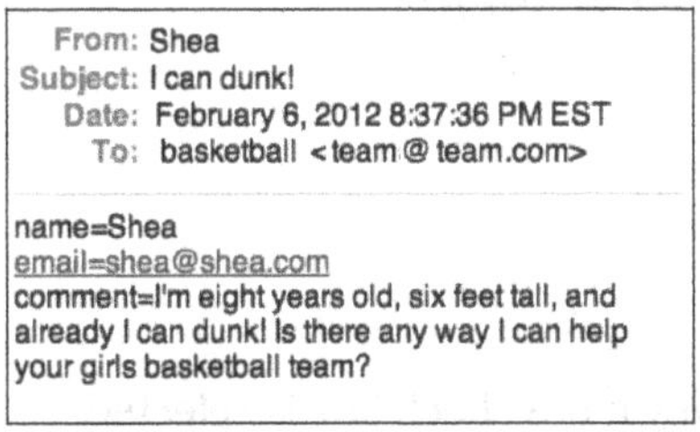

Figure 1-8: Collecting data by e-mail, with content of a password field visible.

From: Shea
Subject: I can dunk!
Date: February 6, 2012 8:37:36 PM EST
To: basketball <team @ team.com>

name=Shea
email=shea@shea.com
comment=I'm eight years old, six feet tall, and already I can dunk! Is there any way I can help your girls basketball team?

Adding a select menu

Select menus, like all form fields, have names and include a set of options (values), along with text that identifies the option for a user. Listing 1-2 creates an `option` menu named `quantity`? that lets users choose how many ribs they want to order:

Listing 1-2:   Option Menu Form Example

```
<p>How many ribs do you want to order?
    <select name="quantity">
      <option value="6">A half dozen</option>
      <option value="12">A dozen</option>
      <option value="24">A slab</option>
    </select>
</p>
```

Added to a form, that select menu looks something like Figure 1-9.

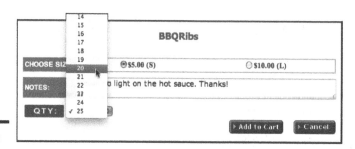

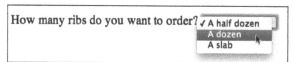

Figure 1-9:
A select
menu
with three
options.

Adding check boxes to a form

Check box fields require three elements:

+ **Input type**

+ **Name**

+ **Value**

> The value is submitted only if the check box is selected.

Unlike a text field, there is no way to indicate within a check box what it is that a visitor is checking, or unchecking. So, check boxes are always accompanied by some regular HTML text that explains what the option is.

The code in Listing 1-3 submits a value of yes for the field name for any and all options a user selects.

Listing 1-3:   Check Box Form Example

```
<h3>How can you help?</h3>
<p><input name="read-books" type="checkbox" value="yes" id="read-books">
  I can read books out loud to school children</a></p>
<p><input name="supervise-play" type="checkbox" value="yes"
    id="supervise-play"> I can help supervise afterschool play activities
    </a></p>
<p><input name="donate-supplies" type="checkbox" value="yes"
    id="donate-supplies"> I can donate office supplies</a></p>
<p><input name="teach-web" type="checkbox" value="yes" id="teach-web">
    I can teach Web design</a></p>
```

A set of check boxes like that in Listing 1-3, with a bit of CSS style applied, looks like the set of choices in Figure 1-10.

How can you help?

☑ I can read books out loud to school children

☒ I can help supervise afterschool play activities

☐ I can donate office supplies

☑ I can teach Web design

Figure 1-10:
Check
boxes can
be selected,
or not,
indepen-
dently.

Using radio button groups

Although other form fields can be used more than once, only radio buttons come in specific groups from which a user can select one, and only one, option. If you ask users to rate your site on a scale of 1–5 (as shown in Figure 1-11), you present them with a group of radio buttons with the same form field name (but with different values). So, because radio buttons are always created in groups, with a common field name (but different values), they are more complicated to create than other form fields. Another downside to radio buttons: Those tiny buttons are difficult to select in mobile devices. For those reasons, their usefulness is near the lower end of form options and sinking, but still functional and worth a quick look.

Book VII
Chapter 1

Collecting
Information
with Forms

Figure 1-11:
Check
boxes can
be selected,
or not,
indepen-
dently.

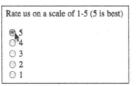

Rate us on a scale of 1-5 (5 is best)

- ● 5
- ○ 4
- ○ 3
- ○ 2
- ○ 1

As noted, radio buttons are defined in HTML with an `input type` (`radio`), a `name`, and a `value`. And, as we alluded to, the trick is that all radio buttons in a group have the same name — but different values. For example, a set of radio buttons that restricts users to choosing option A or option B might look like this:

```
<input type="radio" name="option" value="a" /> Option "A" <br>
    <input type="radio" name="option" value="b" /> Option "B"
```

Tweaking buttons

Earlier in this chapter, when we walk you through the steps involved in cre-ating a simple signup form, we identify that the syntax for a Submit button is

```
<input type="submit" />
```

You can enhance Submit buttons to make them more inviting by adding a value. The only practical impact of changing the value of a Submit button is that different text appears onscreen. So, for example, the code

```
<input type="submit" value="Click here quick, before the world ends!"/>
```

produces a Submit button like the one in Figure 1-12 (which might, or might not, convey a sense of urgency to potential signees, depending on your intended audience).

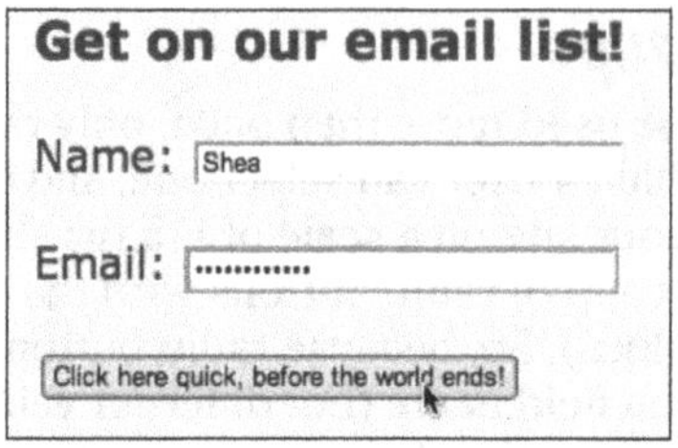

Figure 1-12:
Adding
custom text
to a Submit
button.

> **Get on our email list!**
>
> Name: `Shea`
>
> Email: `............`
>
> `Click here quick, before the world ends!`

And don't forget about the option to add a Reset button to a form. Reset buttons allow users to clear a form of all content. You create a reset button with this HTML code:

```
<input type="reset"/>
```

Making Forms Friendlier with HTML5

A wide range of tools is available for making forms easier to fill out and more accurate in the information they gather. Those tools fall into two categories:

✦ **Tools that make it easier and more inviting to fill out a form:** These include tips that pop up when a user hovers over a field, and place-holder content that suggests the content a user should enter.

✦ **Tools that validate form content:** *Validation* means testing content before it is submitted to check whether it conforms to defined rules. For example, you might validate a user's e-mail address to see whether it meets the criteria of having an @ character.

Sophisticated form validation is done with JavaScript. Dreamweaver, for example, has built-in features that automatically generate validation JavaScript when you create a form.

You can define JavaScript form validation for any form, including the ones we've been working with in this chapter that send form data to an e-mail address.

You can also use server-side scripts to validate form data, written — for example — in PHP. Those server-side validation techniques can't be applied to the e-mail-based forms we create in this chapter.

HTML5 provides a simpler and highly accessible set of validation tools. These tools only work if a user's browser supports HTML5, though, so they can't be relied on to filter all invalid form data. However, they don't cause any harm in other browsers (except that they don't validate data).

Browser support for HTML5 form elements and properties continues to evolve. For an updated chart of which HTML5 form attributes are supported in various browsers, see `http://wufoo.com/html5/`.

Defining placeholder values

HTML5 provides the option of displaying placeholder text to clue a user to what data to enter in a field. Again, this feature doesn't work in older browsers, but users with older browsers can still enter form data, prompted by regular text on the page (like "What's your e-mail address?") — they just won't see the placeholder text.

The `placeholder` parameter can be added to a text `input` element the same way we've shown adding other parameters throughout this chapter to form fields. For example, the following code adds a placeholder to an `email` field that prompts a user with a text hint:

```
<input type="email" name="email" placeholder="Email address goes here"/>
```

And in a browser that supports HTML5, the field looks like Figure 1-13.

Book VII
Chapter 1

Collecting
Information
with Forms

Figure 1-13:
HTML5
placeholder
text in a
form field.

Email: `Email address goes here`

HTML5 validation

HTML5 `input` parameters provide a very easy way to test users' data before a form is submitted.

HTML5 form validation works only in browsing environments that support HTML5, but users without HTML5 support can still submit form data. They just won't have their data validated before it is submitted.

The most basic tool for form field validation is requiring input.

The HTML5 `required` parameter rejects forms that leave a required field blank. The syntax, for example, for a required e-mail field would be

```
<p>Name: <input name="name" required></p>
```

If a user attempts to submit a form without anything entered in a `required` form field, an HTML5-compliant browser will display an error message and prompt, like the one in Figure 1-14. That error message and prompt will vary depending on the browser environment, and will not — of course — display at all in older browsers that do not support this HTML5 feature.

Figure 1-14:
Users can't leave required fields blank.

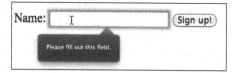

A more sophisticated validation parameter tests for input that looks like an e-mail address. The code for an `email` text field with that parameter is

```
<p>E-mail: <input type=email name="email"></p>
```

If a user tries to enter content that doesn't look like an e-mail address in a form field with an HTML5 `email` type, the error message displayed in Figure 1-15 appears.

Figure 1-15:
An HTML5 e-mail validation at work.

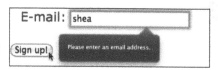

JavaScript-based validation tools are more powerful, and more widely supported in very old browsers than HTML5 validation. They do require JavaScript code. An accessible way to generate that validation code in JavaScript is Dreamweaver's tools, covered in Chapter 4 of this minibook (see "Adding Form Input Validation with JavaScript").

Stylin' Forms

As a general rule, all the CSS style techniques we cover in Book IV apply to HTML pages with forms. Make form pages attractive with color schemes, inviting fonts, and other attributes.

Here, we'll just point to the fact that among the HTML tags you can define styles for the elements used in defining forms. So, for example, any CSS style you define for the `<form>` tag will apply to the appearance of the form.

The style for the `<input>` tag will define how the different input form fields appear: the `text` fields, the `textarea` field, the check boxes, the radio buttons, the select menu, and even the Submit and Reset buttons.

For example, to create a text field with a black background and white text, you can use the following CSS style:

```
input {
    color: white;
    background-color: black;
}
```

And that would create an input field like the one in Figure 1-16.

Get involved!

E-mail:

Figure 1-16:
Applying a
CSS style to
a form field.

shea@shea.ly

And, as a final word of advice, attractive, inviting, accessible forms are going to attract more form input, so don't leave out form elements (like `form` and `input`) when you create the style sheet for your site.

Crafting Form Fields for Mobile Devices

Designing mobile-friendly forms is a particular and increasingly important challenge. Without a mouse to point precisely to a tiny radio button, for example, making a selection from a group of radio buttons is awfully difficult in a small mobile device screen.

Further, it is challenging to type content into form fields in mobile devices. After all, mobile devices are small, with tiny "keyboards." With this problem in mind, there are things to avoid when designing forms for mobile, and techniques that make the experience of filling out a form on a mobile device more accessible.

Mobile-friendly forms

Here are three main themes to keep in mind when designing forms for mobile devices:

✦ **Mobile devices automatically adjust how form fields display to facilitate easy access by mobile users.** The most widely implemented feature is to display drop-down menus more accessibly.

Drop-down menus usually display in a rolling-style box that appears when a select form field is tapped. The simple search box form at Craigslist in Figure 1-4, for example, becomes mobile-friendly when opened in an iPhone, as shown in Figure 1-17.

✦ **Some form fields work better than others in mobile devices.** As we mention earlier in this chapter, we recommend avoiding using radio buttons in forms if a significant part of your intended audience is mobile users (and whose isn't?).

✦ **New ways of collecting and managing data are evolving for mobile devices.** As the need for mobile-friendly input tools takes on ever greater importance, new form fields are evolving in HTML5 and jQuery Mobile. (For a full exploration of jQuery Mobile see the section, "Using jQuery Mobile" in Book VI, Chapter 3.) We explore one of the most useful next.

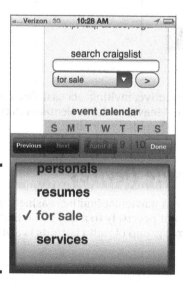

Figure 1-17:
Viewing a
drop-down
menu on
a mobile
device.

Form field display issues in ancient browsers

Until 2005 or so, Internet Explorer 6, 7, and 8 created frustrating issues for web designers for all kinds of reasons. One of them, not the most significant, was that those browsing environments didn't accurately support CSS styles applied to form fields. Today, those browsing environments are moving closer to extinction, and the consensus among web designers is that if CSS styles (like form field background colors) don't appear in those environments, that is acceptable.

Creating a slider

The `slider` form field is an accessible and inviting way to collect form field data in mobile devices, allowing users to input values without having to use the awkward "keyboards" on their devices. Sliders are supported by all mobile devices that support HTML5, and all mobile devices do support HTML5. Figure 1-18 shows a slider in action.

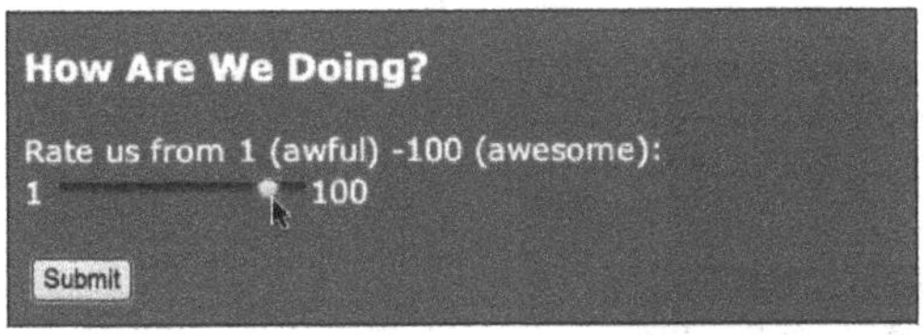

Figure 1-18: Sliders make it easy for mobile users to select a value in a form.

How Are We Doing?

Rate us from 1 (awful) -100 (awesome):
1 ————————— 100

Submit

Before diving right into the HTML code for a slider, step back and survey the emerging terrain of mobile-friendly form fields.

 A limited set of slider-like form fields is emerging from HTML5. As of this writing, those tools are not yet widely supported, flexible, or reliable. Tune into the latest developments in HTML5 form fields and the state of browser support for them at

    http://www.w3schools.com/html5/html5_form_input_types.asp

and

    http://www.w3schools.com/html5/html5_form_attributes.asp

Sliders are created using the `input type range` — referring to giving a user a choice from a "range" of values, such as 1–100.

Listing 1-4 shows you how to create a complete form with the rating slider illustrated in Figure 1-18.

Listing 1-4: Sample Rating Slider HTML for a Form

```
<h3>How Are We Doing?</h3>
<form action="" method="get">
<h4>
<label for="slider">Rate us from 1 (awful) -100 (awesome):</label> <br>
1 <input type="range" name="slider" id="slider" value="0" min="0"
    max="100" />100
</h4>
<p>
<input type="submit" name="button" id="button" value="Submit">
</p>
</form>
```

The HTML, obviously, goes inside the body tags in an HTML page, and will work in browsing environments that support HTML5.

How do sliders (the HTML5 input range type) work in non-HTML5 browsers? In those older browsing environments, visitors simply enter a value in a field with their keyboard, as shown in Figure 1-19, where an HTML5 input range field is being viewed in Internet Explorer 6.

Figure 1-19:
In older browsers, HTML5 slider form fields display as text input fields.

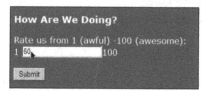

The principle to apply in working with HTML5 form field elements is to use those fields that work better in contemporary browsing environments, but still work fine in older browsers. The HTML5 input range field is a good example of such a solution — providing easy touch accessibility in a mobile phone, while allowing users sitting at a desktop with IE6 (or IE7 or IE8) to enter values from their keyboards.

Chapter 2: DIY PHP Solutions

*I*n this chapter, you enter into the realm of *live data* — namely, content collected from visitors of a web page and sent to a server, or web page content served into a page from a server.

Live data web pages allow you to gather data in forms and send that data to a server without requiring a user to launch an e-mail program. That simple solution will work, and we show you how in Chapter 1 of this minibook, but there are more elegant ways to collect data.

And, live data allows you to embed content from a server within pages. Newspaper articles, header content, navigation bars, and any other kind of page content can be stored in one file on a server, fed into any number of web pages, and updated globally.

If you're creating PHP content in Dreamweaver, there are quirks you should know about regarding how Dreamweaver handles PHP files; knowing these quirks will spare you a lot of unnecessary stress if you work with PHP. Before you start working with PHP in Dreamweaver, review Chapter 4 of this mini-book, especially the section "Scripting PHP in Dreamweaver."

Looking at Live Data — An Overview

If you're thinking that incorporating live data is an awfully powerful way to interact with visitors to a site, and to provide a large volume of frequently updated content, you are correct.

For better or worse, the web as we now know it, dominated by the Facebooks, Tumblrs, and Twitters of the world, is powered by live data. People can instantly share important news, photos, and video without access to technology beyond a digital device and an Internet hookup.

You're used to thinking about live data associated with large-scale sites like Fox, CBS, NBC, and PBS. And it's true that those sites are all managed by feeding data into pages, like the listings for PBS in Figure 2-1.

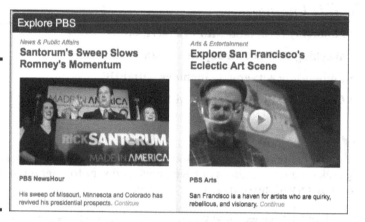

Figure 2-1: Live data is served into pages at huge websites with rapidly changing content.

But live data is accessible to small-scale sites as well — not as accessible as HTML, CSS, or JavaScript, but more accessible than you might think. Take Marc Silber, for example. He sells used stringed instruments online from his studio in Berkeley, California and maintains his inventory with an online database, as shown in Figure 2-2.

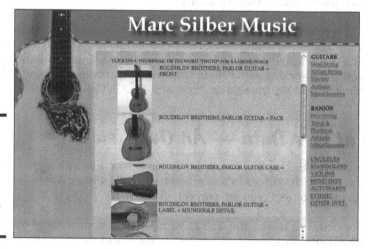

Figure 2-2: Live data can feed inventory into a small-scale website.

Here are two questions to ask in relation to live data and your site:

✦ **Need:** Do you need live data? Or is your content stable and small-scale enough to manage with page-by-page content editing?

This answer is, of course, a judgment call. A publication that comes out biannually might do well to simply post each issue as HTML pages. One that comes out every day might be better served by a live data system.

✦ **Management:** If you do need live data (to maintain updated news, current inventory, timely blog postings, and so on), should you develop your own live data applications, or simply handle your live data needs through a social networking site or other tool?

If and when you do decide you need live data in your site, your options range from going full out with a social network blog system like WordPress or Facebook, to creating a completely do-it-yourself live data setup, to a whole range of inbetween options that combine packaged live data tools with your own custom site.

Live data options

A full exploration of the role of social networking sites in building websites is found in Book VIII, Chapter 2. Here, though, take a minute to explore three possible approaches to collecting and distributing content using live data:

✦ **All by myself:** You create the entire live data setup yourself, collecting data in forms, sending it yourself with a coded server-side script, and feeding easily updated server-side content into pages using scripts you create. (You discover how to do that in this chapter.)

- *Pros:* You have control over your own data, as opposed to handing it over to Facebook, Twitter, and so on.

  You can do it the way you want to do it.

  Cons: You'll be limited in how complex your live data applications can be, and you have to do it yourself.

✦ **Some help:** You can avail yourself of semi–do-it-yourself tools available online that provide generated or updatable live data solutions. We explore that option in depth in the next chapter.

Pros: You can create a relatively powerful online database that manages your data, and do it yourself.

Cons: You'll lose exclusive control over the data you collect, as the services that supply form data tools generally store "your" data at their server.

✦ **A whole lotta help:** You can integrate commercial live-data resources, like YouTube or Vimeo for video distribution, or e-commerce sites for selling things, into a website you build yourself. We explore working with video-serving resources in Book V, Chapter 4, and e-commerce solutions in Book VIII.

Pros: These resources are very easy to use.

Cons: You have almost no control over how your data is saved and made available. For instance, if you rely on YouTube to save and supply video, that video will be available not only at your own site, but through YouTube.

Live data you can manage yourself

For the remainder of this chapter, we walk you through creating two of the most useful and productive things you can do:

✦ Connect a form to a server-side script to collect input from users without forcing them to use their own e-mail program.

✦ Embed data from a server in pages.

This chapter, by the way, is pretty much as technical as we get in this whole big book, but we'll keep things basic and take things step by step.

Having said that, first things first. To develop and test live data, you need to have your website hosted *by* as well as posted *to* a hosting service that supports PHP (most do). PHP is a server-side scripting language.

So, if you plan to actually implement live data at this stage of your site development process, jump over to Book I, Chapter 4 where we explain how to select hosting services, and how to upload your content to those servers.

Keep in mind the difference between a local version of a website (one you create on your own computer), and a remote site hosted by a web-hosting service.

Mixing PHP and Live Data

A variety of server-side scripting languages enable live data: Active Server Pages (ASP; Microsoft's server-side scripting language), Ruby (an open source, server side coding platform), and others. But the one that has emerged as the dominant, most widely available, and easiest to use is PHP.

Once upon a time, PHP was an abbreviation for Personal Home Page. Nowadays, after the language has been modified over the years, the common "definition" is PHP: Hypertext Preprocessor.

PHP has emerged as the most widely applied server-side scripting language. Server-side (also referred to as "back-end") scripts run on servers, and generally are used to manage large amounts of data in commercial applications.

There are many other server-side scripting languages besides PHP. Some of them have been around for a while, and are going to be around for a while. This category includes ASP, a server-side scripting language developed and championed by Microsoft, and the Perl CGI server-side scripting language, which has a large base of installed applications, but isn't as powerful or accessible as more contemporary languages. Emerging server-side scripting languages include the open-source Ruby/Ruby on Rails and Python languages.

Every server-side scripting language has different strengths. Ruby is gaining favor based on the (relative) ease and quickness with which skilled programmers can use it to build apps. Python is close to the Java programming language. *Note:* Neither Python nor Java has any substantial relation to JavaScript, a client-side scripting language that we cover in Book VI.

All that said, PHP is the standard, is free, and is supported by the widest range of hosting services. It is generally considered the fastest running, most reliable and scalable scripting language (meaning it can be used reliably in very large scale projects). The WordPress, Joomla!, and Drupal content management systems (CMS; essentially expanded blogs) are built with PHP, as is Google. The central resource for PHP documentation and downloads is www.php.net.

Because this isn't a programming book, our exploration of actual scripting in PHP goes just deeply enough into coding to create a very basic script to manage form data, and elemental HTML code to embed live data into pages using a PHP script.

After you get the hang of creating some simple, useful PHP applications, you'll be set to work with more complex PHP scripts that you find online, or that are generated using various online tools. We take a look at such tools in Chapter 3 of this minibook.

Making PHP work

Here's a basic parameter for working with PHP: It works when the pages within which it is embedded are saved on a web server that supports PHP.

That carries important implications. If you're developing your site on your own computer (as opposed to a server, where someone else hosts your site) and haven't yet contracted for remote hosting on a web server, you can't test PHP pages. Sure, you can create them, but you can't actually submit a PHP-based form or view embedded live content in your pages.

Book VII Chapter 2

DIY PHP Solutions

If you find yourself in this position, you have three basic options:

✦ **Create PHP content using the discussion and specific models in this minibook and test later.**

✦ **Contract with a web-hosting service that does support PHP.** See Book I, Chapter 4. You can then upload your site to that remote hosting server to test your PHP scripts.

PHP is an open source scripting language. Like all open source projects, it's supported by a community and network of developers. And, like all open source programs, it's free. This is a contributing factor to why even most very low-cost hosting services have PHP installed. So, you won't have a hard time finding a hosting service that supports PHP.

✦ **Install server software — WAMP (for Windows), MAMP (for Macs) — on your own computer.** The free version of this server software (there is also a professional version that costs money) is sufficient to test PHP scripts on your own computer. You download MAMP from `http://mamp.info` and WAMP from `www.wampserver.com`.

The basic steps in installing WAMP, MAMP, or LAMP aren't too hard to follow, but pay close attention to one detail: *Note the login and password you assign yourself during this process, or you'll be locked out of your own server.*

After you install WAMP, MAMP, or LAMP, save your website files to the appropriate folder created during the installation process. In Windows, that folder is www. On Macs the root folder is htdocs.

With WAMP/MAMP running, you can test your PHP pages; open them in your browser from the WAMP or MAMP folders by entering **localhost** in the address bar of your Windows browser or **http://localhost:8888/** in a Mac browser. Figure 2-3 shows the root folder of a MAMP installation viewed in a browser, with all files and folders displayed as clickable links.

Figure 2-3: Viewing saved PHP files at an Installed MAMP server.

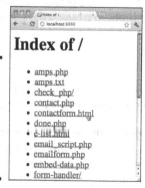

The world of PHP

The basic PHP syntax we explore here will be introduced and explained as you actually build forms that send data to PHP scripts on a server, and as you build HTML pages that embed data supplied by a PHP script. Before you get your feet wet, though, here are a few basic concepts:

✦ **PHP is a full-fledged programming language.**

PHP is much more complicated than HTML or CSS. And what that means for you — and most web designers — is that you can use small chunks of PHP code, but rely on editable libraries and code-generating resources (like the ones covered in Chapter 3 of this minibook) for more complicated applications.

Many editable PHP scripts that you can find online are commented with helpful hints for nonprogrammers. So that you can make sense of those hints and edit the supplied PHP code, though, read through the discussion of PHP in this section.

✦ **PHP files come in two flavors, both of which are "PHP files."**

- *Some basically function like HTML pages and present data to visitors.*

  A PHP *web page* file is like an HTML page except that it can include PHP scripting. When you build pages with *server-side includes* (SSIs; data fed into a page from a server), those pages look and act like HMTL pages, but they're saved with a PHP filename extension instead of an HTML extension.

- *Some are mainly PHP script.*

  A PHP script file is saved to a server. That file also is saved with a PHP filename extension, but it's not set up like an HTML page, and it doesn't (generally) include HTML tags. These server-side scripts are programs that make things happen — not web pages that display content.

Each kind of PHP file can have PHP coding or HTML page structure. Usually, most PHP pages are mainly either page layout documents using mostly HTML, or mainly PHP code, with perhaps a few lines of HTML mixed in. The terminology here can be confusing, so let's break down both kinds of PHP files.

PHP and MySQL

PHP scripts are often paired with MySQL *databases,* which are organized sets of tables that hold a lot of data — anything from names and e-mail addresses to videos and images.

**Book VII
Chapter 2**

DIY PHP Solutions

MySQL?

If you want to work with the folks who design and manage MySQL databases, you'll want to get the pronunciation right, so they think you know what you're talking about. MySQL is pronounced "my-*see*-quell." Factoid: The "my" part comes from the first name of the daughter of the developer of the language, and the SQL is an acronym for Structured Query Language.

You can use PHP without MySQL. For instance, you can store data on a server, like a company mailing address, and embed that data in pages using PHP. But complex, professional level live data involves serving data from online databases into web pages. And that requires adding MySQL to the equation.

Entering data into a MySQL database is doable for a nonexpert. However, setting up and maintaining a MySQL database, and creating scripts that feed data in and out of that database, requires a skillset on the order of what you can learn in a 12-week community college class, or by immersing yourself in a book dedicated to PHP and MySQL, for example *PHP & MySQL For Dummies,* 4th Edition, by Janet Valade.

If you're thinking this might be a direction you want to head, when you're shopping for a web-hosting service, be sure that you find one that provides MySQL as part of the package. As we note earlier, almost every web-hosting service supports PHP, but you also have to check to make sure your hosting service supports MySQL. And, by the way, the WAMP/MAMP/LAMP option we talk about earlier (for installing a server on your own computer) does include a nice MySQL interface. If you're comfortable with defining databases and *relational tables* (sets of related data within a database), you'll find the MySQL interface intuitive.

You might look at MySQL and its relationship to live data and website creation this way: If you want to create substantial live data applications in websites for yourself, your clients, and your company or organization, you can do much with PHP — but without MySQL. However, if your site needs a powerful database manager for uploading hundreds of news articles each day, managing thousands of transactions each hour, or updating traffic reports each minute, you're likely to turn to a packaged PHP/MySQL solution (like the e-commerce options we explore in Book VIII). And if your inclinations and talents lean toward creating that level of powerful web page and database interaction yourself, learning how to integrate PHP and MySQL might be the right path for you.

In sum, when it comes to integrating MySQL databases into your site, you have three options:

✦ **Most complicated:** Study PHP and learn to write your own, more complex scripts.

✦ **Complicated, but within reach of most designers who are comfortable with HTML:** Find resources within the forest of unevenly documented "ready-to-edit" PHP scripts to be found online.

We walk through how to do that, using some of the most valuable available online resources, in Chapter 3 of this minibook.

✦ **Easiest:** Contract for packaged PHP solutions, such as social networking sites, e-commerce resources, and commercial mailing list programs.

Creating a PHP-Ready Form

The PHP-driven input form we show you how to create in the following section is simple, and it works. Visitors can enter their name and e-mail address and submit that information without having to submit that data using their e-mail program (a simpler option we explore in Chapter 1 of this minibook). And, this project displays a "thank you" message when people submit form data.

Book VII
Chapter 2

DIY PHP Solutions

Visitors submitting their info to you won't see your e-mail address, but you will get their submitted content sent to you in an e-mail. As you build up a mailing list, you can simply copy and paste the submitted information to your e-list in a spreadsheet or text file, and then when you're ready to move on up to a commercial e-mail list management program (something we explore in Chapter 3 of this minibook), you can import that list into that mail manager.

You can adapt the form and script we build here to create other forms. The main trick to doing that is to make sure the form fields you collect in your form (like email or name) match those in the PHP script that handles the data. We'll return to that shortly, but keep it filed in the back of your head as you think about how you will adapt this script to suit your own needs.

For now, this simple form lacks the bells and whistles available in more complex forms (like sophisticated validation scripts that test form data before it is sent to the server, to make sure an e-mail address looks like an e-mail address). We explore using more complex PHP mail list applications in this minibook that include data validation (Chapter 3) and tools for generating JavaScript validation for forms (Chapter 4) in the context of looking at some rather sophisticated form design tools in Dreamweaver.

This form example doesn't use sophisticated validation, but we will show you how to incorporate the basic HTML5 validation tools we explore in Chapter 1 of this minibook. Those tools, as we discuss in Chapter 1, work only in contemporary browsers that support HTML5. Users with modern browsers that do support HTML5 will get the assistance of validation scripts that warn them if they leave out required data, or enter an e-mail address that doesn't look like an e-mail address.

Combining Form Actions and PHP

Here is the one basic difference between the mail list form we build in Chapter 1 and one that sends data via a PHP server script.

With an e-mail–based form, the `action` parameter launches an e-mail client; with our PHP-based form, the `action` will be defined by a PHP script at the server.

Defining a PHP-based form action

The form `action` for a form submitted to a server-side PHP script looks like this:

```
<form name="elist" method="post" action="email_script.php">
```

`email_script.php` is the name of the file at the server that manages this form data. If you save a script with a different name, you'd edit the script file name even though you would always have a script with a PHP filename extension. And, if you save your script to a subfolder below the folder holding the page with the form, you have to include a path to that folder. For example, if you save your script to a folder named "scripts," the preceding form `action` would read

```
<form name="elist" method="post" action="scripts/email_script.php">
```

Creating a form for PHP-destined data

Aside from the `action` parameter, forms for PHP scripts are created by using the same techniques we explore in Chapter 1 of this minibook.

Listing 2-1 applies form-design tools covered in Chapter 1 to create an HTML page with a basic form that you can adapt and customize, or just use as-is as an e-list signup form.

Listing 2-1:   Signup Form HTML

```html
<!doctype html>
<html>
<head>
<meta charset="UTF-8">
<title>Get on Our E List</title>
</head>
<body>
<h1>Join our Email List</h1>
<form name="elist" method="post" action="email_script.php">
 <p>Name <input  type="text" name="name" maxlength="50"
   size="30" placeholder="Your name here" required>
  <p>Email <input  type="email" name="email" maxlength="80"
   size="30"placeholder="Email address goes here"  required>
  <p><input type="submit" value="Submit">   </p>
</p>
</form>
</body>
</html>
```

The HTML for our form uses HTML5 parameters for required fields and e-mail type validation as well as the HTML5 placeholder parameter to provide prompt text in the fields. If these features don't display because a visitor's browsing environment is not HTML5-compliant, the form still works — it just lacks validation and placeholder text prompts.

The form will look something like Figure 2-4 in a browser. Of course, you can feel free to spruce it up with CSS styles, as discussed in Chapter 1 of this minibook.

Book VII
Chapter 2

DIY PHP Solutions

Figure 2-4:
Previewing a form that will send data to a PHP script.

Join our Email List

Name [Your name here]

Email [Email address goes here]

(Submit)

With the form defined, take note of a few things that you will need when you create a PHP script to manage the form data:

✦ You have two form fields: `email` and `name`.

✦ You define a form `action` that connects this form data to a PHP file that has to be called `email_script.php`.

Taking a Short Course in PHP Form Scripting

As we discuss earlier, PHP is a complex programming language beyond the scope of this book. Because of that, we're going to present just a small subset of it that provides the syntax you need to create a script to manage your form data.

Defining PHP code blocks

PHP script, whether in a page code or embedded within a web page that's mostly HTML, is enclosed in these tags:

```
<?php
php code goes here
?>
```

All content between the opening `<?php` and the closing `?>` tags is interpreted by browsers as PHP scripting.

Working with string variables

Like all programming languages, a key element of PHP involves defining variables. For example, `name` and `email` can be defined as variables in a program that can handle different values for those variables depending on what a user submits in a form.

In PHP, *string variables* are used to store values that contain characters, such as letters and numbers.

PHP string variables are generally identified with a dollar sign ($) in front of the variable name. Variable names always begin with a letter or an underscore character (_), and you can use only letters, numbers, and underscores. And variable names are case-sensitive.

A variable name can't contain spaces or other special characters.

You assign values to variables using assignment statements, like this:

```
$name = "Shea";
```

Note the full syntax in the preceding example. The variable name is preceded by $, and an equal sign (=) is used to connect the variable to the value assigned to it.

Collecting string values with $POST

The PHP `$_POST` variable collects values (such as Allison, or ali@ali.com) and assigns them to variables (such as `$name`, or `$email`).

The $_POST variable works in sync with form data sent using the POST method. In Listing 2-1, when we define the form action for our signup form, we use the parameter method="post".

The PHP mail ( ) function

The PHP mail() function sends email. The syntax is

```
mail(to,subject,message,headers,parameters)
```

Here's a breakdown of these parameters:

+ to: Required. You enter an e-mail address to which data is to be mailed.

+ subject: Required. This defines what appears in the subject line of the e-mail.

+ message: Required. This defines the message in the body of the e-mail.

+ headers: Not required. You can use this parameter to define what goes in the From, CC, or BCC fields in the e-mail.

+ parameters: The redundantly named parameters parameter is optional, and can be used to custom-configure how data is submitted.

You also need a few additional code bits to make the e-mail message comprehensible, and not just one long run-on line of text:

+ "\n": Creates a new line of text. Think "n" for "new."

+ "\r": Produces a "carriage return" (jump to a new line), but for our purposes, jumps from one field in an e-mail message to another when defining headers. Think "r" for "return."

The PHP script to collect form data

Pshew! With all that under your belt, you now have all the PHP concepts and code needed to create a functional script to manage input form data.

Listing 2-2 holds the code.

Listing 2-2: PHP Script to Collect Form Data

```php
<?php
$email_to = "email@email.com";
$email_subject = "E-list signup";
$name = $_POST['name'];
$email = $_POST['email'];
$email_message = "E-List Signup\n\n";
```

(continued)

Listing 2-2 *(continued)*

```
$email_message .= "name: ".$name."\n";
$email_message .= "email: ".$email."\n";
$headers = 'From: '.$email."\r\n";
@mail($email_to, $email_subject, $email_message, $headers);
?>
<h3>Thanks for signing up! Return to our
    <a href="index.html"> home</a> page.</h3>.
```

That's it? Pretty much.

You do have to replace email@email.com with your e-mail address or the one you set up to receive form data input. And, if your home page is something other than index.html, you should change that link.

The last line of code in our PHP code isn't PHP; it's just a basic HTML heading 3 (h3) element that displays a message on the screen thanking a user for signing up, and offering a link back to the site home page. You'll note that it comes after the PHP script has been closed with ?>.

When a visitor submits the form, he sees the thank-you content (as shown in Figure 2-5), and you get the data sent to you in an e-mail. The formatting will vary depending on your e-mail client, but the data you get should look something like the one in Figure 2-6.

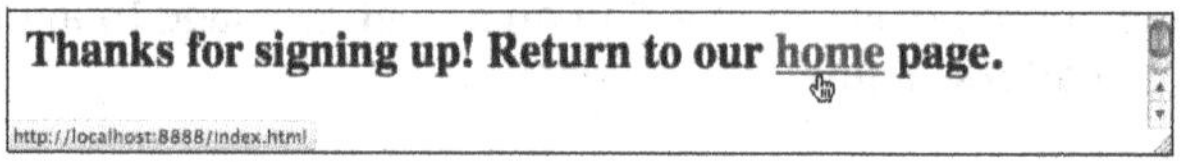

Figure 2-5:
A "thank you" page supplied by a PHP script when a form is submitted

> **Thanks for signing up! Return to our home page.**
> http://localhost:8888/index.html

Figure 2-6:
Form data sent to an e-mail address using a PHP script.

From:	shea@sheastadium.tv
Subject:	E-list signup
Date:	February 9, 2013 1:00:00 AM PST
To:	List Manager <email@email.com>

E-List Signup

name: Shea Stadium III
email: shea@sheastadium.tv

Testing a Form Action Linked to a PHP Script

To test your PHP-linked form and the PHP script, you need to upload (or, if you're using a server like WAMP/MAMP/LAMP on your own computer, save) both the HTML web page with the form and the PHP script to a server.

Because a PHP-ready server is required to test everything in this chapter, here we'll assume (for the moment) that you have a server either on your own computer, or you uploaded your PHP content to a remote server that supports PHP. We show you how to set up a server in more detail at the end of the chapter.

Again, if all this "server" stuff is confusing and annoying, you might jump to the discussion of how to connect to a PHP-ready server at the end of the chapter. We'll still be here when you come back.

Here are the most common trouble-shooting issues you might encounter:

✦ Upload both files to a server.

✦ Make sure both files (in this running example, `emailform.php` and `e-list.html`) are saved in the same folder at your server, unless you're comfortable defining paths between linked files in different folders.

✦ If you're testing your form on a computer with WAMP/or MAMP/, "turn on" your server by launching whichever program you installed.

✦ If all those structural issues are okay, check your code. Did you edit the e-mail address in the model code in Listing 2.2? If not, whatever poor soul has `email@email.com` as his e-mail address has been getting your test form input. But more to the point, you won't.

**Book VII
Chapter 2**

DIY PHP Solutions

You can download the code for both `e-list.html` and `emailform.php` at this book's companion website: `www.dummies.com/go/building websitesallinone`.

Managing Commercial-Level Mail Lists

Our mail list solution in this chapter is obviously one that will work only in a rather small-scale environment, where you are signing up handfuls or dozens of people in a day, and you have time and resources to organize the input into a spreadsheet or your own contact management software.

When your needs outgrow that, opt for one of the two more complex options we allude to in this chapter:

✦ Use a mid-level CMS we explore in Chapter 3 of this minibook.

✦ Move all the way up to a fully professional mail list management system like Constant Contact (`www.constantcontact.com`).

Building Pages with Live Data

Earlier in this chapter, we talk about how exciting and dynamic live data can be. Every site doesn't need to be able to pop new content into pages daily, hourly, or by the minute. But if you do, server-side includes (SSIs) allow you to update blocks of content instantly, and globally, across your entire site.

SSIs have wider applicability in site design. Even if your site doesn't require constant and instant updating, SSIs can hold and supply content for headers, footers, and navigation bars — just to take three examples. If you elect to change your navigation bar, you simply update the SSI file, and new navigation bars instantly appear throughout your site.

Embedding SSIs with PHP is pretty doable. The basic steps involve

1. Create a PHP web page document.

You design and lay this page out just as you would any HTML page, including by styling it with an external CSS style sheet.

2. Define places within the page that will hold SSIs.

3. Create HTML pages that will provide the SSI content.

4. Upload both the PHP page and the HTML pages that hold the SSI content to a PHP-enabled web server.

Our model, and easily customizable project, will create a navigation bar that can be served, as an SSI, into any page. To put together and test the model, we'll create two files:

✦ `ssi-included.html` is the HTML content that will be served into the page.

✦ `ssi-page.php` is the web page that displays the SSI.

Of course, you can give your files different names. The coding we use for SSIs isn't rocket science, and as long as you keep your files in the same folder (or, if you're comfortable with the concept, define paths to your files in different folders), and create both files, you can adapt this model to any SSI.

A more developed model includes a third file, an external style sheet that provides styling for both the page in which the include is embedded, and the embed content itself. To simplify the model (while still making it a working, functional example), we'll skip the styling dimension of the project here.

In many ways, creating and defining SSIs is quite easy, but they work only if all the files involved are uploaded to (or saved to) a PHP-friendly web server. You can test SSIs only by opening them at a server. You can't test them by opening the files themselves on your hard drive, like when testing HTML, CSS, or JavaScript files.

Building includable content

The first step in creating an SSI is to create the HTML content that will be embedded into pages. This might be an updatable "quote of the day," a navigation bar that you want to be able to embed site-wide and later revise, or a copyright notice that appears in the footer of each page that needs to be updated each year.

SSIs can be created as `.txt` (unformatted text) files, HTML files, or any other content supported in browsers (including images, video, or JavaScript). Because they're embedded into larger pages, SSI content tends to be relatively small.

Listing 2-3 creates a very basic HTML document with an editable set of navigation links.

Listing 2-3: Basic HTML Doc with Editable Nav Links

```
<html>
<body>
<a href="/index.html">Home</a> | <a href="/page1.html">
    Page 1</a> | <a href="/page2.html">Page 2</a> |
    <a href="/page3.html">Page 3</a> |
    <a href="/page4.html">Page 4</a>
</body>
</html>
```

**Book VII
Chapter 2**

DIY PHP Solutions

This code should be saved — and in the model we outlined earlier, this would be `ssi-included.html`.

A few notes about this HTML file:

✦ Obviously, you will change the link labels, and replace the placeholder links with real links.

✦ This HTML document has no head section, like a standalone HTML document does. If you create an HTML document to function as an SSI, you don't need to — *and should not* — create head content (like a page title). Such content is supplied by the page in which the content will be included.

✦ To keep the model simple, we created a one-line menu bar. When you're comfortable with the concepts involved, feel free to stretch out and embed the menu in a CSS selector, as we explore in Book VI. And then, define styles for the navigation bar in an external style sheet.

Coding SSIs

The two approaches to coding PHP-based SSIs are

+ The PHP `include()` function

+ The PHP `require()` function

The difference is that if the SSI is corrupted — that is, if something goes wrong, and the SSI doesn't appear in the page like it's supposed to — the `include()` function will generate a warning, but the page will load. If you use the `require()` function, the page won't load in a browser.

For this running example, we use the `require()` option to make sure that pages won't load without included content. Still, which function you opt for is a judgment call. Just remember that using `require()` is "safer" in terms of making sure your pages don't load without important content.

Listing 2-4 holds the code for a PHP document that includes the SSI.

Listing 2-4: PHP Doc with an SSI

```
<!doctype html>
<html>
<head>
<meta charset="UTF-8">
<title>Welcome</title>
</head>
<body>
<h1>Page Heading</h1>
<?php require("ssi-included.html"); ?>
<p>page content goes here</p>
</body>
</html>
```

This page, using our model, is saved as `ssi-page.php`.

A few notes on this PHP code:

+ The document looks and acts like an HTML page, but it's saved with a PHP filename extension. Maybe we could have gotten away with saving this with an HTML filename extension, and counting on browsers to detect the PHP script inside an HTML document. Maybe. But such browser "intelligence" is a mixed bag, and we don't recommend relying on that.

+ The SSI file has an HTML filename extension. That's not a problem. Any file supported by a browser (a JPEG or PNG image, for example), can be used as an SSI.

+ Obviously, you will replace the title and HTML content (the heading one and paragraph tags) with your own content, and add more.

Testing PHP in a Server

We make this point throughout this chapter, but it bears repeating and more explanation: You can use or test PHP script (even PHP SSIs) only on a web server that supports PHP.

If you're creating a website on your own computer — as a way of teaching yourself to create websites, or as a way of developing content before posting it to a server — that's actually a good plan. But it won't work to test PHP on your computer without special *server* software — software that, among other things, runs PHP scripts (usually).

What does that mean? And how do you get one of those PHP servers?

To be clear: You can create PHP files like those in this chapter, but again, you can't test them without posting them to a server.

Your options? Essentially two:

✦ Contract with a web-hosting company that explicitly promises PHP support. If you search through the features offered by web-hosting packages, you'll either find a specific acknowledgment that the hosting service supports PHP, or you won't.

Figure 2-7 shows the kind of wording that tips you off to the fact that a discount hosting service does not support PHP, or requires that you upgrade (for extra money and extra hassle) to enable PHP. If you think there is any chance you might use PHP at any time, including for SSIs, move on to another host provider.

Book VII
Chapter 2

DIY PHP Solutions

Figure 2-7:
This web-
hosting
package
doesn't
support
PHP.

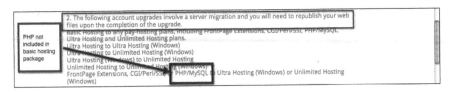

Any hosting service that supports PHP will clearly say so. Figure 2-8 shows a bit of the documentation at the FatCow hosting site, with the current versions of PHP supported. As noted, PHP is a free, open source program, and hosting services that offer PHP are likely to maintain the current version.

Figure 2-8:
Verify that a web-hosting package supports PHP.

Answer/Solution
The current PHP version running on FatCow's servers is PHP 5.0.

✦ Install WAMP or MAMP and save, and test your files in the folder created for web pages.

Earlier in this chapter, we briefly outline the process for doing that, but you'll have to rely on the documentation with those programs (which is not hard to follow) to install them.

For the purposes of using PHP on the level that we address it in this book, including the more complex applications we explore in the next chapter, the free versions of these programs are all you need.

Expect to spend some time installing one of the 'AMPs: This is software aimed at developers (which you are, on a basic level, at this point in this chapter). This is free, open source software, and you aren't going to get the kind of help installing and configuring it that you would expect from an Adobe or Microsoft product. If the prospect of spending some time at online sites looking up error codes and sorting through conflicting advice on how to solve them seems like too much hassle, you might want to opt for a web-hosting service that supports PHP for about $5 (US) per month to host your site and let you test your PHP there.

Tested at a server that supports PHP, our embedded menu bar looks like the one in Figure 2-9.

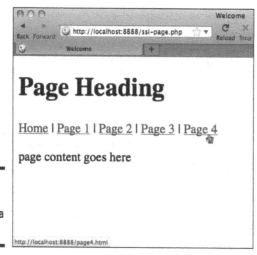

Figure 2-9:
Testing a PHP SSI in a PHP page.

Chapter 3: Gathering and Embedding Live Data

In This Chapter

✔ Making mail lists and blogs fit in your site

✔ Managing a mail list with MailChimp

✔ Embedding external blogs with iFrame

✔ Set up a search box with Google Search

✔ Embedding maps, weather, and RSS feeds

*T*he explosion of social media, video-sharing sites, online photo distribution, blogs, and other online resources that facilitate sharing information has defined the contours of the web. But how do these tools fit into the process of building your website — a site that you build and that is defined by your content and style?

In this chapter, we solve that challenge by walking you through how to collect names and run a powerful e-mail operation sending out announcements and newsletters, how to embed a blog in your own website, and how to embed a search box in your site. We also show you how to embed a map, a weather sticker, and RSS feeds.

But there are also some tips, quirks, and techniques that you should know about how Dreamweaver handles PHP files that will spare you a lot of unnecessary stress if you work with PHP in Dreamweaver, even on the basic level with which we show you how to use PHP in Chapters 2 and 3 of this minibook.

Making a Two-Way Connection with Visitors

Mail lists, blogs, and search boxes are all tools to create a two-way relationship with visitors to your site. Without these tools, you're likely squandering much of what you can accomplish with a website. But with these tools, your website takes on a whole new dimension in what it can do.

For example, with a mail list, visitors can elect to establish a connection with you — to get updates on new products, breaking news, notices of activities, or your band's tour schedule.

Web 2.0 . . . and 3.0?

For a period, the term "Web 2.0" was bandied about to characterize the emergence of two-way interaction online — including the explosion of social networking. Some Internet theorists define increased interactivity (user interaction with websites, like posting a photo or sending a tweet) as a new stage of the Web (2.0, as opposed to the initial stage which would have been 1.0). Others argue that the Web was always interactive, starting with hyperlinks that visitors could click, and forms they could fill out and submit. Web 3.0 gurus identify this emerging phase as one of more integrated, accessible, organized, centralized, and shared information.

With a search box, visitors can find whatever they're looking for at your site. You knew that. The other, and perhaps more valuable, half of the picture is that by studying search reports (lists of what people searched for at your site), you can learn more about who is coming to your site and why — and what they want.

Finally, you know how blogs work and what they can do. You, or those you give posting permission, can use a blog to publish articles, post reader comments, and engage in a two-way conversation with visitors. The challenge we show you how to solve in this chapter is how to integrate blogs into your website so that the experience of interacting with you at your blog is framed by your site content, not Facebook's ads or a WordPress template.

Behind the Curtain: Embedding Live Data Resources

In this chapter, we focus on integrating online resources that collect and manage form data. And in doing so, we build on the tools in Chapters 1 and 2 of this minibook. In those chapters, we explore how to build a form that collects information from visitors that can be used to take orders, sign up people on your mail list, or get feedback from site visitors.

With those foundations in place, you can customize forms that link to powerful database resources.

Their server plus your style and content

As you embed mail lists, blogs, and search boxes — applications that are built with complex programming and hosted on other servers — you can use your HTML and CSS skills (see Books III and IV, respectively) to customize the content and look of those tools.

For example, let Google (or FreeFind — a bit-friendlier search engine you can use on your site) do the hard and dirty work of indexing all the content of your site and figuring out how to present it when someone types a word in a search box. And FreeFind allows you to define how the search form looks.

Likewise, you can rely on Blogger to manage your blog, but you can embed that blog into your own web pages and apply your own CSS style. And then you can look to MailChimp's powerful mail list tools to organize lists and send out e-newsletters — and format how the MailChimp input form looks.

In other words, you can use HTML and CSS to customize search boxes, blogs, and forms. Figure 3-1 shows a page with a search box, a signup form, and a blog embedded in the page, all styled with a consistent CSS style.

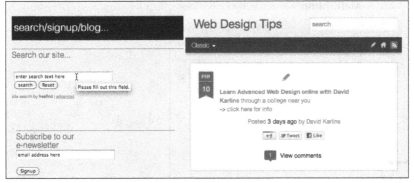

Figure 3-1:
An embedded search box, signup form, and blog.

Mail lists, blogs, and searches: How they do what they do

To understand what you can customize in embedded blogs and forms, start with a basic picture of how mail list managers (like MailChimp), blog software (like Blogger), and search boxes (like Google) work.

The point (beyond general and healthy curiosity) is to understand conceptually what you can tinker with — and what you better be careful about messing with. Sure, you can change the HTML and CSS you get from these resources. However, editing other HTML and CSS code supplied by these tools will prevent the search box, blog, or mail signup form from working.

You can do a lot of editing of the content and style of how these tools look on your Web pages. With a form, for instance (used to enter a search string or sign up for a mail list), you can apply most of the HTML form field parameters that we cover in Chapter 1 of this minibook. You can make form fields longer or shorter. You can define CSS styles for the form itself as well as form fields, including color, background color, borders, font sizes, and so on.

What you *cannot* do is fiddle with the form action and form field names. The form actions in the forms you get when you generate search boxes or sign up forms send content to programs at the servers that make these systems work. And you also can't change the names of the form fields supplied by the application; those, too, are necessary to make the backend programming work.

Before walking through specific examples of implementing mail lists, blogs, and search boxes, take a little time to see how these applications work.

Mail list management

Mail list managers take the information visitors enter into a signup form, and use it to generate targeted e-newsletters. Example: Someone signs up for your e-newsletter and selects the Tell Me about Sales check box, like the one in Figure 3-2, which is a form created and managed by the mail list package MailChimp.

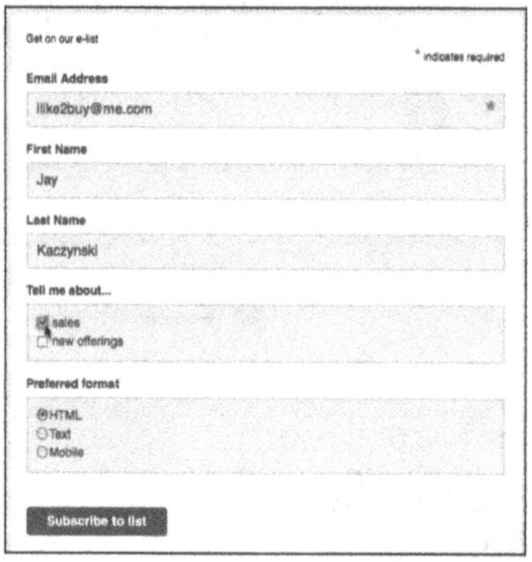

Figure 3-2:
Create mail
list forms
like this.

So now when you have a sale, you can compose an e-newsletter targeted at people who want to know when you're having a sale, and send that newsletter just to them. You might introduce that e-mail with, "You are getting this newsletter because you told us you want to know when we're having a sale. Guess what? We're having one!"

There are all kinds of mail list managers available online, ranging from homemade systems to (at the high end) a commercial product like Constant Contact. MailChimp has many but not all the features of Constant Contact. MailChimp is easier to set up and use, though, and free for lists of less than 500 people. We focus on MailChimp later in this chapter.

✦ **Constant Contact:** http://search.constantcontact.com

✦ **MailChimp:** http://mailchimp.com

✦ **iContact:** www.icontact.com/

A final but important note on mail list managers: They are distinct from spam. Mail list management packages have policies and procedures that weed out spammers. For example, they require that people who sign up confirm that they really want to be on the list by responding to e-mails.

Blogs

Blogs allow you (or others to whom you assign permission) to post articles and then provide comment boxes for users to comment on them. They arrange articles, usually with the most recent listed first.

Blogger.com is a free, Google-owned blogging package you can use to quickly and easily set up a blog. We won't cover setting up or populating a blog, but we do show you how to embed the blog in your website.

Search boxes

There are different options for embedding a search engine in your site, but two of the most widely used and useful are search options from Google and FreeFind. The biggest positive for Google Custom Search is that it employs Google's powerful search engine technology to produce accurate search results. The biggest negative is that it grabs data on who searches for what at your site and markets that data — something FreeFind does not do.

The pros and cons for Google's free embeddable search engine are

✦ **Pros**

- The price. Embedding Google's search box in your site (with ads) is free.

- State-of-the-art accuracy in search results using Google's highly developed search engine.

- Includes an option to let users search just your site, or the entire web.

✦ **Cons**

- Again, the price, but here we're talking about the paid ad-free version. Ad-free Google search boxes for a small-business site can cost several thousand dollars a year, depending on number of searches.

- Search results feature ads (not yours, but ones supplied by Google) at the top of the list of results, and those can well be ads for your competitors.

- Customizing options are limited to formatting themes (colors and layouts) provided by Google, you can't customize the appearance of a Google search form with your own HTML or CSS.

- Google keeps records of searches conducted at your site, and that data becomes part of the data that Google markets.

Figure 3-3 shows an example of how search results from an embedded free Google search box appear.

Figure 3-3:
Search
results
from a free
Google
search box.

As noted, the biggest difference between Google Custom Search and FreeFind is that FreeFind doesn't market data on who searches your site for what. Here's a summary of the pros and cons of FreeFind:

✦ **Pros**

- Free, if you allow FreeFind to display ads in search results.

- Easy to customize results — folders can be excluded from searching.

- Easy to format the supplied search box with your own HTML and CSS.

- Detailed reports to you on who searches for what at your site.

- Ads are slightly less prominent than the display of results with Google's search box.

- The paid (ad-free) version is less expensive than Google's paid service — at this writing, the cost is $19/year for a site with 25,000 pages or less.

- Does not store records of who searches for what and sell that information to advertisers.

✦ **Cons**

- The free version includes ads in search results.

- FreeFind's search box works well for your own site, but if you want to combine searches within your site with searches of the full web, you don't get the power of Google's search engine.

Figure 3-4 shows a web page with a search box from `www.freefind.com`.

Figure 3-4:
Displaying
results of
a FreeFind
search.

Managing a Mail List

As we discuss repeatedly, building a reliable list of people who actually *want* you to contact them is invaluable for almost any business, organization, or cause. Sophisticated mail list programs allow you to

- ✦ Collect names.
- ✦ Sort names into lists: for example, people in a select geographical location or people who volunteered to work with your cause.
- ✦ Design e-newsletters and send them out to selected lists.

Constant Contact and a number of other commercial mail list packages provide these services for a fee. They provide detailed reports on who opened your e-newsletters and what links they followed from those e-newsletters.

For example, Constant Contact will provide you with a list of who opened your e-newsletter and which links within your e-newsletter they followed. You can then specifically target selected groups of users with specialized ads or information based on the history of what kind of links they followed.

Producing and managing mailing lists on that level is a full-time job, or close to it. Organizations that depend heavily on online marketing or outreach will often create a position for a full-time list manager who immerses himself in analyzing responses to e-mailings, feeding that information in marketing teams, and even following up with personalized e-mails at times.

This kind of detailed reporting is one reason why Constant Contact charges a fee. (Prices vary, but we usually figure roughly one cent per person per e-mail for clients with mail lists in the range of 10,000–50,000 names.)

MailChimp provides a great way to get your feet wet with e-lists. It's user friendly and free for your first 500 names. At this writing, unlimited e-mailings to a list of up to 50,000 subscribers costs $240/month at MailChimp.

Here, we won't walk through signing up for an account at MailChimp, creating lists of people who sign up using the form they provide, or composing e-newsletters. Those projects are a bit beyond the scope of creating a website, will vary widely depending on the kind of e-newsletter and lists you are managing, and are coherently documented at the MailChimp site.

What we'll focus on is how to embed the signup form you generate at MailChimp into your own website.

Embed a MailChimp signup form

When you design a form in MailChimp, the Share It tab provides options for how to put that form online. If you don't have the ability to create your own website, you can simply distribute the link they provide to a URL where potential clients, volunteers, fans, subscribers, buyers, and so on can fill out the form.

But you do have the ability to create your own website, so you're interested in the Create Form HTML link.

A wizard, displayed in Figure 3-5, walks you through the process of designing your form.

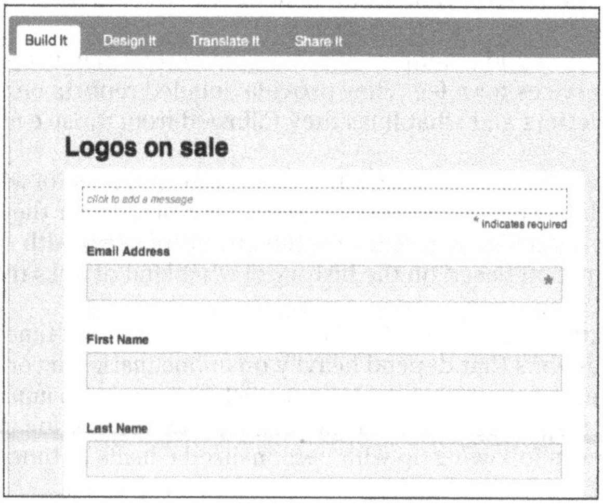

Figure 3-5: Designing a form to sign people up for an e-newsletter at MailChimp.

Click that link and copy the code inside the Copy/Paste into Your Site box, as shown in Figure 3-6. After you copy this code from MailChimp, you paste that code anywhere within the `<body>` element of your web page.

Figure 3-6: Copying form code from MailChimp.

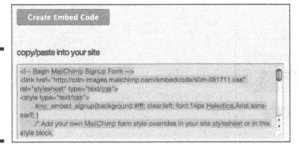

What you can and cannot customize in MailChimp

After you paste the code generated for your form at MailChimp into your own site, you can do many things to customize the appearance and content of that form:

✦ **Invite:** You can edit the HTML that comes with the code to create your own invitation to the mail list.

✦ **Fields:** You can use the techniques that we cover in Chapter 1 of this minibook to edit the form field sizes, fonts, colors, and any other CSS-controlled elements. For example, the line of code below modifies an e-mail field generated by MailChimp to add an HTML5 placeholder attribute that prompts users to enter their e-mail address in the form field. (See Chapter 1 of this minibook for a full exploration of HTML5 placeholders.)

```
<input type="email" value="" name="EMAIL" placeholder="email address here">
```

✦ **Reset button:** You can use the techniques we cover in Chapter 1 to add a Reset button to the form. Here's the code to do that:

```
<input type="reset" value="Reset">
```

In both the preceding examples, make sure you place the code inside the `<form>` element.

Those were two examples, but just about every element of form design we explore in Chapter 1 can be applied to edit how the form looks.

What you cannot do is change the form `action`. Read Chapters 1 and 2 of this minibook to see how forms work and open the door to major control over how embedded form code can be customized.

Figure 3-7 shows a form based on HTML generated in MailChimp but customized with new placeholder text and a Reset button. Most of the code is supplied by MailChimp and customized for your account, but the two lines of edited code in the preceding bullet list create the placeholder text prompt and the reset button.

Figure 3-7:
A customized MailChimp form.

A Full-Featured Do-It-Yourself Mail Form PHP Script

We explore homemade tools for managing form data that we explore in Chapter 1 (e-mailing a form with an e-mail program) and Chapter 2 (using a PHP script to send form data by e-mail) of this minibook. In this chapter, we look at using MailChimp, a full-fledged, professional-level resource for building a mail list and sending out e-mail newsletters.

If your needs fall somewhere between these categories — you want to give people a professional-quality PHP form that validates data and provides services like CAPTCHA (those squiggly letters that prove you are a human) — check out the Free Feedback Form Wizard at TheSiteWizard online. The wizard for generating PHP forms is at

www.thesitewizard.com/wizards/feedbackform.shtml

One note of caution if you're using TheSiteWizard along with Dreamweaver: When you follow the instructions at TheSiteWizard for creating PHP files, make sure to choose None from the DocType popup in the New Document dialog box. Otherwise, Dreamweaver will define the document as an HTML document, and that will corrupt the PHP files you're instructed to create.

Embedding External Blogs with iFrame

Blogger makes it easy to define your own blog. You create the blog, post articles, and allow users to post comments (or not).

As with MailChimp, we won't dissect the features available from Blogger. They are relatively well documented at that site, with a wide range of options that will vary depending on how complex of a blog you wish to maintain.

Unfortunately, Blogger (unlike MailChimp) doesn't provide a way to easily generate HTML code to embed a blog within your own site. The best way to do that is with the iFrame tag.

The iFrame tag is a powerful element in HTML. It allows you to embed the content of another URL within your HTML page. The parameters for an iFrame tag include width, height, border, and pretty much all the same options you have for formatting any box with CSS. We explore those features in depth in Book IV, Chapter 2. And, to emphasize the point, you can format the stuffing out of your iFrame to make it blend into your page so well that visitors won't realize they're looking at content from another page.

If you plan on embedding a Blogger blog (or any other blog) into your site with iFrame tags, you'll want to keep the formatting you choose at iFrame as simple as possible so that it doesn't conflict with the color scheme and styles you define for your site.

The basic HTML code to embed a Blogger blog is

```
<iframe src="http://myblog.blogspot.com/" width="400px" height="600px"></iframe>
```

where *myblog.blogspot.com* is replaced with the URL for your actual blog.

See Book IV, Chapter 2 for all the ways you can format a box with CSS — all of which can be applied to an iFrame tag. Here's an example of an iFrame tag with width and height parameters.

```
<iframe src="http://webdesigntrix.blogspot.com/"
    width="400px" height="600px"></iframe>
```

Book VII
Chapter 3

Gathering
and Embedding
Live Data

The example of a blog embedded in a page with an iFrame in Figure 3-8 uses the following CSS style for the iFrame tag:

```
iframe {
font-family: Verdana, Geneva, sans-serif;
background-color: gray;
margin: 5px;
padding: 5px;
height: 400px;
width: 580px;
overflow: auto;
}
```

There's only one really new thing here that we didn't cover in our exploration of CSS styles in Book IV, Chapter 2: The overflow attribute (and the auto value) mean that if the embedded content doesn't fit in the iFrame, a scrollbar will appear automatically.

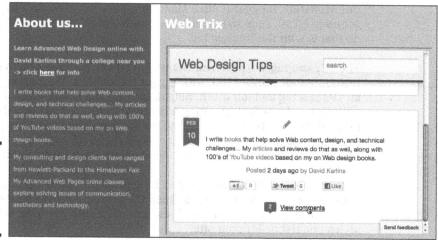

Figure 3-8:
A blog
embedded
in a website
with iFrame.

Beyond that, just to note a couple of things:

✦ The `margin` value creates space between `iFrame` and other page content.

✦ The `padding` value creates space between the blog and the `iFrame`.

Setting Up a Search Box

In the introduction to this chapter, we introduced a couple of options for embedding a search box in your site. But do you need a search box? Probably! Rare is the site of any substance that isn't enhanced with a search box. A search box at your site can be an extremely helpful, inviting, flexible way to give visitors access to site content.

As you build a site, look at a search box as an element in enabling site accessibility and navigation. As we discuss in Book II, the role of a navigation system is not simply to anticipate and respond to what a user might be looking for: It is to "lead" visitors through your site.

In that context, a search box provides an alternative way for people to find things at your site. Search boxes are a more flexible, open way to provide access to your site content. But that doesn't mean you have no freedom, or responsibility, to guide visitors, even as they look for content through your search box.

For example, you might configure your search engine to display only relatively recent content, ensuring that a visitor who searches for a product, medical advice, or an upcoming event finds the most current information.

You might elect to block some folders in your site from being indexed (sorted into the database) used for search results.

Embedding a Google search box

Google packages its free Google Custom Search tools in various ways, but code to create a free Google search box for your site is available from Google Web Elements at `www.google.com/webelements/#!/custom-search`.

The code provided is

```
<!-- Google Custom Search Element -->
<div id="cse" style="width:100%;">Loading</div>
<script src="http://www.google.com/jsapi" type="text/javascript"></script>
<script type="text/javascript">google.load('search', '1');
    google.setOnLoadCallback(function(){var cse = new google.search.
    CustomSearchControl();cse.draw('cse');}, true);</script>
```

You paste this code anywhere in the <body> element of a web page to place the search box.

Essentially, this tool is a JavaScript file loaded and run from Google's site. The search box, embedded in your site with the preceding code, will look something like the one in Figure 3-9. You can apply your own CSS styles to the page that holds the Google search element. And, of course, you can add your own HTML to the page.

Book VII
Chapter 3

Gathering and Embedding Live Data

Figure 3-9:
A search box from Google's Web Elements resource kit.

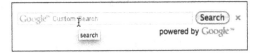

To test the Google Web Elements search, you must then upload your page to the web. You can't test it just saved to your own computer.

The results, when people use the search box, are heavily weighted with external links to Google-advertised products, as you can see in Figure 3-10.

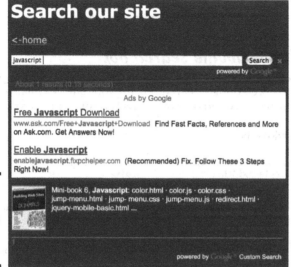

Figure 3-10:
Testing a
Google Web
Elements
search.

Creating a FreeFind search box

FreeFind (www.freefind.com) offers free search boxes, with ads for sponsored products (like Google) as well as ad-free versions that are available for $19/year (for a site with up to 25,000 pages). Either version is considerably more accessible to use and configure than Google's Web Elements tool. The HTML provided by FreeFind creates a form (as opposed to the external JavaScript file that powers the Google search box). And the setup process at FreeFind makes it relatively easy to configure options like excluding some of your pages from search results, or defining the order in which search results appear.

Signing up for a free, or ad-free-but-for-fee, search box at FreeFind is pretty intuitive. You indicate your site URL, and you get an account. The first step is to click the Index Now link at the Welcome page, which generates the index (searchable database) that powers your search box.

You can simply accept the default options for a search box, and then copy generated HTML into your web page to create a working search box. But here are some valuable options to consider when configuring your account:

✦ Use the options in the Build Index tab of the FreeFind site to assign a "weight" to the folders at your site. For example, if you have five pages that you really want to show up at the top of search lists, you could put those in a folder at your site, and then assign a higher relevance value to that folder. For instructions, click the Page Relevance link at the Build Index tab.

✦ Use options on the Customize tab to generate HTML and CSS to format your search box and results pages.

✦ On the HTML tab, you can choose between different search boxes with different options, including adding an "advanced search" link that lets visitors configure their search in more detail, or a search-the-web option to let visitors search either your site, or the entire web.

✦ On the Reports tab, you have easy access to reports on visitor activity so that you can find out what visitors have been searching for.

After you configure settings and generate HTML, you can paste that into your page. As we note earlier, because the generated HTML uses a form and form field tags, you can edit the appearance of the form using the form-editing techniques we cover in detail in Chapter 1, including adding a Reset button, resizing the text input field, and using HTML5 placeholder text and validation parameters. Figure 3-11 shows a FreeFind search box with all those features added. and Listing 3-1 shows the code.

Figure 3-11:
A FreeFind
search box.

Thoughts on search boxes and data integrity

A lot of data is floating around on the web. The questions of who owns that data, and what responsibility they have to protect the rights and privacy of people associated with that data, will continue to be a source of controversy. Here's how some of these issues apply to search boxes you embed in your site — and, by extension, some of these themes apply more broadly to embedded interactive objects in your web pages:

✔ When you embed a search engine from Google, the data generated (who is searching for what, where) becomes the "property" of the search engine provider.

✔ When you generate a search box using a tool like FreeFind, the data that results (who searched for what) becomes your property.

Listing 3-1:   Code for a FreeFind Search Box

```html
<!-- start of freefind search box html -->
  <table width="400" border=0 cellpadding=0 cellspacing=0 >
    <tr>
      <td style="font-family: Arial, Helvetica, sans-serif;
      font-size: 7.5pt;">
        <form  id="ffresult_sbox0" style="margin:0px; margin-top:4px;"
    action="http://search.freefind.com/find.html" method="get"
    accept-charset="utf-8" onsubmit="ffresults.show(0);">
          <input type="hidden" name="si" value="1870143">
          <input type="hidden" name="pid" value="r">
          <input type="hidden" name="n" value="0">
          <input type="hidden" name="_charset_" value="">
          <input type="hidden" name="bcd" value="&#247;">
          <input type="hidden" name="sbv" value="j1">
          <input type="text" name="query" size="32" placeholder = "enter search
    text here" required>
          <br>
          <input type="submit" value="search">
          <input type="reset" name="Reset" id="button" value="Reset">
        </form>
      </td>
    </tr>
    <tr>
      <td style="text-align:left; font-family: Arial, Helvetica,
    sans-serif;font-size: 7.5pt; padding-top:4px;">
        <a style="text-decoration:none; color:gray;" href="http://www.freefind.
    com"
          onmouseover="this.style.textDecoration='underline'"
    onmouseout="this.style.textDecoration='none'" >site search by
        <span style="color: #606060;">freefind</span></a>
        <a id="ffresult_adv0" onclick="ffresults.show(0);" href="http://search.
    freefind.com/find.html?si=1870143&amp;pid=a&amp;
    sbv=j1">advanced</a>
      </td>
    </tr>
  </table>
```

Having Even More Fun with Embedded Content

The complex mathematical formula we've applied throughout this chapter is broadly applicable:

> their PHP + your HTML + your CSS = your custom pages with their complicated stuff

The trick (the concept method and approach, if you want to get formal) is to find content that can be embedded in your site, formatted by you, customized with your own HTML (like the HTML5 parameters we used to enhance a FreeFind search box, for example), and integrated into your site in a way that looks, feels, and acts like it is indeed part of your site.

This trick (method and approach) can be applied to embedding all kinds of content in your page. For example, the iFrame tag can be used to embed *any* web page in one of your own pages.

To be fair and ethical, though, there are aesthetic, functional, moral, and legal issues involved in doing this. Some content just doesn't fit well embedded in your own site, such as Facebook or Flickr. On the other hand, content from places like Vimeo or YouTube is designed to fit well in your own web page.

On the other hand, it does make sense to host your videos at sites like YouTube and Vimeo. And both sites make it easy to generate HTML that uses the iFrame tag to embed videos in your own site. (For more on working with video in your website, see Book VIII.)

Keep reading to see a few elements you might want to embed in your site using iFrame.

Embed a Google map with iFrame

Do you have a business that you want people to find? If so, embedding a Google map in your site with iFrame makes that easy. Here are the basic steps:

1. **Enter your address in the search box at Google Maps** (http://maps. google.com).

2. **Click the Search Maps icon, or press Enter (Windows) or Return (Mac) to display your location on a map.**

3. **Click the Link icon in the panel to the left of the map to display options to link to, or embed, the map.**

4. **Select the HTML option (the second one) to copy the iFrame tag parameters that embed the map; see Figure 3-12.**

   In Figure 3-13, an interactive Google map is embedded in a page.

**Book VII
Chapter 3**

Gathering
and Embedding
Live Data

Figure 3-12:
Select
iFrame tag
parameters
to embed a
Google map.

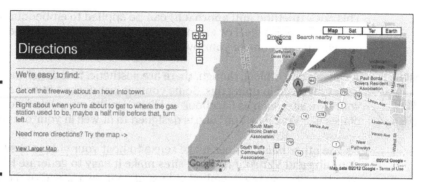

Figure 3-13:
Embedding
a Google
map in a
web page.

Embed the weather

The Weather Underground site provides an embeddable weather forecast sticker (a small box that displays the weather for a selected area) you can embed in your page. You get the code for one of these stickers at www. wunderground.com.

Hey! — no registration, signing up, or anything like that. The technology is super-simple. You get the HTML code to embed an image that Weather Underground updates periodically with your ZIP code's weather forecast.

This example is almost too simple, but it's very useful and provides a good experience with the most basic form of embedded live content — an embedded image that someone else updates.

Here's how you place that sticker on your site:

1. **Go to** www.wunderground.com **and enter your ZIP code in the search box.**

2. **Click the Get Free Weather Stickers link.**

3. **Choose one of the three versions of the sticker, as shown in Figure 3-14, and then copy the generated HTML and paste it into your web page.**

   There are three versions of the weather sticker, the only difference being the design.

Figure 3-14:
Generating
HTML to
embed a
weather
sticker.

4. **Add, edit, and fine-tune your own HTML and CSS so that the weather sticker "fits in" to your page seamlessly.**

In Figure 3-15, the weather sticker is embedded in a page with associated content. And, of course, the weather info itself will be updated by the folks at Weather Underground. When we generated the sticker, we picked the one that best matches our color scheme, and enclosed it in a class DIV tag selector to place and frame it on the page — techniques we cover in Book IV, Chapter 2.

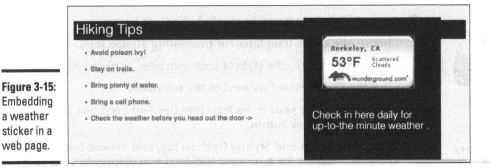

Figure 3-15:
Embedding
a weather
sticker in a
web page.

Book VII
Chapter 3

Gathering
and Embedding
Live Data

Embed an RSS feed

If you've read this chapter to this point, you've picked up on a theme: You can embed just about anything in a web page and customize it to mesh into your page so cleanly it looks, feels, and acts like it *is* part of your page.

Here's one final example you might well be interested in seeing worked through: an RSS feed.

RSS stands for really simple syndication — with *syndication* meaning distribution.

We're not sure what delegate body decided that RSS was *really* simple, but embedding RSS feeds in a web page is certainly doable. However, it requires generating a JavaScript that will format how the RSS *feed* (the content sent out by the RSS source) is presented in your page.

A number of online resources are available for creating code to display RSS feed pages. One is RSSinclude (`www.rssinclude.com`). One advantage of using RSSinclude instead of other online RSS page-generator resources is that you can choose what kind of embedded code to use, and you also get the option of an `iFrame` tag (which you can read about earlier in this chapter).

RSSinclude offers free as well as pay-to-use templates for presenting RSS feeds. We'll stick to the free ones; they work just fine. You do need to register with RSSinclude although you just need an e-mail address. After you register, follow these steps:

1. **Find a feed from any news source.**

   You find these by searching for "news feeds" followed by whatever source or criteria you want to use (such as "news feeds sports" or "news feeds NPR").

2. **Copy the URL for the feed you select.**

   URLs for news feeds begin with `feed://`.

3. **At the RSSinclude home page, click the Start button.**

4. **Choose one of the templates for presenting an RSS feed.**

   Opt for one close to the style of your own site.

5. **Click the Create Now link next to the template.**

6. **Paste the URL for your news feed into the Add Feed box and then click the Add Feed button.**

7. **Click the Content and Styling Options tab, and choose fonts, colors, and other options for how your RSS feed will display in your site.**

   Do your best here to match colors and fonts with your site.

8. **Click the Save and Preview button (at the bottom of the page).**

   This saves (and previews) your selected options, but you haven't generated code yet.

9. **Click the Include tab. Here you can choose from a set of options for how you want to include the RSS.**

   A set of radio buttons on the Include tab provides options for what kind of code to generate: PHP, JavaScript, or an HTML `iFrame` tag.

The `iFrame` tag gives you a lot of freedom to format the content as an HTML element in your page. The `iFrame` option is generally best unless you're embedding the RSS feed in a Facebook (in which case, you choose Facebook) or WordPress (in which case, you select WordPress).

Figure 3-16 shows an `iFrame` tag generated to present the RSS feed.

Figure 3-16: Generating code to embed an RSS feed in your page.

10. **Generated code appears in a box on the bottom of the page. Copy and paste the generated HTML into the body element (the visible part) of your own web page.**

11. **Add, edit, and fine-tune your own HTML and CSS so that the embedded RSS feed meshes nicely with your page seamlessly.**

In Figure 3-17, the feed is embedded in a page with associated content and will update whenever the new source updates.

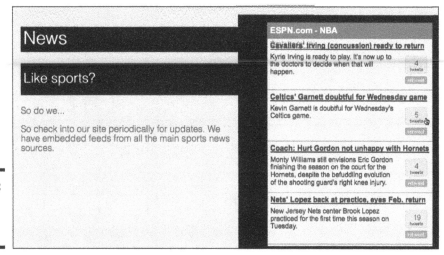

Figure 3-17: An embedded RSS feed.

Chapter 4: Working with Forms and Data in Dreamweaver

Dreamweaver fills two valuable roles in the process of collecting data in forms. One role is pretty much the same role Dreamweaver plays in web design in general: It allows you to quickly and efficiently generate all the HTML and PHP that we explore in the first three chapters of this minibook.

Even more valuable, though, are the Spry form tools built into Dreamweaver that allow you to generate JavaScript-based widgets that enhance the interactivity and usefulness of forms. These include validation scripts, and as of Dreamweaver CS6 (and CS5.5), special form fields that work well in mobile devices.

Scripting PHP in Dreamweaver

If you plan to work with PHP in Dreamweaver at the level we explore it in Chapter 2 of this mini-book, here are a few things you should know.

First, remember that Dreamweaver provides the same professional level of code hinting for PHP that it does for HTML or CSS. You can examine (or change) that color scheme in the Code Coloring panel of the Preferences dialog box in Dreamweaver (choose Edit⇨Preferences in Windows or Dreamweaver⇨Preferences on a Mac).

But there are also some tips, quirks, and techniques that you should know about how Dreamweaver handles PHP files that will spare you a lot of unnecessary stress if you work with PHP in Dreamweaver, even on the basic level with which we show you how to use PHP in Chapters 2 and 3 of this minibook.

First, and foremost — and we know we're beginning to sound like a broken record at this point, but it really is essential — don't do a thing until you've defined a Dreamweaver *site*. If that doesn't ring a bell, jump to Book II, Chapter 4 and review that process.

Color coding and code hints in Dreamweaver

Dreamweaver provides color coding that makes it easier to write PHP. Here's how this works.

To see (or edit) color coding for PHP, open the Dreamweaver Preferences dialog box (Edit⇨Preferences in Windows; Dreamweaver⇨Preferences on a Mac). In the Preferences dialog box, click Color Coding in the Category list on the left. Then select PHP in the Document Type list and click the Edit Coloring Scheme button. The default PHP code coloring appears, as shown in Figure 4-1. By clicking different code elements in the Styles For list, you can see what color means what.

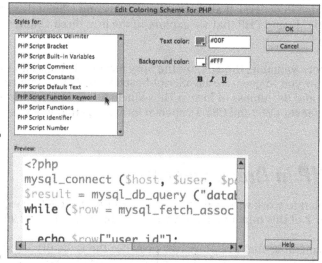

Figure 4-1: Seeing (or editing) color coding for PHP in Dreamweaver.

The value of color-coded PHP is more than just aesthetic (although what coder can't use a bit of color in his life?). What you'll notice right away as you create PHP, again — even at the basic level we explore do-it-yourself PHP coding in Chapter 2 of this minibook — is that colors change as you complete a code fragment. And if they don't change, that's a clue that you've left off a close element (?>) or some other bit of coding.

Other coding packages also present color-coded PHP, by the way. And the colors tend to be standardized across different code editors. TextWrangler (www.barebones.com/products/textwrangler) — a free code editor — for example, provides less comprehensive color code–editing options, but still presents PHP with colors similar to those in Dreamweaver, as shown in Figure 4-2.

Figure 4-2:
Low-budget and free code editors also support limited color-coding.

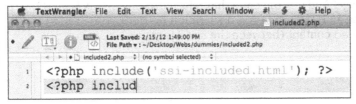

However, Dreamweaver's PHP coding features go beyond just color coding. As you can see in Figure 4-3, Dreamweaver CS6 supplies tooltip code hinting.

Figure 4-3:
PHP code hinting in Dream-weaver.

PHP document types in Dreamweaver

In Chapter 2 of this minibook, we emphasize the two basic types of PHP documents. Some PHP documents are mostly — or at least substantially — HTML files that hold live data, and thus are saved with PHP filename extensions. That PHP filename extension clues browsers to look for PHP code within the document: the kind a visitor would open in a browser with a filename of `index.php`, `about_us.php`, or `search_this_site.php`.

The other kind of PHP document has no or very little HTML at all and is not going to be opened in a browser. Instead, this PHP document contains PHP code to process a form or perform some other server-side scripting function.

If this duality isn't registering with you, read Chapter 2 of this minibook and review the discussion of PHP there before attempting to do much PHP coding in Dreamweaver.

Here's the rather important practical difference: When you tell Dreamweaver that you want to create a PHP file (by choosing File⇨New and choosing PHP from the Page Type category in the New Document dialog box), what you get is really an HTML file with readable PHP. And that file, by default, is saved with a PHP filename extension.

Look, for example, at the code generated automatically when you create a new, blank PHP file from the Dreamweaver New Document dialog box. That code, shown in Figure 4-4, looks just like the code at the top of an HTML page! And it *is* the code that tells a browser, "This is an HTML page," including an HTML doctype declaration (<!doctype html>) and HTML page head content (between the head tags).

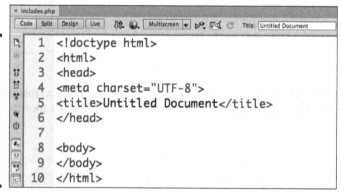

Figure 4-4: PHP documents generated in Dreamweaver come with HTML head content.

```
1  <!doctype html>
2  <html>
3  <head>
4  <meta charset="UTF-8">
5  <title>Untitled Document</title>
6  </head>
7
8  <body>
9  </body>
10 </html>
```

This kind of PHP page works fine — again, as long as you're creating the first kind of PHP page discussed earlier: namely, one that's really an HTML file with a PHP filename extension, and a bit of PHP coding in it (like for a server-side include, or SSI). To put it another way, the PHP pages generated by Dreamweaver work for pages that are really basically HTML pages, with HTML page content, but that have some PHP code embedded within them.

However, this kind of PHP document doesn't work at all if you're creating a server-side code file! Those files have nothing to do with HTML files. They're not, and should not, look like HTML files to browsers. They're coded computer programs, and you want to be sure not to confuse browsers. If a browser sees an HTML doctype declaration at the top of a program file, it will read that content as HTML, not as PHP code. And that will render your server-side scripting dysfunctional.

What does this mean? It means that when you're using Dreamweaver to create a PHP program (as opposed to an HTML page that has some PHP in it), you should start by deleting all the boilerplate HTML code that's created when you generate a new (supposedly) blank PHP page in Dreamweaver.

Again (and we're being a bit redundant because this is confusing and will undercut your project if not handled right): When you're creating a new PHP program (using PHP code) in Dreamweaver, delete everything — yup, everything! — in the "blank" PHP file you generate in Dreamweaver, and then start coding. That way, the PHP you create for the server-side script begins on line 1 of the file, as shown in Figure 4-5.

WARNING!

From the six-degrees-of-separation department: The beginning script you see in Figure 4-5 is from the e-mail–processing PHP script you can generate at thesitewizard.com (as we discuss in Chapter 3 of this minibook). And, in fact, in any scenario where you generate PHP from the tools at thesitewizard.com (or other online PHP-generating resources) and bring them into a Dreamweaver website, you'll want to pay close attention to and apply what we're emphasizing here: Before you copy generated PHP code (or create code yourself), delete all the HTML junk that Dreamweaver places in "blank" PHP files. To check, look at line 1 in your PHP code. It should begin with `<?php`, not `<!doctype html>`.

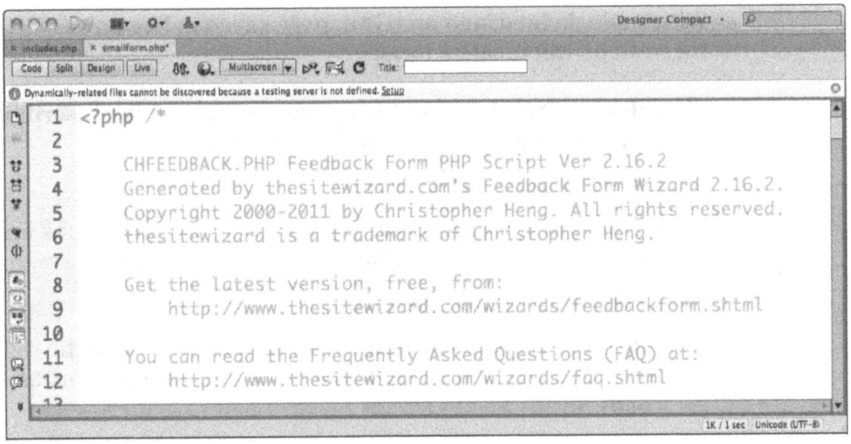

Figure 4-5:
A server-side PHP script coded in Dreamweaver without HTML head content.

```
1  <?php /*
2
3      CHFEEDBACK.PHP Feedback Form PHP Script Ver 2.16.2
4      Generated by thesitewizard.com's Feedback Form Wizard 2.16.2.
5      Copyright 2000-2011 by Christopher Heng. All rights reserved.
6      thesitewizard is a trademark of Christopher Heng.
7
8      Get the latest version, free, from:
9          http://www.thesitewizard.com/wizards/feedbackform.shtml
10
11     You can read the Frequently Asked Questions (FAQ) at:
12         http://www.thesitewizard.com/wizards/faq.shtml
```

Book VII Chapter 4

Working with Forms and Data in Dreamweaver

Having noted helpful tools and at least one dangerous pitfall (generated "blank" PHP files are corrupted with HTML code), you're ready to bring the beginning exploration of PHP in earlier chapters into Dreamweaver.

Creating Forms in Dreamweaver

Someone once said, "Skills build." How true. So as you take the plunge into building a form in Dreamweaver, you need to bring a few skills to the rodeo. First, read about building forms and their elements in Chapter 1 of this minibook. That chapter also covers applying CSS styles to forms, and Book III, Chapter 4 discusses defining CSS styles in Dreamweaver. With those references at your disposal, now it's time to focus on building forms in Dreamweaver.

We'd like to be able to tell you that Dreamweaver makes building a basic form easier than coding it directly in HTML, but it's not that much easier. It's not like typing **<form** takes a lot longer than choosing Insert⇔Form⇔Form. The real value of Dreamweaver lies in seamlessly generating JavaScript for validation scripts and jQuery Mobile form elements. (You use jQuery Mobile to create mobile web pages and forms; we explore it in some depth in Book VI, Chapter 3.) To make those work, though, you need to set up a form correctly in Dreamweaver, so we'll walk through that.

Create a form in Dreamweaver

Here comes the obligatory warning that precedes every discussion of how to do anything in Dreamweaver: *Stop.* If you're not working in a defined Dreamweaver *site* — as defined in the Site Definition dialog box — none of this will work. So, in that case, hop over to Book II, Chapter 4 and come back after you define a Dreamweaver site.

With a site defined, and an HTML page saved in Dreamweaver, following these steps will create a form:

1. **Click in your document to set your cursor at the insertion point in an HTML document where the form will appear.**

2. **Choose Insert⇔Form⇔Form.**

If you're in Code view, the Tag Editor – Form dialog box appears; click OK to make it disappear because you don't need it.

3. **Click OK to embed the form.**

The form appears in Design view in a red box. With the red box selected, the Properties Inspector displays settings for the form, as shown in Figure 4-6.

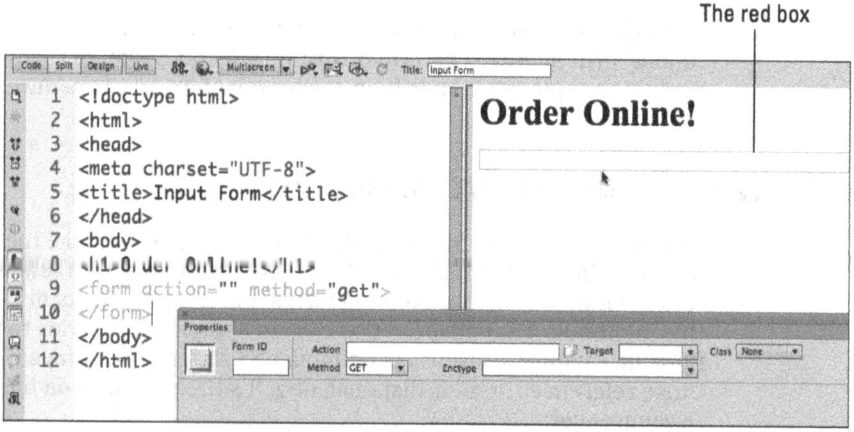

The red box

Figure 4-6:
Form
properties
display
in the
Properties
Inspector
when the
Form tag is
selected.

```
 1  <!doctype html>
 2  <html>
 3  <head>
 4  <meta charset="UTF-8">
 5  <title>Input Form</title>
 6  </head>
 7  <body>
 8  <h1>Order Online!</h1>
 9  <form action="" method="get">
10  </form>
11  </body>
12  </html>
```

Order Online!

4. **In the Action field of the Properties Inspector, enter an action.**

   This could be a link to a PHP script, like the script demonstrated in Chapter 2 of this minibook (see the section "Taking a Short Course in PHP Form Scripting") or an e-mail action (like `mailto:me@me.com`).

   See Chapter 2 of this minibook for a discussion of e-mailing form content through an e-mail client, or Chapter 3 for options for handling form data through server-side scripts.

5. **If you're sending form content by e-mail, enter** text/html **in the Enctype field, as shown in Figure 4-7.**

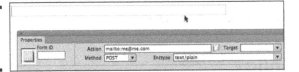

Figure 4-7: Defining a form action.

Red lines in Design view define the beginning and end of the `form` element, and `<form>` and `</form>` tags in Code view do the same thing. Stay inside the `form` element when adding all form elements!

Adding Submit (and Reset) buttons

Every form needs a Submit button. Because you'll be creating more form fields above the Submit button, you can click inside your form in Dreamweaver's Design view (not in Code view) and create a bit of space by simply pressing the Enter (Windows) or Return (Mac) key. This isn't essential, but will make it easier to insert form fields above the Submit button.

Then, add a Submit button by choosing Insert⇨Form⇨Button. The Input Tag Accessibility Options dialog box appears, but you can define all the important button parameters in the Properties Inspector, so just click OK to create the Submit button without worrying about the options in this dialog box. A Submit button appears in your form.

To create a Reset button, insert a second button. Then, with that button selected in the form, select the Reset Form radio button in the Properties Inspector, as shown in Figure 4-8.

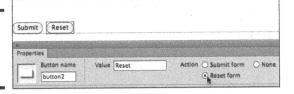

Figure 4-8: Creating a Reset button.

Defining form fields in Dreamweaver

With a form defined, and a Submit (and optional Reset) button, you're ready to explore Dreamweaver's powerful tools for generating JavaScript form elements.

If you want to simply create basic forms in Dreamweaver (like the ones we define using HTML without Dreamweaver in Chapter 1 of this minibook), you can choose between these two methods:

✦ Enter code for different form fields in Code view.

✦ Choose Insert⇨Form, and then choose a form field from the sub menu.

Figure 4-9 shows inserting a Text Field feature in a form.

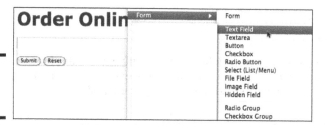

Figure 4-9:
Inserting a
Text Field.

Here, too, you can simply ignore and accept the options in any dialog box that appears (click OK as needed) but then configure form field parameters from the Properties Inspector.

Field IDs and labels in Dreamweaver

When you create a form field in Dreamweaver, the Input Tag Accessibility Options dialog box appears, where you can define a label or an ID. Both labels and IDs are optional for forms although labels are particularly useful in making pages more convenient for vision-impaired users.

✦ **A label:** Text that appears outside, but associated with, the input field, like "Name?" Labels are a way of presenting the text that tells a user what to do (like "Enter your name here") inside a `label` tag, which makes that content more accessible to vision impaired users who rely on reader software to read web pages out loud.

✦ **An ID:** A name for the form field (like "Name"). IDs are more optional than labels in form fields; they're not mainly an accessibility feature, but they're required in some environments where form fields are managed with JavaScript.

Adding Form Input Validation with JavaScript

Having briefly reviewed how the basic techniques for defining forms and form fields that we cover in Chapter 1 apply in Dreamweaver, it's time to get into the really good stuff: Dreamweaver's JavaScript form widgets.

Validation literally means to be strong, substantial, and able to withstand a challenge. In form data handling, validating form data means checking whether that data will pass muster when sent from a browser.

Say someone enters **MC Ferocious2** in a Name field. A modern validation script should be hip enough to understand that this is a legit name and pass the data along to a signup list. Similarly, if someone enters **Sir Mick Jagger II** in a Name field, an effective validation script will be old-school and traditional enough to add him to the e-list as well. In other words, as long as someone enters letters, numbers, and spaces in the name field, a validation script should probably be configured to accept that as valid form field data for a name.

If, however, either MC Ferocious2 or Sir Mick Jagger II enter their names in a field labeled Email Address, or leave this field blank, a competent validation script will display an error message along the lines of, "It doesn't look like you entered a valid email address." And that error message will display instead of the data being submitted to a server.

As such, validation scripts are, well, very valuable. They prevent users from submitting form data that won't accomplish what they want it to accomplish. And they prevent you, the site administrator, from having to deal with submitted form data that doesn't allow you to respond to a complaint, put a user on an e-mail list, or fulfill an order for a custom-designed skateboard.

Dreamweaver uses (creates) JavaScript to validate form data. There are many advantages to that approach. JavaScript is fast and reliable — faster and more reliable than other options.

Before walking through how to create JavaScript-based validation in Dreamweaver, take a minute to briefly review the three ways you can validate form data to situate how JavaScript fits into the big picture:

✦ **HTML:** In Chapter 1 of this minibook, we explore how HTML5 can add form field parameters (like `required`). HTML5 validation parameters are better than nothing and, as the world of browsing environments catches up with HTML5, will be increasingly useful. At this stage of history, though, HTML5 validation falls into the helpful-but-not-foolproof category.

✦ **PHP:** PHP scripts are another technique for validating form data. The options we explore in Chapter 3 of this minibook for collecting and managing mail lists using either MailChimp or the self-generating PHP you can create at thesitewizard.com include PHP code that validates form data at a server, after submission. That's a reliable and powerful way to test form data, allowing PHP coders to create all kinds of tests to make sure something submitted as an e-mail address seems like the appropriate length, has an @ symbol, and so on.

The shortcoming is that data doesn't get validated until it gets to a server, which slows down the process. And, it requires PHP scripting, which adds a level of complexity to collecting form data.

✦ **JavaScript:** JavaScript form data validation offers significant advantages over HTML5 and PHP options. It validates in the client (the browser) before data is sent to a server, so it's considerably faster than PHP, and it's supported even in older browsers that don't support HTML5 form elements.

So, if it's faster than PHP and more reliable than HTML5, why doesn't everyone use JavaScript to validate form input? Answer: Because it's a hassle to write that JavaScript code. You have to know how to code in JavaScript and then, even if you do know how to code in JavaScript, you have to cook up code for your forms.

Enter Dreamweaver. If you have Dreamweaver, you can quickly and easily generate JavaScript to do that validation.

Adding JavaScript Validation in Dreamweaver

Not all form fields really need to be validated. A check box? Either someone checked it or they didn't. A drop-down menu? That often includes a default option, so one way or another, a user is going to select something from the drop-down, consciously or not. A comment box? You'll often leave it optional.

In short, validation usually applies to text fields. And, if you really find it essential to validate other kinds of fields, you'll be able to port the technique we walk through next to other kinds of form fields (like text area fields).

Dreamweaver CS6 also offers a useful tool for validating password data. Because users can't see the characters they enter into a password field (characters show up as asterisks), it is common — and good practice — to require that users submit password data twice, with that data compared to see whether they entered the same password each time.

Validating text form field input

To create a validated text field in a form in Dreamweaver, choose Insert⇨ Form⇨Spry Validation Text Field. Spry is an Adobe-sponsored set of widgets that combine JavaScript and CSS — something we explore in depth in Book VI, Chapter 4.

1. **Use the Input Tag Accessibility Options dialog box to define an ID (say, email) and then a field label ("What's your email address?").**

2. **Click OK.**

3. **With the new tag selected (it's selected by default until you deselect it), view the Properties Inspector.**

4. **In the Properties Inspector, select the Required check box to make the form field required.**

   After all, if an e-mail address is required for the form data to be useful, make the e-mail field required. That way, if someone leaves the selected field blank, he won't be able to submit the form.

5. **Define options for validation in the Properties Inspector.**

   The options are visible and active when the aqua tag above the form field is selected.

   Selecting the form field itself displays a different set of options in the Properties Inspector — options for defining the HTML form field, not the validation script. To define validation options, be sure the aqua tag above the form field is selected.

   • *The Hint field* generates JavaScript that displays a hint in the field to clue users in to what they are supposed to enter. It might be an explanation or an example.

   • *The Type drop-down menu* has options for all the common kinds of validation you might want to collect — e-mail address, ZIP code, credit card, phone number, URL, and more. Choose one (you can choose only one for any particular field).

   Some of these validation options include additional parameters like min chars — for example, requiring that an e-mail address have at least five characters.

   • *The Preview States drop-down menu* lets you look at lots of things:

   How the form field will display initially (Initial)

   What happens if someone doesn't enter anything in a required field (Required)

   What displays if someone enters an e-mail address that doesn't look like an e-mail address (Invalid Format)

   How the form field displays when someone enters valid data (Valid)

• *The Validate On drop-down set of radio buttons* lets you choose any combination of three ways to validate data:

Blur and *Change* are very similar. They validate when a user moves his or her mouse, or otherwise moves out of a form field.

Submit validates the form field data when a user clicks the Submit button in a form.

A validation definition that works well for validating e-mail addresses is shown in Figure 4-10.

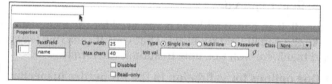

Figure 4-10:
Validating an e-mail address to require five characters that look like an e-mail address.

Validating and confirming passwords

Dreamweaver CS6 tools for collecting and conforming passwords work like this: First you create a password field using a Spry Validation widget, and then you create a confirm field using a Spry Validation widget.

Of course, to create these, or any form fields, your insertion point must be inside a form. With that all in place, follow these steps to create a password/password-confirm form field set:

1. **Choose Insert⇨Form⇨Spry Validation Password.**

The Input Tag Accessibility Attributes dialog box opens.

2. **Enter a form field name (say, "password") in the ID field.**

3. **Enter a descriptive label that tells people what to put in the Label field ("Enter a six-digit or more password here.").**

4. **Click OK.**

5. **Define any necessary form field attributes in the Properties Inspector.**

For example, you might define a width and/or a maximum number of characters a user can enter (in the Char Width or Max Chars boxes, respectively).

6. Click the aqua label above the form field to define validation criteria.

For example, you might make this field required, and require a minimum of six characters, as shown in Figure 4-11.

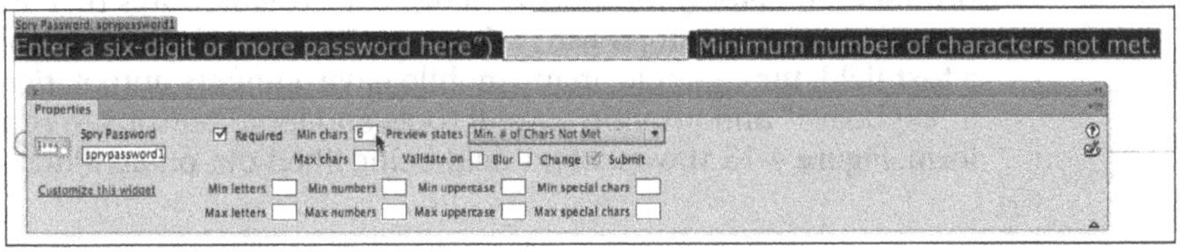

Figure 4-11: Defining a password input field.

Figure 4-11: Defining a password input field.

7. Create the confirmation field by choosing Insert⇨Form⇨Spry Validation Confirm.

You can use the same techniques you used to define the password field to define the confirm field. But because whatever is entered in the confirm form field has to match what was entered in the password field, the only really necessary parameters here are an ID (say, "confirm") and label ("Type your password again.").

Test your validation fields by saving your page, and all the generated JavaScript, and then previewing in a browser. Try "breaking the rules" you defined to test your validation scripts, as shown in Figure 4-12.

For example, you can try entering an e-mail address with only three characters. Or, an e-mail address without an "@" symbol. Or, an e-mail address with no "." (dot) in it. The validation script will reject all these entries.

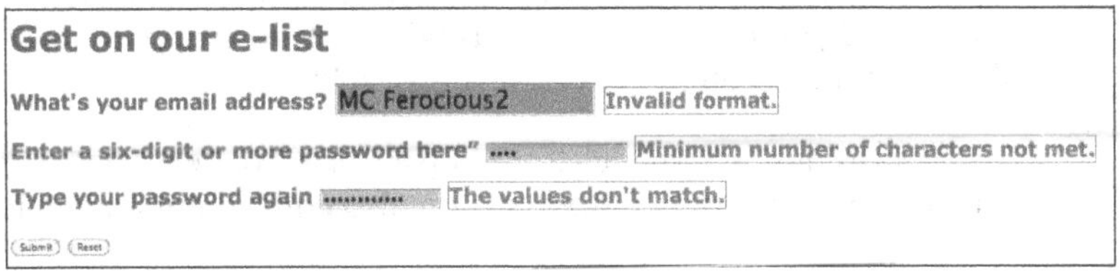

Book VII Chapter 4

Working with Forms and Data in Dreamweaver

Figure 4-12: Testing Spry validation scripts.

Creating jQuery Mobile Form Fields

As we discuss in Chapter 1 of this minibook, building form fields that work well in mobile devices presents special challenges. Envision a visitor to your site trying to send you feedback or follow a link while jogging around the lake, pushing their child's baby carriage, and carrying on a phone conversation. Yes, all at the same time.

So, how can you make it easier for your interacting visitors to enter form data or follow links?

Some of the problem has been solved for you by mobile device manufacturers in league with browser developers. They have configured mobile browsers to display form fields in more accessible ways that are available in desktops and laptops with a (real, physical) keyboard. When a user taps a text field, for example, many mobile environments automatically display a "keyboard" and provide autofill tools and large buttons to return to the form. Figure 4-13 shows a text field being filled out on an iPhone.

Figure 4-13:
Entering
text in a
form field
of a mobile
device.

Still, even with help in the form of text prompts and enlarged text fields, typing in a number with a mobile "keyboard" is quite a bit more hassle than using a real keyboard. Almost all device keyboards require toggling to a set of numbers. So, if you're asking a visitor to select a value between 1 and 100,000 and you're not that concerned about precision, think about using a slider as a workaround instead of a text field.

Toggle switches, where a visitor chooses "yes" or "no," "in" or "out," or from any other set of two options, are also convenient and inviting in mobile devices.

Another form element that makes mobile sites easier to use is creating buttons that serve as links. As opposed to forcing a user to try to land a finger onto a tiny link, use a nice big button with a message along the lines of "Click here to see something new," to provide easier navigation.

Creating jQuery mobile form fields

Dreamweaver CS6 has tools for creating these mobile-handy form elements, but they both require that you first create a jQuery Mobile page. We explain those and how to work with them in Dreamweaver in Book VI, Chapter 4.

If you're going to use sliders, toggle switches, or navigation button links in your site, start by creating a jQuery mobile page.

And, practically speaking, if you're going to create jQuery Mobile forms, you should probably put them on standalone pages without other (non–jQuery Mobile) form fields or at least without Spry validation form fields. The Spry widgets we use earlier to validate form data don't play particularly well in jQuery Mobile pages.

Here's how to create a mobile-friendly form in Dreamweaver, using Dreamweaver CS6's jQuery Mobile features:

1. **Choose Insert⇨jQuery Mobile⇨Page.**

2. **In the jQuery Mobile Files dialog box that appears, choose**

   - Remote (CDN), from the Link Type options

   - Combined, from the CSS options

3. **Click OK.**

4. **When the jQuery Mobile Page dialog box appears, do not select (clear) both the Header and the Footer check boxes.**

   Because you're designing a form for a small mobile screen, you don't want to clutter up the little available space. Instead, you want as simple of a page as you can get, as shown in Figure 4-14.

**Book VII
Chapter 4**

**Working with
Forms and Data
in Dreamweaver**

Figure 4-14:
Building
a mobile-
friendly
form.

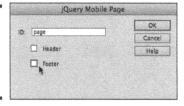

Just like other form fields, jQuery Mobile form elements have to be inside a form. So, the first step in creating jQuery Mobile form elements is to insert a form in the jQuery Mobile page. Do that by choosing Insert⇨Form⇨ Form. (See the earlier section, "Create a form in Dreamweaver" for details on configuring a form.)

When you create form fields in jQuery Mobile, you place them inside both the (red) form field outline in the Design window and inside the (blue) jQuery Mobile page outline. You'll see how this works in detail next, and we'll show you how the Dreamweaver design window is supposed to look as you create jQuery Mobile form fields.

Adding a slider

Sliders, remember, are those bars with a click-and-drag button that a mobile-user can click and drag to choose a value (useful in collecting ratings — "on a scale of 1–100, rate our site" for example). To embed a slider in a form, follow these steps:

1. **With your insertion point inside a jQuery Mobile page, type some text that introduces your slider.**

This text plays the role of a label, but Dreamweaver doesn't prompt you with a label option when you create jQuery Mobile form fields.

2. **Choose Insert➪jQuery Mobile➪Slider.**

The slider just pops onto the page, with preset values of 1–100.

To see how the slider will actually work, jump into Live view. Turn off Live view to edit the slider parameters.

3. **Set slider parameters.**

Click inside the slider field (not the aqua tab for the field that controls the JavaScript) to make sure you have the slider selected. All these parameters are defined in the Properties Inspector, with the slider selected:

a. *In the Value field in the Properties Inspector, enter the default value.*

b. *Click the Parameters button in the Properties Inspector.*

c. *Adjust the minimum and maximum values, as shown in Figure 4-15.*

d. *Click OK.*

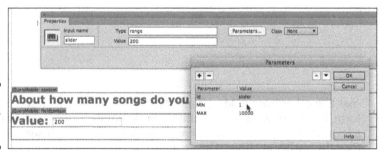

Figure 4-15: Define slider parameters.

4. **Tweak HTML if necessary.**

Most of the control you need over the display of a slider is accessible from the Properties Inspector, but one parameter you might want to add in the HTML is `width="4"` or some other value. The value 4, used here as an example, would display a four-digit number.

Figure 4-16 shows a slider with a width of four.

Figure 4-16:
Testing a
slider in a
browser.

Adding a toggle switch

Toggle switches display two (and only two) options and provide mobile users with a very accessible way to give you information. For example, they can choose "yes" or "no" to be added to your e-mail list with no stress.

To create a toggle switch in a form, follow these steps:

1. **With your insertion point inside a jQuery Mobile page, choose Insert⇨ jQuery Mobile⇨Flip Toggle Switch.**

For whatever reason, when you insert a toggle switch, Dreamweaver *does* generate placeholder label text that you can edit later. So, here, no need for you to type label text.

2. **Replace the placeholder text ("Option") with your own.**

3. **Set the flip toggle switch parameters.**

a. *Click inside the flipswitch field (not the aqua tab for the field that controls the JavaScript).*

b. *In the Properties Inspector, click the List Values button.*

c. *Edit the Item Label (what shows onscreen) and the value (what gets sent with the form data) for the two available options in the List Values dialog box, as shown in Figure 4-17.*

**Book VII
Chapter 4**

**Working with
Forms and Data
in Dreamweaver**

Figure 4-17:
Defining
flipswitch
options.

d. *Click OK.*

e. *In the Properties Inspector, select one of the two available options to be initially selected.*

Because this form field relies on JavaScript, you have to test it in Live view, or preview it in a browser (choose File➪Preview in Browser and select a browser). Figure 4-18 shows the flipswitch in action.

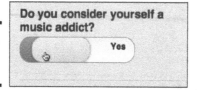

Figure 4-18:
Testing a
flipswitch.

And, when creating forms for an online audience, try to find ways to test the form fields and navigation buttons in different mobile browsing environments; see Figure 4-19. Don't just check out how they look, but how easy they are to use in real-world situations:

✦ Jogging in bright sunlight: Can you enter data without squinting?

✦ Dancing in a dark nightclub: Or, without missing a beat?

Figure 4-19:
Testing a
form on an
iPhone.

✦ Pushing a baby carriage: Remember, one hand on the carriage at all times. So, holding your smartphone in one hand, can you flick the toggle switch with your thumb?

✦ Dribbling a basketball: Maybe you should wait until the game is over to test the form on a mobile device?

Generating button links

As we discuss earlier, buttons in mobile pages often take the place of text links. They're bigger! And thus easier to click.

To create a button link inside a jQuery Mobile page, follow these steps:

1. **With your insertion point inside a jQuery Mobile page, choose Insert⇨ jQuery Mobile⇨Button.**

The jQuery Mobile Button dialog box appears. To create a basic navigation button, all the defaults are fine, as shown in Figure 4-20.

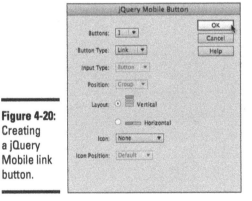

Figure 4-20: Creating a jQuery Mobile link button.

You can experiment with different appearances for the button by choosing different icons from the Icon drop-down menu.

2. **Click OK to create the button.**

3. **Define a link.**

The button appears (with Live view off) as just a link.

4. **Enter a link in the Link field.**

If you want the link to open in a new browser window, choose _blank from the Target drop-down menu. As a general rule, open links to other sites (outside your own site) in a new browser window so when users close that browser window they return to your site. But don't open links in a new browser window if they're within your site — it's annoying to users to have a new browser window pop open each time they follow a link from one page to another in your site.

5. **Define the button text.**

Edit the linked text in Design view to replace the placeholder text ("button") with your own text.

6. **Pop into Live view to see how your button will work.**

Save your page, and test your button in a browser and — if you can — on a mobile device. The following figure shows a button providing your jogging, music-listening, baby-carriage-pushing audience a convenient navigation option on an iPhone.

Click here to return to the Home page

Book VIII

Social Media and Interactive Add-ons

The 5th Wave   By Rich Tennant

"It's web-based, on-demand, and customizable. Still, I think I'm going to miss our old sales incentive methods."

Contents at a Glance

Chapter 1: Adding a WordPress Blog

In This Chapter

✔ Creating a WordPress blog

✔ Creating SEO-friendly posts

✔ Adding multimedia to blog posts

✔ Using a nonhosted blog

*I*f you have something to say, a blog is a wonderful way to get the word out. A *blog* — short for weblog — is an easy way to publish content for viewing on the web. Literally, millions of blogs are out there. Soccer moms use them to brag about their children's athletic prowess, politicians use them to keep in touch with their constituents, and businesses use them to inform their customers. Content runs the gamut from vanity — it's all about "wonderful me" — to useful information. A blog is also a wonderful way to pump up your site's presence with a search engine.

Search engines love blogs because the content changes frequently. So, all other things being equal, a site with a blog will rank higher than a site without a blog. You can also incorporate other social media with your blog. If you or your client has something to say to the world or even just a small circle of Internet friends, we show you how to do it in this chapter.

Adding a WordPress Blog to Your Site

WordPress (http://wordpress.org) is considered the granddaddy of all blogging software, and here's why:

✦ **Free:** It's absolutely free with no strings attached.

✦ **Customizable:** There are lots of ways you can customize a blog, and lots of developers create themes and plugins for the WordPress blog application. Some plugins and themes are available at no cost.

✦ **Your ease:** After you set up a blog on a server, you (or your client) can manage everything online through a web browser.

✦ **Multiple blogs and multiple users:** For example, Doug has three blogs on his site and two authors.

✦ **User ease:** If desired, you can have users create profiles with WordPress. Depending on the template you use, visitors to the blog can leave comments about each post.

About WordPress

WordPress uses a combination of PHP code and a MySQL database to display and maintain the blog. As of this writing, the current version of WordPress is WordPress 3.3.1. You can download the WordPress application at `http://wordpress.org/download`.

Using the WordPress.com blog

If you don't want to go through the hassle of creating a blog and your web-hosting server doesn't have a way to automatically create a blog, you can create a blog at wordpress.com. It's completely free. After you set up a blog at wordpress.com, you have a fully functional blog that you can link to a website. Setting up a blog at wordpress.com is self-explanatory. Use your favorite web browser to navigate to `www.wordpress.com`, press the Get Started Here link, and then fill in a blog address, username, and so on (see the figure). After you set up a blog at wordpress.com, you use the same software as mentioned earlier in this chapter to create your blog posts. As long as you set up your blog as a public blog, the search engines will eventually find it. Optimizing your posts and for that matter the name of your wordpress.com blog will make it easier to get recognized.

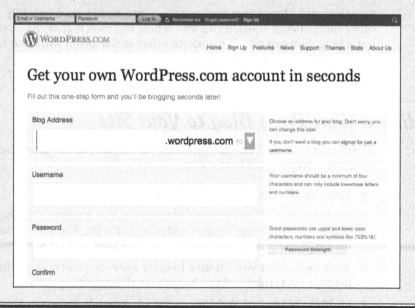

To run WordPress, your web server needs PHP 4.3 or higher and MySQL 4.12 or higher. The designers of the application claim it works best with an Apache or a NGINX server. If you don't have a server yet but are designing a site that will incorporate a WordPress blog, WordPress offers a list of servers that meet its minimum requirements at `http://wordpress.org/hosting`.

WordPress comes with installation instructions. Although the application doesn't have a full-fledged manual, you can find impressive documentation on the application at `http://codex.wordpress.org/Main_Page`. The WordPress website also features an impressive support section (`http://wordpress.org/support`) that covers many installation issues as well as information about how to modify templates. The support section of the WordPress.org website consists of forums that address virtually any issue from installation to plugins.

Installing WordPress

Before you read this section, check with your web-hosting service. The WordPress blogging application is so popular that many web-hosting services give you the option to install WordPress through your site's control panel, which is also known as "cPanel."

If your web-hosting service offers a cPanel that enables you to install a blog, by all means, use it. Our motto has always been: "Why work harder when you can work smarter."

If your web-hosting service doesn't offer WordPress installation through the site's cPanel, start a petition, start a rally outside your web server's office, or write a long letter to your congressman if you're old enough to vote. But seriously, if your server has the necessary features (listed in the preceding section) to run WordPress, you're ready to install the application. Detailed installation instructions can be found here:

`http://codex.wordpress.org/Installing_WordPress`

To give you an idea of how easy it is to install the application, here's a condensed version of the installation process.

1. **Download the application and unzip the files.**

The files needed to run the application are downloaded into a folder called WordPress.

2. **Create a new MySQL database on your server.**

You can easily create a MySQL database through your web-hosting service's control panel or a server application called phpMyAdmin. When you create the database, you're prompted for a name, user name, and password.

Book VIII
Chapter 1

Adding a
WordPress Blog

3. Open wp-config-sample.php in a word-processing application.

You'll find this file in the files you unzipped after downloading WordPress. We recommend using an application like Notepad (Windows) or TextEdit (Mac) to make your changes. We recommend using these applications to modify the code because more sophisticated word processing applications use smart quotes (they look like this: " " ' '), which will cause errors when used to designate the database name, user name, and password.

4. Change the database information.

Modify the file by changing the default name of the database, user name, and password to the names you specified in Step 2 when creating the database on your server.

5. Save the file as wp-config.php.

6. Create a folder on your server.

The logical name for that folder is Blog.

7. Upload the files to this folder.

8. Install the application on your server.

    a. Navigate to the install.php file on your server.

       If you uploaded the files to a folder called Blog, the default location is www.*mywebsite*.com/blog/wp-admin/install.php.

    b. Follow the prompts to install the application.

    c. When installation dialog box prompts you for a name for your blog and your e-mail address, supply that information.

WordPress automatically fills in the table for your database. The application generates a user name and password.

9. Write down your user name and password.

You need these to log in to your blog, administer it, and post entries. If you're not crazy about the password, you can change one or both of them when you administer the blog.

By default, the user name for the person who sets up the blog is *admin*, which cannot be changed. However, in the WordPress Dashboard, you can change the name that blog visitors see attached to the posts you author.

10. Log in to your blog.

You'll find a wp-login.php link at the bottom of the installation dialog box. Click the link to log in and begin blogging.

Modifying a WordPress blog

After you install a WordPress blog, you can modify the blog to suit the website to which it's linked. You can modify an existing theme (skin) or choose one of the alternates that are available after you install WordPress. The alternative is to upload a new theme that you purchase or download for free to your server. You can find all manner of blog templates by entering "WordPress blog template" in your favorite search engine. Make sure that the template you choose looks similar to your main website. However, WordPress is a popular application, and many developers have created themes for the application. If you're using the blog in conjunction with a website, you may be able to find a blog theme that has similar colors, or locate a blog theme that gives you the option to change colors through the WordPress dashboard.

To modify the look and feel of your WordPress blog with a theme, follow these steps:

1. **Open your web browser and navigate to** `http://wordpress.org/extend/themes`.

   The WordPress Free Themes page appears. (See Figure 1-1.)

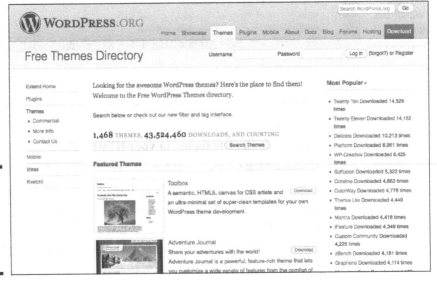

Figure 1-1: Select a new theme for a WordPress blog.

2. **Navigate to a theme you like.**

   As of this writing, you can pick from more than 1,400 themes. You can speed up your search by displaying themes that have color schemes similar to the site to which they'll be linked. You can sort by color by enabling one or more check boxes.

3. **Click the thumbnail to preview the theme in your browser.**

   The test site for the theme you selected appears in a new browser window. (See Figure 1-2.)

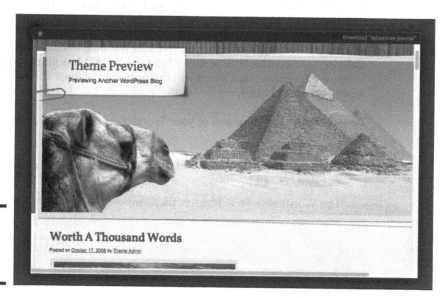

Figure 1-2:
Preview a
WordPress
theme.

4. **When you find a theme you'd like to use, click the Download link and then follow the prompts to download the file to your desktop.**

5. **Unzip the file.**

6. **(Optional) Modify the theme in your HTML-editing application.**

   Modifying a blog theme is not for the faint of heart. If you'd like to have a go at modifying your own blog, make sure you keep a backup of the original blog files on your desktop computer. If you make a mess of the modification, you can upload the original files to make your blog right with the world again.

   Online, here are tutorials that show you how to customize themes:

   ```
   http://codex.wordpress.org/Blog_Design_and_
       Layout#Themes_and_Templates
   ```

7. **Upload the Themes folder to the following directory on your server:**

   `www.`*mywebsite*`.com/blog/wp-content/themes`

This folder is created by default when you install WordPress on your webserver.

Now you can change the look of your blog.

8. Log in to your blog.

When you log in as administrator, the Dashboard section of your blog appears, which is where you administer the blog, write new posts, add new users, and so on. (See Figure 1-3.)

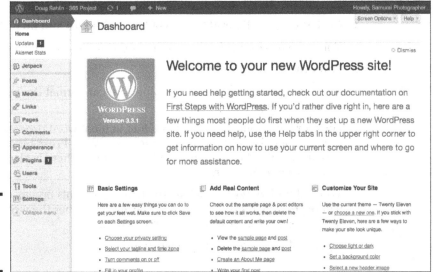

Figure 1-3:
The WordPress Dashboard.

9. From the Dashboard menu, choose Appearance⇨Themes.

Your web browser refreshes and displays default themes and any themes you uploaded to your server. Note the Install Themes tab. There, you can upload and find themes from within your blog instead of going to the WordPress site and downloading a theme.

10. Select the desired theme.

The previously used theme is replaced.

Using a WordPress Blog

After you install a WordPress blog and choose a drop-dead gorgeous theme, you're ready to begin blogging. The WordPress blogging application is very intuitive. If you've not used a WordPress blog before, the following section will get you (or a client) up and running very quickly.

Creating a WordPress blog post

Blogs are all about getting the word out, and WordPress makes it easy for you to post entries to your blog. You can easily add images and hyperlinks when posting a message to your blog. To add an entry to your blog, follow these steps:

1. **Log in to your WordPress blog.**

When you log in as administrator, WordPress displays the Dashboard, which enables you to *administer* — that is, create new posts, edit posts, and all the other fun stuff you can do with — your blog.

2. **Click the + New links at the top of the dashboard and then choose Post.**

Your web browser refreshes to the Add New Post section of your blog.

3. **Enter the desired information.**

When you post an entry to your blog, you can format the text and add images to the post.

Look for icons similar to what you find in most word processing applications. Notice that others are specific to the WordPress blog. You can add links, upload multimedia, and much more. There is also an icon that displays Kitchen Sink mode.

You add hyperlinks by clicking the Links icon. This opens a dialog box where you to enter the URL and determine whether the web page opens in the same browser window or in a new one.

Figure 1-4 shows a post being written.

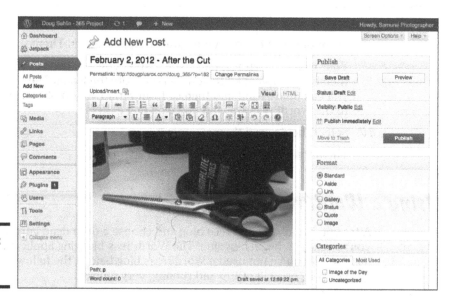

Figure 1-4:
Writing a
post.

4. Click Preview.

This opens a preview of the post in another tab, just as it will appear when you publish it. At this point, you can click Edit to change any part of the post.

5. If the preview looks good, click the Add New Post tab in your web browser, and then click Publish.

Note the Save as Draft option, which enables you to save the post as an unpublished draft on the server. This gives you the option to finalize a long post at a later date. When you save a post as a draft, you can edit and then publish it as shown in the next section. If you choose Publish, WordPress publishes the blog post (see Figure 1-5).

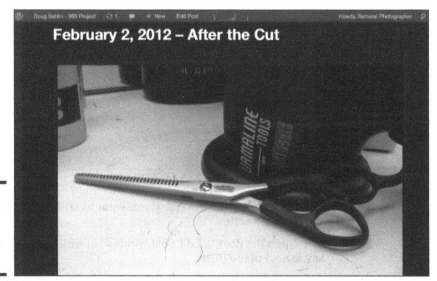

February 2, 2012 – After the Cut

Figure 1-5:
The entry, as it appears on the blog.

If you or your client posts information on several different topics, you can create a category for each topic. This makes it easier to manage your blog.

Managing a WordPress blog

If you're setting up a blog with multiple authors and multiple categories, you can easily manage the blog through the WordPress Dashboard. You can also edit or delete posts. To edit or delete posts in a WordPress blog, follow these steps:

1. Log in to your WordPress blog.

When you log in as administrator, WordPress displays the Dashboard, which enables you to administer your blog. If you have other people creating content for the blog, users with editor status can also edit blog entries.

2. **Choose Posts⇨All Posts.**

   Your browser refreshes to show all entries posted to the blog. (See Figure 1-6.)

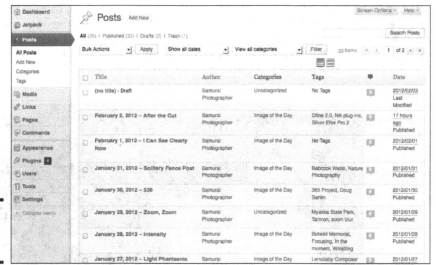

Figure 1-6:
Manage
posts here.

3. **Pause your cursor over the entry you want to edit, and then choose the appropriate action.**

   - *Edit:* Open the post in Edit Post window, in which you can change any aspect of the post.

   - *Quick Edit:* Edit information such as the post title, the date and time the post is published, and so on. This option is handy when you don't need to change the post text or images.

     When you edit a post in Edit or Quick Edit mode, make the desired changes, and then click the Update button.

   - *Trash:* Send the post to the great Cyberspace junkyard.

   - *Preview:* Save the post as a draft.

   - *View:* Take a quick look at the post as it appears in the blog before making your edits.

4. **Click the Update button, if needed.**

   WordPress publishes the edited post.

You can also add categories to the blog, modify comments, and do other tasks from the Manage tab. You can add links to the blog through the Links section, plus add and manage users through the Users section of the Dashboard. And later in "Adding Multimedia Content to Blog Posts," we show you how to add photos and other media.

Creating Search Engine–Friendly Blog Posts

When you create a blog post, it's one of hundreds of thousands created that day. Finding your blog post through a search engine without a bit of SEO wizardry would be a difficult task indeed. Talk about your needle in a haystack. To get your blog post noticed by people other than those who subscribe to your blog, you must take steps to ensure that search engines notice your post.

In your WordPress Dashboard Privacy section, the default Site Visibility option allows search engines to index your blog. **DO NOT CHANGE THIS SETTING.** Yes, we know that caps and boldfaced text is the equivalent of shouting, but this is important. If you do, your blog will be the proverbial needle on the bottom of a 60-foot haystack and invisible to anyone but those to whom you send the URL.

Okay, now that we have your attention, here are a couple of other things you can do to make blog posts more visible on search engine query results pages:

✦ **Create SEO-friendly titles.** When you create the title for your web post, put a bit of thought into it. What is the message of your blog post? Who is your target audience? When you know that information, think of what keywords your target audience would type into a search engine to find that type of information. Use one or two of those keywords in the blog title while still making it look like it was written by an intelligent person instead someone creating a conglomeration of keyword gibberish.

Your blog title will show up in the search results. The title may have all the right keywords, but if it's not compelling, very few people will click through to read the post. If you're writing for multiple audiences, or have multiple keywords, create several posts of the same content with different titles that contain the alternate keywords.

✦ **Link important words to earlier posts.** A search engine ranks a post as more authoritative if it's linked to other content, even content within your own blog. If you've written previous posts about the subject of your current blog post, select keywords in the new post (such as a product name) and use the Link tool to create a hyperlink to the previous post. You can also edit the previous post or posts, and select keywords from those to link to your current post. You can also link keywords to external sites. Creating links to previous posts and external websites with related information creates incoming links. When you create a link to another blog post, or external website, make sure the link opens in another browser window.

✦ **Add relevant tags to your posts.** Tags are a way of organizing your posts so people can find the information they're looking for. You can easily create tags for keywords with WordPress. When you create a post, simply scroll down to the Tags panel when creating or editing a post (see Figure 1-7). You can create new tags, or choose from popular tags you've applied to other posts.

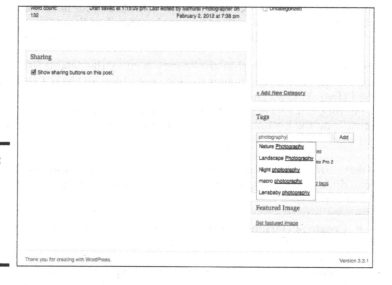

Figure 1-7: Add relevant tags to make a post SEO-friendly.

Make sure the tags are relevant to the post. If you add a popular celebrity's name to a post thinking that it will increase your traffic, it may have the opposite effect. Adding irrelevant keywords is considered SPAM by most search engines.

✦ **Use Google Insights to find relevant search terms.** If you're torn between a couple of search terms and can't decide which one is better for your target audience, Google Insights (`www.google.com/insights/search`) can help you decide which keyword is more popular. The tool lets you compare multiple search terms, and creates a graph that shows the current popularity of each term (see Figure 1-8).

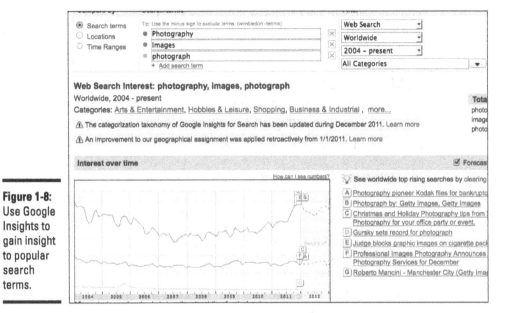

Figure 1-8:
Use Google
Insights to
gain insight
to popular
search
terms.

✦ **Add alt text to images.** *Alt text* is text that describes the image for visually
impaired people using screen readers. (Read more about it in "Adding
an image to a blog post.") You can do this in WordPress when adding
images to a post. Create alt text that contains at least one keyword related
to the post. The keyword should also be relevant to the image for accessibility. To learn more about adding alt text to an image, see the "Adding
Multimedia Content to Blog Posts" section of this chapter.

✦ **Change the default permalink name.** In WordPress, the default permalink for a post has a number. A *permalink* is the permanent URL for a
post. In the Settings section of the Dashboard, you can change the permalink option to the post name. If you give the post a name with a relevant keyword as outlined in the first bullet of this section, the permalink
name also contains this keyword giving your post more relevance for
the search engines. Redundancy works.

Adding Multimedia Content to Blog Posts

A blog post with just words can be very boring indeed. But you can spice
it up by adding multimedia content. The obvious choice is to add images.
Using WordPress, you can add a JPEG image file to your post and automatically upload it to your server as long as it's smaller than 64MB.

You can also add MP3 audio or video files that you host on YouTube. So if you want to spice up your blog posts with multimedia, check out the following sections.

Adding an image to a blog post

A picture is worth a thousand words and adds a lot of punch to any blog post. You can add an image of a product, a company outing, or images from a recent photo shoot. And yup, you can add more than one image to a blog post. To add an image to a blog post

1. **Optimize an image in the JPEG format as outlined in Book V, Chapter 1.**

   Make sure the image file size is smaller than 64MB. You should also optimize the image to the largest size at which images are displayed in the theme you use for your blog. Unfortunately, this information varies depending on the theme you use. Sometimes you can get the dimensions from the website that supports the theme, or from within the Appearance section of the WordPress dashboard.

2. **Create a new blog post (see the "Creating a WordPress blog post" section of this chapter).**

3. **Position your cursor where you want the image to appear and then click the Upload/Insert icon at the top of the Add New Post window.**

   The Add Media dialog box appears (see Figure 1-9). You have three choices:

   - *From Computer:* Upload images from your computer.

   - *From URL:* Insert images that are already on the web.

   - *Media Library:* Add images you've already uploaded to your blog from previous WordPress posts using the Upload/Insert icon.

   The second and third options give you the same options as uploading from your computer.

   The following steps show how to upload from your computer.

4. **Click the Select Files button.**

   The File Upload dialog box opens. Alternatively, you can drag files from the Windows Explorer or Mac Finder directly into the dialog box.

5. **Select the image file and then click Open.**

   A message appears telling you that WordPress is processing the file. When the file is processed, the dialog box refreshes to show a thumbnail of the image and your other options (see Figure 1-10).

Figure 1-9:
Uploading
an image
file.

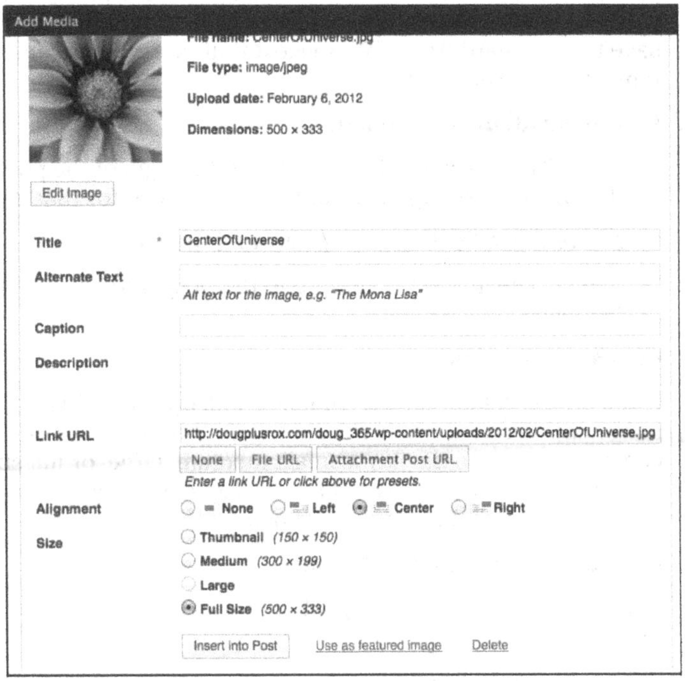

Figure 1-10:
Getting the
image ready
for the post.

6. **You can change the following image parameters:**

   - *Title:* By default, WordPress uses the image title, minus the extension. You can change the image title to any name for the post.

   - *Alternate Text:* As we mention earlier, this is text that describes the image for visually impaired people using screen readers. Search engine robots use alternate (alt) text to determine the contents of a blog post. If you use alt text, be sure to add at least one keyword that's relevant to the post, while still having a readable description for the visually impaired.

   - *Caption:* The text you enter here is displayed below the image. Note that the caption option is not available on all blog themes.

   - *Description:* The text you enter here is displayed below the image if you choose the Attachment Post URL option in the next step.

7. **Accept the default File URL, Attachment Post URL, or None.**

   If you accept the default option, the image opens in another window. If you accept the Attachment Post URL option, the file appears in another window. In either case, it's easy for a viewer to right-click the image and save it to his hard drive. We suggest that you choose None to avoid any temptation at thievery.

8. **Choose an alignment option.**

   - *None:* The image is aligned to the left margin of the post, or accepts whichever text alignment option is specified for that part of the post.

   - *Left or Right:* Post text wraps around the image.

   - *Center:* The image is centered in the post, and text appears above or below it.

9. **Choose a size option.**

   If you chose thumbnail and choose a link option in Step 7, the full size image appears in another window when the thumbnail is clicked. You can also choose to display a small, medium, large, or full-size version of the image in your post. The physical size of the options varies depending on the size of the image you upload.

10. **Click the Insert into Post button.**

    The image is added to your post.

Editing a post image

If you publish a post or preview a post and the image doesn't look right to you, you can easily edit the image. When you edit an image, you can change any of the parameters listed in the previous section, delete the image, or replace the image. If not already, log in; then from the Dashboard, choose All Posts⇨Edit and then choose the desired post.

To edit an image in a post

1. **If the post has been published and you're still logged in as administrator, navigate to the post and then click the Edit link. If you're previewing the post, click the Edit link.**

2. **In the Edit Post window, make sure the Visual tab is selected, and then click the image.**

Two icons appear in the upper-left corner of the image: a red circle and a slash, and a photograph.

- *Delete the image.* Click the red circle with the slash.

  The image is removed from the post, but is still in the Media Gallery.

- *Edit the image.* Click the photograph icon.

  The Edit Image dialog box appears. This is a carbon copy of the dialog box that appeared after you uploaded the image, with the exception that you can now resize the image from 60 percent of its original size to 100 percent of its original size. Change any of the parameters to suit your blog post.

  The Edit Image dialog box also sports an Advanced Settings tab.

3. **(Optional) Click the Advanced Settings tab.**

Here, you can change the size of the image as outlined previously, manually change the size of the image, change the appearance of the image in the post. You can also add a border as well as specify vertical or horizontal space (see Figure 1-11).

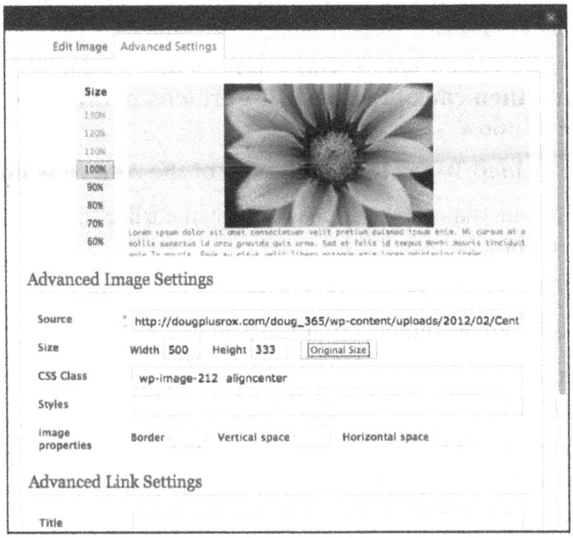

Figure 1-11:
Editing a
post image.

There are also advanced link settings, and you can specify a style. These options are generic to WordPress and the blog theme you use, and are beyond the scope of this book.

If you manually change the size of the image, there is no option to resize the image proportionately. Unless you do the math to get the correct size for the other dimension, you'll end up with a distorted image. We also recommend that you not try to increase the size of an image to larger than the original size you uploaded, or the image will become pixelated.

4. **After making the desired change, click Update.**

   Faster than a speeding bullet, WordPress updates the HTML to display the image as specified.

Adding an audio file to a blog post

The spoken word is a good thing to add to a blog post if you're a politician or a used car salesman. And music is a good thing if you're a musician. You can add an audio file to your blog posts using the upload method outlined in the previous section.

Unfortunately, the audio file isn't embedded in the blog post; it opens up in the web browser, in the same window, which is not a good thing because it takes visitors away from your blog. But there's a workaround with a bit of HTML magic to get the file to open in another window.

The following steps show you how to add audio to a blog post:

1. **Create a new blog post (see the "Creating a WordPress blog post" section of this chapter).**

2. **Position your cursor where you want the link for the audio file to appear and then click the Upload/Insert icon at the top of the Add New Post window.**

3. **Click the Upload/Insert icon at the top of the Add New Post window.**

   The Add Media dialog box appears (shown earlier in Figure 1-10). You have three choices

   • *From Computer:* Upload images from your computer.

   • *From URL:* Insert images that are already on the web.

   • *Media Library:* Add images you've already uploaded to your website from previous WordPress posts.

   The second and third options give you the same options as uploading from your computer. The following steps show how to upload from your computer.

4. **Select the audio file and then click Open.**

   A dialog box appears telling you that WordPress is processing the file. When the file has been processed, the dialog box refreshes to show an icon to represent the audio file and the parameters you can edit (see Figure 1-12).

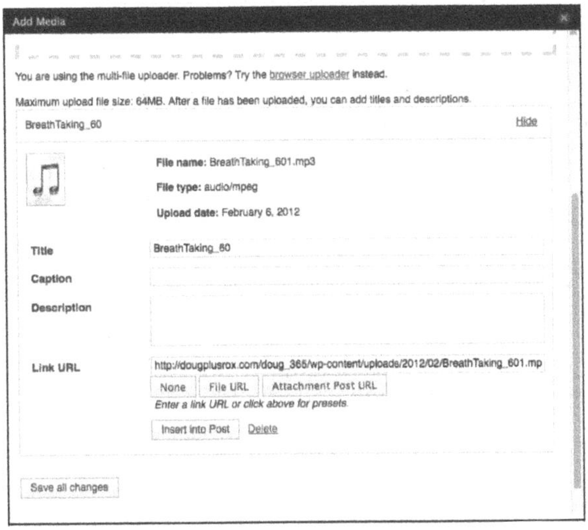

Add Media

You are using the multi-file uploader. Problems? Try the browser uploader instead.

Maximum upload file size: 64MB. After a file has been uploaded, you can add titles and descriptions.

BreathTaking_60   Hide

File name: BreathTaking_601.mp3
File type: audio/mpeg
Upload date: February 6, 2012

Title   BreathTaking_60

Caption

Description

Link URL   http://dougplusrox.com/doug_365/wp-content/uploads/2012/02/BreathTaking_601.mp
                None   File URL   Attachment Post URL
                Enter a link URL or click above for presets.
                Insert into Post Delete

Save all changes

Figure 1-12: I can't hear you!

**Book VIII
Chapter 1**

Adding a WordPress Blog

5. **Accept the default title, or enter a title.**

   Because the title also functions as the name of the link, we suggest that you enter a title that reflects the content of the audio file.

6. **Enter a caption.**

   The caption appears below the audio file link.

7. **Enter a description.**

   The description appears if you choose the Attachment Post URL option in the next step.

8. **Choose a link URL.**

   The default link opens the file in another window. If you choose None, the file will be on your server, but it won't be heard, at least from the blog post. If you choose Attachment Post URL, the entire post opens in the same window, but there's a problem. When the link is clicked, the audio file plays in another window. Our advice is to select the default option and modify the HTML as shown in the following steps.

9. **Click Insert into Post.**

   The link to the audio file is inserted in the post.

10. **Click the HTML tab.**

The HTML for the blog post appears.

11. **Modify the hyperlink for the HTML by adding** `target="_blank"`.

Your hyperlink should now read something like the following; see Figure 1-13:

```
<a herf="//mywebsite.com/blog/wp-content/uploads/2012/02/
    myaudiofile.mp3" target="_blank">My Audio File</a>
```

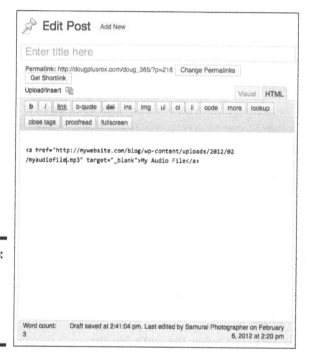

Figure 1-13: The code to play the audio file in another window.

12. **Finish the blog post and then click Publish.**

When you click the link, the audio file will appear in its own player in another window or tab, depending on which browser you're using.

Adding a YouTube-hosted video to a blog post

Video is also a very desirable thing to add to a blog post. You can upload your own videos to your website and create links to them in your blog post. Unfortunately, you have the same issue with video as you do with audio — the link opens in the same window. You can perform the same HTML magic we show you in the preceding section on audio.

If you open the link in another window, it's a distraction. Having an embedded video is so much better. An added bonus is that YouTube takes the bandwidth hit when a visitor plays the video — having your cake and eating it, too. You do need to have a YouTube account set up first. But then you can embed a video in any blog post. Here's how:

1. **Log into your YouTube account.**

You can embed any public YouTube video in a blog post, but unless a business partner created the video, it's best to use your own video.

2. **Click a thumbnail from your channel.**

The video opens in another window and starts playing.

3. **Click the Share button.**

YouTube displays choices for sharing the video.

4. **Click the Embed button.**

YouTube displays the HTML code needed to embed the video in a web page or blog post. The code is selected by default (see Figure 1-14).

Figure 1-14: This puppy's gonna get embedded in a blog post.

Code to copy is selected by default.

5. **Right-click and choose Copy from the context menu.**

   The code is copied to your Clipboard.

6. **Log in to your blog.**

   You know, the old user name, password deal — so many accounts, so many passwords.

7. **Create a new blog post.**

   Give the blog post a search engine–friendly title. (See the "Creating Search Engine–Friendly Blog Posts" section of this chapter.)

8. **Enter the desired text.**

   If the video is the star, the title may suffice.

9. **Position your cursor where you want the video to appear and then click the HTML tab.**

   You see the code required to bring your blog post to fruition in a web browser.

10. **Right-click and select Paste from the context menu.**

    The YouTube HTML code is added to your blog post (see Figure 1-15).

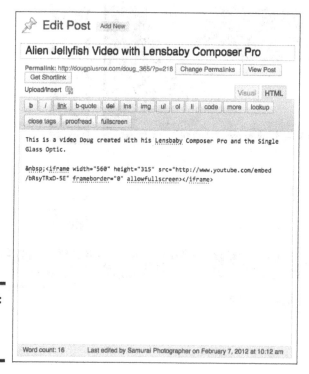

Figure 1-15: From YouTube with Love.

11. **Click Publish.**

The blog post is published complete with the embedded video (see Figure 1-16).

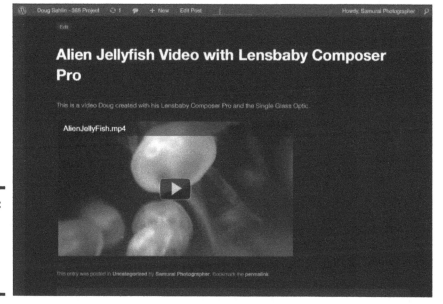

Figure 1-16:
Live and in living color from my latest blog post.

Chapter 2: Integrating Social Media with Your Blog

In This Chapter

✔ Integrating a blog with a website

✔ Creating an RSS feed

✔ Integrating an RSS feed with your blog

✔ Adding social media icons to your blog

*A*fter you get a brand-new, shiny red super-stock blog (see the preceding chapter), it's time to integrate it with your website. And of course you need to integrate your website with your blog. After that's done, you're on your way to getting your message out to the world. And of course, you know how to get your posts found by search engines; if not, we show you how in Chapter 1 of this minibook.

After all, creating a good blog and then populating it with interesting posts that are search engine–friendly are the building blocks of a successful blog. You built it, they came, and now you need them to come back. And the best way to get them back is to feed them your content as soon as it's posted, which you do by creating an RSS (really simple syndication) feed that automatically informs subscribers when a new post is created. Automation is a wonderful thing.

In this chapter, we show you all these things plus how to integrate your other social media with your blog.

Integrating a WordPress Blog with a Website

When you create a blog that will be an integral part of a website, you choose a theme similar to the main website. When you create the navigation for the main website, you create a link to the blog on the navigation menu. You can do this when you create a menu using Adobe Fireworks (as shown in Book V, Chapter 2), or you can create the navigation link using Adobe Dreamweaver.

Whichever method you choose, we recommend that you open the blog in another window — unless you follow our sage advice and create a link from the blog back to the main website. Many blog templates give you the option to modify the code to create your own navigation menus, and the latest version of WordPress (http://wordpress.org) makes it easy to create a menu. So if the theme you're using supports one or more menus, you can easily create a menu using the WordPress Dashboard as follows:

1. **Log in to your blog.**

   You know your user name; just add the correct password.

2. **Choose Appearance⇨Menus.**

   Your browser refreshes to show you the menu options available for your theme (see Figure 2-1).

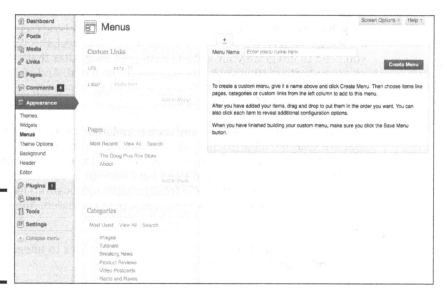

Figure 2-1:
Creating
a menu to
the main
website.

3. **Enter a name for the menu in the Menu Name text box.**

   The name you enter appears in front of the menu.

4. **Click the Create Menu button.**

   The menu is created, and all you need to do is add the links.

5. **Choose the menu name from the Primary drop-down menu. (See Figure 2-2.)**

   You may be tempted to click the Save button now, but you have more work to do before you can save a working menu.

6. **In the Custom Links section, enter the URL for the main website. (See Figure 2-2.)**

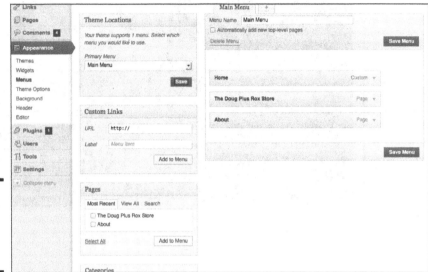

Figure 2-2:
Now all
the missing
links are in
place.

7. **In the Label text box, enter a name for the link.**

Choose a name that's congruent with the main website. For example, you might choose Home, or the name of the website followed by Home.

8. **Click Add to Menu.**

The link is added to the menu.

9. **Add any additional links.**

You could mirror the navigation menu on the main website, or you could create links to pages that you've created for the blog. The pages you add to the blog show up under the Custom Links section. After adding additional links, they show up in the menu dialog box (see Figure 2-2).

10. **Click the Save Menu button, and then click Save in the Main Menu section.**

The menu is saved.

11. **Preview your handiwork.**

Now's a good time to grab a cup of coffee, or give yourself another reward for a job well done (see Figure 2-3).

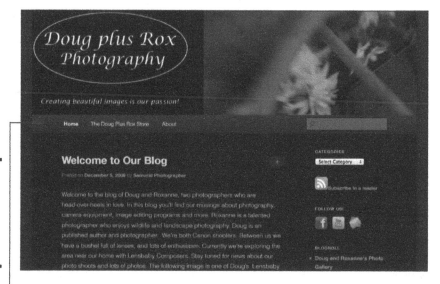

Figure 2-3:
Website
readers
appreciate
a navigation
menu.

The navigation menu

Creating an RSS Feed

After visitors have found you, never let them go, or at least give them a way to find out when you've created new content on your blog. You can do this by creating an RSS feed and by adding a subscription *chicklet* (a feed button with the same shape as the ubiquitous chewing gum) to your blog *sidebar,* that area on the right side of a blog where links and (sometimes) ads appear. An RSS feed is used by people with feed readers, or browsers that can read RSS feeds to show recent titles of blog posts and the first few sentences. From the RSS reader, a Read More link is used to see the full blog post at the actual blog.

Regardless whether you set up a blog for a client, yourself, or your company, WordPress automatically creates an RSS file that you can use for

✦ **Visitors to subscribe to your blog**

✦ **Visitors to be notified when you post new content and read it using**

- *A built-in RSS reader*

- *A free online RSS service, such as Bloglines* (www.bloglines.com)

- *A free desktop RSS reader, such as FreeReader 3* (www.free reader.com)

Either method notifies a subscriber when you create a new blog post. RSS delivers information to RSS feed readers through an XML document: an RSS feed, a webfeed, an RSS stream, or an RSS channel. The RSS feed notifies users when newly released content is added. The type of notification differs depending on the vehicle reading the stream.

The delivery method letting users know of a new feed can vary. Some people don't like to be hassled with auxiliary software, and those folks often opt to do everything through a browser. When those visitors visit a site with an RSS feed, they see an RSS icon. Click that, and they see a page that contains the most recent posts.

For example, if they click the Subscribe to This Feed button in Internet Explorer (IE) 9, the feed can be saved in the default Feeds folder or in a folder specified by the user. After the Subscribe Now button is clicked, Internet Explorer checks the feed on a regular basis and notifies the user when a new post is added to the site.

The popular Firefox browser offers different options for subscribing to a feed. When someone visits a blog with a feed, an RSS icon appears to the right of the address window. If the site has an *Atom feed,* which uses XML data to propagate feeds from a website, the user can subscribe by clicking the icon. After subscribing to the blog, a visitor can specify the desired feed aggregator — also known as a "feed reader" — by choosing an option from the Subscribe to this feed using drop-down menu.

The feed shown in Figure 2-4 enables the user to peruse the newest headlines or all headlines. If a user finds a headline that piques his interest, he can click the headline link to read the article from the website hosting the RSS feed in the actual blog. The visitor can also subscribe to the blog through the Firefox browser.

Many blog applications create feeds. For example, the latest version of WordPress generates a blog feed that can be accessed by IE 9 and the Firefox browser.

Embedding RSS feeds in a web page is something else you can try, and doing so provides even more content for your site's visitors to enjoy. (Another reason to keep them coming back!) You need to generate a JavaScript that will format how the RSS feed is presented in your page, but the process is manageable. See Book VII, Chapter 3 for more information.

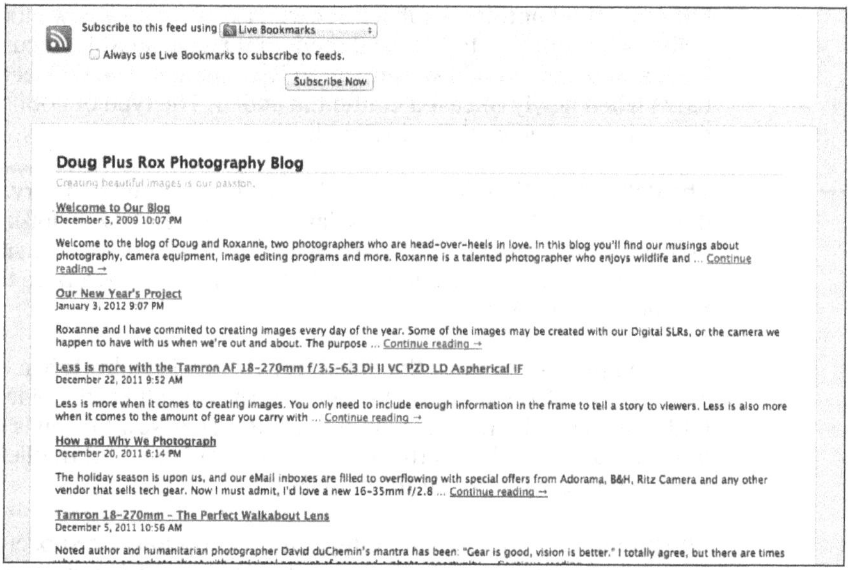

Figure 2-4:
Extra, extra,
read all
about it.

Using FeedBurner

If you really want to err on the side of caution, you can use the online service FeedBurner (www.feedburner.com). After creating a FeedBurner account, you can burn a feed. (*Burn* is FeedBurner-speak for adding your site to its list of feeds.) Setting up a FeedBurner account and feed is self-explanatory. Visit www.feedburner.com and follow the steps to create a free account and then burn a feed. Feedburner is part of the Google empire, so you need a Google account to burn a feed with Feedburner.

After you create a feed, use the FeedBurner feed address to automatically update the feed whenever you create a post. If you or your client uses a blog to host a podcast, Feedburner is the squeaky-clean way to create an iTunes friendly feed. A *podcast* is like a weekly radio show or television show. It contains information about a certain subject or genre. For example, there are several popular photography podcasts. As an added bonus, you can use FeedBurner to view detailed statistics about your feed, such as the number of subscribers for a specific day and over time (see Figure 2-5).

Figure 2-5:
Check your
FeedBurner
stats.

Getting your feed going

After you have an RSS feed, announce it to the world. Of course, you want to let current visitors to the blog know that it's syndicated with an RSS feed. As we mention in the preceding section, we strongly recommend you set up your feed through FeedBurner. Then you get to add the cute little orange RSS chicklet to a blog you created.

To add the RSS chicklet to a blog with a FeedBurner feed, follow these steps:

1. **Log into your FeedBurner account.**

2. **Select the feed for the blog to which you want to add an RSS chicklet.**

   That's right, you can burn multiple feeds with a Feedburner account.

3. **Click the Publicize tab.**

   On this tab, you'll find all manner of ways you can use to publicize your account, such as submitting the site to blog directories or creating an e-mail notification when new posts are written. Feel free to explore them all after you finish doing these steps.

4. **Click Chicklet Chooser.**

   The browser refreshes to show you the different options.

5. **Select the radio button to choose the desired chicklet size (see Figure 2-6).**

You have your big chicklet and your small chicklet. Both should fit on a blog sidebar, so the size you choose is your preference. You also have options to add an icon for popular feed *aggregators,* which are sites that people visit to find interesting blogs. You can add one following these steps and then selecting the desired feed aggregator when applying this step.

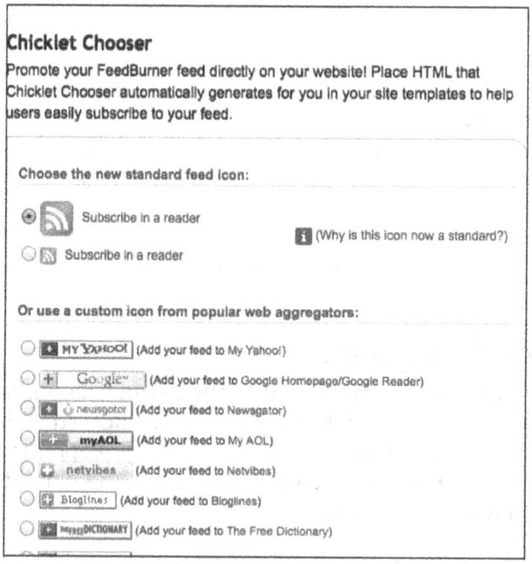

Chicklet Chooser

Promote your FeedBurner feed directly on your website! Place HTML that Chicklet Chooser automatically generates for you in your site templates to help users easily subscribe to your feed.

Choose the new standard feed icon:

◉ 🔲 Subscribe in a reader
ℹ️ (Why is this icon now a standard?)
○ 🔲 Subscribe in a reader

Or use a custom icon from popular web aggregators:

○ 🔲 **MY YAHOO!** (Add your feed to My Yahoo!)
○ 🔲 **Google** (Add your feed to Google Homepage/Google Reader)
○ 🔲 newsgator (Add your feed to Newsgator)
○ 🔲 **myAOL** (Add your feed to My AOL)
○ 🔲 netvibes (Add your feed to Netvibes)
○ 🔲 Bloglines (Add your feed to Bloglines)
○ 🔲 theFreeDICTIONARY (Add your feed to The Free Dictionary)

Figure 2-6: Chew a chicklet for your blog.

6. **Scroll down to the bottom of the web page.**

   You find a text box filled with code.

7. **Select all the code, right-click, and then choose Copy from the context menu.**

   The code is copied to your system Clipboard.

8. **Log into your WordPress blog.**

   To be on the safe side, you might want to do this in another browser window in case you have to go back to the FeedBurner site and copy the code again. Our passwords are very secure and hard to remember, which is why we keep our passwords in a separate document, from which we copy and paste into WordPress when logging in. If you do the same, you'll have to go back to the Feedburner site to copy the code, which is why we recommend using another browser window when logging into your blog.

9. **In the Dashboard, click Appearance, and then click Widgets.**

   The browser refreshes to show you the widgets you have available for your blog.

Most themes support widgets. If the theme you pick doesn't support widget, we suggest you find one that does because this is a powerful feature. Find out by reading the description at whatever website distributes the theme.

10. Select the Text widget and drag it to the desired sidebar.

In most cases, you add the RSS widget to the main sidebar where everyone can easily see it. After you drag the widget to the sidebar, a blank text box appears into which you paste the code.

11. (Optional) Enter a title for the widget.

The code comes complete with a title. Unless you want to delete the title from the code, we suggest that you leave the title blank.

12. Place your cursor in the text box below Title, right-click, and then choose Paste from the context menu.

The code appears in the text box with no fuss or muss (see Figure 2-7).

Figure 2-7:
To add an
RSS chicklet
to your blog,
a little bit of
code will
do ya!

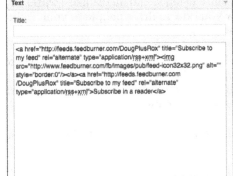

13. Click Save and then click Close.

The RSS chicklet code is added to the text widget, and the dialog box closes.

14. View your blog.

Your RSS chicklet is added to the sidebar (see Figure 2-8). If you don't like the position of the chicklet, modify it in the Widgets section of the WordPress Dashboard. Simply select the widget and drag it to a different position on the sidebar.

There are lots of other ways to spread the word. You can use services like AddThis (www.addthis.com) or ShareThis (www.sharethis.com) to share your posts via social media sites like Facebook, Digg, and Reddit. These tools drive new visitors to your blog and help it grow.

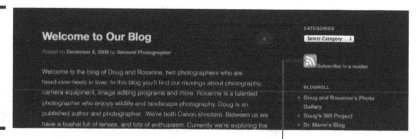

Figure 2-8:
The RSS chicklet after adding it to your blog sidebar.

Your RSS chicklet

Integrating Social Media with your Blog

When you create a blog and use social media, such as Twitter and Facebook, you invite your social media followers to view your blog by tweeting posts, or putting a link to a post on your Facebook page. However, you will get visitors to your blog who find your blog via Google or some other search engine and have no idea that you're using social media like Twitter or Facebook. In this section, we show you how to drive people to your Twitter feed or Facebook page from your blog.

As of this writing, there's a nifty little plugin that you can use to put social media links on your blog to invite users to like your Facebook page, and/or follow you on Twitter. Like an Internet website, however, WordPress plugins can be here today and gone tomorrow.

To integrate social media with your blog using the Social Media widget, follow these steps:

1. **Launch your favorite web browser and then navigate to**

   `http://wordpress.org/extend/plugins/social-media-widget`

2. **Click the Download button.**

   The Social Media Widget file is wrapped in a zip file.

3. **Unzip the file and upload it to your blog's wp-content/plugins folder.**

   This is the humble abode of all the plugins for WordPress.

4. **Log in to your WordPress blog.**

5. **From the Dashboard, choose Plugins⇨Installed Plugins.**

   The Social Media Widget appears on the list (see Figure 2-9).

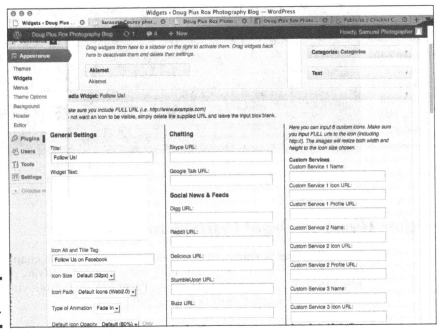

Figure 2-9:
Activate me.

6. **Click Activate.**

   The plugin is ready to rock and roll.

7. **Choose Appearance➪Widgets.**

   The activated widget appears in the Available Widgets column.

8. **Drag the widget to one of the sidebars.**

9. **In the Social Media dialog box that appears, provide the URLs to the social media sites you are a member of.**

   When you add the URL, make sure to include http://.

10. **Click Save.**

    The social media icons for which you provided URLs are added to your blog sidebar (see Figure 2-10).

Figure 2-10:
Social
media icons
are added
to the blog
sidebar.

Social media icons

Other Ways to Draw Visitors to Your Blog

The techniques we mention in the earlier sections of this chapter help integrate social media with your blog and automate notifying people when new blog posts are created. If you use Facebook or Twitter, you have ideal venues to draw other visitors to your blog.

If you use Twitter or Facebook for your business, the people who follow your Twitter posts and like your Facebook page are potential clients. The social media content you create is information that is useful to potential clients. The information isn't a blatant advertisement — it's information that establishes you and your company as an expert, an expert that followers would hire when needed.

The information you post on your blog should be useful information as well. And when you post useful information, add the link to the blog on your Facebook wall along with some pertinent information about the blog. The people who like your page will click the link. If they like the blog post, they'll subscribe to your blog.

The technique with Twitter is similar, but keep in mind that you have but 140 characters to speak your piece. If you're using a desktop client, like TweetDeck (`www.tweetdeck.com`), it automatically shortens a long post and leaves you room to add information pertaining to the post. If you use the Twitter site to send your tweets, you can shorten the URL at Bitly (`https://bitly.com`). This site also gives you the option to track how many people clicked the shortened link.

There is also a WordPress plugin that lets you integrate Google Analytics with a blog. If you'd like to use Google analytics on a blog, visit this web page for installation instructions:

```
http://wordpress.org/extend/plugins/google-analytics-for-
    wordpress/installation/
```

Managing Spam

After you create a blog and follow the steps in Chapter 1 of this minibook to optimize your posts, and then follow the steps in this chapter to create a feed and add social media widgets to your blog, you will get visitors. Most of the visitors wear white hats, but some of them wear black hats. When the visitors with the black hats find a blog, they think it's a place where they can post anything with links to everything from counterfeit Rolex watches to "adult" websites. Never fear, though, because you have a line of defense against spam in a WordPress blog by choosing commenting options in the Discussion section of the Dashboard (see Figure 2-11). A few (important) options you'll want to have enabled include these:

✦ **An Administrator Must Always Approve the Comment:** Enabling this option allows you to review each comment before it's posted.

✦ **E-mail Me Whenever Anyone Posts a Comment:** WordPress notifies an administrator by e-mail when comments are posted.

✦ **Comment Author Must Fill Out Name and E-mail:** Requiring that the person posting the comment adds her name and e-mail address ensures that the comment is posted by a real person, although a CAPTCHA is the only true way to ascertain that a comment is made by a real person. The name and e-mail also gives the post author a chance to thank the person for the comment, which shows the comment author that the blog author is a genuine, caring person.

Book VIII Chapter 2

Integrating Social Media with Your Blog

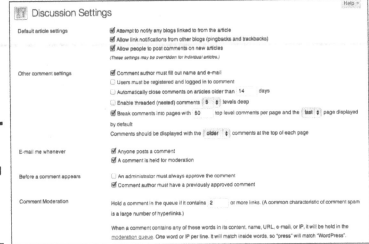

Figure 2-11: Set user commenting options in the Discussion section.

Another powerful option for preventing spam is to use the built-in plug-in Akismet. This plug-in searches posted comments for any known spam words (think Viagra), and quarantines the posts for a site administrator to review. You need to set up an account at WordPress.org, which is free. When you enable the Akismet plug-in, you're prompted to enter your WordPress API (application programming interface) key, which you can retrieve by logging into your account at WordPress.org.

Trust us: As your blog becomes more popular, it will become a target for spammers.

The Akismet plug-in does a remarkable job of thwarting spam, as shown in Figure 2-12. The plug-in filters blog comments through the Akismet web service, which runs hundreds of tests on the comment and detects words or links that indicate the comment is spam. The plugin marks comments detected as spam. The site administrator can delete the comments or let Akismet do it automatically in 15 days. Something that's important to note about spammers is that they basically try to advertise a product of some sort, or post a link to a website that sells a product. Even if nobody clicks the link in the comment, it's still a link back to their site.

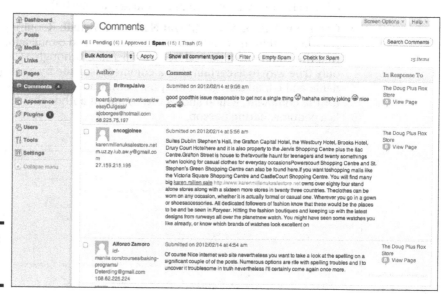

Figure 2-12:
Spam be gone.

Chapter 3: Adding E-Commerce to Your Site

In This Chapter

✓ Choosing a server

✓ Comparing secure and shared servers

✓ Using PayPal to accept payments

✓ Using PayPal Pro

✓ Creating a user-friendly e-commerce site

✓ Adding a shopping cart

✓ Working with customers

Selling merchandise and services online has become commonplace. People can do comparison shopping in the comfort of their own homes and order almost any (legal) nonperishable item from online stores. And in many cases, the prices are less than purchasing items from a brick-and-mortar store.

So how can you cash in on this online bonanza with your website? Set up an e-commerce site. You can use a secure server and integrate the site with an online payment package, but that can be rather costly to set up. Another option is to set up the site and then use PayPal to collect payments for the products or services you sell from the site. PayPal gets a percentage of your sales, but it's pretty painless. Another way to sell online is through eBay.

We explore all these options in this chapter and offer some common sense tips for selling on the Internet. If you or your client has a hot product or service to sell through a website, this chapter is the place to be.

Choosing an E-Commerce–Friendly Server

Web-hosting services are a dime a dozen these days, or so it seems. Choosing the right server can mean the difference between a successful e-commerce site and one that goes the way of the dodo after a few hundred visitors. Web-hosting services offer a variety of features. The following sections offer some sage advice for choosing a web-hosting service for an e-commerce site.

To share or not to share

Most web-hosting companies offer dedicated and shared hosting. The option you choose depends on the website budget and how much traffic you anticipate will be generated for the e-commerce site you're designing. Of course, when it comes to traffic, you'll want all the traffic the site can handle — and then some.

If your company or client is just dipping his toe into the e-commerce tidal pool, using a shared server suffices nicely. When a *shared server* hosts a site, the site information is stored on a host server with several other websites. Shared servers are, understandably, more economical than dedicated servers. The only potential drawback with using a shared server is that if the website you design (or one of the other sites on the server) starts getting a lot of traffic, visitors might not be able to access the site quickly during busy times. Or — the worst-case scenario — visitors might not be able to access the site 100 percent of the time. Another thing to consider is the speed of the server. If the shared server has a T1 line, it might work just fine. A server with a total fiber optic cable connection ensures a fast data-transfer rate.

If your company or client has a successful brick-and-mortar business and you have a stout plan for marketing the site (you do have a marketing plan, don't you?), consider paying the extra to get a dedicated server. When you host a site on a *dedicated server,* the server is dedicated to your client's site. That's right: Your client's site is the only one on the server, which means visitors get faster access — even when the Internet is busy — and with a reliable web-hosting service, they get access 100 percent of the time.

Some web-hosting services have an intermediate package, similar to a dedicated server, known as a "virtual private server." With a virtual private server, you have greater access. You can also create things like private name servers, use more server resources, and so on; these features can make your company appear bigger than it actually is to tech-savvy buyers. If the web-hosting company you're considering offers an intermediate service, compare the price with the additional features you'll be able to use on the site. If the additional cost makes it easier for potential buyers, or for the people who administer the site, the additional cost may be worth it.

If your company or client's initial needs warrant using only a shared server, make sure that the web-hosting company can upgrade the site to a dedicated server without penalty when the need arises.

Getting the best deal

When searching for a service to host an e-commerce site, the best price is not necessarily the best deal. In some instances, the best price is an absolute disaster. As the web designer/builder, you need to be in control and tell your company or client which server you're going to use. So what features do you need for the site? That, like the proverbial well, is a deep subject.

However, here are a few items to consider when shopping for the quintessential, web-hosting service for your e-commerce site:

✦ **Does the web-hosting company provide shared servers or dedicated servers?** If the company provides a shared server, visitors might experience problems connecting to the website during peak traffic periods. Not good.

✦ **Does the web-hosting company provide an intermediate service?** If the web-hosting company is a step above shared servers (but not as expensive as a dedicated server), this may be the best option for a new e-commerce site if it offers a faster connection and better service for site visitors.

✦ **How much hard disk space is included in the hosting plan you're considering?** If the site you're designing is relatively small, you can get by with 300–500 megabytes (MB) of hard disk space. If the site you're designing has copious amounts of multimedia elements — full-motion video, subdomains, and other bells and whistles — you might need up to 20 gigabytes (GB) of space. Choose the hosting plan that allocates the amount of space that best serves the current needs for the site. Just make sure that the hosting service is flexible and also that you can upgrade to a more robust plan when the need arises.

✦ **What is the maximum bandwidth that the service provides?** For a small site, bandwidth probably won't be an issue. If the site goes big time with lots of information and pages, and has a service or product that's in demand causing people to flock to the site in droves, the site will gobble up bandwidth quicker than Donald Trump adds to his considerable net worth. Add a podcast to the mix, and you're talking about gobs of bandwidth. The good news is that web hosting is an extremely competitive business, so most companies offer packages with 15,000GB of data transfer. Now that's a whole lotta bandwidth.

When you're considering a hosting company, ask the salesperson for the URLs of sites they host. Then check with the site webmasters to see whether they've encountered any problems, such as down-time or slow connections.

✦ **What percentage of up-time does the web-hosting service guarantee?** E-commerce sites need to be available 24/7. In an ideal world, there would never be power outages or problems with Internet hub connections. However, these service interruptions are facts of life, and the best web-hosting services have redundancy built into their system to guard against down-time. Choose a web server that can guarantee you near–100 percent availability. Web hosting is a very competitive business, and, with many webhosting services, you sign up online. If possible, talk with a sales rep and ask him to define he considers up time.

✦ **How many e-mail accounts does the web-hosting service provide?** Most web-hosting services provide 50 e-mail accounts with a hosting package. Having an e-mail account linked to a website adds an air of credibility to the site. Most consumers would rather send a query to, say, an e-mail address like info@widgetzrus.com than to fred@aol.com. With 50 e-mail addresses that have your domain name, you can use generic e-mail addresses, such as info@*mysite.com* and sales@*mysite.com* — and, if needed, personal e-mail addresses, such as fred@*mysite.com*.

See Book I, Chapter 4 for more information about choosing and securing a domain name.

✦ **Does the web-hosting service provide a user-friendly method of managing the website?** Most web-hosting services provide a control panel that clients use to manage the website, add e-mail addresses, manage databases, control FTP access to the site, and so on. If you're going to manage the website, make sure you understand how to use the control panel. If your client or another employee in your company is going to manage the site, make sure that the control panel is extremely user friendly.

✦ **Does the web-hosting service provide support? If so, is the support by phone or online?** You need to know whether support is available 24/7 in case of an emergency.

✦ **Can you set up a database for the website?** This feature is especially important if you design a website that receives data from clients for future use. You also want to know what type of database the hosting service supports. Make sure the database is compatible with any applications you intend to use, such as a blog. If you're using a Linux server, a MySQL database can get the job done just fine.

✦ **Does the web-hosting package support pages with PHP code?** If so, make sure the version of PHP offered by the web-hosting service matches the version you'll be using for your code.

✦ **Does the web-hosting service provide web analytics and statistics?** If so, how much information is provided? To gauge the success of the site, your company or you need to know how many visits the site is getting each day, where the traffic is coming from, what keywords are being used to find your site from search engines, what the most popular entrance and exit pages are, and so on. This information is imperative when you fine-tune the content of the site, or when redesigning it in the future. Even though customers may be buying product from the site, analyzing the stats will tell you whether any products that should be selling well are not because of website issues.

✦ **Can you host more than one domain with the hosting package?** This information is important if your company or client is setting up more than one e-commerce site. Many web-hosting services enable you to host up to ten domains with one hosting package at a reasonable cost.

✦ **Does the hosting service enable you to create subdomains?** This feature is useful if the client wants to set up different websites for different aspects of the company's services. For example, you could design pages for the client's customer service and store them in a subdomain that you might name customerservice.*mye-commercesite*.com.

As a web designer/builder, you can opt for hosting your own website with a web-hosting package that permits more than one domain. You can then host your client's websites using your web-hosting service and bill the client for the hosting service, enabling you to add additional profit to your bottom line. If you do host a client's website, make sure that website maintenance is covered in your design contract. Keep the hosting separate from design. You may still get a call from the client if there's a glitch on the server side, but if you choose a reliable web-hosting service, this will only happen on rare occasions. Many web-hosting services also have reseller packages. You can purchase web-hosting for additional domains at a reduced price. You then mark up the hosting service and bill your client.

Planning a user-friendly site

Before you begin designing the site, which we discuss in Book II, sit down with your client or the marketing gurus in your company and define the goals for the site. If the site will be used to dispense information and collect sales leads, you need to create an online catalog and a database that records the names and e-mail addresses submitted by interested parties. You can collect this information, using an online form. Form creation and management is discussed in Book VII.

If the site is used to sell products online, you need additional information to create a successful site. Here are a few important items that must be included when designing an e-commerce website:

+ **An About Us section:** This section gives the company you're designing the site for credibility. Here, you include information about the company and the reasons why visitors should purchase products or services from the site.

+ **A comprehensive description of the company's products or services:** This section of the site should include the features of the products offered and information on how each feature benefits the website visitor. If a product or interactive service is being sold from the site, this section should also explain the function of each feature and its benefit to the customer.

+ **A section that features testimonials and/or success stories from the existing customer base:** This section builds tremendous credibility for the company that you're designing the site for.

+ **FAQs:** An FAQ (frequently asked question) section anticipates and answers questions or concerns potential customers might have.

When you design the site, make it easy for potential customers to gather all the information they need to make an informed buying decision. Add as many graphic elements as you need to add sizzle to the steak. Images are a must when it comes to selling a product. You should include an image with each product description. If an extensive product offering will be sold from the site, you'll display many items on each page, which equates to a small image size. If the products bear close scrutiny, make sure you include links to different views of the product as well as links to larger versions of the image. You can also create thumbnails of different product views that when clicked display a larger version of the image in a pop-up window. For more information on optimizing graphics, see Book V, Chapter 2.

If appropriate, you can also include multimedia elements in your web design. Video clips are great ways to explain complicated details about a product or service. And you can spice up an e-commerce site with the liberal use of videos. We discuss incorporating videos into your site in Book V, Chapter 4.

Don't overload a page with multimedia elements, though, especially if part of the intended audience accesses the Internet with a slower connection. If you feel that multimedia elements are essential for the site, consider creating two versions of the site: one for high bandwidth and one for low bandwidth. Make sure that the multimedia for the low bandwidth version of the site is smaller in size, with higher levels of compression, to ensure that it loads in a reasonable amount of time.

Clean navigation is essential. If you design a site with a cluttered navigation menu with multiple choices, visitors can be confused and have a hard time figuring out what to click to get the information they need. If the product offering is extensive, consider using subdomains to display the different product lines. Each subdomain is like a mini-site with pertinent information to a specific product line or service.

Brainstorming the site

When you and your client or company brainstorm to create the ultimate e-commerce site, your goal is to arrive at a common vision: a marriage of your creative talent and the grand vision for the completed site. During your meeting of the minds, you should strive to take the upper hand. Unless your company or client is familiar with websites and e-commerce, some ideas offered may be over the top or simply undoable. When initially planning the site, consider the following factors:

✦ **Research e-commerce sites of businesses similar the site you're designing.** If you're creating the site for hire, ask your client for the URLs of his fiercest competitors. Most business websites have a common look and feel. It's generally not a good idea to design a site that's considerably different from your client's competitors' sites. Researching your client's competitors' sites gives you an idea of what are considered standard design staples for that type of business.

✦ **Display the company name and logo prominently on each page.** The easiest way to do this is to create a banner and display it at the top of each page.

✦ **Create a separate page for contact information.** On this page, include the company's physical address, phone number(s), fax number(s), and e-mail addresses.

✦ **Create a What's New section to showcase your client's newest products and other pertinent news.** This is also a great place to announce special promotions. This section should be updated frequently to encourage customers to visit the site often.

✦ **In addition to the main navigation menu for the site, add a text-only menu at the bottom of each page.** This information can improve the site's ranking in search engines. It also gives customers a convenient way to navigate when they scroll to the bottom of a page.

✦ **Add a privacy statement that clearly describes the policy for protecting customers' personal information.**

✦ **Keep your navigation simple.** Customers shouldn't have to click more than six times to go from the site's home page to checkout.

✦ **Don't use any trick navigation.** The navigation menu you design should be simple and should not distract the customer's attention from the reason for the site: the product or service being sold through the site.

✦ **Use meaningful link names.** If you or any party involved suggests using obtuse (yet creative) link names, it's your job to become the voice of reason and suggest readily identifiable link names. That is, of course, unless an avant-garde product or service is being marketed through the site, whose target audience consists of eclectic people with a creative bent.

When creating an e-commerce website, set up an `info@`*myecommercesite.*`com` e-mail address. This can be a catchall e-mail for customer queries. Most web-hosting services provide more than enough e-mail addresses with each hosting package. Contact the web-hosting service for more information on setting up new e-mail accounts.

Adding Basic E-Commerce with PayPal

If the site is on a strict budget, or any party involved isn't sure whether the product or service being promoted through the site will take off, PayPal is a viable alternative to hosting with a secure server and purchasing a credit card–authorization package. In fact, many successful e-commerce sites use PayPal to complete transactions. PayPal is the brainchild of the folks who created eBay. Initially, PayPal was used to complete eBay transactions. The buyer could set up a free, personal PayPal account to pay the seller. Online shoppers nowadays with a personal PayPal account can pay for purchases using a debit card or credit card, or by transferring funds from the bank account associated with the PayPal account.

Online merchants can use PayPal to accept payments using either a Premier or Business account. Merchants can sign up for either account for free. The fees for transactions up to $3,000 per month are 2.9 percent plus $0.30 per transaction. The beauty of using a standard PayPal account is that the merchant incurs no set-up fees, no monthly maintenance fees, and no fraud-protection fees. A merchant can transfer money from his PayPal account to his bank account at any time. There is no charge for a wire transfer, but that will take three to four days, depending on the bank account routing.

When you use PayPal to accept payments, you can create a custom payment page. When you create a custom payment page, it looks like the payment is being conducted with your own secure server. To create a custom page in PayPal, follow these steps:

1. **Log on to your PayPal Premier or Business account and navigate to the Profile page.**

   Here is where you specify your account information, financial information, and seller preferences.

2. **Click My Selling Tools and then choose Selling Online⇨Custom Payment Pages.**

   The Page Styles section of the site appears. The default payment style is PayPal unless you already created a custom payment page. In this case, all payment page options are displayed, as shown in Figure 3-1, and a custom style is selected.

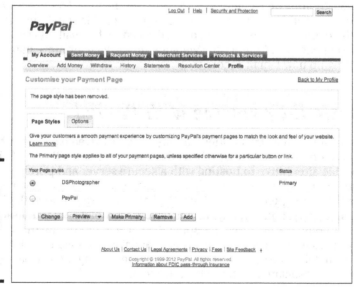

Figure 3-1:
The Custom Payment Page Styles section of the PayPal website.

3. **To create a new custom payment page, click the Add button.**

The Edit Custom Page Style page appears, as shown in Figure 3-2.

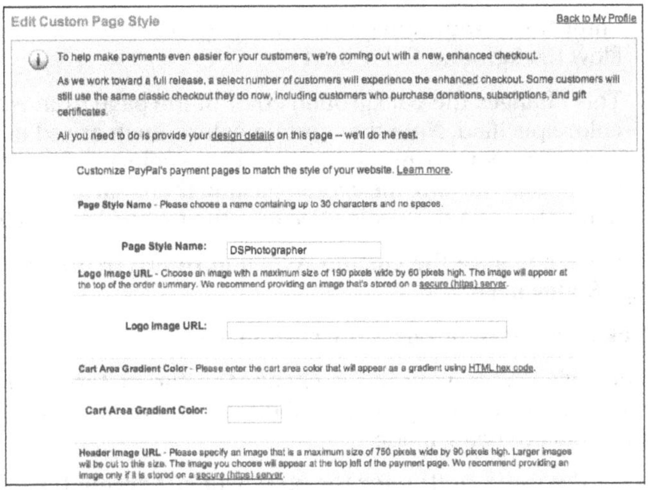

Figure 3-2:
Create a
custom
payment
style.

Edit Custom Page Style   Back to My Profile

To help make payments even easier for your customers, we're coming out with a new, enhanced checkout.

As we work toward a full release, a select number of customers will experience the enhanced checkout. Some customers will still use the same classic checkout they do now, including customers who purchase donations, subscriptions, and gift certificates.

All you need to do is provide your design details on this page -- we'll do the rest.

Customize PayPal's payment pages to match the style of your website. Learn more.

Page Style Name - Please choose a name containing up to 30 characters and no spaces.

Page Style Name: DSPhotographer

Logo Image URL - Choose an image with a maximum size of 190 pixels wide by 60 pixels high. The image will appear at the top of the order summary. We recommend providing an image that's stored on a secure (https) server.

Logo Image URL:

Cart Area Gradient Color - Please enter the cart area color that will appear as a gradient using HTML hex code.

Cart Area Gradient Color:

Header Image URL - Please specify an image that is a maximum size of 750 pixels wide by 90 pixels high. Larger images will be cut to this size. The image you choose will appear at the top left of the payment page. We recommend providing an image only if it is stored on a secure (https) server.

4. **In the Page Style Name text box, enter a name for the custom page style.**

This name is added to the list of custom styles associated with your profile.

5. **Set the banner.**

- *Custom:* Enter the URL for the custom banner that will be displayed at the top of your custom payment page in the Header Image URL field.

The ideal size for the banner is 750 pixels (px) x 90 px. Ideally, the banner should contain your client's logo or the name of the e-commerce site. You can easily create the banner as an image in Fireworks that loads quickly. Unless the banner contains photorealistic images, export the image in the GIF format.

Store the image for a custom payment page on a secure server. If you don't, a warning is displayed in the customer's web browser notifying him that the payment page contains insecure items. The URL for a secure server begins with `https://`. A URL starting with `http://` is used for web pages in which the data is not encrypted. You want customers to feel safe sending financial information online; some will balk and walk away from a transaction if the site is not secure.

- *Not custom:* If you're not using a custom banner, set these parameters.

Enter the hexadecimal value for the *header background color* in the Header Background Color field.

Choose a background color that matches the background color of the e-commerce page from which the payments will be made.

Enter the hexadecimal value for the *header border* in the Header Border Color field.

This places a 2 px border with the specified color around the payment page header.

Enter the hexadecimal value for the *background color* in the Payment Flow Background Color field.

This changes the background color of the page from white to the color specified. Note that certain colors, such as red and fluorescent green, are not permitted because these colors clash with the payment page warning messages, making them hard to read. Of course, don't choose a dark color because the text will be illegible as well.

6. Click Save to save the custom style and return to the Custom Payment Page Styles page.

7. Click Preview to preview the custom style.

If the style isn't to your liking, change the parameters until the custom style matches the look and feel of the e-commerce site from which the payments are being made.

8. Select the radio button for the style you just created.

This makes the selected style the style that displays when payments are made from the e-commerce site.

9. Click the Make Primary button.

The style you created is now the default style for any PayPal transactions. Figure 3-3 shows a custom PayPal payment page.

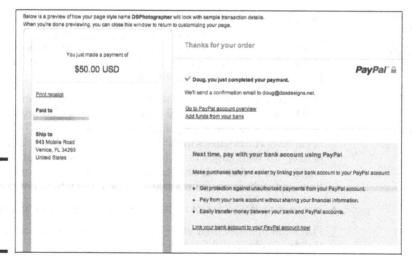

Figure 3-3: A custom PayPal payment page.

A custom PayPal payment page makes it appear as though the payment is being made through the site's secure server, and not through PayPal.

Using PayPal Website Payments Pro

PayPal Website Payments Pro is a package designed for e-commerce websites. The application integrates with existing shopping cards using a developer API. It enables you to take Visa, MasterCard, American Express, and Discover credit cards as forms of payment. In addition, a shopping cart powered with PayPal Website Payments Pro can also accept payments from debit cards, e-checks, bank transfers, and PayPal balances. If PayPal Website Payments Pro is used to handle online transactions, your client won't need another merchant account. Here are some added benefits to using PayPal Website Payments Pro:

✦ No application or setup fees

✦ No cancellation fees

✦ No monthly minimum

✦ No reporting fees

✦ No long-term commitment

When a visitor uses an accepted credit card to make a purchase through a website using PayPal Website Payments Pro, the payment is processed in the background. Here are the pros:

✦ **Payments made using PayPal express checkout transport the visitor to PayPal's secure website.**

✦ **The landing page can be modified to match the look and feel of the website you're designing.**

✦ **Checkout is an innocuous three-click experience.**

✦ **The money from the transaction is immediately deposited to the bank account associated with the PayPal account. (Sweet.)**

✦ **PayPal provides fraud protection.**

According to PayPal, as of this writing, processing payments through PayPal Websites Pro can be up to 14 percent less expensive than other credit card processors. With PayPal Websites Pro, you can set a limit on the maximum purchase amount, country of origin, and so on. As of this writing, Website Payments Pro pricing is as shown in Table 3-1 (all amounts in US dollars):

Book VIII
Chapter 3

Adding E-Commerce to Your Site

Table 3-1	PayPal Website Payments Pro Pricing Schedule	
Monthly Sales	*Per Transaction*	*Per Month (Unlimited Transactions)*
$0.00 to $3,000	2.9% + $0.30	$30
$3000.01 to $10,000	2.5% + $0.30	$30
> $10,000.01	2.2% + $0.30	$30

To qualify for these rates, a merchant must offer his online customers PayPal Express Checkout. If this option isn't offered, rates could be as much as 1 percent higher.

Integrating with Credit Card Authorization Packages

The traditional way to handle transactions from a website is using a credit card authorization package. When you integrate a site with a credit card package, the payments from the site are handled by a number of banking institutions and processes. The service charges a setup fee and a monthly maintenance fee. The maintenance fee is based on the number of transactions handled per month. A thorough review of each of the many authorization packages available is beyond the scope of this book.

Credit card authorization packages enable you to run your online business with minimum overhead. In a traditional brick-and-mortar store, you have to hire salespeople to show customers the product, take orders, and accept payments. With a properly designed e-commerce site and credit card authorization package, these tasks are handled automatically. If the e-commerce site you're designing sells a service, you can schedule regular payments through the credit card authorization package.

Online payments are quite involved, flowing through a complex network of financial institutions and processes. The complexity is exacerbated when you accept payment from foreign countries. Fortunately, technology has simplified this process, and the proper credit card authorization package provides the gateway for this process. When a customer makes an online payment, the process occurs in the background, and the payment process occurs fairly quickly.

Solving the online payment maze

When a customer makes a payment, it's submitted through a gateway. Then the payment must go from the *issuing bank* (the institution that funds the customer's credit card) to your client's or company's bank account. The process appears seamless when a payment is made online, but there are many supporting players in what seems like a one-act play. The following list introduces the various actors in this one-act play that happens when the Checkout button is clicked:

+ **Merchant's online business:** The customer makes a purchase and clicks the Checkout button.

+ **Internet gateway:** The merchant's secure website submits a credit card payment to the payment gateway.

+ **Merchant's bank processor:** The gateway provider receives the secure transaction information and hands it off to the merchant's bank processor.

+ **Credit card processor interchange:** The merchant's bank processor submits the transaction information to the *credit card processor interchange,* which is a network of financial entities that manages processing, clearing, and settlement of credit card transactions.

+ **Credit card issuer:** The transaction is handed off to the customer's credit card issuer, which approves or declines the transaction based on the customer's available credit line. If the transaction is approved, the appropriate funds are sent back through the credit card processor interchange.

+ **Credit card processor interchange:** The credit card processor exchange relays the information to the merchant's bank processor.

+ **Merchant's bank processor:** The merchant's bank processor relays the information to the Internet gateway.

+ **Internet gateway:** The Internet gateway stores the result and funnels the information to the merchant. The process from checkout to sending the information back to the merchant averages less than three seconds.

+ **Credit card processor interchange:** The funds, less any processing fees, are transferred to the merchant's bank account — a process that takes from two to four days.

Fees for credit card authorization packages vary, depending on the institution you choose and the number of bells and whistles included with the credit card authorization package.

Internet fraud: An e-commerce merchant's worst nightmare

Not unlike things that go bump in the night, Internet fraud can rear its ugly head when you least expect it. Online merchants are responsible for fraudulent credit card transactions conducted through their sites. In addition to incurring heavy penalties and fees from the credit card association, there is the matter of product costs and shipping fees incurred by your client or company. Fortunately, you can protect the site against credit card fraud, even with a start-up online business that has limited transactions.

The first and most obvious step in safeguarding against fraud is to choose a secure and reliable payment solution. Choose a payment package that includes standard processing and anti-fraud features such as Card Security Code (CSC) and Address Verification Service (AVS). In addition, the payment solution should have options that enable your client to upgrade to the new buyer verification systems such as MasterCard SecureCode, or Verified by Visa. Your payment solution might have additional options to safeguard against fraud. Ask your representative for details.

SSL — What Is It?

The world is full of acronyms these days, and the wonderful world of e-commerce is no exception. But remember, if it weren't for acronyms, you'd have to type or write a whole lot of words.

In a nutshell, when a site has Secure Sockets Layer (SSL), the transaction is encrypted and cannot be deciphered by a third party. All secure pages are listed as `https`, followed by the rest of the web address. Users can transmit any amount of information from a secure site and know that a third party cannot decipher the information. Sending credit card information via a secure site is safer than whipping out your credit card in a local store where prying eyes — and for that matter, the salesperson — can see the information. When you purchase goods or services from a secure site, the data is *encrypted* when submitted. When the recipient (the bean counter for your client's e-commerce site) receives the data, it's *decrypted*. The bean counter adds the money to your company's or client's P&L (profit and loss) statement, and the goods are shipped to your client's customer.

Using a secure server

When you conduct your e-commerce using a secure server, the SSL certificate is linked to the site from which the transactions are being conducted. The SSL certificate is in your client's or company's name and in the domain name of the e-commerce site.

Hosting an e-commerce site through a secure server is an expensive proposition. To host an e-commerce site on a secure server using an SSL certificate with 128-bit encryption costs several hundred dollars per year — and as much as one thousand dollars and up per year depending on the services included with the package. However, the less-expensive alternative of using PayPal's secure server is always an option. You might pay a bit more per transaction, but the cost of a secure server isn't added to your overhead. The other alternative is sharing an SSL certificate, if your web-hosting service provides this option. Keep reading.

Sharing an SSL certificate

Many web-hosting services allow their customers to share an SSL certificate. This service is included with your hosting, and therefore can be considered free. When you share an SSL certificate, you do so through a third-level domain alias, for example:

www.*yourdomain*.c2.*yourWebhostingserver*.com

When you share an SSL certificate, you must use the domain alias in the code you use to create the buttons for your site's shopping cart. Alternatively, you can purchase a shopping cart package, which you can integrate into the site.

The problem with sharing an SSL certificate is that Internet Explorer issues a warning saying the domain name on the certificate doesn't match the domain name of the site from which the transaction is being conducted. Even so, the data is still encrypted, and the transaction is secure. This might cause a customer to back out of a transaction.

Overviewing E-Commerce Do's and Don'ts

When you create an e-commerce site, your goal is to sell your company's merchandise — or your client's merchandise. In keeping with these goals, there are certain things you should consider as well as certain things you should avoid (such as designing an e-commerce site that looks like a board game). The following list of do's and don'ts can keep you on the straight and narrow:

✦ **Do make the site user-friendly.** Make sure your site navigation is easy to decipher. If your visitors need a manual to figure out how to use your site, it's not a good thing.

✦ **Do include a privacy statement.** If you request the visitor's contact information, make sure you include a link to your privacy statement that is readily visible on any page that requests sensitive information.

✦ **Make sure the site has the look and feel of other e-commerce sites in your company's or client's industry.** Customers shy away from something that looks different from what they've come to expect. After all, no department stores look like the hip boutiques in Haight-Ashbury.

✦ **Avoid using buzzwords and hype, such as *best price* or *highest quality*, in the product descriptions.** These raise a red flag with many buyers.

✦ **Don't write the content.** Your client or the marketing gurus in your company know more about the product or service being offered through the website than you could ever hope to.

Pumping it up with eBay

eBay is without a doubt the largest online merchant in the world. Thousands of people use eBay to auction off their unwanted techno-toys, digital cameras, musical instruments, and so on. One man's trash is another's treasure. A NASCAR driver used eBay to auction a helmet he had thrown at a competitor's car after being forced off the track. The proceeds went to charity. In fact, a section of eBay is devoted to selling cars that sell anywhere from a few hundred dollars to several hundred-thousand dollars.

Savvy owners of e-commerce websites duplicate their efforts on eBay by setting up an eBay store. The fees for selling and setting up an eBay store are reasonable. Many brick-and-mortar businesses that also have websites set up eBay stores. To drive traffic to their eBay stores, they auction popular, fast-selling items. The eBay store features items other than those being offered for auction. After the vendor starts racking up sales on eBay, he can add the buyers to his e-mail list and send them news about specials from their e-commerce website. There's profit in redundancy.

✦ **Spice up the pages.** Many websites have too much text on the page, while others rely solely on graphics. A good design has a nice mix of text and graphics.

✦ **Use Flash content judiciously.** If you need to add some razzle-dazzle, Flash can provide it for you, but don't make your site exclusively Flash. Search engines tend to avoid Flash content like the plague. However, you can safely add a small Flash animation to an otherwise HTML page.

If you use Flash, the animation won't be available to users of certain mobile devices, such as the iPod or iPad.

✦ **Keep it fresh.** Make sure your client or company understands that an e-commerce site needs to be updated frequently to ensure return visitors. Either negotiate a fee for periodic revisions up front, or design the site in such a manner that your client can update it with content management software.

✦ **Don't clutter the home page.** Some e-commerce sites look like the front page of the daily news and are way too busy to be useful. The home page of the e-commerce site should be like the cover of a book: inviting and a reason for the visitor to click a few links to see what your client has to offer.

✦ **Give visitors a reason to return.** Set up the site with a What's New section, or create a small section of the home page devoted to new products or information. Make sure this content is updated at least twice per month.

✦ **Add a blog to the site.** A blog is a wonderful way to update customers to new products that are available. A blog can also be used for customer testimonials, or tutorials about how to use products distributed through the website.

Read about adding a blog in Chapter 1 of this minibook.

✦ **Don't create content that disappoints the visitors.** If your client insists on a section that promises response, such as a section that accepts customer comments, make sure your client is aware that he must live up to the promise and provide feedback.

Selling Items with a PayPal Account

If your client prefers to dip a toe in the e-commerce waters, she can save considerable money by accepting payments with a PayPal account. As we mention earlier in this chapter, the rates are reasonable. All you need is a bank account and an e-mail address to set up a PayPal account. After the account is set up, you can accept payments online. Adding PayPal Add to Cart buttons to any web page you create in Dreamweaver is a breeze, thanks to a free plugin from WebAssist (www.webassist.com). To add PayPal Add to Cart buttons to a web page in Dreamweaver, do the following:

1. **Navigate to**

   ```
   http://www.webassist.com/free-downloads/dreamweaver-
           extensions/paypal-ecommerce-toolkit/
   ```

   As of this writing, this is the URL from which you download the free PayPal eCommerce Toolkit 4.5.4 for Dreamweaver.

2. **Download and install the plug-in.**

   The plug-in, `PayPal454.mxp`, is a Dreamweaver extension. By default, it's downloaded to your desktop (Windows) or the Downloads folder (Macintosh).

3. **Launch Dreamweaver and then choose Commands⇨Manage Extensions.**

   The Adobe Extension Manager CS6 dialog box appears (see Figure 3-4). This dialog box is used to manage all extensions for all Adobe CS6 applications you have installed on your computer.

4. **Click Install, navigate to and select the `PayPal454.mxp` file, and then click Open.**

   You have to accept a disclaimer that the extension is not an Adobe product and that Adobe does not warrant or support the extension. Don't be put off by this: The PayPal extension is a proven performer. Adobe is just dotting every *i* and crossing every *t*. Their lawyers wouldn't have it any other way. After you accept the disclaimer, the extension is installed.

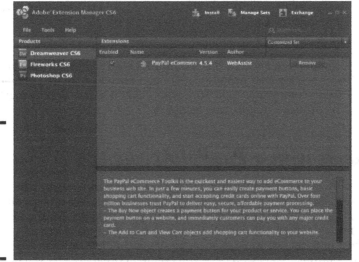

Figure 3-4:
Manage extensions with the Adobe Extension Manager CS6.

5. **Close the Adobe Extension Manager CS6, exit, and then restart Dreamweaver.**

The extension won't work until you do.

6. **Create the page from which the customer will check out.**

Figure 3-5 shows such a page — in this case, a basic HTML page with the image that is being sold. Now it's time to insert the Add to Cart buttons. You have a lot of flexibility here. Many web designers create a page where several products are displayed along with a description, and an Add to Cart button that appears below each product's description.

7. **Choose Insert⇨PayPal⇨Add to Cart Button.**

The first page of the Insert PayPal Add to Cart Button Wizard appears; see Figure 3-6.

The first time you use the PayPal extension, you have to activate it. After you download the extension, you get an e-mail receipt that has the serial number.

8. **Enter the e-mail address of the PayPal account to which the sale will be credited.**

9. **Click Next.**

The second page of the Insert PayPal Add to Cart Button Wizard appears.

Figure 3-5:
An image
that needs
an Add to
Cart button.

Figure 3-6:
Add the
e-mail
address for
the PayPal
account.

10. **Choose the desired button style from the dialog box shown in Figure 3-7.**

You can choose one of the preset styles, or choose a custom button. If you choose the latter option, the Button Image URL field becomes active. In this field, enter the URL where the button image is stored.

Figure 3-7:
Choose a
button style.

11. **Click Next.**

The third window of the Insert PayPal Add to Cart Button Wizard appears.

12. **Enter the product information.**

The product information you enter indicates which product to ship to the customer. You need to use a unique product name for each item. Select Yes or No for the options to request a shipping address from the customer and to include a comments field at checkout time. After the customer pays for the purchase, this information is sent to the e-mail address entered in Step 8. Figure 3-8 shows the dialog box for Step 3 of 4 of the Insert PayPal Add to Cart Button Wizard.

13. **Click Next.**

The fourth page of the Insert PayPal Add to Cart Button Wizard appears, as shown in Figure 3-9.

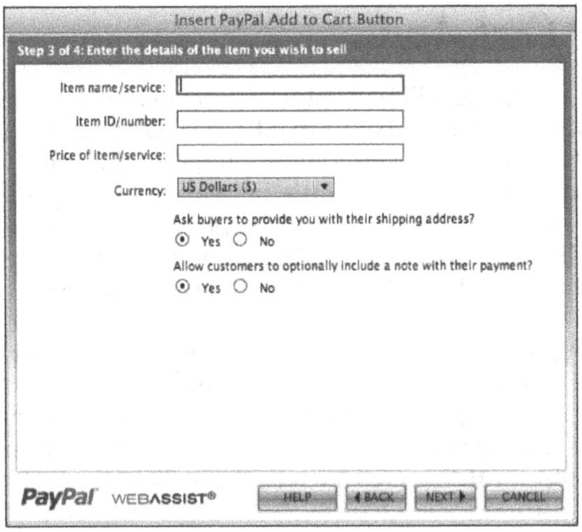

Figure 3-8:
Enter
product
information.

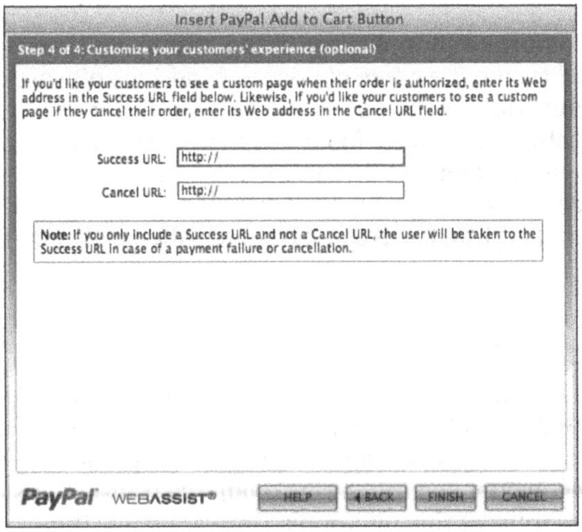

Figure 3-9:
Entering
the URL for
a success
page.

14. **If desired, enter the URL to the success page, which usually thanks the visitor for his purchase.**

    This step is optional. Many designers create a Thank You page for a successful purchase.

15. **Click Finish.**

    And that's all you need to do to add the button to one page. Of course, now you have to perform Steps 6–15 to add the button to other pages of your online store.

Using a Shopping Cart App

If the site you're designing will be hosted at a secure server, integrate the items for sale with a credit card authorization package, as discussed earlier in this chapter. However, if you attempt to integrate the items for sale with the authorization package *without* a little help from a friend, you're a card-carrying geek — also known as a web developer. This means writing code, baby. The thought of writing code sends shivers down most web designers' spines, but you have an alternative. Enter the shopping cart.

You can find shopping cart applications online. In fact, the service hosting the site might include a shopping cart application. Another solution is to purchase an e-commerce shopping cart template that integrates with web design software, such as Dreamweaver. A full-featured shopping cart template gives you complete control with features such as the ability to calculate shipping, integration with a product search page, the ability to add unlimited product features such as size and color, the ability to integrate with popular credit card authorization packages, and much more.

You can find a plethora of shopping cart templates by going to your favorite search engine and typing the name of your web design software followed by **shopping cart template.** When you review the results, look for a template that has all the features you need. Many templates let you design a store from scratch using a generic template that you can integrate with your existing design. These templates include the PHP or ASP code you need to create a functional shopping cart that you can integrate with a credit card authorization package.

Security concerns

The Internet can be a nasty place. Website owners have to contend with hackers, online theft, fraud, and viruses, to name a few. Any owner of an e-commerce site must be prepared for problems. In addition to these security issues, you must consider security for e-commerce transactions as discussed in the previous chapter of this minibook. Here are a few things that you can do to bolster the security of any e-commerce site:

✦ **Add a copyright notice to the bottom of each page.**

✦ **If your client is a photographer or is selling fine art online, make sure each image bears either a copyright symbol and the name of the creator or a watermark.** Furthermore, you can incorporate JavaScript on the page, which prevents visitors from right-clicking an image and downloading it to their computer.

✦ **To prevent high-resolution images from being downloaded, use JavaScript to implement an image swap when users mouse over the image.** The replacement image can either be a warning that copyright laws protect the image, or it can be a low-resolution version of the same image that the visitor would not want to download.

✦ **Copy all your client's website files to CD or DVD.** If the server's equipment crashes or a hacker destroys the site, you can quickly get your client up and running again by uploading the files to the server. Archival CDs or DVDs are the best bet. However, these are quite expensive. If you use them, make sure your rates reflect the added expense. Alternatively, you can use media from a quality manufacturer like Memorex, which should last for a long time. An external hard drive that is used exclusively for backing up images and files is another alternative.

✦ **Make sure the web-hosting service has adequate protection.** Hackers often know how to access hosting service control panels. A successful attack on an e-commerce site through a control panel can be devastating. For example, the hacker can clean out your client's database.

✦ **Advise your client to change his password frequently and to choose one that cannot be easily guessed by competitors or hackers.** This is very important because many hosting services use a combination of the client's e-mail address as the user name and a client-generated password to gain access to the control panel. The best password is alphanumeric and at least eight characters in length.

✦ **To ensure security for all transactions on an e-commerce site, choose a secure server that offers 128-bit SSL encryption.**

Following through on every sale

Businesses that succeed rely on repeat customers to keep the ball rolling. It's expensive to entice new customers to use a product or service. Happy customers who use a product repeatedly and refer friends and business associates are the hallmark of a successful business. The easiest way to get customers to use a product again and again is to treat them like royalty before and after the sale. Here are some tips for following through on a sale:

✦ **Send each customer a thank you letter via e-mail.** The letter also serves as a confirmation of the order.

✦ **Send each customer a copy of the invoice via e-mail.** This is yet another confirmation of the order, and it shows customers that their business is valued.

✦ **Send the customer a message letting her know when her order will ship.** This is another opportunity for the e-commerce company to get its name in front of the customer.

✦ **Send each customer a tracking number when the order has been shipped.** Keeping customers informed is good business.

✦ **Invite each customer to participate in a survey a few days after the order has been received.** Asking customers to participate in a survey makes them feel more important. A discount on future orders can be used as an incentive to ensure that a high percentage of customers participate in the survey.

Book VIII
Chapter 3

Adding E-Commerce
to Your Site

Book IX

Deploying and Managing the Site

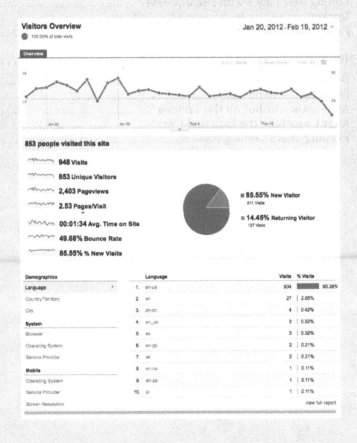

Contents at a Glance

Chapter 1: Optimizing and Testing the Site

In This Chapter

✔ Preparing to launch the site

✔ Ensuring search engines find your site

✔ Researching keywords

You jump through hoops to create a good-looking site that's functional. It's a great feeling to complete the design. At this stage, you may smile and think you're ready to upload your masterpiece to a web-hosting server for an adoring public. But your work is far from done, Sparky. In your humble opinion, you've created the best site in the world, but if the target audience doesn't embrace it, you come up with egg on your face, which is not any fun at all.

So the first task on your To Do list is to make sure that the site is user friendly by testing it on a select audience. After it's been thoroughly tested, you need to tweak your code to make sure the site can be found by search engines. Search engine optimization (SEO) is an art unto itself, and its logic changes by the minute because folks are always trying to "beat the system" to get their site to the top of the search engine results.

In this chapter, we show you how to make sure the site you've lovingly slaved over is user friendly, plus we also show you the latest tried and true SEO techniques.

Look Before You Leap: What to Do Before Launch

Your client is jumpy and anxious to make the site live. Or you built a site for your company or yourself, and you're chomping at the bit to get it out there. If you do so before making sure everything is up to snuff, though, you do yourself and your client a disservice. First and foremost, you damage your reputation as a designer, both with the client and potential clients. Or, if you've built the site for yourself or your company, you do yourself or your company a disservice. If you launch a site that contains code errors, broken links, and so on, you'll get visitors, but they won't stick around for long, and they definitely won't be back. In the upcoming sections, we show you a few things you need to consider before uploading the site to a server.

Develop a checklist

Start by creating a pre-launch checklist to make sure you double-check everything. You can even use the list for all the sites you launch. Write it once; use it countless times. (Like reusable code, a reusable list is a wonderful thing.) Your list should include the following items:

✦ **Check each and every link.** Nothing is more embarrassing than creating a website with links that work on some pages but not on others. You can safeguard against this happening if you create a template that includes the navigation links, and then use this for each page you create. While you're checking links, make sure you have the target right. The *target* is the browser window in which the linked page opens. If the site has links to pages outside your client's domain, good practice mandates opening them in another window.

If you're using Dreamweaver to create your pages, choose Site➪Check Links Sitewide. Press Ctrl+F8 (Windows) or ⌘+F8 (Mac), and Dreamweaver lists any broken links in the Results panel.

From the files of Search and Replace: If you find a link used sitewide that's not configured properly, choose Site➪Change Link Sitewide to open a dialog box from which you can change all instances of the link in one fell swoop.

✦ **Does your fancy code work?** If any of the pages in your site are PHP or ASP, make sure each script works as expected.

✦ **Does the site load quickly?** Web surfers are an impatient lot and won't wait for a site to download. If you did your homework and optimized all your images (as we describe in Book V, Chapter 3) and other interactive content, the site should download in fewer than 12 seconds. And that's 12 seconds for the worst-case scenario in your client's intended audience. If your site loads in 12 seconds for users with a cable hookup but some of the intended audience use DSL (which is slower), you have to go back to the drawing board.

If you feel that your web pages aren't running on all cylinders, consider using Yahoo! YSlow. This tool, which is integrated with Firefox, Chrome, Opera, and Safari browsers, analyzes pages to determine why they're loading slowly. The criterion was developed by Yahoo, and we think it's a useful tool for troubleshooting problem pages. For more information on YSlow, visit `http://yslow.org`.

✦ **Does the site include a call to action?** If your client is selling merchandise or services, Marketing 101 dictates that the site should ask the visitor to do something: a *call to action*. At the very least, the site should include some type of special offer that tempts the visitor into clicking a Check Out button. Another type of call to action might be a form that requests contact information for a mailing list or newsletter. Regardless, every page should have some sort of call to action.

✦ **Is the site easy to navigate?** Make sure that site visitors don't need a PhD to figure out the navigation menu. Try to avoid being cute and designing an *avant-garde* menu that uses only icons. Some people will get it, but the ones who don't will be visiting the site of your competitor — or if you create the site for a client, your client's competitor. If your site design uses graphics in the navigation menu, make sure you have redundant text-only links at the bottom of each page, below the fold. Search engine robots recognize only text-only links when indexing the site.

✦ **Is the content relevant and easy to understand?** If you're working for a client, chances are that she created most of the text for the site and provided images as well. It's your job to put it in a palatable format that visitors can easily digest. Scan each page and make sure the headlines and links provide a message to visitors. This is especially important if the site has a lot of text. If you created the text for your website, and you're not a writer, consider hiring an editor and a proofreader to give the site a critical read.

You can break up a lot of content using headlines, bullet points, bold text, white space, hyperlinks, or images. Internet surfers use these visual clues to quickly find the information they want. You can also plant relevant keywords in headings when optimizing the site for search engines.

✦ **Read each page.** The information provided by you or your client should pique visitors' curiosity and inform them. The home page should grab visitors by the lapel and make them want to click through to other pages on the site. The text should also be relevant and peppered with keywords potential visitors will use when searching for sites similar to your client's. However, when you do optimize the page for search engines, make sure the sentences are readable and not keyword gibberish.

✦ **Make sure that each page has a balance of text and images.** Unless you're doing a portfolio page for a photographer, the images on each page should complement and balance the text. Too much of one or the other presents a confusing message.

✦ **Is the text easy to read?** Make sure the target audience can easily read the text. Even if you or your client is a techie, make sure the text doesn't include jargon. Write the text for the least-common denominator: in other words, for the person who knows nothing about the product or service being marketed by the website. If the content doesn't meet this standard, you or your client needs to make it more clear before the site goes live. Also, make sure that the text font is easy to read and that the font color contrasts well with the background for easy readability.

✦ **Are the paragraphs short?** Long blocks of text might make visitors shy away from the site — that trudging through it is too much work. Send long blocks of text back to your client and ask him to cut out anything that isn't relevant. When all else fails, refer your client to a good copy editor.

✦ **Are the pages consistent?** Each page should have a common look and feel. The navigation menu needs to be consistent on all pages. If it's not, the visitor might think he's clicked away from the site.

✦ **Is the site complete?** In other words, do all or most of the pages have content? It's bad practice to leave a bunch of `Coming Soon` or `Under Construction` messages throughout the site. Missing content frustrates both visitors and your client. If you're under a deadline to launch the site by a certain date and you don't have all the information, it's in your best interest to not launch the site until all pages are complete. If you're creating the site for a client, and she tells you to launch the site before she's given you all the information, you have to be the voice of reason.

✦ **Make sure every image loads.** If you end up with a placeholder with no image, this indicates you might have changed the image's filename or inadvertently moved the image to another folder.

✦ **What's above the fold?** The most important (must-see) information on every page should appear above the *fold,* which is the top portion of a web page visible when the page first loads, without scrolling. Think of a newspaper: its top half. This is the most important part of the entire page, so use it wisely. At the same time, make sure that no images are cut off by the fold, and also that no part of a paragraph is cut off by the fold. When performing this test, make sure to resize your desktop to that of the intended audience.

✦ **How much of the information is below the fold?** If each page of the site has a lot of information that appears below the fold, visitors have to scroll down to access all the information. If this is the case, consider splitting a lengthy page into two or more pages. Alternatively, have your client edit the content.

✦ **Test all forms and other interactive content.** When you submit a form, make sure the data goes to the intended destination or is added to the applicable database.

✦ **Check the spelling.** Most HTML editors come with a spell checker. Don't be unprofessional and upload a site with typos or bad grammar. If you're in doubt of the correct spelling of a technical term, ask your client or find the correct spelling at a reputable online dictionary. Of course HTML editors aren't perfect and may not know whether they're, there, or their is correct for the paragraph being checked. When in doubt, let a second set of eyes proofread the page, preferably a copy editor.

✦ **If the site has options to order merchandise, make sure that transactions can be completed.** You can easily check this before going live by setting the price of items to one cent and then buying the items to make sure you get all the way to the checkout. Also, make sure the confirmation page appears, notifying the buyer that the transaction is complete. You do have a confirmation page, don't you?

Get opinions

A dozen jurors are used in a court of law. You should have at least that many people rendering judgment on your web design. Big caveat: The people who give their opinions on your design should be totally impartial. In other words, don't use your client's employees or your own when you want feedback on your design. For that matter, don't ask any family members or close friends for feedback. You want the truth and nothing but the truth, even if some of the comments are critical.

Do a beta test

If possible, set up a beta test before going live. When you conduct a beta test, you upload your design into a folder on the server and send the URL to your testers. They provide feedback about site usability, aesthetics, and so on. Beta testing is especially useful when you have a really big site with lots of pages and almost as many links as there are Smiths in the New York City phone book. You'll be a candidate for a good hair-coloring product if you tackle testing a huge site by yourself. For more information on beta testing, refer to Chapter 2 of this minibook.

In addition to testing the site for usability, try to use beta testers who are capable of finding bugs that are lurking in your code. Identifying usability issues and other problems greatly enhances the chances of the site succeeding when it goes public. The test can also determine how real-world users react to the site.

In a typical beta test, you contact a potpourri of users to try out the site for a few weeks. Yes, we said weeks, so you have to include this time as part of the total project. During that time, you get feedback on the site design, usability, any potential problems, such as broken links or missing images, and any features that are not clear to the testers. During this time, you monitor the server side to make sure that the data is going to the right places. You also monitor any server scripts (such as mail forwarding) to make sure that data is being forwarded to the proper parties. During a beta test, you typically forward all data and e-mails to one address.

Your best candidates for beta testers are actual users of the product or service for which the website is designed. Your client might be able to supply some beta testers from his customer base. If the website is for your company, contact someone in marketing. If you're building the website for a small company, contact existing customers and ask them to test the site. Bribe them with a discount if you have to. If the website is for a start-up business, or for personal uses, you'll have to coordinate the testing. With a good cross-section of your company's or your client's customer base or intended audience, the test is more effective. The information you receive can give you a good idea of site usability and the value of the site from members of the website's intended audience.

Get feedback

Setting up a beta site and enlisting testers is a lot of work. Your beta testers might have a good time filling in the forms, placing mock orders, and checking out the features of the site, but if you don't get feedback, it's an exercise in futility. When you enlist beta testers, tell them what you're looking for. Any group of individuals has varying degrees of initiative, and beta testers are no exception. Expect some of your testers to give you lots of feedback: others, little or none. Keep tabs on who says what and send reminder e-mails to the people you're not hearing from.

Throughout the course of the beta test, address issues when they come up. If you come across usability issues, tweak your design. Exterminate any bugs as soon as they are reported. After correcting an issue, post the revised page, and then contact the person(s) who reported the bug and ask them whether your tweak resolved the problem.

E-mail is an excellent way to get feedback, but forms enable the designer to create a set of structured questions. With this type of survey, you can target questions that show how often the tester visits similar sites and how often he uses the product or service. Figure 1-1 shows a mini-survey form for beta testers of a hypothetical photography website.

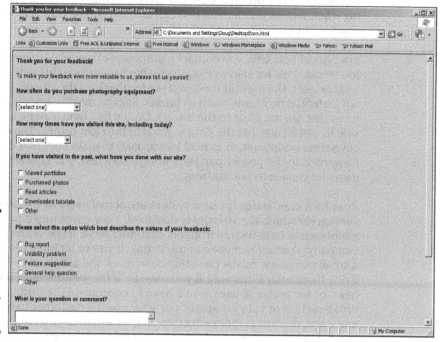

Figure 1-1:
Send
me your
answer; fill
in a form,
mine forever
more....

Follow up with beta testers

After the test is over, you have a lot of data that shows you the best features of the site as well as issues that need attention. However, you can gain some closure, so to speak, by doing a follow-up survey. Send an e-mail to all test participants and ask them about their overall experience with the test site — and, most importantly, whether they liked it and found the content relevant and useful.

In addition to the basic questions, find out how often each participant used the site. You can count on the answers being somewhat inflated (numbers inflated 20 to 30 percent would be the norm), unless you have a meticulous tester who logged everything concerned with the test. When you're compiling your results, you know that the answers from the power users carry more weight than those of casual users.

Another set of pertinent questions is how the testers like specific features or areas of the site. Find out how often they used specific sections of the site plus how they liked the navigation system and any interactive features on the site. If the site includes forms and features, such as a search engine, make sure you get feedback on those as well.

Another set of questions should address the issues most reported by testers. The answers to these questions can enable you to find out whether your beta test tweaks took care of the issues.

Finally, ask your testers to rate the site compared with their experience on similar sites. You can ask users to rate the site on a scale from 1 to 10, or ask them to sum up their experience in a short paragraph. Again, you'll weigh the pertinence of each answer based on how often the tester visited the site.

Tweak your design

The responses from your beta testers enable you to perform last-minute tweaks on the site before it goes live. The issues raised by the beta testers might be related to design, content, or both. If it's design, you have to put on your thinking cap to figure out the best way to overcome the issues. If it's content, your client has to belly up to the table and do some editing. The worst-case scenario would be if you had too many issues to resolve within the current design. If this is the case, postpone the launch and address the issues, perhaps with a major redesign. If so, you'd be wise to do another beta test before launching. Postponing the launch may tick off a few people, especially if you're doing the site for a client. However, it's best to have everything in order before the site goes live. Your client and all parties concerned will be glad you did.

Search Engine Optimization and Marketing

If you build it, they will not come. And that's the truth. There are more sites on the web than Carter has little liver pills — in other words, way too many for people to care about the masterpiece you just designed. If the site you design is to succeed, you have to give your target audience a reason to care. Hopefully, your design and the site content are enough to keep visitors at the website, but first you need to grab that herd of horses by the scruff of the neck and drag them to water. You can achieve part of the task by optimizing the site for search engines. This brings some of the horses to the pond. To search out the thoroughbreds for their sip of Perrier, though, you have to resort to more esoteric marketing techniques. (Note that this discussion is about optimizing your site so that external search engines can find it; in Book VII, Chapter 3, we show you how to generate a Search box for your site that visitors can use to search your site's content.)

Search engine optimization (SEO), like the proverbial well, is deep. We show you how to optimize your site and present some marketing techniques in the upcoming sections. These are really just the tip of the iceberg. For a heaping plateful of website optimization techniques, pick up a copy of *Search Engine Optimization For Dummies,* 4th Edition, by Peter Kent or *Search Engine Optimization All-In-One For Dummies,* 2nd Edition, by Bruce Clay and Susan Esparza.

If you know how to properly optimize a website for search engines, you can make a lot of money — in fact, maybe enough money to give up your day job. Many visits to commercial websites occur as the result of users typing pertinent keywords in a search engine. Your job as a Web designer and builder is to have the site you design show up at or near the top of the first page of results from a keyword search. We know: Easier said than done. Scores of words have been written on optimizing a site for search engines — enough to fill several books. The following tips can help you to optimize your client's site:

✦ **Test keywords.** Brainstorm with your client or other employees of your company and come up with a list of keywords or phrases that you think users enter into search engines to find sites similar to your client's. Test the keywords and phrases in the major search engines such as Google and Yahoo! to test your theory. Discard the phrases or keywords that don't bring up sites that would be visited by your target audience. If a keyword or phrase brings up the website of your client's fiercest competitor, put that keyword at the top of the list.

✦ **Jot down the titles of your client's competitors' websites.** Also include those of similar businesses that are in the top 10 percent of a search result using keywords or phrases that customers use to find sites similar to your client's. Use a variation of these titles for your client's website.

✦ **Create a keyword-rich title for each page of the website.** You can modify the title by changing page properties. Create a unique title with keywords that are likely to be used to find your client's site. A site's title is displayed in the search engine's results page. Some designers think that a series of keywords or phrases will get the job done. However, just because the site's title vaults a site near the top of the first page of search results, it won't necessarily drive traffic to the site. In addition to being keyword rich, the title must make sense and give users a reason to click through to the site.

✦ **Create a keyword-rich description for the website.** This powerful `<meta description>` tag shows up in the search engine results. Mirror some of the keywords in the title, but make sure the description is readable and not a bunch of keyword gibberish. People won't visit a site with a description that doesn't look like it was written by an intelligent adult.

✦ **Make sure that the URLs entice visitors to click through to the site.** The URL can contain a keyword as well. If you design a site for a photography store, and one page is dedicated to telephoto lenses, which page would you visit if searching for "telephoto lenses"?

    www.photosuppliesrus.com/products123.asp

    www.photosuppliesrus.com/telephotolenses.asp

✦ **Mirror the keywords from your title tag in the alt text of each image on the home page.** *Alt text* is displayed in text readers to describe an image. Some browsers also show alt text as a tooltip when the visitors pause the cursor over the image. Make sure the alt text is readable as well.

✦ **Use keywords in the file names of images.** Most digital cameras have their own naming protocol, but those filenames aren't logical or decipherable. Rename the images with a logical name that contains a keyword related to the page on which the image appears. Using the photography store example, if the image depicts a Canon zoom lens, rename the image to reflect the model number of the lens: for example, `CanonEF70-200mm.jpg`.

✦ **Mirror the keywords from your title page in the text on the home page.** The redundancy of keywords gives the site a higher ranking with search engines.

✦ **Create a text menu at the bottom of the page if your design uses images or JavaScript for menu navigation links.** Search engine robots have a difficult time following JavaScript links but can easily follow the redundant text links you place at the bottom of the page. Search engine robots cannot read text on navigation menu images, but you can help the process by adding an `alt` tag to the menu image that tells the name of the page to which the button is linked.

✦ **If possible, include keywords anytime you use a heading style on the home page.** For example, if you're a photographer who photographs weddings, on your wedding photography page, create a headline that includes the words, "Wedding Photography" and perhaps include the area in which you photograph.

✦ **Add content to the meta tags in the head section of each page's HTML.** The `<meta name>` tag enables you to add a keyword-rich description of the website. Limit the description to 250 characters, including spaces; this seems to be the limit that search engine spiders recognize. The `<meta keywords>` tag enables you to add keywords and key phrases that pertain to sites, such as the one you're creating. You can include up to 255 keywords/key phrases. Enter a comma to separate keywords and key phrases. Remember to mirror the key phrases you include in the `<title>` tag. Search engines like redundancy — to a limit.

Don't repeat a keyword more than five times in the `<meta keywords>` tag because many search engines consider this practice as spamming and may remove the site from their index.

When creating keywords for the site, include common misspellings of words in your key phrases. Remember to include the town(s) or regions in which your client does business. You might also want to consider adding all lowercase and all uppercase variations of what you and your client feel are the most popular key phrases, as many people type with all caps or all lowercase.

✦ **Create links to other websites and have them link to yours.** Many search engines increase a site's rank due to its popularity. These search engines include the number of links to your site in that criterion. Read how to do this in the following section.

Don't resort to trickery to try to vault your client's site to the top of the heap. In the past, web designers repeated keywords and key phrases relentlessly beneath the regular site content. To make these invisible to the user, they used the same color as the background, or a color that was one decimal different. Visitors couldn't see the words, but search engine spiders could. Search engines are wise to this trickery and drop a site from their index when they discover a designer's chicanery. Other spamming techniques include adding keywords that aren't related to the site, creating multiple instances of the home page with a different URL and title, or using multiple instances of the same tag.

Using the Google Keyword Tool

Google has a powerful tool you can use to research keywords. You enter a term, the URL for your website, and the type of service or product being promoted from the site, and the Keyword tool lists keywords and shows you the level of competition for each keyword. If you can find a relevant keyword for which the competition is low, your site will appear higher in the search rankings. If you choose a keyword with high competition, your site is the proverbial needle in the haystack. The trick is to find keywords for which there is low or medium competition and that are used frequently as search terms. To use the Google Keyword tool, follow these steps:

1. **Launch your favorite web browser and navigate to Google's Keyword Tool Box (**`www.googlekeywordtool.com`**).**

   In addition to finding keywords, you can use the site for other tasks (see Figure 1-2).

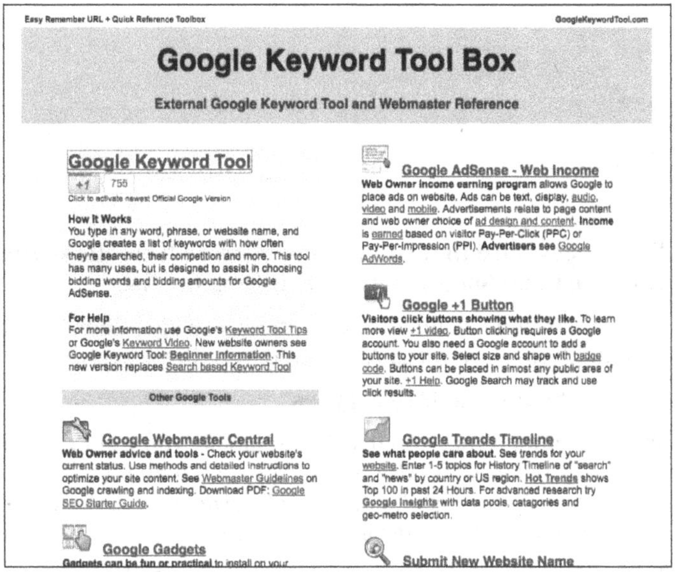

Figure 1-2: We're gonna find some relevant keywords.

2. **Click Google Keyword tool.**

   The browser refreshes and takes you to Google AdWords Keyword Tool (see Figure 1-3).

3. **Enter a keyword you want to include in the search by entering it in the Include Terms text box and then clicking the plus sign (+).**

   You can enter as many keywords as you like. Click the plus sign (+) to add additional keywords to the list. If you type two keywords that you want to appear in a specific order, type a quote before the keywords and one after the keywords ("Sarasota weddings"), and then click the plus sign (+) to add the keyword phrase to the list.

Figure 1-3:
Ye Olde
Keyword
Tool.

4. Enter a keyword that you want to exclude from the search, and then click the plus sign (+) to exclude it from the list.

You can exclude as many keywords as you like. Click the plus sign (+) to add additional keywords to exclude from the search.

5. Choose the desired Match Types.

We recommend that you use Broad unless you want to search for a specific keyword idea, in which case you would choose Exact. If you choose Phrase the search results include all terms that include the keyword word or phrase you enter in the next step.

6. In the Word or Phrase text box, enter the word or phrase for the type of business or service for which you want to find keywords.

You can enter more than one word or phrase. Each keyword or phrase must appear on its own line. Press Enter/Return to put additional keywords or phrases on a new line.

7. In the Website text box, enter the URL for the website.

8. In the Category text box, enter the category for the business or service for which you are attempting to find keywords.

You can choose a category from the drop-down list, or type the category that best describes the business or service for which you are attempting to find keywords.

9. (Optional) Select the Only Show Ideas Closely Related to My Search Terms check box.

This narrows the amount of keywords or phrases that are returned. We suggest you leave this unchecked because you may find a keyword or phrase you never suspected would be useful.

10. **(Optional) Modify the Advanced Options and Filters.**

The default choices are for the part of the world in which you live, the language spoken in that part of the world, and for desktop and laptop computers. To change any term, click it to expand the area and see the additional choices.

11. **Enter the dreaded Captcha terms.**

This is Google's front line defense against robots accessing the site.

12. **Click the Search button.**

The keyword finder thinks about it for a while and returns a list of keywords showing the amount of competition, the number of searches per month both globally and locally (see Figure 1-4).

13. **Make a note of the keywords with Medium and Low competition that have a large number of monthly searches.**

These keywords are more likely to bring success.

14. **Repeat Steps 6–13 as needed to generate a list of keywords for the site you've designed.**

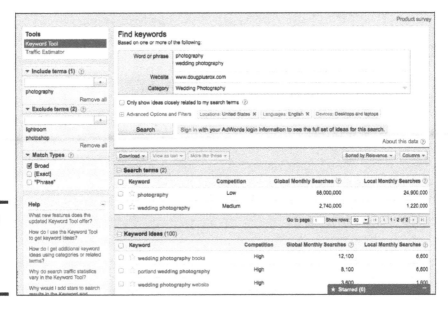

Figure 1-4: Get your red-hot, juicy keywords.

Chapter 2: Uploading the Site

*A*fter you perform your final tweaks on your design, get feedback from beta testers, and optimize the site for search engines (see the preceding chapter), you're ready to upload your design to the server and go live at five — or whatever time you decide to go live. You can upload the site using Dreamweaver, or with a File Transfer Protocol (FTP) client like FileZilla.

After you upload it, you wait for the world to beat a path to your home page. Not. They won't come because the site isn't on anybody's radar screen yet. You solve this problem by submitting the site to popular search engines. If you optimized the site correctly, the site will start getting some traffic.

We show you how to do all these things in this chapter, and the fact that you're here means that you're ready to upload. Read on if you're ready to beam your site into cyberspace — to infinity and beyond.

Going Live

After tweaking the site based on your responses from beta testers or from your checklist, you're ready to go live. If you did your test on the server, it's a simple matter of transferring the files from the beta test folder to the root folder of the website. If you did all your testing on your local machine, upload the pages and related files to the server. You can use an application (such as Adobe Dreamweaver) to upload your content, or you can use an FTP client to upload files to the web server. We use both Dreamweaver and the FileZilla FTP client to handle all our file-transfer needs, depending on whether the site has been defined in Dreamweaver. We cover both options in the upcoming sections.

Uploading the site with Dreamweaver

Dreamweaver features a sophisticated set of commands that enable you to connect to a web server and upload files to that server — in Dreamweaver-speak, "put the files on the server" — or download files from the server —

"get the files from the server." To upload pages using Dreamweaver, follow these steps:

1. **If the Files panel isn't visible, choose Window⇨Files to open the Files panel. (See Figure 2-1.) Alternatively, press F8.**

The Files panel shows the local files associated with the site on which you're working. For your convenience and ease of viewing, Figure 2-1 shows the panel undocked.

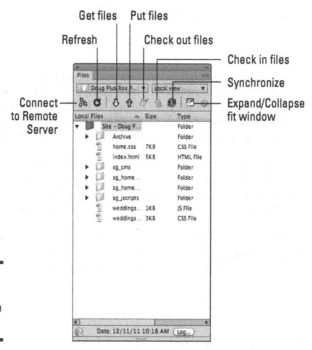

Get files   Put files

Refresh   Check out files

Check in files

Synchronize

Connect to Remote Server

Expand/Collapse fit window

Figure 2-1:
The default layout of the Files panel.

2. **Click the Connects to Remote Host button.**

Dreamweaver connects to the remote server using the credentials you supplied when you set up the site. For information about setting up a site with Dreamweaver, see Book II, Chapter 4.

3. **Click the Expand/Collapse button.**

Dreamweaver increases the size of the panel and splits the panel into two panes. The pane on the left shows the files on the remote server, and the pane on the right shows the files on the local machine. (See Figure 2-2.)

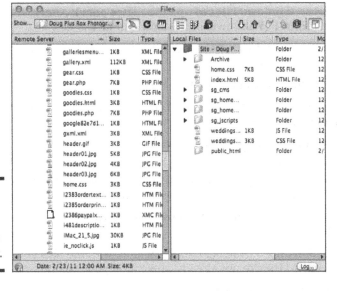

Figure 2-2:
Remote
on the left,
local on the
right. Roger.

4. **Select the files you want to upload to the server from the Local Files window.**

   If you're uploading edited pages on which you haven't changed any associated files, you don't need to select files (such as images) that are associated with the files you're uploading unless they've changed.

5. **Click the Put Files button.**

   Dreamweaver opens the Dependent Files dialog box, from which you can upload files associated with the page, such as images and so on.

6. **Click Yes.**

   Dreamweaver uploads the selected files, along with all files associated with the selected file.

   Alternatively, click No if you know that the files associated with the file you're uploading have not been changed, and no new files have been linked to the file.

You can also upload a page you're editing by clicking the File Management icon (looks like two arrows, one pointing up and one pointing down) and then clicking Put. Alternatively, you can press Ctrl+Shift+U (Windows) or ⌘+Shift+U (Mac).

You can also download files from the remote server by following these steps:

1. **Choose Window⇨Files to open the Files panel. Alternatively, press Ctrl+Shift+F (Windows) or ⌘+Shift+F (Mac).**

The Files panel shows the local files associated with the site on which you're working.

2. **Click the Connects to Remote Host button.**

Dreamweaver connects to the remote server using the credentials you supplied when you set up the site.

3. **Click the Expand/Collapse button.**

Dreamweaver increases the size of the panel and splits the panel into two panes. The pane on the left shows the files on the remote server, and the pane on the right shows the files on the local machine.

4. **Select the files you want to download to the server from the Remote Site window.**

You don't need to select files associated with the files you're downloading unless they're not already present on your computer.

5. **Click the Get Files button.**

Dreamweaver displays the Dependent Files dialog box.

6. **Click Yes.**

Dreamweaver downloads the selected files into the applicable site's folders on your local machine.

Uploading pages with an FTP client

Dreamweaver file management is a wonderful thing. However, if you need to upload files for which you haven't set up a site in Dreamweaver, an FTP client is the ideal solution. An FTP client also comes in handy when you want to download files from a server — for example, when you're doing a site makeover. Quite a few FTP applications are available. We use FileZilla. The current version is 3.5.3, and it's free as of this writing. FileZilla is easy to use, and is flexible enough to upload an entire website at once or upload single or multiple files. You can download a copy of the FileZilla FTP client from http://filezilla-project.org. To upload files using FileZilla, follow these steps:

1. **Launch the application.**

The FileZilla interface is shown in Figure 2-3.

2. **Navigate to the folder on your computer where you stored the files you want to upload.**

The window on the left side of the interface shows the files on your local machine. Click the down arrow to the right of the current folder window in the Local Site window to access your system's directory structure. The window below Local Site displays individual files.

Click to access your system's directory structure.

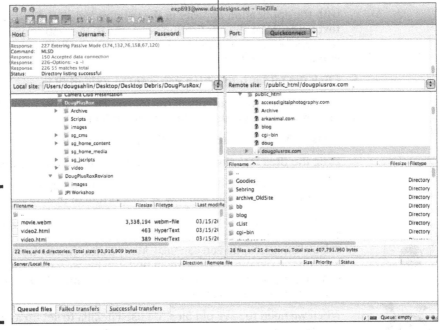

Figure 2-3:
An
innocuous
interface
for an
application
named
FileZilla.

3. Enter the host URL as well as your username and password in the appropriate fields.

You usually don't have to change the default port. Figure 2-4 shows the proper nomenclature for the site URL. Some web-hosting companies are different. If you enter the URL but can't connect, refer to your web-hosting company's technical support. In most instances, all you'll have to change is the port number. Make sure you're using FTP credentials and not the credentials to access your web-hosting account. Most web-hosting services have a cPanel (control panel) in which you set up e-mail, FTP access, and so on.

Figure 2-4:
Beam them
up, Scotty.

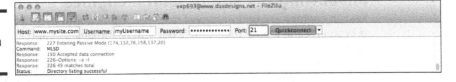

4. **Click the Quickconnect button.**

   FileZilla connects to the website. The status of each task you perform with the application appears in the window below the URL and other text fields. After the application connects to the web server, it displays the remote files on the right side of the interface. Folders have a question mark (?) icon on them.

5. **Click the folder into which you want to upload files.**

   FileZilla reads the contents of the folder. The window below Remote Site displays individual files in the selected folder.

6. **In the left window, select the files you want to upload.**

7. **Drag the files into the applicable folder in the right window.**

   FileZilla uploads the files to the server. When you upload a file, the progress is displayed in the window at the bottom of the application.

If you're uploading edited files with the same name as those on the remote server, a warning dialog box appears telling you that the target file already exists, listing actions you can take. Many times, you do want to overwrite a file on the remote server with an updated file with the same name. In some cases, you might want to save the old file in a different folder in case you ever need to revert to it.

When we need to save old files, we use FileZilla to set up a folder called Archive at the Remote Host. We copy the previous version of a file to this folder before uploading the new one.

What Next? The Launch Is Not the End of the Project

If you think you bask in the glory of a job well done and break out the bubbly after the site goes public, think again. Just because you built it, doesn't mean they will come. Given the number of websites on the 'Net — everyone and his little brother seems to have one — your lovely design will bask in anonymity unless the site is made visible to the search engines. In the following sections, we discuss briefly what needs to be done to make a site succeed.

Submitting the site to search engines

Search engines are technological marvels. Think about it: All you have to do is type in some words regarding what you're looking for, and a few seconds later, you have hundreds of web pages to peruse. Search engines aren't mind readers, though. They don't know when you uploaded the squeaky-clean website you designed that loads at the speed of sound and is turbocharged with enough interactive bells and whistles to keep visitors entertained for hours. To be on a search engine's radar screen, you have to submit the site to search engines.

Submitting the site is like throwing a needle into a haystack, and that needle is going to be hard to find unless you do something to make it stand out. To make a site rank high in search engine results pages, you have to optimize the pages for the keywords and key phrases that the intended audience is likely to use to find the products or services offered on the site. You can either optimize the site yourself or hire a company to optimize the site. Site optimization is a black art that warrants a book of its own. (Visit www.dummies.com for many titles on SEO.)

After you optimize the pages for search engines, you're ready to submit the site to the search engines that your client's intended audience is most likely to use. Many search engines are out there. However, you should concern yourself with only the most popular search engines, such as Google and Bing. If the site you designed caters to a niche market, maybe you can find a search engine dedicated to that market. Your client should be able to tell you whether that's the case.

After you identify which search engines you want to submit to, you can consider several ways of doing that. The topic of search engine optimization and submitting your site to search engines is ever changing, but we cover the current methods of search engine optimization in Chapter 1 of this mini-book. (You can read more about this topic in *Search Engine Optimization For Dummies,* 4th Edition, by Peter Kent.)

Submitting your site to specific search engines

After the website is optimized for search engines, it's time to submit the site to search engines. Submit the site to the most popular search engines. Of course, what's popular now might be *passé* in two or three years. The following is a list of popular search engines and the URLs to the pages where you submit your site:

✦ **Google:** Google is considered the most popular search engine for the masses. You can submit a site to Google at

> ww.google.com/submityourcontent

✦ **Bing Search:** This is another popular search engine affiliated with Yahoo! You can submit your site (for free) to Bing Search at this URL:

> https://ssl.bing.com/webmaster/SubmitSitePage.aspx

Submitting to Google and Bing will help put the site on their radar screen, but site submission doesn't happen overnight. After submitting the site, you may have to wait a couple of weeks before seeing any increase in site traffic. However, a complete tutorial on submitting your site to search engines is beyond the scope of this book.

Don't resubmit the website to a search engine unless you made significant changes to the site or re-optimized pages using a different title or description, or until you have changed the keywords. Continually submitting a site with no changes is considered "spamming the search engine" and can negatively affect the site's rank within the search engine.

You can find services that enable you to submit your site to multiple search engines for no fee by typing **free search engine submission** in your favorite search engine. However, many of the sites that submit for free will try to sell you on using their paid services or will add you to some sort of mailing list. If you decide to use one of these services to submit the website, read the fine print. *Remember:* There are no free lunches.

Using a service to submit your site

If you contract an SEO company to optimize the site, chances are that the company will also submit it for you. If you optimized the site yourself and don't want to go through the hassle of submitting the site to multiple search engines, you can employ a service to submit the site for you.

Like all services, site-submission services come in multiple flavors and varying degrees of initiative. The price charged by the company depends on the number of search engines to which it submits the site, how often it resubmits the site, and other services included in the package, such as sponsored links and so on. Most services use proprietary software to submit the site.

A good search engine–submission company will also know the ins and outs of each search engine and whether the search engine has specialized directories for products and services to which it can submit your site.

You can find a plethora of search engine–submission companies by searching for **search engine submission service**. However, just because a submission service's site is listed at the top of a results page doesn't mean that it's a good service. (Can you say, "Sponsored links"?) Like any other service, make sure that the company is legitimate and that their employees didn't fall off the turnip truck yesterday. A reputable service has testimonials from satisfied customers. Be a savvy buyer. Don't take the service's word for it. See whether the sites listed in the testimonials are still active. If so, see if you can contact the person who wrote the testimonial and ask him for his opinion — off the record, so to speak.

Determining Whether Your SEO Is Working

Even though you submit a site to several search engines or hire a site-submission firm to perform this task, it takes a while to determine what effect SEO is having for your client's website. First and foremost, search engines don't index a submitted site overnight. Depending on the search engine, it might take several weeks to get indexed. The submit page on each search engine usually gives you an idea of how long it takes a submitted site to be added to the search engine's index.

One indication that SEO is working is if your client is getting more orders or inquiries after the site is submitted. However, there are more scientific ways to determine the impact of SEO. Most web-hosting services provide a means by which you and your client can monitor the number of visits to your site and the means by which the traffic was drawn to the site. The following sections provide useful information on website stats, plus what to do with the information you receive.

Accessing your web stats

With most web-hosting services, site stats are accessed through the web service's control panel. In addition to being a wonderful thing, they are artistic and colorful, what with all the bar charts and pie graphs. To read site stats, log on to the site's control panel, click the applicable icon, and . . . *voilà!* Instant stats! Many stat packages show a graphical representation of site traffic, as shown on the left in Figure 2-6. In addition, you'll see other information, such as the number of hits, files, pages, and visits. With most services, you click the desired month to get more details, as shown on the right in Figure 2-5. We know what you're thinking: What does all this stuff mean? Fear not, intrepid designer! Please fast-forward to the next section for nontechnical definitions of web stats terms.

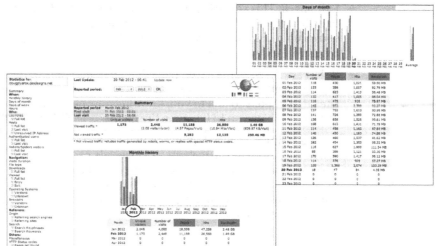

Figure 2-5:
Click a month to get more details about monthly site stats.

Understanding web stats

After you crack open the statistics for a site, you have to decipher what they mean. Unless you're a trained professional, the stats might seem like gibberish. The following list is designed to demystify web stat terms:

+ **Hits:** A *hit* occurs any time the web server delivers a file. The number of hits can be misleading, though, because several files might need to be downloaded for an individual page. For example, in addition to the HTML document for a web page, images, a CSS, animations, and so on must be downloaded as well. A single visit to any page on a site results in multiple hits. Remember that copious amounts of hits do not justify breaking out the bubbly and patting yourself on the back.

+ **Visits:** A *visit* is logged whenever a unique visit is made to the site. This is by far the best barometer you have to determine how successful your SEO efforts are.

   A word of caution: Some stats services tally a visit whenever a new page is accessed on the site. If a visitor navigates back to the home page after initially landing there, the home page has another hit, but it is not a unique visit. If this is the case, the stats service provides a listing for Unique Visitors, which tells you how many visitors have accessed the site.

+ **Entry pages:** This statistic gives the URL for the page on which the visitor first landed. If your client sells many products and services, this information shows you which optimized pages are doing the best job of driving visitors to the site.

+ **Exit pages:** This statistic shows you which page visitors are viewing prior to exiting the site. While everybody has to leave sometime, if one page shows up more than others, it could indicate that the page isn't being received well by visitors.

+ **Referrers:** A *referrer* is a web page that contains a link to one of the pages in your client's site. Referrals may also come from search engines or other sites that choose to link to you. Knowing how people are finding the website enables you to fine-tune the methods used to market the site.

+ **Search strings:** This stat shows which keywords and key phrases the visitor used to find the website. If keywords or key phrases that have been used for a pay per click campaign don't show up, you know that the campaign is not yielding results with the current keywords and key phrases. Marketing (including pay per click campaigns) is covered in Chapter 3 of this minibook.

Adjusting the site and driving traffic

After analyzing the website stats, you'll have a good idea of how much traffic the site is getting and from where the traffic is coming. You'll also know which online marketing techniques are working, how well SEO is working, and how well your traditional marketing is working. The site stats tell you which areas of the site need revision and gives you an idea of what other steps you can take to drive traffic to the site.

If you or your client has employed SEO, take a good look at the search strings that visitors have used to find your site. Do they match the keywords and key phrases you peppered heavily in the title, description, and keywords? If so, your efforts are working. If the search strings are obscure text in any of the head tags or actual text in the body of the page, revise the tags to reflect the keywords and key phrases that people have used to find the site — which, of course, will help drive more traffic to the site.

If you use pay per click marketing to drive traffic to the site, search strings are once again useful. If the search strings match the pay per click words you budgeted with various search engines, the campaign is doing its job. If not, adjust the pay per click campaign, budgeting the keywords and key phrases that show up most frequently in search strings. You can also use referrers to determine the effectiveness of a pay per click campaign. If the referrers are those that your client has employed a pay per click campaign with, your client's money is well spent. If not, advise your client to suspend the pay per click campaign or lower the budget.

Entry pages are another useful statistic to study when a site sells multiple products or multiple services, especially when you use marketing or SEO to draw attention to the site. The most popular entry pages tell you how effective your SEO efforts are. If certain pages aren't being visited and these are popular products or services, optimize these pages again. If you used a pay per click campaign on the pages that aren't getting their fair share of visits, adjust the budget or budget different keywords or key phrases.

Stats on exit pages can tell you whether the content is effective. The pages that visitors exit most frequently might need to be tweaked if the pages are products or services that are vital to the business. In a perfect world, the most frequently used exit page would be the checkout of your client's secure server.

Using Google Webmaster tools

Google is decidedly the king and queen of search engines. More people use Google to find stuff on the 'Net than any other search engine. Therefore, it's imperative that your site rank well in a Google search. You optimize the site for SEO and submit it to search engines, and sometimes hope for the best in spite of the best tools and advice — such as that contained within this book — that money can buy. Fortunately, you don't have to be a rocket scientist to analyze your results if you have a Google account. With a Google account, you can access Google Webmaster tools and get a plethora of information and tools to give you a fighting chance against competing websites. To use Google Webmaster tools

1. **Open your favorite web browser and navigate to** www.google/webmaster/tools.

   The Google login page appears. If you don't have a Google account, you can set one up on this page.

2. **Log in to your account.**

   After you log in to your account, the Google Webmaster Tools page appears (see Figure 2-6). Note that several sites have been added to the account.

3. **Click the Add a Site button.**

   The Add a Site dialog box appears.

4. **Enter the URL of the site on which you want to use Webmaster tools.**

   Be sure to include www. before the domain name.

5. **Click Continue.**

   The Verify Ownership page appears (see Figure 2-7). This page gives you the option of verifying that you are the owner of the website whose URL you entered in Step 4.

6. **Click the link to download the HTML verification file.**

   This is an HTML file that you put in the root directory of your website.

7. **Upload the file to your website.**

   We use the FileZilla FTP client to upload miscellaneous files to a website. See the "Uploading pages with an FTP client" section of this chapter.

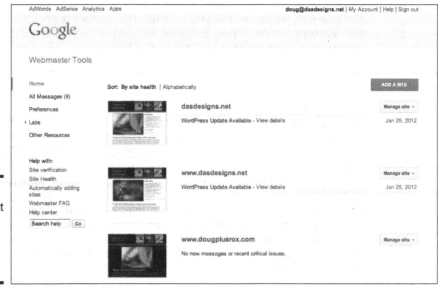

Figure 2-6: This account has several sites associated with it.

Book IX Chapter 2

Uploading the Site

Figure 2-7: Verify that you are the owner of this website.

8. **To make sure the file made it, click the link to navigate to the HTML file you just uploaded to your site.**

Big brother at Google knows whether you've visited the page.

9. **Click the Verify button.**

Google verifies that you're the owner of the site and displays a congratulations page. Make sure you leave the HTML file on the site.

10. **Click Continue.**

The Webmaster Tools for the site are displayed (see Figure 2-8). You can access the tools by clicking the links on the left. An in-depth tutorial on Google Webmaster Tools is beyond the scope of this book. You can, however, find lots of information on the Google Webmaster Tools site that will help you find out all sorts of information about your site, such as who is linking to it and so on.

Google Analytics is another (powerful) tool you can access from Google Webmaster tools. Google Analytics also gives you lots of pertinent information about your site(s). After setting a Google account, Products will be a link on your Google Accounts page. After clicking this link, you have access to all Google services, including FeedBurner, YouTube, and so on. Click the Analytics link to sign up for analytics. After you sign up, you embed some code in the pages you want Google Analytics to track. After a week or so, Google will have statistics for you to examine such as unique visitors, number of page views, and so on (see Figure 2-9). Unfortunately, a full-blown tutorial on Google Analytics is beyond the scope of this book.

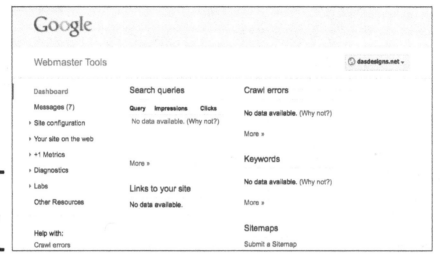

Figure 2-8:
I want my
Webmaster
Tools.

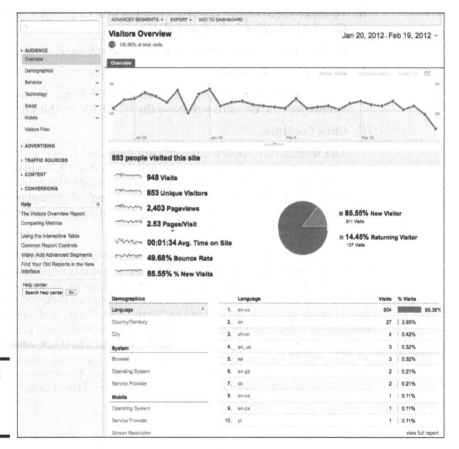

Figure 2-9:
Google
Analytics
at work.

Chapter 3: Maintaining and Marketing the Site

In This Chapter

✔ Archiving the site

✔ Maintaining the site

✔ Marketing the site

✔ Using pay per click advertising

*I*f web design is how you put bread on your table, after you create a site for your company or a client, you may think you're done and can start the next design or another project. But there's more to do before you can add this website to your list of jobs well done. First and foremost, you need to back up the site. This gives you a working copy of the site should there ever be a problem on the web-hosting server. It's also convenient to have a complete backup should you get a request to redesign the site. Keeping the site up to date is also important. We show you how to achieve that task with Dreamweaver. And then there's the matter of marketing the site. We show you how to achieve these tasks in this chapter.

Backing Up the Site

Stuff happens. Server equipment can break down, clever hackers can get past the best security and hack your site, or your server could suffer a natural catastrophe like a hurricane or flood. Hopefully, we've painted the picture that the permanence of your site is not a given. If the worst-case scenario happens and the site disappears, you need to react quickly. The best way to do this is to have a complete backup of the site so that you can re-create it quickly.

We recommend that you back up the site after you upload it to your server. You may think you can just leave the files in a folder on your computer, but your hard drive will eventually go belly-up on you, and you're up the prover-bial creek without a paddle — that is, unless you want to pay a company to restore the data from your corrupt hard drive. We recommend that you back up the sites you design on an external hard drive used only for storing files. After you back up the files, safely eject (Windows) or unmount (Macintosh) the external hard drive and put it away until the next time you need to archive files. Redundancy is also a good thing. Back up your important files to a CD or DVD and store the discs in another location.

Back up the website whenever you make a change to a page. You can back up the site from the server using Dreamweaver or an FTP client like FileZilla. Download the files from the server to your computer, and then archive the latest iteration of the site to an external hard drive and a CD or DVD.

Make a schedule or routine for yourself for making backups. When it's time, make your discs and then label them well. Be clear about what's on the disc and when you made it. That way, when you need to find something, you won't have to dig through lots of discs trying to find a digital needle in a haystack. A good technique is to burn the digital files to discs and put the discs in a folder along with any hard copies of documents pertaining to the project (signed contracts, brochures, and other materials). That way, you can locate all the materials related to one project very quickly if you need to revisit older projects.

Adding New Content

If the website you designed doesn't get updated from time to time, interested visitors will stop by a couple of times to see what's there, but they won't come back if there's no new content. When a site you've designed needs an update, you can use your favorite HTML-editing application to make changes to pages as needed.

If you designed the site for your company, adding new content is usually not a problem. If you design websites for a living, though, we suggest that you not accept jobs to revise only a few items on a page. Time is money, and you can never charge enough for a small update to make it worth your while. If the client wants a major update, that's another kettle of fish.

The following sections cover updating pages in Dreamweaver.

Clients change their minds when you least expect it. It's one of Murphy's Laws — Rule #648, most likely. So what are you to do when your client comes to you with a bunch of updates and then decides — after you created them — that he doesn't like them and wants to revert to the old ones? Well, if you already modified the pages, you're out of luck, Chuck. Whenever a client presents us with the first set of revisions, we do the following in Dreamweaver:

1. **Choose Window⇨Files.**

   This opens the Files panel for the website on which you're working.

 2. **Click the Expand to Show Local and Remote Sites button.**

 3. **Click the Connect to Remote Host button.**

   Dreamweaver connects to the remote host and displays all files and folders on the remote host. (See Figure 3-1.)

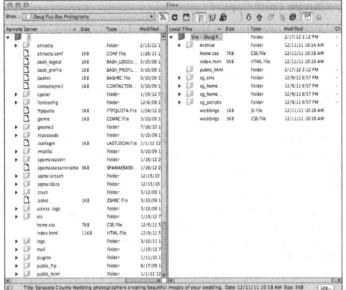

Figure 3-1:
You can
manage
files on
your local
machine
and the
remote host.

4. **Right-click (Windows) or Control-click (Mac) the remote host `root` directory and then choose New Folder from the contextual menu.**

   Dreamweaver creates an unnamed folder.

5. **Change the name of the folder to Archive.**

   This is where you'll store the original HTML files for the website.

6. **Select all the original HTML files for the site, including any CSS (style sheet) files and JavaScript files.**

7. **Choose Edit⇨Copy.**

   Dreamweaver copies the files to the Clipboard.

8. **Select the Archive folder.**

9. **Choose Edit⇨Paste.**

   Dreamweaver pastes the original HTML files into the Archive folder.

10. **Create a subfolder in the Archive folder named Images.**

    This step isn't necessary if you're using the same images in the revised pages. If, however, you're uploading new images with the same file-names, archive the original images so they'll be available if the client ever decides to revert to the original pages.

11. **Select all the images in the site's Images folder.**

    You are storing your images in a separate folder, aren't you?

12. **Choose Edit⇨Copy.**

Dreamweaver copies the images to the Clipboard.

13. **Select the Images folder.**

14. **Choose Edit⇨Paste.**

Dreamweaver pastes the images into the folder.

With the original files and images safely archived, you can modify the website. To revert to the old page, delete the revised file and then drag the page from the Archive folder, which replaces the deleted revision. Do the same with the archived images, and everything is as it was. When you do the next update, create a subfolder of the Archive folder, and name it Revision_1. Store the files from the previous revision in there. Archiving the latest three revisions should be sufficient unless you have a client with a photographic memory. In case of server problems, consider keeping a copy of the archive on your local machine, an external hard drive or on a CD or DVD as outlined in the "Backing Up the Site" section of this chapter.

Editing New Pages with Dreamweaver

If you and your staff have been contracted to manage your client's site, the obvious application for editing is the application with which the pages were created. Dreamweaver is a robust application that enables the savvy web designer to create a way-cool website and edit it as well. This section show you how to edit your pages in Dreamweaver.

The beauty of editing pages in a full-featured HTML editor like Dreamweaver is that you can edit the pages as well as the underlying code. When you edit pages in Dreamweaver, you can work in one of three modes: Design, Code, or the chameleon Split mode, which enables you to view the page and code at the same time, as we describe further in Book III, Chapter 4. Now, how cool is that? To edit pages in Dreamweaver, follow these steps:

1. **In the Files panel, select Local View from the View drop-down menu and then select the site you want to edit from the Site drop-down menu.**

Dreamweaver displays the files associated with the site. (See Figure 3-2.)

2. **Double-click the page you want to edit.**

Dreamweaver opens the page in Design mode. (See Figure 3-3.) Editing pages in Dreamweaver is pretty straightforward. The Properties Inspector is your friend in Dreamweaver. You use it to change links, CSS styles, images, and so on.

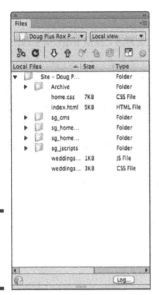

Figure 3-2:
The Files
panel is
your friend.

Choose a view

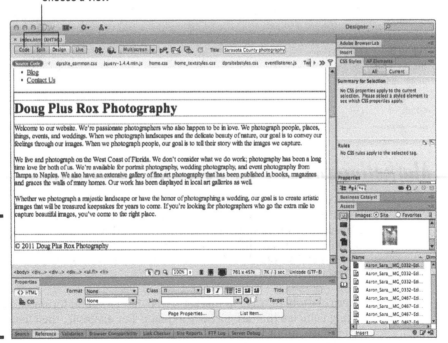

Figure 3-3:
Editing
pages in
Dream-
weaver
is, well, a
dream.

3. **Edit the page as needed.**

If you need to modify the code, click the Code button to display the page in Code view. (See Figure 3-4.)

If you need to view both the code and the page at the same time, click the Split button to display the page in Split view. When working in Split view, you can select items in the Display pane, and the underlying code is displayed in the Code pane.

4. **After editing and saving the page, click the Put button, which looks like an up-pointing arrow.**

Dreamweaver uploads the edited page to the server.

Figure 3-4:
Oh, my. This page has exposed its code.

Marketing the Site by Boosting Its Visibility

After you create the site, back it up, and leap the hurdle of search engine submission, you still have one hurdle to jump: marketing. Very rarely can a brick-and-mortar business survive on word of mouth. The same is true of websites. Granted, the site can get repeat visitors because a friend e-mailed a friend and so on. To achieve the lofty goals for the website, marketing has to be implemented.

There are lots of ways to market a website. First and foremost, use the marketing vehicles that are already in place. For example, the client can add a brief blurb about visiting the website in all his print ads. Of course, the URL should be prominently displayed in all ads — and for that matter, on any printed material that leaves the client's place of business.

Traditional marketing techniques work well for a local business in a local market. However, for the site to be truly effective, your client might have to resort to online marketing as well.

Using reciprocal linking and link exchanges

Like sausages, search engines love links. The more sites that link to your client's site, the higher the site will rank in the search engines. The best way to get sites to link to your client's is to submit a request to the Webmaster of a popular site. Tell the Webmaster that your client's site has content that would be of interest to visitors of his site. Ask the Webmaster to please add your client's URL and a description of the website (which you or your client have previously prepared) to the site's link pages. The Webmaster might ask you to supply a link in return.

Another method of marketing is link exchanges. You can find link exchange services by typing **link exchange** in your favorite search engine. You'll find hundreds of results from which to choose. Typically, a *link exchange* lets subscribers peruse through their directory and choose the sites they'd like to link to, and vice versa. The request is submitted to the site Webmaster, who chooses whether to accept the request and ask for a cross-link. Some link exchange services are free.

However, just as there is no free lunch, a free link exchange service generally comes with strings attached. Before signing up for a free link exchange service, read the fine print and make sure you can live with the service's agreement. For example, you may be required to add a link to the link exchange service's website. You should also make sure that the links propagated by the link exchange are from relevant sites — in other words, sites that relate to your client's business and not competitors'.

If the service randomly generates links to nonrelevant sites, you run the risk of being blackballed from major search engines. Do your homework before agreeing to use the service. You might ask for the URLs of other sites using the service and then contact the webmasters to see whether they're happy with the service.

Search engines pay special attention to the number of sites that link to your client's site. If all other parameters are equal, and one site has more external sites linking to it, the site with more links ranks higher on a results page. In other words: "He who dies with the most links wins."

You can see that it's in your client's best interest to have as many sites as possible linking to his. These are *inbound links*. If your client's site has interesting content and a compelling design (you did give your client a compelling design, didn't you?), it's relatively easy to get other sites to link to his site.

Just ask. That's right — send e-mails to Webmasters of sites that you'd like to link to your client's, telling them you like their site, would like to link to it, and would appreciate it if they'd do the same for your client's site.

Keep at it until you have a slew of sites linked to your client's and then monitor the stats to see which sites are referring visitors to your client's. At the same time, monitor where your client's site appears in search engine results pages. It won't happen overnight, but in a few months, your client's site will rank higher, thanks to the power of reciprocal links.

Navigate to www.yahoo.com or www.google.com and type **Link:** *PopularWebsite*, replacing the phrase *PopularWebsite* with the domain of a popular website that sells the same product or service as your client's. The domain should be in the following format: *PopularWebsite.com* — for example, Wiley.com. You'll get a list of sites that link to the popular website. Send an e-mail to the Webmasters of these sites, requesting that they link to your client's site.

Using a pay per click promotion

Many search engines offer the option of a paid ad that shows up in a results page when users enter a certain keyword or key phrase. Like anything else, he who swings the biggest club gets the game. With most search engines, you specify how much you'll pay for each click on an ad that appears when users enter a specified keyword and specify your maximum budget per month. The placement of your ad is determined on how much you bid per click versus your total budget — which is where the term "pay per click" comes from. In other words, if your bid on a keyword and budget is higher than another advertiser's, your ad appears before hers. If your bid is high but your budget is low, your ad appears lower in the list.

To get a concise idea of how this works, visit the Google AdWords Help Center:

```
https://support.google.com/adwords
```

You can also read *Google AdWords For Dummies*, 2nd Edition, by Howie Jacobson, Kristie McDonald, and Joel McDonald. For a bigger picture, read through *Pay Per Click Search Engine Marketing For Dummies* by Peter Kent.

When you take out an AdWord, you create the content for your ad. The resulting ad appears in a prominent position in the search engine's results pages for the particular keyword(s) you purchase. Figure 3-5 shows the results page for the key phrase, *Sarasota Photographer.* The paid ads are on the right side of the page.

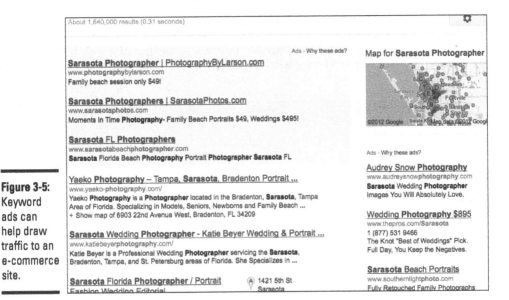

Figure 3-5:
Keyword
ads can
help draw
traffic to an
e-commerce
site.

When you decide to include paid keyword ads in your online marketing campaign, you have four steps to complete before that paid keyword ad is in place:

1. Determine which keywords are relevant to your client's business.

   If your client markets many products, he'll quickly go bankrupt paying for ads for each product he sells. If your client sells multiple products, the key is to break the phrases related to your client's offerings' genres. For example, if your client sells three brands of acoustic and electric guitars, a logical choice would be *acoustic guitars* and *electric guitars*. Your client pays for two key phrases instead of six.

2. Find the most popular keywords and key phrases that relate to the particular genre.

   You can employ an online marketing company to do this work. If your client is on a budget, he can use one of the online tools, such as Google AdWords Keyword Tool (www.googlekeywordtool.com) and then click Google Keyword Tool. After you open the page, simply enter the word or phrase for which you'd like to find keywords, and the site comes up with a page of results.

   Figure 3-6 shows the results for the key phrase, *Sarasota Photographer.* The results page shows the key phrases used most in conjunction with searches for a photographer in Sarasota, Florida. Note that the key phrase, *sarasota wedding photographer,* was used the most times when searching for a photographer doing business in Sarasota. The most popular keyword or key phrase is also the most expensive. Review the list and find a keyword or key phrase that is most relevant to your client's business and will result in customers perusing his website. To take the Sarasota photographer scenario a step further, the eighth keyword on the keyword suggestions page, *photo sarasota*, might be the ideal choice.

Search terms (1)			
Keyword	Competition	Global Monthly Searches	Local Monthly Searches
☆ sarasota photograph	-	-	-

Go to page: 1 Show rows: 50 ▼ 1 - 1 of 1

Keyword ideas (95)			
Keyword	Competition	Global Monthly Searches	Local Monthly Searches
☆ sarasota wedding photographer	High	1,300	1,300
☆ sarasota wedding photographers	High	1,300	1,000
☆ photographers in sarasota	High	2,900	2,900
☆ photographers sarasota	High	2,900	2,900
☆ sarasota photographers	High	2,900	2,900
☆ photography tampa	Medium	22,200	22,200
☆ sarasota photographer	High	3,600	3,600
☆ photo sarasota	Medium	4,400	3,600
☆ sarasota photography	Medium	5,400	5,400
☆ tampa bay photographers	High	★ Starred (0)	

Figure 3-6: You can find suggestions for keywords and key phrases online.

Subscription services for keyword research are also available. Wordtracker (www.wordtracker.com) and Keyword Discovery (www.keyword discovery.com) are available by subscription and also feature free trials.

3. Write the ad that will display in the results page with your client's chosen keyword or key phrase.

Create compelling ad copy that will make people want to click through to your client's site. You should also include the URL to the website in your ad. Even if users don't click-through, they might remember the URL to the site and visit it in the future. But the most compelling ad copy in the world is wasted if the landing page to which the ad is linked is not relevant. For example, if your ad copy is about wedding photography, the wise choice would be to link to the page about wedding photography, not the home page on your client's site.

4. Fine-tune the ad.

Google and Yahoo! enable you to target an ad by language or location. For example, you can target an ad to appear in one or more of the following: countries, territories, regions, and/or cities. Furthermore, you can specify that the ad be available to only a specific language audience. Targeting enables you to get more bang for your buck.

The only way you'll know for sure whether the pay per click campaign is working is to monitor the site statistics. Google and Yahoo! supply statistics with their campaigns. Over time, a thorough review of statistics enables the e-commerce site owner to edit the key phrases and, if necessary, choose new ones. In addition, you can monitor the statistics log supplied by your web-hosting service to see whether a campaign is effective.

Other marketing techniques

If your client has a startup company, her budget might not be able to afford a pay per click campaign. Never fear; there are other ways to get visitors to her site. The following are a couple techniques you and your client can employ:

✦ **Use banner exchanges.** You can publicize your client's site by participating in a banner exchange. Your client's banner is displayed on other sites that subscribe to the service. When clicked, the banner drives visitors to your client's site. Many banner exchange programs are free. When you sign up for a banner exchange program, make sure to read the fine print. Sometimes you have to prominently display the banner exchange company's logo on your client's site in exchange for the free service.

✦ **Offer free content.** If your client is an acknowledged expert in her field, advise her to offer free content, such as articles, to established sites that might be frequented by visitors who would be interested in your client's product or service. In exchange for the content, the site provides a link to your client's site.

Web designers should provide their clients with owner's manuals. Just think about the grief it would eliminate, not to mention the phone calls. In addition to telling clients that they won't get results immediately, the owner's manuals would tell clients the obvious things they can do to promote their sites. When you write your website owner's manual, be sure to include the following advice for your clients: Pump that URL! You'd be surprised how many people jot down the URL of a website when they see it. Add it to:

✦ Your business card and the business cards of your employees

✦ Every piece of stationery for your company, especially note pads and letterheads

✦ Every brochure and catalog you print

✦ Every magazine and newspaper ad you purchase

✦ Notepads that you give away to your customers

✦ Promotional items such as pens, mouse pads, and so on

✦ Every television ad you purchase

✦ Every company vehicle and every sign

✦ Any other type of vehicle used to promote the business, such as billboards and ads on park benches

Promoting a Site with Social Media

Social media is hot. The people for any website's target audience use social media to confer with friends and people who have similar interest. They also use social media to find out information about products. Social media is growing by leaps and bounds. The techniques for marketing will change as the platform matures. If you haven't done so already, jump on the bandwagon now and start reaping the benefits. There are lots of players in the social media game, but in our humble opinion, the two social media sites every business should participate in are Facebook (www.facebook.com) and Twitter (http://twitter.com). You can set up an account at both sites for free.

Twitter is all about micro-blogging. You send a message out to your followers that is 140 characters or less. When you initially join Twitter, you follow people who are related to your industry, and people who are potential clients for your industry.

When you send a message (a "tweet"), it's displayed in your followers' timelines. Many people make the mistake of sending out a tweet that asks people to visit their website. This is blatant advertising that causes people to stop following you. The trick is to send out information that establishes you as an expert in your industry. If you do a really good job, your followers will retweet it to their followers, who may retweet it to their followers. You can see how this could grow exponentially and garner lots of followers for your Twitter presence.

Another way to gain followers is to tweet the URL of an informative blog post. If you use a desktop client (like TweetDeck; www.tweetdeck.com) to send and receive your tweets, you can shorten a long URL. If you send your tweets from the Twitter site, you can shorten long URLs at Bitly (http://bitly.com). This site also gives you the option of tracking how many unique clicks the shortened URL received — valuable marketing information, indeed.

Facebook is another social media site with millions of participants. After you set up a Facebook account, you get a personal page on which you can post information for friends, family, and so on. You can also create a Facebook page for your business. After you set up a Facebook page, you invite your friends to like your page. You also post pertinent information about your business on your Facebook wall.

Facebook is multimedia. You can upload images to accompany a comment you post, create an album of photos, and upload video. You can also benefit by the many apps that are available for Facebook, which enables you to add special tabs on your wall, display blog posts and much more. Figure 3-7 shows the Facebook page for Doug's photography company.

Book IX
Chapter 3

Maintaining and
Marketing the Site

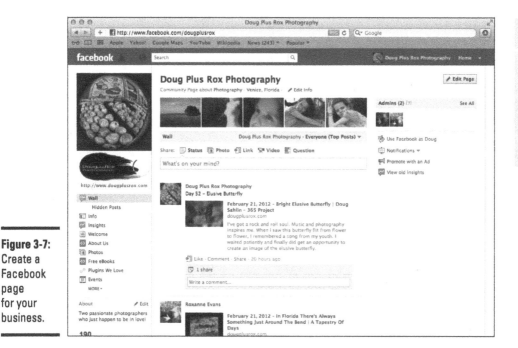

Figure 3-7:
Create a
Facebook
page
for your
business.

Some businesses aren't suited for the social media outlets mentioned previously. However, one social media site every company or businessman should belong to is LinkedIn (www.linkedin.com). LinkedIn is considered "the" social media site for business owners and professionals.

Chapter 4: Redesigning or Expanding the Site

In This Chapter

- ✔ Deciding whether to redesign or add on
- ✔ Redesigning a site
- ✔ Managing a stress-free expansion
- ✔ Knowing what to do after the re-launch
- ✔ Keeping content fresh

*W*hen you design a website, you should keep options open to expand the site as your business or your client's business grows. Expanding a site doesn't need to be rocket science. If you've done your homework and archived the site as discussed in the previous chapter, you have a solid base from which to work. When the marketing kicks in and the site gains popularity, the business associated with the site will grow as well, inevitably leading to a major revision or expansion.

In this chapter, we give you some pointers for revising or expanding a site — and, more importantly, how to tell whether you should redesign the site or add on to it.

Deciding to Redesign or Add On

You designed a wonderful website for your business or a client; you uploaded the design and went on your merry way, designing sites for other clients, or tending to other business. Several months later, the client comes back to you, and guess what? You have another gig. She wants you to do more work on the site. The website is very important to your client, and she wants you to add information about her new products and services. You meet with the client, and she lays out her grand vision for the site expansion. Now, you're faced with an important decision. Do you redesign or add on to your existing design? You might even find yourself taking a middle road approach.

You may face the same dilemma with your own site or your company website. You have new products or service to offer, and the site you so loving designed doesn't include any of these wonderful new products or services, which means it's time to roll up your sleeves and get to work.

Your value as a web designer and builder is your experience, including the sites you've worked on since you created the last iteration of your client's site. You've learned more, experienced more, and grown your skills. After conversing with your client, you'll know whether it makes more sense to add on to the existing content — inherently, the least-expensive option — or to put your expertise and creativity into a total redesign.

And the same is true even if you don't design and build websites for a living. You've seen more websites since then and know the current trends. If you fear that your skills are a little rusty, don't worry: That's what this book is for. In the upcoming sections, we provide information that will help you decide whether it's wiser to redesign the existing pages, or to start from scratch or to just add on.

Regardless of which approach you take, archive the original website before you begin. You might be able to incorporate some of the material from the original design in this and future revisions of the site. If the site's web server allows you to store data, you can archive the old site in a folder on that server. If not, download the old site and save it to DVD or to an external hard drive as outlined in Chapter 3 of this minibook.

Redesigning the site

Redesigning a site is almost the same as designing a new website. The obvious advantage is that you've already worked with the client, so you know her strengths and weaknesses and goals and druthers. And you might be able to repurpose some elements from the existing site.

Here's a real-world example. Figure 4-1 shows Doug's photography site prior to redesign. Doug still does a fair amount of web design, but his major focus is photography. (His web-design work comes from word of mouth and projects with other web designers and developers.) The previous iteration of the site featured a slide show on the home page with a white background (see Figure 4-1). When he redesigned the site, the focus of the business changed, which warranted a new navigation menu. However, he wanted to keep some design elements, such as the banner, but he changed the background to black, which is fitting for a photography company website.

The redesigned site is shown in Figure 4-2. The site and animations also display perfectly on the Apple iPad, which is a major consideration, given the popularity of these mobile devices.

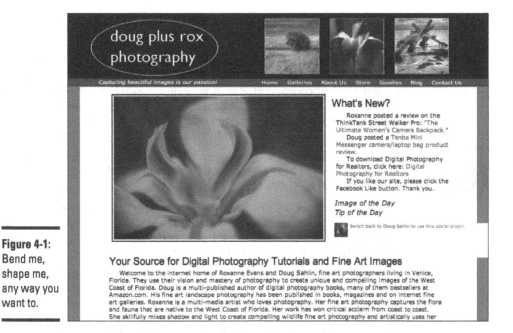

Figure 4-1:
Bend me,
shape me,
any way you
want to.

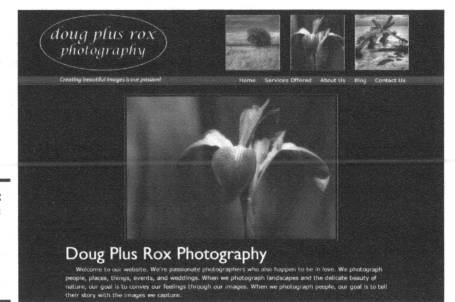

Figure 4-2:
The URL is
the same,
but the
content
has been
changed.

Here are some pretty good indicators for deciding that a site needs to be redesigned instead of just added on to:

+ **The site is more than one year old and appears dated.** You can do an easy test to see whether the site looks like it was designed in the Victorian period: Look at competing sites. If your design still looks fresh, there's no need to reinvent the wheel. On the other hand, if the competing sites look newer and more exciting, or have undergone massive changes since your site was designed, you should think about keeping up with the Joneses.

   If you do web design for a living, make sure you keep track of the time you spend researching competitor's sites and add this to the total cost of your redesign.

+ **The site no longer accurately reflects your client's or company's main focus.** This is another no brainer. If the type of business has undergone a major change, people will visit the website, and nothing will be congruent with the current focus of the company.

+ **The original design was not optimized to play on non–Flash-friendly devices, such as the iPad.** The iPad, smartphones, and other mobile devices are here to stay. If the site's target audience embraces these technologies (very likely), you need to redesign the site to eliminate objects like Flash movies, which will not play on Apple devices.

+ **An expansion will cause usability issues, such as cluttered menus, hard-to-follow navigation, and confusing content.** Envision a store adding new products and trying to stuff them all into the old building.

+ **You already made substantial changes and added new features prior to the client's expansion request.** *Upside:* Redesigning the site enables you to use the latest technology and create a state-of-the-art design for your client or your company. This should strongly be considered if the site is more than a year old, technology has taken a quantum leap, and the budget can stand the burden of a total redesign.

+ **The current website can't easily accommodate your client's or company's expansion plans.** You can't stuff 50 pounds of groceries in a bag that will only hold 30. (Well, maybe you can, but it won't be pretty, and the bag will certainly break. Not the professional look or functionality you want for yourself or a client.)

+ **Your client's intended audience can access the Internet with faster connections.** Faster connections enable you to incorporate more bells and whistles, such as streaming audio and video. Just keep in mind that you may still need to have a version of the site to accommodate visitors that have slower connections.

If you do web design for a living, a previous client might expect a price break because you designed the original site for her. If a price break or discount comes up in the course of discussion, you have to put your foot down and tell the client that a redesign involves just as much work as a new site design. In fact, if it's been more than a year since the initial site design, your price should be higher.

Adding on to a site

Your client has given you some cool new stuff that she wants included on the site, or perhaps your company has some cool new products or services to include on the website. The onus is on you to decide the best way to display the new information. An obvious (and easier) option for you, as a designer, is to simply add on to the site. This route allows you to keep the look and feel of the current website with a virtually seamless expansion (and relatively pain-free for the client or for your business). After all, your website visitors are coming to a place they know, kind of like coming home. They're familiar with the features and the site's bells and whistles — plus, they know how to get around. Consider the following indicators as good signs to know that adding on to an existing site is your best option:

+ **The site is less than a year old and doesn't look outdated when compared with the competition.**

If the site sports outdated features (such as a Flash intro or beveled buttons), remove them. Like beehive hairdos, these features have gone the way of the dodo. If a Flash intro resides on a page (such as `default.htm` or `index.htm`) and links to the home page of the site, simply rename the home page to `default.htm` or `index.htm`. Poof! The Flash intro is gone.

+ **You can do the expansion without a massive renovation to the existing navigation menus.**

+ **Your company or client wants you to only add additional features, such as a forum or blog.** No brainer. You can easily accomplish this by using the existing site framework. (See Book XIII for how to add a blog.)

+ **The current site has been received well by the site visitors, and the expansion can be accomplished by using the existing site framework.**

+ **You can expand the current site without incurring usability issues or otherwise confusing visitors.**

+ **You can redesign the site if warranted and the cost doesn't exceed your company's or client's budget.** You were given a budget for the redesign, weren't you?

Planning the Redesign

When you redesign a site that's been up for a while, you do so because your company or client has new material to show site visitors and because the existing site is getting a bit long in the tooth. When you redesign a site, you need to put the same effort into the redesign as when you created the original site for the client. You need to see what's out there. In other words, do your homework — as we discuss at length in Book I — and visit competing websites.

Just because the first site you designed was state of the art doesn't mean that a redesign that's simply a rehash of the original design will draw "oohs" and "aaahs" from people who visit the new site. Although you do want to keep some continuity, you must examine the content to be included in the redesign so that you can combine the old with the new in a way that satisfies the new goals of the site.

In the following sections, we describe these six phases of a site redesign: consultation, review, analysis, planning, implementation, and testing.

Consultation

If you're doing the redesign for a client, meet with her to get the scope and breadth of the client's expansion. Get as much information as you can. This meeting is very similar to your initial consultation with the client except that you know her better now and can talk frankly with the client based on your previous experience. If you're doing the redesign for your company, hold a fact-finding meeting. In either event, you need the following information.

✦ **Find out everything needed for the site.** What are the goals for the revised site? During your consultation, you also think about future expansion and new products that are coming down the pike. You don't want your redesign to be obsolete in a couple of months.

✦ **Discuss the previous site.** Your client or company is bound to have feedback from site visitors. Find out which pages and sections work and which ones don't. The hosting server's website stats can also give you an idea of which pages are popular and which ones are not.

✦ **Address the current target audience.** Is the intended audience the same as when you did the original site, or is the audience different or expanded based on the new information that will be incorporated in the redesign?

✦ **Address the site's current competitors.** Does the site have different competitors now, or did the list of competitors increase dramatically?

✦ **Address new technology:** Websites can be displayed on everything from mobile phones to tablets, such as the iPad. If the original design isn't compatible with mobile devices, find out whether the target audience use these devices — and if so, get an approximate percentage. This will tell you whether you need to incorporate the new technology in your revision.

✦ **Determine the budget for the redesign.** This is especially important if you're working with a client, or are a web designer for your company. Make sure all parties know the cost involved up front, and get it in writing. And you should create a contract if you're doing a redesign for a client.

✦ **Determine the timetable for going live with the redesign.** You need to incorporate your client's or company's timetable with the other phases of the project and your current workload. If the timetable isn't reasonable, become the voice of reason and tell all concerned parties what the timetable will be based on the scope and breadth of the redesign.

Consider running a brief survey for visitors of the current site and ask them what they like or dislike about the site. If you don't consider the needs and preferences of the target audience, you may create a site that you think is the best thing since sliced bread but doesn't do anything for the current visitors of the site. You can create a link to the survey (a short form is ideal) on the home page or another frequently visited page on the website. If the site has a blog, this is the ideal place to announce that the site is being redesigned and you'd appreciate feedback from the current visitors.

Review

Review the existing site in conjunction with the desired expansion. During this review, you're looking for answers to these questions:

✦ **What does the current site say to the intended audience?** When reviewing the information, make note of which information is concurrent with the new goals and which is not.

✦ **Will the intended audience change based on the new information you'll incorporate with the current site?** If the audience will change, consider what content from the old site is appropriate for the new site and also whether you need to change material and or design elements based on the demographics of the new audience.

✦ **Can you incorporate the current graphics into the redesign?** You might need to change the navigation menu or site banner based on the new goals.

✦ **Does your client or company have a new logo?** If so, incorporate the new logo and colors with your redesign.

✦ **Can you improve navigation and the organization of information?** If the target audience complained about any items on the old site, now is the perfect time to change them.

✦ **Which pages are the most popular, and which pages have the fewest hits?** You can get this information from the site stats. If the pages that have the fewest hits contain important information, you have to tweak these pages during the redesign.

✦ **Which pages have been bookmarked by site visitors?** You have to incorporate a version of bookmarked pages in the new design, and these pages must have the same URL. Your website statistics may include this number. Your client can also use third-party companies to track statistics, or your client or company can sign up for Google Analytics. Google Analytics doesn't show bookmarked pages, but it will give you extensive information about which pages are visited most frequently, how long visitors stay on the site, and so on. As of this writing, the service is free. For more information, visit www.google.com/analytics.

You want to include some familiar items to provide some continuity to people who visited the original version of the site. Two of the most common items in a design are the banner and the footer. If possible, include both in the redesign so your client's website visitors won't think they landed on the wrong website.

Analysis

Analyze the information you gleaned while reviewing the site and then determine whether this information can be incorporated with that presented on the current website or whether you need to create new pages for the material. Analyze the site's intended audience. Has it changed since you originally designed the site? Has the technology used by the intended audience changed since your first design? Has web technology changed since your first design? The answers to these questions shape your redesign.

You also need to know what bandwidth the site's target audience is using to access the Internet, their average computer screen desktop size, and so on. If the technology has changed in leaps and bounds since your last design, chances are the site's target audience is using some of this new technology. Your mission is to figure out how much of the target audience is using the new technology and whether this need to be addressed in the redesign. Your client should have this information. If not, you'll have to use some sort of questionnaire to get this information.

A redesign is more than simply rehashing material from the old site. Although you do want to keep some continuity, analyze the material that is presented to you for the redesign. Analyze the content of the current site thoroughly before examining the material to be included in the redesign. Then review the new content and come up with a plan to marry the old with the new.

Planning

This stage of the redesign process is similar to creating a mockup for client review. Incorporate all the information you gathered to create a user-friendly navigation system that combines the old and new. After you jump this hurdle, consider how you'll organize the information on each page. The information you gathered during the consultation period and other important factors shows you which information is the most relevant in the redesign. This information must be easily accessible to the site's intended audience.

You have to address other issues in your redesign, such as the following:

✦ **Does the current site's server have enough features to implement your redesign?** For example, if your redesign incorporates using a database — say, for example, you're adding a blog to the site — does your web-hosting server have provisions for creating a database? Alternatively, can you upgrade the features on the server side to incorporate the new features in your redesign?

✦ **What software is needed?** For example, if the client asks you to include a site-wide search engine, you need to find the applicable software — and include the cost plus markup of the software in your revision.

✦ **How much of the old can be wed with the new?** Consistency is important to website visitors. Therefore, you should keep some of the old images — and, as we mention earlier, the site banner if possible.

When you plan a redesign, keep the site's intended audience in the forefront of your mind. Your redesign must incorporate the new goals for the site with the intended audience's expectations. In the viewer's eyes, the redesigned site should have value-added services.

✦ **What technology is your client's intended audience using?** Do they have the necessary browser and plug-ins to access the technology you plan on incorporating in the redesign? If not, use different technology or add links to sites where site visitors can download the plug-ins needed to view the redesigned site.

In the long run, your best bet is to plan the redesign around the lowest common denominator; in other words, go with the oldest technology used by your client's intended audience.

Alternatively, you can create two versions of the site: one for the techies who have the latest software plus fast Internet access, and another version for the lowest common denominator. Use a gateway page with links to direct visitors to the site that matches their technology. A *gateway page* describes the resources needed to view each iteration of the site. For example, you can create a Flash site for visitors who have the Flash Player installed on their computer and an HTML site for those who don't. The gateway page has a link to each version of the site.

✦ **Have you incorporated future expansion in the redesign?** Make sure your navigation menus are laid out so that you can easily incorporate additions to the website. Use templates to simplify the construction of each page. Templates will also be indispensable when incorporating future expansion into the redesigned site.

Include search engine optimization (SEO) forethought in your redesign. If you don't, the client's expanded site will be virtually invisible in search engine results pages. See Chapter 1 of this minibook for more information about SEO.

Implementation

At this stage of the process, unless you can use a good bit of the old site, you start with a clean slate in your HTML editor and incorporate your planning to create the actual pages. This is no different than creating a new website. You design a *home page* (a brief overview of the business, service, or organization for which the site is being designed) that's compelling enough to draw visitors to the site. Then you must lay out the ensuing pages in a logical manner with the most important information at the top of the page. The main pages in any section of the site should be short, simple, and to the point. Pages that are deeper in a section can have more text.

If you're incorporating assets (such as images or multimedia files) from the old site, download these to a folder on your computer so you can quickly access them when needed.

Testing

Finally, test the site to ensure a smooth transition from the old to the new. If the site is small, you can test most of it on your local machine. Or, if the site uses ASP or PHP, you can test the pages with a testing server on your local machine. See Book VII, Chapter 2 to read about WAMP/MAMP, which is server software that can help you test PHP scripts on your own computer. Check everything: navigation menus, links, interactive content, and so on. Another option you can choose is doing an online beta test. (Read more about that earlier in this minibook.) After testing the site, evaluate your findings and tidy up any loose ends or faulty code. Then you're ready to go live.

Adding On without All the Trauma

When you add on to a site, everything must go off without a hitch and the finished product must be error free. This is especially important when you're expanding a site because visitors are used to surfing the current site, which (if you did your homework and tested the original design) is error free. (Ahem. You did test the original site, didn't you?) Expanding existing pages is a lot easier if you follow certain steps during the project. Most of this is common sense, but even the best designer might forget a step or take things for granted because he's worked with the client before. Well, the long and the short of it is to *not take anything for granted.* Otherwise, one of Murphy's Laws will come into play when you least expect it. In any event, the following list outlines issues to consider when you're expanding a website:

✦ **Write a proposal for the expansion project.** After you and the client come to terms with the scope and breadth of the project, prepare a proposal and get the client to sign the proposal before you begin work. A proposal is also needed if you're creating a site for your company. Make sure all the players agree on every facet of the proposed redesign. It's very unpleasant to find out someone doesn't agree with an integral component of the redesign at the eleventh hour.

✦ **Work smarter, not harder.** Use the features of your HTML editor to modify the previous work you did for the client as part of the site expansion. If you're using Dreamweaver, read the nearby sidebar, "Making

Dreamweaver work for you," to find out how you can whip through a site expansion without breaking a sweat.

✦ **Archive the original website so you can refer to the old content if you need to.** If the current site is relatively small, download the site to a folder on your computer. If it's a large site, download it to your computer if you have the room, or download it to an external drive.

✦ **Use existing pages as the basis for the site expansion.** When you begin the site expansion, download the old pages from the web-hosting service, or use the pages from your backup CD or DVD. In a worst-case scenario, you may need to create a new navigation menu to incorporate new sections of the site. You can create a new menu in Fireworks and insert it in the proper place in your HTML pages.

✦ **Maintain links and the page's listing in a search engine index.** When revising a page that is currently on the site, begin with the document you downloaded from the web-hosting service. Change the page as needed and save it, using the same name. This keeps all your links intact and preserves the page's listing in a search engine index.

✦ **Change the title of pages and other SEO-related objects, such as** meta **tags and** alt **tags.** When you revise or add on to a site, it's the ideal time to tweak the SEO of the site. As long as you don't change the page URL and other links, the search engines will be able to find the indexed pages. When the site is re-indexed, the search engines will pick up the revised SEO elements, which hopefully will help the site rank higher than the sites you're competing against.

✦ **Keep everyone involved abreast of the project.** If you're uploading your work while you do it, tell the team when the revised work is posted. If you're doing work for a client, get him on each phase of the revision. If you're working on a total redesign, upload the content to a different folder at the web-hosting service and then send the URL to everyone involved, requesting that they review and comment on the work you've done so far.

✦ **Present a mockup for approval.** Just because you've worked with the client before or designed the current version of your company's website doesn't mean that you can take anything for granted. You might be in for a nasty surprise if you assume that your client or company will fall in love with your expansion, sight unseen.

✦ **Set up a testing server.** If you're creating PHP or ASP pages, set up a testing server on your local machine. That way, you can test the pages while you create them.

✦ **Test, test, test — and then test again.** Make sure everything on the pages you're creating or revising works perfectly. That includes links and any code. A site expansion should be handled with the same kid gloves as a new design. Consider doing a full-blown beta test. In lieu of a beta test, use your friends, employees, or the client's employees to test the revised site.

Making Dreamweaver work for you

Whether you're revising the old site or redesigning it, there's no sense in reinventing the wheel. Here are ways to repurpose your hard work:

✔ The **Assets panel** is chock-full of items you used on the old site: images, Flash movies, URLs, and so on. To use them in the revision or redesign, simply open the Assets panel and then drag the Asset into the new or revised page.

✔ **Snippets** can also be a great timesaver, especially if the site uses a lot of code. If you added items to the Library (such as footers and copyright notices), you can use these in the site expansion as well.

✔ Recycling **templates** you used when creating the site is a no-brainer. If you're undertaking a total redesign, you might be able to get by with revising templates. To revise a template, open the document as a DWT file. You can then edit locked regions of the template and make other necessary changes to suit the revision. As an added bonus, when you save the template, you have the option of updating all pages that were designed with the template.

✦ **Upload the revised site *after* getting every team player's approval.** Never upload pages to the root directory of the web-hosting service until after you test the pages to ensure that no problems exist and also that everyone involved agrees that the work is acceptable. Your best bet is to upload the new pages to a different folder on the server and send the URL to the team and anyone else who is testing the pages.

After Launching the Expanded Site

You might think the work is done after you upload the revised or redesigned site to the server. Nay, nay, Nanette! Your work — or your client's work — has just begun. Sure, you posted something new (and hopefully exciting) for the world to see. However, like anything else, nobody will know what you did unless you tell them about it. That's right: You've got it, so flaunt it. The following is a list of things you or your client should do to publicize a revised or redesigned site:

✦ **Send a press release to the local media.** The press release should include the reason why the website was redesigned. Don't forget to include information about the business or organization for which the site was redesigned. Be sure to include the URL to the site in the press release. If the website enjoys a worldwide audience, several services are available on the Internet that you can use to create a press release. You can find a service that suits your needs by typing **"Internet Press Release"** in your favorite search engine.

✦ **Notify members of the website mailing list that the site has new content.**

✦ **Send a newsletter to existing subscribers telling them about the expanded website.**

✦ **Request link exchanges.** If the expanded website contains information pertinent to websites not currently linked to the site, request a link exchange.

✦ **Include an invitation to visit the expanded website in all printed media, including advertisements.**

✦ **Re-register the site with the search engines.**

✦ **Use other online marketing techniques, such as pay per click ads, to draw visitors to the expanded site.** See Chapter 3 of this minibook for more information about pay per click ads, which can help you (and your client) bring a steady flow of potential customers to your client's site.

Book IX
Chapter 4

Redesigning or
Expanding the Site

After you launch the redesigned or revised site, pay careful attention to the site statistics to determine the overall success of the expanded site. Notice which pages are getting the most visits and from which pages visitors exit the site. If viewers are exiting the site from pages that contain important new content, you need to revise the pages. The information you learn from site statistics will drive future changes, revisions, and redesigns.

Convince your client or company to add an online survey with your redesign or revision. The survey should ask visitors what they like and dislike about the redesigned site. If the survey is long, consider including a special offer as a reward for submitting the completed survey. The information garnered from the survey can determine the overall success of the revised site. You can also require the visitor's e-mail address, which can then be added to the website mailing list.

Keeping Them Coming Back

Even after you do your best to launch an informative website, you have to keep looking ahead. If you don't, the site can quickly lose popularity, and business can dwindle. The best way to keep visitors returning to a site is to keep the content fresh. In this regard, think ahead and plan for future content. In the upcoming sections, we give you a few tips to ensure a steady stream of visitors to your website.

Ongoing content development

A successful website should have new information at least once every two weeks. That's not really as difficult as it seems. If your client is an expert in his field, he can post articles or tutorials on the website. A blog is also a wonderful way to post new content. The articles or blog posts should be compelling enough to ensure that visitors will look forward to bi-weekly installments. If the client uses a blog, tell him to make a post at least twice a week, and to post on the same day. Visitors will get used to the regular post and anticipate them.

The articles or blog posts should include hyperlinks to the product or service the client is featuring in the article. For example, if the website's purpose is to sell art supplies, an article could show visitors how to mix colors. You've likely seen websites with a headline that gives a short introduction to an article with a Read More link at the bottom of the blurb. Savvy web surfers know that this content is usually updated on a regular basis. If your client isn't a writer, perhaps someone on his staff can write the articles. In lieu of that, perhaps the client's vendors can create content. Alternatively, you can find websites that offer free material for reprint, in exchange for an ad.

As of this writing, you can find an index of free web content at FreeSticky (`www.freesticky.com/stickyweb`). Note that this material is available to everyone, and an article you choose may be seen on a competing site.

The best way to plan for ongoing content is to know the demographics of the audience that are likely to visit the site. Knowledge of your client's intended audience is the key to developing the revised site. Advise your client to find interesting new stories that relate to her product or service. Include links to these articles on the client's Home or What's New page. A blog for your client (which we discuss in further detail in Book VIII, Chapter 1) is an excellent place to mention interesting news articles or product developments.

Another way to keep customers returning is to post success stories on the Home or What's New page. This takes a bit of planning on your client's part. If the client has an established brick-and-mortar business, advise her to solicit customers for testimonials or success stories. For example, if your client is promoting a weight-loss service, before-and-after pictures are great testimonials.

Advise your client to obtain a release from her customer before posting the pictures and success story. Contact your lawyer for more information on what information a model release should include. If your client is a savvy marketer, she can exchange goods or services in exchange for a good article or success story.

When planning new content, your client should be on the prowl, visiting industry-specific websites in search of new material. Your client can set up alliances with websites that sell similar products or services to her intended audience. Your client can find articles on these websites that interest her customers, and she probably has content that is of interest to other websites. This information can be exchanged between sites with a short ad and hyperlink to the marketing partner's website.

On the home page, add some text that tells visitors the site content is updated on a regular basis and ask them to bookmark the page.

Another way to develop content for the site is to recycle. As long as the information is timely, there's no reason your client can't post an article again in another three or four months. If your client uses this tactic, though, make sure he keeps track of when the articles are posted and that he mixes them up. In other words, advise him not to repost the articles in the same order they were originally posted. Your client can also do a bit of creative cutting and pasting to create a new article from information that's already been posted on the site.

Keeping content fresh

In addition to creating articles and tutorials, you can employ other devices to ensure that visitors want to return. This type of content is the fun and informative stuff. The following are a few time-honored techniques that can be used to have visitors flocking to the site on a regular basis:

✦ **Add short-term specials to the home page.** The specials can be on new products or services. Make sure the special is really a value and not just an attempt to get rid of old inventory. If the visitor perceives the short-term special as a value, he's likely to purchase the product or service. Or even if he doesn't make the purchase, the seed is planted, and the visitor is likely to return when the special expires to see what's offered next. Make sure the short term special includes a call to action, such as a link to a page on the site where the visitor can find more information about the product that's being featured on the home page.

✦ **Provide tutorials.** If your client has a service that includes instructional material, consider giving away a short tutorial in PDF format. When you give something away, make sure you ask for something in return — say, the visitor's e-mail address so you can inform her of the next, free tutorial. Another option is to create video tutorials, upload them to YouTube, and embed them in blog posts.

✦ **Give away stuff.** If the business associated with the website has promotional material, such as t-shirts or baseball caps, give the materials away to every 25th visitor who registers contact information on the website or signs up for the newsletter.

✦ **Create a What's New page and update it frequently.**

✦ **Create a newsletter.** Have visitors register their e-mail addresses, and notify them when the newsletter is updated. You can also use a service like MailChimp (http://mailchimp.com) to create newsletters that are delivered via e-mail. MailChimp maintains a database of web visitors who sign up for the newsletter.

✦ **Hold a contest related to your client's products or services.** The grand prize can be a product or a discount. The visitor submits his contact information when registering for the contest.

Book X

Case Studies

The 5th Wave   By Rich Tennant

"Okay-looks like the 'Dissolve' transition in my presentation needs adjusting."

Contents at a Glance

Chapter 1: Photographer's Portfolio

In This Chapter

↳ **What a photographer needs**

↳ **Less is more**

↳ **Fleshing out the site**

↳ **Adding the gallery**

*L*ike the proverbial plumber with the leaky faucets in his own house, our websites need some TLC. Doug has a couple of websites, and when he gets a chance, he revises them in conjunction with the latest technology. In this chapter, we focus on a site that Doug is revising — the website for his business — in conjunction with this book. Doug runs a photography business with his significant other, Roxanne. Photography websites have certain needs. They need to be state of the art and artistic, but not so artistic that the site distracts viewers' attention from the images displayed. In this chapter, we give you a behind the scenes look at the revision of Doug's website. Of course, by the time this book is in print, he may decide to do something totally different.

Deciding What a Photographer Needs

When a photographer creates an image, he decides what stays in as well as what stays out of frame. A photographer is a visual storyteller. He uses light and shadow to create images viewers will give more than just a casual glance. A competent photographer can create a properly exposed image, but a photographer who has transcended digital technology creates something that is a work of art. A photographer's website is the frame for his artwork.

In many instances, the images that photographers create are minimal: a collection of shapes or colors that are artistically arranged in the viewfinder. Less can definitely be more. The site for Doug's company underwent a transformation shortly before the first words of this book were written. That site featured a slideshow on the home page (see Figure 1-1), and a thumbnail gallery on the portfolio pages. The site had white text on a black background with minimum intrusion from menus and other devices. The images were definitely the focal point of the site.

Figure 1-1:
A minimalist
photogra-
pher's
website.

Knowing When Less Is More

While pondering a site revision, Doug was reading a book about the innovation secrets of Apple founder Steve Jobs. Apple products are sleek, with minimal intrusion from switches, keyboards, and other appendages. An iPod has one button and two camera lenses. The iPod and iPad navigation systems are accessed by touching the screen, an extension of the user. Doug decided to try a sleek minimal approach for his site and made the decision to use an off-white background. He created the header and menu in Adobe Fireworks CS6 (see Figure 1-2) and exported it as images and HTML. For more information on creating graphics in Fireworks CS6, read Book V, Chapter 2.

He created the site in Adobe Dreamweaver CS6 by creating a new HTML document and then importing the HTML he exported from Fireworks (see Figure 1-3).

After laying out the site with placeholders for text and other content, Doug saved the file as a Dreamweaver template in the DWT format. Then, all remaining pages would be created from this template.

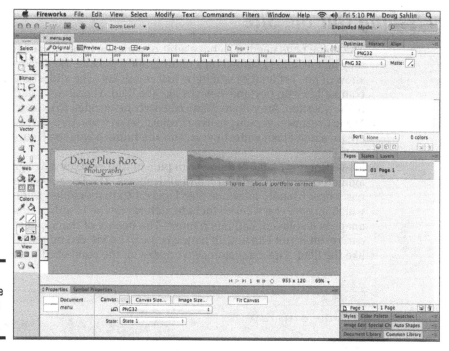

Figure 1-2:
Creating the
header and
menu.

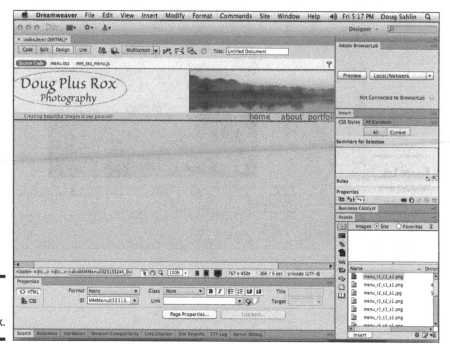

Figure 1-3:
Laying the
groundwork.

Fleshing Out the Site

The home page needed to have a bit of panache to announce to visitors that they had definitely landed on a photography website. He decided that a slideshow of fine art images would be just the ticket. The slideshow needed to be compatible with portable devices like the iPad. Therefore, using Flash was out of the question. After doing some research, he decided to use the Image Rotator Magic Dreamweaver plug-in from Project Seven (www.projectseven.com) to create a non-Flash slideshow on the site home page (see Figure 1-4).

Image Rotator Magic is a powerful plug-in that enables a designer to create animated banners, sidebars, and slideshows. The Dreamweaver extension has a user-friendly interface (see Figure 1-5) that enables you to choose which images you want to include, determine the length of time for which an image is displayed, and much more. The beauty of the application is that the end result is not Flash, which means it can be viewed on portable devices like the iPad. The extension also creates all the code used to switch images.

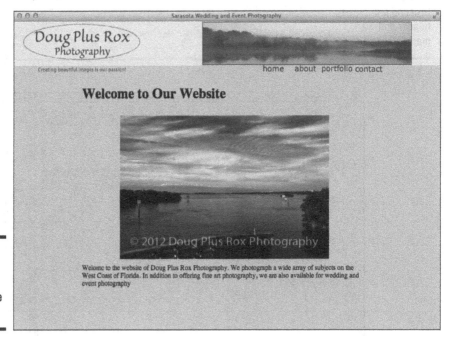

Figure 1-4:
Adding a slideshow to the home page.

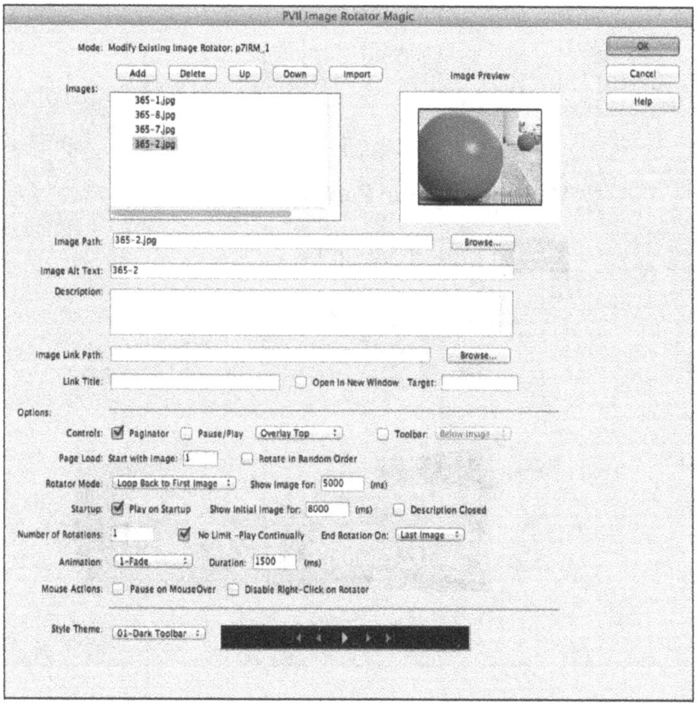

Figure 1-5:
The Image
Rotator
Magic
extension at
work.

Creating the Gallery

Every photography website needs a gallery of some sort. Doug's company
creates images in a couple of different genres. Rather than have a separate
drop-down menu for each gallery, Doug wanted to create a single gallery that
featured all genres of his company's work. Project Seven was the source for
yet another elegant solution. A combination of the Horizontal Glider extension, which was used for the gallery menu, and Image Rotator Magic, which
was used to create the individual galleries, proved to be the ideal solution
(see Figure 1-6).

Figure 1-6:
Multiple galleries displayed on one page. Sweet!

Finishing the Site

After creating the gallery, Doug designed the About and Contact pages based on the template he created when he started the project. He was thinking about search engine optimization (SEO) when he created the home page and the other pages. He used the Google Keyword tool to find the optimum keywords for his photography business and peppered them in the text, page titles, and alt tags.

Alt tags — accessibility options used by people with screenreaders as descriptions of the image — are picked up by search engines.

As this book comes to a close, Doug is putting the finishing touches on the site. At the end of a project, Doug typically lets a client site breathe for a couple of days before adding his finishing touches and then presenting it to his client for final approval. In this case, he's going to set the design aside for a couple of weeks before tweaking the design. Then he's going to present it to his business partner for final approval. So, the site that is uploaded to his server may be different than what you see on these pages.

In designing this site, Doug's goal was to create a simple site that was aesthetically appealing and showcases his company's photography. Did he achieve his goal? That will be decided after he uploads the site and starts getting some visitors. He will also carefully monitor the site's stats from month to month to see whether he needs to fine-tune the new content.

Chapter 2: E-Commerce Site

*A*uthor and web designer, Janine Warner is a busy lady. She writes books about web design, teaches web design, and designs websites. She has two websites: one to promote her speaking and writing, and another site that she uses to sell books and videos. In this chapter, we feature the site she uses to sell products. Ms. Warner is the author of more than a dozen books on web design and the presenter of more than 50 hours of video training. We discuss her e-commerce site in this chapter.

Assessing Needs

When Janine decided to create a website to promote and sell products, such as training DVDs, she had to find a reliable hosting service with lots of features. The hosting service she chose enables her to add features like blogs without having to create databases or upload software. In addition, the hosting service features unlimited bandwidth and economical pricing.

When you choose a web-hosting service for e-commerce, get the best bang for your buck. For more information on choosing a web-hosting service for an e-commerce website, check out Book VIII, Chapter 3.

In addition to choosing a reliable web-hosting service, she needed to determine which technologies she was going to use for her e-commerce site. She used standard HTML with some CSS magic and templates she created in Adobe Dreamweaver CS5 to create the basic site. She used a combination of PayPal and Google Checkout to flesh out the e-commerce portion of her site.

Designing the Site

Janine designed the site using Adobe Dreamweaver. The flexibility of the software enabled her to create a template that she used on the entire site. The header of her site contains the site logo, a drop-down navigation menu, and links to her social media (see Figure 2-1).

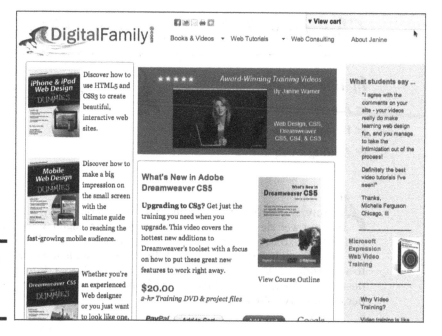

Figure 2-1:
The Digital
Family
website.

She had a lot of information to post on the site, which made creating a navigation system a challenge. She solved the problem by using drop-down menus and also by adding a column on the left side that contains links to other information on her site. On the Web Tutorials page, she added a third column with links to her online training and links to specific book pages at Amazon.com (see Figure 2-2).

When Janine created DigitalFamily.com, she had three concerns:

✦ Create a site that's easy to update with her new books, videos, and tutorials.

✦ Create a site that makes it easy for visitors to discover the many tips, tutorials, and other resources. She also wanted a site to promote and sell her books and training videos.

✦ Use state-of-the-art web technology, such as Dreamweaver templates and CSS, to design a site that's easy to expand or redesign in the future.

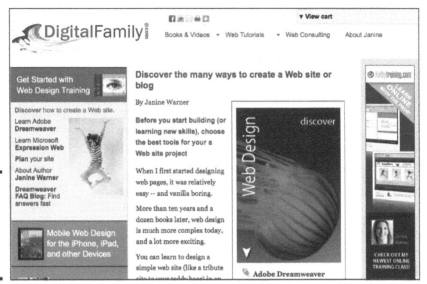

Figure 2-2:
Solving
navigation
challenges
with
columns.

Integrating E-Commerce

One of Janine's goals was to sell merchandise from her website. She could
have used a secure server and purchased an expensive e-commerce package to accept credit card payments, but she shares the philosophy of your
intrepid authors and decided to use inexpensive but secure services to
handle her transactions. She also wanted to provide a comfort level for her
visitors, so she employs two services to handle online payments: Google
Checkout and PayPal.

The Web Tutorials section of her site is where the e-commerce magic happens. The products are displayed in the center column. Each product has
a PayPal Add to Cart button (read about that in Book VIII) and a Google
Checkout Add to Cart button (see Figure 2-3). Note that the tutorials are for
Dreamweaver CS5. As of this writing, Ms. Warner is working on video tutorials for Dreamweaver CS6.

Both systems work well. With PayPal, you add the button to a product
description by adding a few lines of code to the desired position in your
HTML page. You get the code by logging into your PayPal account and then
navigating to the Merchant Services page. Click the Buy Now Button, or the
Add to Cart Button, and then follow the easy prompts to create the code that
you add to your HTML document. You don't even have to host the button
images; PayPal does that for you. When PayPal introduces new button
designs, your site is automatically updated. You can also create a custom
checkout page, as outlined in Book VIII, Chapter 3.

Janine's site offers visitors the option to check out with Google Checkout. The service is very similar to PayPal. The most notable difference for the visitor is needing to sign up for a Google account before the transaction can be completed.

We must admit that the Google Checkout system is more seamless than PayPal's system. However, some web designers may decide not to create a Google account, and some website visitors may decide they don't want to create a Google account to purchase an item, which is why we prefer PayPal, even though a transaction momentarily takes a visitor from the site. When a site visitor purchases with Google Checkout, she stays on the site.

When a purchase is made through Google Checkout, it is noted in the View Cart button on the vendor's website (see Figure 2-4). The visitor can add additional items to the cart as she peruses the site. When she's ready to check out, she clicks the Checkout button. If she has a Google account, she's prompted to sign in. If not, she'll have to set up a Google account before she can complete that transaction.

To find out more about Google Checkout, launch your favorite web browser, and mosey on over to checkout.google.com.

The PayPal transaction isn't quite as seamless. When the buyer clicks the Add to Cart button, he ends up on a PayPal payment page (see Figure 2-5). He has the option to complete the transaction using a credit or debit card, even if he doesn't have a PayPal account. However, if he wants to purchase more items, he'll have to click the Continue Shopping button to return to the vendor's site.

Janine's site has been around for a while, and she intends to update the site sometime in 2012. So don't be surprised if you visit the site and see something entirely different than you see in this chapter. She assures us she'll use the same technology for the e-commerce section of the site.

Figure 2-4:
Google
Checkout at
work.

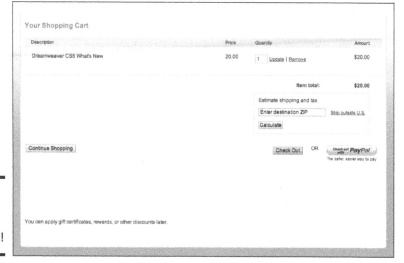

Figure 2-5:
PayPal
checkout.
Cha-ching!!!

Chapter 3: Blog Site

*W*hen Doug revised his company's photography website, he knew he wanted to include a blog with the site. As we mention in Book VIII, adding a blog to your site helps with search engine optimization (SEO) because posts are added to a blog site frequently.

Then shortly after he added the blog to the site, Doug and his business partner Roxanne decided that they were going to do a "365 project." That 365 project would test their visual acumen as photographers by committing to photograph every day of the year and upload the best picture of the day to a website. A blog was the obvious answer for this project as well. In all, Doug added three blogs to the main website.

In this chapter, we show you the whys and wherefores behind Doug's choices as well as share a few tips for modifying a blog to suit the website and blog material.

Creating the Main Blog Site

When Doug decided he needed three blogs to compliment his company's main website, opting for a WordPress blog was the obvious choice. The blogging software is easy to install and use. As an added bonus, the web-hosting service for his website has the option to automatically install a WordPress blog and create a directory for the blog in one fell swoop. Talk about convenience!

The main blog site needed all the WordPress bells and whistles. Doug wanted to use the sidebar feature to publicize a book of fine art photographs created by his company. Another requirement was the addition of icons: for the company's social media and for an RSS feed. The blog also needed to have a similar look and feel to the main website, which required choosing the right blog template.

Then, creating the site with Fantastico was pretty much child's play. *Fantastico* is a feature that may be available through your website cPanel (control panel); read all about it in Book VIII, Chapter 3. All you need to do is specify the directory, admin-access data, configuration, and so on. If you're setting up a blog through a web-hosting service that uses Fantastico, the installation process is very much self-explanatory. It's a three-step process (see Figure 3-1).

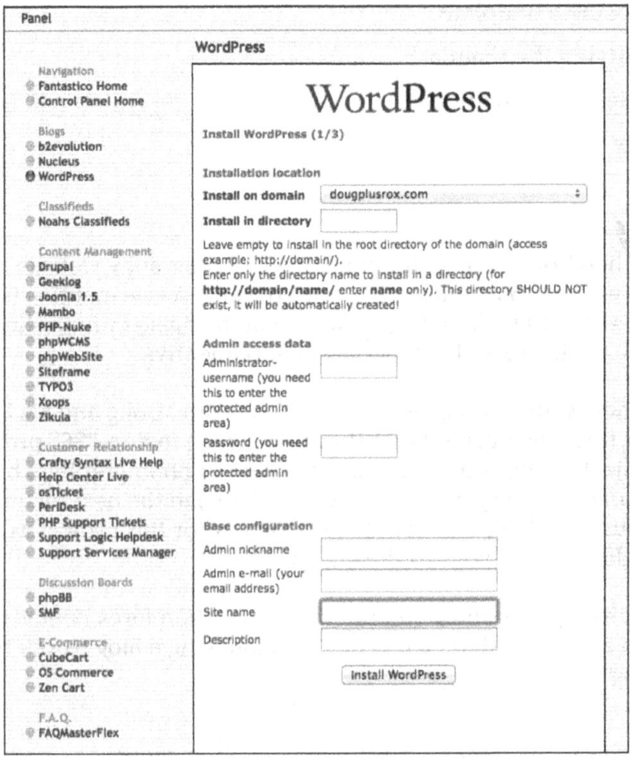

Figure 3-1: Creating the blog.

After setting up the site through Fantastico, you have a generic blog with the default image for the template you chose (see Figure 3-2). This is the point where you roll up your sleeves and customize the blog to suit your website, which is exactly what Doug did immediately after the blog was created.

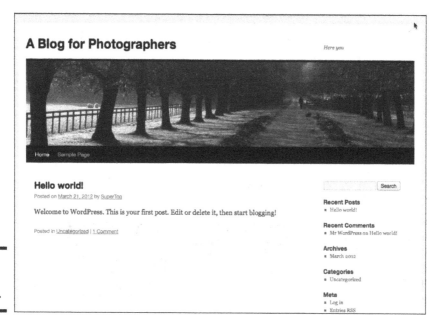

Figure 3-2:
The bare-
bones blog.

Modifying the Blog Template

After you create a blog, you customize it to suit the main website. Alternatively, you may have created a blog-only site, in which case you customize the blog to suit your (or your client's) taste. You can find free custom blogs at http://wordpress.org/extend/themes. The templates you find at this web page are pretty sophisticated. You can search for specific parameters, such as the number of columns, sidebar placement, colors, and so on. For more information on modifying a blog, see Book VIII, Chapter 1.

Doug decided to use the Twenty Eleven 1.3 template, which was created by the WordPress team. The reason he went with this template is because it's customizable, and the WordPress team should keep it up to date with future releases of WordPress.

When you choose a third-party blog template, the developer might lose enthusiasm and not update the template when a new version of WordPress is released. This can definitely be a problem when the template is free and is created by an independent developer.

Doug got his fingernails dirty and got under the hood of WordPress — um, actually into the Appearance section of the WordPress Dashboard (see Figure 3-3). Notice that the Appearance section for this template gives you options to work with widgets, create menus, modify theme options, change the background color, and modify the header.

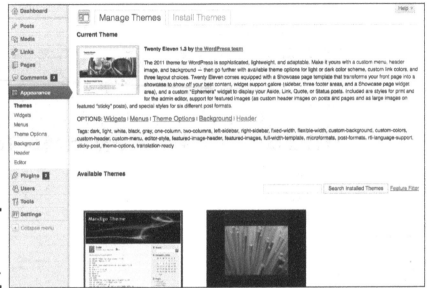

Figure 3-3:
Modify
your blog's
appearance.

For the blog that accompanies the main website, Doug chose the dark background and the default link color. Alternatively, he could have specified a specific color for links by entering a known hexadecimal value or by clicking the Select a Color link and then choosing a color from the color wheel (see Figure 3-4). We define hexadecimal values in Book II, Chapter 3.

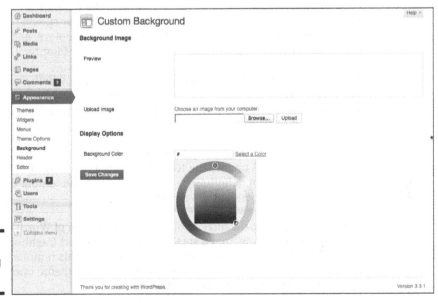

Figure 3-4:
Set the blog
link color.

The Twenty Eleven 1.3 blog template also gives you the option to create a menu. This is a wonderful option when you need to create a link back to the main site, or if you're creating a standalone blog and want to create pages and menu links. Doug took advantage of this option to create a custom menu with a link to an online store, an About page, and the blog Home page (see Figure 3-5).

The number of menus you can use varies depending on the template you use. The Twenty Eleven 1.3 blog supports one menu.

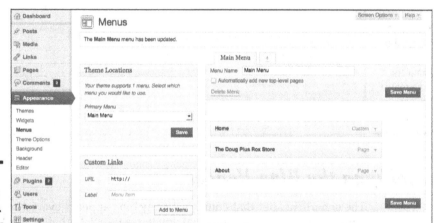

Figure 3-5:
Add a menu
to your blog.

Using Widgets

Widgets give you the power to add items to the sidebar, such as an RSS feed, custom text, and social media icons. You add widgets in the Appearance section. Widget support varies depending on the template you use.

One of the reasons why Doug chose the Twenty Eleven 1.3 blog template was its robust widget support. Doug wanted links from the blog to his company's social media, an RSS feed, and a link to a book of fine art photography (*Pieces of a Dream*) his company created. He used the Social Media widget (procured at the WordPress site), a text widget for the blog's RSS feed, and a text widget for the HTML code for a book badge and link to the website from which the print-on-demand book could be purchased. In addition, he used the Cloud widget to display a cloud of tags from blog posts on the blog home page. Figure 3-6 shows the Widgets section of the Twenty Eleven 1.3 blog template.

Modifying the Blog Header

The generic header that comes with any blog appears everywhere the blog template is used. We suggest that you find a template that supports changing the blog header. The Twenty Eleven 1.3 template supports this option. With some templates, you have to upload the header image file to a specific folder on your server. You also need to know exactly what size to make the image for it to properly fit inside the blog template. The template Doug chose does everything but create the header.

The first thing Doug did was to visit the Header section of the Dashboard. The size of the image was clearly listed as 1000 x 288 pixels (px). Armed with that info, half of your intrepid author team ventured into Photoshop CS5 and created a new document, 1000 px x 288 px, with a resolution of 72 pixels per inch. The header featured the logo from the main website, the company tagline, and an image. After saving the image as a JPEG file, Doug logged into the blog site, navigated to the Header section of the Dashboard, and uploaded the image (see Figure 3-7).

After uploading the header, Doug was ready to start blogging. The customized blog is a good fit for his company's website (see Figure 3-8).

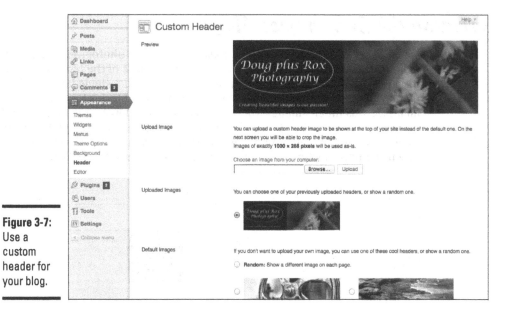

Figure 3-7:
Use a
custom
header for
your blog.

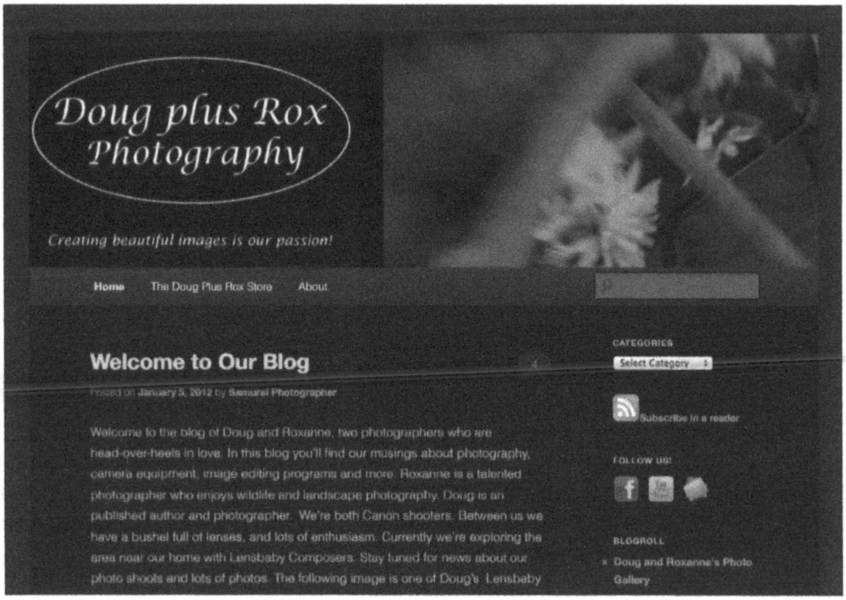

Figure 3-8:
The finished
blog.

Creating the 365 Project Blogs

When Doug and Roxanne decided to showcase their photography with a 365 project, they knew the photos would be the highlight of the blog with very little text for each daily post. Therefore, they wanted a single image to be displayed at a width of 1000 px. The default Twenty Eleven 1.3 blog space for an image was much smaller, though, because the sidebar took up a lot of the screen real estate. Then Doug discovered the theme had a template option to display one column and no sidebar. This change can be made in the Theme Options section of the Appearance section (see Figure 3-9).

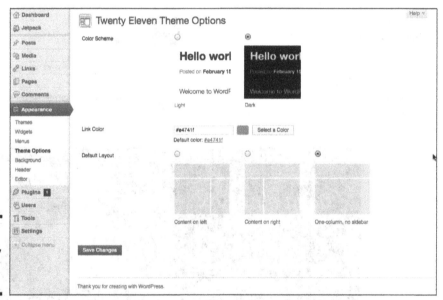

Figure 3-9:
One column,
easy on the
sidebar.

Doug thought this would be the ideal solution, but the default image size was the same size as the column in the one column with a sidebar option. He scratched his head a bit, put on his thinking cap, and realized he'd have to change some code in the default layout but had no idea of which code to change. Instead of working harder, he let his fingers do the walking and typed a query into his favorite search engine. He found the answer rather quickly, and the answer was to change the code in the styles.css document. We uncover the murky depths of CSS in Book IV. To get the images to display at a maximum width of 1000 px in the Twenty Eleven 1.3 blog template, perform the following steps:

1. **Log in to your blog.**

2. **In the Dashboard, navigate to the Editor section of the Appearance section.**

3. **Click the Stylesheet link on the right side of the page.**

   The `styles.css` document loads in the Edit Themes window.

4. **Change the #page code to the following:**

   ```
   #page{
       margin: 2em auto;
       max-width; 1000 px;
   }
   ```

   Your revised style sheet should look like Figure 3-10.

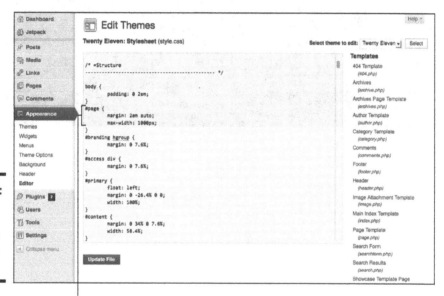

Figure 3-10: Revise the style sheet to increase the column size.

Adjust the code here.

5. **Click the Update File button.**

   Your revised style sheet is changed.

Make sure you change the code exactly as described in the previous steps. If you change the wrong lines of code, you will probably make a mess of your pretty blog.

Now that the blog was displaying one image with no sidebar, Doug had to create a menu with links to log in, navigate to Roxanne's 365 blog, navigate to the main blog, and navigate to the main website. Figure 3-11 shows a post from Doug's 365 project blog.

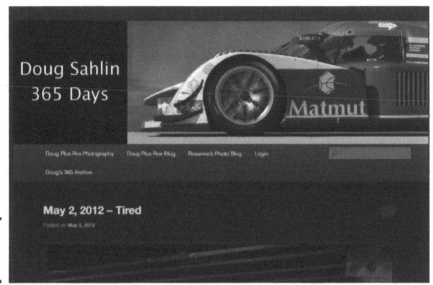

Figure 3-11:
The finished
365 blog.

Chapter 4: Online Newsletter

In This Chapter

✔ The value of a newsletter

✔ Choosing a newsletter service

✔ Creating a newsletter

✔ Integrating a newsletter subscription opt-in with a website

*W*hen you create a website for a product or a service, there are many ways you can keep clients and potential clients up to date on new products, services, or events. You can use social media such as Facebook and Twitter to spread the word, write about new products or events in your blog — or you can send a newsletter to clients or potential clients on a regular basis. When you opt for the latter, you're sending a newsletter via e-mail that's been requested by site visitors who have opted into the newsletter. In this chapter, we give you a behind-the-scenes look at a newsletter that gets sent out to visitors of a veterinary clinic website.

Why Send a Newsletter?

Whenever you or a client decide to take on another project associated with a website, a time factor is involved. In fact, with any type of media that you or your client needs to spend time creating, there's a time factor. The return on investment (ROI) must justify the time (the investment) you or your client spend creating the newsletter. If you create an HTML newsletter from scratch and embed it in an e-mail, you have a fairly large time expenditure. However, if you use an online newsletter service to compose your newsletter, your time expenditure is less, and the resulting quality of the product is considerably higher, which means better retention of newsletter subscribers.

When you send a newsletter to visitors who subscribe through your website, you have the recipient's permission to send the newsletter. Here are other benefits to sending a newsletter to clients and potential customers:

✦ You can update newsletter subscribers on a regular basis. In fact, after a few compelling fact-filled newsletters, your subscribers eagerly anticipate the arrival of the next newsletter.

✦ Newsletters keep your company or service on a subscriber's radar screens. Out of sight, out of mind. A well-written newsletter keeps your product or service on subscribers' minds.

✦ If a subscriber is not yet a customer, informative newsletters will place your company or service near the tops of the subscriber's list when they are ready to purchase.

✦ A newsletter is a quick and convenient way to notify subscribers about a new product or service your company is offering.

Choosing a Newsletter Provider

Ark Animal Hospital in Venice, Florida changed ownership in late 2011. The hospital had been using a paid newsletter service to send newsletters to roughly 800 subscribers on a regular basis. The newsletters informed clients about new advances in veterinary medicine and provided useful tips and information about pet care and health. The new owner realized the value of the newsletter but wanted to keep marketing expenses to a minimum without losing any marketing benefits. The hospital manager was given the job of finding the best newsletter service at the most economical cost.

Of the many newsletter services from which to choose, after careful consideration, the hospital manager decided that MailChimp (`http://mailchimp.com`) was the best service. MailChimp offers several levels of service, including a free service. For a new company, or a company with a limited number of clients, the free service is ideal. With the free MailChimp service, a customer can store as many as 2,000 subscribers in the MailChimp database. In addition, the free account allows a customer to send 12,000 e-mails per month, with a limit of sending 2,000 e-mails in a 24-hour period.

MailChimp makes it possible for a client to quickly create a newsletter using its online interface and templates. The client can add images to the newsletter, which are stored on the MailChimp server. And after a newsletter is sent, it's archived in HTML format on the MailChimp server.

MailChimp has an extensive library of information online. If you're thinking of starting an e-mail marketing campaign, you can find a treasure trove of information at `http://mailchimp.com/resources`.

Creating a Newsletter

When you decide to send e-mail newsletters, you decide which clients will receive your newsletter. Ark Animal Hospital already had a mailing list, which was imported to MailChimp. Ark Animal Hospital also had the option to manually add clients to the list and delete clients. After importing the list, it's time to create the first "new" newsletter. You can, however, create multiple lists for different segments of the website target audience, which we show you in upcoming sections of this chapter.

Creating a newsletter shouldn't be a hassle. A good newsletter provider has templates you can use as the basis for your newsletter. All you need to do is add the text and images.

When you log in to MailChimp, the first thing you see is the Dashboard (see Figure 4-1). This displays information about recent campaigns. MailChimp users can also select individual campaigns, modify current mailing lists, check reports, create an auto-responder message to thank subscribers for signing up, and manage the account.

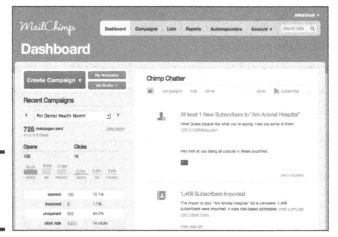

Figure 4-1:
The
MailChimp
Dashboard.

To create a newsletter, you begin by creating a "campaign." So in MailChimp, the first step is to click the Create Campaign link. A campaign in MailChimp-speak is a single newsletter sent out to a list. Then, use a MailChimp template to create the newsletter, or use a saved template. A newsletter can be created from scratch, or a draft can be edited to completion.

Creating a newsletter campaign is a six-step process:

1. Decide which list the newsletter will be sent to.

MailChimp gives you the option of creating multiple lists. You can also fine-tune the recipients by sending the e-mail to a segment of the list.

2. Enter information about the campaign.

Enter the name of the newsletter, the message subject, the name of the sender, and the reply to e-mail (address). In this step, you can also add the capability to track how many recipients open the e-mail, use Google Analytics to monitor traffic from the campaign to your website, and also integrate the newsletter with Twitter and Facebook.

3. Create the newsletter.

   You can change templates, preview the newsletter, save the newsletter as a template, or use the style editor to fine-tune the look of the newsletter. Figure 4-2 shows the newsletter Ark Animal Hospital sent to subscribers after client pets were photographed with a local Santa Claus by a professional photographer.

4. Enter a plain text message.

   This step allows the newsletter author to create a plain text message that will be displayed to those recipients with e-mail applications that don't support HTML. Another option is to let MailChimp copy the plain text from HTML.

5. Confirm the campaign.

   Preview all your choices and edit anything prior to sending the campaign.

6. Send the campaign immediately, or schedule the delivery for a later date or time.

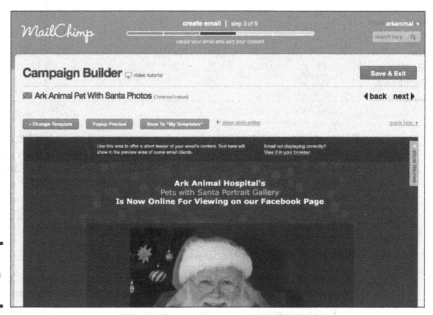

Figure 4-2:
Creating the
newsletter.

Analyzing Campaign Results

When you take the time to create an e-mail campaign, it's important to know whether your time is well spent. To get an idea of what type of return you're getting on your time investment, you can analyze reports about all your campaigns or an individual campaign. The response to a campaign helps you to fine-tune the content for future campaigns. MailChimp reports show you a graph for all your campaigns (see Figure 4-3), or you can select an individual campaign.

When you analyze results for an individual campaign (see Figure 4-4), pay attention to how many people actually opened the newsletter. MailChimp gives you an industry comparison on the graph. If the percentage of people who opened the e-mail newsletter is higher than the industry standard, you're doing something right. If that rate slips below the industry standard for one newsletter, review the content of the newsletter. If you did something radically different than previous newsletters, you know that it wasn't received well. On the other hand, if the percentage is higher than the industry standard and higher than your average, you're moving in the right direction.

MailChimp also gives you performance advice at the bottom of each report. If you decide to add a newsletter to your online marketing arsenal, we advise that you review the report for every newsletter to deliver meaningful content to your subscribers.

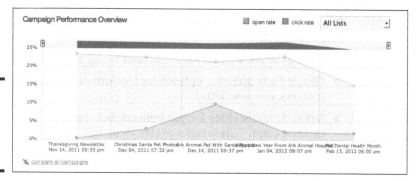

Figure 4-3:
Analyze
results
for e-mail
campaigns.

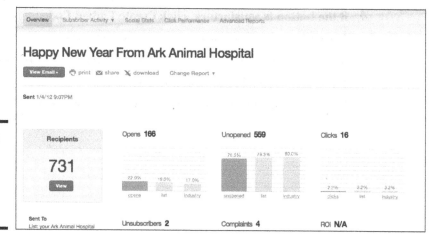

Figure 4-4:
Analyze
results for
a specific
e-mail
campaign.

Adding an Opt-in Form to Your Website

When you use a service like MailChimp to deliver information to your clients and potential clients, increasing the number of subscribers increases your potential reach. MailChimp makes it possible to easily add a Subscribe form to your website or blog. To add a subscribe form to your website, just copy MailChimp's HTML code and add it to the desired web page. We suggest that you add the subscribe form to your home page. If you have a WordPress blog, you can use the Text widget to add the form to your sidebar. To get the MailChimp code for a subscribe button

1. **Log in to your MailChimp account.**

2. **Click Lists.**

   Your lists are displayed.

3. **Click View.**

   The page refreshes and shows information about the list.

4. **Click For Your Website, and then click Signup Form Embed Code.**

   The page refreshes to show you a preview of what the button will look like. You get three options:

   - *Super Slim Form* includes a text field for an e-mail address.

   - *Classic Form* includes options for the format in which the recipient receives the newsletter.

   - *Naked Form* includes format options, but the code contains no CSS or JavaScript. This is not a pretty form, but if you have a bare-bones site, it will get the job done.

5. **Choose the desired form option.**

   The preview changes.

6. **If the button is satisfactory, click Create Embed Code.**

   The code in the Copy/Paste into Your Site text window changes.

7. **Select the code and then press Ctrl+C (Windows) or ⌘+C (Macintosh).**

   The code is copied to your Clipboard.

8. **Paste the code into the desired web page or your blog.**

Index